Theories of the Arts in China

Theories of the Arts in China

EDITED BY
SUSAN BUSH AND CHRISTIAN MURCK

Princeton University Press
Princeton, New Jersey

Copyright © 1983 by Princeton University Press

Published by Princeton University Press, 41 William Street, Princeton, New Jersey
In the United Kingdom: Princeton University Press, Guildford, Surrey

All Rights Reserved

Library of Congress Cataloging in Publication Data will be found on the last printed page
of this book

This book has been composed in Monophoto Bembo by
Asco Trade Typesetting Ltd., Hong Kong

Clothbound editions of Princeton University Press books are printed on acid-free paper,
and binding materials are chosen for strength and durability

Printed in the United States of America by Princeton University Press,
Princeton, New Jersey

Designed by Laury A. Egan

To our families

Preface

A conference on "Theories of the Arts in China" was held under the sponsorship of the Committee on Studies of Chinese Civilization of the American Council of Learned Societies from June 6 to 12, 1979, at the Breckinridge Public Affairs Center of Bowdoin College at York, Maine. The purpose was to stimulate interest in Chinese aesthetics. For five days, two philosophers and two cultural historians, along with ten historians of Chinese literature and eight of Chinese art, met to comment on eighteen papers.

Many people were responsible for the realization of the conference. The editors would like to express their appreciation first to the Subcommittee on Thought and Religion of the ACLS Committee on Studies of Chinese Civilization which initiated this project under the chairmanship of Donald J. Munro. Richard Barnhart and John Timothy Wixted offered invaluable suggestions and practical help during the planning stages. J. T. Wixted was responsible in large part for the drafts of several proposals and for the choice of the site, which contributed greatly to the success of the conference. Geoffrey Stanwood of the staff of Bowdoin College was most helpful in the final planning of the conference program. The three rapporteurs, Steven Van Zoeren, Louisa A. McDonald, and Louisa Shen Ting, coped effectively with all the benefits and inadequacies of modern machines for oral and written communication to produce transcripts and summaries of the proceedings. These were put to good use by the participants when they revised their papers along the lines suggested by the discussions.

The "unity experience" of the occasion, in which topics seemed to strike sparks off each other in harmonious progression, led to expressed wishes that the papers be published together. This wish has a large extent been fulfilled with the publication of this symposium volume. Regretfully, two of the papers were judged incomplete by their authors and were withdrawn from consideration. They were "Literature, Art, and the Tao in Pre-T'ang Writings" by James J. Y. Liu, and "The Role of Figurative Language in Early Texts on Calligraphy" by Marilyn W. Fu and Shen C. Y. Fu. The editors hope that some of the fine perceptions in these papers have been assimilated in our introduction, and we are confident that full presentation in published form will follow in due course.

All the authors are grateful to the four discussants. In addition to participating usefully in our conversations throughout the conference, at mid-point they produced considered and impromptu remarks on overarching issues. Since these untitled comments may be of some interest to our readers, their contents are briefly indicated here. (Full transcripts are available in the depository sets of conference papers at major research libraries.) Donald J. Munro discussed certain specific characteristics of the nature, Tao, cosmos, or universe on which the artist patterned himself, and emphasized that such patterning or manifesting was a step toward the unity of self with other, a unity that could be sought in a variety of ways through structural, functional, or empathetic approaches. Furthermore, he noted that it was equally effective for an artist to emulate a master who himself manifested the Tao, and that emulation of this sort need not be limited to a strict form of copying since again a variety of attitudes allowed for the play of creativity. As a literary historian, Stephen Owen stressed that art theory is after all a program, an indication of what art or literature should be, not what it is, and he urged that Chinese critical texts be read as discourse, that is as responses to the conditions of their time. Similarly, as an art historian, James Cahill underlined the differences between the theory and practice of art, and, taking aesthetic statements as ideal views, he preferred a pluralistic approach to both art and theory, one that examines fine distinctions. He favored a parallel development model for art and religion or any outside factor, and thus highlighted the difficulty of identifying the specific symbolism of any artistic work. As a philosopher, Mary Mothersill formulated in precise terms some of the questions raised and answered in the papers. She cautioned against relying on imported philosophical concepts as props, and outlined steps toward a systematic theory of aesthetics that would link the discrete areas covered by our papers. Bald summaries can convey little of the discussants' response to our work; if this volume succeeds in pointing the way for future students, it will be in large measure due to their penetrating critiques.

In conclusion we would like to thank Christine K. Ivusic and her colleagues at Princeton University Press for their skill in guiding a large manuscript through the process of publication. We are also indebted to Pramod Chandra for his help in checking certain Sanskrit terms.

SUSAN BUSH
CHRISTIAN MURCK
October 1981

Contents

Abbreviations

A. PERIODICALS

AA	*Artibus Asiae*
AAA	*Archives of Asian Art*
AM	*Asia Major*
AO	*Ars Orientalis*
BEFEO	*Bulletin de l'Ecole française d'Extrême Orient*
BMFEA	*Bulletin of the Museum of Far Eastern Antiquities*
CCBK	*Chūgoku chūsei bungaku kenkyū*
CLEAR	*Chinese Literature: Essays, Articles, Reviews*
HJAS	*Harvard Journal of Asiatic Studies*
JAOS	*Journal of the American Oriental Society*
JAS	*Journal of Asian Studies*
JOS	*Journal of Oriental Studies*
MN	*Monumenta Nipponica*
MS	*Monumenta Serica*
NPMQ	*National Palace Museum Quarterly (Ku-kung chi-k'an)*
OA	*Oriental Art*
TP	*T'oung Pao*

B. *Ts'ung-shu* OR COLLECTIONS OF TEXTS

CTPS	*Chin-tai pi-shu*, comp. Mao Chin, 1628–1643 (rpt. Shanghai, 1922).
HLTK	*Hua-lun ts'ung-k'an*, comp. Yü An-lan, 2 vols. (pagination cont.) (Peking, 1960).
HSTS	*Hua-shih ts'ung-shu*, comp. Yü An-lan, 10 vols. (Shanghai, n.d.).
ISTP	*I-shu ts'ung-pien*, comp. Yang Chia-lo, I, 36 vols. (Taipei, 1962).
MSTS	*Mei-shu ts'ung-shu*, comp. Teng Shih, 20 vols. (rpt. Taipei, n.d., of Shanghai, 1947 ed.).
PWCSHP	*P'ei-wen-chai shu-hua-p'u*, comp. Sun Yüeh-pan, 4 vols. (rpt. Taipei, 1969, of 1708 ed.).
SPPY	*Ssu-pu pei-yao*, comp. Kao Yeh-hou et al. (Shanghai, 1927–1931).
SPTK	*Ssu-pu ts'ung-k'an*, comp. Chang Yüan-chi et al., 3 series (Shanghai, 1919).
TSCC	*Ts'ung-shu chi-ch'eng*, comp. Wang Yün-wu (Shanghai, 1935–1939).
WSHY	*Wang-shih hua-yüan*, with *Wang-shih shu-yüan*, comp. Wang Shih-chen, in *Wang-shih shu-hua-yüan* (rpt. Shanghai, 1922).

Theories of the Arts in China

Introduction

An interest in Chinese art and aesthetics, broadly understood, led the Committee on Studies of Chinese Civilization of the American Council of Learned Societies to sponsor a conference on "Theories of the Arts in China" in June of 1979. The essays in this book were originally presented for discussion at that conference. Serious scholarly interest in the Chinese literature on art has been pursued in recent years largely within separate disciplines: art history, comparative literature, the history of literature, musicology, philology, philosophy, and intellectual history. The division of humanistic scholarship into disciplines is in general a fruitful approach to our experience of the past and its rich wholeness. An analytical and critical framework inevitably requires the specification of a body of material for controlled exploration. Those who study the past may tend to recreate it in the light of their own intellectual concerns, but the pride of the contemporary scholar is that his work displays awareness of this fact by making explicit the assumptions and hypotheses which guide it. But as methods harden into methodologies, the primary source material at hand—a painting, a poem, a critical text—can become relevant only as potential data advancing the theoretical position of the discipline. At times the quiddity of the past may seem overwhelmed by the weight and power of the apparatus brought to bear on it. Yet we would contend that scholars usually come to their fields through an empathetic response that in the first instance stands beyond analysis, and leaves a sense that any single approach has its limitations. Indeed, if a method were as open-ended and as various as the past itself, it could provide no "discipline" at all. Consequently, dialogue among scholars of related disciplines, and similar but distinct interests, can be extraordinarily rewarding. With that in mind, a group of students of Chinese thought, literature, and art convened.

The conference addressed the problem of the historical development of indigenous discourse on the arts in China. We asked ourselves such broad questions as: When did the Chinese become aware of the aesthetic response to nature and to human artifacts as an intellectual problem? What arts became the vehicles within the high culture for cultivating and expressing aesthetic responses? What were the terms of discourse on the arts, and how were theories of the arts articulated in relation to other concerns? Historically, writing about the arts in China tended to draw heavily on the common values of its period; therefore, even when dealing ostensibly with a single art form, such literature was relevant to other arts, and often to social, political, moral, and spiritual ideas as well. That is to say, the arts were appreciated within the holistic culture of the traditional Chinese elite, and rarely considered as a separate province of their own. It is not surprising, therefore, that we found that our broad focus evoked papers on specific problems in various periods which repeatedly isolated the same issues and texts and stimulated constructive debate.

In the initial section, "Comparative Perspectives on Literary Theory," two papers treat questions of historical grouping and critical definition. In "Periodization in the Arts and Patterns of Change in Traditional Chinese Literary History,"

Maureen Robertson underlines the cultural values implicit in the "code" through which a writer explains and defines different periods. Robertson's point of view is comparative, and certain characteristics of traditional Chinese criticism become clearer in contrast with Western models. For instance, a Western critic might consider political periodization an extrinsic type of classification when applied to the development of the arts, but in China art was generally viewed as an integral part of government and society, and there was no initial distinction between ethical and artistic standards of judgment. The *Book of Odes* was an anthology of songs which embodied ideal values; hence *pien*, "to change," is to decline when used in the evaluation of the songs by the Han critic Cheng Hsüan. In the Six Dynasties, when belles-lettres were appreciated in their own right and a concern for technique came to the fore, *pien*, as "changes" or "turning points," could be used in a neutral sense, whether a critic's organizational model was a cyclical decline from a Golden Age or a progressive linear development. It was nonetheless still necessary to legitimatize the aesthetic by assimilating it to the ethical and the quasi-metaphysical. In the light of the Confucian renewal of late T'ang and Sung times, change began to seem more threatening, and *pien* resumes its pejorative meaning in the writings of the Ming archaists. In tracing such patterns in critical periodization, Robertson's essay stresses the importance of the Six Dynasties of the third to the sixth centuries A.D. as a formative period of literary and art criticism. In the process of classifying and evaluating writers, and preparing anthologies, specific genres were established, lineages and critical terminology were invented, and sources of artistic authority were defined. This emphasis is echoed by many of her colleagues, as will be seen below.

If a method of demarcating the passage of time is fundamental to critical thought, it is certainly equally important to know, for example, what a poem is. As in the West, Chinese critics focused on technique as a distinguishing feature of literature and poetry, and the question of form was a major concern. Pauline Yu's paper, "Formal Distinctions in Chinese Literary Theory," compares the theories of modern, Western Formalists with definitions of Chinese writers of the Six Dynasties, and the later Ming and Ch'ing periods, the two most productive eras for literary criticism in China. Her point is not to search for a strictly formalist position that focuses on the text to the exclusion of reader, author, and world; rather it is to consider the Chinese critical literature in the light of the formalist problematic. Thus her attention is drawn to the delimitation of the all-inclusive term *wen*, "culture, civilization, pattern, embellishment, scholarship, writing." By the first half of the sixth century A.D. in the writings of Six Dynasties critics and anthologizers, *wen* is used in the sense of "pattern" or "embellishment" to label the broad category of belles-lettres appreciated for aesthetic effect, as opposed to *pi*, unrhymed "plain writing," didactic in intent and of practical use. But in the *ku-wen* movement of T'ang prose writers, *wen* becomes associated with literature in general, and specifically with prose. Distinctions based on technique are blurred from then on by the Neo-Confucian insistence that all literature is didactic in function, and properly serves "to convey the Way." By Ming times, the only grounds of argument against this all-encompassing formulation were purely formal ones. Hence Li Tung-yang (1447–1516) revives the T'ang distinction between *wen*, or prose, and *shih*, "poetry," and emphasizes the difficulty, and superiority, of the latter. Like the Western formalist critics, he opposes poetic language to nonpoetic prose to define differences both in form and function, with the aim of freeing poetry from didactic restrictions. Unfortunately the concern with form led his followers, the Ming archaists, to stress rules and strict imitation. In an ironic twist, the Ch'ing scholar Juan Yüan (1764–1849) returns to a Six Dynasties concept of *wen* as rhymed literature (or parallel prose) as the definition of poetry, again an attempt to defend the aesthetic function of writing. Juan's position on the meaning of literature foreshadows Yu's own general critique of formalist theories of art: "Divorcing literature from any utilitarian or communicative function in effect robs it of any potential significance." Yu's essay brings the development of theories that distinguished literary writing or poetry on the basis of formal considerations into sharp focus. The contrast with Western formalists not only defines the problem more clearly, it also highlights the traditional heritage of the Chinese critic, the pervasive and lingering influence of earlier formulations and terminology. Our problem as readers is often to chart the shifts in meaning of familiar terms, and to understand which among a complex layering of associations is being drawn on in a given passage, and how new ideas can be expressed in old and powerful words.

Whereas Robertson and Yu surveyed the Chinese critical literature from a cross-cultural point of view, in the second chapter, "The Human Body and Artistic Values," Tu Wei-ming and John Hay examine the relation between ideas of the physical self and the emergence of aesthetic values within the Chinese tradition. The term *i*, "art," originally meant "to sow, plant, or cultivate." In "The Idea of the Human in Mencian Thought: An Approach to Chinese Aesthetics," Tu explores the traditional concept that self-cultivation is central to artistic creativity in the context of the ethical thought of Mencius, the pre-Han philosopher of the fourth century B.C. There, *Tao*, the Way, is a process of development and an inspiration for self-transformation through the total experience of learning. *Shen*, the body, is the starting point for self-realization, the ground in which the seeds of the self are cultivated, initially through physical discipline in the practice of the six arts of the Chou period: ritual, music, archery, charioteering, writing, and arithmetic. Yet the meaning of an act and the understanding of it lie within the heart, *hsin*. According to Mencius, the way of learning is a quest for the "lost heart," and the six arts are also mental training that will "preserve the heart." The heart as the "great body" may be contrasted with brute physical form as the "small body," but the reclamation of our original nature by the ethical nourishing of the heart leads to a transformed physicality. Similarly, *shen*, the "spiritual," refers to a state of human perfection derived from humane potentialities, and its achievement is aided by *ch'i*, "vital spirit," a floodlike physical force generated by moral self-cultivation. Thus, in a stimulating reading of Mencius, Tu traces the use of body language to chart the stages of cultivation of the self, and argues that the underlying concepts are equally applicable to the arts in Confucian learning. The arts take their place as both method and expression of physical, as well as spiritual, cultivation.

John Hay's paper on "The Human Body as a Microcosmic Source of Macrocosmic Values in Calligraphy" notes the abundance of physiological terminology in Han and Six Dynasties appreciations of calligraphy and literary criticism, and suggests that these terms need to be understood in the perspective of contemporary medicine, which has been studied by Manfred Porkert. Chinese medical theory generally identifies functions rather than organs, and is quite distinctive in its focus on energy, describing a system of flow and transformation integral to the Chinese world view. In the concept of the body as an energized network, *ch'i*, or "matter-energy" (Tu's "vital spirit"), and the arterial system are the most important features. The relationship between inner and outer is also fundamental in Chinese medical thought, as is the focus on change, transformation, and resonance. Critical terminology in calligraphy and literary theory, as well as painting theory, can be reinterpreted in the light of these ideas. Hay concludes that the search for life was central in early Chinese physiology and not less so in art, considered as inseperable from life. These resonances between images of configurational energy in all areas of traditional culture must lay down pathways for explorations of the inevitably distanced past.

The religious background to the Six Dynasties appreciation of landscape in nature and art is emphasized in the chapter on "Images of Nature," which contains papers by Kiyohiko Munakata, Susan Bush, and Lothar Ledderose. Munakata focuses on the concepts *lei* and *kan-lei*, familiar in a variety of religious and philosophical texts, but not often given their full range of implication when encountered in an art text. As it occurs in the commentaries of the *I ching* (Book of Changes), *lei*, "kind" or "category," refers to the active force of a category of being, whether substantial or phenomenal, that responds to its like by inclination, thus setting in motion the fundamental cosmic order of harmonious interaction. *Kan-lei*, or "sympathetic responsiveness," has been described for Han times by Joseph Needham as a "symbolic correlation system" of magical efficacy structuring the cosmos, that "ordered harmony of wills without an ordainer." The principle of *kan-lei* influenced early Chinese rituals such as rainmaking ceremonies. In a particularly stimulating section of his paper, Munakata analyzes the design of a late Chou bronze vessel with inlaid ornament in the light of this pervasive principle. The earliest application of this concept in an art text is said to occur in the early fifth century A.D. in Tsung Ping's essay on painting landscape, in which *lei* is a basic requirement.

Hitherto scholars have taken this term to mean "resemblance" to nature, but Munakata interprets it as "nature of the kind" and understands it to refer to the category of sacred mountains. Tsung's thought is seen as an amalgamation of Buddhist and Taoist beliefs, a "Buddhist animism," since early animism underlies the concepts of sacred mountains and sacred rivers. If the *lei* of a sacred mountain were to be incorporated into a landscape painting, the effect would be the same as in nature. Hence the "sacredness" of a sacred mountain would be more important than formal details of appearance, and indeed Tsung's essay is wholly theoretical in approach rather than a practical guide to painting.

Many of Munakata's conclusions hinge on questions of interpretation or translation, some of which are brought up again in the paper that follows by Susan Bush, "Tsung Ping's Essay on Painting Landscape and the 'Landscape Buddhism' of Mount Lu." She notes the Confucian aspects of Tsung's thought, labeling his stress on the guiding role of the Buddha or the sages as "Confucian Buddhism," and does not discern specific animistic tendencies in his expansive view of nature. Tsung's approach to landscape painting is seen as shaped primarily by Buddhist attitudes toward icons, since the painted image is an aid to meditation of the same order as the natural scenery. The paper underlines the basis of Tsung's Buddhism in the teaching and practices of the monk Hui-yüan's community on Mount Lu, and studies the essay on painting landscape in conjunction with an anonymous preface to poems on wandering at the Stone Gate mountain of this range, which documents the "landscape Buddhism" of A.D. 400. This preface explicitly describes the meaning of the new appreciation of nature in the Mount Lu community, and is likely to have been known by Tsung Ping. Historical background and commentary introduce the translations of these two texts in which variant interpretations are cited. Significant terms discussed are *shen*, the human or cosmic spirit, *ling*, spiritual intelligence or the numinous, and *li*, ultimate "truth" intuited, a source of authority for Buddhist images. *Lei*, in the controversial usages, is considered to have the basic verbal sense of "to be like" but translated as "to correspond (in type)" in deference to probable Buddhist concerns with iconography. In the milieu of Mount Lu, the aesthetic experience of the work of art still remains the handmaid of religion.

Intense discussion of the Tsung Ping essay at our conference showed that it can be interpreted from Confucian, Taoist, and Buddhist points of view. Its vocabulary, as Munakata and Bush show, is particularly rich in words already carrying evolving traditions of meaning when Tsung wrote that will reoccur frequently in subsequent times. To understand the context in which he wrote, and place his work within Chinese cultural history generally, requires meticulous and imaginative scholarship. We hope that others will be encouraged by these papers to explore these problems themselves.

The connection between religious attitudes toward nature and the birth of landscape art is also the focus of a third paper in this section, "The Earthly Paradise:

Religious Elements in Chinese Landscape Art,'' by Lothar Ledderose. The art he is concerned with is three-dimensional representations of nature in imperial parks and tomb compounds, in imperial paradise gardens and later "natural" gardens, and in miniature in incense burners and tray landscapes in the period from Ch'in through T'ang. Ledderose's thesis is that the religious significance of such material underlay the aesthetic appreciation of landscape painting, then in its initial stages. In later periods painted landscape continued to have the function of serving as imaginative retreats for contemplation. In conclusion, Ledderose suggests links of religious role and formal motif between fully developed landscape painting and the earlier tradition of physical transformations or representations of nature.

If the Six Dynasties was a period when religious impulses were important in the Chinese view of art, it was also the moment when the gradual process of secularization led to purely aesthetic responses to nature and art, prized and self-consciously practiced by an aristocratic elite. The arts of music, poetry, literature, and calligraphy were fully developed as high arts. Music, the first of the arts, had long been considered an essential attribute of government because of its role in ritual. It now also became the solitary pleasure of the cultivated recluse, who strummed on his lute in order to resonate in harmony with nature. Poetry, as canonized in the classical anthology, the *Book of Odes*, had long been revered as expressing the ethical nature of the social order, and had provided many of the rhetorical figures of speech employed in politics and diplomacy. Attention now turned to criteria of literary and artistic merit. The cultivated individual was the ideal type, and criticisms of styles developed out of evaluations of personalities. Writers focused on the relation of the viewer or the artist with nature, and on the art of viewing or appreciation; they were thus concerned both with perception and creativity. Vitality, naturalness, and spontaneity were the qualities sought in aesthetic experience, qualities that emphasize the dynamic relationship between the artist and nature, on the one hand, and the artist and his audience, on the other.

The most sophisticated early theory of the arts was inspired by music and poetry, as is noted in the fourth chapter, "Music Theory and Poetics of the Six Dynasties." Kenneth DeWoskin's paper, "Early Chinese Music and the Origins of Aesthetic Terminology," traces the influence of music on the development of criticism generally. The link between music and the emotions inspired the most highly evolved philosophical investigations of the Wei-Chin period, to judge from the extant "Discourse on the Non-emotional Nature of Sound" by the poet Hsi K'ang (223–262). He argued that in the aesthetic context of music, sound will coincide with the emotional content of the mind of a given listener. This emphasis on inner response demanded an "overriding order of which the performer's mind, the sound, and the listener's mind are part." Hence ideas of the stringless lute and the soundless performance came into vogue, stressing the pure aesthetic experience as such, the effort rather than the outcome, and indicating the role of music in the sage's integration with nature.

As DeWoskin notes, critical evaluation on the practical level was initiated in appraisals of the technique of music, since the songs of the *Book of Odes* were considered sacrosanct by later writers. When lyric poetry reached a new height in post-Han times, criticism of poetry became an established genre, and it often took the form of a poetic appreciation. The other two papers in this chapter deal with early poetics and criticism of the period, considering the "lyric mode" and the process of evaluation. In "Chinese 'Lyric Criticism' in the Six Dynasties," Kang-i Sun Chang distinguishes "lyric criticism" from "commentary" as two distinct modes of post-Han writing on poetry. Developing the ideas of Yu-kung Kao, she stresses that the basis for this mode lies in the aesthetic experience itself, an empathetic union of self and world difficult to conceptualize, as Chuang Tzu noted, and hence nearly impossible to communicate to others. Chinese literary criticism insists on the supremacy of the lyric experience and the inexpressible moment. In representative works, single lines or couplets are selected to stand for the piece as a whole, and poetic styles are given impressionistic characterizations through the evocative use of descriptive phrases. Critical appreciation itself was an aesthetic experience, and reading criticism demanded no less sensitivity than reading poetry itself. Critics sought to suggest the "meaning beyond words" just as musicians of the period found their deepest satisfaction in the resonant silences between notes, or just after finishing playing.

Though criticism in the lyric mode may have been resolutely undiscursive, it nevertheless proposed to evaluate poets and poems. John Timothy Wixted offers a cogent analysis of this largely implicit process in his paper "The Nature of Evaluation in the *Shih-p'in* (Gradings of Poets) by Chung Hung (A.D. 469–518)." The text classifies poets into three evaluative grades, "upper, middle, and lower," drawing its language from contemporary rankings of talent. Yet Chung's evaluations also describe a poet's traits perceptively and objectively. Clear critical standards are to be inferred from the prefaces, where Chung stresses the expressive function of poetry and argues against the use of allusions and formal rules, but these standards are loosely applied in his individual critiques, where he attempts to be unbiased in judgment by focusing on particular traits. This is precisely where Wixted would locate Chung's own value as a critic. Rankings of poets in broad groupings are likely to have been influenced by extra-artistic factors such as social position or political career, but the identification of specific features of style forms the basis for later critical appreciation and analysis. Wixted therefore shows how a critic writing within and for the literary world described by Chang and DeWoskin can nonetheless be an important guide for critical scholarship responding to the needs of our own day.

In the Sung period, the striking group of talents in the circle around Su Shih (1037–1101) provided artistic and critical models of enduring influence, thus establishing a dominant ideal of the cultivated scholar expressing himself in arts such as poetry, painting, and calligraphy. This ideal and the taste associated with it were counterposed against the values of professional artists or specialists, who worked in a more limited range. The professionals' great technical skills were increasingly seen by critics as reflecting mere craftsmanship, hence as lacking in depth of sensitivity and creativity. The tensions between these two views of art were translated into practical and theoretical problems in later periods.

Another fundamental issue for the scholar-official elite centered on the purpose of artistic practice. According to Confucius, the gentleman should roam, or amuse himself, in the arts. If the cultivated man did not pursue the arts as a vocation, what was his aim? The Confucian revival which began in the late T'ang found brilliant and committed leadership in the Northern Sung, and was consolidated by Chu Hsi (1130–1200) in the Southern Sung into what is commonly termed Neo-Confucianism. This school placed the arts within a specific framework of moral self-cultivation. The various arts were accepted insofar as they served as a means of enhancing spiritual and moral development along the path outlined in the *Ta hsüeh* (The Great Learning), but they were also regarded with caution as tending to distract the practitioner from his greater end. Su Shih rejected this view and the concept of self-cultivation upon which it was based. His artistic practice and its relation to the intellectual issues of the day is explored by Christian Murck in "Su Shih's Reading of the *Chung Yung*." In interpreting this classic, Su Shih emphasized the spontaneity and naturalness of man. Faced with the unceasing, ever-shifting rhythms of the cosmos, the sage responds on the basis of his feelings, and the aesthetic ordering of this response is not merely a means of self-cultivation, it is itself an ideal end. From the point of view of intellectual history, Su Shih's essay on the *Chung yung* is a curiosity; unpersuasive as a hermeneutic reading, his argument did not carry the day. Yet in the broader context of Su Shih as artist and personality, and the enormous attraction he held and still holds for Chinese scholars, the essay has interest for the modern reader.

The second of the two papers on Sung figures is "Chiang K'uei's Treatises on Poetry and Calligraphy" by Shuen-fu Lin. Chiang K'uei (ca. 1155–ca. 1221) struggled in his poetics with a classic problem. Admiring Su Shih's genius, and inspired by Chuang Tzu's comments on attaining the Tao of an art, the mastery beyond any skill, Chiang K'uei maintained that "great poetry must be spontaneous and natural." On the other hand, Chiang was self-consciously heir to a long tradition of poetry within which Su Shih was only one of the more recent exemplars, and there was no doubt that extensive training in the methods of past masters was necessary before one could "forget the fish trap," in Chuang Tzu's analogy. Thus Chiang K'uei also said: "A true poet must attend to self-cultivation and to learning the methods." Hence there was a need for critical guides such as his *Shih shuo* (A Discourse on Poetry), even though ultimately they were only to be relied on temporarily as a means to an end. A key term in this text is *ch'i-hsiang*, "atmosphere," which is conceived of in Sung writings as "aura" or "outward manifestation" of style or personality. In Chiang K'uei's criticism, it is something that an author can manipulate, and therefore one sign that a poem is considered apart from its maker as an entity in itself. Lin believes that this attitude underlies Chiang's relatively lucid and direct analysis of the craft of composition. Similarly, in his colophons and treatises on calligraphy written between 1202 and 1209, Chiang is able to think of characters as objective entities, each with an "authentic form" not to be violated by "subjective opinion," and his critiques of specific styles and strokes are rigorous descriptions of calligraphic structure. Chiang K'uei's treatise on poetry has long been recognized as an important forerunner of Yen Yü's *Ts'ang-lang shih-hua* (Ts'ang-lang's Discussion of Poetry), the monumental thirteenth-century work which guided the orthodox school of poetics in the Ming dynasty. Lin Shuen-fu has now convincingly related both the literary and calligraphic criticism to a single ideal conception of the arts, and to the belief that the appropriate methodology can bring a full realization of that conception. Lin thus argues that Chiang K'uei was poised at an important watershed in cultural history, astride the divide between the traditional emphasis on self-realization and artistic expression, and the emergence of detached, pragmatic, and systematic criticism typical of later "academic" writings.

The last chapter, "Issues in Ming Criticism," presents the thrust and counter-thrust of archaism and anti-archaism, as well as of orthodoxy and individual-ism, frequently recurring in the literature on poetry and painting of the period. Richard John Lynn's "Alternate Routes to Self-Realization in Ming Theories of Poetry" sets out the major positions. The archaists, following the basic tenets of Yen Yü, were the poet-officials who dominated the literary world of fifteenth- and sixteenth-century China. They are associated in particular with the dictum formulated by Li Meng-yang (1472–1529) that prose (*wen*) must be that of the Ch'in and Han dynasties, and poetry (*shih*) that of the High T'ang period. These tenets were countered by various Ming expressionists, but the anti-archaist position was most strongly formulated by the Kung-an school, whose leader was Yüan Hung-tao (1568–1610). These writers did not insist on the distinction between poetic diction and prosaic diction, and appreciated Sung poets, or Su Shih in particular, for spontaneous, honest expression. As Lynn notes, for both sides poetry was a route to self-realization and spontaneity was the goal, but for the archaists poetry came from without and should be internalized, whereas for the expressionists poetry was to be revealed from within. The two poetic schools can be understood more fully against the political and cultural background of the period. "Authoritarian state ideology and archaism seem to have had a great deal in common," as Lynn remarks, and the most extreme attempt to free the individual from tradition by defining an autonomous self occurs in the radical philosophy of Li Chih (1527–1602), an associate of the Kung-an poets. Finally, on a general level, Lynn points out certain parallels between the Chinese archaists and Western neoclassicists, since both identify and emulate the works of particular periods, and both tend to view the mind as an entity to be shaped or conditioned. In this last respect they contrast with the Chinese individualists and Western romantics, who consider the mind to be spontaneously creative, and emphasize the role of expression in art.

The second parallel has been elaborated by several modern critics, and in opposition to their views, in "The Panoply of Images: A Reconsideration of the Literary Theory of the Kung-an School," Jonathan Chaves argues against applying the term "romantic" to the Kung-an poets. He emphasizes that Yüan Hung-tao and his followers recognized the quality of the major archaist poets at least, and shared certain of their beliefs, in particular the concept that poetry should contain ineffable reality. Although the Kung-an poets rejected any strict imitation of the formal aspects of earlier styles, they still accepted the principle of emulation, approving of inspiration drawn from the individualistic spirit of T'ang masters. As for their views on creativity, they did not simply advocate self-expression or "art for art's sake," but believed that a poem must reflect the concrete reality of actual places, at times embodying the fusion of the poet's emotion with the scene experienced. Chaves believes that the range of these opinions, their links to the orthodox mainstream, and their true value as criticism will be obscured if the Kung-an writers are merely dimissed as "romantics."

Questions of mislabeling or historical distortions in traditional Chinese art theory are taken up in the last two essays. In "The 'Wild and Heterodox School' of Ming Painting," Richard Barnhart offers a penetrating reevaluation of Ming professional artists. Discussing the values implicit in the art and lifestyles of the individualist followers of Tai Chin (1388–1462) and Wu Wei (1459–1508), Barnhart traces the gradual hardening of their image in sixteenth-century criticism. These artists aimed at heroic boldness and vigorous spontaneity in painting and calligraphy, as well as in life and personality. Their popularity was simply unacceptable to literati critics, who were full of contempt for their crudeness, and stressed the importance of an orthodox tradition in landscape painting. The only notable critic who could to some extent appreciate the alternative culture of boldness and originality, in art at least if not in thought and literature, was Wang Shih-chen (1526–1590). By the time of Tung Ch'i-ch'ang, all Ming painters except the scholar-artists were declared to be "heterodox." Barnhart argues that modern critics must gain a perspective on Ming art criticism by referring to the extant works of the professionals and to the fragmentary information about their lives. His hypothesis is that such a perspective reveals both the bias inherent in the judgments of most literati critics, and the artistic worth of the professionals' oeuvres. Barnhart therefore attempts to break apart the nexus between extant works, and the received view of historical development and standards of quality that perhaps unfairly shapes our understanding of Chinese painting.

An inside view of the evolution of literati taste can be gained from Susan E.

Nelson's study, "*I-p'in* in Later Painting Criticism." The term *i*, "free" or "untrammeled," was used to characterize the lofty recluses of the Six Dynasties period, with the associations of independence and high-mindedness. It entered painting criticism in the mid-ninth-century *T'ang-ch'ao ming-hua lu* (Records of Famous Painters of the T'ang Dynasty), where the category *i-p'in*, or "untrammeled class," was established to accommodate three wild and sketchy stylists who rejected orthodox methods. In Ming and Ch'ing times, the term *i* was generally restricted to the exceptional art of Mi Fu (1052–1107) and Ni Tsan (1301–1374) or their imitators. The earlier *i-p'in* masters were forgotten, and the "untrammeled" *i* of T'ang became the "relaxed" *i* of post-Yüan criticism. Basically, the idea of freedom associated with *i-p'in* painting was subsumed within the broader category of "scholar's painting." This quality now indicated a transcendence of historical limitations, an attaining of a self-created extreme in art. Although it did not refer originally to an artistic manner, it came to be associated with the specific styles of Mi and Ni, polarized opposites in their use of "ink" and "brush." These two artists were said to be inimitable, and critics stressed the complex resonances of the hidden "bone" in Mi's wetness and the concealed richness in Ni's aridity. Hence it is interesting that works by their followers, recognizably after the masters' styles, are also thought to contain the unlearnable quality of "untrammeledness." By the end of Ming, the concept is largely remade in the image of Ni Tsan: its range is thus limited to the balanced aspects of "refinement, subtlety, appropriateness, and understatement." It has become a scholarly *i* indeed, far removed from the unconventional wildness of the T'ang masters. This study of a shift in the meaning of critical terminology complements Barnhart's focus on the limitations of literati art criticism vis-a-vis the professionals. Both papers highlight the strength of the tradition that sustained and constrained artists and critics by the end of Ming.

Traditional Chinese criticism speaks from the center of a holistic culture and is increasingly aware of its inheritance from the past. Coming to it from another culture, and across the gulf of a fundamental discontinuity between the assumptions of the tradition and those of the modern world, one who seeks to understand it must essentially attempt an imaginative recreation. These essays are presented to the reader as efforts to contextualize various problems in the literature on the arts. The writers have tried to read sympathetically and yet to stand outside the tradition described in delineating historical relationships, in estimating the shifting usage of key terms, and in relating the theories of different arts and art criticisms to each other, and in turn to broader currents of thought. Despite the variety of strategies employed here, and the complexity of the subject matter, strands of continuity are evident. Lacking a compelling belief in an active Creator in anthropomorphic form, the Chinese critic tends to describe artistic creativity in terms of the transformations of natural creation, often taking the spontaneous, self-generating universe as a model. Basically this implies a mutuality between nature and man: throughout the classic formulations of Confucian and Taoist philosophers runs the common insistence that the sage has grasped and may yet again grasp the Way. From this source stems the deeply humanistic orientation of the Chinese artistic tradition, its focus on such key problems as the nature of self-expression, its approach to defining formal generic criteria, and its stress on the role of past masters as models. We hope that these essays support our original judgment that it is an appropriate moment to launch an interdisciplinary venture, and that readers will be stimulated by agreement or disagreement to pursue these themes further in their own roamings in the arts.

Susan Bush
Christian Murck

I / Comparative Perspectives on Literary Theory

Periodization in the Arts and Patterns of Change in Traditional Chinese Literary History

By Maureen Robertson

> Draw a blade and break the water—
> the water still flows on.
> (Li Po, "Giving a Farewell Dinner for
> Collator Shu-yün at the Hsieh T'iao
> Villa in Hsüan-chou."[a])

A universal physical analogue for the concept of time's process is the river, an unbroken flow which, though it may indeed have a main current, crosscurrents, and even an undercurrent, is known in its nature to be without segmentation. The segmentation of time by historians relies, in its simplest form, upon calendrical schemes, producing the chronicle. The writer of narrative history tells a story with a plot in which motivation and causality serve to explain relationships among pieces of historical data; he segments his tale as a collection of related episodes, each episode or period a cluster of more closely related micro-segments (for even events must be isolated from the "flow" and defined).[1]

Topical histories within the field of political or cultural history may employ a purely formal segmentation: units of one hundred years,[2] units determined strictly by what Collingwood has called "accidents of regal mortality," or units determined by a belief in immutable laws, expressed as regularity generalizations, which produce invariable sequences, regardless of the force of human purposefulness or natural disaster. Such sequences inform the historical writings of Oswald Spengler (*The Decline of the West*) and Arnold Toynbee (*A Study of History*). A more synthetic approach has consisted in the use of the period as a critical concept; specific periodizations emerge when a body of historical data is viewed in terms of both hypotheses about the subject of study and concepts of change in time (e.g. Marxist historians hypothesize that human history is best told as a history of economics and that economic arrangements will follow a fixed series of changes in time). A specific pattern of change is thus "discovered" to be intrinsic to the data, and this pattern is codified in the making of temporal cuts, periodizing.

Three simple models for the process of change in time are recognized in historiographical study: (1) cyclical, (2) directional or linear, and (3) irregular.[3] The cyclical

[a] 李白，宣州謝脁樓餞別校書叔雲

model is realized in narratives based upon the concept of recurrence (the "dynastic cycle" or repeated cycles of youth, maturity, and decline), periodicity (as in the "eternal return" of Mircea Eliade and, earlier, Friedrich Nietzsche), or oscillation between two poles or two complementary conditions (in the arts, Ernst Gombrich's "classical and nonclassical"; Roman Jakobson's metaphoric and metonymic poles as applied by him to arts history; or the universally useful poles, vigor and exhaustion, as in Wang Kuo-wei's summary of literary history).[4] Directional models are realized in periodizations which trace the linear development of "progress" (with evolutionary and revolutionary versions) or its inversion, decline from a Golden Age. Directional periodizations in the West have had a teleological character; movement is toward an anticipated end—the perfection of human reason, the Last Judgment, utopian social order, or the triumph of technology. In the arts, this model is represented by, for example, early modern histories of fiction based on the implicit premise that earlier works exhibit a slow but sure "advance" toward realism and the effaced narrator,[5] or histories of painting which describe the progressive "conquest" or solution of technical problems (e.g. the "problem" of perspective). The concept of a dialectical process has produced a cyclical model with linear development, a spiral.[6] The irregular periodization claims strict dependence upon the configurations of the data studied and does not, in its structure at least, display a belief that change obeys laws of regularity or directionality. Nevertheless, that the historian is likely to discover patterns he is culturally predisposed to see is to be expected. When historians claim a close fit between their patterned or periodized accounts and actualities of the past, it is often easy to forget how highly selective a body of historical data is, how compelling the need to construct meanings is, and how processes of historical generalization and cultural coding work to shape that body. In his story "Funes the Memorius," Jorge Luis Borges portrays a man who, by a freak accident, is condemned to perfect recall, an inability to remember selectively. Certainly, he could accurately reconstruct an entire day (it required an entire day); however, Ireneo Funes was unable to forget differences, to generalize. In fact, he had difficulty forming the classifications upon which abstract thought depends: "... it bothered him that the dog at three fourteen (seen from the side) should have the same name as the dog at three fifteen (seen from the front)."[7] We accept the generalizing process in historiography and the periodizing activity which is a part of it, as a function of thought itself. However, as a corrective for necessarily limited, though valuable, individual solutions, it is desirable to have a plurality of periodizations of the historical subject, each based upon differing criteria of selection and ordering, each with a slightly different plot.

Why periodize at all? Indeed, this subject of periodization is of little interest to more recent theorists of synchronic modes of historical study, and it has shared in the general decay of interest in traditional historiographical approaches. (As a part of the methodology of history, it has in fact not often been a subject upon which historians themselves have had much to say, either because they regarded it simply as a convenience and not a theory-based tool, or because they did not feel it necessary to spell out the model implicit in their own periodizations.[8]) Remote in time is St. Augustine, whose linear, epochal periodization based on the six days of creation began with the five epochs prior to Christ's birth and was to end after the sixth with the Last Judgment. Similarly remote is a Chinese counterpart, Shao Yung (1011–1077), whose grand scheme contained fixed periods in a hierarchical arrangement, culminating in cycles of 129,600 years, each segment exhibiting the *yin-yang* rhythms of the seasonal cycle.[9] Yet these efforts remind one that aside from fulfilling the desideratum of convenience for the treatment of a large mass of data viewed diachronically, periodization in any of its forms is one response to the necessity of recovering an intelligible pattern from what seriously threatens to remain formless and meaningless—the processes of change in time. The propensity of earlier historians and philosophers to reconstitute the history of practically anything as an enactment of divinely or naturalistically founded laws of change alerts one to the urgency of the desire for coherence. In a time of greater intellectual and religious pluralism, this urgency is still with us, though modes of interpreting change have themselves changed. Systems analysis, structuralist models, and the tracing of the permutations of a *problematique* have provided nonteleological, nonlinear models which now suggest new bases for periodization.[10]

At a more functional level, it is the historian's business to tell "what happened" and, in so doing,

> ... to produce an account that will make sense as a single account, and one in which he and others can take an interest. He must either tell a story that will hold together as a narrative with causal and purposive connections ... or explain some phenomenon ... that is presumed to be puzzling or otherwise in need of explanation.[11]

Historical reconstructions must be convincing, and the marking of significant temporal units within a history is one means by which the writer implies that he has a reasoned command of *all* the relevant temporally conditioned events that fall within the span he treats. When marking period boundaries, the writer is likely to use an explanatory "code" or myth which is already culturally validated to such a degree that, as a code, it is transparent (not recognized as merely one possible construction or reading of the available data), providing what seems a bright, clear window on the truth about processes of change in time.

The foregoing has been intended as a general background to more specific remarks on the special concerns of periodization in the arts and, following that, a consideration of approaches to periodization and models of change in some premodern discussions of, primarily, literary history in China.

Periodization in the arts has in varying degrees shown reliance upon the efforts of historians in other areas of culture. Frequently, the arts have simply borrowed a segmentation and plot from political or intellectual histories; this has been especially true for earlier periods in the West, and strong ideological, aesthetic, and formal links between the arts and the rest of culture continued to be recognized later by historians of art such as Heinrich Wölfflin, who felt that one could speak of a "spirit of the times," perceptible in social behavior, artistic styles, philosophical ideas, and political activity.[12] From a modern Western point of view, period schemes borrowed from political and intellectual history are to be termed "extrinsic," not being based on evidence taken exclusively from the art objects themselves. From a traditional Chinese point of view, the political periodization cannot be seen as wholly extrinsic to arts history; even a writer as interested in stylistic features as T'ang dynasty anthologist Yin Fan (fl. 740) felt he could attribute the glory of T'ang poetry to the reigning emperor's having rejected one style and favored another.[13] In such a situation it is difficult to speak precisely of "histories of the arts." (Indeed, there are no full-scale histories of literature in traditional China, though the same is not true for calligraphy and painting.) Artistic activity was not felt to take place in isolation from the complex and powerful forces set in motion by the character and authority of individual reigning sovereigns, and periodization by political periods serves not only descriptive but explanatory functions in traditional historical thinking. As Arthur Wright has said,

> ... the persistent holism that was part of the self-image of Chinese civilization meant that the phases of the [dynastic] cycle were thought to be reflected in all areas of culture—creativity in poetry and painting, the ethos of the peasant villages, the morals and mores of the elite, the rise and fall of the price level. It is not surprising, therefore, to find regularity generalizations that correlate effete or over-ornamented literary style with dynastic decline.[14]

The concept of *shih*, [b] "configurational dynamics," was another support for holistic approaches. The profile of change in time was thought to be a material and social realization of all-inclusive processes of interaction and change that animated the world; one was therefore compelled to view each human activity and natural happening in a larger context. While historical writing on calligraphy and painting has seemed more comfortable with intrinsic criteria for both marking and explaining change, views of the literary past, even those using stylistic criteria to mark change, may explain change by relating it to the phases of the dynastic cycle.

Periodizations of the arts have been said to involve special problems because of the nature of the attitude of art historians toward their data. Social and political historians can, with a degree of confidence, refer description and explanation to

b 勢

"facts." In their reconstitution of the past, they may turn to documentary evidence the significance of which is rarely in dispute (birth certificates, treatises, legal records); the institutionalized authority behind such data tends to inspire a general agreement as to its validity. But in histories of the arts, a critical attitude toward the data and aesthetic judgments inevitably play a larger role, not only in the business of describing what happened but also in the authentication and interpretation of the data themselves. The authority for statements appears to reside more fully in the art historian's personal claims to sound artistic judgments in the discrimination of styles and assessments of value and influence. If the writer is not a professional historian of the arts (retaining the quasi-institutional authority of his profession) but simply a person of cultivated taste, as in traditional China, the personal nature of the claim is even more pronounced. Out of such a situation comes historical writing that is more clearly interpretive or critical, inviting debate and new interpretation.

In an integrated, full history of an art, the job of the scholar who marshalls data to provide a narrative account of the past, structured so as to suggest a meaningful pattern of change, and that of the critic concerned with the description of technique and medium, with judgments regarding indebtedness, quality, and authenticity, require a coordination of great delicacy. An otherwise well-supported theory of change may, for instance, be seriously undermined by its inability to account for the appearance of major figures who, though they may form the very center of interest of the history of an art, may yet sit like alien beings among those many others whose works collectively yield up the norms thought to identify periods in question. Their own norm-giving influence will be felt in subsequent periods. Indeed, some writers will prefer to periodize in terms of the dominating influence of the major figures, placing them at the beginning of periods, rather than in terms of the dominance of period styles, genres, technical innovations, or leading themes. The idea of a span of dominance, whether of collective norms or of the influence of major figures, is a crucial critical concept governing periodizations in the arts which rely more heavily upon intrinsic criteria. Whether the source of the dominating influence is single or multiple, whether the boundaries marking either side of the time span are indeterminate or distinct, and whether the entire geographical area under consideration is seen to be uniformly affected—these are the more problematic issues.[15]

René Wellek has argued, in writings on general literary history, the baroque, romanticism, and symbolism, for the usefulness of period concepts and terms. He has rejected conceptualizations of literary periods seen as ideal or psychological types (the romantic, the classical) not linked to specific historical contexts, and he has implied that dominance should be determined on a basis of not one stylistic feature, theme, genre, or "metaphysical essence which must be intuited" but by a "system of literary norms, standards, and conventions, whose introduction, spread, diversification, integration, and disappearance can be traced."[16] This definition appears to point to formal and thematic criteria as the basis of the norms in question; elsewhere, however, Wellek seems to suggest that ultimately ideas, not works themselves, are the sources of these norms: " 'Period' demands the dominance (but not the total dictatorial rule) of a set of norms which, in the case of romanticism, are provided sufficiently by similar or analogous concepts of the imagination, nature, symbol and myth." [17]

Thus, one arrives at a problem faced particularly by historians of literature. The history of an art may be told as a story of successive alterations in masters and schools or developments in skills, styles, genres, and technical conventions; it may on the other hand be wholly or partly told as a drama of ideas, or conflict of ideals, deriving from general philosophy or philosophy of the arts. Formal and thematic elements of the works in question are, in the latter case, seen to have a meaning principally in terms of some ideologically or philosophically validated pattern. It is especially historians of literature who tend to combine the two modes, due to the nature of the literary medium as a vehicle for the relatively more explicit expression of ideas and states of mind. While initially historians of calligraphy and painting in China, writing mainly in chronicle format, were freer than those discussing portions of literary history to focus on intrinsic criteria and to explain change in terms of individual genius, direct influence of predecessors, master models, and technical innovations, in later centuries, styles and style models themselves became more complexly referential, carrying moral, philosophical or social implications; at the same time, historical writing about calligraphy and painting became more informed with the explanatory myths used by social historians and philosophers, as these arts came fully into the orbit of the Confucian life. Thus, from late T'ang onward, accounts of calligraphy and painting, like those of literature, are often histories which mix two modes.

Periodization of verse and music in China could be said to begin in connection with an evaluation of what were termed in the *Mao shih* preface and Cheng Hsüan's commentary the *pien*,[c] "transformed" or "deviate", songs among the odes, those attributed by Cheng Hsüan to the reign of the Chou king I and after. Occurring in the prehistory of literature as belles-lettres, the judgment that at a certain juncture in Chou political history some *shih* became inferior as models of song because they expressed in their melodies, language, moods, and themes a change for the worse in the mores of Chou society is important in its complete identification of what we usually distinguish today as ethical and artistic standards of judgment. In such a context, the notion "artistic" is relatively meaningless. Cheng Hsüan places *cheng*,[d] "correctness," in opposition to *pien*, and the latter must be understood in context to mean "deviance, departure from the correct standard." As Chu Tzu-ch'ing has demonstrated, *pien* had in pre-Han and early Han times a history of usage which did not require that it be used in a pejorative sense.[18] However, with literary history

[c] 變   [d] 正

subsumed to social and ethical history, the decline ascribed to Chou culture as a whole must necessarily be shared by all its parts. Lo Ken-tse has called attention to a passage in the *Tso chuan* (Hsiang 29) in which we see clearly that those songs regarded as beautiful were felt to be expressive of order and social harmony; ethical and aesthetic values are one precisely because of the predominantly functional value of the *shih*. Music and poetry were numbered among those activities that contributed to personal development, social unity, and the stability of the state; they could thus naturally be appreciated in terms of how successfully they fulfilled those functions. Change could be defined as a difference in the manner or extent of their functionality. The nobleman from Wu who appears in the *Tso chuan* passage just referred to enjoys a performance of songs, *ko*,[e] from the various feudal states. He comments on each in turn: "Beautiful!"; "Great!"; "Reflective, but not timid!"; "As with heaven, there is nothing they do not cover; as with earth, there is nothing they do not sustain!"; "If there *is* some other music, I would not venture to request it!" When the music of the (degenerate) state of Ch'en is played for him, he says, "When a state has no ruler, how can it endure for long?" The text observes that he did not inquire into the remainder of the songs (*feng*[f]).[19]

Writers during Han and after, who increasingly appreciated fine writing for its demonstration of language skills and as an instrument of distinctive personal expression, were obliged to come to terms with the functional view of written literature. The new literary forms and the interest in formal aesthetic values needed to be given sanction by being integrated theoretically, to find their place within the holistic vision of human activity. Essays offering descriptions of the origin and development of the new verse and of calligraphy, along with critical treatises and letters drawing terminologies of value from canonical sources were the instruments by which artistic activity was given a place and a meaning within the larger cultural context.

The vigorous emergence of belle-lettristic writing from the third to the sixth centuries was an event which included the recognition of generic categories, the creation of literary lineages, the coining or borrowing of descriptive and value-weighted terms for styles, the evaluation and ranking of writings and writers, the preservation of a specifically literary past in anthologies, and, most important, the identification of the sources of the authority (the classics, the natural world order, Tao) which had to be claimed for belles-lettres if they were to be recognized as a worthy pursuit. This legitimatizing effort in all its intensity and variety provided for the development of an art-historical writing in which stylistic and generic criteria were employed in the marking of change, while the patterns of change perceived and the explanatory material reflected writers' reliance upon structures and ideas found in historical and philosophical writings. Alterations of styles and themes could

[e] 歌　　　　　　[f] 風

still be viewed in terms of moral values, and change (despite recognition of direct literary influence) could be felt to have its ultimate source in natural or social forces.

Binomes used to characterize styles, through the centuries when fine writing was establishing its claims, were often value-weighted in terms of their reference (or lack of it) to the classics (e.g. *tien-ya*,[g] *chih*[h]), attributes of the *chün-tzu*[i] (*pin-pin*,[j] *pu-yüan*[k]), or attributes ascribed to nature or Tao (*tzu-jan*,[l] *wen-hou*[m]). Describing literature in terms applied to the classics, cultivated men, or nature, of course transferred the values and authority inherent in these to literature and established fine writing as itself a source of such values. The newer linguistic complexity and ornament might derive its sanction from an association with the flourishing of plants and flowers in nature, however such a defence was risky; all were aware of the classical passages which advised one to seek fruits, *shih*,[n] not flowers, *hua*.[o] *Hua* could thus be, and was, used pejoratively, while "new and different," *hsin-ch'i*,[p] having no authority behind it at all, was nearly always a term of strict disapproval, at least until the T'ang.

For calligraphy and poetry, the legitimatizing efforts began in late Han, when both lyric poetry and the grass script began to offer highly personalized modes of expression. The very terms of Chao I's attack on grass script made it clear that the wide interest in this art would need to be sanctioned by writings which might invoke the authority of the classics, say, by comparing calligraphic forms to the hexagrams of the *I ching*: "Above it is not that which was conferred by the signs of Heaven; below it is not that which was given forth by the Yellow River or the Lo; in the middle it is not that which was fashioned by the sages."[20] Though early writers on painting, such as Hsieh Ho (fl. A.D. 500–535) and Yao Tsui (A.D. 535–602) refer to the ethical functions of painting and the parallel between nature's process and that of the painter, it is Chang Yen-yüan's *Li-tai ming-hua chi* (finished in 847) which places painting legitimately within the context of the established world order, just as Liu Hsieh's *Wen-hsin tiao-lung* had shown, through an elaborate argument, that all of literature, including belles-lettres, was written in the stars.

The interest in analysis of formal elements in poetry during T'ang does not significantly displace the view of poetry as more than an art, in the modern sense, though it certainly helps to increase the tension between those primarily concerned with the effects of poetry on its audience and those more interested in artistry and in turning the expressive and revelatory functions of poetry to more personal uses. Analysis of the components of poems simply adds another dimension to critical activity, an interest in composition and individualized artistry which was to be integrated at a higher level in later critical writings when a choice of technique was

g 典雅　　　　　　　k 不怨　　　　　　　n 實
h 質　　　　　　　　l 自然　　　　　　　o 華
i 君子　　　　　　　m 溫厚　　　　　　　p 新奇
j 彬彬

felt to carry stronger moral or philosophical implications. However, a reaction to the intensified interest in more strictly artistic values and in stylistic variety or novelty helped stimulate further change in literary historical writing and criticism; partisan support of particular early figures and a stronger evaluative character distinguish accounts of the literary past from the eleventh century on. The importance attached to positions on literary issues increases as literature assumes a more important role in the process of personal self-cultivation; an atmosphere of debate surrounds much of the historical and critical discussion of later centuries.

Several models for marking the stages of change in literary history appear in premodern writings on the arts in China.[21] A review of these will show that the cyclical, linear (with directional subtypes), spiral, and irregular patterns are all represented. Few sources aim at such extensive and detailed accounts of their past as are to be found in Chung Hung's *Shih p'in* and Chang Yen-yüan's *Li-tai ming-hua chi*; most writers summarize the stages of change in a way that makes the model relied upon and the criteria used to measure change immediately evident. On the whole, writers will be seen to be more interested in the operations of change as a continuous "flow" (*liu*[q]) than in isolating and labeling unitary time blocs, in contrast to the greater reliance of Western arts historians upon unitary period concepts such as classic, baroque, or romantic.

The simplest form of periodizing is division into two or three large segments (or "megaperiods," a term suggested by Erwin Panofsky in describing the Renaissance as one great period separating the Middle Ages from the Modern Age). The tripartite "ancient, medieval, and modern" is a staple of Western and of modern Chinese literary histories. In the third and fourth centuries, Chinese writers recognized two vaguely defined periods, that of the ancients and that of the moderns. For Chih Yü (?–ca. 312) in his *Wen-chang liu-pieh lun* the ancients were the authors of pre-Han prose works, the *Shih* poets, and Ch'ü Yüan, but by T'ang the Chien-an (A.D. 196–220) poets could be called ancients; and from later Sung onward, the poets of High T'ang (ca. 713–766) were included among the ancients. For Ch'ih Yü, as for his successors in criticism, the relationship between the literary products of the two ages was a matter of intense interest. He defines the classical genres and traces changes in each up to his own time. These changes are not used to mark period subdivisions however, a fact which is in keeping with the author's view of change in a given genre as a linear "flow," a continuous "transformation from past to present" (*ku chin chih pien*[r]).[22] Using an analogue from Buddhism, Sung critic Yen Yü (ca. 1200) effectively divided the history of poetry down to his own time into two segments. The "superior vehicle" (*shang sheng*[s]) or "first principle" (*ti-i i*[t]) (Mahāyāna teaching) represented poetry from Han through High T'ang (with a few later stragglers), while "the inferior vehicle" (Hīnayāna teaching) was

q 流
r 古今之變

s 上乘
t 第一義

poetry from the T'ang Ta-li period (766–779) onward.[23] In the Ming, Hu Ying-lin (fl. 1590), author of the critical miscellany *Shih sou*, summarized the history of poetry to show that the *shih* genre exhausted itself in T'ang, giving way to *tz'u* and to *ch'ü*. Finally, as verse writing lost its resources altogether, narration became the focal point of literary interest.[24] Hu's megaperiods are established on the basis of generic dominance; failure to dominate, or generic exhaustion, opens the way for the emergence of new, if lesser, forms. His two periods could be labeled "*shih*" and "other." Indeed, all of the many other critics who repeated—in virtually the same words—that in T'ang the expressive and compositional aspects of *shih* had reached their fulfillment (*pei*[u]) were effectively confirming a division into two great periods, with High T'ang as a pivotal point in the history of poetry, the end of a long era of development after which writers of *shih* sought in various ways to preserve the values and high standard of their T'ang predecessors and after which only the appearance of a literary giant such as Han Yü or Su Shih makes a significant historiographical ripple. The outlines of this general scheme reappear in modern writings; the following description by Wen Fong of two stages in Chinese arts history provides an example:

> A brief survey of the histories of figure painting, calligraphy, and thought in China will show that they shared a common pattern of development: after a primary evolutionary phase, they each went through successive *fu-ku* or "return to the archaic" movements.[25]

Linear models of change, from simpler two-stage schemes to more elaborate accounts of successive "transformations," are the most numerous of the types in early Chinese writings. A distinguished representative of an important variety of the linear model, the *Shih p'in* by Chung Hung (fl. 505) establishes dual literary lineages for pentasyllabic verse, using stylistic affinities and influence as the criteria for relatedness. The two major lineages have their separate sources in the *Shih* and the *Ch'u tz'u*. Chung Hung's model here is one found in historical biography, the family saga in which, starting from an ancestral family head, generation begets generation, good forebears are followed by descendants who can be recognized by family resemblances (but who often carry the features in a coarsened form). There are strong figures and many others who should not serve as models for the younger generation. Using political period markers, Chung Hung singles out reign eras (not mentioning individual emperors) and notes a revival (*chung-hsing*[v]) during the T'ai-k'ang era of Chin (280–289), followed by exhaustion (*chin*[w]) after the Yung-chia (307–312) era—specifically, exhaustion of the affective power (*feng li*[x]) in verse for which poets of the Chien-an era were the models. However, revival and exhaustion

[u] 備　　　　　　　[w] 盡
[v] 中興　　　　　　[x] 風力

in the *Shih p'in* are not portrayed as periodic, remaining isolated events in the account of stylistic descent. In Chung Hung's preface, major figures are declared but their dominance does not form the basis of literary periods. Here the model for the relevant passages appears to be, again, historiographical; one sees a literary version of a chronicle of heroes.

> Ts'ao Chih is the great eminence of Chien-an, with Kung-kan [Liu Chen] and Chung-hsüan [Wang Ts'an] second in command; Lu Chi is the glorious figure of T'ai-k'ang, with An-jen [P'an Yüeh] and Ching-yang [Chang Hsieh] second in command; Hsieh the Guest [Hsieh Ling-yün] is the hero of the Yüan-chia era (423–453), with Yen Yen-[chih] second in command.[26]

The successive terms *chieh, ying,* and *hsiung*[y] suggest a mildly declining order of greatness, and though Chung Hung goes on to call these figures "the crowns of pentasyllabic verse," there is a hint of the rhetoric of decline. The story of decline, though it has its place in the family saga as a topos, is not, however, the main theme of Chung Hung's account.

The tracing of lineages based primarily upon shared stylistic modalities and common links with early models became one of the most important ways of structuring historical accounts of literature and the arts in China. In the Sung dynasty, Yen Yü transposed the family saga, with its potential for multiple lines of descent, into the realm of the sacred, with the transmission of esoteric religious teaching and the true Buddhist patriarchal succession analogues for the lineage of true artistic excellence down through the T'ang. In this version, the two lineages given are not equally acceptable. Similarly in Ming, literary critics such as Kao Ping (fl. 1393) and art critics such as Chan Ching-feng (ca. 1545–ca. 1600) and Tung Ch'i-ch'ang (1555–1636) identified canonical models and traced out lineages so that the correct (*cheng*) models for emulation were established. As James Cahill points out, Tung follows Chan in using a dual-lineage structure; however Tung incorporates a judgmental aspect by means of discussing the two lineages in terms of the "orthodox" and "heterodox" Northern and Southern schools of Buddhism, as Yen Yü had done with poetry (though Yen Yü's two literary lineages were not concurrent or parallel in time as Tung's lineages for painting were).[27]

Linear models of change in China include both progressive and retrograde directional forms. Hsiao T'ung (501–531), in his preface to the *Wen hsüan,* advances the "ice is colder than water" concept of progressive change. Again, there is little interest shown in marking out a series of stages of change in fine writing; it is the nature and direction of change which require explanation. The humble oxcart of antiquity, he reasons, loses its clumsiness in an evolved form, the imperial carriage,

[y] 傑，英，雄

while ice keeps the original form of water but water undergoes an internal change, an increase in density which transforms it into something new, different, and valued. In each case the derivative item has a superior value.[28] The optimistic view which Hsiao T'ung took of innovation and departures from the standard (*hsin pien*[z])—words often used pejoratively by late Six Dynasties and early T'ang critics such as P'ei Tzu-yeh and Li Ao—must have had considerable influence upon T'ang readers of the *Wen hsüan*. Echoing Hsiao T'ung's confidence, Sun Kuo-t'ing, author of an early T'ang work on calligraphy, argues against the belief that earlier models are necessarily superior models. He asks, "Who would change his sculptured palace for a cave dwelling or his jade chariot for a clumsy cart?"[29]

The retrograde directional model is represented in chapter 29 of Liu Hsieh's early sixth-century *Wen-hsin tiao-lung*. There he gives succinct descriptions of the songs and written literature of nine successive ages; the ages are defined in dynastic terms. The songs of the first ages have vitality and worth, but since successive ages all model themselves upon immediate predecessors and not on the "source," the disparity in quality between the first, best model and the products of succeeding ages increases. Literature thus becomes, he claims, weak and artificial, having lost touch with the natural poetic expression it had in its early beginnings. Using Liu's own analogue, we can call this the "blue comes from indigo" syndrome. ("Blue comes from indigo, red comes from madder; though [the reds and blues] may go beyond the original color, they themselves are incapable of further transmutation."[30]) In an attempt to reconcile the ideal of an ancient source with the reality of change, Liu employs the sense of *pien*, "transformation," found in the early philosophers in his concept of "transforming while carrying through," *t'ung pien*.[aa] Recognizing that there are constants in literary genres (*yu ch'ang chih t'i*[ab])—the principles embodied in the classics—while at the same time there are an unlimited number of possible changes (*pien wen chih shu wu fang*[ac]) he argues that generic names and principles should be consonant with established past models but that literary language and the force of personality (*wen-tz'u ch'i-li*[ad]) should admit of variety and newness. By this means, the writer does not lose contact with the wellsprings; he may travel a "road without end" and simultaneously "drink from the inexhaustible source."[31] This early argument for intertexuality, for the continuous interfolding of sameness and difference, suggests how Chinese writers might have been less satisfied with static, bloc periodization of the arts than were their Western counterparts.

In chapter 45 of the *Wen-hsin tiao-lung*, Liu tells quite a different story, one with a much more detailed but less regular plot development. This chapter contains a history of imperial influence upon letters. Using dynastic, reign, and era markers, Liu describes the fate of literature in successive political periods. The account is quite close from Han on, and in specifying the nature of each sovereign's involvement in

---

| z 新變 | ab 有常之體 | ad 文辭氣力 |
| aa 通變 | ac 變文之數無方 | |

the literature and scholarship of his time, Liu has provided a brief but complete history of imperial literary sponsorship or patronage. There is a hint of periodicity in his description of Emperor Ming of Chin as the Emperor Wu of Han of his day, however the entire account must be seen as an irregular procession of slumps, revivals, regressions, and surges in the fate of letters, all dependent upon the personal will of rulers and the climates they fostered, rather than upon collective moral slippage, loss of contact with the source, or impersonal cosmic forces. This plot, the more interesting and valuable for its untidiness, ends not with a call for reform but on a note of triumph, as Liu celebrates the enlightened ruler of the current dynasty.[32]

A concern with decline, whether periodic or cumulative, seems to be characteristic of literary critics and historians in every tradition, in varying degrees. In accounts of the literary past in China, decline was a persistent thematic element; some merely deplored the failures of their immediate predecessors in time-honored fashion, but others believed that true poetry, having suffered a gradual diminution over the centuries, was about to vanish altogether. In the early years of a new dynasty, complaints about the decline of literary excellence may be to some extent rhetorical signals that the stage is being set for a new dynastic and cultural enterprise and that scholar-officials are declaring their essential function as preservers of fundamental cultural values at a time when it is important to firmly establish this role in relations with the new ruling house. Not motivated by such factors, however, T'ang poet Po Chü-i sincerely believed that poetry must recover its ancient admonitory function and put itself directly in the service of society as a whole. He makes decline the dominant theme of his summary of *shih* history. In his view, the *sao* and early pentasyllabic lyrics still retained a measure of the quality of the classical songs, but from Chin and Sung on, "people went from the profundity and learnedness of Hsieh Ling-yün to an obsession with landscapes, and from the noble, archaic style of T'ao Ch'ien (372?–427) they proceeded to indulge themselves exclusively in rusticism. Those writing after the manner of Chiang Yen (444–505) and Pao Chao (405–466) were even more narrow."[33] Increasingly limited in seriousness and scope, poetry finally loses its link to the six principles of the *Shih* completely. In T'ang, even Tu Fu's (712–770) collection contains too few *yüeh-fu* satires to qualify him for unreserved praise, and Po Chü-i concludes that if the situation is to be remedied, a personal commitment is required. "I have always been keenly unhappy over the collapse and ruin of the proper way of the *shih*, and in sudden moods of passionate concern I sometimes fail to eat and sleep, thinking that, whether I have the ability or not, I shall undertake to sustain it myself."[34] In Po's account, decline is located in such aspects as genres, prominent figures, and stylistic modes, while the model is one of progressive loss, marked formally in dynastic terms. Decline is not explained with reference to dynastic succession, however.

If change in time is viewed as a continuous process, there are moments when a change which has been gradually taking place may suddenly appear to us in its aspect of completeness or fulfillment. Something once known is no longer there, and something else stands in its place; a transformation, *pien*, has occurred, a turning point in history. The linear account of literary history in which periods are effectively created through a focus upon these moments of completed transformation is one of the staples of historical discussion of the arts in China. The transformation itself may be regarded as a positive, negative, or neutral event. Down through the early T'ang historians, there is general agreement on the major turning points in literature: the appearance of *sao*; Su Wu and Li Ling's pentasyllabic lyrics in Han; the Ts'ao family's leadership in and patronage of poetry in the third century; the burst of major talent in the T'ai-k'ang era of Chin; the rise of a new subject, the natural world, in the fifth century; the advocacy of prosodic rules by Wang Jung, Hsieh T'iao, and Shen Yüeh in the late fifth and early sixth centuries; and the falling off into shallowness and language play during the fifth and sixth centuries.[35] Criteria for locating turning points recognize the variety of factors in literary activity: genres, dominant figures, patronage, topics, and stylistic and prosodic features. Further concensus was reached, as mentioned above, in regard to the complete development or fulfillment, *pei*, of forms of *shih* during the K'ai-yüan era of T'ang (713–742). Writing in the early 750s, Yin Fan precisely dates this consummation as having taken place after the sixteenth year of K'ai-yüan, when "melodic and harmonic elements, affective and compositional aspects were, for the first time, brought to fulfillment!" (*sheng-lü feng-ku shih pei i*[ae]).[36] This dictum is echoed for centuries afterward in summaries describing the major transformations. Ming critic Hu Chen-heng (fl. 1630) reduced the story of development to four chapters, with the final chapter set in T'ang.

> From the *feng* and *ya* onward, *shih* underwent a complete transformation and the *Li sao* came into existence; it transformed again to become the pentasyllabic *shih* of Western Han; when it transformed a third time, the songs, ballads, and assorted styles came into being; then it transformed a fourth time to produce the tonally regulated *shih* of T'ang. When *shih* reached T'ang, its embodiments achieved their great fulfillment.[37]

A belief in the inevitable succession of genres (sometimes associated strictly with the succession of dynasties), is also widely expressed in critical writings. Ming critic Hu Ying-lin, confining his comment to *shih*, wrote:

> After the four-syllable line, a transformation took place and there was the *Li sao*; after the *Li sao* a transformation took place and there was pentasyllabic verse [and so on with septasyllabic verse, tonally regulated verse, and the quatrain appearing in turn]: the embodiments of *shih* transformed in successive stages.[38]

[ae] 聲律風骨始備矣

The concept of *shih-yün*,[af] "the coursing of the times," referring to the continual processes of temporal movement, is often used to explain that change is inevitable and need not be considered either strange or undesirable. Ch'ing critic Yeh Hsieh (1627–1703), for instance, rejects the principle he believes implicit in Ming archaists' elevation of the literature of Han and High T'ang by alluding to this idea.

> Ever since there was a world, the coursing of the generations and the diverse forms of vital energy have continuously transformed and shifted, so that one thing has given way to another....[39]

> It is not that what is earlier is bound to be in a situation of flourishing and what is later is bound to be in a situation of decline.[40]

The analogues used in critical writings to make this concept of continuous change more vivid reflect the underlying organismic structures and integrative processes implicit in much of traditional Chinese thought. They include that of the river (with its flow, currents, rapids, calms, tributaries, blind channels, pure and muddy waters, dwindling side-streams, and sources) and the topographical analogue of peaks and valleys (*shih*[b]), representing the configuration of high and low points of achievement in which the dominance of important figures is like that of mountain peaks rising over the landscape, visible from afar. There is also, of course, the analogue of the tree, springing from a root which provides endless nourishment for the successive growth of trunk, branches, flowers, fruits, and twigs. Yeh Hsieh observes,

> If poetry has a source (*yüan*[ag]), it necessarily has an outflow (*liu*[ah]). Having a root (*pen*[ai]), it must extend itself to branch-tips (*mo*[aj]). Moreover, there is such a thing as being based in the outflow and going upstream to the source, or following back along the branch-tips so as to return to the root. There is no end to the study and practice of it [poetry]; its ordered pattern (*li*[ak]) emerges every day. Thus we know that the way (*tao*[al]) of poetry is something in which every single day one thing succeeds another, one thing gives way to another....[41]

When the concept of *shih-yün* is used to explain changes in literature, the markers of change are likely to be major figures, whose differing but equally extraordinary achievements give expression to the inexhaustibility and dynamism of change in time.

Should the larger forces that propel change in time be viewed as periodic, the writer in question will draw upon a cyclic conception of change culturally available

af 時運，世運
ag 源
ah 流

ai 本
aj 末

ak 理
al 道

in theories of *yin-yang* dynamics. Cyclic models of the periodic or oscillating type, in which the old/new, the austere-and-simple/ornate-and-refined, or the vigorous/exhausted pairs alternate, propose that literature, in its own way, exhibits the universal, cosmic rhythms. As Yeh Hsieh explains,

> The familiar and the new—these two, with regard to their functioning principle, are interdependent (*tui-tai*[am]) [or complementary]. And as for the principle of interdependence, from the time the Grand Ultimate generated the Two Primal Processes (*liang i*,[an] *yin* and *yang*), onward, no event or thing has been exempt from it. Sun and moon, cold and heat, day and night, and also the great variety of human affairs such as life and death, noble birth and low estate, poverty and wealth, loftiness and baseness, the superior and the inferior, the far and the near, the novel and the familiar, large and small, sweet and foul, deep and shallow, bright and dim—these various poles (*tuan*[ao]) are so numerous that they are impossible to calculate.[42]

> ... if we take up a single time period for discussion, then after there is flourishing there is bound to be a decline. Speaking in terms of a thousand years, then there may be flourishing, but [a given thing] is bound to reach a period of decline. However, it is also bound to start from the decline and return to a state of flourishing.[43]

Yeh incorporates the theme of alternate flourishing and decline in his argument against the archaist belief in a directional pattern of change.

> If we examine in turn the poetry from Han and Wei on and follow the ups and downs of source and outflow, we cannot declare that the correct is the source, ever flourishing, and that with transformations as the outflow, poetry then begins to decline. The fact is that what is correct exhibits a gradual decline and, therefore, the transformation can initiate a [new] flourishing. For example, the poetry of Chien-an is truly correct, truly flourishing! But after people had written in the same fashion for a time, poetry flowed into a decline. Those among later figures whose powers (*li*[ap]) were great brought about major transformations and those whose powers were lesser made minor transformations. Various poets of the Six Dynasties were on occasion able to bring about minor transformations, but none of them by himself could present an unfamiliar face. Early T'ang went along with their vulgarly overdone and superficially beautiful mannerisms, with lines cut to their patterns and words paired with theirs. Such poetry was neither "ancient" nor "regulated." This was a point of

am 對待　　　ao 端
an 兩儀　　　ap 力

extreme decline for poetry! And yet the vulgar insist upon saying: "Poets emulate their predecessors and attain correctness (*cheng*)." They do not realize that actually this is a case of [the early T'ang representing] a decline due to a progressive deterioration of correctness. Only with the advent of the K'ai-yüan and T'ien-pao eras was there a complete, major transformation. But again, the vulgar say: "This is a case of attaining correctness in poetry." They do not realize that actually it was due to an extreme decline in correctness that poetry transformed and enjoyed a period of extreme flourishing.[44]

According to Yeh Hsieh, each major transformation represented by one or several dominant figures (Chien-an poets, High T'ang poets, Han Yü, Su Shih) occurs because the decline phase has come to its full development. The interdependence or complementarity inherent in decline and vigor create a cyclic process.

Anciently it was said: "The processes of nature undergo a complete transformation every ten years." This is a matter of inherent pattern (*li*, "principle"). It is also a matter of configurational dynamics (*shih*).[45]

The dialectical model of change, cyclical with linear development, is seen in the following example as a refinement of the notion of interdependence. In Yüan Hung-tao's (1568–1610) analysis change in literary modes occurs due to a given generation's attempt to correct the follies of its predecessors. However, each new mode has its own characteristic, potential defects which will show themselves as the vigor of the new phase declines. The underlying structure of this process recalls that of the interdependent *yin-yang* phases; however, here a multivalency in relationships occurs, with each follower also a predecessor and interacting as a member of two sets of complementary pairs.

Given methods (*fa*,[aq] or "rules") have as their cause some deficiency and end by producing some kind of excess. Those who reformed the Six Dynasties habit of splendid, artificial arrangements and elaborate, empty displays used a free-handed ornamental beauty (*liu-li*[ar]) to overcome it. Without question, elaborated and empty display was the basis for the free-handed beauty; however, the latter's excess lay in triviality and overrefinement (*ch'ing-hsien*[as]), and so the various figures of High T'ang used a wide-ranging and grand (*k'uo-ta*[at]) manner as a remedy. But having achieved the wide-ranging, they went on to produce from it the vague and confused (*mang*[au]). Thus it was that those who succeeded to High T'ang remedied [the excess] with actualities (*ch'ing-shih*[av]). They were true to the facts all

aq 法
ar 流麗

as 輕纖
at 闊大

au 莽
av 情實

right, but also out of this realistic approach they produced the pedestrian (*li*^{aw}). Thus, those who came after the writers of mid-T'ang used the strange and eccentric (*ch'i-p'i*^{ax}) as a remedy. When they did so, their poetic settings were necessarily too narrowly limited and idiosyncratic and each one labored to produce something unprecedented so as to outdo the others. As a result, by late T'ang the way of poetry was greatly diminished. When Ou-yang Hsiu, Su Shih, and their peers emerged in Sung, they brought about a major transformation of the mannerisms of the late T'ang. With respect to things (*wu*^{ay}), there was none they failed to include in their verse; in the matter of methods (*fa*), there was none they did not have; as for feelings (*ch'ing*^{az}), there was none they failed to express; in regard to settings (*ching*^{ba}), they made use of every kind.... People at present notice only that the Sung poets do not write with T'ang methods; they do not realize that Sung poets' methods have their basis in the T'ang. For example, what is bland and neutral (*tan*^{bb}) is not richly flavored (*nung*^{bc}), and yet rich flavor actually depends upon the existence of blandness. However, when the practices of the Sung poets declined, they made poetry out of prose, out of Confucian doctrine, and out of songs and formulaic declarations. This sort of thing kept spreading until they were making poetry out of liturgical chants and the degeneration of poetry was such that there is no way to express it in words. Literary men of recent times initiated a theory of "returning to the ancients" (*fu-ku*^{bd}) in order to overcome it. Now "returning to the ancients" is certainly well and good. However, they have gone so far as to take plagiarism to be "returning to the ancients," matching lines and copying words, laboring to get a close correspondence; rejecting the scenes before their very eyes, they collect phrases overflowing with staleness.[46]

The vegetal cycle might be thought to have been a convenient and durable model for periodizations marking a repeated pattern of sprouting, flowering, withering, and death. However, it is difficult to find, in Chinese critical writings on literature, an account that describes more than one full linear sequence of stages. The most famous of the many limited periodizations based upon the stages of organic life is the periodization of T'ang poetry. Interest in T'ang achievements was so strong that from late Sung to late Ming the periodization of T'ang poetry is a recurrent critical topic. During Yüan, Yang Shih-hung's *T'ang yin* reworks the five T'ang poetic periods Yen Yü had defined, making four (Early, High, a Middle which combines Yen's Ta-li style and his Yüan-ho style, and Late). Kao Ping, stating in

aw 俚	az 情	bc 濃
ax 奇僻	ba 境	bd 復古
ay 物	bb 淡	

Ming that during the three hundred years of T'ang poetry's numerous embodiments were brought to fulfillment, describes an organic pattern of rise (*hsing*[be]), completion or maturity (*ch'eng*[bf]), a "flowing into decline" (*liu yü pien*[bg]), and dissolution.[47] With Kao, an important source of archaist ideas, *pien* is used in its negative sense. He applies evaluative labels to poets' work, such as "correctness within decline" (*pien chung cheng*[bh]) and "decline within correctness" (*cheng chung pien*[bi]) to permit himself more flexibility in making distinctions among writers of each period, thus softening considerably the concept of division into period blocs. Period terms for Kao Ping had a clear evaluative character because of his use of the life-cycle model. Whether or not he viewed this pattern as ultimately cyclical is debatable; he was apparently not inclined to periodize Sung poetry in terms of this model. In late Ming, Shen Ch'i's preface to the *Shih-t'i ming-pien* continues the quadripartite division of T'ang poetry, referring to the "four great master-periods" (*ssu ta tsung*[bj]) and focusing more sharply on dominant figures. Shen for the first time includes the first T'ang emperor Kao Tsu's reign in the early T'ang period and also slightly extends Middle T'ang, establishing the fixed periods which have been accepted generally ever since. Chu Tzu-ch'ing states that the periodization resulting from this long cooperative effort is the only fixed periodization in Chinese literary history.[48]

Views of what happened in literature and the other arts in China reveal reliance upon all of the primary models mentioned at the beginning of this discussion, the cyclic, the linear with directional variants, the irregular, and the spiral or dialectical. The patterns themselves were ready to hand, as in the West, by virtue of their currency in traditional historical and philosophical discourse. What seems distinctive in the materials examined here is the emphasis upon continuities, such as style lineages, rather than upon period boundaries; upon cumulative changes with their turning points; and upon the identification and explanation of the forces at work in the process of change, not upon the formulation and naming of isolating, unitary time blocs. Political time blocs were the most stable points of reference and provided a background structure often for the discussion of literary activity, yet even dynasties participated in the living rhythms of change—the organic life cycle, familial descent, and the progression of the seasons—and their changes, as well, could be rung in these terms.

The foregoing review of Chinese critics' perceptions of the patterns of literary change in time is highly selective and cannot fully represent the actual variety that exists in the treatment of this subject, despite what may seem to be a remarkably uniform agreement on the major turning points in literary history through the Sung. More problematic is the difficulty, in the format used here, of illustrating adequately the way in which individual writers, in discussing the literary past,

| be 興 | bg 流於變 | bi 正中變 |
| bf 成 | bh 變中正 | bj 四大宗 |

tended to engage their subject from multiple perspectives. A cultural predisposition to appreciate the multirelational nature of every human activity allows individual writers such as Liu Hsieh or Yeh Hsieh to view and explain the same historical sequence in a variety of contexts. Observations on a seemingly deterministic pattern of vigor and exhaustion or flourishing and decline for genres may be followed by a discussion of stylistic influence in which conscious choices or personalities appear to be deciding factors; moreover, it may become necessary for the same writer to attribute certain developments to a shift in the social climate or to the sudden appearance of a literary genius. This openness to complexity, an ability to forego a complete reduction of complexity to an isolating, unilinear analytical program, is one of the features of the best traditional literary critical and historical writings, and it is a feature which can be unsettling to those trained to bring analytical approaches to these materials. But an accomodation to such freely shifting perspectives in the exploration of a complex reality will surely promote a fuller appreciation of the traditional Chinese vision of literary activity and its history. The simple analytical categories offered in this study have a heuristic value in the initial attempt to define fundamental patterns; held to rigidly, however, they could work to obscure the protean quality of the materials themselves.

1. For the explanatory function of histories, see William Dray, *Laws and Explanation in History* (Oxford, 1957). An interesting discussion of story, plot, and argument in historical narratives is Hayden White, "The Structure of Historical Narrative," *Clio* (1972), 1:5–20.

2. Called "hectohistory" by David Fischer in his *Historical Fallacies: Toward a Logic of Historical Thought* (New York, 1970), p. 145. Historians using this approach will speak of "the ninth century" or "the eighteen hundreds" in a way that ascribes a genuinely unitary character to centuries.

3. Jerzy Topolski, *Methodology of History* (Boston, 1976), p. 594.

4. On the dynastic cycle, see Arthur Wright, "On the Uses of Generalization in the Study of Chinese History," in *Generalization in the Writing of History*, ed. Louis Gottschalk (Chicago, 1963), pp. 41–43, and Lien-sheng Yang, "Towards a Study of Dynastic Configurations in Chinese History," *Studies in Chinese Institutional History* (Cambridge, Mass., 1961), pp. 1–17. Portions of both essays are reprinted in *The Pattern of Chinese History* ed. John Meskill (Boston, 1965), a collection of essays on the periodization of Chinese social and political history. Wang Kuo-wei offers a succinct version of the vigor and exhaustion pattern in his *Jen-chien tz'u hua*: "When four-word poetry became worn-out, the *Songs of Ch'u* came into existence; when the *Songs of Ch'u* became worn-out, it was followed by the five-word poetry. When the five word poetry declined, seven-word poetry began to flourish.... When a literary genre has been popular for a long time and practiced by many it naturally becomes stale.... each literary genre flourishes for a time and finally declines." *Poetic Remarks in the Human World*, trans. Tu Ching-i (Taipei, 1972), pp. 37–38.

5. An attitude discussed at some length by Wayne Booth, who cites Ian Watt as a modern critic for whom "properly speaking, the novel ... begins only when Defoe and Richardson discover how to give their characters sufficient particularity and autonomy to make them seem like real people." *The Rhetoric of Fiction* (Chicago, 1961), p. 41. The pitfalls of such assumptions are illustrated in John L. Bishop's essay, "Some Limitations of Chinese Fiction," *The Far Eastern Quarterly* (1956), 15:239–247.

6. For literary history in China, clearly illustrated in a discussion by Ming poet-critic Yuan Hung-tao (1568–1610); a portion of the discussion is translated below.

7. Jorge Luis Borges, *Labyrinths: Selected Stories and Other Writings* (New York, 1962), p. 65.

8. Topolski, *Methodology*, p. 594. John Meskill, in his introduction to *The Pattern of Chinese History*, says: "Most regrettable is the difficulty of presenting in this book much original Western history of China, since Western scholars of Chinese history have paid little attention so far to periodization." This volume, published almost two decades age, remains the most helpful source in English on the problems and varieties of periodization in traditional Chinese historiography and in modern studies of Chinese history.

9. Shao's scheme is discussed in Fung Yu-lan, *A History of Chinese Philosophy*, trans. Derk Bodde, 2 vols. (Princeton, 1952, 1953), 2:451–476.

10. Summarizing Louis Althusser's fusion of Marxist and structuralist concepts and their applications to the history of ideas, Frederic Jameson notes how historical change would be treated with this model: "If ... philosophical positions are little more than systematic variations on a given paradigm or model, then what counts is not so much the individual position itself ... but rather the conceptual limits of the model in question, which thus becomes a kind of bed-rock of thought, of 'theoretical praxis,' where it functions as a type of infrastructure to the history of ideas. This reality of the model or of the ideational infrastructure Althusser calls the *problematique*, or problem-complex. The latter determines the thinking done in it in the sense in which it serves as an ultimate limitation on thought, on the conscious problems which thought poses itself, as well as on their solutions. This is ... the 'cloture' or conceptual ceiling inherent in the model or paradigm which governs the thinking of a given generation; the implication is that a given generation will take its place as a whole within a given *problematique* and that the latter is at one with the historical moment itself. Genuine historical change will therefore be felt, not so much as development—for given a model, intellectual work will simply consist in its application or exploration—as a sudden replacement of an old problematique by a new one." *The Prisonhouse of Language* (Princeton, 1972), p. 135. The idea of the "paradigm" was elaborated earlier in Thomas S. Kuhn's *The Structure of Scientific Revolutions* (Chicago, 1962). New perspectives on change in time are offered also by George Kubler in *The Shape of Time* (New Haven, 1962).

11. F. E. Sparshott, "Notes on the Articulation of Time, *New Literary History* (1970), 1:315–316.

12. Heinrich Wölfflin, *Kungstgeschichtliche grundbegriffe* (Munich, 1915), trans. as *Principles of Art History* (New York, 1929).

13. Preface to the *Ho-yüeh ling-ying chi*, contained in *T'ang-jen hsüan T'ang-shih* (Peking, 1958), p. 40. Allowances may need to be made here, it is true, for the rhetorical piety considered appropriate to a preface.

14. Wright, "On the Uses of Generalization," *The Pattern of Chinese History*, p. 4.

15. In an article on the periodization of ancient American art (4000 B.C.–A.D. 1500), Geoge Kubler presents a simple but innovative periodizing diagram which shows differing rates of change, according to area, within a single period. The ideas of "fast centers" and "slow margins," especially for early periods, provides a basis for an alternative to charts full of areal columns which are divided into strict periods. See Kubler's "Period, Style and Meaning in Ancient American Art," *New Literary History* (1970), 1:131.

16. Rene Wellek and Austin Warren, *Theory of Literature* (New York, 1949), p. 55.

17. Rene Wellek, "Romanticism Reconsidered," in *Concepts of Criticism*, ed. Stephen Nichols, Jr. (New Haven, 1963), p. 200.

18. Chu Tzu-ch'ing, *Shih yen chih pien* (A Critical Inquiry into "poetry verbalizes intent") (Peking, 1956), pp. 132–136. For Cheng Hsüan's interpretation, see *Mao-shih cheng-i* (The *Mao Odes* Correctly Interpreted), "Tsung hsü," (Collected Prefaces) (*SPPY* ed.) 3a.

19. Lo Ken-tse, *Chou Ch'in Liang-Han wen-hsüeh p'i-p'ing shih* (History of Literary Criticism in the Chou, Ch'in, and Two Han Dynasties) (1942; rpt. Taiwan, 1966), pp. 51–52.

20. *Fei ts'ao-shu* (Against Draft Calligraphy), trans. in W.R.B. Acker, *Some T'ang and Pre-T'ang Texts on Chinese Painting*, 3 vols. (Leiden, 1954–1974), 1:lv. Acker translates the entire essay.

21. This paper restricts itself to consideration of premodern views of literary history and patterns of change. For a study of attempts by modern scholars and critics to periodize Chinese literary history, see Tak-wai Wong, "Period Style and Periodization: a Survey of Theory and Practice in Histories of Chinese and European Literature," *New Asia Academic Bulletin* (1978), 1:45–67. Wong's essay also contains useful references to recent articles in English and European languages which reflect current thinking about the problems of periodization in Western arts history.

22. *Ch'üan Chin wen* (Complete Chin Dynasty Prose), in *Ch'üan Shang-ku San-tai Ch'in Han San-kuo Liu-ch'ao wen* (The Complete Prose of High Antiquity, the Three Epochs, the Two Han Periods, the Three Kingdoms, and the Six Dynasties), ed. Yen K'o-chün (Taipei, 1963), 4:7b–9b.

23. *Ts'ang-lang shih hua* (The Ts'ang-lang Comments on Poetry) in *Li-tai shih-hua* (Comments on Poetry Through the Ages), ed. Ho Wen-huan, 2 vols, (Taipei, 1956), 2:442.

24. *Shih sou* (Thicket of Poetry) (Peking, 1962), "Nei p'ien," p. 1.

25. Wen Fong, "Archaism as a 'Primitive Style,'" in *Artists and Traditions: Uses of the Past in Chinese Culture*, ed. Christian Murck (Princeton, 1976), p. 89.

26. *Shih p'in chu* (A Commentary on the *Shih p'in*), ed. Ch'en Yen-chieh (Hong Kong, 1959), p. 3.

27. I am indebted to James Cahill for the opportunity to read the introduction to his then unpublished history of late Ming painting, in which he discusses new attempts in that period to formulate histories of painting. The relationship between Chan's dual lineage, the *tso-chia* 作家 and the *i-chia* 逸家, and Tung Ch'i-ch'ang's evaluative lineages is particularly interesting. In Cahill's astute analysis, Tung's formulation of "orthodox" and "heterodox" lineages allowed him to address himself, from a single theoretical position, to the major issues in painting being debated in his day.

28. "*Wen hsüan* hsü" (Preface), *Wen hsüan* (Hong Kong, 1936), p. 1.

29. Quoted by Alexander C. Soper in "The Relationship of Early Chinese Painting to Its Own Past," in *Artists and Traditions*, ed. Murck, p. 27.

30. *Wen-hsin tiao-lung hsin-shu* (A New Edition of the *Wen-hsin tiao-lung*) ed. Wang Li-ch'i (Peking, 1951), p. 85.

31. *Wen-hsin tiao-lung hsin-shu*, p. 84.

32. *Wen-hsin tiao-lung hsin-shu* p. 118. That Liu may not be insensitive to having created two periodizations with concluding chapters that contradict each other is suggested by his use of the phrases "ten ages" (*shih tai* 十代) and "nine changes" in literary artistry (*tz'u ts'ai chiu pien* 辭采九變) in his summation to chapter 45, "Shih hsü" (The Times and Their Order) 時序. Not only does the phrase "nine changes" serve a larger justifying purpose by placing literature (including belles-lettres) on a par with other important activities that exhibit "nine changes" (such as the ancient music referred to in the *Chou li*; military deployments in the *Sun Tzu*; the Tao itself, as in the *Chuang Tzu*); the phrase could also recall a belief expressed in the *Lieh Tzu* ("T'ien shui" 天瑞) concerning cosmic patterns of change in which, after nine changes, things go back to their beginnings. Thus the reigning dynasty may have come at the end of a long literary decline, but as the last in a series of "ten ages," it must also be the first in a new series of "nine changes" and could be expected to usher in a new sagely era. The story of progressive decline in one chapter and the optimistic conclusion in the other thus seem "reconciled."

33. From the letter to Yüan Chen quoted in Po's biography, *Chiu T'ang shu* 166 (Peking: Chung-hua ed., 1962–1976), p. 4346.

34. *Chiu T'ang shu* 166, p. 4347.

35. Critics from Chung Hung and Liu Hsieh on agree in considering these the major turning points; they do not, however, always agree upon the relationships and values of the elements in this sequence.

36. *T'ang jen hsüan T'ang shih*, p. 40.

37. *T'ang yin kuei ch'ien* (On T'ang Poetry, Tenth Collection) (Taipei, 1964) 1, p. 1.

38. *Shih sou*, "Nei p'ien," p. 1.

39. *Yüan shih* (Going to the Source of Poetry) 原詩 "Nei p'ien," in *Ch'ing shih hua* (Ch'ing Dynasty 'Comments on Poetry'), ed. Ting Fu-pao (Peking, 1963), p. 566.

40. *Yüan shih*, p. 565.

41. *Yüan shih*, p. 565.

42. *Yüan shih*, "Wai p'ien," p. 591.

43. *Yüan shih*, "Nei p'ien," p. 565.

44. *Yüan shih*, p. 569.

45. *Yüan shih*, p. 566.

46. "Hsüeh-t'ao-ko chi hsü" (Preface to the Snowy Waves Lodge Collection) 雪濤閣集序, *Yüan Chung-lang ch'üan chi* (Complete Works of Yüan Hung-tao) (Taipei, 1964), pp. 6–7.

47. A summary of the categories, with extensive quotation from Kao's *T'ang shih p'in hui* (An Evaluation and Classification of T'ang Poetry), is available in Chu Tung-jun's *Chung-kuo wen-hsüeh p'i-p'ing shih ta-kang* (Outline of the History of Chinese Literary Criticism) (Hong Kong, 1959), pp. 218–224.

48. For discussion, see Chu Tzu-ch'ing, *Shih yen chih pien*, p. 164. The periods are defined as Early, 618–713; High, 713–766; Middle, 766–835; and Late, 836–906. There were

other attempts to create precise periods in literary history, though none of them achieved the degree of acceptance given to the T'ang periodizations. A Ch'ing writer, Ku Ssu-li, proposed three periods for Yüan poetry: Early, 1234–1297; Middle, 1297–1335; and Late, 1335–1367. This segmentation has been adopted recently by Pao Ken-ti in a work on thirteen important Yüan poets, *Yüan shih yen-chiu* (Studies in Yüan Poetry). (Taipei, 1978).

Formal Distinctions in Chinese Literary Theory

By Pauline Yu

Given the eclectic, syncretic, and nonsystematic nature of most Chinese literary criticism, it is possible to find support for virtually any theory of literature in the works of a particular critic. Thus, for example, the opening lines of the *Ta hsü* (Great Preface) to the *Shih ching* (Book of Odes)—"Poetry is where the intent of the heart/mind goes: what in the heart is intent is poetry when emitted in words. An emotion moves within and takes form in words. If words are insufficient, then one sighs; if sighing is insufficient then one prolongs it [the emotion] in song; if prolonging through song is insufficient then one unconsciously dances it with hands and feet"[1]—reappear through the centuries as an almost obligatory dictum in the writings of people with whom one would not ordinarily associate the expressive theory inherent in the passage. This is even more true of formalistic notions of literature, particularly if one defines formalism as focusing on the form or manner in which a work is presented, something to be distinguished from thought or subject matter, and as "making art consist essentially in the skillful handling of words and phrases, verse and rhyme, style and diction."[2] Accepting this definition, one would be hard-pressed not to discover formalistic tendencies in works from Lu Chi's (261–303) *Wen fu* (Rhymeprose on Literature) onward, given the persistent penchant of critics for including discussions of method, rules to be obeyed, examples to be imitated, or infelicities to be avoided. All of these, one might argue, suggest a view of literature as craft, primarily concerned with the technique of manipulating the formal, linguistic materials of the work of art.

We can narrow the field significantly, however, by redefining formalism along the lines drawn by Roman Jakobson several decades ago, as a theory positing that "the object of study in literary science is not literature but 'literariness,' that is, what makes a given work a *literary* work."[3] Seen in this light, formalist writings can be singled out as those which, while still interested in practical problems of craftsmanship, also attempt, on a more theoretical level, to define the nature and scope of literature itself on the basis of specific properties of the text. Whether or not such an enterprise is possible or legitimate, of course, is subject to question.

In the West, formalist discussions center on the differences to be discerned between two kinds of language, one designated as "poetic" or "literary" and the other labeled variously as "nonpoetic," "nonliterary," "ordinary," "practical," etc. While the general effort to set off the domain of the purely literary from other activities and concerns begins with the romantics, the focus on formal criteria becomes acute only in the writings of the French symbolists, Russian formalists, and Czech structuralists. Their apparent lack of interest in other aspects of the literary experience is encapsulated in the following anecdote recorded by Valéry:

> The great painter Degas often related these words of Mallarmé to me, which are so apt and so simple. Degas sometimes wrote verses, and he has left some delectable ones. But he often encountered great difficulties in this work which was ancillary to his painting.... One day he said to Mallarmé: "Your profession is an infernal one. I'm not successful at doing what I want to and yet I'm full of ideas." And Mallarmé answered: "It is not at all with ideas, my dear Degas, that one writes verses. It is with *words.*"[4]

Or, as Viktor Žirmunskij puts it, "The material of poetry is neither images nor emotions, but words.... Poetry is verbal art."[5]

In their view, poetry neither discusses ideas, teaches a lesson, nor expresses feelings; it is the craft of words, so that the answer to what makes a given work "poetic" must at least begin for these critics as an essentially linguistic one. Osip Brik provides us with a dogmatic formulation of their position: "The correct point of view sees in poetry a specifically verbal complex created on the basis of special laws which are not identical to those of ordinary speech."[6] He regards poetic and ordinary language as formally distinct because the former exploits available auditory resources, such as repetition, rhythm, stress, and intonation, while the latter does not. Since Brik assumes, as Mary Pratt points out, "that rhythmic organization is alien to nonliterary discourse,"[7] he believes that the transformation from a poetic to a nonpoetic text necessitates but a few simple operations on the level of form. As he describes it, "by rearranging words we can deprive any line of poetry of its poetic shape and convert it into a phrase from the sphere of ordinary speech. This is not hard to do, if for certain words we substitute equivalent ones, introduce ordinary conversational intonation, and smooth out the syntactic structure."[8]

Although few critics define the essence of poetic language as narrowly as does Brik, formalists agree that it represents a "distortion" or "disruption" of the form of ordinary speech, thus creating a denser texture among its various elements.[9] Symbolist poets describe the transformation as the construction of "a language within language"[10] or of "a total word, new, stranger to language and incantatory."[11] In the following letter, Rilke not only stresses the distinctiveness of the poetic word and its more intricate connection to other words, he also employs the analogy of writing to craft and points to the logical consequences of a formal distinction:

> No one would think of pushing ropemaker, cabinetmaker, or cobbler away from their handicrafts "into life," so that they could become a better ropemaker, cabinetmaker, or cobbler; even the musician, painter, and

sculptor are sooner left alone with their activities. Only with the writer does the handicraft seem so paltry, so *possible* from the very beginning (anyone can write), that many people (and among them, occasionally, even [the poet Richard] Dehmel) are of the opinion that the person involved with it would slip into empty play if he were left too much alone with his career! But what an error! To be able to write, God knows, is no less a "difficult handicraft," more so, in fact, because the material of the other arts is removed from the beginning from daily use, while the poet's task is intensified by the unusual obligation to differentiate in a fundamental way *his* word from the words of mere intercourse. *No* word in the poem (I mean here each "a," or "the" or "those") is *identical* with the same sounding word of daily usage and conversation; the purer regulation by laws, the greater relationship, the constellation that it occupies in the verse or in artistic prose, alters it to the very heart of its nature, makes it purposeless, useless for mere intercourse, untouchable, and enduring....[12]

This passage demonstrates how the isolation of poetic language on formal grounds ultimately serves as the springboard and justification for an even more important distinction in function, which of course only exists because of the formal one. As Edward Stankiewicz suggests, this is a fairly recent phenomenon in the West, deriving from Kant's characterization of art in his *Critique of Judgment* as "purposiveness without purpose"; in other words, "poetic language is purposiveness in terms of the internal organization of the message, and purposelessness in terms of the external reference."[13] Hegel in turn, according to Heinrich Anz, related the Kantian formulation more directly to literature by positing a difference between *"poetic expression* and the *practical and theoretical prose of normal life and consciousness*," attributed to the latter's conception of language as "a mere *means of communication*."[14] Poe thus proclaimed the self-sufficiency of poetry: "this poem *per se*—this poem which is a poem and nothing more—this poem written solely for the poem's sake."[15] Symbolist poets followed him with their persistent envy of the musician's resources, unsullied by any prior communicative, practical function: witness Verlaine's "Art poétique," which opens with a declaration for "Music first, before everything." Valéry employs an analogy to another art in contrasting two different uses of, and attitudes toward, language, one of which aims for comprehension of its message and thus demands the substitution of meanings for its "system of sonorities, durations, and signs," the virtual abolition of the words themselves, the transformation of language into "nonlanguage." The other, however, insists on the primacy of its very form and demands that it be not only noticed but also respected, desired, and repeated, thus leading us into "the poetic universe."[16] He compares the relationship between poetry and prose to that between dancing and walking—both begin with the same materials but are directed toward opposite ends and experience different fates. Prose is transitive, poetry intransitive:

The language that has just served to express my plan, my desire, my command, my opinion, this language that has fulfilled its purpose, vanishes as soon as it is spoken. . . . On the contrary, the poem does not die for having lived: it is made expressly to be reborn from its ashes and to become again indefinitely what it has just been. Poetry can be recognized by this property of tending to cause itself to be reproduced in its form: it inspires us to reconstitute it identically.[17]

This notion is couched in noticeably different terms by formalist critics, but it remains the same. When Viktor Šklovskij, for example, writes that "Poetic language is distinguished from prosaic language by the palpableness of its construction. The palpableness may be brought about by the acoustical aspect or the articulatory aspect or the semasiological aspect,"[18] he is providing the groundwork for a contrast between the behaviors and uses of literary and nonliterary language. The greater palpability of poetic language increases what he calls its "perceptibility," which, since aesthetic perception is defined in almost exclusively formal terms,[19] entails a focus on the medium rather than the message. This is what Jan Mukařovský terms "foregrounding," which aims to prevent the reader's attention from slipping immediately to the content of the message:

The function of poetic language consists in the maximum of foregrounding of the utterance. . . . In poetic language foregrounding achieves maximum intensity to the extent of pushing communication into the background as the objective of expression and of being used for its own sake; it is not used in the services of communication, but in order to place in the foreground the act of expression, the act of speech itself.[20]

In other words, poetic language differentiates itself on the formal level of sound, rhythm, and syntax in order to establish its autotelic nature, its freedom from the various utilitarian functions of ordinary language. Conversely, since the poetic function is defined as establishing this autonomy and focus on the text for its own sake, only formal elements remain as legitimate objects of consideration. Such distinctions would, in theory, have been impossible for traditional Chinese literary critics to draw, given the all-embracing notion of *wen* (culture, civilization, pattern, embellishment, scholarship, writing) and of the cosmological and social harmony which it was felt to constitute and embody. Certainly, no writer at any time would, if questioned, have denied the didactic function of literature or asserted its independence from other than formal concerns. Nevertheless, although it is difficult to define them strictly as "formalist" in the Western sense, attempts were made to set off one class of writings as "literary" or "poetic" on formal grounds, with a concomitant emphasis on a resulting difference in function. These occurred first during the Six Dynasties, and later during the Ming and Ch'ing dynasties, although the situations out of which they arose were quite dissimilar. Not surprisingly, definitions were blurred by shifts in terminology, and again not surprisingly, they hinged on the protean word *wen*.[21]

During the Six Dynasties, efforts to break down the large category of literature centered around the words *wen* and *pi*, "plain writing," literally "writing brush." The two terms had been used in combination during the Han to refer to a person's writings in general, and they did continue to be employed in this way, as various quotations from biographies in the dynastic histories demonstrate.[22] But other passages from the histories suggest some kind of distinction between the two: "Sung Wen-ti asked Yen-chih about the talents and abilities of various writers. Yen-chih said: 'Chün's *pi* is as good as mine; Ts'e's *wen* is as good as mine'";[23] "He wrote both *wen* and *pi*"; and "He was good at both *wen* and *pi*."[24]

On what basis were these two categories, literature and "plain writing," being distinguished? The answer varies throughout this period, but evidence suggests that an early criterion was an exclusively formal one: the presence or absence of rhyme. Fan Yeh (398–445) includes one of the first examples of such a differentiation in an oft-cited letter. After apologizing for his own deficiences at *wen*, he stresses the primacy of meaning (*i*), but then goes on to place equal emphasis on auditory, formal aspects:

> By nature I could discriminate between [the first and second notes on the pentatonic scale] *kung* and *shang*; that I could recognize clear and turbid [sounds] also came naturally. But when I observe both past and present-day literati, most of them do not completely comprehend these elements, and even if there are some who understand them, they do not always work from the fundamentals.... Prose is deficient because the writing is not restricted by rhyme.[a][25]

Although this final comment uses the term *wen* to refer to writing in general rather than to a particular class thereof, it is clear that Fan Yeh is opposing unrhymed to rhymed works and asserting, furthermore, the greater "literariness" and superiority of those meeting greater formal demands.

A well-known passage from Shen Yüeh's (441–532) biography of Hsieh Ling-yün (385–433) indicates that it was this latter category, defined by its adherence to considerations of sound and form, which in fact constituted what was to be called *wen* or literature:

> Now if one discusses matters openly, in evaluating the skill and clumsiness of former writers, the following can be said. The five colors (blue-green, yellow, red, white, and black) highlight one another, and the eight sounds

[a] 性別宮商，識清濁，斯自然也。觀古今文人，多不全了此處；縱有會此者，不必從根本中來⋯⋯手筆差易，文不拘韻故也。

(of musical instruments—metal, stone, silk, bamboo, gourd, earthenware, leather, and wood) harmonize with each other: this is because dark and light colors and the notes on a pitchpipe all have their proper places. If you wish to alternate [the first and fifth notes of the pentatonic scale] *kung* and *yu*, and make low and high modulate each other, then if you have a floating tone first, you must have a piercing tone afterward. Within a single line, the rhymes should be completely varied, and within a couplet, light and heavy sounds should all be different. Not until one grasps these subtle principles can one discuss *wen*.[b26]

Shen Yüeh thus clarifies the opposition suggested in Fan Yeh's letter: what can truly be characterized as *wen* or literature is that which adheres to rules of rhyme and intonation; to paraphrase Verlaine in the last line of his "Art poétique," all the rest is *pi*.[27] The following passage from the biography of Shen Yüeh's contemporary, Lu Chüeh, also implies that the definition of *wen* hinges on these formal considerations:

> At the end of the Yung-ming period (483–493), literature flourished. Shen Yüeh, Hsieh T'iao (464–499), and Wang Jung (467–493) were similar in spirit and promoted each other; Chou Yung (d. 485) of Ju-nan had a good knowledge of tones and rhymes. In their *wen* they all employed *kung* and *shang* and called *p'ing* (level), *shang* (rising), *ch'ü* (leaving), and *ju* (entering) the four tones. They used these to regulate rhymes and had [the rules of] level head, rising tail, wasp's waist, and crane's knee. Within the five words [of a line in a pentasyllabic poem] the rhymes had to be different; within a couplet [the third and fourth notes of the pentatonic scale] *chiao* and *chih* could not be the same.[c28]

Liu Hsieh (ca. 465–523) also indicates the widespread acceptance of this formal distinction between *wen* and *pi* in the opening of chapter 44, *Tsung-shu* (Summarizing the Art) of his *Wen-hsin tiao-lung* (The Literary Mind: Dragon-Carvings): "A common saying at present is that there is *wen* and there is *pi*; what is unrhymed is considered to be *pi*, and what is rhymed is considered *wen*."[29] Of course, the comprehensive thrust of the *Wen-hsin tiao-lung* as a whole would suggest that he himself would not agree with a purely formalist distinction. Nevertheless, as Liu Shih-p'ei pointed out, Liu Hsieh at least implicitly regarded rhyme as some sort of distinctive feature in organizing his treatment of specific genres: chapters 5

b 著夫敷衽論心，商榷前藻，工拙之數，如有可言。夫五色相宣，八音協暢，由乎玄黃律呂，各適物宜。欲使宮羽相變，低昂舛節，若前有浮聲，則後須切響，一節之內，音韻盡殊，兩句之中，輕重悉異，妙達此音，始可言文。

c 永明末，盛爲文章，沈約，謝朓，王融，以氣類相推轂，汝南周顒善識聲韻，爲文皆用宮商，以平上去入爲四聲。以此制韻，有平頭，上尾，蠭腰，鶴膝。五字之中，音韻悉異，兩句之內，角徵不同。

through 15 examine various types of rhymed composition, whereas those discussed in the following ten chapters are all unrhymed.[30]

During the fifth century, then, the previously all-embracing category of *wen* or *wen-chang* was subdivided by many writers into two groups, the very choice of the highly charged word *wen* to label those works obeying rules of rhyme and intonation suggests that this involved an attempt at defining ''literariness' itself on formal grounds. The criteria did, however, become somewhat broader. This is evident in the *Wen hsüan hsü* (Preface to the Anthology of Literature) of Hsiao T'ung (501–531), crown prince Chao-ming of Liang, although he does not actually use the dichotomy of *wen* and *pi*. Explaining why the Confucian classics and works of other philosophers have not been included in his anthology, he writes:

> As for the writings of the Duke of Chou and the books of Confucius, they are suspended as high as the sun and moon and vie in mystery with ghosts and spirits. As the models for filial respect and the guides to human relationships, how could they be improved by weeding or cutting? The works of Lao Tzu, Chuang Tzu, Kuan Tzu, and Mencius focus on establishing a theory and do not regard *wen* as fundamental. I have also omitted them from my anthology.[d][31]

Nor has he selected "the beautiful words of worthy men, the righteous remonstrances of loyal ministers, the speeches of strategists, or the arguments of sophists," both because they have been recorded elsewhere and because "their matter is different from that of literary compositions."[32] Thus neither the classics and philosophy nor political, public writings can be included in a collection defined as literature, the former because of their didactic function and the latter because of their inappropriate subject matter. Hsiao T'ung finally presents his standards in a more positive form when explaining why he has omitted a third class of writings:

> As for histories and chronicles, they praise and blame right and wrong and distinguish like and unlike and are also not the same as literary writings. But as for the concentrated verbal beauty of appreciations and disquisitions and the organized rhetorical flourish of prefaces and accounts—their subject matter derives from profound thought and their purport places them within literary elegance, thus I have collected them with the other pieces.[e][33]

---

[d] 若夫姬公之籍，孔父之書，與日月俱懸，鬼神爭奧，孝敬之准式，人倫之師友，豈可重以芟夷，加以剪截？老莊之作，管孟之流，蓋以立意爲宗，不以能文爲本。今之所撰，又以略諸。

[e] 至於記事之史，繫年之書，所以襃貶是非，紀別異同。方之篇翰，亦已不同。若其讚論之綜緝辭采，序述之錯比文華，事出於沈思，義歸乎翰，故與夫篇什，雜而集之。

In other words, *wen* in his eyes must meet several criteria at once: it can embrace neither the classics nor works of philosophy or history because of their didactic and evaluative purposes; it can include certain types of public, expository writing, but only those which result from deep thought (political arguments, presumably, do not) and display beauty, polish, and elegance of style. Formally perceptible qualities and their effects remain his primary means of discrimination: he defines literature as belles-lettres mainly on the basis of its aesthetic properties and intents, placing renewed stress on the meaning of *wen* as "pattern" or "embellishment."

Hsiao T'ung's younger brother Hsiao I, who ascended the Liang throne as Emperor Yüan in 552, subscribes to a similar definition and returns to the *wen-pi* terminology as well. In his best-known discussion of literature, he opens by mentioning that the Han dynasty had separated it into two parts, scholarship and literature, and that this division had been further broken down in recent times:

> Among the ancients there were two types of scholars, and among the moderns there are four. The disciples of the philosophers who transmitted what they received from their masters and understood the classics of the sages were called scholars. The followers of Ch'ü Yüan (343?–278 B.C.), Sung Yü (third cent. B.C.), Mei Sheng (d. 141 B.C.), and [Ssu-ma] Ch'ang-ch'ing [Hsiang-ju] (179–117 B.C.) only wrote rhymeprose, which was called *wen*. Among the scholars of today, those who have read extensively in philosophy and history but only know the facts and do not understand the principles are called pedants. As for those who are not practiced at writing memorials, like Po-sung [Chang Sung]—this group's [work] is called *pi*.[f]

In other words, there are now two kinds of scholars—true thinkers and mere pedants, and two kinds of written compositions—*wen* and *pi*. The value judgment implied by this analogy is confirmed in Hsiao I's description of two:

> What is chanted and intoned like ballads and habitually given to [the expression of] mournful thoughts is called literature.... On the one hand, plain writing cannot be said to be a truly literary composition, nor, on the other, does it have the purport [of true scholarship]; all it can do is demonstrate [the author's] intelligence and [skill at] organizing. As for *wen*, it but demands the diverse beauties of fine silk, the lingering excellence of *kung* and *chih*, refined language, and aroused emotions.[g] [34]

[f] 古人之學者有二，今人之學者有四。夫子門徒，轉相師受，通聖人之經者，謂之儒。屈原，宋玉，枚乘，長卿之徒，止於辭賦，則謂之文。今之儒，博窮子史，但能識其事，不能通其理者，謂之學。至如不便爲詩如閻纘，善爲章奏如伯松，若此之流，汎謂之筆。

[g] 吟詠風謠，流連哀思者，謂之文……筆退則非謂成篇，進則不云取義，神其巧惠，筆端而已。至如文者，惟須綺縠紛披，宮徵靡曼，脣吻遒會，情靈搖蕩。

Hsiao I thus distinguishes literature formally by its aesthetic patterning and its association with music, whence derives its emotional and affective power; he relegates *pi* to some undefined twilight zone between scholarship and belles-letters.

To what do we owe the appearance of the *wen-pi* distinction and subsequent variations in its interpretation? It seems to me that the answer lies in the efforts of Six Dynasties literary critics to reduce the overly inclusive category of *wen* to an entity of somewhat more definite and manageable proportions. To turn first to formal considerations must have seemed an obvious step to take in the light of current interests and discoveries. In the first place, the decentralization and uncertainty of politics fostered a de-emphasis on orthodoxy or didactic function, manifested in many fields. Second, on the literary scene the proliferation of new genres of writing created a demand for some kind of classifying, selective principle, a need which became particularly acute with the growing popularity of anthologizing. Simply assigning a different function, content, or origin to each individual genre would not reduce the chaos of multiple forms; rhyme, however, would offer at least one means of establishing tangibly discrete categories. And finally, the new awareness of tonal properties of the language and the resulting refinement of prosodic rules also suggested considerations of sound and rhythm as likely distinguishing features of one class of writing, with rhyme again the clearest exploitation of these auditory elements, an obvious first choice.[35] Critics like Hsiao T'ung and Hsiao I introduced somewhat broader criteria of content and function, but these were still based on formal qualities.

The opposition of *wen* to *pi* did persist beyond this period, for the *Bunkyō hifuron* (The Literary Mirror: Secret Repository of Discussions) of Kūkai (774–835) contains the following passage from an unknown T'ang dynasty text:

> The *Wen-pi shih* (forms of *wen* and *pi*) says: The way of composition lies only in *pi* and *wen*. *Wen* includes lyric poetry, rhymeprose, inscription, eulogy, admonition, appreciation, condolence, dirge, and the like. *Pi* includes proclamation, strategem, dispatch, summons, memorial, proposal, letter, report, and the like. To speak of them more directly, what is rhymed is *wen*, and what is unrhymed is *pi*. *Wen* is completed by joining two lines; *pi* takes shape by using four lines. *Wen* is bound together by rhyme, for the two verses are linked by their mutual harmony. *Pi* does not use rhyme, and the formation of the four lines [into a whole] rests in the way they follow one another. Thus the four lines of *pi* are comparable to the two lines of *wen*: on examination *wen* and *pi* are approximately as described.[h][36]

h 文筆式云：製作之道，唯筆與文。文者，詩，賦，銘，頌，箴，讚，弔，誄等是也；筆者，詔，策，移，檄，章，奏，書，啓等也。即而言之，韻者爲文，非韻者爲筆。文以兩句而會，筆以四句而成。文繫於韻，兩句相會，取於諧合也；筆不取韻，四句而成，佳於變通。故筆之四句，此文之二句，驗之文筆，率皆如此也。

This text not only retains the Six Dynasties terminology but also employs the earlier formalistic distinguishing criterion of rhyme. But this is an anomalous instance, for other evidence shows that these two terms were no longer being employed in contrast to one another.

Instead, the *wen-pi* dichotomy was replaced at times by that between *shih* and *pi*, poetry and prose, which had already come into use. Two examples include the saying describing the poet Wang Wei (701–761) and his younger brother Wang Chin (d. 781?): "In court, the prose of the Minister on the Left; under heaven the poetry of the Secretary on the Right," and Chao Lin's *Yin-hua lu*: "Han Wen-kung [Yü] (768–824) and Meng Tung-yeh [Chiao] (751–814) were good friends. Han's official writings were extremely lofty and Meng's strong point was pentasyllabic verse, so at the time people spoke of 'Meng's poetry and Han's prose.'"[37] More persistent, however, was a new distinction between *wen* and *shih*. *Wen* in any case could no longer be used to denote lyric poetry or other rhymed, tonally regulated, parallel, embellished, or emotionally expressive writings, since it had been appropriated by Han Yü and followers of his *ku-wen* movement to refer, on the contrary, to prose; the term *pi* largely fell into disuse. This demise of the Six Dynasties terminology can be seen from the following statement of Lu Yu (1125–1210):

> The poets of the Southern Dynasties called *wen, pi*. Thus the biography of Shen Yüeh says: "Hsieh Hsüan-hui [T'iao] was good at poetry, and Jen Yen-sheng [Fang] (460–508) was skilled at prose; Yüeh could do both." Also the biography of Yü Chien-wu (fl. 520) [includes] letter of emperor Chien-wen [Hsiao Kang] (503–507) to the prince of Hsiang-tung [Hsiao I]. In discussing the degradation of literature, it says: "Poetry having reached this state, prose will also follow." It also speaks of "the poetry of Hsieh T'iao and Shen Yüeh and the prose of Jen Fang and Lu Ch'ui (470–526)." The biography of Jen Fang also has the saying "Shen's poetry and Jen's prose." Tu [Fu's] (712–770) poem, "Sent to Chia Chih and Yen Wu," says: "Chia's prose expounds a solitary zeal; / Yen's poems extend to several works." Tu Mu (803–852) also writes: "Tu [Fu's] poems and Han [Yü's] prose I read when sadness comes; / It's like borrowing Ma-ku's claw to scratch an itchy spot." They have also appropriated the terms of the Southern Dynasties. When these past dynasties talked of poetry as *shih* [versus] *pi*, they were wrong.[i][38]

---

i 南朝詞人，謂文爲筆。故沈約傳云，謝玄暉善爲詩，任彥昇工於筆，約兼而有之。又庾肩吾傳，梁簡文與湘東王書。論文章之弊曰，詩既若此，筆又如之。又曰，謝朓沈約之詩，任昉陸倕之筆，任昉傳。又有沈詩任筆之語，老杜寄賈至嚴武詩云，賈筆論孤憤，嚴詩賦幾篇。杜牧之亦云，杜詩韓筆愁來讀，似倩麻姑癢處抓。亦襲南朝語爾，往時諸晁謂詩爲詩筆，亦非也。

Moreover, despite voices like Ssu-k'ung T'u's (837–908) attesting to the greater demands, and by implication the superiority of poetry—"Prose (*wen*) is difficult, but poetry is even more difficult,"[39] the formal distinctions were no longer being used to establish dissimilarities in function. Instead, they were simply recognized and attibuted to differences in canonical ancestry, thus blurring the neat division into four fields (classical scholarship, history, philosophy, and belles-lettres) so carefully established by Six Dynasties theorists. Liu Tsung-yüan (733–819), for example, at the beginning of one of his prefaces, clearly distinguished between two types of language according to their differing classical origins. After observing that literature (*wen-chang*) has two paths, one based on compiling and recounting (*chu-shu*) and the other on comparison and association (*pi-hsing*), he writes:

> The tradition of compiling and recounting derives from the maxims of the *Book of History*, the Images and Appended Words of the *Book of Changes*, and the corrections of the *Spring and Autumn Annals*. It demands loftiness, strength, breadth, and sincerity; the language must be proper and the reasoning complete, what is best preserved in records and documents. The tradition of comparison and association derives from the songs of Shun and Yü and the airs and elegances of the Shang and Chou dynasties. It demands beauty, pattern, clarity, and transcendence, lucidity of word and excellence of meaning, best handed down in songs. When one examines the principles behind these two types, they are not the same at all, so that scholars who wield the brush can generally master one only, and rarely both.[j][40]

Liu includes poetry under the general rubric of *wen* or *wen-chang*, but he also emphasizes the formal, linguistic differences between poetry and prose; this is what the Six Dynasties would have called *wen* versus *pi*, but Liu's distinction is no longer an invidious one. Now, *all* writing was once again viewed as fulfilling the same purpose, an explicitly didactic one which was intensified from the statement attributed to Han Yü by Li Han—"*Wen* is for connecting the Way," to that of Chou Tun-i (1017–1073)—"*Wen* is a means of conveying the Way."[41] Chu Hsi (1130–1200), for example. asserts the unity of function shared by the two forms when he writes: "When have students of literature today wasted much energy in writing a work? If one focuses on learning in order to elucidate principle (*li*), then one will naturally produce a good literary composition (*wen-chang*). It is the same with poetry."[42] This Neo-Confucian orthodoxy came to be codified in the writings

j 著述者流蓋出於書之謨訓，易之象繫，春秋之筆削。其要在於高壯廣厚，詞正而理備，謂宜藏於簡册也。比興者流蓋出於虞夏之詠歌，殷周之風雅。其要在於麗則清越，言暢而意美，謂宜流於謠誦也。茲二者考其旨義乖離不合，故兼筆之士恆偏勝獨得，而罕有兼者焉。

of various Sung dynasty critics as method, to be learned through meditation on the works of past masters and regarded as a means of achieving self-cultivation, self-transcendence, and enlightenment.[43]

Given this identity of function, which would admit none superior to it, the only criteria by which later critics could hope to assert the distinctiveness or independence of any type of writing were formal ones. This was the situation confronting the Ming writer Li Tung-yang (1447–1516), who therefore repeatedly stressed the purely formal distinction between poetry and prose: "When words form a pattern, that is prose (*wen*), and prose that forms musical sounds is poetry (*shih*). Both poetry and prose are called words, but each has its own form (*t'i*) and should not be confused."[44] Like Western formalist critics, Li maintains that the fundamental differences between poetry and prose lie in the former's auditory and specifically musical features and its greater degree of regulation, and he emphasizes the restrictions imposed on poetry; although prose is also subject to certain standards, it nevertheless allows the writer a greater degree of freedom:

> Now prose is words formed into a pattern, and in poetry they are further formed into musical tones. The usefulness of patterns is to be found in their capacity to record and make detailed statements, while developing and embellishing, restraining and letting go, and doing what one wants to do, but there must be a fixed standard. As for songs and chants, hums and sighs, which flow and move, their usefulness lies in the musical sounds, but the regulation of high and low, long and short, must be definite and unconfused.[k][45]

Li's mention of the narrative expository function of prose recalls Liu Tsung-yüan's distinction between two different types of discourse, and while Li focuses on the musical rather than the metaphorical nature of poetic language here,[46] he nevertheless goes on to agree with the T'ang critic's opinion that not only are the two literary forms quite distinct, they also require two equally distinctive types of talent that are rarely found in the same person. In a passage from his *Lu-t'ang shih-hua*, for example, he opens by concurring with Huang T'ing-chien's (1045–1105) emphasis on the differing forms of poetry and prose, though disagreeing with the earlier's poet's extreme interpretation of the methods of Tu Fu and Han Yü ("Poetry and prose each has its form. Han uses prose to write poetry, and Tu uses poetry to write prose, thus neither is skilled"[47]). Li Tung-yang then develops the implication of the formulations cited above that since poetry goes one step beyond prose in its manipulation of language, it is the more difficult of the two.

k 夫文者言之成章，而詩又其成聲者也。章之爲用，貴乎紀述鋪敍，發揮而藻飾，操縱開闔，惟所欲爲，而必有一定之準。若歌吟咏歎，流通動盪之用，則存乎聲，而高下長短之節，亦截乎不可亂。

> The forms of poetry and prose are not the same. Someone in the past said that Tu Tzu-mei used poetry to write prose and that Han T'ui-chih used prose to write poetry. This is certainly not so, yet in what they attain, each has his own strong points and unique areas of achievement. As for the famous writers of today, when those self-proclaimed prose writers come to write poetry, they miss the mark entirely, though to the ends of their lives they will never realize [their errors[l 48]].

Among other things, this passage not only distinguishes between *shih* and *wen*, but it also in effect separates poetry from writing as a whole, by using the term *wen-chang* to refer to prose alone. In any case, like his Western counterparts, Li is certainly arguing for the greater difficulty—and, by implication, the superiority—of poetry, for he avers later that "when poetry is too clumsy, it approaches prose."[49]

Li supports this distinction by tracing it back to the Confucian canon, setting off the *Shih ching* from the other five texts: "Of the Six Classics of antiquity, the *Changes, History, Spring and Autumn Annals, Ritual,* and *Music* are all prose, and only the *feng, ya,* and *sung* (airs, elegances, and hymns) can be called poetry."[50] As is the case with poetry in general, so the essence of this difference lies in the odes' ties to music. Elsewhere Li again emphasizes this connection and bemoans its general dissolution in latter-day works:

> The *Shih* is one of the Six Classics but contains its own teaching, which is none other than music, one of the Six Arts (ritual, music, archery, charioteering, writing, and mathematics). Music begins with poetry and ends with rules. . . . In later generations poetry and music were separated into two, and though there were formal rules, there was no music and rhyme. This is nothing more than prose written in parallel lines.[m51]

In other words, poetry consists not only in the mastery of structural parallelism, but also in the full exploitation of the acoustical features of the language—intonation and rhyme—which link it with music. Li also writes that "if you contemplate the *Yüeh chi* (Record of Music) and discuss the aspects of musical sound, then you will recognize the method of poetry."[52]

Although Li criticizes the mere observance of rules without a corresponding music throughout the *Lu-t'ang shih-hua,* he nevertheless underlines the importance of understanding and being able to manipulate all of the formal elements of poetry. Distinctions between the two major forms, for example, must be clearly observed,

---

l 詩與文不同體，昔人謂杜子美以詩爲文，韓退之以文爲詩。固未然，然其所得所就，亦各有偏長獨到之處。近見名家大手，以文章自命者，至其爲詩，則毫釐千里，終其身而不悟。

m 詩在六經中，別是一教，蓋六藝中之樂也。樂始於詩終於律……後世詩與樂判而爲二，雖有格律，而無音韻，是不過爲俳偶之文而已。

although there is a certain degree of flexibility: "Ancient and regulated verse are not the same forms; with each, one must use the proper form in order to adhere to the style. Although regulated verse may contain some elements of ancient verse, no qualities of regulated verse may slip into ancient verse."[53] In general, he writes further on, one should master all styles and sounds: "In poetry one must have a perfect eye and one must also have a perfect ear. The eye focuses on formal styles and the ear focuses on musical sounds. If you can hear which string on a zither has just been stopped, then you have a perfect ear. If under moonlight you can discern five different colors of thread through the window, then you have a perfect eye." He continues by explaining that this would enable a person to recognize the periodic formal style (*shih-tai ko-tiao*) of an unidentified poem and relates an anecdote in which he impresses two friends with his own ability to do so.[54] A familiarity with musical aspects can also enable one to distinguish among works of different geographical areas: "The sounds and melodies of the songs and poems of today are different in being light or heavy, clear or turbid, long or short, high or low. Someone who listens to them can know without asking whether they are from Wu or from Yüeh."[55]

Despite this emphasis on the distinctiveness of periodic or regional formal styles, however, Li Tung-yang does not, unlike both earlier and later critics, recommend the imitation of any one of them. At several points in his *Lu-t'ang shih-hua* he argues against straining to copy old models faithfully or becoming "mired in rules." This idea also underlies his blunt estimation that "The T'ang poets did not talk of poetic method—that is largely a phenomenon of the Sung, yet the Sung poets didn't accomplish much in the way of poetry."[56] Despite this preference for T'ang poetry, and for that of Tu Fu in particular, however, Li never insists on declaring them as models to be imitated, summing up his position in one of his prefaces:

> Some people say that one must write like the T'ang or write like the Sung; they bow their heads in bewilderment and walk with shortened steps, not daring to change one word or produce one saying. Even if they resemble [the past models], they are worthless; how much more so if they don't resemble them! It has been said that poetry involves a different talent from that concerned with books and that poetry has a different interest from that concerned with principle, but unless one reads extensively and thoroughly understands principle, then one cannot write it.[57] One must have extensive learning in order to accumulate principle and select objects to broaden one's talent, match these with sounds and rhymes, harmonize them with rhythm and measure, and then one's words can be chanted aloud and recited for a long time, can record what is current and transmit

what is past. How can it be that a certain poet must be copied or a period imitated in order to be called poetry?[n 58]

In other words, Li advocates neither an exclusive interest in rules and method nor the imitation of a particular poet who might embody those rules, both of which are part of the often narrow interest in form of the *ko-tiao* school of Chinese criticism with which Li is generally associated. Instead, like the Western proponents of such distinctions, he is interested in setting off a class of writing as "poetic," on linguistic, formal grounds, emphasizing poetry's distinctive use of the auditory resources of the language and suggesting that it is superior to prose because of its adherence to different and more stringent laws. He also focuses on the musical qualities of poetry to underscore the differences in content and function between the two: one records facts and events, the other expresses emotion and elicits a specifically aesthetic appreciation.

To be sure, this interest in subject matter and emotion was anathema to Western formalists, and Li certainly does not share their conception of poetic language as an opaque object focusing attention on itself alone. Nevertheless, the similarities between them are striking, especially when we consider the situations implicit in their explicit formulations. In contrasting poetic to nonpoetic, ordinary, or practical language, the Western theorists were attempting to delineate something which both obeyed different formal laws and fulfilled different functions from writing as a whole. In fact, the primary motivation for the formal distinction seems to have been to support their notion of poetry as liberated from established considerations of content and communication. For Li Tung-yang the situation is much the same: language and literature have become tied to communicative and explicitly didactic purposes (in contrast to the more flexible and belle-lettristic notions of the Six Dynasties), so that by opposing *shih* to *wen* on formal grounds, he is trying to assure it some breathing room in other respects as well; his nods in the direction of poetry's political usefulness seem little more than token gestures. Where the pre-T'ang theorists were making formal distinctions in a groping effort to delimit the notion of *wen*, Li is moving poetry out from under the umbrella of *wen* altogether. But this focus on formal considerations alone, which he extends even to poetry's canonical ancestor, had more far-reaching practical consequences in China than in the less historically conscious West, for it supported an already established tendency toward a backward-looking hypostatization and enshrinement of past eras

[n] 或者又曰，必爲唐，必爲宋，規規焉俛首縮步，至不敢易一辭出一語，縱使似之，亦不足貴矣；況未必似乎。說者謂詩有別才非關乎書，詩有別趣非關乎理，然非讀書之多，識理之至，則不能作。必博學以聚乎理，取物以廣夫才，而比之以聲韻，和之以節奏，則其爲辭，高可諷，長可詠，近可以述，而遠則可以傳矣。豈必模其家，效其代，然後謂之詩哉。

and masters, which Li himself opposed. Both he and his Western counterparts were trying to guarantee a certain autonomy to poetry, but in practice, at least, archaism, imitation, and the dangers of triviality remained stronger in China than did the self-reflective hermeticism of the symbolists in the West.

Later Ming dynasty critics were in fact less interested in extending Li Tung-yang's theoretical remarks on the formal differences between poetry and prose than in encouraging some of these logical, practical consequences. Li Ming-yang (1472–1529) does, however, distinguish between the two on similar grounds in one of his prefaces:

> By the time poetry reached the T'ang, ancient melodies had been lost. But there were singable melodies during the T'ang, and the lofty ones could still be played on pipes and strings. The people of the Sung emphasized principle and did not emphasize melody, so that T'ang melodies were also lost.... When has poetry ever not had principle? But if you solely use the language of principle, then how will you not be writing prose? And what will be poetry?[°][59]

Like Li Tung-yang, he emphasizes the musical qualities specific to poetry and its correspondingly minor communicative or didactic function: it is the task of prose, not poetry, to emphasize such matters as *li*. But generally, along with other of the Seven Former and Latter Masters (*ch'ien-hou ch'i-tzu*) of the Ming, Li Meng-yang is more concerned with developing the groundwork laid by Yen Yü and other Sung critics, focusing on such matters as rules, method, and the study of ideal models of the past.[60] Indeed, he is said to have been responsible for coining a call to imitation that became a virtual given for subsequent generations: "Prose must be like the Ch'in and Han, and poetry must be like the high T'ang; nothing else is worth discussing."[61]

Wang Shih-chen (1526–1590), one of the Seven Latter Masters, agrees with Li Meng-yang on the necessity of imitation and the role played by rules in even the most ancient of texts. In his lengthy collection of remarks on literature and other arts, for example, he writes that "When people say that the three hundred airs and elegances [of the *Shih ching*] and the *Ku-shih shih-chiu shou* (Nineteen Ancient Poems) do not have syntactic rules, they are wrong. Of course they have rules—there are just no differences in level to be traced,"[62] and he goes on to criticize the *Book of Odes* for some of its formally clumsy aspects. Like Li Tung-yang, he is also interested in distinguishing poetry from prose on formal grounds, and he uses the differing roles of rules as one basis for making this distinction: "Poetry has constant forms; its skill naturally comes from working within these forms. Prose does not

○ 詩至唐，古調亡矣，然自有唐調可歌詠，高者猶足被管絃。宋人主理而不主調，於是唐調亦亡……詩何嘗無理，若專作理語，何不作文，而詩爲耶？

have established rules; its artistry moves beyond rules."[63] He harks back to Six Dynasties parlance by suggesting that one specific distinctive feature of poetry is the presence of rhyme and also anticipates a later trend by claiming that this extends even to the *I ching* (Book of Changes): "Eight-tenths of the Hexagrams, Remarks, and Images in the *Changes* are rhymed, thus it is also poetry."[64]

But it is not until the Ch'ing dynasty that a more extensive theoretical discussion of formal distinctions, as opposed to the concern with practical matters of craft, once again emerges—in the writings of the critic Wu Ch'iao or Wu Shu (ca. 1660), who at several points in his *Wei-lu shih-hua* (Wei-lu's Remarks on Poetry) explores the differences between *shih* and *wen*. Recalling Huang T'ing-chien, he feels that they certainly exist: "The prose of Li [Po] (701–762) and Tu [Fu] is, in the end, the prose of poets and not the prose of prose writers. The poetry of Ou [-yang Hsiu] (1007–1072) and Su [Shih] (1037–1101) is, in the end, the poetry of prose writers and not the poetry of poets."[65] More often than not, he regards the latter situation as the more egregious of the two, taking various Sung poets to task for "using prose to write poetry."[66]

Wherein do the differences lie? In general, Wu Ch'iao focuses on specifically linguistic areas of differentiation. One passage which cites with approval a remark from Su Shih bridges Wu's interests in form, content, and function:

> Tzu-chan said: "The fundamental principle of poetry is unusual interest. What is out of the ordinary and accords with the Way is interest." This saying is excellent. Without unusual interest, how can one write poetry? What is out of the ordinary and does not accord with the Way is confused babble. What is not out of the ordinary and accords with the Way is prose.[P67]

And what causes poetry to be "out of the ordinary," he suggests in several other passages reminiscent of the Western emphasis on "deviance" and "distortion," is its use of language. These discussions often employ quite vivid metaphors and center around comparisons among the poetry of the T'ang, the Sung, which he has criticized for being too much like prose, and the Ming, which falls even wider of the mark. Early in his *shih-hua*, for instance, he writes that poetry should have meaning, but there are different methods of presenting it:

> T'ang poetry has meaning but relies on comparison and association to manifest it in various ways. Its language is indirect and subtle, like a person wearing clothes and cap. Sung poetry also has meaning, but uses description and rarely comparison and association. Its language is direct and straightforward, like a person completely naked. The Ming imitates the

P 子瞻云，詩以奇趣爲宗，反常合道爲趣。此語最善，無奇趣，何以爲詩。反　　常而不合道，是謂亂談，不反常而合道，則文章也。

high T'ang; its words are brilliant on the surface but lack both meaning and rules, just like a puppet covered with patterned embroidery.[q][68]

Wu reiterates these opinions when he writes that poetry is like "a secluded orchid in an empty valley: it does not seek to have anyone appreciate it." T'ang poets come closest to this ideal because they are concerned neither with their readers' grasp of the meaning nor with their approbation; Sung poets are worried about the former and thus are overly direct, and Ming poets about the latter and thus too "jangling," "glittering," and imitative.[69] As far as poetic language is concerned, then, it should be subtle and indirect, primarily through the use of metaphor, thus "in poetry the meaning generally emerges from the side," whereas "in prose it emerges from the front."[70]

Wu Ch'iao's point is that the linguistic or formal distinctions between poetry and prose are directed toward an even more important difference in effect. This becomes especially clear in a long passage whose central metaphor recalls that of Valéry between dancing and walking:

> Someone asked: "What are the realms of poetry and prose?" and I answered: As for their meanings, how can they be different? Their meanings are the same but their functions are not. This is why the forms and structures of poetry and prose are different. The language of prose must communicate,[71] whereas the language of poetry is indirect. The *History* speaks of political affairs, thus it is fitting that its language communicates. The *Odes* speaks of personal nature, thus it is fitting that its language is indirect. This can be compared to the way grain produces both cooked rice and wine. Prose is like steaming it to make rice, and poetry is like fermenting it to make wine. When prose employs words, they must serve the meaning; it is like cooked rice which does not alter the outward form of the grain, and once you've eaten it, then you are satiated. When poetry employs words, they do not have to serve the meaning; it is like wine which completely alters the grain's outward form, and once you've drunk it, you are tipsy.[r][72]

Since prose is useful in human affairs, he continues, its language must "reach" or communicate, whereas since poetry is useless, its language must be beautiful and indirect. In particular, it is poetry's link with song and music that distinguishes it

q 唐詩有意，而託比興以雜出之，其詞婉而微，如人而衣冠。宋詩亦有意，惟賦而少比興，其詞徑以直，如人而赤體。明之瞎盛唐詩，字面煥然，無意無法，直是木偶被文繡耳。

r 問曰，詩文之界如何。答曰，意豈有二，意同而所以用之者不同，是以詩文體製有異耳，文之詞達，詩之詞婉。書以道政事，故宜詞達。詩以道性情，故宜詞婉。意喻之米飯與酒所同出，文喻之炊而爲飯，詩喻之釀而爲酒。文之措詞，必副乎意，猶飯之不變米形，噉之則飽也。詩之措詞，不必副乎意，猶酒之變盡米形，飲之爲醉也。

from prose; as Wu notes later, since "poetry is originally music and song, it certainly must have rhyme."[73] In other words, Wu Ch'iao stresses the formal distinctiveness of poetic language in order to support his notion of its nonutiliarian, noncommunicative function. Although he does not deny the importance of meaning, his call for its indirectness in poetry certainly dislodges it from the focal point it occupies in prose; the interest in poetry resides instead in the manner in which it is presented and apprehended. Thus, as was the case with his counterparts in the West and with Li Tung-yang, these claims for the distinctiveness of poetry are made at the expense of diminishing its overall significance.

Indeed, the seriously devalued position which poetry came to occupy during the Ch'ing is implicit in the writings of the classical scholar Juan Yüan (1764–1849), who rejects the opposition of *shih* to *wen* and revives the Six Dynasties conception of *wen* instead. In his *Shu Liang Chao-ming t'ai-tzu Wen hsüan hsü hou* (Postface to Prince Chao-ming of Liang's Preface to the Anthology of Literature), for example, he begins with the earlier text's separation of *wen* as belles-lettres from three other areas of learning: the Classics, philosophy, and history were not included in the anthology, he recalls, because they were not characterized by "profound thought" and "literary elegance," nor did they "regard embellishment as fundamental" (both quotations from Hsiao T'ung), hence they could not be called *wen*. In true archaistic fashion, however, Juan immediately jumps from the sixth-century text to the *Wen-yen* (Embellished Words) commentary on the *I ching*, which he attributes erroneously to Confucius. This work, he argues, is the ancestor of all *wen* and suggests by its own example that *wen* should be defined by the use of parallelism and rhyme. Since the *ku-wen* movement of the T'ang, these two features have been scorned, and *wen* has been used to denote nonparallel, unrhymed prose. But "Confucius himself called his words *wen*, and within the work, eight out of forty lines are parallel, and five out of thirty sayings are rhymed. How could he be regarding [parallelism and rhyme] as unorthodox or inferior form?"[74]

Implicit in this rhetorical question is the fact that those very formal features by means of which Li Tung-yang and other critics had asserted the distinctiveness of poetry were now misprised, because they had resulted in its trivialization. Only ancient prose was now defined as conveying meaning, and all other forms were by implication inconsequential. Juan is thus attempting to defend rhymed writings by tracing their features to the sage himself, and by lending them the ancient mystique of *wen* through the revival of Six Dynasties terminology. He therefore concludes in this preface that what is currently labeled as *ku-wen* should more correctly be classified with the three non-belle-lettristic areas of learning, and he echoes Hsiao T'ung's content-based criteria (classical scholarship elucidates the Confucian canon; history records facts; and philosophy establishes a doctrine). When someone asks him what his own "Postface" should be called, he answers, quite consistently, that since it is unembellished it is a work of philosophy.

Juan's efforts to legitimize the devalued formally distinctive features are equally clear in his *Wen-yen shuo* (Interpretation of the Embellished Words). Once again he describes the commentary on the hexagrams *ch'ien* and *k'un* as the ancestor of all literature and asserts, furthermore:

> When those who write literary compositions do not bother to match sounds in order to form rhymes or polish their words so that they will go far,[75] which enables men to easily recite and remember them, and when they use single [nonparallel] language, recklessly writing up to thousands of words, then they do not realize that this is what the ancients called straightforward words or disputative language, and not words with embellishment. This is not what Confucius called literature. Of the several hundred words in the *Wen-yen*, many of the lines are rhymed.[s][76]

As this passage demonstrates, unlike Western formalist critics, Juan Yüan emphasizes the specifically communicative and didactic usefulness of the formal features in question: they are handy mnemonic devices for propagating a doctrine. He goes on to note that Confucius

> wanted to make [his commentary] easily recitable both near and far and easily transmittable both then and now; all ministers and scholars can remember and recite it. In order to communicate to the myriad things on heaven and earth and admonish states and individuals, not only did he use much rhyme, but he also used much parallelism.[t]

Then after citing several four-character parallel phrases he concludes that "all parallelism is *wen*."[77]

Although these two essays do not explicitly oppose *wen* to *pi*, in his *Wen-yün shuo* (Interpretation of Literary Rhyme) Juan discusses the pre-T'ang distinction and broadens his conception of rhyme. In responding to his son Juan Fu's (b. 1802) query as to why, if *wen* and *pi* were distinguished in the past on the basis of rhyme, the *Wen hsüan* contains so many unrhymed works, Juan Yüan explains: "What during the Liang dynasty was commonly called rhyme meant, of course, end-rhyme, but it also referred to the intonation and rhyme (*yin-yün*) within a line. This is what the ancients called *kung* and *yü* and what people today call level and oblique [tones]."[78] All true works of literature (*wen*), from the *Shih ching* and *Li sao* onward, have employed these musical principles and parallelism, if not pure end-rhyme. Juan cites the famous passage from Shen Yüeh's biography of Hsieh Ling-yün to support his

---

[s] 爲文章者，不務協音以成韻，修詞以達遠，使人易誦易記，而惟以單行之語，縱橫恣肆。動輒千言萬字，不知此乃古人所謂直言之言，論難之語，非言之有文者也，非孔子之所謂文也。文言數百字，幾於句句用韻。

[t] 要使遠近易誦，古今易傳，公卿學士，皆能記誦，以通天地萬物，以警國家身心，不但多用韻，抑且多用偶。

expanded definition of rhyme and once again holds up the *Wen-yen* commentary as the precedent for defining *wen* by the use of all of these structural and auditory features. This is further reinforced, he argues, by the *Great Preface*, which relates *wen* and music, and he uses the first poem in the *Shih ching* as an example of both end-rhyme and musical patterning. In conclusion, he writes: "All literature in sound uses *kung* and *shang* and in appearance displays elegant flourish." Thus the nonparallel, unrhymed prose written at present "is none other than the plain writing (*pi*) of the ancients, and not their literature (*wen*)."[79]

In sum, whereas Li Tung-yang was simply using formal features as a means of distinguishing poetry and prose, the intervening centuries, with their emphasis on the often sterile imitation of ancient method and rules, have forced Juan Yüan to defend rhyme and parallelism in his efforts to rehabilitate the aesthetic function of literature. Ironically, however, he can do this only by giving them an orthodox heritage and stressing their mnemonic usefulness, thus reversing the very thrust of Li's distinction by justifying formal features on the basis of their didactic function. His revival of the *wen-pi* dichotomy represents an attempt to shift the balance between rhymed and unrhymed writings and restore the aura of *wen* to the former, but with grounds quite different from those of his Six Dynasties predecessors.

Juan's position demonstrates both the problems and the dangers inherent in making formal distinctions and definitions, in China and the West. For one thing, the fallacy of positing literature as formally distinct from other kinds of utterances and thus linguistically autonomous has been persuasively demonstrated by both linguists and critics: there is too much evidence that "nonliterature" displays the same formal qualities as does what is defined as literature. William Hendricks, for example, argues against establishing a dichotomy between poetic and ordinary language because, among other things, "this differentiation assumes that words in scientific texts do not undergo contextual modification," i.e. interact with each other in the manner formalists describe as characteristic of poetry. He feels that "emphasis needs to be shifted from considerations of poetic LANGUAGE to considerations of poetic TEXTS. Strictly speaking, there is no such thing as poetic language, there are only poems."[80] Mary Pratt also criticizes the formalist distinction, primarily by means of an extensive analysis of so-called "nonliterary" speech. She points out that literary language is not privileged in its exploitation of rhythm and sound values or deviations from syntactic norms, and that ordinary language is not solely concerned with communication and grammaticality but also with what Hendricks called the "contextual modification" of its verbal materials, with *how* something is being said. Formalist criticism, however, despite its exhaustive examination of literary devices, never considers their possible role in utterances outside literature:

> Examples from literature are virtually never accompanied by data from extraliterary discourse. Instead, devices observed in literature were as-

sumed to be "literary," to constitute "literariness" (the term is Jakobson's) because nonliterature was assumed a priori not to possess the properties of literature. Hence even terminologically, the right-hand term of the poetic/ nonpoetic dichotomy scarcely mattered at all. "Nonpoetic" could be specified variously as "practical," "utilitarian," "spoken," "prosaic," "scientific," "everyday," "communicative," "referential," or any combination of these without in the least disturbing the notion of what "poetic" was.[81]

More importantly, we need accept neither Hendricks' suggestion to concentrate on individual texts nor Pratt's use of speech act theory to realize the limitations this poetic/nonpoetic language opposition places on literature itself. Not only does it assume the superiority of the one over the other on spurious grounds, but, as Pratt observes, "a definition of literature which impoverishes and misrepresents nonliterature equally impoverishes and misrepresents literature."[82] This is not the place for me to attempt to provide an alternative definition of literature; perhaps, as Tzvetan Todorov has argued in his debunking of the formalist dichotomy, it does not even exist.[83] Certainly the formalist/structuralist focus on the text alone impoverishes literature by eliminating such factors as reader, author, and world, and the interactions among them, from consideration. The world of the formalists is a self-enclosed, exclusively linguistic-literary one, although even the intraliterary development of forms over time is given short shrift. They are unable to conceive of literature in human terms, as presenting a vision of reality which arises out of and is intimately connected to that reality. Nor, by definition, do they allow literature to have any effect on that world. Despite the insistence of many formalists on the "indissolubility of sound and sense," their notion of literature diminishes, if not eliminates altogether, the role of the second member of that pair. Divorcing literature from any utilitarian or communicative function in effect robs it of any potential significance: if its purpose is to shortcircuit meaning, then it has no meaning at all.

1. Included in the *Chao-ming Wen hsüan* (Taipei, 1969) 45, p. 636. All translations are my own.

2. Alex Preminger et al., ed., *Princeton Encyclopedia of Poetry and Poetics* (Princeton, 1974), p. 286.

3. Roman Jakobson, *Recent Russian Poetry, Sketch 1* (Prague, 1921), p. 11, quoted in Boris M. Ejxenbaum, "The Theory of the Formal Method," trans. I. R. Titunik, in *Readings in Russian Poetics: Formalist and Structuralist Views*, ed. Ladislav Matejka and Krystyna Pomorska (Cambridge, Mass., 1971), p. 8.

4. Paul Valéry, "Poésie et pensée abstraite," in *Oeuvres*, ed. Jean Hytier, 2 vols. (Tours, 1959), 1:1324.

5. Viktor Žirmunskij, "The Aims of Poetics," quoted in Victor Erlich, *Russian Formalism: History—Doctrine* (The Hague, 1969), p. 175. Erlich later points out that the emphasis on words and "devices" or "materials," rather than "means of expression," represented part of a large aim of avoiding unscientific psychologism: "... the Formalist theoreticians were intent on side-stepping the vexing issue of the creative personality. Literary technology seemed to them a much firmer ground than the psychology of creation. Hence the tendency to treat literature as a suprapersonal, if not impersonal, phenomenon, as a deliberate application of techniques to "materials" rather than a self-expression, as a convention rather than as a confession" (p. 190).

6. Osip M. Brik, "Contributions to the Study of Verse Language," trans. C. H. Severens, in *Readings in Russian Poetics*, p. 125.

7. Mary Louise Pratt, *Toward a Speech Act Theory of Literary Discourse* (Bloomington, 1977), p. 13.

8. Brik, "Contributions," p. 124.

9. For descriptions of the metamorphosis effected on "ordinary" language as a "distortion," "violence," "infraction," or "disruption," see Jan Mukařovský, "Standard Language and Poetic Language," ed. and trans. Paul L. Garvin, in *Linguistics and Literary Style*, ed. Donald C. Freeman (New York, 1970), p. 42; Roman Jakobson, *On Czech Verse* (Berlin, 1923), quoted in Erlich, *Russian Formalism*, p. 219; Jean Cohen, *Structure du langage poétique* (Paris, 1966), p. 149, quoted in Gérard Genette, "Langage poétique, poétique du language," in *Essays in Semiotics/Essais de sémiotique*, ed. Julia Kristeva et al. (The Hague, 1971), p. 436; and Cleanth Brooks, "The Language of Paradox," in *The Well-Wrought Urn* (New York, 1947), pp. 3, 8–9.

10. Valéry, "Situation de Baudelaire," in *Oeuvres*, 1:611.

11. Stéphane Mallarmé, "Crise de vers," in *Oeuvres complètes*, ed. H. Mondor and G. Jean-Aubry (Paris, 1945), p. 368.

12. Rainer Maria Rilke, letter of March 1922 to Gräfin Margot Sizzo-Noris Crouy, in *Briefe*, 2 vols. (Wiesbaden, 1950), 2:339–340. Michael Riffaterre also writes: "Poetry is language, but it produces effects that language in everyday speech does not consistently produce ...: the poem follows more rules (e.g. meter, lexical restrictions, etc.) and displays more conspicuous interrelationships between its constitutive elements than do casual utterances.... The poem is like a microscosm, with its own system of references and analogies." From "Describing Poetic Structures: Two Approaches to Baudelaire's *Les Chats*," *Yale French Studies* (1936), 36–37:200, 206.

13. Edward Stankiewicz, "Poetic and Non-poetic Language in Their Interrelation," in *Poetics*, ed. Donald Davie et al. (The Hague, 1961), p. 15. Stankiewicz uses the term "interiorization" to describe the "orientation towards the verbal material" itself that is characteristic of poetic language.

14. Heinrich Anz, "Poetische Sprache: Überlegungen zu ihrer ontologischen Bestimmung," *Euphorion* (1976), 70:346.

15. Edgar Allan Poe, "The Poetic Principle," in *The Complete Works of Edgar Allan Poe*, ed. James M. Harrison, 17 vols. (New York, 1965), 14:272.

16. Valéry, "Poésie et pensée abstraite," in *Oeuvres*, 1:1325–1326.

17. Ibid., 1:1331.

18. Viktor Šklovskij, "Potebnja," quoted by Ejxenbaum, *Readings in Russian Poetics*, p. 14.

19. In a 1914 pamphlet, *The Resurrection of the Word*, Šklovskij wrote: "If it is a definition of 'poetic' perception or of 'artistic' perception in general we are after, then we must surely hit upon this definition: 'artistic' perception is a perception that entails awareness of form (perhaps not only form, but invariably form)." Quoted by Ejxenbaum, *Readings in Russian Poetics*, p. 12.

20. Jan Mukařovský, "Standard Language and Poetic Language," pp. 43–44.

21. For discussions of the various meanings of this word and its compounds over time, see Kuo Shao-yü, *Chung-kuo wen-hsüeh p'i-p'ing shih* (History of Chinese Literary Criticism) (rpt. Hong Kong, n.d.), esp. pp. 2–4, 8–10, 23–25, 56–65, 92–96; Lo Ken-tse *Chung-kuo wen-hsüeh p'i-p'ing shih* (rpt. 3 vols. in 1, Hong Kong, n.d.), esp. pp. 45–49, 81–85, 140–145; and James J. Y. Liu, *Chinese Theories of Literature* (Chicago, 1975), pp. 7–9.

22. Several examples are given in Liu T'ien-hui, *Wen-pi k'ao* (Examination of *Wen* and *Pi*), in Juan Fu, ed., *Wen-pi k'ao* (*TSCC* ed., vol. 2623), p. 15.

23. Biography of Yen Yen-chih (384–456) (*Nan shih* [Southern History] 34); quoted, *inter alia*, in Kuo Shao-yü, *Chung-kuo wen-hsüeh p'i-p'ing shih*, p. 59.

24. These are taken from the biographies of Pao Ch'üan (*Liang shu* [Liang History] 30) and Liu Fan (534–581) (*Chou shu* [Chou History] 22), respectively, and are quoted in Hou K'ang, *Wen-pi k'ao*, in Juan Fu, p. 18. As Hou points out, if *wen* and *pi* were being considered here as one category, then the word "both" world have been unnecessary.

25. Fan Yeh, *Yü-chung yü chu sheng-chih shu* (Letter Sent to All My Nephews from Prison), *Sung shu* (Sung History) 69; included in abridged form in Kuo Shao-yü, *Chung-kuo li-tai wen-lun hsüan* (Anthology of Discussions of Literature in China through the Ages), (rpt. Hong Kong, 1978), p. 178.

26. From *Sung shu* 67; included in Kuo Shao-yü, *Chung-kuo li-tai wen-lun-hsüan*, pp. 170–171. Although not all commentators are in agreement here, Kuo feels that "floating" or "light" and "piercing" or "heavy" refer to level and oblique tones, respectively (p. 175).

27. For Verlaine, of course, "all the rest is Literature," as opposed to poetry, which alone adheres to his injunction that one must have "Music first, before everything."

28. From *Nan shih* 48; quoted by Huang K'an in Fan Wen-lan, ed., *Wen-hsin tiao-lung chu* (rpt. Taipei, 1975), p. 668.

The rules alluded to are the first four of Shen Yüeh's "Eight Faults of Poetry." "Level head" refers to the mistake of having the first and sixth and the second and seventh syllables of a pentasylabic couplet share the same tone. "Raised tail" refers to the use of identical tones in the last syllable of the first line of a couplet and the first syllable of the second. A line with "wasp's waist" employs words of the same tone in the second and fifth positions of a line. A poem with "crane's knee" has syllables with the same tone at the end of the first and third (i.e. unrhymed) lines.

29. Fan Wen-lan ed., *Wen-hsin tiao-lung chu*, p. 655.

30. In chapter 5 of his *Chung-kuo chung-ku wen-hsüeh-shih chiang-i* (Comments on the

History of Literature in Medieval China), quoted in Kuo Shao-yü, *Chung-kuo wen-hsüeh p'i-p'ing shih*, p. 57. As Kuo points out, Liu Shih-p'ei actually neglects to include Liu Hsieh's fifth chapter and begins his count of chapters on rhymed genres with the sixth instead.

31. Hsiao T'ung, *Wen hsüan hsü*, included in the *Wei Chin Nan-pei-ch'ao wen-hsüeh-shih ts'an-k'ao tzu-liao* (Research Materials for the History of Literature in the Wei, Chin, Northern and Southern Dynasties) (Peking, 1961), p. 572. Cf. translation by James Robert Hightower, in "The *Wen Hsüan* and Genre Theory," *HJAS* (1957), 20:529–530.

32. Ibid., pp. 572–573.

33. Ibid. p. 573.

34. *Li-yen p'ien hsia* (Words Handed Down, pt. 2), in *Chin-lou-tzu* (Master of the Golden Tower) (*Ssu-k'u ch'üan-shu chen-pen pieh-chi* ed. [rpt. Taipei, 1975], vol. 523) 4:32a–b; excerpted in Kuo Shao-yü, *Chung-kuo li-tai wen-lun hsüan*, p. 301.

35. The role of these latter two developments in the evolution of the *wen-pi* distinction has been noted, respectively, by Kuo Shao-yü, *Chung-kuo wen-hsüeh p'i-p'ing shih*, p. 58, and Huang K'an, quoted in Fan Wen-lan, ed., *Wen-hsin tiao-lung chu*, p. 667.

36. *Wen-pi shih ping te-shih* (Poetry and Prose: Ten Faults, and Success and Failure), in *Bunkyō hifuron*, ed. Chou Wei-te (Peking, 1975), pp. 219–220. Also quoted in Lo Ken-tse, *Chung-kuo wen-hsüeh p'i-p'ing shih*, p. 194, and Wang Li-ch'i, "Wen-pi hsin-chieh" (A New Explanation of *Wen* and *Pi*), *Kuo-wen yüeh-k'an* (Nov., 1948), 73:6.

37. The first is alluded to by Hou K'ang in Juan Fu, *Wen-pi k'ao*, p. 19, and the second is quoted by Juan Fu, p. 12.

38. *Lao hsüeh-an pi-chi* (Notes from an Old Cottage of Learning), in *Lu Fang-weng ch'üan-chi* (Collected Writings of Lu Yu), 2 vols. (rpt. Taipei, 1975), 1:9:59. Shen Yüeh's and Jen Fang's biographies are included in *Nan shih* 59, and Yü Chien-wu's in *Liang shu* 49. The poem by Tu Fu is in the *Tu-shih yin-te* 42 (Concordance to Poems of Tu Fu) (Harvard-Yenching Sinological Index Series, supp. no. 14 [rpt. Taipei, 1966]), p. 336, l. 69.

There is some dispute about the authorship of the poem about Tu Fu and Han Yü. Whereas Lu Yu, Hou K'ang (in Juan Fu, *Wen-pi k'ao*, p. 19), and Fan Ning ("Wen-pi yü wen-ch'i" [*Wen* and *Pi* and the *Ch'i* of Literature], *Kuo-wen yüeh-k'an* [June, 1948], 68:19) all agree that it is Tu Mu's "Tu Tu Han chi" (Reading the Collections of Tu Fu and Han Yü) (*Ch'üan T'ang shih* [The Complete T'ang Poems], 2 vols. [1706 ed., rpt. Taipei, 1977], 2:5955), both Juan Fu (*Wen-pi k'ao*, p. 12) and Liu T'ien-hui (in Juan Fu, *Wen-pi k'ao*, p. 13) attribute it to Yüan Hao-wen (1190–1257). Moreover, all of them differ from the text in the *Ch'üan T'ang shih*, where the first lines reads: "Tu's poems and Han's collection (*chi*) I read when sadness comes." Ma-ku was a Taoist immortal who had birdlike claws.

39. *Yü Li-sheng lun-shih shu* (Letter to Master Li Discussing Poetry), in Tsu Pao-ch'üan, *Ssu-k'ung T'u shih-p'in chu-shih chi i-wen* (Ssu-k'ung T'u's Classification of Poetry: Notes and Translations) (Hong Kong, 1966), p. 68.

40. *Ta-li p'ing-shih Yang-chün wen-chi hou-hsü* (Postface to the Collected Writings of Judge Yang of Ta-li Temple), in *Ch'üan T'ang wen* 577 (The Complete T'ang Prose), 20 vols. (1814 ed., rpt. Taipei, 1961), 12:7407. Also quoted in Lo Ken-tse, *Chung-kuo wen-hsüeh p'i-p'ing shih*, p. 427.

41. The first phrase is attributed to Han Yü by Li Han in his *Ch'ang-li hsien-sheng chi-hsü* (Preface to the Collection of Master Ch'ang-li); Chou's is from his *T'ung-shu, wen-tz'u*

(Comprehensive Book: Letters) 28. Both are quoted by Kuo, *Chung-kuo wen-hsüeh p'i-p'ing shih*, p. 167.

42. *Chu Tzu yü-lu* (Sayings of Master Chu) 139; quoted by Lo Ken-tse, *Chung-kuo wen-hsüeh p'i-p'ing shih*, p. 712.

43. For a discussion of the relationship of Neo-Confucianism to Sung dynasty poetics, see Kuo, *Chung-kuo wen-hsüeh p'i-p'ing shih*, pp. 189–196, 207–213; Richard John Lynn, "Orthodoxy and Enlightenment: Wang Shih-chen's Theory of Poetry and Its Antecedents," in *The Unfolding of Neo-Confucianism*, ed. W. T. de Bary (New York and London, 1975), pp. 217–269; and Lynn's paper in this volume.

44. *P'ao-weng chia-ts'ang chi-hsü* (Preface to the Familial Collection of Old Man P'ao), in *Huai-lu-t'ang chi wen-hou-kao* (Second Manuscript of the Collection from Mountain Woods Hall) 4; quoted by Kuo, *Chung-kuo wen-hsüeh p'i-p'ing shih*, p. 290.

45. *Ch'un-yü-t'ang kao-hsü* (Preface to the Manuscript from Spring Rain Hall), in *Huai-lu-t'ang chi wen-hou-kao* 3; quoted by Kuo, *Chung-kuo wen-hsüeh p'i-p'ing shih*, p. 291. Also trans. Liu, *Chinese Theories of Literature*, p. 90.

46. Elsewhere, however, Li Tung-yang does echo Liu Tsung-yüan's emphasis on metaphor rather than description: "There are three principles of poetry, and description (*fu*) is only one of them; the other two are comparison and association (*pi-hsing*). What is called comparison and association consists in lodging your feelings in objects, for if one's words are direct and straightforward, then they will be easily exhausted." From his *Lu-t'ang shih-hua* (Lu-t'ang's Remarks on Poetry) (*TSCC* ed., vol. 2576), p. 6.

47. Quoted in Ch'en Shih-tao (1053–1101), *Hou-shan shih-hua* (Hou-shan's Remarks on Poetry), in *Li-tai shih-hua* (Remarks on Poetry through the Ages), ed. Ho Wen-huan (rpt. Taipei, 1974), 6:3; p. 182. Quoted in Lo Ken-tse, *Chung-kuo wen-hsüeh p'i-p'ing shih*, p. 633.

48. *Lu-t'ang shih-hua*, p. 4.

49. Ibid., p. 10.

50. *Ch'un-yü-t'ang kao-hsü*, quoted in Kuo, *Chung-kuo wen-hsüeh p'i-p'ing shih*, p. 291.

51. *Lu-t'ang shih-hua*, p. 1.

52. Ibid., p. 4.

53. Ibid., p. 1.

54. Ibid., pp. 2–3.

55. Ibid., p. 10.

56. Ibid., p. 3.

57. Li Tung-yang is paraphrasing a famous passage from Yen Yü's *Ts'ang-lang shih-hua* (Ts'ang-lang's Remarks on Poetry), in *Ts'ang-lang shih-hua chiao-shih*, ed. Kuo Shao-yü, (Peking, 1961), pp. 23–24.

58. *Ching-ch'uan hsien-sheng shih-chi-hsü* (Preface to the Collected Poetry of the Master from Ching-ch'uan) in *Huai-lu-t'ang chi wen-kao* (Manuscript of the Collection from Mountain Woods Hall) 8; quoted in Kuo Shao-yü, *Chung-kuo wen-hsüeh p'i-p'ing shih*, p. 295.

59. *Fou-yin hsü* (Preface to Sounds of the Crock), in *K'ung-t'ung hsien-sheng chi* (Collected Works of Master K'ung-t'ung) (*Ming-tai lun-chu ts'ung-k'an* ed.; 4 vols., rpt. Taipei, 1976) 51:4b; p. 1462. Also quoted in Kuo, *Chung-kuo wen-hsüeh p'i-p'ing shih*, p. 304.

60. For a discussion of these concerns, see Liu, *Chinese Theories of Literature*, pp. 90–92; Lynn, "Orthodoxy and Enlightenment," pp. 217–237; and Lynn's article in this volume.

61. *Ming shih* (Ming History), *Wen-yüan* (Garden of Letters), 286; quoted in Kuo Shao-yü, *Chung-kuo wen-hsüeh p'i-p'ing shih*, p. 298.

62. *I-yüan chih-yen* (Scattered Remarks from the Garden of Art) 1:18a, in *Yen-chou shan-jen ssu-pu-kao* (Four-part Manuscript of the Mountain Man from Yen-chou) (*Ming-tai lun-chu ts'ung-k'an* ed., 15 vols., rpt. Taipei. 1976), 13:6615.

63. Ibid. 1:17b; p. 6614.

64. Ibid. 1:20b–21a; pp. 6620–6621.

65. *Wei-lu shih-hua* (*TSCC* ed., vols. 2609–2610) 1:8.

66. Ibid. 2:40 and 5:126.

67. Ibid. 1:5.

68. Ibid., 1:2. (Also quoted in Kuo, *Chung-kuo wen-hsüeh p'i-p'ing shih*, pp. 476.)

69. Ibid. 1:2–3.

70. Ibid. 3:72.

71. Wu Ch'iao is alluding to a passage from the *Lun-yü* (Analects) 41.

72. *Wei-lu shih-hua*, 1:8. (Also quoted in Kuo, *Chung-kuo wen-hsüeh p'i-p'ing shih*, p. 476.)

73. Ibid. 1:11.

74. *Shu Liang Chao-ming t'ai-tzu Wen hsüan hsü hou*, in *Yen-ching-shih san chi* 8 (Collection from Yen-ching Hall, III) (*TSCC* ed., vols. 2197–2208), 2:570.

75. Juan is alluding to a passage from the *Tso chuan* (Commentary of Master Tso), *Hsiang-kung* (Duke Hsiang), twenty-fifth year (547 B.C.).

76. *Wen-yen shuo*, in *Yen-ching-shih san chi* 8, 2:567. (Also trans. Liu, *Chinese Theories of Literature*, p. 104.)

77. Ibid., 2:568.

78. *Wen-yün shou*, in *Yen-ching-shih hsü-chi* 2 (Second Collection from Yen-ching Hall) (*TSCC* ed., vols. 2209–2211), 3:126.

79. Ibid., 3:128.

80. William O. Hendricks, "Three Models for the Description of Poetry," *Journal of Linguistics* (April, 1969), 5(1): 18, 17.

81. Pratt, *Toward a Speech Act Theory of Literary Discourse*, pp. 5–6.

82. Ibid., p. 96.

83. Tzvetan Todorov, "The Notion of Literature," *New Literary History* (1973), 5:5–16.

II / The Human Body and Artistic Values

The Idea of the Human in Mencian Thought:
An Approach to Chinese Aesthetics

By Tu Wei-ming

In his *Chung-kuo i-shu ching-shen* (Spirit of Chinese Aesthetics), Hsü Fu-kuan states that Confucians and Taoists share the belief that self-cultivation is basic to artistic creativity.[1] This is contrary to the trite and commonplace observation that the essential purpose of art is to assist in the perfection of the moral and spiritual personality. It suggests a way of perceiving what art is rather than what its function ought to be. Art, in this sense, becomes not only a technique to be mastered but also an articulation of a deepened subjectivity. It moves and touches us because it comes from a source of inspiration which humanity shares with heaven, earth, and the myriad things. Proponents of this view assert that the manifestation of true subjectivity depends on a complete transformation of the self, which they attempt to achieve by various methods: the establishing of the will, the emptying of the mind, the fasting of the heart, and the nourishing of the great body. Deepened subjectivity centers upon the "great foundation" (*ta-pen*[a]) of the cosmos. As a result, it harmonizes different forms of life and brings humanity into tune with nature, so that the distinction between subject and object is dissolved.

Hsü Fu-kuan adds that a root idea in Chinese aesthetics is precisely this insistence that the dichotomies of subject/object, self/society, and man/nature are unreal and thus transformable.[2] True subjectivity opens up the privatized ego so that the self can enter into fruitful communion with others. The ultimate joy of this communicability allows us, in Chuang Tzu's phrase, to roam around with the Creator.[3] Since even the gap between Creator and creature is bridgeable,[4] when human beings create art they participate "in the transforming and nourishing process of heaven and earth."[5]

Hsü maintains that philosophically and historically the *Chuang Tzu* text epitomizes the emergence of aesthetic subjectivity in China. He is critically aware, of course, that the moral subjectivity established in Confucian teachings is also laden with far-reaching aesthetic implications, and he alludes to Confucius' fascination with music and the relevance of the six arts to the development of Chinese aesthetics.[6] However, he says little about Mencius. In the present essay, I would like to examine the ways that the Mencian perception of self-cultivation is pertinent to theories of art in China.

My purpose is twofold: to explore the idea of the human in classical Confucian

[a] 大本

thought with particular emphasis on Mencius, and to suggest that such an exploration could be fruitful for an understanding of Chinese aesthetics. I intend neither to offer a thorough analysis of the Mencian image of man nor to argue that Mencius, rather than Chuang Tzu for example, is particularly relevant to Chinese aesthetics. I do hope to show, however, that in China philosophical anthropology has provided much of the symbolic resources for the development of theories of art. As I focus on some of the insights found in a text which is central to ethics and hitherto ignored in aesthetics, my immediate concern is simply to present an orientation or a method of analysis. It is possible that such an approach will eventually lead us to belief that Chinese arts have deep humanist roots.

Tao[b] (the Way). The principle of the human way in its all-embracing fullness underlies Mencian thought.[7] As a metaphor in Mencian language, the Way is never a static category, signifying something external and objective. It is a process, a movement, and, indeed, a dynamic unfolding of the self as a vital force for personal, social, and cosmic transformation. Rather than a norm to be conformed to, Mencius sees the Way as a standard of inspiration that must be reenacted by ceaseless effort. We do not achieve humanity purely and simply by being alive. We must learn to cultivate ourselves so that we can fully realize those humane possibilities inherent in our nature. Only then can we say that we are on our way to becoming authentically human. This unending process led Tseng Tzu to describe the mission of a resolute scholar as a long road and a heavy burden: "For humanity (*jen*[c]) is the burden he has taken upon himself; and must we not grant that it is a heavy one to bear? Only with death does his journey end; then must we not grant that he has far to go?"[8]

What will we become, if we commit ourselves to this long and strenuous task of learning to be human? There must be people who have no interest whatsoever in this sort of effort. Is there really any serious deficiency in their lives, if they never entertain the possibility of self-improvement? Mencius does not speculate on what kind of miserable creatures human beings can degenerate into. The rampant inhumanity among men during the period of the Warring States was probably indication enough of the lower end of the scale. Mencius is acutely aware of the internecine struggle for wealth and power throughout the country, but he maintains that ordinary human beings can become sages by directly applying the inner resources of their hearts (*hsin*[d]) for their own moral and spiritual cultivation. He asserts that the sages and we are the same in kind.[9] Even if we learn to become sages, we do not ascend to a different kind of being. We are still human to the core. Even though Mencius denounces those who choose not to improve themselves as committing inexcusable self-abasement,[10] he fully recognizes their right to be human. Between sagehood and self-deprivation, the range of humanity is truly vast.

A defining characteristic of Mencian thought is the belief that human beings are

b 道　　　　　　　　　c 仁　　　　　　　　　d 心

perfectible through self-effort.[11] He appeals neither to the existence of God nor to the immortality of the soul, but sees the spontaneous feelings of the heart as sufficient for the task. It seems that there is a moral "deep structure" inherent in human nature that can be fully developed, without forcing, as a natural process of growth.[12] This deceptively simple and easy way of self-development is, however, not a quest for isolated inner spirituality. Rather, it is a holistic process of learning through which the privatized ego is transformed into a feeling and caring self. We have here, in addition to the idea of a deep structure, also the image of natural growth. Learning so conceived not only encompasses the sudden emergence of one's innate qualities but also unhurried nourishment of "buds" and "sprouts" of humanity. For example, we are all capable of feelings of commiseration when suddenly confronted with the tragedies and misfortunes of other human beings, as seen in our immediate response to a child who falls into a well.[13] But unless we cultivate our sense of commiseration, it will be limited in its capacity and it will not flow beyond a small circle of close associates. Often, it takes an unusually powerful impact from outside to awaken us from our ordinary insensitivity. Developing the deep structure, like learning a moral language or acquiring a ritual form, requires a balanced ("neither forgetting nor assisting")[14] approach. Just as the usefulness of the five kinds of grain depends upon their ripeness, "the value of humanity depends upon its being brought to maturity."[15]

Even the mature person does not cease to learn, for the development of our innate qualities necessitates continuous refinement. To learn a moral language proficiently or to acquire a ritual form thoroughly is a perpetual challenge. Just as we require daily practice in order to develop the ability to generate new linguistic patterns or to create new modes of human interaction, we must constantly cultivate the capacity of the self in order to enter into fruitful communion with others. Maturity, as a value in human learning, thus includes an authentic possibility for further growth. There is a multiplicity of paths to be pursued in the process of moral development, but they converge at various states to give us standards of inspiration that we can look up to, not as fixed models but as ways of witnessing the excellence in humanity.[16] This leads us to the following characterization in *Mencius*:[17]

He who commands our liking is called good (*shan*[e]).
He who is sincere with himself is called true (*hsin*[f]).
He who is sufficient and real is called beautiful (*mei*[g]).
He whose sufficiency and reality shine forth is called great (*ta*[h]).
He whose greatness transforms itself is called sagely (*sheng*[i]).
He whose sageliness is beyond our comprehension is called spiritual (*shen*[j]).

e 善　　　　　g 美　　　　　i 聖
f 信　　　　　h 大　　　　　j 神

From the good to the spiritual there are numerous degrees of subtleties. A sophisticated appreciation must also take into consideration the dynamic process that underlies all of them, as a more detailed explanation of the idea of the human in classical Confucian thought will make clear.

Shen[k] (*Body*). It is often assumed that the Confucian method of self-cultivation (*hsiu-shen*[l]) is sociological, since it teaches a child to be obedient to his parents, to respect authority, and to accept societal norms. This common-sense observation fails to account for a large amount of literature in the Confucian tradition that repeatedly stresses the importance of taking care of one's body as a necessary condition for learning to be human. Tseng Tzu's symbolic gesture of showing his hands and feet to his disciples shortly before he died clearly indicates the reverence he had for what was given to him by his parents.[18] It is not merely out of a sense of filial piety that one must respect one's physical body as a sacred vessel, to borrow an image from the *Analects*.[19] The self as a concrete living reality is inseparable from the body. Since self-cultivation in its literary meaning refers to the cultivation of the body, there is a rich reservoir of body-related language in the Confucian classics. Indeed, without an awareness of the importance of the body, we can hardly appreciate the significance of the six arts (*liu-i*[m])[20] in classical Confucian thought.

Etymologically the character "*i*,"[n] which is commonly rendered as "art," signifies the activity of planting of cultivating fields.[21] It seems that the agricultural origin of the character later gave rise to its meaning of acquired skills. Thus a man of *i* is a talented person capable of performing unusual tasks.[22] The Confucian emphasis on literary accomplishments may have provided the impetus to define *i* in terms of fine arts.[23] In the classical educational context, however the six arts are disciplines that have particular reference to physical exercises. They are activities to be performed as well as subjects to be mastered mentally. The learning of the six arts seems to be a deliberate attempt to allow civilizing influences to work through our bodies as well as our minds. Of course, we are not necessarily aware of the underlying philosophical import of these disciplines. But the idea that the arts implant prosocial attitudes in us as a one-way subjugation is misleading. For we are not simply being socialized; we are actively engaged in our own socializing by planting and cultivating the "buds" and "sprouts" within us. This is part of the reason for Mencius' insistence that "rightness" is not drilled into us but is inherent in the deep structure of our human nature.[24]

Accordingly ritual, the first of the six arts, is a discipline of the body. It is intended to transform the body into a fitting expression of the self in our ordinary daily existence. The practice of ritual, which involves such simple activities as

k 身

l 修身

m 六藝

n 藝

sweeping the floor and answering short questions,[25] trains us to perform routine functions in society as fully participating members. We learn to stand, sit, walk, and eat properly so that we can live in harmony with those around us. We do so not to seek their approval but to respond to the standards that have inspired us to become an integral part of the community. Some of those around us may use ritual language in a clumsy way. That should not discourage us from trying to perfect our own arts, however, because we ourselves are primarily responsible for what we can and ought to become. On the other hand, if we fail to live up to the expectations of our community, it should be a grave concern for us, because we cherish the reciprocal relationship as a necessary condition for our own moral and spiritual self-cultivation. Thus, we emulate those who are worthy of our admiration and turn our gaze within to scrutinize ourselves in the presence of a bad man.[26] The Confucian golden rule— "Do not do to others what you would not want others to do to you!"[27]—supports the attitude of altruism as a corollary of being honest with oneself.

Confucian thought values the heuristic function of ritual so highly that it seems to have characterized ritualization as the concrete process whereby we learn to become mature human beings.[28] In fact, even though verbal instructions are common in Confucian teachings, the preferred method is to conduct them in an atmosphere suffused with nonverbal forms of communication. Exemplary teaching (*shen-chiao*°), which is superior to teaching by words (*yen-chiao*ᴾ), literally means to teach by one's body. Finely executed ritual acts as performative demonstrations of what one should do in given situations have greater educational force than verbal descriptions of them can ever have. The *Analects* is full of vivid examples of Confucius in action. The *Hsiang-tang* chapter, for instance, portrays in delightful detail how the master dressed, sat, stood, bowed, walked, and ate. The care with which it depicts even the slightest gestures of the master on solemn occasions is particularly illustrative:

> When carrying the tablet of jade, he seems to double up, as though borne down by its weight. He holds it at the highest as though he were making a bow, at the lowest, as though he were proffering a gift. His expression, too, changes to one of dread and his feet seem to recoil, as though he were avoiding something. When presenting ritual-presents, his expression is placid. At the private audience his attitude is gay and animated.[29]

If ritualization disciplines the body, music (the second of the six arts) is intended to harmonize the body so that it can appropriately express our emotions in tune with the rhythm of life. The importance of music in Confucian education cannot be exaggerated. Together with ritual it symbolizes the civilizing mode, the proper way of learning to be human. Since all authentic music is said to arise from the human

° 身教   ᴾ 言教

heart,[30] it can shape the movements of the body into a graceful manifestation of the inner self. In Confucian literature, not only the performances of the court dancers but also the demeanors of cultured men are thought to be melodious.[31] Musical instruments, ranging from weighty stone chimes to the delicate lute, produce an infinite variety of sound patterns to channel all our "seven feelings" into their proper courses.[32]

One learns to play the lute or to sing lyric songs in order to communicate with others and, more importantly perhaps, to experience the internal resonance one shares with nature. Far from being a mere fleeting impression on our senses, the sound of the great music that we hear is an enduring virtue (*te*q).[33] As harmony of heaven and earth, it brings us into accord with the primordial order. Music—the right kind of music, and not the excessively sensuous songs of the state of Cheng[34]—can transform the human body into an articulation of beauty. As the *Analects* reports, after being exposed to the charming music of Shao, Confucius was in such a state of beatific enchantment that he did not notice the taste of meat for three full months.[35]

Although the arts of archery and charioteering may not have comparable cosmic significance, the physical exercises involved are, nevertheless, laden with far-reaching implications. An exemplary archer, for example, is not merely a skillful marksman but a "profound person" (*chün-tzu*r) who, having mastered all the techniques of the art, constantly turns inward to examine himself, especially when he fails to hit the target.[36] If the case of Wang Liang in *Mencius* is any indication, the art of charioteering also involves complex rituals of self-mastery.[37] The discipline required builds one's sense of developing the proper forms of conduct as well as one's physical strength. By analogy, calligraphy and arithmetic can also be conceived as ways of refining one's body by acquiring the necessary dexterity with the brush or abacus to use it resourcefully.[38]

The "six arts" are therefore ways of planting and cultivating the body. They transform the body from its original state where, like the rustic Shun before he was exposed to good words and good deeds,[39] it has merely the "buds" and "sprouts" of human possibility, into a center of fruitful relationships. As a center, a person never loses his proper location whenever and wherever he happens to be: the profound person always feels at home.[40] At the same time, he is sensitive and responsive to the human network around him. Through dialogical encounters, he deepens his self-awareness and enriches the lives of those who have entered into communion with him: "A man of humanity, wishing to enlarge himself, enlarges others."[41] To him, the "six arts" are not merely acquired skills; they are instrumental in establishing and enlarging himself. In the Mencian perspective, the person whose body is transformed by ritual, music, archery, charioteering, calligraphy, and arithmetic has

q 德   r 君子

created truth and beauty in and for himself. And as he is both a producer and an appreciator of the idea of human, he is eminently qualified to be called a "good," "true," and "beautiful" person.

Yet, self-cultivation involves much more than the transformation of the body. It is true that Mencius explicitly states, "Form and color (our body) are nature endowed by heaven. It is only the sage who can fully realize his physical form."[42] But "physical form" (*hsing*[s]) here symbolizes the self as a whole. The body is often a limited figure of speech in which the subtler and finer aspects of the self are deliberately relegated to the background. Paradoxically the sage can fully realize his physical form precisely because he has transformed and transcended it. The possibility of self-transformation and self-transcendence leads us to the language of the heart.

Hsin (Heart). If the body is a spatial concept, occupying a specific location, a distinctive character of the heart is its remarkable ability to wander: "It comes in and goes out at no definite time and without anyone's knowing its direction."[43] Since the body is observable, it is possible for us to establish behavioral criteria to describe it. Exemplary teaching is, in a sense, model learning. The student learns proper ritual, right music, or good calligraphy by imitating the movements of the hands, feet, and body of the master. An outsider observing a Confucian student's learning the six arts may easily conclude that he is engaged in a sort of mimetic dance. But, presumably, the Confucian master is interested not only in the correctness of the form but also in the mental attitude behind it. He is keenly aware of the difference between a rote performer and an active participant, even though both follow instructions correctly. There is something missing in the rote performer. We might say that his heart is not in it. How does the master know that form-likeness is not the real thing? If the student knows exactly how ritual acts are to be performed and does so proficiently, how can we not conclude that his heart is in it all the time? Yet the master, with his discerning attentiveness, is able to pick up signs here and there that enable him to conclude that the student still lacks the intensity necessary for a virtuoso execution of the ritual. This seems to imply that form itself can be a sufficient basis for judging the truth and beauty of a performer. The Confucian master does not focus solely on the result, however, but also on the whole process by which the result is attained. His primary concern is the well-being of the student as a total person in transformation.[44]

In moral education, knowing manifests itself in acting, and through action one authenticates one's knowledge. It is inconceivable for one to will oneself to be polite, courteous, respectful, and humble yet not have the inner strength to learn to be so. The Mencian distinction between "inability" (*pu-neng*[t]) and "unwillingness" (*pu-*

---

s 形   t 不能

*wei*ᵘ) is particularly relevant here. One may excuse oneself for one's inability to move a mountain single-handedly, but one cannot say that one is incapable of showing deference to an elder.⁴⁵ Since behavioral criteria are dificient in matters of intention, the master is never content simply to show his students the correct form. He tries to enable the student to create his own style and his own interpretation. A truly inspired student should be like Yen Hui, who perceived Confucius' teaching in mystic terms:

> The more I strain my gaze up towards it, the higher it soars. The deeper I bore down into it, the harder it becomes. I see it in front; but suddenly it is behind. Step by step the Master skillfully lures me on. He has broadened me with culture, restrained me with ritual. Even if I wanted to stop, I could not. Just when I feel that I have exhausted every resource, something seems to rise up, standing out sharp and clear. Yet though I long to pursue it, I can find no way of getting to it at all.⁴⁶

As words (*yen*ᵛ) can never fully explain the hidden meanings of intentions (*i*ʷ), the body can hardly express the inner feelings of the heart.

Although the body, no matter how ritualized, melodious, strong, and dexterous, is not able to encompass the activities of the heart, it is the proper place for the heart to reside. Mencius emphatically states that the way of learning consists of none other than the quest for the lost heart.⁴⁷ In this sense, the six arts are efforts to "preserve the heart" (*ts'un-hsin*ˣ). They are training for the heart as well as discipline for the body. While the body requires a long and gradual process to assume a proper form, the transformation of the heart appears to be swift, since the heart is amorphous: "Hold it fast and you preserve it. Let it go and you lose it."⁴⁸ It is misleading, however, to believe that an act of willing is by itself sufficient to preserve the heart. Mencius does appeal time and again to the king's "unbearing heart" (*pu-jen chih hsin*ʸ) to establish "humane government" (*jen-cheng*ᶻ), as if we could solve the problem of tyranny by a natural extension (*t'ui*ᵃᵃ) of the king's inability to bear the suffering of others.⁴⁹ But we must not confuse this strategic attempt to pinpoint a basic feeling shared by all members of the human community, even by an insensitive king, with Mencius' philosophy of the heart. As the parable of the farmer in the state of Sung points out, the cultivation of the heart is a delicate matter. If we exert too much artificial effort to help a plant grow, it will soon wither. In the same way, there is a natural course for the development of the heart. One should neither forget (*wang*ᵃᵇ) nor assist (*chu*ᵃᶜ) in one's daily effort to preserve it.⁵⁰ "Hold it fast and you

ᵘ 不爲	ˣ 存心	ᵃᵃ 推
ᵛ 言	ʸ 不忍之心	ᵃᵇ 忘
ʷ 意	ᶻ 仁政	ᵃᶜ 助

preserve it" should therefore be understood as the art of steering, involving a process of adjusting and balancing on unpredictable currents.

Despite its changing configuration, Mencius asserts that the structure of the heart is knowable through direct experience. He tells the story of I Ch'iu, a superior chess player who failed to instruct an absent-minded student, to show that the mere presence of "buds" and "sprouts" of humanity in us cannot guarantee our actually knowing and preserving our hearts.[51] Since "even a plant that grows most readily will not survive if it is placed in the sun for one day and exposed to the cold for ten," without sustained effort of cultivation, nothing much can be done with the few new shoots that come out.[52] To use a different analogy, the spring that is about to dry up can hardly overflow a small pond. On the other hand, in times of flooding, water can be extremely powerful. It is a matter of quantity as well as quality. Here lies a unique Mencian insight about the structure of the heart: if cultivated, it is capable of virtually unlimited expansion. This is the reason that, to Mencius, the heart is the "great body" (*ta-t'i*[ad]), whereas our physical form is only the "small body" (*hsiao-t'i*[ae]).[53] To know and preserve the heart is therefore to hold fast to a dynamic and an ever-enlarging structure. The growth of the heart, unlike the maturation of the body, is infinite. Between self-deprivation and sagehood, the range of humanity is indeed vast. It is not the body but the heart that makes the real difference. Just as we eat to nourish the whole body rather than just a small portion of the belly, Mencius claims, self-cultivation allows the development of the "great body" rather than just the small.[54]

Mencius suggests that we can best nourish the heart by making our desires few.[55] What he advocates is not a kind of asceticism but a sense of priority. He fully recognizes the importance of such instinctual demands as the appetite for food and sex, but he insists that human fulfillment requires a holistic vision in which other equally compelling propensities—notably humanity, rightness, the rites and wisdom—ought to be satisfied as well. While the same instinctual demands we share with other animals define us in terms of what we are born with, the moral propensities inherent in our nature make us uniquely human.[56] This observation leads to two interrelated ideas: (1) the uniqueness of being human is a moral and spiritual question which cannot be properly answered if it is reduced to biological or social considerations; and (2) the actual process of self-development, or the nourishment of the heart, far from being a quest for pure morality or spirituality, necessarily involves the biological and social realities of human life. Consequently, if we satisfy only our instinctual demands, we can never realize the potential of the human heart. If we cultivate the "great body," however, our physical form will also be fulfilled:

ad 大體   ae 小體

> That which a profound person follows as his nature, that is to say, humanity, rightness, the rites and wisdom, is rooted in his heart, and manifests itself in his face, giving it a sleek appearance. It also shows in his back and extends to his limbs, rendering their message intelligible without words.[57]

The sage dwells in the peaceful abode of humanity and walks on the path of rightness.[58] Mencius claims that we learn to appreciate the greatness of such a person by an analogical reflection of the germinations of the four basic human feelings inherent in our own hearts: commiseration, shame and dislike, deference and compliance, and right and wrong. The germinating power of these feelings provides us with an intellectual intuition to perceive truth and beauty in ourselves as well as in sages and worthies.[59] The body-language must now ascend to the language of the heart to explain the educational functions of moral excellence in the human community: "A profound person transforms where he passes, and works wonders where he abides. He is in the same stream as Heaven above and Earth below."[60]

This cosmic reference opens up a new vista, adding a transcending perspective to the heart. Indeed, the Mencian heart is both a cognitive and an affective faculty, symbolizing the functions of conscience as well as consciousness. It not only reflects upon realities but, in comprehending them, shapes and creates their meaningfulness for the human community as a whole. In this way, the person who realizes his "great body" and "whose sufficiency and reality shine forth is called great." However, Mencius also maintains that "the great man does not lose his child-like heart"[61] and that the "great body" is, in the last analysis, our original nature. This twofold assertion that the great man has become a spiritlike being flowing with the cosmic transformation of heaven and earth and that, at the same time, what he manifests is no more than authentic humanity gives rise to what some sinologists call mysticism in Mencian thought.

Shen (Spirit). We may recall that Mencius characterizes those whose greatness transforms itself as "sagely" and those whose sageliness is beyond our comprehension as "spiritual." Sageliness and spirituality are therefore, like goodness, truth, and beauty, symbols of human perfection. These are standards of inspiration to be continuously enacted as we learn to realize ourselves. In the Mencian perspective, they are not objective criteria for judging human worth but aesthetic appraisals of what human beings can attain and, by implication, what we ought to learn to become. Since sages and we are the same in kind, we should applaud Yen Hui's courage: "What sort of man was Shun (a sage-king)? And what sort of man am I? Anyone who can make anything of himself will be like that."[62] Indeed, it is not only the great man whose sufficiency and reality shine forth, for we possess the same internal resources:

All the ten thousand things are there in me. There is no greater joy for me than to find, on self-examination, that I am true to myself. Try your best to treat others as you would wish to be treated yourself, and you will find that this is the shortest way to humanity.[63]

Profound insight into the human condition, rather than naive moral optimism, prompts Mencius to articulate his philosophical anthropology. Human beings "survive in adversity and perish in ease and comfort." [64] We learn to mend our ways only after we have made mistakes. "It is only when a man is frustrated in mind and in his deliberations that he is able to innovate. It is only when his intentions become visible on his countenance and audible in his tone of voice that others can understand him." [65] We learn to know ourselves, to communicate with others, and to assume responsibility for humanity through endeavor. Mencius observes that many of the ancient sages and worthies experienced personal ordeals before they emerged as spiritual models:

> That is why Heaven, when it is about to place a great burden on a man, always first tests his resolution, exhausts his frame and makes him suffer starvation and hardship, frustrates his efforts so as to shake him from his mental lassitude, toughen his nature and make good his deficiencies.[66]

In addition to the mandate of heaven, Mencius fully acknowledges that both the social and the psychological environments play important roles in human growth, but his faith in the possibility of moral and spiritual self-development leads him to perceive the matter in a hopeful light:

> For a man to give full realization to his heart is for him to understand his own nature, and a man who knows his own nature will know Heaven. By retaining his heart and nurturing his nature he is serving Heaven. Whether he is going to die young or to live to a ripe old age makes no difference to his steadfastness of purpose. It is through awaiting whatever is to befall him with a perfected character that he stands firm on his proper destiny.[67]

The profound person, accordingly, steeps himself in the Way in order to be able to find it within his own heart. "When he is at ease with it, he can draw deeply upon it; when he can draw deeply upon it, he finds its source wherever he turns." [68] The spring that did not have enough water to overflow a small pond before is now in a state of abundance: "Water from an ample source comes tumbling down, day and night without ceasing, going forward only after all the hollows are filled, and then draining into the sea." [69]

To continue the water analogy, self-cultivation in Mencian terms is an attempt to cultivate one's "floodlike *ch'i*." [af] At this level it does not consist merely of

af 氣

developing the proper form or the right mental attitude. It aims, rather, at nourishing the inner resources, enhancing the power of the will and building up the reserve of one's psychic energy. The character *ch'i*, variously rendered as "material force" (W. T. Chan), "matter-energy" (H. H. Dubs), and "vital spirit" (F. W. Mote), denotes a kind of psycho-physiological power associated with breathing and the circulation of the blood. In the Mencian usage, it refers to a "strong, moving power" generated by moral and spiritual self-cultivation.[70]

Mencius' discourse on the "floodlike *ch'i*" was occasioned by Kung-sun Ch'ou's question about the method of attaining the state of the "unperturbed heart" (*pu-tung-hsin*[ag]). At the outset, Mencius asserts that "the will is commander over the *ch'i* while the *ch'i* is that which fills the body." Ordinarily the *ch'i* follows where the will directs. It is therefore important to "take hold of your will and do not abuse your *ch'i*." However, it is conceivable that when the *ch'i* is blocked, it also affects the will. Even though "the *ch'i* rests where the will arrives," nourishing the *ch'i* is essential to the well-being of the heart. What, then, is this floodlike *ch'i*?

> It is difficult to explain. This is a *ch'i* which is, in the highest degree, vast and unyielding. Nourish it with integrity and place no obstacle in its path and it will fill the space between Heaven and Earth. It is a *ch'i* which unites rightness and the Way. Deprive it of these and it will collapse. It is born of accumulated rightness and cannot be appropriated by anyone through a sporadic show of rightness. Whenever one acts in a way that falls below the standard set in one's heart, it will collapse. . . . You must work at it and never let it out of your mind. At the same time, while you must never let it our of your mind, you must not forcibly help it grow either.[71]

As we can see, even in this brief passage, Mencius claims that within the structure of the human body and the human heart, there is the real potential and great possibility of enlarging the self to become one with heaven and earth. Humanity so conceived is not an unrealizable ideal but an inexhaustibly abundant power of moral and spiritual transformation. To use an image found in *Chung yung*: Since humanity can assist in the transforming and nourishing process of heaven and earth, it can form a trinity with them.[72]

Does such an approach to self-perfection suggest that there was a deep humanist base for the arts in China? Since neither Mencius nor Chuang Tzu was interested primarily in aesthetics, we must resort to interpretive reconstruction to discover what theory of art, if any, lies in these rich sources. Hsü Fu-kuan's successful effort to show by recontextualizing the text that there are indeed aesthetic insights in *Chuang Tzu* has encouraged me to raise questions about truth and beauty in terms of the human self-images in works such as *Mencius*. This kind of endeavor may ultimately

[ag] 不動心

broaden the scope of aesthetic studies. But my real purpose has not been to explore the possibility of a Confucian aesthetics, in contrast with or complementary to, a Taoist aesthetics. Rather, I have sought to tap those symbolic resources that are common to both traditions. To pursue Hsü's analysis further, self-cultivation as a mode of thinking may have predated any systematic attempt to formulate a tradition later identified as either Taoist or Confucian. In one of the most significant events in classical Chinese intellectual history, Mencius creatively appropriated some of these early insights to develop his integrated idea of the human.

We can easily see how the use of Mencius' definition of the human way affects aesthetic terminology. The body and "the sentience that infuses the human frame"[73] become primary points of reference in conceptualizing the idea of beauty, and any impulse to objectify a norm of beauty as a static category is relegated to the background. Beauty, like all good and true qualities of human growth, exists as a standard of inspiration. It informs our sense of sufficiency and reality not as a fixed principle but as a dynamic interplay between the experiencing self and the perceived entity. We see beauty in things. In describing it, we move from its physical existence to its underlying vitality and, eventually, to its all-embracing spirit. The thing can be a tree, a stream, a mountain, or a stone. Its aesthetic effect on us, however, is not that of a silent object, but a living encounter and, indeed, a "spiritual communion" (*shen-hui*[ah]). This is not simply a form of anthropomorphism, and to interpret such encounters as the imposition of human characters on the external world limits and distorts the dialogical relationship that underlies the aesthetic experience. The idea of the human in *Mencius* is not anthropocentric. It does not subscribe to Protagoras' principle that man is the measure of all things. Instead, it intends to show that self-realization, in an ultimate sense, depends on a mutuality between man and nature. As Hsü Fu-kuan points out, a basic assumption in Confucian thought is that the completion of the self (*ch'eng-chi*[ai]) necessitates the completion (*ch'eng*[aj]), rather than the domination (*ts'ai*[ak]), of things (*wu*[al]).[74]

Perhaps this is the reason that auditory perception features so prominently in classical Confucian thought. As I have noted in a different context, the Confucian Way is not perceptible if we cast our gaze outward;[75] the objectifying act of visualization alone cannot grasp the subtle manifestations of cosmic transformation. To be sure, the brilliant insight of a sage-king, such as that of the Great Shun, is capable of penetrating the incipient activation of the universe by probing into minute signs of nature.[76] But, it is through the art of hearing that we learn to participate in the rhythm of heaven and earth. The "virtue of the ear" (*erh-te*[am]), indeed the "virtue of hearing" (*t'ing-te*[an])[77] enables us to perceive the natural process in a nonaggressive, appreciative, and mutually supportive mode. Through the

ah 神會

ai 成己

aj 成

ak 宰

al 物

am 耳德

an 聽德

mental as well as physical discipline of listening, we open ourselves up to the world around us. By broadening and deepening our nonjudgmental receptivity, rather than by projecting our limited visions onto the order of things, we become co-creators of the cosmos.

Mencius' choice of music as a metaphor to characterize the sageliness of Confucius, in the light of the above discussion, seems to have been a deliberate attempt to present the Master's form of life in auditory images:

> Po Yi was the sage who was unsullied; Yi Yin was the sage who accepted responsibility; Liu Hsia Hui was the sage who was easygoing; Confucius was the sage whose actions were timely. Confucius was the one who gathered all that was good. To do this is to open with bells and conclude with jade tubes. To open with bells is to begin in an orderly fashion; to conclude with jade tubes is to end in an orderly fashion. . . .[78]

Bells and jade tubes, or chimes, are musical instruments symbolizing the proper way of opening and concluding a ritual performance. A performance that accords with the highest standard of excellence requires both the "strength" to carry it out and the "skill" to make it right. It is not only the power and ability to complete the whole process but also the "timing" at each moment as the music unfolds that gives the quality of "an orderly fashion" to the performance. Thus Mencius further comments:

> To begin in an orderly fashion is the concern of the wise while to end in an orderly fashion is the concern of a sage. Wisdom is like skill, shall I say, while sageness is like strength. It is like shooting from beyond a hundred paces. It is due to your strength that the arrow reaches the target, but it is not due to your strength that it hits the mark.[79]

To return to the earlier metaphor, the perfect "timing" of Confucius' sageness goes beyond the unsullied, the responsible, and the easy-going, precisely because it symbolizes a great concert, "gathering together all that is good." If the single note properly produced can enlighten the mind—"Hence, hearing of the way of Po Yi, a covetous man will be purged of his covetousness and a weak man will become resolute" or "hearing of the way of Liu Hsia Hui, a narrow-minded man will become tolerant and a mean man generous"[80]—how much more so can a great concert inspire us?

The followers of this kind of approach would consider analogical thinking and the lyric mode, with their emphases on internal resonances, to be the supreme forms of aesthetic communication. They would deliberately deprecate the art of argumentation, seeking beauty in understanding. A smile between two resonating hearts or an encounter between two mutually responding spirits cannot be demonstrated to the insensitive eye or the unattuned ear. Aesthetic language is not merely descriptive:

it suggests, directs, and enlightens. It is not the language itself that is beautiful. Indeed, words need not be eloquent or ingenious, for they merely carry and convey (ta[ao]) the meaning (i).[81] It is the extralinguistic referent—the inner experience, the joy of the heart, or the transforming spirit—that is the real basis of beauty, either in artistic creativity or in aesthetical appreciation.

1. Hsü Fu-kuan, *Chung-kuo i-shu ching-shen* (Taichung, 1966), p. 132.

2. Ibid.

3. *Chuang Tzu* 6. See Wing-tsit Chan, trans., *A Source Book in Chinese Philosophy* (Princeton, 1973), pp. 196–198.

4. F. W. Mote observes: "The basic point which outsiders have found so hard to detect is that the Chinese, among all peoples ancient and recent, primitive and modern, are apparently unique in having no creation myth; that is, they have regarded the world and man as uncreated, as constituting the central features of a spontaneously self-generating cosmos having no creator, god, ultimate cause or will external to itself." Even if we believe that this claim is too strong, it is undeniable that the perceived gap between man and heaven is bridgeable. See Mote, *Intellectual Foundations of China* (New York, 1971), pp. 17–18.

5. *Chung yung* 22.

6. Hsü Fu-kuan, *Chung-kuo*, pp. 1–40, 48–49.

7. See Tu Wei-ming, "On the Mencian Perception of Moral Self-Development," *The Monist* (January, 1978), 61(1):72–81.

8. *Analects* 8:7.

9. "The sage and I are of the same kind" and "The sage is simply the man first to discover this common element in my heart" (*Mencius* 6A:7). For this translation, see D. C. Lau, trans., *Mencius* (Middlesex, 1970), p. 164.

10. *Mencius* 4A:10.

11. For a critical reflection on this Mencian claim, see Donald J. Munro, *The Concept of Man in Early China* (Stanford, 1969), pp. 72–77.

12. For a classical formulation of this belief in the goodness of human nature, see *Mencius* 6A:6.

13. *Mencius* 2A:6.

14. Ibid. 2A:2.

15. Ibid. 6A:19.

16. Tu, "On the Mencian Perception of Moral Self-Development," pp. 80–81.

17. *Mencius* 7B:25.

18. *Analects* 8:3.

19. For a perceptive analysis of this, see Herbert Fingarette, "A Confucian Metaphor— the Holy Vessel," in his *Confucius—The Secular as Sacred* (New York, 1972), pp. 71–79. See *Analects* 2:12, 5:3.

20. *Chou-li chu-shu* (Shih-san-ching chu-shu ed., 1815) 10:24b and 14:6b.

ao 達

21. This is the original meaning found in Hsü Shen's *Shuo-wen*. See Morohashi Tetsuji, *Dai Kan-wa ji-ten*, 13 vols. (Tokyo, 1955–1960), 9:987.

22. *Analects* 6:6.

23. For example, the early Yüan scholar Liu Yin (1249–1293) observes that the meaning of the "arts" has undergone a fundamental change since the time of Confucius: While the Master used it to refer to the practices of ritual, music, archery, charioteering, calligraphy, and arithmetic, nowadays the arts mainly include poetry, prose, calligraphy, and painting. See "Hsü-hsüeh" 叙學, in *Ching-hsiu hsien-sheng wen-chi* (1897 ed.) 1:3b–10b.

24. *Mencius* 6A:6.

25. For a vivid description of some of the daily ritual practices, see Wang Meng-ou, *Li-chi chin-chu chin-i*, 2 vols. (Taipei, 1970), 1:1–39.

26. *Analects* 4:17.

27. Ibid. 15:23.

28. For an interpretation of ritual from this point of view, see Tu Wei-ming, "Li 禮 as Process of Humanization," *Philosophy East and West* (April, 1972), 22(2):187–201. For a thought-provoking analysis of ritual, see Erik H. Erikson, *Toys and Reasons: Stages in the Ritualization of Experience* (New York, 1977), pp. 67–113.

29. *Analects* 10:5. For this translation, see Arthur Waley, *The Analects of Confucius* (London, 1938), p. 147.

30. See the beginning line of the "Yüeh-chi" 樂記, in Wang Meng-ou, *Li-chi chin-shu chin-i*, 2:489.

31. For an interesting description of the demeanors of the *chün-tzu* by using jade as a metaphor, see Wang Meng-ou, *Li-chi chin-shu chin-i*, 2:827.

32. See Hsü Fu-kuan, *Chung-kuo*, pp. 1–8.

33. Ibid., pp. 12–33.

34. *Analects* 15:10.

35. *Ibid.* 7:13, 3:25.

36. *Chung yung*, 14.

37. *Mencius* 3B:1.

38. Of course, there is no historical evidence to support the view that the abacus, or a kind of calculating machine, was actually used then. This apparently anachronistic observation is intended to note that it is highly likely that arithmetic was not conceived of only as a mental activity but also as a technique to be mastered. The term *suan-shu* 算術" technique of calculating"—to be sure, a later coinage—seems to convey this sense well. A form of finger exercise may have been involved in the study of arithmetic.

39. *Mencius* 4B:1, 7A:16.

40. *Analects* 9:13; *Chung yung* 14.

41. *Analects* 6:28.

42. *Mencius* 7A:38.

43. Ibid. 6A:8.

44. For a relevant study on this subject, see Herbert Fingarette, *The Self in Transformation* (New York, 1965), pp. 244–293.

45. *Mencius* 1A:7.

46. *Analects* 9:10 (see Waley, p. 140).
47. *Mencius* 6A:11.
48. Ibid. 6A:6.
49. Ibid. 1A:7.
50. Ibid. 2A:2.
51. Ibid. 6A:9.
52. Ibid.
53. Ibid. 6A:14, 15.
54. Ibid. 6A:14.
55. Ibid. 7B:35.
56. Ibid. 6A:3.
57. Ibid. 7A:21.
58. Ibid. 6A:11.
59. Ibid. 2A:6.
60. Ibid. 7A:13 (see D. C. Lau, p. 184).
61. Ibid. 4B:12.
62. Ibid. 3A:1.
63. Ibid. 7A:4.
64. Ibid. 6B:15.
65. Ibid.
66. Ibid.
67. Ibid. 7A:1.
68. Ibid. 4B:14.
69. Ibid. 4B:18.
70. See Wing-tsit Chan, *Source Book*, p. 784, and F. W. Mote, *Intellectual Foundations*, p. 60.
71. *Mencius* 2A:2 (see D. C. Lau, pp. 77–78).
72. *Chung yung*, 22.
73. Huston Smith, *Forgotten Truth: The Primordial Tradition* (New York, 1976), p. 63.
74. Hsü Fu-kuan, *Chung-kuo*, pp. 132–133.
75. Tu Wei-ming, "The Confucian Perception of Adulthood," *Daedalus* (April, 1976), 105(2):110.
76. *Mencius* 4B:19.
77. It should be noted that these two terms do not appear in *Mencius*; they are found in the so-called "Lost Confucian Text" in the newly discovered Ma-wang-tui silk manuscripts. However, a preliminary investigation indicates that the "Lost Confucian Text" may very well have been in the Mencian tradition. For a brief reference, see Tu Wei-ming, "The 'Thought of Huang-Lao': A Reflection on the Lao Tzu and Huang Ti Texts in the Silk Manuscripts of Ma-wang-tui," *The Journal of Asian Studies* (November, 1979), 34(1):96, n. 5.
78. *Mencius* 5B:1 (D. C. Lau, p. 150).
79. Ibid. (D. C. Lau, pp. 150–151).
80. Ibid. (D. C. Lau, pp. 149–150).
81. *Analects* 15:50.

The Human Body as a Microcosmic Source of Macrocosmic Values in Calligraphy

By John Hay

With Chinese calligraphy the art historian commonly meets two kinds of explanatory challenge. Why was calligraphy of such great and enduring importance to the Chinese? How should we, lacking both the cultural milieu and the technical training, perceive calligraphy? At the same time and in contrast to the apparent inaccessibility of this art, some people having no previous acquaintance with Chinese culture react to calligraphy with immediate, even visceral, excitement.

There are many ways of analyzing a piece of calligraphy. One method anciently and effectively used by the Chinese themselves is the imagery of organism, of physiology as we would classify it. Brush strokes have "bones" and "arteries," characters have "skeleton" and "sinews." I would like to explore this fact, for it involves both a mode of analysis and the conceptual and experiential framework of that analysis. The issues lead directly to the roots both of calligraphy's cultural particularity and of its universality. In pursuing these issues, we meet questions of the what, how, and why of art, which are fundamental to much broader phenomena of Chinese art. This in return may help us in more productively reformulating our enquiry. To ask what is a "Chinese theory of art" is perhaps to ask after something that never existed.

The broadest context for our chosen problem is the great richness and the universality of physiological imagery. It is characteristically systematized through the coherence of the human body. The Hermes of Praxiteles and the descending nude of Duchamp are but two instances toward chronologically opposite ends of an extraordinarily varied spectrum. A poet can speculate that "the only way to escape History of Styles is not to have a body."[1] Ernst Kris writes that "the 'bodily' experience with which we react in front of representations of the human figure suggests a formula of wide application.... All perceptual reactions, according to Schilder, are to some extent influenced by the image of the body."[2]

It is appropriate to look to Chinese painting for some reference points with which to map our approach to body imagery in calligraphy. But where is the physically sensible body image in Chinese painting? One might say that the court ladies of Ku K'ai-chih's "Admonitions of the Palace Instructress" (fig. 1) or the emperors of Yen Li-pen's procession (fig. 2) are a sociological, rather than a somatic theme. There is certainly a close association between society and its body, in both a corporate and corporeal sense. In the words of Mary Douglas:

> The social body constrains the way the physical body is perceived. The physical experience of the body, always modified by the social categories through which it is known, sustains a particular view of society. There is a continual exchange of meanings between the two kinds of bodily experience so that each reinforces the categories of the other.[3]

We are clearly in a complex network of factors, through which we could work in a variety of directions.

We might be tempted to use the figures of Ku and Yen as evidence that Chinese art had an innate and ancient tendency toward nonphysicality—toward abstraction as commonly understood—and that the importance of calligraphy is the supreme expression of this. I think this would be wrong.

The complement to the *apparently* disembodied figures of Ku and Yen is the frequency of good and solid, flesh and blood terms appearing in texts on calligraphy. Many are physiological, but there is wide variety of the most vigorously sensory metaphors, such as "a stone falling from a high peak, bouncing and crashing, about to shatter."[4]

The, in turn, complementary tendency for theories of painting to use sensorily less specific metaphors and to subordinate "formlikeness," *hsing-ssu*,[a] has, in colliding with the alien terminology of the modern West, contributed much to the unfortunate shibboleth that Chinese (and Japanese) art is concerned with spirit and not with matter. The metaphors of calligraphy seem not to count.

One could say simply that the plethora of metaphor in Chinese art texts makes for colorful reading but is otherwise a snare and a delusion. I think, however, that there has been sufficient study of metaphor to reveal its validity and its potency as an instrument of knowledge: "Metaphor is the root of reason, science and art. It is the root of feeling as understood beyond the immediate sensations of the self and of all expression of feeling . . . : in human feeling, reason, imagination, play, experiment, judgment and decision is embodied. . . ."[5] The metaphors of art texts are far more than picturesque embroidery, they are the most effective mode of understanding.

The physiological metaphors in calligraphy texts are immediately sensible. This in itself is an important indicator. It is immediately effective to ask someone, in their first meeting with calligraphy, to look at the characters as though they were a body structure—as supporting skeletal structures made beautiful with flesh, and strong with muscle and sinew—to suggest they grasp kinesthetically the implications of movement, so that they can perceive the tensions and balance within the writing through these same functions within their body. It is valid also. But for the historian the situation is far more complicated. Within calligraphy texts, physiological

[a] 形似

1. Attributed to Ku K'ai-chih (ca. 344–ca. 406), "Admonitions of the Palace Instructress," seventh section: "No one can please for ever; affection cannot be for one alone." Handscroll, ink and colors on silk, height 24.5 cm. Courtesy of the Trustees of the British Museum.

晋武帝司馬炎

2. Attributed to Yen Li-pen (d. 673), "Portraits of the Thirteen Emperors," sixth portrait: Emperor Wu of the Chin. Handscroll, ink and colors on silk, height 51.3 cm. Museum of Fine Arts, Boston.

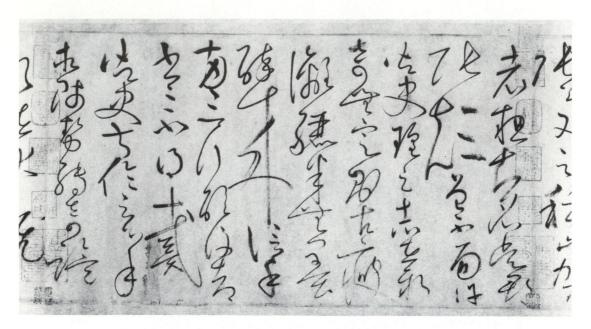

3. Huai-su, "Autobiography," dated 777. Section of a handscroll, *ts'ao-shu*, height 28.3 cm. National Palace Museum, Taipei, Taiwan, R.O.C.

metaphors are applied more to the cursive styles (fig. 3) than to the seemingly more somatic structures of regular script (fig. 4). As soon as we move outside calligraphy, we find the same terms in almost every conceivable context. Their occurrence in the sixth-century *Wen-hsin tiao-lung* is a well-known case in literary theory. Thus, to maintain any value to this metaphorical set, we must find a conceptual matrix very different from that to which we would naturally refer.

How do we elucidate the meaning of terms such as *jou*,[b] *chin*,[c] *ku*,[d] *hsüeh*,[e] *mo*,[f] *feng*,[g] *ch'i*,[h] and *shen*[i]? I will leave aside the justification of the last three for the moment. Do we examine their immediate context, as does David Pollard in his excellent article on *ch'i* in Chinese literary theory?[6] Essential though such an enterprise be, it tends to dissolve the root of the concept in the foliage of its application. Why was the term used in the first place? Do we look them up in a dictionary and find "flesh," "sinew," "bone," "blood," "vein," "wind," "breath," and "spirit"? But how do we know the signification of these terms which we can now write in a different language?

We have a distinct awareness of the things to which these names are applied, an

b 肉
c 筋
d 骨

e 血
f 脈
g 風

h 氣
i 神

4. Chao Meng-fu (1254–1322), "Record of the Miao-yen-ssu Temple in Hangchou." Section of a handscroll, *k'ai-shu*, height 35.3 cm. Anonymous Loan, The Art Museum, Princeton University.

awareness of their existence and importance. But we would be almost completely at a loss to say anything of their nature, function, and relationships without at least a simple knowledge of our contemporary physiology, anatomy and, in the broadest sense, cosmology. I use "cosmology" according to Karl Popper's statement that, "All science is cosmology, I believe, and for me the interest of philosophy, no less than of science, lies solely in the contributions which it has made to it."[7] Physiological and anatomical knowledge is not a simple product of common sense; it is a very complex product of sophisticated science, seeping down into common awareness. This is startlingly apparent to a layman, such as myself, perusing a history of the medical sciences.[8]

At this stage, the important realization is that the meaning of terms such as those just mentioned spread through many areas of human activity. They are integral to all humanity, but they radiate out from centers of particular knowledge. In this case the knowledge is that of medical practice. The history of medicine in China specifically supports this approach. Anyone studying the pattern of China's intellectual history must be struck by the interpenetration of what, for us, would be distinct areas of thought and activity. Parenthetically, we should emphasize that this applies most profoundly to art.

Medicine is no exception to this interpenetration and this is true at an early date. The *Tso-chuan* commentary on the "Spring and Autumn Annals," covering the period from 722 to 481 B.C., contains over forty-five medical consultations and descriptions of diseases. The most important occurred in 540 B.C., when Ho the Physician lectured the Prince of Chin on the fundamental principles of medicine.[9] The equivalent of the Hippocratic corpus is the *Huang-ti nei-ching* (Yellow Emperor's Classic of Corporeal Medicine), the core of which is thought to have taken its present form by the beginning of the Western Han (206 B.C.–A.D. 9).[10] It is considered as synthesizing the experience and theory of the preceding four or five centuries. Physicians at the Han court are well recorded.[11] As important as the early dates, roughly contemporary with developments in Greece, is the manner in which medical practice became integrated into the bureaucratic system and everyday life. The reorganization of the Imperial University, *T'ai-hsüeh*, completed probably in A.D. 493, included a Regius Professor of Medicine and a Regius Lecturer in Medicine.[12] This suggests that examinations in medicine were already part of the university curriculum. With other items of evidence, it also indicates that Confucian gentlemen had long been at home with medical theory. On the other hand, Chinese alchemy from pre-Han times onward had merged interests in aurifaction, iatro-chemistry, and macrobiotics. Many of those loosely labeled as "Taoists" were closely involved with matters medical.[13] To a degree unique in the ancient world, medical knowledge and practice were dispersed through society.

This knowledge and practice were distinctive. Needham writes: "We like the saying of Keele that 'it would seem probable that the first civilized people to free themselves from the purely magico-religious concepts of disease were the ancient

Chinese,' but we cannot follow him in his belief that this liberation was achieved only briefly until the acceptance of Buddhist thought from India."[14] Indeed, the theory and practice of traditional Chinese medicine are remarkable for their empirical basis, their systematic coherence, their inextricable integration with the broadest patterns of thought, and their pragmatic reading of concepts absolutely central to these patterns. We should note, at the same time, that theory and terminology remained compatible with religious and daemonic references which could readily reassert themselves. But we will leave this aspect aside. The remarkable work on pathological symptoms, especially the late second century A.D. *Shang-han lun* (Treatise on Febrile Diseases), by Chang Chung-ching, is an expression of critical and classificatory thought with the broadest significance.[15] The monograph by Manfred Porkert, *The Theoretical Foundations of Chinese Medicine*, is an intensive exploration of these issues in their specific application and broad extension. It demonstrates, first, that Chinese medical theory can be understood only if fundamental concepts are clarified in a broader context and, secondly, that understanding of these concepts may be significantly advanced through an examination of their function in medical theory. I will rely upon it extensively.

In this theory, we do not find the various divisions arising out of post-Renaissance science in the West. There is, for example, no division between anatomy and physiology. This is of major significance and affects radically our sense of basic terms such as *ku* and *mo*. The situation may be highlighted by comparison with the Western tradition, in which the development of anatomical studies played a major role. As Arturo Castiglione writes:

> In medicine it was the new anatomy that led the rebellion against scholasticism and gave a huge impulse to the development of the arts and sciences. . . . In this preparation for the renaissance of medicine, it is highly significant that the greatest precursor of the movement should have embodied in his marvelous personality all the characteristics of the Renaissance—we refer to Leonardo Da Vinci.[16]

Leonardo's anatomical studies were buried in obscurity, being perhaps too original. But it is equally significant that the most influential monument of anatomical investigation emerged from the cooperation of a physician and the studio of Titian.

> The work of Andreas Vesalius of Brussels constitutes one of the greatest treasures of Western civilization and culture. His masterpiece, the *De Humani Corporis Fabrica*, and its companion volume, the *Epitome*, issued at Basel in 1543, established with startling suddenness the beginning of modern observational science and research.[17]

There are at least three separate subjects of these studies: the skeleton, the tissues and organs, and their functions. Roughly speaking, the importance of their roles in man's discovery of himself succeeded each other in that order.

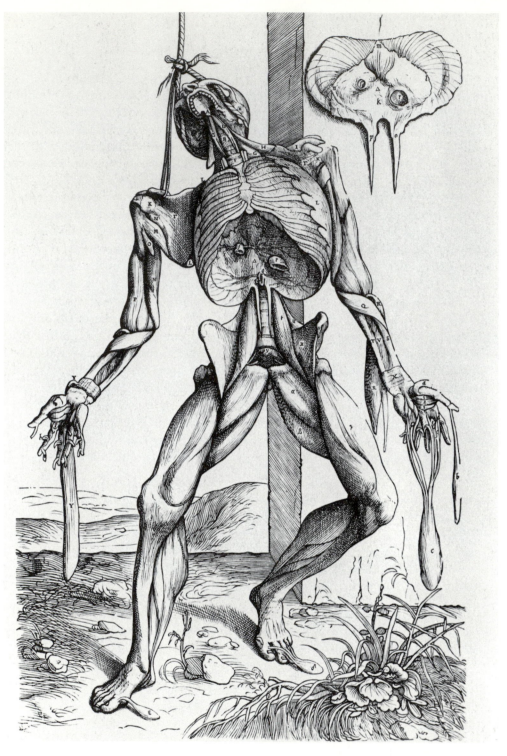

5. Andreas Vesalius, Seventh Plate of the Muscles, from *De Humani Corporis Fabrica*, published in 1543. After *The Illustrations from the Works of Andreas Vesalius of Brussels*, ann. J. B. de C. M. Saunders and Charles D. O'Malley, Dover Publications, 1973, pl. 30.

One hardly needs to be reminded how different is the illustration to Vesalius's work (fig. 5), or the art of his contemporary, Michelangelo, from anything ever done in China (fig. 1). Equally, even though there are interesting similarities between pre-Renaissance (and modern!) medicine and Chinese medicine, from the fifteenth century to the present they have differed fundamentally. This is certainly not due to any inability of the Chinese to observe reality.

The purpose of anatomy is the differentiation and identification of separate organs. Organs, as discrete physical objects, barely exist in traditional Chinese medical theory (its present situation is more complex). Instead, it identifies functions. This is our first essential factor. As Nathan Sivin writes in his introduction to Porkert's book:

> ... the classical (Chinese) understanding of the interior of the body, which he calls "orbisiconography," is not the counterpart of Western anatomy but its antithesis. Anatomy is concerned with the organism as a structure of parts, and orbisiconography (tsang-hsiang[j]) with the dynamic interplay of what is best described as a number of functional systems. Any normal Chinese-English dictionary, for instance, will define kan[k] simply as "liver." In medicine (as opposed to, say, cooking) this word seldom refers to the physical organ, but rather to the energetic sphere ("orb") which the organ serves as a material substratum.[18]

Porkert himself writes of these seemingly anatomical terms that:

> ... they refer on the one hand to a bodily substratum with ill-defined material and spatial contours, and on the other hand to a physiological function associated with the substratum and qualitatively defined in time with precision and subtlety.... The qualifiers used in orbisiconography must be understood as definitions of effective relations or functions, not simply as expressions of crude anatomical insights. That is why statements bearing on a certain orb can under no circumstances be made to agree completely with statements bearing on the corresponding organ in Western thought.[19]

The only principal orb that figures prominently in art theory is the hsin.[l] Porkert describes its specific function as:

> "Sovereign": seat of the configurative force (shen), conditions the character and the cohesion of the personality.[20]

j 臟象   k 肝   l 心

Much more common are several of the *ch'i-heng chih fu*[m] (Porkert: "paraorbs"). *nao*,[n] *sui*,[o] *ku*, *mo*, *tan*,[p] and *pao*.[q] Their essential function is the storage of energy.[21] Both *ku* and *mo* are: "'Stem': framework of the body; moves active and structive physiological energies."[22]

It is impossible to understand the nature of the "paraorbs" without reference to the "orbs." In general, they are specific "unfoldments," *ch'ung*,[r] or secondary extensions of the orbs.[23] In the *Nei-ching* we read:

> The functional dominions of the five orbs: *Hsin* dominates [is unfolded in] *mo* (commentary: which, obstructing the constructive energy,[24] moves in response to respiration). *Fei*[s] dominates *p'i*[t] (commentary: which, enwrapping the sinews and flesh, defends the body from noxious influences). *Kan* dominates *chin* (commentary: which, binding together the segments, operate in accordance with configurative force, *shen*). *P'i*[u] dominates *jou* (commentary: which covers and keeps the sinews and bones, and distributes the defensive, structive energy). *Shen*[v] dominates *ku* (commentary: which, stretching the sinews and transforming the marrow, forms a stem so that the body may stand). These are what are termed the five functional dominions.[25]

There are many overlapping systems, and the *wu-chu*[w] listed here only partly overlap with the six *ch'i-heng chih fu*. The essential point is that everything is knit into a dense web of functions. The bones are indeed a support for the body, or rather an organic "stem," but they share this function with the arteries and they can fulfill it only because they are a concretion and storage of energy transmitted from the *shen* orb ("kidneys and testes"). Porkert writes of *jou* and *chin*:

> *Chi-jou*,[x] or simply *jou* designates the flesh of the muscles, connoting not so much its motor function as the somatic element which gives the body its characteristic shape and which, by its changes, permits inferences to be drawn about the individual's nutrition and reserve capacities. In contradistinction *chin* (*nervus*, muscles and sinews) points to the mechanical elements, sometimes concealed, of the locomotive system.[26]

Unlike *ku*, the *chin* and *jou* do not store energy, but they do transmit it; and the defensive energy, *wei-ch'i*,[y] transmitting through the *jou*, has an essential role in protecting the inner organism from heteropathic influences.

m 奇恆之腑	r 充	v 腎
n 腦	s 肺	w 五主
o 髓	t 皮	x 肌肉
p 膽	u 脾	y 衞氣
q 胞		

At a somewhat less specific level, these values are immediately tangible in a passage such as this from the *Pi-chen-t'u* (Battle Array of the Brush):

> Calligraphy by those good in brush strength has much bone; that by those not good in brush strength has much flesh. Calligraphy that has much bone but slight flesh is called sinew-writing; that with much flesh but slight bone is called ink-pig. Calligraphy with much strength and rich in sinew is of sage-like quality; that with neither strength nor sinew is sick. Every writer proceeds in accordance with the manifestation of their digestion and respiration of energy, *hsiao-hsi*.[z][27]

There are several further points to note about this passage. First, there is the equating of quality with health. The term "sickness," *ping*,[aa] for a shortcoming is common in calligraphy and elsewhere. The probable role of medical practice in developing critical apparatus has already been mentioned. Sagehood is also an ultimate state of health, as the *Nei-ching* states repeatedly.

> The Sages attained harmony with Heaven and Earth and followed closely the laws of the eight winds.... Their bodies could never be harmed, nor their faculties be dispersed.[28]

Nathan Sivin has called the state of *hsien*[ab] "immortality ... thought of as the highest kind of health."[29] Needham has drawn attention to the importance of the Chinese concern for *physical* immortality.[30] Secondly, there is the element of strength, *li*,[ac] out of which these qualities materialize. Thirdly, and related to *li*, is the concept of *hsiao-hsi*, which I have tried to emphasize through a rather clumsy translation.

These matters turn our attention to other terms, such as *hsüeh*, *ch'i*, and *mo*, which all belong at another level of medical theory. They are all concepts of energy. It is as a system of energy flow and transformation that Chinese medical theory was most distinctive in its achievements and most fundamentally integrated with the Chinese universe as a whole. This is our second essential factor.

Ch'i has long since been translated by Homer H. Dubs as "matter-energy."[31] The concept of energetics as the core of an organismic world view has been fundamental to works such as Needham's *Science and Civilization in China*. No one who looks in general at man's attempts to understand the universe from the earliest times onward can fail to be struck by the importance and the variability of the concept of energy.[32] Similarly, once one has begun to look for the role of energy in traditional Chinese thought, it becomes nearly impossible to get away from it. Porkert has discussed at length the question in relation to medicine,[33] detailing a dozen basic forms of energy and over two dozen accessory forms.

z	消息	ab	仙
aa	病	ac	力

The body is a complex network of patterns of energy. The most general state of energy is *ch'i*, which, in Porkert's words,

> ... comes as close as possible to constituting a generic designation equivalent to our word "energy." ... And yet, unlike our concept of energy, ch'i, whatever the context and absolutely without exception, always implies a qualitative determination of energy.... For this reason we use for the technical term *ch'i* the standard definitions "configurational energy"—i.e., energy of a definite direction in space, of a definite arrangement, quality or structure—and "energetic configuration."[34]

Hsüeh was another form of energy. Porkert defines it in a technical medical sense as "structive physiological energy of individual quality":[35]

> *Hsüeh* is but one of several forms of energy occurring in the microcosm, not simply a moving fluid. The vital functions depend not on the presence of *hsüeh* but on its particular intrinsic quality and its harmony with the other forms of energy, especially *ch'i*.[36]

We should note how modern our own conceptions of breath and blood. There are a number of earlier Western views, such as that of Francis Bacon (1561–1626), who considered air as "a form of mercury that united with flame to become the pneumatical component of living tissue."[37] Robert Boyle (1627–1691), with his vacuum experiments, was the first to challenge the established Galenic belief that respiration was for the removal of waste vapors.[38] An understanding of oxygen and its role in respiration did not mature until the eighteenth century.

Down to the time of the great Roman physician Galen (A.D. 130–200), it had been thought that the arteries carried not blood but air. Later, in medieval times, it was thought, as Owen Barfield describes, that the heart:

> ... drew the blood into itself, in order to replenish it with *pneuma* or "vital spirits," after which the blood passed of its own motion back again into the system of the body. Instead of a circulation, there were two kinds of blood; the arterial, whose function has just been described, and which contained those vital spirits to which we unknowingly refer when we speak of "high" or "low" spirits; and the venous, which flowed back and forth in the veins, conveying nourishment.[39]

When William Harvey (1578–1657) discovered the circulation of the blood, in the sense of the heart's mechanical action, he still wrote of blood in these words:

> Now I maintain the same thing of the innate heat and the blood [as does Aristotle of semen]: I say that they are not fire, and neither do they derive their origin from fire. They rather share the nature of some other, and that

> a more divine body or substance. They act by no faculty or property of the elements; but as there is something inherent in semen which makes it prolific, and as, in producing an animal, it surpasses the power of the elements—as it is a spirit, namely, and the inherent nature of that spirit corresponds to the essence of the stars, so there is a spirit, or a certain force, inherent in the blood, .. and the nature, yea, the soul in this spirit and blood is identical with the essence of the stars.[40]

I think it worth noting Western analogies, partly because the Western evolution is much better studied, and partly because a realization of these analogies may lead us to reflect more carefully on the broader implications of these patterns of thought. The Neo-Confucian philosopher Ch'eng I (1033–1107) wrote that the exhaled *ch'i* is produced from the "*ch'i* of the true source" within the body. It is not the same as the inhaled *ch'i*, which simply nourishes the internal *ch'i*:

> To say that the retracted ether, *ch'i*, (breathed in) is again required as the material of the extending ether (breathed out) is a complete misunderstanding of the transformations of heaven and earth.[41]

This is remarkably similar to the concept of arterial and venous blood. Some implications of these views will be considered later.

In a diatribe against the draft script, *Fei ts'ao-shu*, by Chao I of the Eastern Han, we read:

> The nature of *ts'ao* is easy and quick, but nowadays it has contrarily become difficult and slow. What a loss of principle. All men differ in their *ch'i* and *hsüeh*, and vary in their sinew and bones; the heart-mind, *hsin*, may be dispersed or dense; the hand may be skilled or clumsy. The beauty or ugliness of calligraphy is in the heart-mind and the hand. Can it be forced?[42]

The syntactical parallelism here clearly differentiates between the forms of energy and their material substances, between the orb-function, *hsin*, and the mechanical extension, *shou*.[ad] The systematic relationships are characteristic. The ninth-century author Chang Huai-kuan wrote of the *ts'ao* script:

> The body and force-form, *t'i-shih*,[ae] of a character is complete with a single stroke. There may happen [a passage] where [the brush line] is not continuous but the blood-artery, *hsüeh-mo*,[af] is uninterrupted. Where there is continuity, then the energy, *ch'i-hou*,[ag] communicates through from one line to the next. Only Wang [Hsien-chih] understood this profound

ad 手   af 血脈
ae 體勢   ag 氣候

principle, thus the character at the top of a line in his calligraphy often continues [the energy] from the character at the bottom of the preceding line. What is called the "one-stroke writing" which originated with Chang [Chih] [Eastern Han] is this.[43]

Ch'i is the more generic category of energy flow, and appears thus in a wide variety of contexts in calligraphy texts. The blood arteries are energy functioning at a more specific level, embodying the structure within and between characters.[44] Since the arteries can now extend through a succession of characters, and since the body is defined functionally, a line of calligraphy can be even more "bodily" than a single character.

The concept of arteries is one of the most revealing of all. It developed very early, having already a well-articulated role in the *Nei-ching*. The classic texts of Huang-fu Mi on acu-moxi-therapy and Wang Shu-ho's "Classic of the Pulse" were written during or before the fourth century A.D.[45]

Mo, or "pulse," is defined by Porkert as both "the active aspect of *hsüeh*,"[46] and "the energetic conduits (sinarteries, the internal substratum of the pulse)."[47] This ambiguity of a materialized movement is characteristic. From our point of view, the interest of the evolution of *mo* is twofold. It presents the patterns of energy, first, in their more systematic and topological form and, secondly, in their most sensible form so that they are literally palpable to the outsider.[48] Such an understanding may have had its source as early as the second millenium B.C., in the experience of how disease could be influenced from known points on the body's surface. By the mid-Han dynasty, an increasingly large number of these points had been integrated into a theoretical system of energy conduits. This combination of tangible, empirical knowledge with a highly sophisticated theoretical system remained characteristic. The conduits connect the orbs and carry endogenous energy from the interior to the surface, and may also carry exogenous energies from the surface inward. These latter are the heteropathic *ch'i*, *hsieh-ch'i*,[ah] absorbed through the skin. There are twelve cardinal conduits, *ching-mo*,[ai] which provide a supporting framework for an extensive and complex arterial system and, with the bones, form the stem of the body.

If there is any single, fundamental characterization of calligraphy, it is that of a line of energy, materializing through the brush into the ink-trace. Hence many terms, such as "brush-strength," *pi-li*,[aj] are essentially aspects of energy. The characterization is so natural and effective that it is easy to take it for granted. But in fact, it should count as one of the most original and effective achievements in all of art theory. Why should the Chinese have produced it? Clearly it has a kinesthetic component in the actual movements of the calligrapher's arm, hand, and fingers. But such movement is in some degree common to all material arts. The source of the

ah 邪氣   ai 經脈   aj 筆力

theory is much more complex. This is emphasized by the extension of the theory to less material arts, such as literature.

There is no doubt whatever that the *ching-mo* system in medicine provides an extremely close analogy. The facts that the human body *is* so vividly a source of both perceptions and values, that the Chinese medical theory articulated so precisely the very tangible energetics of the body, and that it seems this articulation and its sophisticated terminology were roughly contemporary with but probably slightly earlier than corresponding developments in art theory, make it likely that the former is a major source for the latter. A principal theme in the evolution of first the medical and then the art theory is the increasing differentiation and integration of energy-flow into energy-pattern. One may note two of the most splendid of these configurations of energy evolving in a broader context, the dragon itself and its transformation into the mountain-dragon, which eventually found a prominent home in the visual arts. In figure painting, paradoxically but not surprisingly, it was clothes rather than flesh which proved the most suitable medium for representing patterns of energy.

The analogies could be pursued at length. One of the most important is the relation of inner and outer, *nei-wai*,[ak] and *li-piao*.[al] It is absolutely fundamental to medical theory, appearing on almost every page of the *Nei-ching*.[49] The whole sinarteriological system depends on the patterns of energy deep in the body's interior being palpable at its surface. It is surely more than a coincidence that the same word, *ts'ang*,[am] "to store," is at the root of *tsang-hsiang*,[an] "orb" or "visceral-store-image," and *ts'ang-feng*,[ao] "stored or hidden brush tip."[50] Both the viscera and the brush-core tip are a store and source of energy. As the bone tip in calligraphy should not be overmanifested at the surface, so the strongest pulse in the body, that of the *shen* orb, which unfolds through the bones, should not be overmanifested.[51] The relation between inner store and outer manifestation is a concept of very wide application, and is the third of our major factors.

Both the chronological sequence of texts on calligraphy and the descriptions of successively evolving scripts given in single texts, such as Chang Huai-kuan's "Judgments of the Ten Forms of Script,"[52] indicate that the criteria of calligraphic value developed from image-making of the *I-ching* type, to a concern for energy and its transformations. But the role of image-making is not supplanted, for the process itself becomes increasingly explicit in the nature of transformation, *tsao-hua*,[ap] and *pien-hua*.[aq] The view of *ts'ao-shu* as a sequence of changing images, such as in Wei Heng's *Ssu-t'i shu-shih* (The Forms of Force in Calligraphy in the Four Scripts),[53] is increasingly focused in the process of *pien-hua* itself. This may be seen in Chang

ak 內外
al 懷素
am 藏

an 臟象
ao 藏鋒

ap 造化
aq 變化

Huai-kuan's discussion of *ts'ao*, which "takes the wind and bone as its embodiment and transformation as its instrument."[ar][54]

The process of transformation was crucial to medical theory. Bone is a transformation of *ch'i*, and ultimately everything was transformation. Indeed, it was perhaps in medicine that transformation received its most immediate and intensive study. The processes of respiration and digestion that are a major concern of the *Nei-ching* form the somatic core of the perception that "the self is change."

Through the brush of the calligrapher, the actual understanding of transformation received its most vivid expression. Later, in painting, the "dragon vein" which often appears as an essential structural principal in the landscapists' mountains, embodies on the largest scale the process of materializing energy. In literature, the *fu* is often a transformational sequence of images equivalent to the pattern of change in *ts'ao-shu*. Later literature explores the phenomenon more directly.

In connection with these patterns of energy transformation, we should note the remarkable prevalence of resonance in Chinese art. Whether it be the rhythmic repetition of strokes in calligraphy, the reverberating forms of painting, the multiplication of basic units such as pillars and brackets in architecture, the constant echoes of parallelism in literature, or even the psychological echoing of one artist representing, *fang*,[as] another, in all of these we can identify resonance as a constant factor. It is noticeably weaker in Japanese derivations of these Chinese forms.

In China, it is surely a function of the self-generating transformations of energy and the broader habits of correlational thought in an organismic world. In physiological theory we find exactly the same sense of constant reduplication and resonance. Resonance is a constant image in Chinese cosmogony, being inherent in the very nature of these energetic processes. In sinological studies, the themes of transformation and resonance will be found prominently exactly where we should expect them, in Needham's *magnum opus*. He writes: "Concentrating their interest upon Nature as they did, it was inevitable that the Taoists should be obsessed by the problem of Change,"[55] and remarks how, in contrast, the Western tradition of Aristotelian logic "provided the natural sciences with an inadequate tool for the handling of the greatest fact of nature, so well appreciated by the Taoists, Change."[56] The evolution of the concept of *li*[at] amongst Neo-Taoist thinkers such as Wang Pi (226–249) and Kuo Hsiang (d. 312), although with widely varying emphasis, is clearly related to patterns arising out of change.[57] Change becomes fully integrated into the Neo-Confucian system. This complex of change, transformation, and resonance is our fourth principal factor.

These considerations take us into such broad issues that we can only touch them. But I think it very important to make an initial stretch. The transformations

ar 「以風骨爲體，以變化　　as 倣　　　　　　　at 理
爲用」

of energy occurred within a distinctive framework, that of the microcosm within the macrocosm. Although this is a very general truth, nowhere could it be clearer than in medical theory. This is only natural, since the principal basis of the pre-modern understanding of the micro/macrocosmic relationship is the human body within the grandeur of its environment. It is the most recurrent theme in T. S. Hall's *History of General Physiology: From Pre-Socratic Times to the Enlightenment*. When Harvey revealed the mechanical circulation of the blood, he still thought of the heart as a microcosmic sun.[58]

No theme is stronger in the *Nei-ching*, from beginning to end. At the beginning of section 3, we read:

> The Yellow Emperor said: "From earliest times the communication with Heaven has been the very foundation of life; this foundation exists between Yin and Yang and between Heaven and Earth and within the six [cardinal] points. The (heavenly) breath prevails in the nine divisions, in the nine orifices, in the five viscera [orbs], and in the twelve joints; they are all pervaded by the breath of Heaven.[59]

At the beginning of section 9, we read:

> Man is formed of 365 segments, which have long been considered as Heaven and Earth.[60]

The habit of reading destiny in physical patterns is a direct expression of the micro/macrocosmic belief. The main thrust of anthroposcopic works such as the third-century A.D. *Jen-wu-chih*, by Liu Shao, is to understand man as a microcosm, integrated into the macrocosm through the correlations of Yin-yang polarity and the energy phases of the *wu-hsing*.[au] Landscape became subject to similar divination.[61] The empirical and pragmatic nature of this divination is shown by the texts on assessment of horses, *hsiang-ma*,[av] prevalent in the Han. It is not surprising that both painting and calligraphy became "divinable" in this sense. The physiological derivation is shown by Chang Huai-kuan, when he writes:

> A horse is considered superior when it has much sinew and little flesh, inferior when it has much flesh and little sinew. Calligraphy is also like this.[62]

Calligraphy, like every other activity, occurred within the micro/macrocosmic framework. Much of the imagery in textual descriptions emphasizes this. Specific reference is common. We may note, parenthetically, that the puzzling term *feng*[aw] ("wind") should probably be explained in this context. In medical theory it occurs

au 五行   av 相馬   aw 風

with increasing frequency as the exterior aspects of *ch'i* which surround the body and are also *intermediate* between the macro- and the microcosm. Usually they are heteropathic.[63] In areas such as calligraphy and literary theory, whilst *ku* is the interior store and pattern of energy, *feng* seems to be flow of energy between the art work and its audience. If this is so, it offers a remarkable approach to an endemic problem of aesthetics.

The "Discussion of Brush Marrow," *Pi-sui lun* (nice title!) attributed to Yü Shih-nan (558–638), states:

> Although characters have material traces, their root is in non-being; given being by the [polarity of] Yin-yang the quiescence is stirred; embodying the myriad phenomena they take form; the realization of its energetic character goes through all changefulness, *ta-hsing t'ung-pien*, its constant nature has no contrary check, *ch'i-ch'ang wu-chu*; thus we know the recondite transcendancy of the Tao of calligraphy. One must entrust oneself to the operation of configurative force, *shen-yü*, and not seek it by corporeal strength, *li-ch'iu*.[ax][64]

In the polarity of heaven and earth, heaven was Yang and earth was Yin. Certainly the dynamics of Yin-yang operated in calligraphy, which in its execution was probably seen as Yang. The *Pi-lun* attributed to Ts'ai Yung (132–192) states that calligraphy is "dispersing," *san*.[ay][65] *San* is a Yang function.[66] The formal structure of the character, *hsing*,[az] was of the earth, structive rather than active, and therefore Yin. But the transformations of energy within the process of polarity were a constant Yin-yang reaction.

It is easy to pay lip service to the ideas seen in the Yü Shih-nan text and everywhere else, but then to leave them aside as empty conventions. My personal conviction is that they were tangibly vital and essential to comprehension. The micro/macrocosmic reality is the fifth of our principal factors.

The dynamics of polarity within this reality must be seen as a perception of potentiality and actuality in an inescapable nexus of existence itself. Again, it is notable how this appears as a natural element in the writing of scholars such as Needham:

> [The *Li* of the Neo-Confucianists] was thought of as a kind of four-dimensional pattern in the universe, according to which things were brought from potentiality to actuality.[67]

However, it is curiously absent from much writing on Chinese cultural history. I think this is perhaps a case where an analogy with Western history is helpful in

---

ax 「字雖有質跡，本無爲，稟陰陽與動靜，體萬物以成形，達性通變，其常不主，故知書道玄妙，必資神遇，不可以力求也。」

ay 散

az 形

alerting us to fundamental shifts of cognitive modes. Owen Barfield, a remarkable student of Western literature and thoughts, has written of the medieval world:

> . . . a whole book, instead of a chapter, would not be too much to give to the philosophy alone of that lost world. Once again, it *is* a lost world . . . in which both phenomenon and name were felt as representations. On the one hand "the word conceived in the mind is representative of the whole of that which is realized in thought" [Aquinas]. But, on the other hand the phenomenon itself only achieves full reality (*actus*) in the moment of being "named" by man . . . the name or word is not mere sound, or mere ink. For Aquinas, as for Augustine, there are, anterior to the uttered word, the intellect word, the heart word and the memory word.[68]

> . . . knowledge was defined, not as the devising of hypotheses, but as an act of union with the represented behind the representation.[69]

> We must forget all about our "laws of nature," those interposed, spectral hypotheses, before we can understand the "forms" of medieval scholasticism . . . for we have not even a transmuted survival of that *actus: potentia* polarity which was the very life-blood of Scholastic thought. . . . Being is potential existence; existence actualizes being. . . . Everywhere around us we must see creatures in a state of *potentia* being raised to *actus*: and yet, behind the appearances, the *actus* is already there. What is the intellectual soul but the potentiality of determining the species of things? And what are the phenomena themselves? *Actually* the likenesses or representations of all sorts of "species"—but *potentially* immaterial in the soul itself.[70]

> Thus the polarity of *actus* and *potentia* had carried perhaps half the weight of the Western mind through all the centuries that elapsed between Aristotle and Aquinas.[71]

I apologize for quoting at such length, but I see no better way of conveying an absolutely crucial point. Despite the distinctive nature of the Chinese tradition, we should not be surprised at such fundamental similarity between two worlds. They are both divided from us by the revolution of Renaissance science. And as Nathan Sivin comments, "man's prodigious creativity seems to be based on the permutations and recastings of a rather small stock of ideas."[72] I think the essential polarity carried an even greater weight of thought in China. But the terms *potentia* and *actus* are not Chinese. In China, it is *T'ien* and *Ti*,[ba] with a number of related pairs such as *wu* and *wei*,[bb] *shen* and *hsing*.[bc] *Tao* is the *process* of the polarity, a process on which all depends. Hence the perennial emphasis on process is a concern that *hsing* (*actus*) should not become divorced from *shen* (*potentia*). As a statement of this polarity, it would be hard to improve on the opening passage of the *Lao Tzu* text:

ba 天地   bb 無爲   bc 神形

The way that can be spoken of
Is not the constant way;
The name that can be named
Is not the constant name.
The nameless was the beginning of heaven and earth;
The named was the mother of the myriad creatures.
Hence always rid yourself of desires in order to observe its secrets;
But always allow yourself to have desires in order to observe its manifestations.
These two are the same
But diverge in name as they issue forth.
Being the same they are called mysteries,
Mystery upon mystery—
The gateway of the manifold secrets.[73]

It should be unnecessary to say that the *potentia/actus* polarity is fundamental to pre-modern Western physiology, just as the analogous *T'ien-ti* polarity is fundamental to the Chinese. Any page of the *Nei-ching* will reveal it. Porkert, in his important chapter on "basis standards of value," discusses specifically the "polarity of potentiality/actuality."[74] One must watch the terminology when he enlarges upon the "active" role of *T'ien/Yang* and the "structive" pole of *Ti/Yin*. "Active" here is not equivalent to *actus*, but initiative of it. It is of great value when he clarifies Yang as signifying

> something incipient, something inchoative—in Chinese, *sheng*,[bd] ... identical with some action.[75]

and Yin as signifying

> something completing (something perfective)—in Chinese *ch'eng*,[be] Struction, the substantiation of effects ... initiated actively.[76]

The images, *hsiang*,[bf] of the *I-ching* are clearly symbols of passage from potentiality to actuality. Calligraphy inherited this immense power. With sharpening epistemological focus, the *Tao* of its actualizing process, its direct line to potentiality, became increasingly explicit. The *Chiu-shih* (Nine Forms of Calligraphic Force) attributed to Ts'ai Yung states:

> Calligraphy originates in thus-ness. When thus-ness is established the Yin-yang is produced therein. When Yin-yang is produced, then shape and force-form emerge.[bg][77]

Many criteria of calligraphy must be understood by direct reference to patterns of energy transforming out of potentiality/actuality polarity within a micro/

bd 生
be 成

bf 象
bg 「夫書肇於自然，自然

既立，陰陽生焉，陰陽
既生，形勢出矣。」

macrocosmic reality. Thus, when Chang Huai-kuan in his *Wen-tzu-lun* (Discussion of Scripts) says:

> The *chen-shu* of Chung Yu and the *hsing-shu* of Wang Hsi-chih, one ancient and the other modern, each have the heaven-bones of thus-ness; like traces [stretching] a thousand *li*, remote beyond pursuit....[78]

we may sense profound and potent resonances. The frequent image of distance is clearly one that evokes the great depths of potentiality, summoned by art from remoteness into immediacy. This relationship is the sixth of our principal factors.

In this world, art cannot be isolated. As man-made nature, like alchemy, it distills the essence of reality. It is man's chosen image of the process between potentiality and actuality, the *Tao*. It becomes, in fact, an image of intensely comprehended life. Just as a search for life was the mainspring of physiology, so was it also the heart of art. The classic formulation states exactly this:

> In the resonating of the [primal Yang] energy, life is set in motion. In the patterning of structure, the instrument is the brush.[bh][79]

Of the eight characters in the original phrases, probably brush, *pi*, is the only one with a significance close to our contemporary English words. Perhaps not even that one. For some time it has hardly been fashionable, barely possible, for art to be equated with life in this sense. But the Chinese certainly did; and should we, as historians, deny them?

There is a level in the structure of human thought that we can no longer consider simply in terms of the analysis and classification of ideas. The entire matrix out of which ideas arise, the whole pattern of human consciousness, also has its evolution. Study of history in the full sense, including the history of art theory, and going beyond rewriting the past in terms of the present, must deal with the history both of ideas and their consciousness. The relationships between micro- and macrocosm may be the major theme in this history. I would like to conclude by stressing that the factors to which I have been trying to draw attention are not merely vague matters of the spirit, but tangible realities subject to historical change.

When Vesalius was raiding the charnel house at the Cemetery of the Innocents in Paris and allowing himself to be locked outside the city gates at night so that he could plunder a gibbet and subsequently reassemble the first artificially articulated skeleton, something was happening to the image of man. In the early seventeenth century, the mystic Jakob Boehme could still describe this image as "a complete abridgement of the whole universe ... a living emblem and hieroglyph of eternity and time."[80] But its days were numbered.

Curiously enough, something analogous had almost happened in China. In 1054, the first recorded Chinese dissection was carried out on fifty-six executed bandits.

bh 氣韻生動，骨法用筆

These studies were published and eventually transmitted to the West through Arab intermediaries. There are other signs of the discipline of anatomy developing during the Sung.[81] In this period, the ancient hold of microcosm and macrocosm was almost broken. China led the world in many sciences and if this remarkable impetus had carried through, then the course of world history would certainly have been different.[82] The course of Chinese art would have been different also. A Yüan dynasty writer, Ch'en I-ts'eng, wrote:

> Characters are born from ink, ink is born from water; water is the blood of characters. . . .

> Characters do not have bones. What acts as the bone of a character is the second segment of the thumb. When it is raised, the "bone" of the character is strong.[83]

The language seems familiar, but this is an extraordinarily literal, pseudo-anatomical interpretation of an ancient formulation. During the Southern Sung there developed a style of painting that was the antithesis of both earlier and later ideals. Like the contemporary poet Lu Yu, who wished that his "poet's mind was sharp as the blades of Ping, to bring a slice of the Autumn scene to his page,"[84] many painters developed the sharply analytic, fragmenting eye of an observer who was fast becoming his own measure. Accordingly, the scope of time and place in landscape painting rapidly became more specified and limited. Its images were of perfection, of a structure finalized and frozen.

The impetus of this age did not carry through, although many of its achievements survived and it exerted great influence. The art most characteristic of the time fell into disrepute. The calligraphy of some of its greatest hands, such as that of Chang Chi-chih (1186–1266), was described as degenerate. Its painting was thought of as *merely* beautiful. I do not know whether this period produced its own theory of art. But within the ancient context, its theory may have been written a thousand years earlier. Attributed to Chung Yu (151–230) are the words:

> Using the brush is Heaven; streaming forth beauty is Earth.[85]

Beauty isolated is the material earth, objectivity divorced from potentiality, *hsing* without *shen*. Although much of later Chinese art is beautiful, no one could claim that beauty was ever its ideal. All the great painters of landscapes whose ideas can also be traced through their words, Ching Hao, Kuo Hsi, Huang Kung-wang, Tung Ch'i-ch'ang, Kung Hsien, Tao-chi, and Wang Yüan-ch'i, for example, all were acute perceivers of transformation within the micro/macrocosmic polarity. The paintings may all be most effectively described as configurations of energy. These configurations became increasingly purified, until Tung Ch'i-ch'ang (1555–1636) had the "powers of transformational creation at his brush tip."[86] But they are not

6. Tao-chi (1641–ca. 1710). Leaf from an album of landscapes and calligraphy, ink and colors on paper, 24.2 × 27.8 cm. C. C. Wang Collection.

abstractions, for they come closer to life rather than farther away from it. They could be miscalled "abstractions" only in something approaching Rudolf Arnheim's sense of the generative principles of conceptual vision.[87] However, the whole question of "abstraction" is one wherein angels might fear to tread. The words of Piet Mondrian are salutary:

> In removing completely from the work all objects, "the world is not separated from the spirit," but on the contrary *put in a balanced opposition* with the spirit, since the one and the other are purified.... To love things in reality is to love them profoundly; it is to see them as a microcosmos in the macrocosmos. *Only in this way can one achieve a universal expression of reality.*[88]

Relationships have changed profoundly and Mondrian sees duality rather than polarity, but the resurgence of the microcosm and the macrocosm in contemporary thought is a major reason for elucidating it in the traditional Chinese context.

Perhaps the ultimate vision of configurational energy in the world we have suggested is the work of Tao-chi (1641–ca. 1710). Here we come as close to potentiality as may be possible (fig. 6). The images of physiology had often appeared in the texts of landscape painting. Kuo Hsi provides a notable example. Tao-chi, as we would expect from his painting, is the most involved instance. The most powerful and elusive statement is section 18 of his *Hua-yü lu* (Talk of Painting). To quote Lin Yutang's footnote:

> This is the strangest discourse I have ever translated. In this whole section, the artist identifies himself with the universe and its various manifestations. He must justify and maintain the proper "functions" of the myriad things. . . . The artist's creation is compared with the creation of the world of forms out of chaos and life out of forms. When the first vague shapes take form in ink, this is comparable to the awakening and growth of a child's consciousness.[89]

In his chapter on "Transformations," Tao-chi makes his famous remark that:

> The ancients had their ancient hair and eyebrows. They can grow only on the faces of the ancients. They cannot grow on my face. The "lung" viscera of the ancients can grow only within the bellies of the ancients. They cannot grow in mine. I myself will express my own "lungs" and flourish my own hair.[bi][90]

Tao-chi doubtless knew his medical theory and was aware that the "lung" orb, *fei-fu* was the "prime minister" of rhythmic order and the root of *ch'i*.[91] Its specific outward manifestation was the hair of the head.[92] Where was Tao-chi going? Back to the source, to the original *ch'i*. Not out into abstraction. His message was clear:

> The Remote Antiquity is devoid of *fa*, or methods;
> *T'ai-pu*, or the Primordial Substance, has not dispersed.
> Once the Primordial Substance is dispersed;
> Methods are thereby established.
> Whereupon are the methods established?
> They are established upon I-hua, "One Stroke."[93]

He returned to the most potent function of calligraphy, its transformational flow of energy. This function depended not only on the practice of calligraphy, but also on the articulation of its principles. Life, art, and thought were not to be divided.

bi 「古之鬚眉不能生我之　　入我之腹腸，我自發我
　　面目，古之肺腑不能安　　之肺腸，揭我之鬚眉。」

1. Frank Bidart, in "Ellen West" (*The Book of the Body*), quoted in a review by Robert Kent, *The Boston Review* (February–March, 1979). I am grateful to Professor Marie Adams for drawing my attention to this.

2. Ernst Kris, *Psychoanalytic Explorations in Art* (New York, 1952), p. 55, referring to P. Schilder, *The Image and Appearance of the Body* (New York, 1935). See further, *The Body as a Medium of Expression*, ed. J. Benthall and Ted Polhemus (London, 1975).

3. Mary Douglas, *Natural Symbols: Explorations in Cosmology* (New York, 1970), p. 93.

4. Cf. Richard M. Barnhart, "Wei Fu-jen's *Pi-chen T'u* and the Early Texts on Calligraphy," *ACASA* (1964), 18:16. This important article deals with the question of dating these texts, a question which obviously should be pursued much further. Since I have been concerned with broad issues, I have ignored this complication for the present.

5. Donald MacRae, "The Body and Social Metaphor," in *The Body as a Medium of Expression*, p. 59; cf. also E. D. Hirsch, Jr., *Validity in Interpretation* (New Haven, 1967), p. 10; Owen Barfield, *Saving the Appearances: A Study in Idolatry* (New York, 1965), p. 73 et passim; Ernst Kris, *Explorations*, p. 258; Susanne K. Langer, *Feeling and Form* (New York, 1953), chap. 14; and the oeuvre of Ernst Cassirer, for a variety of approaches.

6. David Pollard, "*Ch'i* in Chinese Literary Theory," in *Chinese Approaches to Literature from Confucius to Liang Ch'i-ch'iao*, ed. Adele Rickett (Princeton, 1978), pp. 43–66. Pollard does investigate briefly the cosmological sources. This present paper could be greatly expanded by incorporating a large amount of secondary, as well as primary, sources. But although its concerns are broad, its material is deliberately restricted. Therefore no direct reference has been made to valuable studies such as: Kiyohiko Munakata, *Ching Hao's Pi-fa-chi: A Note on the Art of the Brush* (*Artibus Asiae Supplementum* 31 (Ascona, 1974); the same author's "The Rise of Ink-wash Landscape Painting in the T'ang Dynasty" (Ph.D. dissertation, Princeton, 1965); William R. B. Acker, *Some T'ang and Pre-T'ang Texts on Chinese Painting* (Leiden, 1954); Nakamura Shigeo, *Chūgoku garon no tenkai* (Kyoto, 1956); Tanaka Toyozō, "Chūgoku bijutsu shisō," in *Chūgoku bijutsu no kenkyū* (Tokyo, 1964); Tseng Yu-ho Ecke, *Chinese Calligraphy* (Philadelphia, 1971); Roger Goepper, *Shu-p'u: der Traktat zur Schriftkunst des Sun Kuo-t'ing* (Weisbaden, 1974); comments in various volumes of *Shodō zenshū* (Tokyo, 1961); the considerable literature of Hsieh Ho's *liu-fa* (see Munakata, "Landscape Painting," pp. 123–124, n. 24); an excellent bibliography of Chinese sources is given in Pollard, "*Ch'i*"; and in a broader context, Donald J. Munro, *The Concept of Man in Early China* (Stanford, 1969); Susan Bush, *The Chinese Literati on Painting: Su Shih (1037–1101) to Tung Ch'i-ch'ang (1555–1636)*, Harvard-Yenching Institute Studies 27 (Cambridge, Mass., 1971); Andrew March, "Self and Landscape in Su Shih," *JAOS* (1966), 86(4):377–396; and James J. Y. Liu, *Chinese Theories of Literature* (Chicago, 1975).

7. Karl Popper, *The Logic of Scientific Discovery* (New York, 1959), p. 15.

8. Cf. Thomas S. Hall, *History of General Physiology*, vols. 1 and 2 (Chicago, 1969); Arturo Castiglione, *A History of Medicine* (Cleveland, 1950); Karl Rothschuh, *History of Physiology* (New York, 1973).

9. Joseph Needham, "Medicine and Chinese Culture," in *Clerks and Craftsmen in China and the West* (Cambridge, 1970), pp. 284–285.

10. See ibid., p. 270; Manfred Porkert, *The Theoretical Basis of Chinese Medicine* (Cambridge, Mass., 1974), p. 42. The *Huang-ti nei-ching* (*Nei-ching*) is translated in Ilza Veith,

The Yellow Emperor's Classic of Internal Medicine (Berkeley and Los Angeles, 1966). The translation is full of problems, but still useful. For further medical bibliography, see *Chinese Science: Explorations of an Ancient Tradition* ed. Shigeru Nakayama and Nathan Sivin (Cambridge, Mass., 1973), pp. 302–308.

11. Needham, "Hygiene and Preventive Medicine," in *Clerks and Craftsmen*, p. 347; also "China and the Origin of Qualifying Examinations in Medicine," in ibid., pp. 380–381.

12. Ibid., pp. 383–384.

13. Ibid., pp. 283–284, 342.

14. Ibid., p. 266.

15. See Porkert, *Theoretical Basis*, p. 42; Needham, *Clerks and Craftsmen*, pp. 270, 274.

16. Castiglione, *History*, p. 410.

17. J. B. de C. M. Saunders and Charles D. O'Malley, *The Illustrations from the Works of Andreas Vesalius of Brussels* (New York, 1973), p. 9.

18. Porkert, *Theoretical Basis*, pp. xiii–xiv.

19. Ibid., p. 107.

20. Ibid., p. 164. Porkert's understanding of *shen* as the force which shapes the materialization of energy, in a process from active states (*yang*) through structured states (*yin*), seems to me exceptionally valuable. If used with care it makes excellent sense in a wide range of contexts, in all of which, of course, it must be seen in relation to the phenomena of energy.

21. Ibid., p. 112.

22. Ibid., p. 165.

23. Ibid., pp. 114, 116.

24. Reading *ying-ch'i* for *jung-ch'i*, see ibid., pp. 188–190.

25. *Huang-ti nei-ching su-wen* (hereafter *Nei-ching*), in *I-t'ung cheng-mo ch'üan-shu* (Chekiang, 1875–1907 era edition), 23, 7:4a.

26. Porkert, *Theoretical Basis*, pp. 131–132.

27. In the *PWCSHP* (rpt., Taipei, 1969) 3:2b.

28. Veith, *Internal Medicine*, p. 101.

29. Preface to Nakayama and Sivin, *Chinese Science*, p. xxi.

30. Needham, "Elixir Poisoning in Medieval China," in *Clerks and Craftsmen*, p. 337.

31. H. H. Dubs, "Mencius and Sun-dz on Human Nature," *Philosophy East and West* (1956), 1:219; see also Pollard, "*Ch'i*"; and Wing-tsit Chan, *A Source Book in Chinese Philosophy* (Princeton, 1963), Appendix, p. 784. For reasons that will appear, I find Dubs's "matter-energy" better than Chan's "material force."

32. Cf. Max Jammer, *Concepts of Force* (Cambridge, Mass., 1957).

33. Porkert, *Theoretical Basis*, pp. 166–196.

34. Ibid., pp. 167–168.

35. Ibid., p. 185.

36. Ibid., p. 186.

37. Hall, *Physiology*, p. 272.

38. Ibid., p. 290.

39. Barfield, *Appearances*, p. 80.

40. Hall, *Physiology*, p. 247.

41. A. C. Graham, *Two Chinese Philosophers: Ch'en Ming-tao and Ch'eng Yi-ch'uan*

(London, 1958), p. 42. This is an excellent example of how basic perceptions permeated different areas of thought (different according to our lights). Another very interesting example, particularly relevant to this paper, is Su Shih's description of expression in painting in terms of the *kan* and *fei* visceral orbs (see March, "Su Shih," p. 385).

42. *Fei ts'ao-shu, PWCSHP* 5:2b.

43. Chang Huai-kuan, *Shih-t'i shu-tuan, PWCSHP* 1:29a.

44. There is a paragraph on *hsüeh-mo* in Chiang K'uei's *Hsü Shu-p'u*, representing a view from the period of ca. 1200 (*PWCSHP* 8:10a–b).

45. Porkert, *Theoretical Basis*, pp. 5, 201.

46. Ibid., p. 186.

47. Ibid., p. 187.

48. Ibid., ch. 4 is devoted to the subject.

49. See also ibid., pp. 25, 114 et passim.

50. See ibid., p. 110, for etymology of *tsang-hsiang*.

51. Cf. *Mo-ching* (*Wan-yu wen-k'u* ed.) 1:6, and *Nei-ching* 18 (Veith trans., p. 174).

52. In *PWCSHP* 1:23b–29b.

53. *PWCSHP* 1:8a–b.

54. In *Fa-shu yao-lu* (*Mei-shu ts'ung-shu* ed.) 4:68.

55. Joseph Needham, *Science and Civilization in China*, vol. 2: History of Scientific Thought (Cambridge, 1956), p. 74.

56. Ibid., 2:201.

57. See Wing-tsit Chan, "The Neo-Confucian Concept of *Li*," *Tsing-hua Journal of Chinese Studies* (1964), n.s. 4(2):129–131.

58. Barfield, *Appearances*, pp. 80–81; Hall, *Physiology*, pp. 244–245.

59. Veith, *Internal Medicine*, p. 105.

60. *Nei-ching* 3:3b.

61. There is a considerable literature on geomancy. Among the most recent works is Hong-key Yoon, *Geomantic Relationships between Culture and Nature in Korea* (Asian Folklore and Social Life Monographs 89) (Taipei, 1976).

62. *Yao-shih-lun*, in *PWCSHP* 6:4a. This text, "Treatise on Medicinal Minerals," is a discussion of calligraphic criteria that is of considerable interest in the present context.

63. Cf. *Nei-ching* 5.

64. *PWCSHP* 5:20a, in the section titled *ch'i-miao*, "The tally of transcendance."

65. *PWCSHP* 5:1b.

66. Porkert, *Theoretical Basis*, p. 16.

67. Needham, *Science and Civilization*, 2:446.

68. Barfield, *Appearances*, p. 85. There are tremendous differences between the thought of medieval Europe and that of prescientific China, some of which cluster around the Chinese attitudes toward creation and divinity. Nevertheless, I believe that Barfield's observations hold great value for the Sinologist. I broached this question in chapters 2 and 4 of my thesis, "Huang Kung-wang's 'Dwelling in the Fu-ch'un Mountains': The Dimensions of a Landscape" (Ph.D. dissertation, Princeton, 1978). For a critical essay on the question of micro/macrocosm in art history, see Fritz Saxl, "Macrocosm and Microcosm in Medieval Pictures," in his *Lectures* (London 1957), vol. 1, pp. 58–72.

69. Ibid., p. 87.

70. Ibid., pp. 87–88.

71. Ibid., p. 93.

72. Forward to Porkert, *Theoretical Basis*, p. xi.

73. D. C. Lau, trans., *Lao Tzu: Tao Te Ching* (Middlesex, 1963), p. 57.

74. Porkert, *Theoretical Basis*, pp. 48ff.

75. Ibid., p. 14.

76. Ibid., p. 9.

77. *PWCSHP* 3 : 1a. "Force-form" is my translation of *shih*. It is the form of becoming, process and, by extension, movement. Shape, *hsing*, is the outer shell of manifested process, fixed yet transient.

78. *PWCSHP* 6 : 1a.

79. A paraphrase of the first two principles of Hsieh Ho (early sixth century A.D.). The first appears as a yang function, the second a yin. For the distinction between active (yang) and structive (yin) which seems appropriate here, see the passages from Porkert quoted in notes 74 to 75 above. In premechanistic societies, movement tends to be perceived as an essence of life in both physical and psychological states. In relation to the Chinese view of art as life created by craft, it is not surprising that life, movement, energy and then physical instruments are so closely interwoven in their aesthetic formulations.

80. Quoted by Stephen Jay Gould, review of Lewis Thomas, *More Notes of a Biology Watcher*, in *New York Times Review of Books* (April, 1979).

81. See Saburo Miyasita, "A Link in the Westward Transmission of Chinese Anatomy in the Late Middle Ages," in *Science and Technology in East Asia*, ed. Nathan Sivin (New York, 1977), pp. 200–206; and Mark Elvin, *The Pattern of the Chinese Past* (Standford, 1973), p. 186.

82. See, for example, ibid.; Sivin and Nakayama, *Chinese Science*; and the oeuvre of Joseph Needham for an immense volume of material bearing on this question.

83. *PWCSHP* 4 : 8a–b.

84. Trans. Burton Watson, in *Sunflower Splendor*, ed. Irving Lo and Wu-chi Liu (New York, 1975), p. 380.

85. *PWCSHP* 5 : 3b.

86. Specifically, "Rise in the dawn to watch the transformations and visions in the cloud-energy; you can gather them into the tip of your brush." In *Hua-chih*: see *Chung-kuo hua-lun lei-pien*, ed. Yü Chien-hua (Taipei, 1962), p. 71.

87. As elucidated, for example, in Rudolf Arnheim, *Visual Thinking* (Berkeley and Los Angeles, 1966).

88. Piet Mondrian, from *Plastic Art and Pure Plastic Art*, anthologized in *Theories of Modern Art*, ed. Herschel B. Chipp (Berkeley and Los Angeles, 1968), p. 359.

89. Lin Yutang, *The Chinese Theory of Art: Translations from the Masters of Chinese Art* (New York, 1967), p. 154. I am grateful to Professor R. M. Barnhart for drawing my attention to this comment.

90. Yü Chien-hua, ed., *Shih T'ao Hua-yü-lu* (Shanghai, 1962), p. 28.

91. Porkert, *Theoretical Basis*, p. 164.

92. Ibid., p. 138.

93. Ju-hsi Chou, *The Hua-yü-lu and Tao-chi's Theory of Painting* (Arizona State University Occasional Paper 9) (1977), p. 9.

III / Images of Nature

Concepts of *Lei* and *Kan-lei* in Early Chinese Art Theory

BY KIYOHIKO MUNAKATA

INTRODUCTION

In magic and religious rituals, dance, music, and ritual objects have been essential tools in communications between man and the supernatural powers. Even when art is secularized and its communicative power is directed toward fellow human beings, it still retains a certain mystical quality. Throughout the long history of Chinese art the basic requirement for first-rate artists has been to achieve *ch'i*[a] (vital force) or *ch'i-yün*[b] (resonance of the vital force) in their works of art. As late as the seventeenth century, Tung Ch'i-ch'ang (1555−1636) said. "*Ch'i-yün* cannot be learned. One has to be born with it. It is the endowment of the Heaven." [1] First-rate artists share with sorcerers a mystical ability to capture and use heavenly powers. It is only natural that the people of ancient days, when the distinction between the realms of the supernatural and the natural was less clear, had a strongly mystical view of art.

The terms *lei*[c] (kind or category) and *kan-lei*[d] (lit. response of the kinds) which I deal with in this paper seem to have had a bearing similar to that of *ch'i* and *ch'i-yün* on ancient Chinese thinking about cosmic phenomena and, as an extension of it, about artistic matters. But unlike *ch'i* and *ch'i-yün*, concepts of *lei* and *kan-lei* were ignored or very lightly handled in later Chinese philosophy and were completely forgotten in later theories of art. In this paper I shall try to establish the importance of these concepts in ancient Chinese thinking and find their significance in the early theories of art, especially in interpreting *Hua shan shui hsü* by Tsung Ping (375−443), the earliest extant philosophical treatise of painting ever written in China.

CONCEPTS OF *lei* AND *kan-lei* DURING THE CHOU AND HAN DYNASTIES

The situation of "Nine in the Fifth place" in the *I ching* is stated as "Flying dragon in the heavens: It furthers one to see the Great man." [2] This is the most felicitous among all the situations which can possibly take place in the universe. But, what does it signify? This question, according to the "*Wen-yen* commentary," was explained by Confucius as follows:

a 氣   c 類
b 氣韻   d 感類

Things that accord in tone vibrate together. Things that have affinity in their inmost natures seek one another. Water flows to what is wet, fire turns to what is dry. Clouds follow the dragon; wind follows the tiger. Thus, the sage rises, and all creatures follow him with their eyes. What is born of heaven feels related to what is above. What is born of earth feels related to what is below. Each follows its kind (*lei*).[3]

Here we find several very basic concepts concerning the term *lei*: namely, (1) it does not mean "a categorical unit" in the static sense, but rather is the active nature or force of that unit; (2) it includes both substantial and phenomenal existence, such as water and wetness, clouds and dragons, and the sage and the myriad things; (3) as an active force, it has a particular inclination to respond to another kind of sympathetic nature, such as clouds to dragons and wind to tigers. This notion of *lei* as the active components of the universe is extremely important for our present discussion. The basic Chinese cosmology as developed into the *I ching* is that every existence, substantial as well as phenomenal, is a product of a certain combination of the basic forces of *yin* and *yang*. Thus it is very natural to think that a thing or a phenomenon is at once a physical being and a force which interacts with other forces.

The same idea can explain the process of the evolution of the universe from primordial chaos to ordered entity. The Great Commentary (*Hsi tz'u*) of the *I ching* begins its opening passage as follows:

Heaven is high, the earth is low; thus the Creative and the Receptive are determined. In correspondence with this difference between low and high, inferior and superior places are established.

Movement and rest have their definite laws; according to these, firm and yielding lines are differentiated.

Events follow definite trends, each according to its nature (*lei*). Things are distinguished from one another in definite classes. In this way good fortune and misfortune come about. In the heavens phenomena take form; on earth shapes take form. In this way change and transformation become manifest.[4]

In this passage the process of cosmic evolution is described in terms of the hexagram system of the *I ching*. It consists of four stages; (1) the setting of the value levels of heaven and earth, and those in between; (2) the differentiation of the firm (i.e., *yang*) and the yielding (i.e. *yin*) forces; (3) the distribution of the two forces into different value levels, according to the rules that "similar natures (*lei*) respond to each other" and that "similar things tend to group together"; and (4) the resulting formation of all the phenomena and things which interact with each other and keep changing with a certain harmony and order. We observe here that the sympathetic responses between similar kinds of existence was considered one of the very basic principles underlying cosmic evolution. It is also notable that this principle was taken to be responsible for the good fortune and misfortune of the events of the world. For the sake of simplicity of rendering, from now on throughout this paper, I shall use the term *kan-lei* (lit. response to kind) for this principle, after Wang Ch'ung (27– ca. 97 A.D.) of the Han. It must be noted, however, that many other similar terms, such as *chao lei*[e] (inviting similar kinds) or the more descriptive *i lei hsiang tung*[f] (according to kinds [things] mutually influence), were commonly used for this principle in the late Chou and Han writings.

It was Joseph Needham who called this principle of *kan-lei* a "symbolic correlation system" and suggested its relationship to ancient magical practice.[5] One of Frazer's basic principles of magic is "like produces like, effect resembling cause." Indeed, as Needham says, "one can immediately see how the Chinese symbolic correlations would have worked in this respect, and one begins to visualize some of the motives which led to their establishment."[6] I shall come back later to this aspect of magic involved in the principle of *kan-lei*. For now, I would simply point out that it already had deep roots in the long history of Chinese thought prior to the time of completion of *I ching* commentaries. The actual dates of the completion of the *I ching* commentaries are matters of dispute. Fung Yu-lan, for example, dates the commentaries as late as the early Han dynasty.[7] It is evident, however, that whenever they were actually put together, most of the concepts expressed must go back much earlier. Whatever the case may be, there are many Ch'in and Han writings which refer to the concept *lei* in discussing cosmological, moral, political, religious or artistic (musical) issues. Among the pre-Han writings, *Hsün Tzu* and *Lü-shih ch'un-ch'iu* (both from the third century B.C.) are the ones which clearly base some of their discussions on the principle of *kan-lei*.[8] Under the influence of these two writings, as well as that of the *I ching*, this concept found its way into most of the major writings of the Han dynasty, which include notably *Ch'un-ch'iu fan-lu* by Tung Chung-shu (179?–104? B.C.), *Shih chi* by Ssu-ma Ch'ien (145?–90? B.C.) and *Huai nan Tzu* compiled by Liu An (died 122 B.C.).[9] In fact, the section of the *Ch'un-ch'iu fan-lu* called "*Wu lei hsiang tung*"[g] (Similar Kinds Mutually Influence) is, as Needham points out, the discourse which, based upon *kan-lei* principle, formed the basis of the traditional Chinese causation theory.[10]

Among the writings of the Han dynasty, the *Huai-nan Tzu* is probably the most extensive in expounding the principle of *kan-lei*. A section of the chapter called "*T'ien wen hsün*"[h] (Discourse on the Cosmic Happenings) reads as follows:

[e] 召類

[f] 依類相動

[g] 物類相動

[h] 天文訓

Birds and animals are the kind (*lei*) which fly or run, thus they belong to *yang*. Insects and fish are the kind (*lei*) which lie flat on the ground or in the water, thus they belong to *yin*.... The moon is the master of all the *yins*. Therefore when the moon half wanes, the amount of brains in fish is reduced, and when the moon completely wanes, the meat of the clam gets thin.... The many kinds (*lei*) move (or behave), mutually responding to each other; and the basic (such as the sun and moon) and the peripherals (such as birds and clam) mutually correspond. Therefore, when a bronze lens (which is *yang*) meets the sunlight, it starts burning and produces fire, and when the bronze cup in the form of a large clam shell (which is *yin*) meets the moonlight, it gets wet and produces water. When a tiger roars, the wind from the gorge comes out, and when a dragon rises, the felicitous clouds gather around it.... The spirit of the ruler of the people is associated with the heaven above. Therefore, when he collects taxes relentlessly and beyond reason, tornados result.[11]

Following these passages, the *Huai-nan Tzu* goes on to explain how the cycle of the year is related to the four cardinal directions, the positions of the constellations, activities and events of human beings—especially those of the rulers of states—behaviors and occurrences of animals and vegetables, and the musical tones to be played in harmony with the seasons. The *Huai-nan Tzu* apparently uses the same logic as the *I ching*, including examples of the dragon-clouds and tiger-wind relationships in the *Wen-yen* commentary quoted above. The *Huai-nan Tzu* simply expands the number of examples, with the intent of explaining every occurrence of the mystical heaven-earth relationship.

One important point to be noted here is that mysticism underlies the concept of *kan-lei*. We must recognize that most of the pre-Han and Han intellectuals, Confucian or non-Confucian, had reverence for the mysterious power, call it heaven or Tao, regulating or causing cosmic evolution. There is a general tendency among modern cultural historians to emphasize strongly the rational aspects of the Confucian scholars of pre-Han and Han and ignore or play down greatly the religious aspects of their thinking.[12] It is certain that Confucian scholars of this time emphasized human nature and the moralistic implication of their cosmic view. But it is a matter of emphasis. We must remember, for example, that Tung Chung-shu, the most influential Confucian scholar of the Former Han, stressed the importance of sacrificial rituals in many sections of his *Ch'un-ch'iu fan-lu*.[13]

Needham, irritated by some Western scholars' notion that the Chinese way of thinking was primitive, took great pains to explain that Chinese coordinative thinking was not "an alogical or pre-logical chaos," but "was a picture of an extremely and precisely ordered universe," and further "was an ordered harmony of wills without an ordainer." Thus, for him, the sacrifices performed by the Chinese emperors were symbolic acts "which signified the unity of heaven and earth."[14] I certainly agree with him on the point that Chinese thinking was not primitive, but cannot agree with his antimysticism bias.

Man, whether he be Tung Chung-shu or the modern physicist, must first accept the very existence of unexplainable force(s) behind many occurrences. For Tung Chung-shu this force is *ch'i* (ether or vital force), which is differentiated in a sequence from the force of the Origin (*yüan*[i]) into first that of two (*yin* and *yang*), then five (*wu-hsing*,[j] or Five Elements), and finally into that of the numerous kinds (*lei*).[15] One of the major differences between the world views of the pre-Han and Han thinkers and that of modern physicists is that the Chinese attached different values to the differentiated components of the world and arranged them in a certain hierarchy of values between heaven and earth. Here we find the difference between religion and science. Needham was probably right in a general sense when he said that "in such a system (of Chinese cosmology) causality is reticular and hierarchically fluctuating, not particulate and singly catenarian."[16] But, fluctuating though it may be, causality in the system, at least in that of the Han thinkers, was clearly hierarchical. Further, if we look at the system in a historical perspective, we can see it at the end of a long process of systematizing and theorizing the earlier animistic beliefs into a semi-monotheistic system. As such, the system justifies the traditionally accepted miracles and magico-religious rituals, probably with certain modifications. In other words, the original magical notion of the "symbolic correlations," which Needham pointed out, can survive and actually survived in this system of thinking.

During the Chou dynasty *lei* was the name of a certain type of sacrificial ritual. Unfortunately this term, as the name of a ritual, had been dropped from actual use before the Han dynasty, when the records of Chou rituals were put together and studied.[17] Thus, the information concerning the *lei* sacrifice in the *Chou li* (both in the main text and in Cheng Hsüan's commentaries) is contradictory and uncertain.[18] However, comparing the ritual practices of the Shang dynasty reconstructed from oracle bone inscriptions and the descriptions of the Chou rituals in the *Chou li* and other Han writings, we can conjecture the following points: (1) *lei* sacrifices were performed at regular *chiao*[k] altars located in the vicinity of the royal court and aimed at reporting to and asking favor of the Supreme Deity (Shang Ti); (2) in most cases this sacrifice was performed in conjunction with military campaigns, but also done in times of natural calamities, such as long droughts; (3) although the sacrifice itself had its origin in the Shang, the specific term *lei* for this sacrifice became common usage possibly in the early Chou. My reasons for the above conjectures may be too complex to discuss and beyond the scope of this paper. But one thing should be clear; the term *lei* was used not only for the influences of the forces of higher value over those of lower value as we have seen in the conceptions

---

i 元   j 五行   k 郊

expressed in the *I ching* and the *Huai-nan Tzu*, but also for man's efforts to get influence over the forces of the higher value.[19]

The clearest and best documented ancient ritual of China is "rainmaking." Since this ritual is not only well documented historically, but has been continuously performed until modern times in China, there have been many studies on the subject by historians and anthropologists.[20] Nonetheless, in order to make my point, I shall introduce here the case of the rainmaking ritual of the Former Han period which Tung Chung-shu described in the section *"Ch'iu yü"*[1] (Asking for Rain) of the *Ch'un-ch'iu fan-lu*.[21] The basic structure of the ritual remained constant throughout the year, but some of the components varied according to which one of the five seasonal divisions (spring, summer, late summer, autumn and winter) it was performed in. The constant features were the use of a platform on which trees were planted, the so-called "toad pond," clay dragons, animal sacrifices, prayers, and dancing. The seasonal variables were the deities to be invoked, through whose good offices, I assume, men tried to reach the force of the Supreme Deity; the leading colors used for the clothes of the performers, clay dragons and so forth, which were blue, red, yellow, white, and black respectively, corresponding to the seasonal progress from spring to winter; the numbers designating the sizes and numbers of the components of the rituals, such as the sizes and numbers of the clay dragons. The leading principle in organizing this ritual was apparently that everything in the ritual should be of "similar kinds" in order to get a "sympathetic response." Since the basic nature of rain is "water" with the force of *yin*, the things related to water, and things which are *yin*, feature prominently in the components of the ritual.

The rituals that Tung Chung-shu described were performed during the second century B.C. and done on the local level. We can expect certain variations of the ritual according to the time and the social level of the performing institutions, such as the imperial court of the Han or the feudal lords of the Chou dynasty. However, we have every reason to believe that these rituals were all organized with the same intense desire to utilize the principle of *kan-lei* for maximum efficacy, as in Tung Chung-shu's example. And we can safely assume that the same rule is applicable to other so-called *lei* sacrifices, including those performed at the time of military campaigns.

The arts, whether visual art, music, dance, or poetry, were important elements of magico-religious rituals. Thus, the principle of *kan-lei*, which was the basic rule for organizing sacrifices, should have had a strong bearing on designing, composing, and choreographing the artistic components of the rituals. Unfortunately, at the present stage of our study, we have very little knowledge of the relationship between the specific rituals and their artistic components. Only gradually and through intensive interdisciplinary studies can we proceed to unveil the creative process

[1] 求雨

behind ritualistic art. One of the necessary approaches to this problem is the analytical study of the motifs used in designing bronze ritual vessels. Many of the late Chou ritual vessels seem to be made for general use in the various rituals, often using abstracted dragon and bird motifs. But some of them seem to have been made for very specific purposes. For example, a study of the so-called "pictorial bronzes" by Hayashi Minao reveals that the genrelike scenes which appear on the bronze vessels were actually scenes of specific court rituals.[22] The vessels with such particular motifs must therefore have been made in conjunction with the rituals depicted, to be used either for such rituals or for related rituals.

I would like to discuss here one example of a ritual bronze vessel of late Chou design, in order to illustrate my point. My example is the well-known bronze ritual vessel, a ting[m] from the Warring States period, in the Minneapolis Institute of Art (fig. 1).[23] The inlaid designs decorating the surface of this vessel have been vaguely called a combination of dragon motifs and geometric patterns. Karlgren, however, pointed out that the so-called geometric patterns were derived from animal motifs, and specifically those of birds and dragons. He suggested also that the three small animals in the round attached on the lid and the three legs of the vessel in the form of animal's legs show the influences of the art of the Ordos region.[24] I partially agree with Karlgren, but differ largely about the identity of the motifs and the major significance of the design as a whole. As I see it, the "geometric" motifs appearing on the vessel are all derived from the dragon motif. On the lid, a pair of dragons facing each other is repeated three times. Superimposed upon them, a hexagonal pattern is placed as if to tie all the six images of dragons together. The motifs at the corners of the hexagon appear to be abstract patterns derived from two dragons: those which are located between two facing dragons are abstracted images of two dragons facing each other; those which are located between two dragons placed back to back are the abstracted image of two dragons grouped together back to back. The band on the upper part of the body of the vessel is a combination of two zig-zag patterns, one of which is an abstraction of two dragons meeting face to face, the other of two dragons grouped back to back. The heartlike motif on the lower part of the body of the vessel, repeated six times, two on each of the spaces between the legs of the tripod, is the simplest form of the two dragons facing each other. The identity of this motif is confirmed by the fact that it is a part of the corner motif of the hexagon appearing between the two dragons facing each other on the lid. The basic component of the total design of this vessel is a dragon, or rather the two aspects of force of the dragon, shown by the two ways of combining two dragons, face to face and back to back. The shape of this vessel is also quite suggestive. The shortness of the animal-shaped legs and consequent low position of the belly of the vessel, which Karlgren pointed out matter of factly, appear to me expressive of dragons, with their

m 鼎

1 (a and b). *Ting* tripod with a design of dragons inlaid with gold and silver from Chin-tsun, Loyang, Honan. Bronze vessel, height 15.3 cm., fourth to third century B.C. Courtesy of the Minneapolis Institute of Arts, Minneapolis.

reptilian characteristics of low-hanging, heavy bellies supported by short legs. Each of the ears of this vessel, with its upward bend which is not necessarily a feature particular to this vessel, fits nonetheless well with the upward projections from the rear part of the heads of the dragons represented on the lid. Thus the two ears of the vessel suggest the two heads of dragons facing each other.

We notice that throughout this design three numbers play important roles, that is 2, 3, and 6 as the combination of them; 2 dragons, 2 ways of combining two dragons, 3 repetitions of the unit motifs, resulting in 6 images and a hexagon, or the 2 ears and 3 legs of the vessel, and so forth. At this point we may take note that the two forces represented by the two ways of combining two dragons, face to face and back to back, could well be meant to be, respectively, the firm (*yang*) force and the yielding (*yin*) force. Then we realize that the basic way of thinking in creating this

design has a clear parallel to that of the "Images" of the *I ching*. We are certainly tempted to look into what the *I ching* says about that "Image" which consists of evenly distributed firm and yielding forces with the firm line at the bottom; in this vessel the "firm" and "yielding" patterns are evenly distributed and the "firm" is at the bottom. The hexagram of this situation in the *I ching* is *Chi chi*[n] (After Completion, or Accomplishment), and its "Image" is, interestingly, "Water over Fire," exactly the image of the *ting* cooking vessel.[25] Its meaning as "After Completion, or Accomplishment" is not too good from the philosophical point of view of the *I ching*, since it maintains that accomplishment always implies decline afterward. However, for a magico-religious ritual aiming at achieving a specific result, such as causing rain, "Accomplishment" should be the message to send to the

[n] 既濟

supernatural power, or, if we use the language of the *kan-lei* conception, the *lei* (nature of happening) to achieve through sympathetic response. It is for future studies to verify or discredit this interpretation. But I can at least assert here that we are confronted with superbly intelligent designers when we deal with the designs of a late Chou ritual object. Another important aspect of this *ting* is that it represents a composite image of a dragon, or force of dragon, in an abstract way. The *lei* of the dragon was supposed to attract that of clouds, as discussed above, and consequently of rain. This is why the images of dragons made of clay were the important components of the rainmaking ritual that Tung Chung-shu described. It is very likely that this *ting* was specifically designed to be used in the rainmaking ritual.

The small figure of an animal repeated three times on the lid of this vessel should be considered too. This animal is not identified, but it is possibly a "wild boar."[26] "Wild boar" (*chia chu*[o] or *chia t'un*[p]) was, together with cock, one of the most common sacrificial animals used during the late Chou and Han. In Tung Chung-shu's rainmaking ritual, "wild boars" together with cocks were offered in the *fan*[q] (roasting) sacrifice.[27] According to the *Li chi*, "wild boar" was used for the *chin*[r] (blood smearing) ritual to consecrate newly made important ritual vessels.[28] In order to enhance further the magical power of the vessel, attaching images of "wild boars" on its lid is not in any way outside the basic logic of its design.

I have tried in the above discussion to illustrate the methodological importance of understanding the concept of *kan-lei* in order to be able to interpret the designs of ritual objects in early Chinese art. As I stated before, this type of study involves complex and extensive interdisciplinary studies. My argument still remains largely hypothetical. But I believe that it is enough to discredit a commonly held opinion that late Chou designs of ritual bronzes are largely decorative, i.e. made with the intention of pleasing viewers' eyes. Another point is that early Chinese art forms were essentially indications of the forces of various qualities (*lei*) of objects or phenomena. The importance of the abstracted forms, as well as the figurative images of dragons in the design of the Minneapolis *ting*, clearly illustrates this point.

Unfortunately there exist no treatises on visual art from the Chou and Han dynasties. But there are quite a number of discussions of music extant from this period, including chapters on music in the *Hsün Tzu*, the *Shih chi* and the *Li chi*.[29] Although these theories are very much moralized, they nonetheless assume the basic notion of mystical relationships between the music used in rituals and the Cosmic powers, between divinely created music and its listeners, or between the music created and its composer. For example, about the magical power of music the *Li chi* says as follows:

o 豭豬   q 燔
p 豭豚   r 釁

Ceremonies and music resemble the nature of Heaven and Earth, penetrate to the virtues of the spiritual Intelligences, bring down the spirits from above, and raise up those whose seat is below.... Therefore, when the great man uses and exhibits his ceremonies and music, Heaven and Earth will in response to him display their brilliant influence.... The genial airs from above and the responsive action below will overspread and nourish all things. Then plants and trees will grow luxuriantly; curling sprouts and buds will expand; the feathered and winged tribes will be active; ... and all will have to be ascribed to the power of music.[30]

And about the mutual relationships of the music and the environment within which it is produced, both the *Li chi* and *Shih chi* have the same passages, quoted, with little modification, from the *Hsün Tzu*. I quote here from Legge's translation of the *Li chi*.

Whenever notes that are evil and depraved affect men, a corresponding evil spirit responds to them [from within]; and when this evil spirit accomplishes its manifestations, licentious music is the result. Whenever notes that are correct affect men, a corresponding correct spirit responds to them [from within], and when this correct spirit accomplishes its manifestations, harmonious music is the result. The initiating cause and the result correspond to each other. The round and the deflected, the crooked and the straight, have each its own category; and such is the character of all things, that they affect one another severally according to their class (*lei*).[31]

Here what Legge translated as "note" is *sheng*[s] which, according to the definition given in the *Li chi*, is meant to be an exclamatory voice uttered in response to outside things (happenings).[32] The last sentence in Chinese is *wan wu chih li, ko i lei hsiang tung yeh*.[t] It is nothing but a reassertion that the *kan-lei* principle is behind all evolving processes in the world, including the creation of music. The original passage in the *Hsün Tzu* does not include this last sentence. And the intention of the original passage, although the sentences are almost exactly the same as the quotations appearing in the *Li chi* and the *Shih chi* with only very slight changes, was actually to describe an opposite situation, i.e. that evil music causes a disorderly society to develop and correct music, a peaceful society.[33] The idea of the influence of music over listeners and consequently on society, however, was found in many other places in discussions in the *Shih chi* and *Li chi*.[34] I cannot go any further into the theory of music here. But it should be clear that the concept of *kan-lei* was very much an integral part of the theory of music during the late Chou and Han periods.

We can expect a similar way of thinking in the Han people's attitudes toward

s 聲   t 萬物之理，各依類相動也

visual art, which seems to move gradually toward the secular, or at least the nonritualistic, sphere. Since we have no treatise on visual art, as stated before, we have to skip to the post-Han period and see how the matter had developed by then.

TSUNG PING'S *Hua shan shui hsü* AND THE CONCEPT OF *lei* AND *kan-lei*

Tsung Ping's *Hua shan shui hsü*, or "A Preface to the Painting of Mountains and Rivers" (hereafter referred to as "Landscape Essay"), is not only the earliest extant theory of landscape painting, but the earliest systematic treatise on visual art in the history of China. It is quite significant that we find *lei* used as very basic requirement for attaining a good painting. This term *lei* has been taken, by virtually every scholar who has studied the essay, to mean "verisimilitude" or "to attain verisimilitude or resemblance"; that is, as an indication of Tsung Ping's naturalistic inclination toward the representation of natural objects. This notion is a direct contradiction to what is observed by Chang Yen-yüan of the ninth century who claimed that the landscape paintings of the pre-T'ang period were conceptional and did not closely depict the appearances of the natural objects, a claim which is generally supported by extant monuments.[35] However, if we take the meaning of *lei* used by Tsung Ping in the sense of "nature of the kind" discussed above, we get quite a different interpretation of his essay. In this section I would like to analyze Tsung Ping's way of thinking concerning the concept of *lei* and to propose a new interpretation.

Tsung Ping's "Landscape Essay" has already been studied by many scholars. Yet its precise meaning in the history of Chinese art, or in a broader sense of Chinese cultural history, still remains unclear. For one thing, many scholars in interpreting this essay have simply ignored the fact that Tsung Ping was a devout Buddhist layman and a defender of Buddhism from Confucian and Taoist critics.[36] Some scholars even insisted that his essay was based upon Taoistic mysticism.[37] Since Susan Bush presents this problem, together with an extensive bibliography, in this book, I shall avoid duplicating her discussion. However, a few points essential to my arguments must be given here.

One of the basic problems concerning Tsung Ping's essay is that he was one of the so-called "apologists" or "apologetes" who discussed Buddhist doctrines using traditional Chinese terms, names, and even philosophical idioms. Thus, in their writings a statement which appears innocently traditional can have a Buddhistic connotation. And there were different types of "apologists." For example, Sun Ch'o (ca. 300–380), a predecessor of Tsung Ping in the debates concerning Buddhism, was truly eclectic. He wrote *Yü tao lun* (An Elucidation of the Way), in which he claimed that Buddhism and Confucian thought were both meaningful and to be accepted side by side, since one is concerned with "what is beyond the world (*fang wai*[u])" and

u 方外

the other with "what is within the world (*fang nei*ᵛ)."[38] Indeed, his writings, such as *Yü tao lun*, can be taken simply, as Zürcher says, to be an "extreme hybridization of Buddhist and traditional Chinese ideals."[39] In contrast, Tsung Ping accepted Buddhism in a much more fundamental sense. In the *Ming fo lun* (Discourse on Enlightening Buddhist Doctrine), Tsung Ping's major writing in defense of Buddhism, Tsung states:

> Those Buddhist scriptures wrap within themselves the virtues of the Five Classics and possess additional wider and larger truth. They also include the conception of void in [the teachings of] Lao Tzu and Chuang Tzu, and exhaustively pile [on top of them] further layers of the theories of the complete void.[40]

Apparently for Tsung Ping, Buddhism was not a supplemental philosophy that took care of the area not covered by traditional philosophy, but one containing ("wrapping within it") the traditional values. Moreover, it was for him a religion to which one should commit oneself. As Leon Hurvitz has observed, Tsung Ping brought "a new dimension, that of faith," to the defense of Buddhism.[41] It should be clear that the use of traditional names and terms in the "Landscape Essay" cannot possibly warrant such interpretations of its philosophical bases as "Taoistic mysticism." It is imperative for us to compare carefully the "Landscape Essay" with the *Ming fo lun* in order to decide what Tsung Ping meant in certain passages.

There are three scholars who in their interpretations of Tsung Ping's "Landscape Essay," refer to the *Ming fo lun*. They are, in the order of the publication of their studies on this topic, Nakamura Shigeo, Hatano Takeshi and Fukunaga Mitsuji.[42] Nakamura compares Tsung Ping's two essays and concludes that Tsung's theory of landscape is based upon Buddhistic karmic theory. As I shall discuss later, I agree with Nakamura on this point. Nakamura's arguments, however, are very conceptual, and his comparisons of Tsung's two essays remain on a general level, missing specific parallels existing between the two essays, and thus fall short of proving his points. Hatano, who follows Nakamura's lead, has made detailed comparisons of the two essays, but somehow he has not pursued Nakamura's point that karmic theory was the basis of Tsung Ping's ideal of painting. Fukunaga's study is also quite detailed in finding the sources of Tsung's use of terms and conceptions in the essay among Taoistic writings and in the *Ming fo lun*. He is, however, more concerned with Taoistic (*hsüan-hsüeh*ʷ) logic in Tsung's thinking, which he points out both in the "Landscape Essay" and in the *Ming fo lun*, thus minimizing the importance of the essay's Buddhistic elements. This group of Japanese scholars has contributed greatly to the advancement of our understanding of Tsung Ping's theory of landscape painting. Yet all of them, as has everybody else who has studied

ᵛ 方內 ᵂ 玄學

Tsung's essay, take the conventional meaning of "verisimilitude or resemblance" from the term "*lei*," and argue that for Tsung Ping, obtaining naturalistic images of objects is the way to attain the spiritual effect he expects from a painting. Hatano, in fact, has gone further, saying that one of the two basic points of Tsung's theory was the attainment of verisimilitude (*hsing-ssu*[x]) and that this was in conformity with the trend of poetry at the time.[43]

The basic philosophical standpoint of Tsung Ping is expressed in the opening statement of the "Landscape Essay":

> The sage embodies the Way and illuminates things, while the worthy purifies his heart and savors the images [of things]. As for the mountains and rivers, their physical nature (*chih*[y]) is being (*yu*[z]), but their spiritual orientation (*ch'ü*[aa]) is numinal (*ling*[ab]). Thus people like Hsüan-yüan (Yellow Emperor), Yao, Confucius, Kuang-ch'eng-tzu, Ta-wei, Hsü Yu and (the man of) Ku-chu all wandered on [the mountains such as] K'ung-t'ung, Chü-tz'u, Mo-ku, Chi, Shou and T'ai-meng. They are to be called (the ones who) have had "the pleasures of the virtuous and the wise" [in the words of Confucius].
>
> Now the sage, with his spirit (*shen*[ac]) realizes the Way; thus the worthy can pass through (*t'ung*[ad]) it. Mountains and rivers [likewise], with their forms, relish the Way; thus the virtuous can enjoy it. How similar they are to each other![44]

In this passage Tsung Ping aims to show a parallel between the sage and the (sacred) mountains and streams. But who did Tsung mean to be the sage(s) and what to be the Way? Sun Ch'o says in the *Yü tao lun* that "Buddha is the one who embodies the Way, and the Way is the one which guides things."[45] Sun Ch'o's definition of Buddha literally coincides with Tsung's words for the sage. Furthermore, Tsung himself says in the *Ming fo lun*:

> [What Lao Tzu called] "invariable non-being" (*ch'ang-wu*[ae]) is [same as the] Way. Only Buddha, with his spirit, realizes the Way. Therefore his [Buddha's] virtue (*te*[af]) and the Way become "one." While [with others] their spirits (*shen*) and the Way remain "two." Being "two," therefore, those spirits can pass through (*t'ung*) [the Way] and achieve their transformations, only when [the Way] is illuminated [by Buddha]. [As for Buddha] since [his spirit] is one [with the Way], [he is one with] the "invariable causation" (*ch'ang-yin*[ag]) and does not will to do.[46]

x 形似	ab 靈	ae 常無
y 賢	ac 神	af 德
z 有	ad 通	ag 常因
aa 趣		

This paragraph is written as Tsung's defense of Buddhism against the question why so many tragedies have happened to people who have done nothing wrong, if there are indeed buddhas who have the ability to see things widely and penetratingly and the power to do things freely. Tsung's explanation is, in essence, that Buddha is not destined to do things by his own initiative, because his virtue is one with the "mysterious virtue" (*hsüan-te*[ah]) of the Way (*Tao*).[47] This virtue, according to Lao Tzu, nourishes all things in accordance with universal Way, but without conciousness or self-will. This thesis itself is an amazing amalgamation of Buddhism with Lao-Chuang philosophy. Nevertheless, if we compare this statement with the sentence in the second paragraph in the previous quotation, we realize that the ideas expressed and the wording of the major parts are the same, except that the "Landscape Essay" version is more succinct and uses the words "the sage" and "the worthy" in place of "Buddha" and unspecified "other spirits." Undoubtedly Buddha and the sage are same in Tsung Ping's mind. The Way is also Buddha's way, which is none other than Cosmic Way, and can be equated with Lao Tzu's "primeval all-inclusive eternal non-being." Tsung Ping simply wanted to avoid using Buddhistic terms in the "Landscape Essay."

The list of the names of the legendary and historical figures, and the places where they wandered, in the above quotation from the "Landscape Essay," also appear in the *Ming fo lun*.[48] In the *Ming fo lun* version the list is only slightly expanded. Tsung Ping's point in emphasizing the associations of these figures with the mountains in the *Ming fo lun* was that by retiring from the secular world and associating with such lofty places, they proved themselves to have known and followed the Way of Buddha. Furthermore, Tsung claimed that the Five Emperors (including the Yellow Emperor in the "Landscape Essay" list) were endowed with superhuman qualities, as described by Ssu-ma Ch'ien in the *Shih chi*, and thus belonged to the same category as the bodhisattvas of the Great Vehicle who transformed and revealed themselves as human beings.[49]

The major issue in the opening passage of the "Landscape Essay" is that there exists a parallel between the sage and the sacred mountains and rivers; both reveal Tao, one with the merit of his spirit and the other with their forms. But how could Tsung Ping justify giving such high spiritual value to landscape features? In the *Ming fo lun*, Tsung Ping explained the Buddhist karmic theory that a spirit, or soul (*shen*), is indestructible and that it transmigrates eternally. According to him, "the spirits of the numerous creatures are equal in their origin, but through the karmic interactions and other events in their process of transmigration they acquire their own distinctive qualities of fineness and coarseness. Yet they are essentially indestructible."[50] Explaining this basic karmic theory, Tsung introduces the case of the mountains and rivers as an example. His arguments are as follows:

ah 玄德

Can one say that the Five Great Mountains and the Four Great Rivers have no sacred spirit (*ling*)? No one has yet been able to say that in any definitive way. But what are those spirits? The mountains are simply great piles of earth and the rivers only collections of water. How can the sacred spirit that attains oneness [with the Way] be born from the coarse substance of water or earth? Rather, [the spirit] responds to and lodges in the cliffs and streams and thus forms their awesome entity. Yet, even if the mountains collapse or the waters dry up, this spirit is not destroyed together with the water or earth. Spirit is not bound by forms and is indestructible. Human beings are the same way.[51]

Tsung Ping's argument here may sound somewhat strange to modern readers but was based upon the fact that the sacredness of the great mountains and rivers was one of the basic presumptions in traditional Chinese religion. Sacrifice to the sacred mountains and rivers was one of the institutionalized religious rituals of imperial courts from the Chou dynasty onward throughout the history of the successive dynasties in China. This belief, apparently based upon early animism, was certainly not a monopoly of the so-called "Taoists," as some people hastily assume, but was shared by Confucian scholars and everyone else. As Tsung said, "no one has yet denied it in any definitive way."

Tsung Ping, in another section of the *Ming fo lun*, discusses the merit of the karmic interactions. In the following passage he brings up the problem of the karmic interaction between the spirit of the great mountains and those of the visitors.

If we travel through wild nature and climb to the top of the peak, we can view the great span of the marvelous landscape, the expansion of Cosmic space which is clear and pure, and the miracles of the sun and moon which illuminate the darkness. How could we fail to find in them the nobility and dignity of the sages and the powerful sacred spirits? [The world] is not simply filled with scattered people and the busy chores of daily life. This is a matter of contemplating infinity and thus being open to the thought of the divine karmic Way, of perceiving the [great] quietness and thus being enlightened about the interactions of the bright spirits [of Buddhas and other higher spiritual beings].[52]

These lines convey a sense of the excitement, or ecstacy, that Tsung Ping had experienced in climbing the great mountains and still felt at the time of writing when he recalled these experiences. We can compare his thought and sense of exhilaration in the *Ming fo lun* with what he expects from the paintings of the great mountains. The latter is clearly stated in the concluding part of the "Landscape Essay."

> I make my place secluded, regulate my vital force, clean the wine cup and strum my lute. [After this preparation of mind] I shall open the painting and face it quietly. Then, while sitting, I can reach the limits of the four remote corners of the world, without failing to face a host of supernatural forces, and alone respond to the wilderness where no human forms can be seen. There, with peaks of various shapes towering high and with the cloud-covered forest mysteriously stretching afar, I will sense the sages and worthies shining through the innumerable ages and their divine thoughts clearly showing through the myriad spiritual effects [of the great nature]. Then what have I to do? I will just let my soul be exalted. When one's soul is exalted, there is nothing more left to do.

Apparently what Tsung Ping expects from a landscape painting is the same effect that the actual visitors to the great mountains were supposed to experience.

Now, how could the karmic effects of the sacred mountains be achieved in a painting? Tsung Ping's answer to this question is to attain the *lei* of the sacred mountains in the painting. As I have already stated in the beginning of this section, all the scholars who have studied the "Landscape Essay" take *lei* in Tsung Ping's usage as "verisimilitude, likeness or resemblance." But is it really so?

Let us start with a practical question; if Tsung Ping was really after naturalistic representation, what kind of images did he paint? Reading through his essay, we realize that Tsung Ping is not using the term *shan-shui*[ai] in the general Western sense of "landscape painting," but in the sense of "mountains and streams" with the traditional reverent feeling attached to it; and practically, he is concerned only with the paintings of the sacred mountains. A sacred mountain in China is a complex of many peaks, cliffs, gorges, water falls, and streams covering a large area. To get a likeness of a sacred mountain in China is not as simple as drawing, say, Mt. Fuji of Japan. Just diminishing the size of actual topographic features, which many scholars insist was Tsung Ping's method of obtaining verisimilitude, cannot produce a painting of a "sacred mountain." A paragraph in the "Landscape Essay" which is directly related to this problem should be discussed first. It reads, in Leon Hurvitz's translation, as follows.

> ... furthermore, Mount K'un-lun is so great, and the pupil of the eyes so small, that if the former presses upon the eye at a range of an inch, then its form cannot be seen, while, if it is distant by several leagues, it can be encompassed within a pupil measuring an inch. Truly this is because, the greater the distance, the smaller it appears. If now one stretches fine silk taut and therewith reflects [things] at a distance, then the form of K'un

---

ai 山水

[-lun]'s height may be encompassed within a square inch. By drawing a vertical [line of] three inches, one can represent a height of a thousand fathoms, and, by extending a horizontal [line of] three feet, one can embody a distance of a hundred leagues.[53]

In this passage Tsung's expression, "to reflect [things] at a distance (*yüan-ying*[aj])" on silk, raises a problem. Some Western scholars seem to take it to mean "sketching *in situ*," and consider the whole passage as an expression of Tsung's idea of "proportional or convincing diminution of scale."[54] On the other hand, most Chinese and Japanese scholars take it to mean "to see the scene through the stretched silk."[55] The latter interpretation seems to me a gross overextension of the original sentence, especially since the next sentence clearly mentions the vertical and horizontal brush strokes. In order to cope with this incongruity of interpretation, scholars who take this view consider the sentence concerning the brushwork to refer to the drawing obtained in copying the image seen through the stretched silk. If this is the case, Tsung Ping is certainly a pioneer of Western-type perspective, as some scholars have claimed. I can hardly agree with such an interpretation. To start with, it is physically not possible to get a clear view of a scene through stretched silk in broad daylight, unless the silk is very thin and is so located that the viewer can see a bright scene through the silk from a very dark place. And even if this difficulty is overcome, it is not possible to apply this method to a sacred mountain as a whole, which, as I mentioned above, is a complex topographic feature occupying a huge area.

I don't think "reflection at a distance" in this instance means the immediate optical transfer of the image of an object onto the silk, not even in the sense of "sketch *in situ*" as Western scholars seem to think. As we know from his biography and from the content of this very essay, Tsung Ping painted the sacred mountains after he became too old to visit them. And such a painting, painted in a studio far from the actual scene, should be a "reflection at a distance." We should note that the uses of the term *yüan-ying* quoted in the *P'ei-wen yün-fu* have all nothing to do with the optical reflection of images.[56] In those examples, the term was used either in the sense of the virtues of a person "glowing at a distant [time]," or birds or branches of willow "shining against a distant [object]." Generally speaking the term *ying* has a positive connotation, such as illuminating, and even in the sense of "reflection" it means the glow of reflected sunlight or some other sort of light. And for the negative sense of "reflection" in the sense of cast shadow or a cast image on the water, another character of *ying* tends to be used.

It is logical to assume that Tsung Ping used the term *yüan-ying* in a positive and, most possibly, spiritual sense, i.e. in the sense of "to let the image glow [with the virtue or force of the sacred mountain depicted] at a distance." This interpretation

aj 遠映

can explain why Tsung Ping cited as an example Mt. K'un-lun, a legendary mountain, instead of an actual mountain, such as Mt. Lu, with which he was most familiar. There is, needless to say, no way to get a realistic painting of Mt. K'un-lun through diminution of scale. Thus, we can see that in the passage from the "Landscape Essay" quoted above, Tsung Ping was discussing not a technical matter at all, but a highly theoretical problem, that is, how a painting in small scale and a necessarily abbreviated form can achieve the same effect on the viewer as the effect he would get from a real sacred mountain. The logic in Tsung Ping's argument is that both experiences are obtained through the eyes, or more correctly, as he expounds in the later section of the essay; "through the response of the eye, realizing [truth] in the heart (*ying mu hui hsin*[ak])."

It is now time to examine Tsung Ping's uses of the term *lei*. The term *lei* is used three times in the "Landscape Essay." When it is used alone, it can be interpreted in various ways, including to mean "verisimilitude." However, if it is used as a part of the compound *kan-lei*, it clearly means "kind" as in the concept of "sympathetic response of similar kinds," or "nature" of such kind, discussed in the previous section. The third instance of Tsung Ping's use of *lei* is as *kan-lei*. Let us start our discussion with this most concrete case. The passage which includes the term *kan-lei* reads, in my translation, as follows:

> Spirits (*shen*) are in essence eternal and they dwell (temporally) in forms and respond sympathetically (*kan*) to the [similar] kinds (*lei*).

This sentence is a succinct summary of the karmic principle which, as I have already discussed above, is one of the basic themes of the *Ming fo lun*. The first half of the sentence is concerned with the point that existing beings, in this case the sacred mountains, are a combination of forms and the eternally transmigrating karmic spirits. The second half is concerned with the karmic interactions between the spirits dwelling in the forms, such as between those of a sacred mountain and the visitor, or the painted image of it and the viewer. An important point is that Tsung Ping uses the term *kan-lei* for karmic interaction, thus equating the traditional and the Buddhistic concepts of mystical interactions between two independently existing units. We find Tsung Ping's very interesting and ingenious discussions of this matter in the *Ming fo lun*. The pertinent section reads:

> When the dipper and the moon change [their positions of forms], the tones of music [harmonious with the cosmic movement] change accordingly. When the moon waxes or wanes, the clam responds [by getting fat or thin]. [At the points marking the cycle of year such as] equinoxes, solstices and the beginning days of the four seasons, swallows, hawks, dragons and snakes mysteriously appear and disappear. In these pheno-

ak 應目會心

mena, (karmic) transformations first take place in the mysterious realm, then are revealed through the kinds (*lei*) of the [visible] things. All the corporeal things which appear as belonging to one class or the other are revelations of mysterious (karmic) transformations. [These changes] are not limited to a few special cases but are the limitless transformations of all things.[57]

In this statement, Tsung Ping accepts those phenomena which are claimed to be examples of the *kan-lei* principle in the traditional writings, such as the *Huai-nan Tzu* quoted in the previous section, and reinterprets its meaning from a standpoint based upon Buddhistic karmic theory. According to him, the traditional examples of *kan-lei*, the sympathetic interactions between the kinds (*lei*), are the revelations of the mystical karmic responses which take place in the spiritual realm. Here is Tsung Ping's consistent attitude which, while accepting traditional thought and "facts," takes Buddhism as fundamental. For Tsung, then, the most important example of *kan-lei* is the assembly of the celestial spirits in Buddha's land, which is the revelation of the highest kind of karmic interactions. In one section of the *Ming fo lun*, Tsung says:

> With his extreme power of influence, yet without trying, [Buddha] let things straighten by themselves. This is like Emperor Yao's extraordinary way of interacting [with others]. Musical tones get response from the sympathetic nature (*lei*) [of the listeners] who through their hearts attain a mystical realization [of the content of music]. This is even more so for the sages of the sacred spirits (i.e. those of the buddhas and bodhisattvas) whose common nature (*lei*) is the divine principle. All of those who meet mysteriously in Buddha's land share a strong wish [for good], pure spirits, accumulated [good] deeds and increased brightness [for seeing truth]. Therefore they are able to respond to the ultimate spiritual state and penetrate into the ultimate truth.[58]

It must be clear that the concepts of *lei* and *kan-lei* are very important with regard to the karmic theory in Tsung Ping's thinking. As I discussed above, karmic theory was the very basis of Tsung Ping's theory of landscape painting. Logically, then, the term *lei*, which is the basic requirement for the painting of the sacred mountains, should be taken in this particular sense; that is, as the essential nature of the sacred mountains which causes a specific karmic response in the viewer.

One of the cases in which Tsung Ping uses the term *lei* in the "Landscape Essay" concerns the quality of painting. In my interpretation it reads:

> One who views the painting is only concerned with how the essential nature (*lei*) is skillfully achieved, and not with the matter of smallness of size and of impairment in "verisimilitude (*ssu*[al])." This is the natural way

al 似

[of cause and effect]. And in this way, the majesty of the Mt. Sung and Hua as well as the sacred spirit of the Mysterious Female of the Valley can all be captured in a single picture.

The essential nature (*lei*) of the sacred mountains to be achieved in painting is the "sacredness of mountains," which is common to all in the category of sacred mountains. As such, it is very different from the "verisimilitude" of a specific sacred mountain. This does not mean that Tsung Ping did not paint an image of a specific mountain. He might have. But when he painted, or was faced with a painting of, a sacred mountain, he considered that the most important thing to be captured is not the correct details of that mountain but its "sacredness." This is exactly what he insists on in the part which follows the above quotation. It reads:

> Now, those who take as their principle "the realization of [truth] in the heart, through the response of the eye" can achieve the essential nature (*lei*) [of the sacred mountains] skillfully [in their paintings]. Then [the viewer's] eye can get the same response, and his heart reaches the same truth [as he gets from real nature]. This is the experience of the mystical communion and the spiritual [karmic] interaction [of the man and the great mountains], with which the viewer's spirit achieves transcendence and his mind attains the truth. Even if we seek [real] solitary cliffs here and there, what can we gain that adds [to the experience of the painting]?

We find in Tsung's argument here a striking parallel to his statement on music that he brought into his discussion of karmic theory in the *Ming fo lun*, quoted previously; namely that "musical tones get responses from the sympathetic nature (*lei*) [of the listeners], who through their hearts attain a mystical realization [of the content of music]." The mystical quality of the "sacredness" of the sacred mountains, attained in a painting, is evoked in the viewer, "through his eye reaching his heart," as the spiritual quality of sacred music effects the listener through his ear.

We now face a question: how, then, did he think the actual way of the *lei* of the sacred mountains might be achieved? My point is that his discussion is limited to the theoretical level and does not touch upon the problem of practical representation at all. The concluding section of the "Landscape Essay," which I have already quoted, describes Tsung Ping's reaction in confronting one of the paintings of the sacred mountains. The first part of it reads, if I may quote it again: "I can reach the limits of the four remote corners of the world, without failing to face a host of supernatural forces, and alone respond to the wilderness where no human form can be seen." The concept expressed in this description is close to that in the *Shan-hai ching*, a pre-Han compilation of fantastic descriptions of the sacred mountains within and outside Chinese territory; it describes "the four remote corners of the world," "a host of supernatural forces" in the form of fantastic animals, and as a whole "the sense of wilderness where no human forms are to be found."[59] The second part of Tsung

2. Drawing of part of a landscape inlaid in gold on a bronze tube of the Han dynasty. Tokyo Academy of Arts, Tokyo. After William Willetts, *Foundations of Chinese Art*, Thames and Hudson, London, p. 149, fig. 26.

Ping's reaction to the painting can be taken to describe its naturalistic content, since the description mentions "peaks of various shapes towering high" and "cloud-covered forests mysteriously stretching afar." But these elements can also be taken to describe Tsung Ping's imaginings provoked by the painting, or possibly to reflect peaks and forests represented in a very conceptional way. In fact, the fantastic landscape representations often shown in the inlaid designs on the bronze objects from the Han dynasty can serve Tsung Ping's purpose very well. They are, in my opinion, representations of the sacred mountains following the conception of the *Shan-hai ching*. For example, the design on a bronze tube in the Tokyo National Academy of Arts, ascribed to the late Former Han, (fig. 2), is a fantastic representation of a mountain scene with "peaks of various shapes" and "forests" and fantastic animals in their various activities.[60] The mountain ranges and forests are shown in a linear pattern integrating the so-called "cloud scroll (*yün-ch'i*[am]) motif" within it.[61] Both the *yün-ch'i* motif, which is derived from the abstracted birds and dragon motifs, and the fantastic animals are indications of the presence of the supernatural forces, the "nature" or *lei*, of the sacred mountains. In short, Tsung

am 雲氣

Ping's exaltation of spirit could just as well have come from a painting resembling this design.

Major points of this section may be summarized here. Tsung Ping's "Landscape Essay" is closely related to his own participation in climbing the great mountains of China and experiencing an "exaltation of spirit," the common practice of the Buddhists at the time, which Richard Mather once termed "Landscape Buddhism."[62] Tsung explains these experiences in the *Ming fo lun* in Buddhistic terms as one's realization of "the thought of the divine karmic Way" and "the interactions of the bright spirits [of Buddhas and other higher spiritual beings]." Further, he theorizes that the sacred mountains and streams provide such experiences because they simulate the Way with their forms, which, in turn, result from a union of the divine karmic spirits with earth and water. In this thinking of Tsung's we observe that the traditional animistic belief in the sacred mountains was still very much alive; it was about half way in the process of transformation into the humanistic approach to nature of the later period. We may call Tsung Ping's standpoint Buddhistic animism.

Tsung Ping's theory of landscape painting is an application of his karmic theory about the sacred mountains to the paintings of them. The purpose of such a painting is to provide the same mystical spiritual experience to the viewers that they would have had in the actual mountains. Here, Tsung Ping brings in the traditional concept of *kan-lei*. For Tsung Ping, the *kan-lei* phenomena are mystical manifestations, visible in this world, of the spiritual karmic interactions which are behind all occurrences in the universe. Thus, the requirement for the artists in the paintings of the sacred mountains, "icons" so to speak, is to attain the essential nature (*lei*) of the mountains, so as to cause a mystical karmic interaction between the spirit of the viewer and the spirit of the sacred mountain depicted. It is interesting that Tsung Ping in this theory is perfectly in conformity with the traditional theory of art which in the previous section we observed in the music theory of the Han dynasty. In art theory, as in the fields of religious belief and philosophy, Tsung Ping's attitude is to incorporate the traditional viewpoint into the new inclusive Buddhistic theory.

My interpretation of Tsung Ping's "Landscape Essay" is that his discussion is on the theoretical level and does not deal at all with the problem of practical representation. I have argued that Han representations of the sacred mountains in the designs on bronze objects fit well what Tsung required in painting. It was to illustrate my point that almost any landscape representation in China, to the extent that it conveys the power of nature—from the Han representations to a later painting such as the *Waterfall at Mt. Lu* by Tao-chi (1641?–1707?) in the Sumitomo collection—can satisfy Tsung Ping's requirement for the paintings of the sacred mountains.[63] To determine what was the most likely style for Tsung Ping's time is a problem for a separate study.

It is a historical irony that in spite of his great ingenuity in formulating new theories, Tsung Ping, with his inclusive way of thinking, became a preserver of the traditional, say, conservative, approach to art based upon the *kan-lei* principle. A new trend of art theory with an emphasis on more abstract forces than the iconic force of *lei*, for example, *ch'i* (vital force), *shih*[an] (kinetic force) and *ku*[ao] (structural force), was developing at the time in the line of theorists from Ku K'ai-chih (ca. 344–ca. 406) to Hsieh Ho (active ca. A.D. 500). This new trend, parallel to the development of the theory of calligraphy, which is essentially an abstract art, eventually became the main stream of Chinese art theory. Tsung Ping's theory, on the other hand, was left as a "last glory" of the pre-Han and Han theory of art, and was destined to be forgotten in its true meaning.

1. Tung Ch'i-ch'ang, *Jung-t'ai chi* (*Ming-tai i-shu chia-chi hui-k'an* ed.) *Pieh-chi* 6:1b.

2. *Chou i* (*Shih-san-ching chu-shu* ed.) 1:15a. Translation, quoted from Richard Wilhelm, (tr. Cary Baynes), *The I Ching* (Princeton, N.J., 1967; hereafter Wilhelm/Baynes), p. 382.

3. Ibid.

4. Wilhelm/Baynes, p. 280. For the original text, see *Chou i*, 7:1b–2b.

5. Joseph Needham *Science and Civilization in China*, vol. 2: History of Scientific Thought, (Cambridge, 1956), pp. 279–280.

6. Ibid., 2:280. For Frazer's original statement, see Sir James George Frazer, *The New Golden Bough*, ed. T. H. Gaster (New York, 1961), p. 5.

7. Fung Yu-lan, *A History of Chinese Philosophy*, trans. D. Bodde, 2 vols. (Princeton, 1952, 1953), 1:381–382.

8. For specific uses of the term *lei* in discussions, see, for example, *Hsün Tzu* (SPTK ed.) 1:9a–b, and *Lü-shih ch'un-ch'iu* (SPTK ed.) 13, 20, 21, 25.

9. *Shih chi* (SPTK ed.) 23, 24, 25, 26, 28. For the *Ch'un-ch'iu fan-lu* and the *Huai-nan Tzu*, see below.

10. *Ch'un-ch'iu fan-lu* (SPTK ed.) (hereafter *CCFL*) 13:3b–5a. Needham, *Science and Civilization*, 2:281–282.

11. *Huai-nan Tzu* (SPTK ed.) 3:1b–2a.

12. Some scholars, although still a minority, are now expressing strong opposition to this traditional trend. For example, see C. K. Yang, *Religion in Chinese Society* (Berkeley and Los Angeles, 1961), pp. 244–277. Huston Smith, "Transcendence in Traditional China," *Religious Studies*, (1966), 2:185–196; Yamashita Ryūji, *Yōmeigaku no kenkyū*, 2 vols. (Tokyo, 1971), 1:25–62.

13. *CCFL* 66, 67, 68, 69, 15:1a–5b.

14. Needham, *Science and Civilization*, 2:286–287.

15. Tung's stated enumeration stops at five (*CCFL* 59, 13:7–8), or at ten in a somewhat illogical way (ibid. 81, 17:8b). See Fung/Bodde, *Chinese Philosophy*, 2:19–23. However,

an 勢   ao 骨

Tung's discussions of the basic elements in the chapters included in *chüan* 13 clearly imply that from these elements all the categorical beings (*lei*) of the world result.

16. Needham, *Science and Civilization*, 2:289.

17. In the *Li chi* (*SPTK* ed.) 4:5a, Cheng Hsüan's comment says: "*Lei, i* and *tsuo* are the names of sacrifices. However, the rituals are now lost."

18. *Chou li* (*SPTK* ed.) 5:19b, 23a, 25b. See also *Erh ya* (*SPTK* ed.) 1:1b, 2:8b.

19. Bilsky in Lester James Bilsky, *The State Religion of Ancient China* (Taipei, 1977) discusses in detail the evolution of the practices of sacrificial rituals from the early Chou through the Han dynasty. However, his treatment of the *lei* sacrifice is unfortunately too brief. I owe some of my thinking here to Shirakawa Shizuka's excellent summary of the magic oriented world of the Shang people based upon information obtained from the oracle bone inscriptions. See Shirakawa Shizuka, *Kōkotsubun no sekai* (Tokyo, 1972; hereafter Shirakawa). About the term *lei* as a sacrifice, he quotes from the *Li chi*, but does not quote examples of its use in the oracle bone inscriptions. Academia Sinica, ed., *Chia ku wen pien* (Peking, 1965) does not include the character *lei*. Needham lists in Table 11 a reconstructed ancient script form of *lei*, with a note saying that "no early [i.e. oracle bone] forms known" (Needham, *Science and Civilization*, 2:226).

20. One of the most recent studies with an extensive bibliography is Alvin K. Cohen, "Coercing the Rain Deities in Ancient China," *History of Religions* (1978), 17:244–266.

21. *CCFL* 74, 16:3a–6a.

22. Hayashi Minao, "Sengokujidai no gazōmon," *Kōkogaku zasshi* (1961–1962), 47:190–212, 264–292; (1962), 48:1–21.

23. Bernhard Karlgren, *A Catalogue of the Chinese Bronzes in the Alfred F. Pillsbury Collection* (London, 1952), No. 47 (pls. 66, 67).

24. Ibid., p. 129.

25. *Chou i* 6:21a–b. Wilhelm/Baynes, pp. 244–245.

26. The identification of this animal as a "wild boar" is by no means certain. Its relatively long neck testifies against such an identification if *chia chu* was the same species as the present-day wild boar.

27. For the *fan* sacrifice in the rainmaking ritual, see CCFL 16:4a.

28. *Li chi* 12:18a–b.

29. *Hsün Tzu* 20 ("Yüeh lun") 14:1a–7b. *Shih chi* ("Yüeh shu") 24:1a–41b. *Li chi* 19 ("Yüeh chi") 11:5b–22b.

30. *Li chi* 11:14b. Translation by Legge. See *Li chi*, Book of Rites, 2 vols. (rpt. New York, 1967), 2:115.

31. Ibid., p. 110. The text is in the *Li chi* 11:12a–13a.

32. The definition of *sheng* is given in the *Li chi* 11:5b.

33. *Hsün Tzu* 11:4a–b. Its English translation is in Burton Watson, *Basic Writings of Mo Tzu, Hsün Tzu and Han Fei Tzu* (New York and London, 1967), p. 116.

34. For example, see *Li chi* 11:11a–b, and *Shih chi* 24:38a–39b.

35. See William R. B. Acker, *Some T'ang and Pre-T'ang Texts on Chinese Painting*, 2 vols. (Leiden, 1954, 1974), 1:154–156.

36. See E. Zürcher, *The Buddhist Conquest of China*, 2 vols. (Leiden, 1959, 1:218–219, 268–271. Kimata Tokuo, "Eon to Sōhei o megutte," in *Eon kenkyū*, ed. Kimura Eiichi, 2 vols. (Tokyo, 1962), 2:295–302, 341–360.

37. For example, see Hsü Fu-kuan, *Chung-kuo i-shu ching-shen* (Taichung, 1966), pp. 241–360); Michael Sullivan, *The Birth of Landscape Painting in China* (Berkeley and Los Angeles, 1962; hereafter Sullivan, *Birth*), p. 102.

38. Sun Ch'o, *Yü tao lun* (*Taishō Shinshū Daizōkyo* ed., vol. 52), p. 16 middle. For Sun's life and thought, see Zürcher, *Buddhist Conquest*, 1:132–134.

39. Ibid., 1:132.

40. *Ming fo lun* (*Taishō Shinshū Daizōkyo* ed., vol. 52), p. 9 middle.

41. Leon Hurwitz, "Additional Observations on the 'Defense of the Faith,'" *Essays on the History of Buddhism, Presented to Professor Zenryu Tsukamoto* (Kyoto, 1961), pp. 28–40, especially 31–32.

42. Nakamura Shigeo, *Chūgoku garon no tenkai* (Kyoto, 1965), pp. 59–81. Hatano Takeshi, "'Sō Hei gasansui jo' no tokushitsu," *CCBK* (1968), 7:37–54. Fukunaga Mitsuji, *Geijutsu ronshū* (*Chūgoku bunmei sen*, vol. 4) (Tokyo, 1971), pp. 147–164.

43. Hatano, *CCBK* 7:47–52.

44. For the text of Tsung Ping's "*Hua shan shui hsü*," I used the collated edition in Yü Chien-hua, *Chung-kuo hua-lun lei-pien*, 2 vols. (Peking, 1956), 1:583–584. All the names of the people and places are identified by Leon Hurvitz. See Leon Hurvitz, "Tsung Ping's Comments on Landscape Painting" *AA* (1970), 32:148–150.

45. *Yü tao lun*, p. 16 middle.

46. *Ming fo lun*, p. 13 top. The term *ch'ang-wu* is in *Lao Tzu tao te ching* (*SPTK* ed.; hereafter *Lao Tzu*) 1:1. Hatano also quotes this passage and suggests that *fa tao* 法道 in the text connotes "being together with the Way." See Hatano, *CCBK* 7:40.

47. Discussions of virtue (*te*) or mysterious virtue (*hsüan-te*) are found in *Lao Tzu* 1, 10, 21, 28, 51. Also see Fung/Bodde, *Chinese Philosophy*, 1:179–181.

48. *Ming fo lun*, p. 12 middle. For a discussion of this problem, see Hatano, *CCBK* 7:39–40.

49. *Ming fo lun*, p. 12 middle.

50. Ibid., p. 10 top.

51. Ibid.

52. Ibid., p. 15 top.

53. Hurvitz, *AA* 32:152.

54. In translating the passage of the "Landscape Essay" in question, both Alexander Soper and Michael Sullivan use the term "convincing diminution." See Alexander C. Soper, "Early Chinese Landscape Painting," *Art Bulletin* (1941), 23:164, and Sullivan, *Birth*, p. 103.

55. Kobayashi Taichirō is one of the earliest propagators of this theory of Tsung Ping's method of "see-through perspective." Most Japanese scholars seem to follow Kobayashi's lead. See Kobayashi Taichirō, "Shinaga no kōzu to sono riron," *Chūgoku kaigashi ronkō* (Kyoto, 1947), pp. 64–65. Yü Chien-hua is not as graphic as Kobayashi, but insists that the idea of proportional diminution coincides perfectly with the present day one-point perspective method. See Yü Chien-hua, *Chung-kuo hua-lun lei-pien*, 1:584.

56. *P'ei-wen yün-fu* (*Shang-mu yin-shu kuan*, indexed ed.; Taiwan, 1965), p. 3286 bottom.

57. *Ming fo lun*, p. 10 middle.

58. Ibid., p. 13 middle.

59. For the relationship between Tsung Ping and the *Shan-hai ching*, see Zürcher, *Bud-*

dhist Conquest, 1:271. It is possible that when Tsung Ping talked about Mt. K'un-lun, he might have had an image of it from the *Shan-hai ching*.

60. William Willetts *Foundations of Chinese Art* (London, 1965), pp. 148–149, fig. 26.

61. Ibid., pp. 146–148, and Mizuno Seiichi, "Kandai no senkai ishō ni tsuite," *Kōkogaku zasshi*, (1937), 27:501–507.

62. Richard Mather, "The Landscape Buddhism of the Fifth-Century Poet Hsieh Ling-yün," *JAS*, (1958), 18:67–79.

63. See Richard Edwards, *The Painting of Tao-chi* (Ann Arbor, 1967), p. 151 (Catalogue No. 22).

Tsung Ping's Essay on Painting Landscape and the "Landscape Buddhism" of Mount Lu

By Susan Bush

I

Tsung Ping (375–443) is a key figure in Southern Dynasties aesthetics, and his writings are of interest to specialists in Chinese thought and religion, as well as to historians of art and literature. Since the T'ang dynasty, the *Hua shan-shui hsü* (Introduction to Painting Landscape) has been bracketed in anthologies with the *Hsü hua* (Discussion of Painting) by Wang Wei (415–443) as exemplifying a Taoist approach to landscape painting.[1] In modern times, both texts have been translated under the heading of "Landscape Taoism," and taken to reflect different aspects of Neo-Taoist thought.[2] The Tsung Ping essay has been studied as well in conjunction with fourth- and fifth-century poetry and poetics that emphasize the role of feelings in the new appreciation of natural scenery.[3] However, besides being a noted recluse and mountaineer, Tsung Ping was also a devout Buddhist layman who once studied briefly with Hui-yüan (344–416/7), the famous abbot of the Tung-lin monastery in the Lu mountain range, and was profoundly influenced by his teachings.[4] The majority of Tsung's extant writings are Buddhist polemics such as the *Ming fo lun* (Discourses Illuminating the Buddha), written around A.D. 433.[5] Since the "Introduction to Painting Landscape" was evidently composed in the last decade of Tsung's life and contains phrases found in his Buddhist tracts, certain Japanese scholars have recently suggested that it also reflects a Buddhist point of view.[6] Some of their interpretations will be presented below, and further information will be given in an attempt to place Tsung's essay in the context of the "landscape Buddhism" of Mount Lu. For this purpose, the "Introduction to Painting Landscape" will be considered in connection with the '*Yu Shih-men shih* [*hsü*]' (Introduction to Poetry on Wandering at the Stone Gate), which is said to have been composed at the beginning of the fifth century by laymen at Hui-yüan's monastery.

Certain questions about this material should be raised initially, to be answered at least in part in the discussion that follows. Even if it is a known fact that Tsung Ping was a devout Buddhist, should he be labeled a Buddho-Taoist because of the syncretic nature of early Chinese Buddhism? More specifically, can any significant distinctions be made between "landscape Taoism" and "landscape Buddhism" in as far as these terms apply to the "Introduction to Painting Landscape"? Do such labels really indicate different types of perceptions or distinctive world views? It is difficult to produce clear-cut answers to these questions, since there are variant interpretations of the relevant texts. In my opinion, Tsung Ping's stress on the guiding role of the Buddha or the sages is closer to a kind of "Confucian Buddhism" than a "Buddho-Taoism," and his appreciation of the vast expanse of the universe and the emptiness of unpeopled nature is distinctively Buddhist in cast, lacking in animistic tendencies.[7] Like Hsieh Ling-yün (385–433), another fearless mountaineer and a disciple of Hui-yüan, Tsung Ping ventured into uninhabited wilderness to experience a type of "landscape Buddhism," which in his case was associated with the sages of the past.[8] When this was no longer possible because of his infirmities, Tsung traveled in his mind through painted scenery, meditating in front of his own landscapes. The experience of nature promoted a detachment from worldly concerns and reinforced the purification of the karmic spirit or immortal soul. Thus Tsung's essay on art is infused with his religious aims.

Paul Demiéville has written of the new interest in natural beauty that appears in the writing of the Southern Dynasties:

> C'est qu'à ce moment la Chine commence a découvrir l'art pour l'art; l'esthétique se degage des servitudes de la religion, de l'éthique, de la politique. C'est là une tendence générale. . . .[9] [It was at this time that China began to discover "art for art's sake"; aesthetics detached itself from the bonds of religion, ethics, and politics. This was a general trend then . . . .]

However valid this statement may be for the period as a whole, it does not apply to the Tsung Ping text, in which painting is still the handmaid of religion and aesthetic experience is directed toward Buddhist ends. At this time, due to the interpretation of Indian Buddhism in Chinese terms, the Buddhists were the chief exponents of the preservation of individual life, a concept earlier espoused by popular Taoism that no doubt originally stemmed from the cult of ancestor worship. In the *Ming fo lun* and in a correspondence with Ho Ch'eng-t'ien (370–447), Tsung Ping was a noted defender of Hui-yüan's doctrine of the immortal spirit,[10] and a prime example of a Chinese thinker who enthusiastically adopted the expansive universe of Indian cosmology. As Wolfgang Bauer has written of this early form of Chinese Buddhism:

> . . . it envisaged a world of incomprehensibly enormous dimensions where, across equally enormous temporal and spatial distances, all creatures were connected in all directions by the threads of karma. Precisely due to the erroneous belief that the soul passed through a number of existences, it seemed that the individual lives of all these creatures were set on a course that was nothing short of majestic, for it had begun eons ago and led through all the forms of creation. What was central in Buddhism

paled before the profound impression these conceptions of enormous magnitudes, mostly traceable to Brahmin influences, made on the Chinese mind, accustomed as it was to "human," historical dimensions. The notion of a wholly personal retribution continuing to be effective through an endless chain of rebirths gave Buddhism a nighty impetus as a religion.[11]

Among the Buddhist laymen in Hui-yüan's circle, Tsung Ping was especially noteworthy for his belief in the possibility of directly experiencing this limitless universe.[12] Unlike Pascal, he was not daunted by the emptiness of vast immensities, conceivably in part because his imagination was buoyed by the spirit journeys of earlier shamanistic mythology. From Indian Buddhist teachings, he derived the conception of a world ordered by the law of karma and by the exemplary role of a Buddha in each era. A "Confucian" strain is also evident in Tsung's writings, particularly in the significance of earlier sages as models in religious life. As for his approach to landscape, the importance of sacred mountains and the belief in a purified spirit separate from gross matter count as "Taoist" elements rooted in the Chinese past. These various aspects of Tsung Ping's thought can be studied in more detail in connection with the *Hua shan-shui hsü*, preserved in *Li-tai ming-hua chi* 6.[13] As has been noted, this work is generally thought to represent Taoist inspiration in landscape painting of the Six Dynasties, and it mentions such typical "Taoist" activities as lute playing, wine drinking, and breath control. Nonetheless, Tsung's literary references are strictly Confucian: he seeks for precedents for his love of landscape in the lives of sages and virtuous recluses of antiquity, and quotes from *Lun-yü* (the Analects) to buttress arguments. Although he writes of responding in solitude to the uninhabited wilderness, thoughts of the great men of the past who had also experienced such scenery never seem to leave his mind. Instead of communing solely with nature, he seems to be attuned to the spirits of these sages and worthies. It is conceivable that Buddhism, which is never explicitly mentioned, is the most important frame of reference in the essay.

Analogies drawn between Taoism and Confucianism and the recently imported Buddhism were common in this period. Nakamura Shigeo has argued that Tsung Ping's essay expresses Buddhist thought dressed in Neo-Taoist garb and supported by references to the Confucian *Analects*. The sages who play such a prominent role in the text do so as Buddha figures even though they function like Neo-Taoist saints. The distinction made between the sages and virtuous men reflects the separation between Buddhas, whose minds are identified with the universe, and bodhisattvas, who still perceive the world in terms of a dichotomy between subjective and objective.[14] That the few textual references are to the *Analects* is not surprising, since contemporary Buddhist centers like Mount Lu continued to foster Confucian learning. Tsung Ping himself evidently studied the rites during his sojourn there, and, like many other laymen of the period, even in Buddhist

1. "'Flying Emperor' on a Spirit Journey." South quadrant of the ceiling of Tun-huang Cave 249. Early sixth-century colored mural. Courtesy of James C. M. Lo.

polemics, Tsung refers largely to Chinese sources.[15] Moreover, in the *Ming fo lun*, he consciously promotes a syncretic point of view: thus the ruler should "rely on the Duke of Chou and Confucius to nurture the people, and savor the Buddha's law to nurture the spirit."[a][16] For Tsung, as for the Neo-Taoists Wang Pi (226–249) and Kuo Hsiang (d. 312), whose philosophical speculations were a branch of Confucian learning, Confucius remained the prime example of the sage because of his ability to travel in both the mundane and transcendental worlds.[17] Tsung could compare the empty landscape of the mountain top to the purified mind of the sage, detached from illusory forms and projected into infinite space, and he wrote of Confucius, who had gazed afar on the world from Mounts T'ai and Meng and thought the state of Lu to be small, "was it not because his spirit had fused with the eight distances that he rose above his age?"[b][18] As described in the preceding passage of the *Ming fo lun*, the ascent on high could afford the experience of cosmic space in a Buddhist sense: "instead of there being any lack therein of the awesome dignity of the ranked sages' powerful spirits, is there not simply nothing more than a detachment from humankind, an indifference to worldly affairs? Thus one should harbor distance to establish an image of the divine Way, and respond to stillness to perceive the echo of spiritual intelligence."[c][19]

The view from on high diminished worldly attachments and led to an appreciation of limitless space and time. As Tsung remarked of the sage-rulers who ascended sacred peaks, "[when they were] roaming in sublime freedom, how do we know that they did not follow the Way of the Tathagata."[20] (For an illustration of one such "flying emperor," see fig. 1.) He believed that the purified spirit of the sage had magical power and could literally travel to the ends of the earth like the earlier shamans of Ch'u mythology or the adepts of Indian Buddhism.[21] In a similar fashion, the individual spirit could be developed by mind-expanding exercises, and the sense of self be undercut through the direct experience of the universe in meditation. The *Ming fo lun* advocated this practice as a way of understanding essential Buddhist doctrine (in Erik Zürcher's translation):

> Stroke your body from the heels upward to the top of the head and continue [this movement] with your thought without [ever reaching] a final point, then [you will realize] the infinity of the four quarters, upward and downward. Life is not independently created: it is always transmitted .... This [my] person makes daily use of that endless substance; it comes from a beginningless past, and will be transmitted into an endless future.[22]

This exposition is not unrelated to Tsung's belief that he could purify his mind by visualizing the Tao, traveling from his bed in the painted scenery.

---

[a] 依周孔以養民，味佛法以養神……
[b] 豈非神合於八遐，故超於一世哉？
[c] 寧無列聖威靈，尊嚴乎其中，而唯離離

人羣，念念世務而已哉？固將懷遠以開神道之想，感寂以昭明靈之應矣。

Tsung's love of landscape and use of painting as a substitute for actual nature were noted in *Sung shu* 93, as translated by Alexander Soper:

> He loved mountains and waterways, and delighted in excursions to faraway places. In the west he made his halting place Mount Lu in Ching-chou and on the south he climbed up Mount Heng. There he made himself a hut in the hope of following the example of the hermit [Shang] Tzu-p'ing; but instead fell ill and had to return to Chiang-ling. He said with a sigh: "I am old and ailing: I fear that I can no longer wander among famous mountains. Now I can only purify my heart by contemplating the Tao, and do my roaming from my bed." All that he had visited he depicted in his chamber. He told someone: "I strum my *ch'in* with such force because I want all the mountains to resound." [23]

To judge from the *Hua shan-shu hsü*, it is possible that Tsung's approach to landscape painting was conditioned by Buddhist attitudes toward icons, since he considered painted scenery to be as effective an aid to meditation as the natural landscape. The concern for the correct canons of proportion in Buddhist images may underlie his stress on the exact correspondence of small-scale forms with distant views. Of relevance here is a Buddhist usage of *li* as absolute "Truth" that gives validity to reflections and traces such as the icon of the Buddha's Shadow or Reflection. [24] According to Tsung's essay, if such correspondence, or *lei*, was skillfully achieved, the very essence of a landscape could be captured in painting and the viewer would react to it as to the natural scene.

Certain questions are raised for modern readers by the references in the opening and closing passages of the essay to sages and worthies who respond or reflect light from the distant past. Why should they occur so prominently in a text on painting? If their appearance at the beginning can be explained as a device to legitimize the new subject of landscape, why should they be brought in again at the end? Here even Nakamura Shigeo felt obliged to interpret them as painted figures in a landscape scene. What is their exact relationship to the painter or viewer? Should the perceptions of adepts be linked specifically with those of painters in the initial passage, as William Acker thought? Does the conclusion imply that the viewer is communing with the sage artists of antiquity, as Leon Hurvitz would have it? [25] The commentaries of Japanese scholars have emphasized the significance of such figures for Tsung as potential Buddhas able to experience the universe directly with their purified spirits. Conceivably, these sage rulers or recluses are presented as models of action or ideal viewers, to be emulated through the proper appreciation of landscape.

Something of the importance of such mythical or historical figures in art can be inferred from the biography of Tsung Ping's grandson Tsung Ts'e, a recluse who refused office toward the beginning of the Southern Ch'i dynasty (479–502). In words that echoed his grandfather, he spoke of his love of nature where he abandoned himself to the point of madness, unaware that old age had arrived. Like

Ping he was a calligrapher, painter, and lute player, and he traveled to both Mount Heng and Mount Lu, writing records of these famous spots. Tsung Ping had hoped to follow the example of the Eastern Han recluse Shang Tzu-p'ing, or Hsiang Ch'ang, and live out his life on sacred peaks apart from worldly affairs.[26] To express a similar desire to visit noted mountains, Ts'e copied on his wall a painting of Shang Tzu-p'ing said to be by his grandfather. Furthermore, he evidently retired to live in Ping's former house, which is now placed on Mount Lu rather than on Mount Heng. There he painted the meeting of the poet Juan Chi (210–263) with Sun Teng on Mount Su-men, and faced this movable screen when sitting or lying down. Sun Teng was the third-century Taoist adept whose whistling technique was so developed that it evoked a response from nature. For Tsung Ts'e, who had studied Taoist texts, he must have represented the ideal of harmony with nature. Presumably Shang Tzu-p'ing's portrait had a similar significance, since it was painted for inspirational purposes. No true landscapes are attributed to Ts'e, although background motifs could have been included in these historical portraits.[27] Since Ts'e is said to have done paintings for the Buddha's Shadow Terrace at the Yung-yeh monastery near Mount Lu, he also shared his grandfather's Buddhist interests. The original image of the Buddha's Shadow or Reflection was commissioned by Hui-yüan in 412, around the time when recent scholarship would place Tsung Ping on Mount Lu. And it has even been suggested by Zürcher that Ping himself might have painted this icon, which was displayed to advantage against the scenery of Mount Lu.[28]

Mountain settings were certainly considered to be appropriate places to meditate on the sages and recluses of antiquity, with or without the benefit of paintings. It was common to think of the spirits of great men when ascending heights, and also fitting to portray their likenesses in rustic retreats.[29] Although Tsung Ping's essay mentions "the uninhabited wilderness," like other contemporary painting, his work probably included certain mythical or historical figures as a focal point. In general, the titles of works attributed to him in T'ang texts are of figure subjects, such as portraits of contemporaries and Confucian disciples, and illustrations of the *Chou li* (Book of Rites). He is not credited with any Buddhist works nor any landscapes apart from one unlikely genre scene.[30] Furthermore, the likeness of Shang Tzu-p'ing is given by T'ang critics to the earlier and more famous Tai K'uei (d. 396), whose work is of relevance and should be mentioned here.

Since Tai K'uei's interests were similar to Tsung Ping's, this attribution is quite plausible. Tai is said to have produced influential images of sages and worthies, and portrayed two of the "Seven Sages of the Bamboo Grove," Hsi K'ang (223–262) and Juan Chi, no doubt in the style seen in contemporary tomb reliefs (see fig. 2). Like Tsung Ping and Tsung Ts'e, members of the Tai family of K'uai-chi in modern Chekiang were professional recluses, landscape enthusiasts, and Buddhist devotees, known for their skills in calligraphy, painting, and lute-playing. It is noteworthy

2. "Hsi K'ang with Lute and Juan Chi Whistling." Rubbing of a section of a molded-brick relief from a fifth-century tomb at Hsi-shan Bridge, Nanking, height 80 cm. The Nanking Museum. Courtesy of Nicholas Cahill.

that they were recorded specifically as Buddhist sculptors and painters, and that landscape subjects were listed under their names in T'ang texts.[31] A younger son, Tai Yung (d. 441), recommended for office at the beginning of the Liu-Sung dynasty (420–478) along with Tsung Ping, was especially praised for his fine judgments of the proportions of Buddhist images.[32] Works attributed to Tai K'uei and Tai Po suggest that landscape painting might have been more fully developed in the eastern coastal region than at Chiang-ling or Mount Lu, where the two Tsungs were the chief exponents of the appreciation of nature. The activities of the Tais could have influenced Tsung Ping and Tsung Ts'e; similarly it is likely that the initial cult of landscape in Hui-yüan's community was stimulated by practices in the vicinity of the southern capital. Questions of possible influence and of regional distinctions will be raised again in connection with devotions on Mount Lu.

Tsung Ping's *Hua shan-shu hsü* has been translated into English not only by Osvald Sirén, Shio Sakanishi, William Acker, and Hsio-yen Shih, but also by Alexander Soper, Michael Sullivan, Lin Yu-t'ang, and Leon Hurvitz.[33] Since the translations by Acker and Hurvitz are extensively annotated, yet another English version of Tsung Ping's essay may seem unnecessary. However, none of these translators were able to draw on the research of Japanese scholars like Nakamura Shigeo, who has studied the essay in a Buddhist context. Leon Hurvitz, who noted Tsung's association with Hui-yüan and underlined the existence of the *Ming fo lun*, did not discover any significant Buddhist overtones in the essay on painting. But by pointing out parallels in the language with phrases in Tsung's polemics, Nakamura has argued for a Buddhist interpretation of the content. Hatano Takeshi has duplicated this approach and reached a similar conclusion, relying as well on Kimata Tokuo's investigation of Tsung's Buddhist thought. The essay has also been placed in a wider frame of reference by Hatano, who cites certain fourth-century appreciations of landscape.[34] On the other hand, a more limited study of the text by Fukunaga Mitsuji cites a few passages from the *Ming fo lun* but primarily stresses parallel phrases to be found in earlier Taoist texts and similar lines that occur in the syncretic "Yu T'ien-t'ai-shan fu" (Fu on Roaming on Mount T'ien-t'ai) by Sun Ch'o (fl. 330–365).[35] These scholars' interpretations will be referred to in connection with the translation presented below, which will be preceded by a discussion of important terms and a summary of central ideas.

Traditional Chinese terminology was used to translate imported Buddhist concepts and in turn often shaped these doctrines. In the essay on painting, it was *shen*, originally the deified human spirit, that characterized the sages and was roused in the viewer of scenery. When this spirit is described as boundless, resting in forms temporarily and affecting different types of beings, it seems analogous to the "world soul" that early Chinese Buddhists posited to explain the phenomenon of transmigration after death. If *shen* for Hui-yüan and Tsung Ping was a cosmic spirit that when aroused to intention was bound in individual entities by karmic law, it was not to be thought of as existing in all matter. Hui-yüan distinguished between things that have *ling*, spiritual intelligence or the will that leads to reincarnation, and things that lack it and simply die or disintegrate.[36] In what category did landscape fall?

Tsung Ping's position on this matter is hard to define, since somewhat varying attitudes are expressed in this writings. In one passage of the *Ming fo lun*, he discusses the proposition that the Five Sacred Peaks and Four Sacred Rivers are without *ling*, noting that this has not yet been determined:

> [But] if we do assume that there is spirit (*shen*) therein, mountains are simply heaps of earth and rivers merely collections of water, and how can the spiritual intelligence (*ling*) that "attains unity" be produced from the coarse substance of water or earth? Moreover, even if it responds to and lodges in cliffs and streams, and is completely unified with them, should the mountains collapse or the waters dry up, it is not destroyed along with water or earth. Spirit is not created of forms and hence does not die with them.[d][37]

Here Tsung's line of argument stresses the Buddhist doctrine that spirit is separate from matter in which it lodges temporarily, indicating that this would be true even in the case of tutelary deities of sacred sites, granting that they existed. Elsewhere in the text he expresses his belief in a cosmic spirit permeating the universe: "it is clear that heaven and earth have spiritual intelligence (*ling*) and that the quintessential spirit is not extinguished."[e][38] *Ling*, which is variously translatable as spiritual intelligence or "soul," the numinous or the "ethereal," is definitely associated with landscape and its pictorial image in the essay on painting, which may be more "Taoist" in its orientation. As the gateway to the Void, landscape is thought to be near the immaterial plane of existence; hence it was appreciated by those purified adepts closest to the cosmic spirit. In the *Ming fo lun*, Tsung noted that the love of mountains, like the ideals of the virtuous, was still an attachment that could lead to karmic entanglement.[39] Nonetheless, in the "Introduction to Painting Landscape," he seemed to have no doubt that a disinterested appreciation of nature could stimulate the spirit and set it on the path toward enlightenment. Here landscape, in its vastness and emptiness, was more than a symbol of the mind of the sage; it functioned literally as a "vale of soul-making."[40]

If *ling* alone, as interpreted in the translation below, described the immaterial or spiritual aspect of landscape in the essay, *shen* and *li* in the fifth paragraph remain ambiguous terms. *Li* often poses problems of translation in this period. At the end of the paragraph it does seem to represent the absolute Truth of the Buddhists, while in

[d] 若許其神，則岳唯積土之多，瀆唯積水而已矣。得一之靈，何生水土之粗哉？而感託巖流，肅成一體，設使山崩川竭

必不與水土俱亡矣。神非形作，合而不滅。
[e] 夫天地有靈，精神不滅明矣

the beginning phrase it appears to have the underlying traditional meaning of "natural law" or "principle," a common truth. The meaning of the intermediate *li* in the second sentence is more difficult to judge. It occurs in conjunction with the character *shen*, which presents a similar problem and also is used three times in the paragraph. In the last instance it is likely to be Hui-yüan's universal Spirit; elsewhere it may have the meaning of the spiritual intelligence of individuals as can be documented in the *Ming fo lun*.[41] It is possible to read the second sentence as referring solely to a viewer's faculties; then *shen ch'ao li te*[f] might be translated "as his spirit soars his reason is satisfied." However, this reading seems unlikely in the context of the paragraph as a whole. When, as below, the phrase *li te* is given as "truth is attained," the question of what *li* means here is still to be answered. Conceivably, "truth" is a mental state that is the goal of the viewer, an intuitive understanding of the natural order. This is one meaning of the *li* that early Chinese Buddhists came to equate with *prajñā*, or transcendental Wisdom, after the interpretation of Chih Tun (314–366). That *li* is used in this sense is plausible, because in the fourth sentence it is again paired with *shen*, here the cosmic spirit that descends into forms according to karmic law. Similarly, "Truth enters into reflections and traces," and will be attained if the artist describes with skill. Understood in a Buddhist context, this phrase might refer to the efficacy of icons: *ying*, "reflections" or "shadows," and possibly *chi*, "traces," although the latter may indicate Buddhist teachings.

Li occurs in two stanzas of Hui-yüan's inscription on the Buddha's Shadow image, which has been translated by Zürcher:

> How still and vast is the Great Image!
> [In it] the Truth is hidden and nameless.
> The body, spirit-like, enters [the world of] transformation,
> and the shadow cast by it becomes separated from the form....
> [These visible] traces serve to symbolize Reality
> and the principles [hidden behind it] make its purport profound.[42]

Hui-yüan's initial definition of *li*, "Truth," is derived from Chih Tun's exposition of the *Prajñāpāramitā*: "the highest Principle is dark and empty like a ravine, in which everything is reduced to a state of being nameless."[43] Paul Demiéville, who has traced the development of *li* as an absolute in Neo-Taoism and early Chinese Buddhism, notes its eventual association with mystical insight: "L'absolu n'est pas un concept abstrait, c'est un absolu vécu, qui a pour sanction et pour couronnement l'expérience mystique." [The absolute is not an abstract concept: it is a *lived* absolute, with its justification and highest achievement being the mystical experience.][44] The

f 神超理得

very fact that *li* is such an important term in Tsung's essay makes it likely to have been used with Buddhist overtones, as also seems the case in Hsieh Ling-yün's poetry.[45]

If Tsung was thinking of Buddhist icons in the conclusion of this paragraph, the inference would be that when an artist draws forms correctly his image will be successful. For Tsung, the *dharmakāya* still meant "pure existence of spirit" apart from matter.[46] In the introduction to the inscription on the Buddha's Shadow, Hui-yüan expounded his belief in the underlying unity of the Buddha's *dharmakāya* (law or eternal body) and *nirmaṇakāya* (transformation or manifestation body) "as manifestations of the Original One:" "originally the *dharmakāya* did not take two courses; the [proposed] distinction between his [real] body and its shadow cannot mean the denial of his [essential] unity."[47] Thus the Shadow or reflection of the Buddha's transitory body was an effective representation of his Reality, the *dharmakāya*. For Tsung, the painted landscape may have stood in a similar relation to nature and ultimately to the Tao.

Another term that should be considered in this connection is *lei*, which occurs as "species" or "kind" toward the end of the fifth paragraph, but appears to have its verbal meaning of "to be like" or "to resemble" elsewhere in two other phrases: "unskillfulness in correspondence" and "when correspondence is achieved with skill."[48] However, in these it has been rendered as "correspondence" to avoid the inference of naturalistic imitation or "formal likeness." Tsung may have been less concerned with the details of external appearance than with the correct type or category of an image as a whole, as is argued in this volume by Kiyohiko Munakata.[49] From a slightly different point of view, it is noteworthy that the use of *lei* is rather unusual here and remains problematic in translations.[50] It is conceivable that it should be understood against a Buddhist background. William Acker has speculated that the phrase *sui-lei* in the fourth of the *liu-fa*, or "six laws" of painting, transmitted by Hsieh Ho (act. ca. 500–535?) is relevant to the first of the Sanskrit *sadaṅga*, or "six limbs" of painting, presently known only in a thirteenth-century commentary to the *Kāmasūtra*.[51] In a review of Acker's book, Zürcher has underlined this surmise by suggesting that Tsung Ping is likely to have gained a knowledge of Indian Buddhist iconography when on Mount Lu, where he may even have put it into practice; hence this connection might explain Hsieh Ho's comment on Tsung Ping's excellent understanding of the six laws.[52] In any case, the first two of the *sadaṅga*, *rūpa-bheda* and *pramāna*, are concerned with issues touched on in the essay on painting landscape, appropriate iconography and proportion. Furthermore, it is indeed possible that *rūpa-bheda*s, "variety of manifestations (or forms)," could have been translated into contemporary Chinese as *sui-lei*, "according to different types." A similar expression, *sui-chi*, or *āsaya-bhedana* in Sanskrit, again refers to the teaching of Buddhas "according to individual capacities" in *sūtras* of relatively early date.[53] As in the case of *li*, although no firm proof can be given, the term *lei*, "to correspond [in type]," should perhaps also be interpreted in a Buddhist context.

The general punctuation of the following translation is after Hatano Takeshi, and the paragraphs have been numbered to facilitate references.[54] The initial paragraph justifies the love of mountains through landscape's association with the Tao, and compares the appreciation of nature with the understanding of the virtuous drawn from images, or the phenomena of the universe. A distinction is made between physical and spiritual planes of being in landscape as in a passage quoted from the *Ming fo lun*; there the sages and worthies who climbed or lived on various peaks were considered analogous to Buddhas and boddhisattvas.[55] In the second paragraph, Tsung speaks of being unable to roam on famous peaks, and hence turning to painting. A reference to the Stone Gate on Mount Lu and to the men who climbed, meditated, and wrote poems there is in keeping with the personal tone of this passage. The opening statements in the third paragraph bring to mind Tsung's arguments in the *Ming fo lun* to the effect that silence in Confucian scriptures about Buddhism does not prove that it did not exist in antiquity, since certain remarks of the sages, when rightly understood, indicate that it did.[56] From the context of the essay as a whole, it should be clear that the sights which Tsung hoped to reproduce in painting were presumably the same as those enjoyed by the ancients. The fourth paragraph goes on the describe the practice of painting a landscape "form for form," with the concern for proportion appropriate to an icon. In turn, the fifth paragraph focuses on the effectiveness of a painting for the viewer as a substitute for scenery. Although there are different interpretations of the initial phrase, it has simply been taken here to state a common truth about the appreciation of nature. In a typically Buddhist fashion, the psychology of viewing is emphasized, and like the landscape itself, a painting is thought to reflect ultimate reality. Finally, the last paragraph, which mentions Taoist techniques of achieving harmony, describes Tsung's own practice of purifying his heart, while meditating in front of landscape paintings. The translation presumes that the sages, who reappear at this point, simply provide models for the ideal expansion of the purified spirit that fuses with all things in the universe.

Introduction to Painting Landscape[A]

1. Sages, harboring the Tao, respond to things. The virtuous, purifying their thoughts, savor images.[57] As for landscape, it is substantial, yet tends toward the ethereal plane.[58] Therefore, men like the Yellow Emperor, Yao, Confucius, Kuang-ch'eng, Ta-k'uei, Hsü Yu, and Po-i and Shu-ch'i insisted on roaming in the mountains K'ung-t'ung, Chü-tz'u,

Miao-ku, Chi, Shou, and T'ai and Meng.[59] These have also been praised as the delight of the humane and the wise.[60] Now, sages model themselves on the Tao through their spirits and the virtuous comprehend this. Landscapes display the beauty of the Tao through their forms and humane men delight in this.[61] Are these not similar?

2. When I was deeply attached to the Lu and Heng mountains and roamed with abandon on the Ching and Wu peaks, I did not realize that old age was approaching.[62] Ashamed at being unable to concentrate my vital breath and attune my body, I am afraid of limping among those at the Stone Gate.[63] Therefore, I paint images and spread colors, constructing cloudy peaks.

3. If truths that were lost before the period of middle antiquity may be sought by the imagination a thousand years later, and if meaning that is subtler than the images of speech can be grasped by the mind in books and records, what then of that where the body has strolled and the eyes rested repeatedly when it is described form for form and color for color?[64]

4. However, the K'un-lun mountains are immense and the eye's pupils small. If the former come within inches of the viewer, their total form will not be seen. If they are at a distance of several miles, then they can be encompassed by inch-small pupils. Truly, the farther off they are, the smaller they will appear. Now, if one spreads thin silk in order to reflect from afar, the form of K'un-lun's Lang Peak can be encompassed in a square inch. A vertical stroke of three inches will equal a height of thousands of feet, and a horizontal ink-stretch of several feet will embody a distance of a hundred miles.[65] That is why those who look at paintings are only troubled by awkwardness in correspondence and do not consider that diminution detracts from verisimilitude, since it is a natural effect. In this way, the lofty elegance of the Sung and Hua mountains and the soul of deep valleys can all be included in one picture.[66]

5. If response by the eye and accord by the mind [to nature] is considered a universal law, when correspondence is achieved with skill, eyes will also respond completely and the mind be entirely in accord.[67] As this response and accord affect the spirit, the spirit becomes transcendent and truth is attained.[68] Even though one should again futilely seek out remote cliffs, what more could be added? Furthermore, the essence of spirit, being limitless, resides in forms and responds to species, and truth enters into reflections and traces.[69] One who can truly describe with skill will also truly achieve this.

6. Thus, I live at leisure, regulating my vital breath, brandishing the wine cup, and sounding the lute. As I unroll paintings and face them in solitude, while seated I plumb the ends of the earth.[70] Without resisting a

multitude of natural dangers, I simply respond to the uninhabited wilderness, where grottoed peaks tower on high and cloudy forests mass in depth.[71] The sages and virtuous men shed reflected light from the distant past, and a myriad delights are fused into their spirits and thoughts.[72] What then should I do? Freely expand my spirit, that is all. What could be placed above that which expands the spirit?[73]

In this text, appreciation of nature is justified on spiritual grounds. The gist of this argument is in the conclusion of the first paragraph. Sages and landscapes are united or linked with the Tao, and their close association is understood and appreciated respectively by the virtuous who "savor images" or natural phenomena, and the humane who delight in the mountains. Thus the enjoyment of landscape is at least loosely comparable to a step toward enlightenment. No longer able to have the beneficial effect of roaming in the mountains, Tsung Ping has turned to painting landscapes and tries to recreate the places he has experienced in exact, small-scale images. If correspondence to type-forms is skillfully achieved, the viewer will respond imaginatively to the scene, which can be thought of as containing the essence of nature. Meditation before such a painting will bring one closer to the frame of mind of the sages and worthies who experienced nature in the past.

Here painting is not discussed as an art form in itself but as a means to an end, the achievement of enlightenment. As a devout Buddhist, Tsung Ping believed in practicing meditation to diminish worldly attachments and assure rebirth on a higher plane of existence. A distant view from on high also effectively diminished the sense of self and could be thought of as analogous to the empty mind of the sage. Although there was a danger of karmic attachment inherent in any love of mountains, contemplation of the vastness and emptiness of a landscape could stimulate the immortal spirit toward a state of purity. It is conceivable that Tsung's approach was partially fostered by the use of Buddhist icons as aids for visualizing, a common form of meditation in the community on Mount Lu. There is also some evidence that Hui-yüan had formerly directed the aesthetic appreciation of nature into Buddhist channels as can be seen in the "Introduction to Poetry on Wandering at the Stone Gate."

II

If Tsung Ping's "Introduction to Painting Landscape" can be more fully understood in relation to his Buddhist writings, it can also be seen as an off-shoot of a new appreciation of nature, the "landscape Buddhism" of Mount Lu. This aspect of Tsung's essay may be highlighted by a study of the relatively unknown preface to poetry composed by members of Hui-yüan's community after an excursion to the

Stone Gate Gorge in A.D. 400.[74] The preface and its accompanying poem have been associated with Hui-yüan and his *Lu-shan lüeh-chi* (Brief Notes on Mount Lu), because both texts were recorded by title as being engraved in stone at the Tung-lin monastery in the eleventh century.[75] Since Hui-yüan is referred to in the preface as "the Master of the Doctrine," he could have been responsible only for the concluding poem, but this has also been excluded from his writings by modern scholars.[76] The preface and poem generally appear in gazeteers and anthologies as anonymous works by laymen (*tao-jen*) of the Mount Lu community, and are sometimes placed in conjunction with other poems that may have been written on this occasion. The latter have been studied as examples of nature poetry in which descriptions of landscape are mingled with Taoist references.[77]

Like other sacred sites where spectacular scenery and fantastic rock formations were taken as a sign of the supernatural, Mount Lu had been hallowed by popular Taoism before it became a center of Buddhist learning. It harbored local divinities and was associated with a pre-Han recluse K'uang Su.[78] Appreciation of its views were already being written in the Han period, and during Hui-yüan's residency the relatively unknown Chan Fang-sheng wrote his "poems of the Gods and Fairies on Mount Lu" with a preface of A.D. 386, which reports the miraculous ascension of a monk. Chan's characterizations of nature have been thought to be unusually realistic for this time, and may have stimulated the later literary efforts of members of Hui-yüan's community.[79] However, the preface on the expedition to the Stone Gate, which affords an explicit definition of the experience of nature in a Buddhist context, was modeled after the "Preface to the Festival in the Orchid Pavilion" written by Wang Hsi-chih (303–379) at the gathering of A.D. 353 in the K'uai-chi district.

The "Introduction to Poetry on Wandering at the Stone Gate" was probably known to Tsung Ping, and may be echoed in his essay on painting landscape. It is even conceivable that Tsung Ping, like his grandson Ts'e, was responsible for preserving descriptions of scenery, in this case by Hui-yüan and his associates. In *Kao-seng chuan* 6, Tsung is said to have had an inscribed stele erected at the entrance to the Tung-lin monastery in memory of Hui-yüan. According to Ch'en Shun-yü in the eleventh-century *Lu-shan chi* (Records of Mount Lu), this monastery was the site where the correct text of the preface was engraved in stone after Hui-yüan's "Brief Notes on Mount Lu" that ends with a mention of the Stone Gate. As Hui-yüan stated in *Yu-shan chi* (Notes on Wandering in the Mountain) of A.D. 403, he made two trips to this gorge.[80] Tsung Ping may well have had these excursions in mind when he referred to a Stone Gate in his essay. Another mountain climber, Hsieh Ling-yün, had also heard of this scenic spot, since he mentioned it in connection with his friend T'an-lung, who had studied on Mount Lu.[81] Two phrases of some importance in Tsung's essay, *chih-yu* and *ch'ang shen*, also occur in some form in the earlier preface and poem on ascending the Stone Gate.[82] Whether *chih-yu* is or is not read as a compound, the eighth line of the poem indicates that substantial being diminishes in the climb toward immaterial heights, a view of landscape that tallies with Tsung's. "Spirit was thereby exhilarated" (*shen i chih ch'ang*) is not an emphatic statement in the preface, but it does appear in a passage on the selfless, hence soul-expanding, enjoyment of nature. Tsung Ping might have recalled this discussion as he concluded the essay on painting.

There *ch'ang shen*, translated as "freely expand the spirit," contained the gist of Tsung's approach to viewing landscape. Its use in the essay and in the earlier preface on climbing the Stone Gate would seem to derive from the circle of Wang Hsi-chih and the Orchid Pavilion poets. Hatano Takeshi believes that this phrase parallels *san huai*, the therapeutic "release of feelings" in nature experienced at the spring purification festival. Obi Kōichi lists several similar phrases beginning with *ch'ang* that occur in poems by Wang Su-chih, Wang Yün-chih, and Sun Ch'o composed on this occasion.[83] The characterization of the landscape and of communal emotions during the Stone Gate expedition has also been compared to Wang Hsi-chih's summary of the circumstances at the Orchid Pavilion.[84] Knowledge of this literature would certainly have reached Mount Lu by way of gentry connections at the southern capital. Hui-yüan and his brother Hui-ch'ih are known to have been in contact with members of the eminent Wang clan from Lang-yeh such as Wang Mi (360–407), and a certain lay disciple on Mount Lu, Wang Ch'iao-chih or Ch'i-chih (d. ca. 417), must have been a close relative of Wang Hsi-chih himself. In his associations with laymen, Hui-yüan was presumably emulating the Buddhist theologian Chih Tun, whose conversation was so admired by the gentry of the southern capital and whose climbing expeditions in the K'uai-chi district were undertaken with writers such as Sun Ch'o and Wang Hsi-chih.[85] However, under Hui-yüan's guidance the aristocratic cult of landscape was directed toward devotional ends.

What was the "landscape Buddhism" of the preface on climbing the Stone Gate? Like the poetry-writing contest during the spring purification festival at the Orchid Pavilion, it was a communal experience of emotional release in a natural setting of great beauty. Two features of the occasion are especially characteristic of activities on Mount Lu. Aesthetic impressions served to stimulate meditation in a manner somewhat analogous to the devotional practice of visualizing the Buddha's body. In effect, Hui-yüan made use of the setting as an aid to realization just as he would focus the minds of his congregation on the images of Amitābha or the Buddha's Shadow.[86] His writings reflect a continuing interest in the process of visualization and the concrete manifestations of the Buddha. The visionary aspect of Hui-yüan's teaching is directly connected with the use of icons for meditation, which had a great appeal for lay devotees. As Zürcher notes, "This urge to have a concrete object of worship, perceptible by the senses, characterizes the Buddhism of the Lu-shan."[87]

Another aspect of this Buddhism was the strong feeling of community among the lay disciples on Mount Lu. In the collective vow for rebirth in the Western Paradise of 402, all those present expressed their intention to help each other ascend to the supernatural realm of the mountain paradise, "mindful of the principle of 'marching together.'"[88] The smaller group of men who climbed the Stone Gate two years earlier were moved to express their shared joy in a communal hymn in honor of the occasion. It is conceivable that this side of the devotional practices on Mount Lu touched even such a rugged individualist as Hsieh Ling-yün, who was at least a long-distance disciple of Hui-yüan's.[89] A belief that shared understanding enhanced the appreciation of scenery was an integral part of Hsieh's own "landscape Buddhism." Elevated by a mystical insight into the natural order, he could still regret the lack of an empathetic mind to validate his religious experience.[90] And, unlike Tsung Ping, he felt alone in his communion with the universe, quite cut off from the sages of antiquity.

The occasion described in the "Introduction to Poetry on Wandering at the Stone Gate" requires little explanation. Interestingly enough, Hui-yüan and his companions are inspired to climb by poems on landscape. Through their efforts they gain a view, which is initially characterized in general terms; then they note the layout of mountain and rock formations that seem to indicate the palace grounds of the immortals. Illusory qualities of shapes are underlined by shifting light and atmospheric effects, and a feeling of spatial disorientation is given by the blurring of sense impressions. These unsought-for perceptions arouse a selfless delight, which is then analyzed by the group as the correct response to phenomena. At sunset the view from on high suggests the vast scale of the universe; in turn this stimulates thoughts of eternal time and the remoteness of the Buddha. After meditating on him for a while, the group is moved by a shared emotion to compose a poem on their experience. Despite a few Taoist references, it treats the climb up the cliffs of the Stone Gate as a stage in a spiritual ascent that leads through meditation to Nirvāna. In the preface, purification of the mind through the perception of emptiness allows it to respond correctly without emotion and to seek the merging with the universal spirit that was the aim of Hui-yüan's teaching. A gradual detachment from illusory forms and an enlarging perspective that diminishes personal concerns are the dramatic equivalents of qualities that Tsung Ping valued in the landscape experience. Since the text itself is relatively untrodden ground, it can be presented without extensive commentary.

Introduction to Poetry on Wandering at the Stone Gate
by the Laymen of Mount Lu[B91]

The Stone Gate is over ten *li* south of the *vihāra* [Tung-lin monastery], and is also known as Screen Mountain. Its base joins the great range [of Mount Lu], and its form rises above the clustered hills. It founds the juncture of three streams; standing close together, it initiates their currents. The inclining cliffs darkly gleam from above; they receive their external shapes from Nature. On this account it was named [the Stone Gate]. Although this spot is but one corner of the Lu range, nonetheless it is the most extraordinary view of the region. All this was known through earlier accounts, but there were many who had never seen it themselves. This was perhaps due to the fact that the waterfall was so precipitous that trails for men and beasts were cut off, and, since paths wind about twisting hills, access was blocked and walking difficult. Hence few people have visited it.

In the second month of spring in the fourth year of Lung-an (A.D. 400), Shih [Hui-yüan], the Master of the Doctrine, who had been hymning the landscape, accordingly took up his ringed abbot's staff and wandered off. On this occasion there were some thirty men of like mind among his companions. Together we donned our robes and set off at dawn, our doubts only increasing exhilaration. Although the forests were gloomy and valleys deep, we still broke through a path and vied to push forward. And ascending the heights and treading on rock we were wholly at ease through what gave us pleasure. On reaching [the gorge], we pulled ourselves up by trees and grasped for creepers, traversing the perilous and plumbing the precipitous; only when arms stretched apelike were extended to each other did we advance to a summit. Thereupon, leaning against the cliff, we seized the view and clearly saw what was below, experiencing for the first time the beauty of the seven ridges and the gathering of exceptional sights in this spot.

The twin gatetowers soared up in opposition before us, while layered precipices gleamed about behind; peaks and hills twisted and turned to form a screen, and high cliffs built up on all sides to support the roof of heaven. Within there was a stone tower and a rocky pond, semblances of palace halls and representational shapes; it was all most pleasing.

Limpid brooks ran separately and poured together; pellucid depths were of a mirrorlike translucency in the Heavenly Pond.[92] Patterned rocks displayed their colors, tangibly present in their glory, while tamarisks, pines, plants, and herbs dazzled the eyes with their luxuriance; all that constitutes spirited beauty was present.

On this day, various emotions hastened our enjoyment and we gazed at length without tiring. We had not looked about for long before the weather changed several times. In the dusty gathering of mist and fog, all things concealed their forms; in the reflected illumination of radiating light, the myriad peaks were inverted as mirrored scenery. At intervals of clearing, appearances had a numinous quality yet could not be fathomed.

When we went on to climb, hovering birds fluttered pinions and crying apes harshly clamored. Homing clouds driving back called to mind the visitations of feathered men; mournful cries blended in harmony like the embodiment of mysterious tones. Even though they were heard only faintly, one's spirit was exhilarated. And although in enjoying one did not expect delight, nonetheless happiness lasted throughout the day. At that time, this experience of empty pleasure truly had subtleness yet was not easy to define.

We then withdrew to seek an explanation. For, as the assembled beings in these cliffs and valleys lacked conscious selves, response was not through emotions.[93] Yet they awakened an exhilaration that drew us onward to such an extent. Could it not be that emptiness and luminosity clarify reflections, and quietness and distance deepen the emotions? Altogether we repeated this discussion several times and its subtlety was still inexhaustible.

Suddenly the sun announced evening, and this world was gone. We then became aware of the mysterious perception of world-renouncers and comprehended the true nature of enduring things: could it be merely the landscape that caused such divine pleasure? Thereupon, as we roamed on cliffs and precipices, shifting our gaze to scan all sides, the nine rivers [of Kiukiang] were like a belt and foothills formed anthill mounds. From this one could deduce that as in forms there are large and small, so understanding is also proportionate.[94]

We then sighed deeply, lamenting that though the universe is of long duration, ancient and modern are of a piece. The Vulture Peak is far away, and the overgrown path is daily more impassable. Without the Sage [Śākyamuni], even though His influence and traces [of His teaching] still remain, His profound enlightenment must necessarily be remote.[95] With feeling we reflected for a long while. As each of us was enjoying the shared happiness of a rare time, moved by an auspicious moment that would be hard to recreate, emotions burst forth from our midst, and we accordingly hymned them together:

Super-mundane exhilaration is without root cause;
When one is moved by insight, exhilaration comes of itself.
Suddenly, as we heard of roaming at the Stone Gate,
These unusual lays brought forth our hidden feelings.
Plucking up our robes, we thought of cloud-charioteering [immortals];
And gazing at precipices, we envisaged the tiered city [of K'un-lun].
Spurring forward, we climbed up the great cliffs
Without perceiving the diminishing of substantial being.
Lifting up our heads, we ascended the cloudy gatetower
As remote as if it reached to the Great Purity [of heaven].

Seated upright, we turned the empty wheel [of the mind],
Setting in motion the Norm from within Profundity.
Spirits and immortals share in the changes of all beings;
It is better that both [self and others] be altogether darkened [in
    oblivion].[96]

CONCLUSION

It has been noted that by the fourth century mountains lost their aura of sacred
terror and became accepted sites for philosophical and aesthetic appreciations.[97] In
the "landscape Buddhism" of Mount Lu, the world of man effectively expanded to
include all of nature. Communal devotion was directed toward the Buddha at the
end of the "Introduction to Poetry on Wandering at the Stone Gate." Similarly, the
sages and worthies of antiquity shone from afar as guides in the concluding
paragraph of Tsung Ping's essay on painting landscape. To appreciate nature in the
Mount Lu community was to attempt to experience the mind of the sage who had
ultimately merged with the universe. Gazing from a height into the empty distance
was analogous to the detached view that diminished worldly concerns and achieved
insight into the natural order. Sages and virtuous men played important roles in
Tsung's writing as models for the viewing of landscape with mental clarity.
Through meditation in front of nature or a painted landscape, the onlooker could
purify his heart as did the climbers at the Stone Gate. When scenes are depicted for
religious ends, the main concern is to achieve the correct image of Reality; the
landscape experience itself validates the painting of landscapes. Theoretically it is an
"unpeopled" wilderness that is appreciated in art as in life, but nature is rendered
more accessible through the intermediary figure of the sage, the center of a rational
universe ruled by karmic law. In these texts, as in contemporary scenes of nature, the
human image seems to loom over the landscape setting.

1. Chang Yen-yüan, *Li-tai ming-hua chi* (Records of Famous Painters in History) in
William R. B. Acker, *Some T'ang and Pre-T'ang Texts on Chinese Painting* (hereafter *T&PT*),
2 vols. (Leiden, 1954, 1974), 2:131–132.

2. See Wm. Theodore de Bary et al., *Sources of Chinese Tradition* (New York, 1960),
pp. 292–293; James Cahill, "Confucian Elements in the Theory of Painting," *The Confucian
Persuasion*, ed. Arthur F. Wright (Stanford, 1960), p. 120.

3. See J. D. Frodsham, "The Origins of Chinese Nature Poetry," *AM* (1960–1961),
n.s. 8:101–103.

4. Tsung Ping, who consistently refused posts offered to him by prominent men of the

late fourth and early fifth centuries, is classified as a recluse in *Sung shu* 93 and *Nan shih* 75; also see *Li-tai ming-hua chi* 6, trans. in Acker, *T&PT*, 2:115–129. Tsung was noted for his calligraphy and painting as well as for his philosophical discussions and lute-playing. His interests were shared by his wife, and after her death he sought consolation in Buddhism. In Hui-yüan's biography in *Kao-seng chuan* 6, Tsung is recorded as a member of what was later to be called the "White Lotus Society," but it is unlikely that he was present on Mount Lu when the joint vow for rebirth was taken in front of a statue of Amitābha. His stay of some fifty days probably took place ten years later, before family affairs forced him to return home to Chiang-ling, another noted Buddhist center. Over a decade later, Tsung acknowledges his indebtedness to Hui-yüan's teachings in the *Ming fo lun*. See Susan Bush, "Two Fifth-Century Texts on Landscape Painting and the 'Landscape Buddhism' of Mount Lu" (paper written for the ACLS sponsored conference on "Theories of the Arts in China," June, 1979), pp. 24–26, available in depository sets). For material dealing with Hui-yüan and the Buddhist aspects of Tsung Ping's life, see Erik Zürcher, *The Buddhist Conquest of China* (hereafter BCC), 2 vols. (Leiden, 1959), 1:15, 143, 218–219, 252–253, 263–264, 268–271; 2:406, n. 46. The sequence of narration in the *Sung-shu* suggests that Tsung's stay took place after a battle of 412: see Kimata Tokuo, "Concerning Hui-yüan and Tsung Ping" (in Japanese, English summary), in *Eon kenkyū* (Hui-yüan Studies), ed. Kimura Eiichi, 2 vols. (Kyoto, 1960–1962), 2:297. For a summary of the historical events at Chiang-ling and Mount Lu in 412, see J. D. Frodsham, *The Murmuring Stream: The Life and Works of the Chinese Nature Poet Hsieh Ling-yün (385–433), Duke of K'ang-lo*, 2 vols. (Kuala Lumpur, 1967), 1:15–20; also Paul Demiéville, "Présentation d'un poète," *TP* (1970), 56:260–261; also in *Choix d'études sinologiques* (Leiden, 1973).

5. The first section of the *Ming fo lun* is translated in Walter Liebenthal, "The Immortality of the Soul in Chinese Thought," *MN* (1952), 8:378–394. The Chinese text is included in *Ch'üan Sung wen* 21 (Complete Sung Prose; hereafter *CSW*), in Yen K'o-chün, *Ch'üan Shang-ku San-tai Ch'in-Han San-kuo Liu-ch'ao wen* (Complete Prose Writing of Ancient Antiquity, the Three Dynasties, the Ch'in and Han Dynasties, the Three Kingdoms, and the Six Dynasties) [1894]. As a Buddhist treatise, it was transmitted in the *Hung-ming chi* (Collection for Propagation and Clarification), compiled in the early sixth century by Seng-yu (445–518): see Jimbun Kagaku Kenkyūjo, Chūsei Shisōshi Kenkyūhan, ed., *Gumyōshū kenkyū* (Studies on the *Hung-ming chi*), 3 vols. (Kyoto, 1973–1975), 2:81–143.

6. See Nakamura Shigeo, *Chūgoku garon no tenkai* (The Development of Chinese Painting Theory) (hereafter *CGT*) (Kyoto, 1965), pp. 59–81; Hatano Takeshi, "'Sō Hei gasansui jo' no tokushitsu" (Two Characteristics of Tsung Ping's Preface on Landscape Paintings), *CCBK* (1968), 7:37–54.

7. The intepretation of the *Ming fo lun* passage cited below in note 37 is based in part on correspondence with Professor Whalen Lai in the fall of 1979.

8. For Hsieh Ling-yün's approach to landscape, see Richard Mather, "The Landscape Buddhism of the Fifth-Century Poet Hsieh Ling-yün," *JAS* (1958), 18:67–79.

9. Paul Demiéville, "La montagne dans l'art littéraire chinois," *France-Asie/Asia* (Autumn, 1965), 20:17; also in *Choix d'études sinologiques*.

10. For Ho Ch'eng-t'ien, see Zürcher, BCC, 1:15; 2:415, n. 42. Hui-yüan's influential statement "Spirit Does Not Perish" was the third section of his treatise of A.D. 404, *Sha-men*

pu ching wang-che lun (A Monk Does Not Bow Down Before a King), summarized in Zürcher, *BCC*, 1:238–239. For a revised version with explanation, see Richard Robinson, *Early Mādhyamika in India and China* (Madison, Milwaukee, and London, 1967), pp. 102–108. For a translation of the whole treatise, see Leon Hurvitz, "'Render unto Caesar' in Early Chinese Buddhism," *Sino-Indian Studies* (1957), 5(3–4):2–36.

11. Wolfgang Bauer, *China and the Search for Happiness: Recurring Themes in Four Thousand Years of Chinese Cultural History*, trans. Michael Shaw (New York, 1976), p. 156. Used by permission of The Continuum Publishing Corporation.

12. See Kimata, *Eon kenkyū*, 2:343–344.

13. The version of Tsung's essay in *CSW* 21 is taken from *Li-tai ming-hua chi* 6 but contains some misprints.

14. See Nakamura, *CGT*, pp. 72, 74.

15. He quotes mainly from Taoist works as well as Confucian classics in the *Ming fo lun*, and also cites some phrases from Buddhist *sūtras*: see Liebenthal, *MN* 8:378–394. Hui-yüan is said to have lectured on the Rites to Tsung Ping and Lei Tz'u-tsung (386–448): see Zürcher, *BCC*, 1:218, 252–253.

16. Tsung Ping, *Ming fo lun*, *CSW* 21:16a; see Zürcher, *BCC*, 1:263–264.

17. For this point, see Wing-tsit Chan, *A Source Book in Chinese Philosophy* (Princeton, 1963), p. 333.

18. Tsung, *Ming fo lun*, *CSW* 21:13b; also *Gumyōshū kenkyū*, 1:63–64, 2:134; see Liebenthal, *MN* 8:394.

19. Ibid. This rather obscure statement is evidently an expression of "landscape Buddhism:" see Nakamura, *CGT*, p. 79.

20. Zürcher, *BCC*, 1:270. For the theme of the "spirit journey," see Susan Bush, "On Beyond the Thunders: Some Problems in Han and Six Dynasties Iconography" (conference paper for "China's Past Unearthed: The Reconciliation of New Discoveries and the Historical Records of the Early Imperial Period," San Francisco, March 26–28, 1980), pp. 51–54 (available in the set of conference papers).

21. These magical powers are stressed in some *Ming fo lun* passages translated in Liebenthal, *MN* 8:388–391.

22. Zürcher, *BCC*, 1:268; again see *Eon kenkyū*, 2:343–344.

23. Alexander Soper, *Textual Evidence for the Secular Arts of China in the Period from Liu Sung through Sui* (Ascona, 1967) (hereafter *Textual Evidence*), p. 16. Shang Tzu-p'ing, or Hsiang Ch'ang, was a Taoist recluse of the first century A.D. who absolutely refused gifts even from friends, once accepting only the hooves of a horse cooked for him. He left his family after his children were married to roam on the Five Sacred Peaks: see Huang-fu Mi, *Kao-shih chuan* (*Ts'ung-shu chi-ch'eng* ed.) 2:83–84.

24. See the opening stanza of Hui-yüan's inscription on this icon cited in part in n. 42 below: Zürcher, *BCC*, 1:243. Needless to say, this sort of inscription is extremely difficult to translate. Dr. Raoul Birnbaum prefers to interpret *ying* as "reflection," since this conveys the idea of light streaming from the Buddha's body.

25. See Nakamura, *CGT*, p. 79; Acker, *T&PT*, 2:116, 119, ns. 9, 10; Leon Hurvitz, "Tsung Ping's Comments on Landscape Painting," *AA* (1970), 32:154.

26. For Shang Tzu-p'ing, see n. 23 above.

27. See *Li-tai ming-hua chi* 7; Acker, *T&PT*, 2:151. It was Ping, rather than Ts'e's father, who is said to be responsible for the picture of Shang Tzu-p'ing. For the practice of whistling, see Douglass Alan White, "Ch'eng-kung Sui Poetic Essay on Whistling: The Hsiao-fu" (Harvard University Honors Thesis, 1964).

28. See Erik Zürcher, "Recent Studies on Chinese Painting, I," *TP* (1964), 51:292; also Acker, *T&PT*, 2:126–127; n. 4 above. Tsung Ts'e's biographies are in *Nan-Ch'i shu* 54 and *Nan-shih* 75. Hsio-yen Shih notes that the former places the Yung-yeh monastery in the vicinity of Mount Lu.

29. See Soper, *Textual Evidence*, p. 20: Frodsham, *AM* 8:75.

30. This was a painting of "Villages in Yung-chia," probably the name of a region in modern Chekiang associated with Wang Hsi-chih and Hsieh Ling-yün. There is no indication that Tsung traveled in the eastern coastal provinces, and this painting title was once attributed to a minor Southern Ch'i artist: see Michael Sullivan, *The Birth of Landscape Painting in China* (Berkeley and Los Angeles, 1962), pp. 119–120.

31. See ibid., pp. 116, 119, 121, 123–124; Acker, *T&PT*, 2:94–102.

32. See the biography of Tai Yung in *Sung-shu* 93.

33. See Osvald Sirén, *The Chinese on the Art of Painting* (Peiping, 1936), pp. 14–16; Shio Sakanishi, *The Spirit of the Brush* (London, 1939), pp. 37–40; Acker, *T&PT*, 2:116–117. Also see de Bary, *Sources of Chinese Tradition*, pp. 292–293. Hsio-yen Shih's version is for an anthology of early Chinese painting texts now in preparation. For the separate English translations of Tsung Ping's essay, see Alexander Soper, "Early Chinese Landscape Painting," *Art Bulletin* (1941), 23:164; Sullivan, *Birth*, pp. 102–103; Lin Yutang, *The Chinese Theory of Art* (New York, 1967), pp. 31–32; Hurvitz, *AA* 32:148–154. Since this text is included in *PWCSHP* 15, Arthur Waley's reason for suspecting its authenticity is invalid: see James Cahill, "Wu Chen, A Chinese Landscapist and Bamboo Painter of the Fourteenth Century" (Ph. D. dissertation, University of Michigan, 1958), p. 6, n. 6.

34. See Nakamura, *CGT*, pp. 59–80; Hatano, *CCBK* 7:37–54; Kimata, *Eon kenkyū*, 2:287–364 (English summary, pp. 17–18).

35. See Fukunaga Mitsuji, *Geijutsu ronshū* (A Collection of Essays on Fine Arts) (*Chūgoku bunmei sen*, vol. 14) (Tokyo, 1971), pp. 147–164; Richard Mather, "The Mystical Ascent of the T'ien-t'ai Mountains: Sun Ch'o's *Yu T'ien-t'ai-shan fu*," *MS* (1961), 20:226–245.

36. See Walter Liebenthal, "Shih Hui-yüan's Buddhism as Set forth in His Writings," *JAOS* (1950), 70:248, n. 23; 251, n. 53.

37. Tsung, *Ming fo lun, CSW* 21:3a; *Gumyōshū kenkyū*, 1:41–42; 2:89.

38. Tsung, *Ming fo lun, CSW* 21:10b; *Gumyōshū kenkyū*, 2:118.

39. For a definition of *ling* in contemporary Buddhist texts, see Walter Liebenthal, *The Book of Chao (Chao lun)* (*Monumenta Serica Monograph* 13) (Peking, 1948), p. 27, n. 99; also see n. 36 above. For the dangers of attachment, see Tsung, *Ming fo lun, CSW* 21:5a; Liebenthal, *MN* 8:392.

40. In a Western context, Keats' phrase refers of course to the building of character through harsh experience: see Douglas Bush, *John Keats: His Life and Writings* (New York and London, 1966), pp. 125–126.

41. See Liebenthal, *MN* 8:394; *CSW* 21:5b.

42. Zürcher, *BCC*, 1:242–243, (verse 1, ll. 1–4; verse 4, ll. 9–10).

43. Ibid., 1:124; also 88, 90, 125–126.

44. Paul Demiéville, "La pénétration du Bouddhisme dans la tradition philosophique chinoise," *Cahiers d'histoire mondiale* (1956), 3 (1):30; also see 28–35.

45. See nn. 89 and 90 below.

46. See Zürcher, *BCC*, 1:143.

47. Liebenthal, "Shih Hui-yüan's Buddhism," *JAOS* 70:257–258; see Nakamura, *CGT*, pp. 78, 177, 361 n. 19.

48. *Lei* is used at least once in the meaning of "to be like" in the *Ming fo lun*: see *Gumyōshū kenkyū*, 1:47, 2:100; Liebenthal, *MN* 8:394.

49. See Kiyohiko Munakata, "Concepts of *Lei* and *Kan-lei* in Early Chinese Art Theory," in this volume. Elsewhere he explains *lei* as "the mystic quality intrinsic to a certain category of objects": Kiyohiko Munakata, "Some Methodological Considerations," *AA* (1976), 38:310.

50. For example, in the controversial phrases an emendation of *hui*, "to paint," for *lei* has sometimes been preferred: see Hsü Fu-kuan, *Chung-kuo i-shu ching-shen* (The Chinese Aesthetic Spirit) (hereafter *CKISCS*) (Taichung, 1966), pp. 240–241; James J. Y. Liu, "Literature, Art, and the Tao in Pre-T'ang Writings" (paper written for the ACLS conference on "Theories of the Arts in China" available in depository sets at research libraries), p. 15. For different interpretations of the syntax of the sentences in which *lei* occurs, see Bush, "Two Fifth-Century Texts on Landscape Painting," pp. 49–50.

51. See Acker, *T&PT*, 1:xliii–xlv.

52. See ibid., 2:126–127. Here Acker, who goes on to discuss Hsieh Ho on Tsung Ping, quotes estensively from Zürcher, "Recent Studies on Chinese Painting," pp. 389–392.

53. For example, both *sui-chi* and *sui-lei* occur in *Erh-chiao lun* (Discussion of the Two Teachings) of A.D. 570/571: see *Taishō issai kyō kankō kai*, ed. Takakusu J. and Watanabe K., 100 vols. (Tokyo, 1924–1934) (hereafter T), 77:375b–380c; also Zürcher, BCC, 1:272. I am indebted to Professor Victor Mair for these references and for the opinions on the first of the "six limbs" given in correspondence of August, 1979.

54. See Hatano, *CCBK* 7:38–47. Note that this text is more an essay than a traditional preface.

55. See Zürcher, *BCC*, 1:279.

56. Ibid., 1:269–271.

57. Nakamura notes that in the *Ming fo lun* Tao is identified with the non-activity or void of the Taoists as well as with the *Dharmakāya* or *Nirvāna* of the Buddhists. In the second phrase, the *CTPS* edition followed by Hatano has *ying*, "to reflect light" or "to shine," a character that also appears in the concluding phrases of the essay. The *WSHY* and *PWCSHP* editions have *ying*, "to respond," which has generally been preferred by most commentators and translators. The Neo-Taoist saint who was one with nature, embodying the Tao and the responding to things without involvement, was often identified or confused with the Buddha in this period: Zürcher, *BCC*, 1:90–91, 133, 225–226, 310. In the *Ming fo lun*, purification of thoughts through contemplation on the void and the "daily diminishing" of actions and desires (see *Lao Tzu* 48) is the course that should be followed by those who aspire

to *Nirvāna* or the pure existence of spirit: see Nakamura, CGT, pp. 68–69, 72; Liebenthal, *MN* 8:388, 392–394.

58. Although the general meaning of the third sentence can be grasped, the grammar of *chih yu erh ch'ü ling* is difficult to determine. *Chih yu* is a phrase where the expected order of the characters is reversed, and *chih* has been taken as the equivalent of a modifier, noun, or verb. Nakamura prefers to understand *chih-yu* as a compound analogous to *wei-yu,* "false existence" or "illusion," in the *Ming fo lun.* Following the *PWCSHP* version of the text, he accepts the variant of *ch'ü,* "to hasten," which he interprets as "hataraku" or "function" in this reading: "As for landscape, it is substantial yet its functioning is spiritual" (Nakamura, *CGT,* pp. 70, 73). Hatano, on the other hand, prefers the more common *ch'ü* of the *WSHY* and *CTPS* editions, which can also mean "to tend toward," as well as "interest" or "charm." He notes two possible readings of the phrase corresponding roughly to: "its substance is existence and its charm is spiritual;" "it is based in existence but tends toward the spiritual." See Hatano, *CCBK* 7:39; also Kimata, *Eon kenkyū,* 2:346. The last reading, preferred both by Kimata and by Kohara Hironobu, has been translated more precisely by Hurvitz as "having the existent as their basic stuff, yet they tend toward the numinal realm": Hurvitz, *AA* 32:148. It is supported by a verbal usage of *chih* as "to take as substantial" or "to have as a basis" in the *Ming fo lun*: see Liebenthal, *MN* 8:393, n. 297; also Nakamura, *CGT,* p. 69. It is also possible that *ch'ü,* toward the end of the phrase, is used verbally in a Buddhist sense as "to tend toward a future plane of existence" predestined by karmic law: see Morohashi Tetsuji, *Dai Kan-Wa ji-ten* (Tokyo, 1955–1960), 10:885, no. 37207:2.

59. In the text, the Yellow Emperor is referred to as Hsien-yüan, a personal name based on the name of a hill, and the clan name Kung identifies Confucius. For the legendary rulers, the Yellow Emperor and Yao, and the hermit sages, Kuang-ch'eng-tzu and Ta-k'uei (or -wei), see B. Karlgren, "Legends and Cults in Ancient China," *BMFEA* (1946), 18:212–214, 279, 289–295. The lives of Hsü Yu, who refused the empire, and Shu-ch'i and Po-i, the brothers from "Ku-chu," who declined their father's inheritance and starved to death, are in *Shih chi* 61. For their stories, and the locations of the listed mountains, along with a line-up of the sages and recluses associated with them, see Hurvitz, *AA* 32:148–150. The text has *ta-meng,* a place where the sun sets according to *Huai-nan Tzu* 13, instead of Mounts T'ai and Meng, from which the world looked small to Confucius, or to Confucius and Yao respectively, as noted in the *Ming fo lun*: see Liebenthal, *MN* 8:381; n. 18 above.

60. According to *Lun-yü* 6:21, "The wise find pleasure in water; the [humane] find pleasure in hills:" James Legge, *The Chinese Classics,* 5 vols. (Hong Kong, 1960), 1:102. Note that the *jen* of *jen-che* could be used in early Chinese Buddhism as a transliteration of *muni,* or "holy man," as in Śākyamuni: see *HJAS* (1957), 20:379–380.

61. *Fa tao,* "to take the Tao as a model [or law]," occurs in *Lao Tzu* 25; the *Ming fo lun* states that only the Buddha can do this by means of his spirit or spiritual insight: see Nakamura, *CGT,* p. 74; Hatano, *CCBK* 7:40. As for *mei tao,* the word *mei,* "to charm, to captivate, to pay homage to," has been interpreted as "*to display the beauty of the Tao*" by analogy with Hsieh Ling-yün's usage: see Liu, "Landscape, Art, and the Tao," pp. 12–13.

62. The mountains mentioned are those located in the modern provinces of Kiangsi, Hunan, Hupei, and Szechwan, and presumably indicate the scope of Tsung's travels. In the

second phrase of the first sentence, the term *ch'ieh-k'uo*, found in Ode 48 of the *Shih ching* is usually taken either as "separated from" or "attached to," but can also be read as "toil and suffering." Hatano prefers the last reading because of a passage in the *Ming fo lun*: see Hatano, *CCBK* 7:41. Nakamura, on the other hand, interprets it as "to stroll about," a meaning of the term in the Chin and Wei histories. It has been translated as "roamed with abandon" because of the sixth meaning given in reference to this line in Morohashi, *Dai Kan-Wa ji-ten*, 6:590, no. 5917:14. The first sentence ends with a well-known phrase about the approach of old age from *Lun-yü* 7:18, to emphasize the depth of Tsung's devotion to mountain climbing: see Legge, *The Chinese Classics*, 1:200.

63. The next sentence may simply refer to Tsung's illness and subsequent inability to climb mountains. *Ning ch'i*, "to concentrate vital breath," is probably comparable to *ning yü shen* of *Chuang Tzu* 19, the "concentration of spirit" achieved by a Taoist immortal, and hence may indicate Taoist health practices (although it could also refer to Buddhist yoga): see James Legge, *The Sacred Books of China: The Texts of Taoism*, 2 vols. (New York, 1962), 2:15. The following phrase with the term "Stone Gate" is problematical, and Hatano does not even hazard an interpretation of the verbs. A Stone Gate is mentioned in *Lun-yü* 14:41, where the gatekeeper comments on the futility of Confucius' actions in inauspicious times to one of his disciples: see Legge, *The Chinese Classics*, 1:290. In English translations, "those at the Stone Gate" have generally been thought to be people who continue to attempt the impossible like Confucius, or, alternatively, people who withdraw from action like the gatekeeper. Hurvitz would have the term refer to the Confucian tradition as opposed to the Taoist practices of the previous phrase: see Hurvitz, *AA* 32:151. Hsü considers the Stone Gate to be the name of a mountain that Tsung feared he could no longer climb, but does not try to identify which of the various Stone Gate mountains it might be: see Hsü, *CKISCS*, p. 139. Kimata also seems to favor such an interpretation, although his summary of the text is extremely abbreviated at this point: see *Eon kenkyū*, 2:347. Only Nakamura identifies the Stone Gate as the name of a gorge in the Lu Mountain range, climbed and celebrated in writing by members of Hui-yüan's community at least once in A.D. 400 (see below). This Stone Gate should not be confused with the mountain in modern Chekiang that Hsieh Ling-yün describes: see Nakamura, *CGT*, p. 75; Frodsham, *AM* 8:84-85, 98-99.

64. Like most English versions, the translation accords with Hatano's interpretation that *i* and *hsin* are the "imagination" and "mind" of later men, not the "intention" and "heart," for example, of "truths" and "meaning" respectively, as in Nakamura and Kimata's readings. Hatano notes that the *Ming fo lun*'s descriptions of the powers of the human spirit, or *ching-shen*, support this view: see Hatano, *CCBK* 7:41-43; also Liebenthal, *MN* 8:380-381, 384-385.

65. The phrase "form a distance" is introduced by *shih*, "actually," in *T'ai-p'ing yü-lan* (*SPTK* ed.) 750:10b. Following Kobayashi Taichirō, the Japanese commentators believe that Tsung advocates holding up thin, unglazed silk and sketching the outlines of a view seen through it to ensure the correct proportions in a landscape composition: see Kobayashi Taichirō, *Chūgoku kaiga shi ronkō* (Studies on Chinese Painting History) (Kyoto, 1947), p. 65. They also generally take "K'un Lang" as referring to the K'un-lun mountains and the Lang gardens of the Immortals; however, Lang-feng was the name of the central peak of the K'un-lun range: see Yü Chien-hua ed., *Li-tai ming-hua chi* (hereafter *LTMHC*) (Shanghai, 1964),

p. 130; David Hawkes, *Ch'u Tz'u: The Songs of the South* (London, 1959), pp. 29, 136. These semimythical mountains to the west were noted for their great size, and may stand here for hypothetical large-scale mountains.

66. Mounts Sung and Hua are two of the Five Sacred Peaks often paired in poetry: here they evidently indicate the *yang* element of height. *Hsüan-p'in* is "the mysterious female" of the *Lao Tzu* 1:6—"the valley spirit dies not.... The female mystery thus do we name": Legge, *The Texts of Taoism*, 1:51. Its "soul," or *ling*, seems to refer to the *yin* side of landscape, associated with the vagina-like aspects of valleys. Nakamura's text (*CGT*, p. 71) has an extra possessive *chih* in the phrase discussing the effects of diminution.

67. Hatano's commentary on paragraph 5 notes specific phrases that occur in connection with the viewing of nature in the *Shih-shuo hsin-yü*. Thus *hui-hsin*, "accord by the mind," appears in a remark that can be translated: "The spot which suits the mind isn't necessarily far away:" Richard Mather trans., *Shih-shuo Hsin-yü: A New Account of Tales of the World* (Minneapolis, 1976), p. 60. This is a common truth about about the appreciation of scenery, the subject taken as the topic of the initial sentence by Hsü Fu-kuan in *CKISCS*, p. 241. An alternative interpretation is favored by Nakamura in *CGT*, pp. 76–79. He would have the first phrase refer to the painter's perceptions of landscape, gained through spiritual communion with nature, which are to be lodged in painting. His Japanese paraphrase might lead to James Cahill's English translation: "Now, if one who considers the right principle to be *response to his eyes and accord with his heart* perfects his skill in keeping with this [principle], then all eyes will respond to, and all hearts be in accord with [his paintings]": Cahill, "Confucian Elements in the Theory of Painting," p. 119. Cahill's translation again points up the problematic aspect of *lei*, which he takes as a preposition in the second phrase. Questions of translation also arise in connection with the introductory phrase. Should the *che* be taken as a pronoun or as a particle marking off an impersonal statement for explanation, as in paragraph 3? Hurvitz interprets it as a pronoun, "someone who," that refers to the painter (*AA* 32:152), the subject of the following phrase as in Nakamura's Japanese version. Acker, whose English rendering of the whole sentence is more literal, understands the first phrase as an impersonal topic and translates *che* as "thing" (*T&PT*, 2:117). In the English version given above, it has been taken as an untranslatable particle. Another problem is the rendering of *li*, a key term in this paragraph, as has been discussed above in the text.

68. *Shen ch'ao*, "the spirit becomes transcendent," could simply describe the effect of a landscape poem on a reader: "I always feel my spirit transported and my body far removed": Mather, *Shih-shuo hsin-yü*, p. 133. The succeeding phrase, *li te*, "truth is attained," occurs in the "Great Appendix" of the *Book of Changes*, where it indicates the sage's "mastery ... of all principles under the sky": see Z. D. Sung, *The Text of the Yi King* (James Legge's translation with Chinese text) (New York, 1969), p. 273. Hence Hatano identifies *li* as *shen-li*, here Divine Principle, Absolute or Truth. His reading of the second sentence of the paragraph is based on the *Ming fo lun*'s assertion of the relation between the cosmic spirit and individual souls. The viewer's response is to the transcendent spirit of the painter's perception, and when his own spirit in turn transcends, Truth is attained; see Hatano, *CCBK* 7:44–46. For Nakamura, who favors a similar interpretation, the *shen* and *li* of a landscape should have been transmitted by the painter along with its external forms for the response to be effective. Purification in accord with the laws of *karma* could lead to Enlightenment, and the direct

perception of emptiness in the landscape could stimulate this process: see Nakamura, *CGT*, pp. 77–78. Hsü Fu-kuan, whose frame of reference for this essay is Taoist not Buddhist, also understands the second sentence and the paragraph as a whole as involving the response of the viewer's spirit to the spirit of the landscape, which has entered the painting in a kind of sympathetic responsiveness in accord with universal laws (*tao-li*). It is the *shen* and *ling* of a landscape that the painter will be able to attain if his spirit is in harmony with nature: see Hsü, *CKISCS*, pp. 240–241. For Fukunaga Mitsuji, it is also a matter of a sympathetic response attained between the *shen* of a landscape and the *shen* of the painting, which in turn affects the *shen* of the viewer: see Fukunaga, *Geijutsu ronshū*, p. 161. On the other hand, T'ang Chün-i would simply have the passage describe an individual viewer's reaction in a natural manner: see T'ang Chün-i, *Yüan tao* II, *Chung-kuo che-hsüeh yüan-lun* (Discussion of the Sources of Chinese Philosophy), 3 vols. (Taipei, 1966–1973), 3:971–972. As noted in the text, there are widely differing interpretations of this crucial sentence.

69. At the suggestion of Masatoshi Nagatomi, *pen* is taken as a noun, "essence," rather than as an adverb, "fundamentally." *Pen* stands in opposition to *chi*, "traces," in the preface to the *Vimalakīrti-nirdeśa* by Seng-chao (374–414) in a passage that also mentions the response of the sages: "Thus subtle connections are difficult to explain and the response of sages is not identical. If essence is lacking, there is no way to send down traces; if traces are lacking, there is no way to manifest essence." 然幽關難啓，聖應不同。非本無以垂跡，非跡無以顯本。 (*Chu Wei-mo-chi ching* [T 38:327b]).

Tsung Ping may have conceived of forms and images in nature as in painting as operating on different levels as reflections of truth. In another interpretation, Raoul Birnbaum would take *ying-chi* as a compound, "reflection-traces," and, perhaps by analogy with the Buddha's Reflection Image at Nagahāra, have these be embodiments of Spirit to be copied by the painter, whose properly proportioned image of landscape could serve as an aid in meditation. He also notes that Tsung Ping must have been aware of the use of Buddhist icons for the purpose of visualizing, even if Tsung never actually painted such an image, and suggests that some inspiration might have come from Kālayaśas, a Central Asian master who specialized in this type of meditation: see Raoul Birnbaum, "Vision and Image: The Influence of Buddhist Meditation Teachings on Early Chinese Landscape Painting" (a paper presented at the International Association of Buddhist Studies at Columbia University, September 15–18, 1978), pp. 13–18.

70. *Ssu-huang*, "the four wildernesses," are "the ends of the earth" at the extremities of the four directions according to the *Erh ya*. Hatano notes a parallel to this phrase in the *Ming fo lun*'s description of the transcending spirits of the sages: "seated, they penetrate the universe": *CSW* 20:3a; cf. Liebenthal, *MN* 8:384–385, Hatano, *CCBK* 7:47.

71. *Wu jen chih yeh*, the "uninhabited wilderness" of *Chuang Tzu* 22, was the place where a marquis of Lu was advised "to cleanse your heart, to put away your desires, and to enjoy yourself:" Legge, *The Texts of Taoism*, 2:29–30. *T'ien-li* in the preceding phrase is problematical. Yü Chien-hua suggests that it be interpreted as "natural inclinations:" see Yü, *LTMHC*, p. 30. Nakamura would read *li*, "to incite," as *li*, "to oppress" or "cruel," and have *t'ien-li* be "natural dangers" such as fierce animals, commonly associated with the wilderness along with demonic dangers: see Nakamura, *CGT*, p. 79.

72. Nakamura (ibid.) considers the remote sages and worthies of the past, and the

myriad charms of nature, to be those depicted in the painting and hence accessible to the viewer. Leon Hurvitz believes that *ch'ü*, rendered as "delights" above, is used in a special Buddhist sense as *viṣaya*, and hence translates it as "object": see Hurvitz, *AA* 32:153–154.

73. *Ch'ang shen*, "to [freely] expand, or release, the spirit," which occurs at the end of the paragraph, can be traced back to the correspondence between Liu K'un (271–318) and his follower Lu Ch'en in *Wen hsüan* 25. Hatano considers Tsung Ping's usage to be closest to Lu Ch'en's, which has been translated as "Dein Geist hat schon alles durchdrungen." Erwin von Zach, *Die Chinesische Anthologie*, 2 vols. (Cambridge, Mass., 1958), 1:424; see Hatano, *CCBK* 7:47.

74. The Stone Gate gorge is "the ravine with the waterfall" located on the western side of Mount Lu near the Tung-lin monastery: see Zürcher, *BCC*, 1:241; Alexander Soper, *Literary Evidence for Early Buddhist Art in China* (Ascona, 1959) (hereafter *Literary Evidence*), p. 32; Wu Tsung-tz'u, *Lu-shan chih*, 2 vols. (Shanghai, 1933), 1:51a; map inset 47b–48a.

75. See Ch'en Shun-yü, *Lu-shan chi* (*Ts'ung-shu chi-ch'eng* ed.), p. 11. This text reports the vicissitudes of Hui-yüan's complete *K'uang-shan chi*. For Hui-yüan's *Lu-shan lüeh-chi*, see Kimura, *Eion kenkyū*, 1:72–74, 321–326.

76. See ibid., 1:320–321; cf. Wu, *Lu-shan chih*, 10B:4a; Ch'en San-li, *Lu-shan ku-chin yu-chi ts'ung-ch'ao* in *Lu-shan chih fu-k'an* 4 (Shanghai, 1934), A:6a–b. The preface to the poem was quoted as Hui-yüan's in the late seventeenth century in Ku Tsu-yü, *Tu-shih fang-yü chi-yao* (Shanghai, 1899), 83:6b.

77. See Frodsham, *AM* 8:98–99. These poems are collected along with Hui-yüan's extant writings on Mount Lu under the title of *Lu-shan chi-lüeh* (*Ts'ung-shu chi-ch'eng* ed.), p. 3; also see Kimura, *Eion kenkyū*, 1:319–320.

78. As "Hut Mountain," Mount Lu was considered the natural dwelling place of recluses and immortals. Taoist legends concerning it are reported in *Lu-shan lüeh-chi*: see Zürcher, *BCC*, 1:207–208; also see Mather, *Shih-shuo hsin-yü*, p. 288. Taoist attitudes toward landscape are treated in Paul Demiéville, "La montagne dans l'art littéraire chinois," pp. 7–32, especially pp. 10–18.

79. See *Ch'üan Chin-wen* (Yen, *Ch'üan Shang-ku San-tai Ch'in-Han San-kuo Liu-ch'ao wen*) 140:7a; Frodsham, *AM* 8:95–96; cf. Zürcher, *BCC*, 1:208. The landscape description in the preface on climbing the Stone Gate is quite full, as noted in Liu [Ch'ung-ch'un] Ta-chieh, *Chung-kuo wen-hsüeh fa-chan shih* (A History of the Development of Chinese Literature) (Shanghai, 1973), p. 327. Later prefaces written for poems composed on court outings are quite different in tone: see *Wen hsüan* 46; von Zach, *Die Chinesische Anthologie*, 2:848–858.

80. See n. 46 above; Zürcher, *BCC*, 1:253. For Hui-yüan's *Yu-shan chi*, see Kimura, *Eion kenkyū*, 1:74, 326; Mather, *Shih-shuo hsin-yü*, p. 288.

81. See Frodsham, *The Murmuring Stream*, 1:44.

82. See nn. 58 and 73 above.

83. See Hatano, *CCBK* 7:53–54; Obi Kōichi, *Chūgoku bungaku ni arawareta shizen to shizenkan-chūsei bungaku o chūshin to shite* (Nature and the Concept of Nature as They Appear in Chinese Literature—with the Emphasis on Medieval Literature) (Tokyo, 1963), pp. 210–213. For a discussion of the Orchid Pavilion gatherings and translations of some of the literature, see Frodsham, *AM* 8:88–93. For a translation of the Sun Ch'o couplet in which

ch'ang, glossed in the commentary as *t'ung* or "to penetrate to," is rendered as "inspired by," see Mather, *MS* 20:238–239.

84. See Teng Shih-liang, *Liang-Chin shih-lun* (Discussion of Chin Poetry) (Hong Kong, 1972), pp. 180–181. The style and phrasing of these two prefaces is also comparable.

85. For the literary circle of K'uai-chi which included the Tais, see Frodsham, *AM* 8:86–88. For Hui-yüan's connections with the Wangs, see Zürcher, *BCC*, 1:211, 213–214, 219.

86. For the practice of *buddhānusmrti* and the concern with the "body of the Buddha," see ibid., 1:219–229, 242–245. Wang Ch'i-chih's poem on this practice is translated in Liebenthal, *The Book of Chao*, pp. 193–195. The actual character of the Buddha's Shadow, which was modeled on the miraculous "reflection" of the manifestation body at Nagarahāra, is clouded by literary descriptions. Hui-yüan's biography seems to indicate that it was a painting on silk placed in a shrine or grotto; Hsieh Ling-yün's inscription of 413/4, written from afar, is more suggestive of a colored bas-relief: see Alexander Soper, *Literary Evidence*, pp. 32–33; Mather, *JAS* 18:70–72.

87. Zürcher, *BCC*, 1:220. Hui-yüan's "concrete and empiric" concerns emerge in his correspondence with Kumārajīva, see ibid., 1:226–229; Robinson, *Early Mādhyamika in India and China*, pp. 108–109.

88. Zürcher, *BCC*, 1:220, 245.

89. Hsieh Ling-yün may have visited Mount Lu only in A.D. 431, some fifteen years after Hui-yüan's death: see Paul Demiéville, "Présentation d'un poète," pp. 248–250, 260. His hymn on the Buddha's Shadow and his epitaph for Hui-yüan indicate a deep interest in the Mount Lu community; his Buddhist studies were influenced by monks who had lived there, principally by the eminent Tao-sheng (ca. 360–434), the exponent of sudden enlightenment in whose writings *li* or *prajña* is a key concept: see Fung Yu-lan, *A History of Chinese Philosophy*, trans. Derk Bodde, 2 vols. (Princeton, 1952, 1953), 2:273–282; David C. Yu, "Skill-in-means and the Buddhism of Tao-sheng: A Study of a Chinese Reaction to Mahāyāna of the Fifth Century," *Philosophy East and West* (1974), 24:414, 417.

90. *Li* is also an important term in Hsieh Ling-yün's landscape poetry and may not be unrelated to the concept of sudden enlightenment. Appreciation of scenery is a prerequisite for insight into the natural order, but ideally this appreciation (*shang*) should be shared. For the meaning of *li* in certain poems and its relation to *shang*, see Francis A. Westbrook, "Landscape Description in the Lyric Poetry and 'Fuh on Dwelling in the Mountains' of Shieh Ling-yunn," (Ph.D. dissertation, Yale University, 1973), pp. 108, 119, 136–140, 142–143, 149. For Hsieh's "cult" of friendship and the term *shang hsin*, "to delight the heart," see Demiéville, "Présentation d'un poète," pp. 253–254. For *shang* as applied to the appreciation of nature by Hsieh Ling-yün and others, see Obi, *Chūgoku bungaku ni arawareta shizen to shizenkan*, pp. 542–552.

91. Lu-shan chu tao-jen, "Yu shih-men shih-hsü" is extensively annotated in Hoshigawa Kiyotaka, *Koshi gen* (Investigations of Early Poetry), 2 vols. (Aoki Masaru [ed.], *Kanshi taishi* 5) (Tokyo, 1965), 2:113–120. I should like to express my appreciation to Dr. Achilles Fang and Professors Masatoshi Nagatomi, Victor Mair, and Stephen Owen, who have gone over this translation at different stages; any errors of interpretation that remain are, needless to say, my own.

92. For the Heavenly Pond on Mount Lu, see Ch'en, *Lu-shan chi*, p. 16.

93. In the phrase *wu chu*, "to lack an owner," *chu* may correspond to *ātman*: see Liebenthal, *MN* 8:384, n. 215.

94. A different moral is drawn from the view on high in *Mencius*, 7A:24: see Legge, *The Chinese Classics*, 2:463–464.

95. Alternatively, "His response is [impenetrably] deep and His enlightenment is remote."

96. In certain gazetteers, the fourth character of the eighth line of the poem, the *yu* of *chih-yu*, is replaced by *tzu*, "naturally," and the fourth of the ninth line, *yün*, "cloudy," by *ling*, "ethereal:" see Wu, *Lu-shan chih*, 10B:4a. Of some relevance to this poem is a letter to Seng-chao (384–414) by Liu Ch'eng-chih (354–410), Hui-yüan's first lay disciple. According to Liebenthal, meditation on Mount Lu was understood as a sublimation of the material in a Taoist manner, and *Nirvāna*, or the merging with nature, was a positive goal to be sought at the end of a career. In his passive state, the Sage was the cosmic meditator: see Liebenthal, *The Book of Chao*, pp. 90–93; Walter Liebenthal, *Chao Lun: The Treatise of Seng-chao* (Hong Kong, 1968), pp. 25–26, 85–87.

97. See Demiéville, "La montagne dans l'art littéraire chinois," p. 15.

A　畫山水序 　　　　　　　　　　　　　　　　　　　宗炳

　　聖人含道應物，賢者澄懷味像。至於山水質有而趣靈，是以軒轅堯孔廣成大隗許由孤竹之流，必有崆峒具茨藐姑箕首大蒙之遊焉。又稱仁智之樂焉。夫聖人以神法道，而賢者通，山水以形媚道而仁者樂，不亦幾乎？

　　余眷戀廬衡，契闊荆巫，不知老之將至。愧不能凝氣怡身，傷跕石門之流，於是畫象布色，構茲雲嶺。

　　夫理絕於中古之上者，可意求於千載之下；旨微於言象之外者，可心取於書策之內。況乎身所盤桓，目所綢繆，以形寫形，以色貌色也。

　　且夫崑崙山之大，瞳子之小，迫目以寸，則其形莫覩，迥以數里，則可圍於寸眸。誠由去之稍闊，則其見彌小。今張絹素以遠暎，則崑閬之形，可圍於方寸之內。豎劃三寸，當千仞之高；橫墨數尺，體百里之迴。是以觀畫圖者，徒患類之不巧，不以制小而累其似，此自然之勢。如是，則嵩華之秀，玄牝之靈，皆可得之於一圖矣。

　　夫以應目會心爲理者。類之成巧，則目亦同應，心亦俱會。應會感神，神超理得，雖復虛求幽巖，何以加焉？又神本亡端，棲形感類，理入影迹，誠能妙寫，亦誠盡矣。

　　於是閒居理氣，拂觴鳴琴，披圖幽對，坐究四荒，不違天勵之藂，獨應無人之野。峯岫嶢嶷，雲林森渺。聖賢暎於絕代，萬趣融其神思，余復何爲哉？暢神而已，神之所暢，孰有先焉！

B　廬山諸道人
　遊石門詩「序」

　　石門在精舍，南十餘里，一名障山。基連大嶺，體絕衆阜；闢三泉之會，並立而開流。傾巖玄映其上，蒙形表於自然；故因以爲名，此雖廬山之一隅，實斯地之奇觀，皆傳之於舊俗，而未覩者衆。將由懸瀨險峻，人獸迹絕，徑迴曲阜，路阻行難；故罕經焉。

釋法師以隆安四年仲春之月，因詠山水，遂杖錫而遊。於時交徒同趣，三十餘人。咸拂衣晨征，悵然增興。雖林壑幽邃，而開塗競進。雖乘危履石，並以所悅爲安。既至則援木尋葛，歷險窮崖；猿臂相引，僅乃造極。於是擁勝倚巖，詳觀其下，始知七嶺之美，蘊奇於此。

雙闕對峙其前，重巖映帶其後；巒阜周迴以爲障，崇巖四營而開宇。其中則有石臺石池，宮館之象，觸類之形；致可樂也。

清泉分流而合注，淥淵鏡淨於天池。文石發彩煥若披面，檉松芳草，蔚然光目；其爲神麗，亦已備矣。

斯日也，衆情奔悅，矚覽無厭；游觀未久，而天氣屢變。霄霧塵集，則萬象隱形；流光迴照，則衆山倒影。開闔之際，狀有靈焉，而不可測也。

乃其將登，則翔禽拂翮，鳴猿厲響。歸雲迴駕，想羽人之來儀；哀聲相和，若玄音之有寄。雖髣髴猶聞，而神以之暢；雖樂不期歡，而欣以永日。當其沖豫自得，信有味焉；而未易言也。

退而尋之。夫崖谷之間，會物無主，應不以情；而開興引人，致深若此。豈不以虛明朗其照，閒邃篤其情耶？並三復斯談，猶味然未盡。

俄而太陽告夕，所存已往。乃悟幽人之玄覽，達恆物之大情；其爲神趣，豈山水而已哉？於是徘徊崇嶺，流目四矚，九江如帶，邱阜成垤。因此而推，形有巨細，智亦宜然。

迺喟然歎，宇宙雖遐，古今一契；靈鷲邈矣，荒塗日隔。不有哲人，風迹雖存，應深悟遠；慨然長懷。各欣一遇之同歡，感茲辰之難再，情發於中，遂共詠之云爾：

超興非有本，理感興自生。忽聞石門遊，奇唱發幽情，褰裳思雲駕，望崖想曾城。馳步乘長巖，不覺質有輕。矯首登雲闕，眇若臨太清。端居運虛輪，轉彼玄中經。神仙同物化，未若兩俱冥。

The Earthly Paradise:
Religious Elements in Chinese Landscape Art

By Lothar Ledderose

The present paper is based on the conviction that there are definite links between religious and aesthetic values. Aesthetic values generally originate in a religious sphere; they develop and gain autonomy as religious values decline. Similar developments can be observed in many areas of human culture, for example in the emancipation of science from religious domination. Indeed, the process that is discussed here seems to be a universal one in cultural history. It is called secularisation.

During the gradual and complex metamorphosis that turns religious values into aesthetic ones, the former do not disappear without trace. Religious concepts and connotations tend to persist and continue to influence aesthetic perceptions to a more or less explicit degree. For a better understanding of many aesthetic phenomena it is therefore helpful to trace their religious roots.

An example is the art of landscape painting. Even nonspecialists admire landscape painting as one of the greatest and most characteristic achievements of Chinese culture. It comes less readily to mind that the Chinese created landscapes also in other, three-dimensional media. The origin of most of these types of landscape art antedates the birth of landscape painting, and their form and function is largely determined by religious factors.

In the following paper, attention will be drawn to some of these types of three-dimensional landscape art. They are, as discussed in a sequence of diminishing size, imperial parks, imperial tomb compounds, paradise gardens, natural gardens, miniature landscapes in trays, and incense burners. With the exception of incense burners this order corresponds by and large also to the sequence in which these types made their historical appearance.[1]

In China, as in many other cultures, since antiquity it has been a privilege of the ruler to have a park at his disposal. According to tradition, the Yellow God (Huang Ti) still raised dragons in his park.[2] His followers in the less golden ages of Shang and Chou had to content themselves with more earthly beasts. A major purpose in keeping them was a religious need. Animals had to be available continuously for ritual sacrifices, and such sacrifices could take place within the precinct of the park.

It is only in the Han period that we begin to have more detailed accounts about this early type of landscape shaped by man. In 138 B.C., two years after he ascended to the throne, Emperor Wu expanded the imperial park south of his capital Ch'ang-an to the enormous area of four hundred *li* in circumference. Formerly the First Emperor of Ch'in had established his Supreme Forest (*shang-lin*[a]) in the same region. It had housed his legendary *O-pang*[b] palace, perhaps the most imposing building to have been erected in China up to that time.[3]

Emperor Wu's Supreme Forest, like its predecessors, was used for the private enjoyment and recreation of the ruler, for the entertainment of guests of state, for regular religious sacrifices, and for the famous annual winter hunt, a ritual spectacle of enormous proportions.[4]

Despite its size the Supreme Forest was not left throughout as complete wilderness. Contemporary descriptions[5] dwell on the awe-inspiring grandeur of untouched nature as well as on the many sights that were testimony to human effort. The park contained thirty-six "detached palaces and separate hostels" (*li-kung pieh-kuan*[c]) with "divine ponds and numinous pools" (*shen-ch'ih ling-chao*).[d][6] It was populated by rare and precious animals that had been brought together from the corners of the world, from places as far away as Mesopotamia, India, and northern Vietnam. The range of plants was equally inclusive. According to one source there were more than three thousand species.[7] Moreover, valuable and exotic stones had been gathered there, among them a coral tree with four hundred and sixty-two branches.[8] With these tangible specimens of every kind of thing in the universe, the park was not merely an image of the cosmos, but its replica: a microcosm.

The symbolic quality of the park as a mandala of the universe was also apparent in the orderly arrangement of its components. Animals were placed in different quarters of the park depending on their place of origin. The vegetation was planted according to the same principle, and even the rivers are said to have frozen only in the northern, not in the southern part.[9]

Certain spots were given the names of famous places far away in the empire or even beyond its borders. An artificial lake dug in 120 B.C. was called *Kun-ming*[e] lake. It had a circumference of forty *li* and was a replica of a lake measuring three hundred *li* in the southern kingdom of Kun-ming or Tien. Emperor Wu had long harbored a plan to conquer the kingdom of Kun-ming which blocked the trade routes to India and in 107 B.C. he was finally able to subdue its king and turn him into a vassal. By building a *Kun-ming* lake in his park beforehand he had symbolically anticipated this conquest.

Behind this act of political demonstration one detects an archetypal idea which is one of the basic reasons for man to create images at all, the magical belief that by artificially making a replica of something one wields power over the real object. The First Emperor of Ch'in had acted in a similar way when he built in his capital Hsien-yang replicas of all the palaces of the feudal lords whom he had defeated.[10] Still,

a 上林
b 阿房

c 離宮別館
d 神池靈沼

e 昆明

Emperor Wu profited from his *Kun-ming* lake not only in a magical but also in an enormously practical way: he used it as the training ground for the upcoming naval battles on the real *Kun-ming* lake.[11]

Besides the Supreme Forest of Emperor Wu there were other parks in the Han dynasty, but they could not compare, neither in size nor extravagance. During the centuries of political division following the Han no great parks were being built, and when the Sui and T'ang emperors established large imperial parks again they did not try to attain the archaic grandeur of the Han Supreme Forest. One reason for this was the influence of a new genre of landscape design that had developed in the meantime and directed attention to detail and intimacy, the genre of gardens. However, before discussing these, we will take a look at imperial tomb compounds.

In China, as in many other cultures, the tumulus of a ruler's tomb was one of the most elementary forms of landscape design. Tumuli began to appear during the last centuries B.C. Probably the best known is the tomb mound of the First Supreme Emperor of Ch'in, who died in 210 B.C. With an original circumference of two and a half kilometers and a height of one hundred and sixty-six meters, it was also the biggest of its kind in this period. Yet the artificial hill was only the center of a large layout comprising numerous buildings and other architectural structures. This particular precinct must have been exceptionally elaborate, as was suggested by the spectacular discoveries of an army of approximately seven thousand terracotta figures larger than life-size that were buried underground in three casemate-like structures at a distance of about one and a half kilometers from the tumulus.[12]

Tomb compounds like the First Emperor's were enclosed by a wall. The segregated precinct was only accessible on certain occasions and to specific people. Officials lived there who were responsible for the maintenance of the tomb and for the sacrifices, which the descendants of the buried ruler in particular had to perform at regular intervals.[13] The tomb compound centering around the artificial mound thus was a separate area, a world by itself, within which the owner of the tomb enjoyed immortality as it were.

Moreover, in the case of the First Emperor of Ch'in's tomb there was beneath the tumulus still another separate world in the form of a miniature landscape. According to the description in *Shih chi*,

> ... the tomb was filled with models of palaces, pavilions and offices, as well as fine vessels, precious stones and rarities. Artisans were ordered to fix crossbows so that any thief breaking in would be shot. All the country's streams, the Yellow River and the Yangtse were reproduced in quicksilver and by some mechanical means made to flow into a miniature ocean. The heavenly constellations were shown above and the regions of the earth below.[14]

The tumulus of the First Emperor's tomb as well as those of the tombs of the Han emperors were artificially constructed hills. A few centuries later, when the T'ang emperors built their tombs again in the vicinity of Ch'ang-an, they used already existing mountains as centers of gigantic layouts. A natural elevation was thus turned into an element in an architectural precinct, an area of untouched nature became a landscape formed by man. Even today tomb layouts like that of T'ang T'ai-tsung or that of T'ang Kao-tsung and Wu Tse-t'ien impress the observer by their almost megalomanic dimensions.

In garden design one may differentiate between two basic types, the paradise garden and the natural garden. For the history of the paradise garden one has again to turn to Emperor Wu. He built a garden with a specific religious symbolism in his *Chien-chang*[f] palace. It was designed as a replica of the islands of the immortals. The belief in these islands was very popular. Sailors had been looking for them some centuries before the First Emperor of Ch'in dispatched his famous children's expedition into the Eastern Sea.[15] They were thought of as mountains, looking from afar like clouds and floating on the water or carried by giant turtles. Stocked with exquisite animals and plants as well as full of precious minerals, adorned by palaces built of the most costly material, the islands were the dwelling place for lofty immortals. Their names are generally given as *P'eng-lai*,[g] *Fang-chang*,[h] and *Ying-chou*.[i] [16]

Early in 104 B.C. Emperor Wu had traveled to the coast and sacrificed to the immortals whom he envisaged beyond the horizon. Immediately after his return the *Chien-chang* palace was built. Behind its Hall of State a large pond was constructed, called *T'ai-yeh ch'ih*.[j] In its center rose four islands, *P'eng-lai*, *Fang-chang*, *Ying-chou*, and *Hu-liang*,[k] and at its shore a tall platform, more than two hundred feet high, called *Chien-t'ai*.[17]

Concerning these four artificial islands the sources state explicitly, that they were made "to look like" (*hsiang*)[m] the holy mountains in the sea. The use of the term *hsiang* implies clearly that this garden architecture was meant to *represent* something. The similarity of the artificial islands with the real islands of the immortals was enhanced by a lush vegetation containing numinous herbs and mushrooms, and by the use of selected metals and stones for the construction of steep cliffs.[18] At the rim of the pond lay the stone sculpture of a whale, thirty feet long, looking as if it had just leaped out of the water,[19] and even the movement of the waves of the sea is said to have been imitated.

Han dynasty authors describing the artificial islands of the immortals in the *Chien-chang* palace dwell in detail on the exciting sights that startled their eyes. They

f 建章	i 瀛洲	l 漸臺
g 蓬萊	j 太液池	m 象
h 方丈	k 壺梁	

use a language similar to that of later writers trying to convey the appearance and aesthetic qualities of landscape paintings. There can be no doubt, however, that the Han creations were not primarily made for aesthetic enjoyment. Rather they still served a definite religious purpose. Although it is not known exactly what kind of ritual was performed there, Emperor Wu apparently could use the place for sacrifices to the immortals instead of going to the coast and praying to them from afar. He also cherished the concrete hope that immortals would come to visit his islands and that he might meet them there. The *Chien-t'ai* platform was the intended meeting ground. It was suitable because with its soaring height of two hundred feet it was the highest elevation in the entire precinct.[20]

The *Chien-t'ai* moreover was not the only lookout from which the emperor hoped to establish contact with the supernatural world. He also built a *Shen-ming t'ai*[n] with the bronze statue of an immortal on top. It held a basin in its palm to collect dew from the pure sphere beyond the clouds. Immortals who like high elevations as well as to drink dew were thus to be lured to the scene.[21]

Emperor Wu's replica of the islands of the immortals did not remain an isolated case. In the centuries following the Han dynasty several emperors built paradise gardens in their palace compounds. In A.D. 224 Emperor Wen of Wei had a pond dug in the great imperial garden in Loyang,[22] and two years later a platform (*t'ai*) was erected in the pond.[23] When the decayed compound was restored by the emperors of the Northern Wei:

> Emperor Hsiao-wen (r. 471–499) constructed a *P'eng-lai* mountain in the pond. On top was the "Hostel of the Immortals" (*hsien-jen kuan*[o]).[24]

In A.D. 235 Emperor Ming of Wei started digging an artificial pond in his imperial park[25] and again two years later:

> . . . he constructed an earthen mountain. . . . He asked all of his high officials and courtiers to contribute some earth to built the mountain. On top he planted pines, bamboo, and various trees as well as fine vegetation, and he also caught mountain birds and various quadrupeds and placed them there.[26]

This mountain was a microcosm in the additional sense that it was put together by the emperor's subjects, and thus demonstrated his claim to power. Apparently the posession of an artificial earthen mountain was a privilege which rulers—at least until the Han dynasty—did not like to share with common people. This was made clear to the merchant and millionaire Yüan Kuang-han, who owned a lavish park with an artificial stone mountain more than one hundred feet high that was stocked with exquisite plants and animals.

[n] 神明臺   [o] 仙人館

Later when Yüan Kuang-han was sentenced to death, the park was confiscated and turned into an official garden. Its birds and beasts, plants and trees were all transferred into the Supreme Forest.[27]

What happened to these animals and plants prefigures the fate of many art collections in later centuries. When collectors fell in disgrace, their scrolls of calligraphy and painting were also incorporated into the imperial collection.

Emperor Yang of Sui again demonstrated that building extensive palace gardens was a suitable duty for a powerful and cultivated emperor. In A.D. 605, the first year of his reign, he started construction of the Western Park with a circumference of two hundred *li* and sixteen smaller precincts (*yüan*[p]) in it:

> In the garden he also constructed a mountain and made a [pond like the] sea with a circumference of more than ten *li*. The water was several dozen feet deep and in its center were the mountains *Fang-chang*, *P'eng-lai*, and *Ying-chou*. Between each of them was a distance of three hundred steps and the mountains rose from the water to a height of more than a hundred feet. On top were the "Lookout for Reaching the Perfected" (*t'ung-chen kuan*[q]), the "Platform for Assembling the Spirits" (*chi-ling t'ai*[r]), and the "Place for Gathering the Immortals" (*ts'ung-hsien kung*[s]), respectively.[28]

When Ch'ang-an was the T'ang capital a compound in its eastern part housed a *P'eng-lai* hall, a *P'eng-lai* mountain, and a pond which, as in Emperor Wu's garden, was called *T'ai-yeh ch'ih*.[29]

A famous paradise garden of a later age was the one built by Emperor Hui-tsung in the *Hsüan-ho* period (1119–1125). It was situated in the northeastern corner of his capital, K'ai-feng, and was equipped with all the familiar paraphernalia. There was an "impregnable mountain" (*ken-yüeh*[t]), consisting of several peaks. The highest rose to ninety steps and had a pavilion on top, and beneath there was a large pond. Different parts of the garden were made to represent different places in the empire. The compound was enriched with rare animals and plants and with those famous rocks for which Hui-tsung felt a special love.[30]

Many of the gardens with a "spiritual mountain" (*ling-shan*[u]), a "holy mountain" (*shen-shan*[v]), or an "artificial mountain" (*chia-shan*[w]), were designed by magicians of Taoist affiliation (*fang-shih*[x]). Yet Buddhists also built some of these mountains, calling them representations of the cosmic mountain *Sumeru* which was already well known in India. This is another example of the sinicization of Buddhism. The Chinese replicas of mount *Sumeru* apparently looked similar to the replicas of mount *P'eng-lai*. Their construction also involved building steep cliffs. Precious

p 院
q 通眞觀
r 集靈臺

s 總仙宮
t 艮岳
u 靈山

v 神山
w 假山
x 方士

animals and extraordinary vegetation could be seen there, and they were filled with Buddhist images and figures of immortals.[31] Similar artificial mountains like those in China were erected in Korea, and even in Japan two such constructions are known from the Asuka period.[32]

Mention should be made in this connection also of the peculiar layout of Buddhist temples of the Pure Land school (chin. *ching-t'u*; jap. *jōdo*).[y] These temples are designed as representations of the Western Paradise of Buddha Amitābha, in a similar way as, for example, a gothic cathedral is the representation of the Heavenly Jerusalem. In China precincts of this type are not preserved but they can still be studied in Japan.[33] The most famous example is the *Hōōdō*, Phoenix Hall, in the *Byōdōin* in Nara, which was started in 1052, in the year of the expected end of the world, *mappō*.[z].

The characteristic feature of this type of temple layout is a lotus pond in front of the icon hall. In pictorial representations of the Western Paradise one sees how the deceased are reborn in this pond. Modern scholarship tends to emphasize the similarity with aristocratic mansions of the *shinden zukuri*[aa] type, where the main building is also placed behind a pond. Yet the tradition seems to lead further back to the pre-Buddhist paradise gardens of the Han dynasty, with their two constitutent elements of pond and mountain. A mountain is, iconologically speaking, always represented in a Buddhist temple in the form of the throne of Buddha.

Even today gardens of the traditional paradise type still exist in China. An example is the compound to the west of the imperial palace in Peking, comprising three artificial lakes with islands. The northernmost lake is called *Pei-hai*, Northern Sea.[34] It was enlarged to its present shape when in 1267 Kubilai Khan established the capital of his empire in Peking. As reported by Marco Polo, the island was filled with rare trees and azurite stones, which gave it the typical paradise color.[35] Its present appearance is largely determined by Ch'ing architecture, and it is dominated by a building of religious heritage, a pagoda of the Lamaist type, the so-called Dagoba of 1652.

The largest extant paradise garden lies a few miles further west. It is the *I-ho yüan*, generally known as Summer Palace. The artificial lake is again called *Kun-ming* lake; its area is about five times the size of the man-made mountain in its northern part. The history of this compound goes back to the twelfth century, but it owes its present character also largely to architectural remains of the Ch'ing period. Both, *Pei-hai* and *I-ho yüan* are public parks today, but notwithstanding this change of function they still convey a very concrete idea of what traditional paradise gardens must have looked like.

In summary one may say that the basic design of a paradise garden is of striking simplicity. A hole is dug in the ground and filled with water; the earth gained in this

y 淨土
z 末法
aa 寢殿造

way is piled up into a mountain. A landscape is the thus created with its two complementary elements, mountain and water, shan[ab] and shui.[ac] Through selected minerals, plants, and animals this piece of landscape is moreover turned into a microcosmic replica of the universe. The paradise garden thus is essentially the same as a cosmic park, but it is in a more concentrated form.

A decisive phase of aesthetic emancipation in the history of the visual arts in China was the period of the Six Dynasties (third to sixth centuries). Among the symptoms of a rising aesthetic awareness are the beginnings of an art theoretical literature, the formation of artistic traditions among members of the educated elite, and the establishment of art collections.[36] New approaches to garden design were also developed during this period.[37] Besides the traditional paradise garden centering around a main mountain, a "natural" type of garden came into vogue. It was less formal and less ostentatiously stuffed with rare animals and plants. Rather the design was subtle, aiming at the quality of tzu-jan.[ad] These gardens were built with an unprecedented aesthetic consciousness.

The new attitude is discernible in a passage in the Shih-shuo hsin-yü that records the words of Emperor Chien-wen of Chin (r. 371–372) on entering the imperial garden:

> The spot that suits the mind isn't necessarily far away. By any shady grove or stream one might quite naturally have such thoughts as Chuang Tzu had by the rivers Hao and P'u,[38] where unselfconsciously birds and animals. fowls and fish, come of their own accord to be intimate with men.[39]

This garden is also a small model of an ideal sphere, in this case the area, where Chuang Tzu roamed and declined to accept political office. The garden is again a place beyond the confinement of the common world. But rather than being a meeting ground between immortals and men, it becomes a "spot that suits the mind" (hui-hsin-ch'u[ae]) and a place for political retreat. It is still stocked with animals, but they now symbolize man's intimacy with nature. Rather than the imperial court, it was the educated elite which cultivated these new designs. The place where the Seven Sages of the Bamboo Grove met must have been such a garden. The famous gathering at the Orchid Pavilion in A.D. 353, during which Wang Hsi-chih wrote his immortal Lan-t'ing hsü probably also did not take place in untouched nature but rather in a garden setting.[40]

The growing consciousness for the aesthetic qualities of gardens is exemplified by Tai Yung (378–441). He was a typical member of the southern intelligentsia who

ab 山
ac 水

ad 自然
ae 會心處

kept apart from government service and indulged in the enjoyment of the arts and of nature. His biography is included among the "recluses" in the dynastic histories, and the great painting compendium of A.D. 847, the *Li-tai ming-hua chi* has a long paragraph on him. He is praised as well versed in many arts such as lute-playing, calligraphy, and painting, and it is told, how he gave technical advice on casting a Buddhist bronze figure.[41] Both his brother and his father made themselves names as painters. His father Tai K'uei (died 396), furthermore, became a famous figure for the emerging artistic ideology of the literati class; he broke his lute rather than play for the amusement of a prince.[42] In his own time Tai Yung was renowned for his appreciation of gardens:

> When he went to live in Wu, the nobles there joined to build an abode for him, collecting stones and directing the flow of water, planting trees and digging a gorge. Within a short span of time the place had become lush and dense and looked like nature (*tzu-jan*).[43]

Tai Yung was a contemporary of Tsung Ping, the author of a famous early treatise on landscape painting. Emperor Wen of Sung (r. 424–452) said about the two of them that "their minds were set on intimate gardens".[44] Yet Tai Yung's garden connoisseurship was not confined to the natural garden. He was also expected to appreciate the traditional design with the mountain in a pond. When he had died before the construction of a new paradise garden in the imperial palaces could be finished, "the emperor sighed and said: 'What a shame that I did not get a chance to have Tai Yung see this'!"[45]

As a result of the new aesthetic attitude, members of the educated elite did not only appreciate gardens but also no loner considered it below their dignity to design gardens themselves. Consequently garden architecture ceased to be an anonymous craft. It began to be practiced by individuals whose names and activities are included in the historical records. This is a phenomenon that had close parallels in the fields of calligraphy and painting.

For example, the name is known of the man who built the paradise garden that Tai Yung failed to see before his death. It is Chang Yung (d. 475), who is characterized as follows:

> Chang Yung was widely read and could himself compose literary texts. He was good at writing clerical script and had an understanding for the rules of music. Horsemanship and archery and various other skills he all mastered by analogy and his technical gifts again and again came to the attention of the emperor. He manufactured his own paper and ink, and everytime the emperor got a written memorial from him, he always kept it with a sigh of admiration as an object of value, lamenting that those who had to supply the court were not all up to the same level. When in the year

446 A.D. the emperor built the *Hua-lin*[af] garden and the *Hsüan-wu*[ag] pond, he asked Chang Yung to take charge of these works.[46]

It is remarkable how many among the early garden designers either painted themselves or had famous painters among their close relative, like Tai Yung. Another example is Chiang Shao-yu (d. 501) who restored the imperial garden of the Northern Wei between A.D. 493 and 495. He is called an accomplished calligrapher and figure painter by the author of the *Li-tai ming-hua chi*, who adds somewhat disapprovingly, "although he had talent and learning he was always surrounded by his carving chisels and [carpenter's] string and ink."[47]

Both Yen P'i and Yen Li-te, the father and brother respectively of the famous T'ang painter, Yen Li-pen (d. 673), knew how to paint and also supervised the construction of imperial palaces.[48] Yen Li-pen himself painted or designed figures for the tomb of T'ai-tsung of T'ang that has been mentioned above.[49] The depiction of palace gardens had by then become a familiar subject for painters of the period.[50]

In this survey of some gardens two basic types have been singled out: the paradise garden with its specific religious symbolism, and the natural garden, where the symbolic meaning is less definite. However, the difference between the two types is not as great as it might perhaps seem. The two important innovations of the Six Dynasties period mentioned here, the rise of an aesthetic attitude toward gardens and the end of anonymity in garden design, apply not only to the new natural garden, but to the paradise garden as well. Although the natural garden is not layed out as a cosmic mandala, it also has all the essential elements of a microcosm: earth and water, stones, plants, animals, and pavilions. And even if the natural garden is not arranged with the concept of a specific paradise in view, it is still a place where one is sheltered against political and other turmoil: in the words of Li Po, "a complete world apart, not among the people."[51] Even if the urbane intellectual does not expect to contact flying immortals in his garden, he will meet there with another type of genius (*hsien*[ah]), the lofty scholar. In short, the natural garden is a secularized version of the paradise garden.

In the wake of parks and gardens a new type of artificial landscape appears in the T'ang dynasty, the miniature landscapes in trays, *p'en-ching*.[ai] An early example is seen on a wall painting in the tomb of Li Hsien, who was reburied in A.D. 706.[52] Miniature landscapes have been discussed at length in a path-breaking study by Rolf Stein; I therefore will confine myself here to a few summarizing remarks. Whereas parks and gardens could be built and owned only by a privileged few, miniature landscapes were cultivated in many different segments of society. One saw them in the imperial palaces as well as in the houses of common people, in Buddhist as well as

af 華林

ag 玄武

ah 仙

ai 盆景

in Taoist establishments; they formed an indispensable element in every mountain retreat but were also to be found in the courtyards of city mansions. They have a long history; best known in the West is the Japanese variety called *bonsai*.[aj]

As a result of the wide distribution, many different types in the design of miniature landscapes have evolved, but they can all be regarded as variations on the theme of the paradise landscape with the constituent element of a main mountain rising from the water. Like parks and gardens containing specimens from various parts of the universe, tray landscapes were also conceived as a microcosm in a very concentrated form. The small stones used for the mountains were rare and exquisitely shaped, imbued with the power of mighty rocks. The essence of giant old trees was concentrated in the dwarf versions that were planted on the mountains and cultivated with great care. As was the case with gardens and parks, miniature landscapes could also be designated as replicas of famous scenes.

The tray landscape is also a refuge and retreat, a realm separated from the common world. There are stories of magicians like a certain Hsüan Chieh, who lived at the T'ang court and was able to disappear in a miniature landscape when he chose to.[53] But less adept owners could also draw comfort from their trays. They participated in the essence enclosed in the dwarfed plants, so that their skin remained supple even in old age, and in the morning they collected dew from the herbs and used it to moisten their eyes.[54]

Every single one of the motives in the "iconography" of tray landscapes is fraught with a cluster of magical connotations. Stones are the finest essence of the earth; they are incredibly old; their unusual shapes are an outgrowth of their inherent *ch'i*.[ak] Special attention is focused on stalactites and stalagmites because they "grow" in caves (which themselves are also a separate world). Corals are appreciated for similar reasons. There is no essential difference between stones and plants. Old trees will be invigorated when the powder of stalactites is put into the tray, and after thousands of years they will turn into stones themselves. Old trees are not thought of as creatures approaching death, but on the contrary as beings filled with accumulated vital energy. By keeping them small and by contorting their trunks and branches, the flow of sap is slowed down and their energy is thus concentrated and preserved. Particularly important are evergreen plants, whose roots grow out of rocks. They let out some of their energy in the form of precious resin, and miraculous mushrooms will grow at their feet. Mushrooms, again, are only one type of smaller beneficial plants that are seen in a tray landscape paradise. Sometimes miniature landscapes could also be enveloped in clouds. In the Sung period, in particular, small rocks were constructed or found with openings for smoke from incense burned inside. Su Shih owned such a rock.

Whereas the early parks were only cursorily modified areas of nature, gardens

[aj] 盆栽   [ak] 氣

1. *Po-shan hsiang-lu*. Bronze incense burner inlaid with gold, height 26.1 cm. Courtesy of The Cultural Relics Bureau, Beijing and The Metropolitan Museum of Art.

樹緣微葉溪
澗凍搖闖仙
居客上層不
蕗杜桅澗點
級春山早見
氣如蒸
己卯春月
尚題

2. Kuo Hsi, "Early Spring," dated 1072. Hanging scroll, ink and light colors on silk, 158.3 × 108.1 cm. National Palace Museum, Taipei, Taiwan, R.O.C.

are the result of a more directed human effort, and in a tray landscape every single pebble and blade of grass is especially arranged and attended to. The concentration in size inevitably leads to an increase in artificiality, but at the same time it entails a more intensive dealing with nature and fosters its aesthetic appreciation. In front of tray landscapes it becomes evident that in Chinese aesthetics there is no simple border line between objects created by nature and works of art created by man: they are both considered "natural."

The earliest entirely artificial representations of landscape in China are incense burners in the form of the Universal Mountain, *po-shan hsiang-lu* (fig. 1). [al] A typical *po-shan hsiang-lu* of the Han period consists of a bowl resting on a stand that emerges from a basin filled with water. The bowl is covered by a cone in mountain form with several outlets for the smoke from the incense which is burned in the bowl. The shape of a *po-shan hsiang-lu* thus closely corresponds to the image of islands of the immortals that emerge from the sea and are shrouded in clouds. The mountain cone contains precious metals like silver and gold, it is embellished by inlaid stones and filled with immortals, men, and animals, some of which are being hunted.[55]

Descriptions of *po-shan hsiang-lu* sound similar to descriptions of paradise gardens and minature landscapes. In the Taoist text *Hsi-ching tsa-chi* (ca. fifth century) an incense burner is described as follows:

> In Ch'ang-an there was a dexterous artisan, a certain Ting Huan [first century B.C.].... He built a *po-shan hsiang-lu* in nine tiers with carvings of rare birds and unusual beasts, and complete with all those exceptional objects which possess religious power. Everything moved in a natural way.[56]

Numerous incense burners have been found in tombs. Apparently they were indispensable in religious ceremonies and they may have been used in particular to aid prayer and meditation. With his mind and vision absorbed in the clouds of incense, the pious believer would transcend into the paradise in front of him. When Buddhism entered China it also incorporated incense burners of the *po-shan hsiang-lu* type among its ritual implements.

Some of the magical qualities associated with miniature landscapes in trays may also be heritage from the *po-shan hsiang-lu* which seem to disappear just at the time that tray landscapes come into vogue. The fact that some rocky tray landscapes were constructed in such a way that they could be used as incense burners seems to be a symptomatic one. There must have been still other roots leading back into the sphere of religious practice.

[al] 博山香爐

In conclusion I should like to return to landscape painting, and suggest ways in which it may be connected to the three-dimensional landscape creations discussed in this paper.

This rise of autonomous landscape painting during the period of the Six Dynasties was a most remarkable step in the history of Chinese art. It required, among other things, that landscape become something that a painter might want to represent, and also something which might be judged according to aesthetic criteria. Both conditions had already been fulfilled in garden design. Real or ideal landscapes had long been represented in parks and paradise gardens, and the recent natural garden was shaped in such a way as to conform to aesthetic standards. The birth of autonomous landscape painting was thus facilitated and encouraged. It was the application of established designs in a different creative medium.

In terms of subject matter landscape painting owes much to gardens. It certainly is no mere accident that a handscroll with the depiction of his garden villa became the most famous painting of the great poet-painter Wang Wei (701–761).[57] That he appeared to be the archetype of a literati painter in later times is probably not so much due to his stylistic innovations (as Tung Ch'i-ch'ang wants us to believe), but rather due to the fact that he immortalized in his painting one of the great creations of the literati class, the natural garden. Also many later paintings which at first glance seem to represent a lonely landscape are in fact garden settings. Untouched nature is added in the background as "borrowed landscape" (*chieh-ching*[am]) which is a well-known principle in garden design.

The stylistic relationship between landscape painting and other landscape creations is a complex one. One hears of miniature landscapes in trays in the styles of Ma Yüan (active about 1190–1225) or Huang Kung-wang (1269–1354), and in turn the style and composition of many paintings seem to owe much to three-dimensional landscapes. Many of the bizarre rock formations piled up in a precarious balance that are found so often in later Chinese painting look as if they had been transferred directly out of a tray.[58] Gardens centering around a main mountain had already been designed for centuries when in the tenth century a new type of pictorial composition emerged in which a central mountain dominated the scene. A famous example is Kuo Hsi's "Early Spring" of 1072 (fig. 2). From the middle of the water below rise some boulders supporting, as it were, a world landscape. Thus there is a striking relation between the composition of this painting and the shape of a *po-shan hsiang-lu*, especially if one envisions the clouds of incense eveloping its upper part.

Connections between three-dimensional and two-dimensional landscape representations may also be traced in the theoretical literature on landscape painting. For example, the magical concepts that are associated with paradise gardens and minia-

am 借景

ture landscapes in trays have their analogy in painting. The "square foot" of a painting may serve as the substitute for a real landscape which can thus be brought into the painter's study, in the same way that Emperor Wu brought the *P'eng-lai* islands into his palace. Just as a magician was thought to have entered a miniature landscape, painters are also said to have disappeared in their painted landscapes. The tiny figures that one finds so often in later paintings remind the viewer that such a possibility might still exist. Indeed, if one were to explore the numerous historical, biographical, iconographical, stylistic, and functional links that tie landscape painting together with three-dimensional landscape creations, it might appear that to a larger extent and in a more concrete sense than generally recognized, landscape painting in China is the representation of an earthly paradise.

1. It is hoped that this preliminary survey will be followed by a more detailed investigation.

2. Wang Chia, *Shih-i chi* (fourth century A.D.), in *T'ai-p'ing yü-lan* (Imperial Readings from the T'ai-ping period) 196:7a. Quoted in Edward H. Schafer, "Hunting Parks and Animal Enclosures in Ancient China," *Journal of the Economic and Social History of the Orient* (1968), 11:318–343; 321, n. 1 in particular.

3. *Shih chi* 6, p. 256 (all dynastic histories are quoted in the new edition of Chung-hua shu-chü, Peking).

4. For descriptions of the hunt, see also Michael Sullivan, *The Birth of Landscape Painting in China* (Berkeley and Los Angeles, 1962), pp. 28–30; Derk Bodde, *Festivals in Classical China* (Princeton, 1975), pp. 381–386.

5. Apart from the relatively sober comments on the Supreme Forest in the *Shih chi* and *Han shu*, flowery descriptions are found in six *fu* (prose-poems) in the *Wen hsüan*:

Pan Ku, *Hsi-tu fu* (Description of the Western Capital)

Pan Ku, *Tung-tu fu* (Description of the Eastern Capital)

These two poems are translated in Georges Margouliès, *Le "Fou" dans le Wen-siuan: Etude et textes* (Paris, 1926), pp. 31–74:

Chang Heng, *Hsi-ching fu* (Description of the Western Capital)

Chang Heng, *Tung-ching fu* (Description of the Eastern Capital)

These two poems are translated in Erwin von Zach, *Die chinesische Anthologie: Übersetzungen aus dem Wen-hsüan* (Harvard-Yenching Institute Studies 18) (Cambridge, Mass., 1958), pp. 1–37.

All four poems are dealt with at length in E. R. Hughes, *Two Chinese Poets: Vignettes of Han Life and Thought* (Princeton, 1960).

Yang Hsiung, *Yü-lieh fu* (The Hunt) (von Zach, pp. 117–125)

Ssu-ma Hsiang-ju, *Shang-lin fu* (The Supreme Forest) (von Zach, pp. 108–117). This is the most detailed account; it is also contained in *Shih chi* 117, pp. 3016–3043.

Additional information—sometimes apparently exaggerated—can be found in the later and less reliable *San-fu huang-t'u* (See n. 7 below).

6. Pan Ku, *Hsi-tu fu* (*Wen hsüan* 1, p. 4). Quoted in Schafer, "Hunting Parks," p. 328, n. 1.

7. *Chiao-cheng san-fu huang-t'u* (*Chung-kuo hsüeh-shu ming-chu* ed., 6) 4, p. 29.

8. Ibid. 4, p. 35. See also Schafer, "Hunting Parks," p. 328, n. 4, and *Hsi-ching tsa-chi* (Miscellaneous Records of the Western Capital) (*Han-Wei ts'ung-shu* ed.) 1:6a.

9. Ssu-ma Hsiang-ju, *Shang-lin fu* (*Wen hsüan* 8), p. 108.

10. *Shih chi* 6, p. 239.

11. *Han shu* 6, p. 177; *Chiao-cheng san-fu huang-t'u* 4, pp. 31–32: *Hsi-ching tsa-chi* 1:1a.

12. See Maxwell K. Hearn, "The Terracotta Army of the First Emperor of Qin (221–206 B.C.)," in *The Great Bronze Age of China*, ed. by Wen Fong (New York, 1980), pp. 353–373. For bibliographical references to the Chinese excavation reports, see ibid., p. 386.

13. Cf. the excellent study by Yang Shu-ta, *Han-tai hun-sang li-su k'ao* (A study of Customs and Rites in Funerals and Marriages of the Han Dynasty) (Shanghai, 1933).

14. *Shih chi* 6, p. 265. Translation by Yang Hsien-yi and Gladys Yang, *Selections from Records of the Historian* (Peking, 1979), p. 186.

15. *Shih chi* 6, p. 247.

16. Descriptions in *Shih chi* 28, p. 1369 and *Han shu* 25, p. 1204, and a more fanciful account in *Lieh Tzu, T'ang-wen pien*. Several descriptions of a paradise have been translated by Wolfgang Bauer in his admirable *China und die Hofnung auf Glück* (Munich, 1971).

17. *Shih chi* 12, p. 482 and 28, p. 1402; *Han shu* 25, p. 1244. Cf. also Maggie Keswick, *The Chinese Garden* (New York, 1978), p. 40.

18. Pan Ku, *Hsi-tu fu* 1, p. 7; Chang Heng, *Hsi-tu fu* 2, p. 22.

19. Ibid., and *Chiao-cheng san-fu huang-t'u* 4, p. 33

20. In A.D. 22 the usurpator Wang Meng chose the *Chien-t'ai* as his last retreat and was killed there. See *Han shu* 99c, p. 4191.

21. *Shih chi* 12, p. 459; *Han shu* 25, p. 1220; *Chiao-cheng san-fu huang-t'u* 3, p. 23.

22. *San-kuo chih* 2, p. 84.

23. Ibid., 2, p. 86.

24. *Lo-yang ch'ieh-lan chi chiao-shih* (Records of Buddhist Establishments in Lo-yang; Edited and Explained) (Peking, 1963), 1, p. 67. (Quoted in Nagahiro Toshio, *Rikuchō jidai bijutsu no kenkyū* [The Representational Art of the Six Dynasties Period] [Tokyo, 1969], p. 169.)

25. *San-kuo chih, Wei-shu* 3, p. 104. (Quoted in Nagahiro, *Rikuchō*, p. 161.)

26. Ibid. 3, p. 110. Nagahiro, *Rikuchō*, p. 161.)

27. *Hsi-ching tsa-chi* 1:3a–b. (Quoted in Sugimura Yūzo, *Chūgoku no niwa* [Tokyo, 1966], p. 24. Cf. also Keswick, *The Chinese Garden*, pp. 42ff.)

28. *Ta-yeh tsa-chi* (Miscellaneous Records of Great Yeh) (*Pai-pu ts'ung-shu* ed.) 8b–9a. Cf. also Lorraine Kuck, *The World of the Japanese Garden* (New York and London, 1968), pp. 19–22.

29. *Chiu T'ang shu* 17A, p. 529. (Quoted in Murakami Yoshimi, "Tōtō Chōan no ōshitsu teien," *Kansai gakuin shigaku* (June, 1955), 3:50.)

30. *Shou-san ken-yüeh* in *Yün-ku tsa-chi* [Chang] Yün-ku's Miscellaneous Records) (*Shuo-fu* ed.) 30:19b–23b. See also Rolf Stein, "Jardins en miniature d'Extrême-Orient," *BEFEO* (1943), 2:1–104, here p. 21; and Sugimura, *Chūgoku no niwa*, pp. 50ff.

31. For a discussion of two early Northern Wei examples, see Kosugi Kazuo, "Asuka jidai ni okeru zōzan no genryū ni tsuite," *Hōun* (1935), 13:73–100.

32. Ibid.

33. See Sugiyama Shinzō, *Fujiwarashi no Ujidera to sono inke* (Temples and Monasteries of Fujiwara Family: An Architectural Study) (*Nara kokuritsu bunkazai kenkyūjo gakuhō* 19) (Tokyo, 1986); and *Jodō no niwa* (*Taiyō niwa to ie shiriizu* 3), ed. by Matsumoto Tamotsu (Tokyo, 1980).

34. Hou Jen-chih, "Pei-hai kung-yüan yü Pei-ching ch'eng," *Wen-wu* (1980. 4), pp. 10–12; and Sun Hsiao-hsiang, "Pei-hai kung-yüan ti yüan-lin i-shu," ibid., pp. 13–22.

35. Henry Yule, *The Book of Ser Marco Polo* (London, 1903), p. 365.

36. Cf. Yü Ying-shih, "Han-Chin chih chi shih chih hsin tzu-chüeh yü hsin ssu-ch'ao," *Hsin-ya hsüeh-pao* (August, 1959), 4(1):25–144. Cf. also my *Mi Fu and the Classical Tradition of Chinese Calligraphy* (Princeton, 1979), pp. 28–44.

37. Wu Shih-ch'ang, "Wei-Chin feng-liu yü ssu-chia yüan-lin," *Hsüeh-wen yüeh-k'an* (1934), 1(2):80–114; Murakami Yoshimi, "Rikuchō no teien," *Kodaigaku* (1955), 4(1):41–60; Keswick, *The Chinese Garden*, pp. 73–90.

38. *Chuang Tzu* 17.

39. Richard B. Mather, *Shih-shuo Hsin-yü: A New Account of Tales of the World* (Minneapolis, 1976), p. 60 (Mather's translation).

40. Ch'en Tsung-chou, "Shao-hsing ta-yü-ling chi Lan-t'ing t'iao-ch'a chi," *Wen-wu* (1959. 7), pp. 40–43.

41. *Li-tai ming-hua chi* (HSTS ed.) 5, p. 75; translated in William R. B. Acker, *Some T'ang and Pre-T'ang Texts on Chinese Painting*, 2 vols. (Leiden, 1954, 1974), 2:100–102.

42. Robert H. van Gulik, *The Lore of the Chinese Lute* (Tokyo, 1979), p. 158.

43. *Sung shu* 93, p. 2277. (Quoted in Nagahiro, *Rikuchō*, pp. 164ff.)

44. Ibid.

45. Ibid., 93, p. 2278.

46. Ibid., 53, p. 1511. (Quoted in Nagahiro, *Rikuchō*, p. 165.)

47. *Li-tai ming-hua chi* 8, p. 95; Acker, *Some T'ang and Pre-T'ang Texts*, 2:188 (Acker's translation). Mentioned in Nagahiro, *Rikuchō*, p. 168. See also Alexander C. Soper, "South Chinese Influence on the Buddhist Art of the Six Dynasties Period," *BMFEA* (1960), 32:75ff.

48. *Li-tai ming-hua chi* 8, pp. 97ff,; 9, p. 103. For architecture of the Sui dynasty and for biographies of architects, see Tanaka Dan, "Zuichō kenchikuka no sekkei to kōshō," in *Chūgoku no kagaku to kagakusha*, ed. Yamada Keiji (Kyoto, 1978), pp. 209–306.

49. *Li-tai ming-hua chi* 9, p. 105; Acker, *Some T'ang and Pre-T'ang Texts*, 2:216 and 221, n. 51.

50. Michael Sullivan, *Chinese Landscape Painting of the Sui and T'ang Dynasties* (Berkeley, 1980), pp. 94ff.

51. *Li T'ai-po ch'üan-chi (SPPY* ed.), 19:2b.

52. Jan Fontein and Wu Tung, *Han and T'ang Murals* (Boston, 1976), p. 99, pl. 120. Stein, who could not yet know this painting, estimated that miniature landscapes in trays existed at least by the end of the early period of the T'ang dynasty ("Jardins," p. 36).

53. Su Ngo, *Tu-yang tsa-pien (Pi-hai* ed.) 2:6a. Quoted in Stein, "Jardins," pp. 40ff. and in Sullivan, *Chinese Landscape Painting*, p. 85.

54. Stein, "Jardins," pp. 24, 38.

55. Cf. A. G. Wenley, "The Question of the *Po-Shan-Hsiang-Lu*," *ACASA* (1948–1949), 3:5–12.

56. *Hsi-ching tsa-chi* 1:7b. Quoted in Stein, "Jardins," p. 37. Mentioned in Alexander C. Soper, *Literary Evidence for Early Buddhist Art in China* (*Artibus Asiae Supplementum* 19) (Ascona, 1959), p. 90.

57. Cf. the many versions in *Ōi* (*Bunjinga suihen* 1), ed. Kaizuka Shigeki, Kohara Hironobu et al. (Tokyo, 1974).

58. See James Cahill, *Fantastics and Eccentrics in Chinese Painting* (New York, 1967). Some miniature rocks were juxtaposed with paintings in this exhibition.

IV / MUSIC THEORY AND POETICS OF THE SIX DYNASTIES

Early Chinese Music and the Origins
of Aesthetic Terminology

By Kenneth DeWoskin

Music presents unique problems in the investigation of aesthetics and the arts. For the historian, there is no artifact except for instruments, little in palpable remnants to reveal song or dance as they were actually performed in their times. Music is the lost facet of ancient ritual, poetry, and drama, even where the texts remain to be studied. Historically, music can be pursued only so far as recovered bells and stone chimes provide insights into tone gamuts, scales, and timing, and early texts provide descriptions of performances and dances and provide hints to the contexts of musical presentations. The scholar of early thought must face the same difficulties that discussions of music presented the early philosophers and present contemporary aestheticians. Of all the arts, music seems the least congenial to verbal description of its processes or translation of its "content." From an analytical perspective, there is still very little understood of the relationship between a song and lyrics carried by it and a rhythm and action governed by it beyond the blunt claim that music increases the aesthetic impact of a presentation. The situation is aptly described by Susanne Langer in her compelling contemporary analysis. Music is said to be preeminently nonrepresentative, having "practically nothing but tonal structures before us, no scene, no object, no fact."[1]

Music appears to play some role in all cultures, in the odd case as an object of proscription if nothing else. In the cultures with which I am familiar, music is a persistent object of philosophical inquiry, both prior to and following recognition of its artistic import.[2] Thus, while unyielding before analytic and descriptive efforts, music has held a lasting fascination for speculative thinkers. Among its attributes, it is first and most widely credited with a purity of form that finds expression in such concepts as "music of the spheres," "music without sound," "choirs of angels," "nature's fundamental tone," "pipings of the winds," and the like.

As a human activity, music is variously perceived as a medium of communication between man and man or between man and nature or supernatural forces. In either case, it differentiates itself from other arts in that it is not necessarily burdened by mundane referents or obviously constrained by the limitations of human rational processes, language, or intellect. As a medium, therefore, music is perceived as having potential for greater scope or greater purity than art forms based on language or visual image. In scope it may be truly cosmic, achieving the largest imagined forces and forms. In purity, it has perfectability equal to the finest imagined sagely or paradisiacal existence. In many traditions, the perception of music as a human artifact, operating in a social or social-ritual context, is eclipsed by the perception of it as a medium of communication between man and God, heaven, or nature. In this latter context, which arises in sources as diverse as Aristotle, Plato, Horace, the Hindu Purāṇas, Bharata, Śārṅgadeva, Confucius, Mo Tzu, and Chuang Tzu, the gist of music's communicative power is its bearing on the spiritual shaping of man and society. Music is seen as the primary means of bringing to man, in apprehensible form, the ideals, norms, or perfected processes of realms beyond him.

Even in discussions where music is associated with divinities or other forces beyond man, the key issues are diverse. Discussions may focus on the origins of music, as in early Chinese myths relating the extraction of intervals from cosmic processes or the invention of key instruments. They may focus on the ultimate, ongoing sources of music and musical inspiration, as in Chuang Tzu's discussion of the piping of heaven. Confucius and his disciples discussed types, modes, and their varying effects on man, praising the orthodox ritual music while deploring the lewd music of Cheng. During the Han, typical discussions of music were eclectic, being primarily concerned with establishing the significant correspondences between music as a system and other orderly systems, and integrating discrepancies among the pre-Han philosophical record. The eminent Han texts in this group, including the *Huai-nan Tzu*, and the *Han shu*: "Lü-li chih"[a] (History of the Han: "Treatise on the Pitchpipes and Calendar"), bring acoustics, metrology, geography, and calendrics together in a numerological web that bears serious implications for all questions of politics, ritual, and morality.[3] In early China, the discussions of music stop short of arguments for music as a representation or incarnation of superior beings, as one finds, for example, in the *Viṣṇu Purāṇas*, but there seems a complete consensus among all schools that discuss music that there is something extraordinary about it, about the pitches, and about orderly sounds, that ordinary discourse cannot reach. There are ineffable facets to music in both the superhuman and human contexts. Naturally, where music is associated with realms beyond man it partakes of their mysteriousness. Where seen in largely human terms, as is the case with most discussions of aesthetics, music is described as divorced from the rational, and the process by which it works on men's minds is likewise mysterious.

Perhaps of ultimate interest to most aestheticians are the problems of music and mind. By what process does it emanate from the composer and performer? By what process does it work on the mind of the listener? These questions are more readily evaded than answered, but are the omnipresent background to all but the most technical analyses of music. Generally speaking, music can be found in the company of other irrational or ineffable dimensions of human existence, including the achievement of extraordinary mental composure or enlightenment, the creation and appreciation of art, and the development and curing of madness. It contributes

[a] 律曆志

terminology (we speak of harmony and discord of mind), it serves as a metaphoric referent, and often is presented as an actual factor in achievement of sanity, enlightenment, madness, and artistic creation. There is endless variety in the lore of music and the irrational. A Brahmanic lawbook states, "One attains the Supreme Being by practising continuous *sāmans* in the prescribed manner and with mental concentration."[4] In Ancient Greece, both the Pythagorean and Peripatetic schools of healing practiced forms of musical catharsis or therapy, with one physician of the first century B.C., Asclepiades, treating his mentally deranged patients with "symphonia."[5] There were similar ideas explored by early Chinese thinkers. Confucius labeled as indispensable the singing of the *Odes*, knowledge of ritual music, and the discipline of the *ch'in*[b] zither in the regimen of self-cultivation. Though the power of music is acknowledged to be of great significance by Confucius and his disciples, the precise matter of process is left untouched in Confucian discourse up to the Han. Chuang Tzu provides engaging reflections on the mysteries of music, nature, and mind, and attributes a particularly musical nature to his favorite fool, Chieh-yü. The musical ditty that constitutes Chieh-yü's fool's talk reveals that his mind responds to an order beyond the rational.[6] For Chuang Tzu, the presence of certain music can be an obsessive, and welcome, distraction from rational activities.[7] But Chuang Tzu, like Confucius, does not venture into analysis of the music and mind problem. In sundry narratives from the earliest times through the Six Dynasties, order is associated with proper music, while illness and other banes are associated with improper music.[8] In the narratives of the early Six Dynasties, music plays a role in the exorcism of madness and possession-induced illnesses of various descriptions.[9]

Our focus is on music and the arts and those thinkers who took music and earlier discussions of music as an aid in developing theories of the arts. Music was the first art to be given serious philosophical consideration, hence its concepts and terminology occupied a central position when generalized theories of aesthetics were evolving. Lu Chi's (261–303) *Wen fu* (Rhymeprose on Literature) is the pivotal text for our discussion, and it is thought by many scholars to be the earliest, well-unified discussion of an art form that might be termed a theory of aesthetics. Lu Chi's rhymeprose is a brilliant exploration of the nature of poetry from its conception in the poet's mind to its reception in the world. In a central and influential section of the rhymeprose, describing the making of the object, Lu Chi relies heavily on what he inherited from the tradition of music theorizing to build terminology for his poetry criticism. Before analyzing Lu Chi's chapters at length, it will be useful to review some specific texts and ideas about music that were the foundation for his work.

As I have suggested above, discussions of music and dance of great variety reach back to the earliest Chinese texts. In modern scholarship, these have generally been

b 琴

treated singly and *in situ*, with little effort to illuminate them as moments in an evolving body of knowledge or against the background of contending views. The lack of a comprehensive treatment of Chinese music to bring the complex evolution of ideas into focus has still not obscured recognition of the importance of these ideas. Of the many modern studies on particular aspects of Chinese music, several can be counted as highly significant contributions to our knowledge of early China.[10]

During the Han, scholars asserted that a *Yüeh ching*[c] (Classic of Music) had existed in the middle Chou, and that the text was to be regarded as equal in importance to the *Li ching*[d] (Classic of Rites). The compilation of the *Li chi* (Book of Rites) during the Han paid a restrained tribute to this belief by including a lengthy chapter entitled *"Yüeh chi"*[e] (Book of Music) and several other chapters concerned with music.

There is no verifiable music classic from pre-Han China, but a sampling of extant texts suggests what ideas one might have contained, or at the very least the ideas that Han ideology would have liked it to contain. The earliest historical accounts attribute to music the power to "regulate" both nature and man and, hence, to be an instrument of order in the universe. "K'uei said, 'Oh' when I strike the stone, when I knock on the stone, all of the animals follow (it) and dance, all of the governors, (i.e. officials) become truly harmonious.'"[11] Maspero has attempted to explain the sometimes peculiar structure of the *Shu ching* (Book of Documents) by arguing that it is a collection of libretti for ritual performances. The *Kao-yao mo* would, by this account, be itself a musical composition for "regulating" an event. By pre-Han accounts, we know that ritual drums were assigned the important task of beginning and regulating the pace of the highly formal religious performances.[12] In the social prescriptions of the *I li* (Ceremonial Rites), which I would prefer to translate as *Cermonial Programs*, and the administrative scheme of the *Chou li* (Rites of Chou), preferably translated *Programs of Chou*, earlier mythic accounts are distilled and formalized. Music and music masters are fully and exclusively employed in the service of social or political order.[13]

When belief in the influential power of music was established, the concern turned to determining what was correct, that the influence might be conducive to order and harmony. Confucius speaks repeatedly in the *Analects* of the need for correct music. It plays a broad role in the process of self-cultivation, from the refinement of inner qualities to the acquisition of social graces. In the Confucian ideology as it later developed, the musical content of the *Odes*, chanted texts, and ritual music play the subtler side in a complementary relationship to *li*:

> To make peaceful the powers above and regulate the people, nothing surpasses *li*. To change ways and transform customs, nothing is better than music.[14]

c 樂經　　　　　　　　d 禮經　　　　　　　　e 樂記

Confucius had already begun the identification of what was correct music and what was not, and had begun to identify specific qualities that defined correctness. Closely related to the idea of a musical orthodoxy was the idea that an absolute value attached to particular pieces of music or even particular pitches. As early as the *Tso chuan* (Commentary of Tso), certain pitches are associated with colors, measures, seasons, and other systems of signifiers in what ultimately emerges as a semasiology of music and pitch during the Han. The *Huang-chung*[f] note, first in the standard gambit of twelve tuning notes, is named after the color yellow and associated with the earth, the garb of the superior man, and the center. In the fragmentary apocrypha remaining from the Han, we can see that the significance of the pitches was felt to be precise, enduring, and that it was believed partially translatable into other language systems. Hence the texts elaborated on the prognosticatory and metaphysical import of music.[15] These and other interpretive traditions in the corpus of musical theory share the premises of the Confucian view, trusting not only to the significance of music, its specificity and durability, but also to man's ability to comprehend it, relate it to other systems of signification, including speech and writing, and ultimately to make use of it in improving himself and his world.

We can see sailent points of contrast in Chuang Tzu's thoughts on the subject. For Chuang Tzu, music provides a bridge from man's mind to nature, but it is a mystical rather than intelligible communication. Man is no more capable of comprehending the greatest music rationally than he is capable of using his tools of rational expression, speech and writing, to comprehend or express the greatest truths. Music is not significant in a particular and translatable way. What was significant music for Confucius is the "trivia of music" for Chuang Tzu, namely the ritual songs and feathered dances.[16] For Chuang Tzu, great music is something to which men can only listen, and listen with confusion.

> Ch'eng of North Gate said to the Yellow Emperor, "When Your Majesty performed the Hsien-ch'ih music in the woods around Lake Tung-t'ing, I listened, and at first I was afraid. I listened some more and felt weary, and then I listened to the end and felt confused. Overwhelmed, speechless, I couldn't get hold of myself."
>
> "It's not surprising you felt that way," said the emperor. "I performed it through man, tuned it to heaven, went forward with ritual principle, and established it in Great Purity...."[17]

The divergence of views turns on disagreement over what music signifies, how it signifies, how it affects man, and to what use it might be put. Between Confucius and Chuang Tzu, two positions were established that served later aestheticians well, for whom an abiding tension continued between two parallel inclinations, on one

[f] 黃鐘

hand to see art as a means of personal expression and communication of the ineffable, and on the other to see art as an instrument of education, maintenance of social order, and a repository of normative social values.[18]

In this swift review, there are materials outside of the philosophical texts that deserve mention. The various narrative and anecdotal texts that coalesced in pre-Han times treated music often in a way that synthesized some aspects of the contending philosophical positions. Early narratives, which focused largely on the *ch'in* zither, made their own contributions to late aesthetic theory. Because the *ch'in* played an important part in the life of the superior man, the early narratives contributed to a lasting literati ideology in traditional China.[19]

The association between the *ch'in* and the literatus and aesthete was such that by the early Six Dynasties the *ch'in* had become an emblem for a sage or superior man. By the Sung Dynasty possession of a fine *ch'in* was a widespread affectation, even among those who had no ability to play it. The history of the instrument is documented in detail in a substantial body of *ch'in* lore texts. The texts themselves had their origins in pre-Han China, but were subject to frequent revision and expansion, especially in the Six Dynasties, Sung, and Ming, with the result that the date and origin of much of the materialis difficult to ascertain with any degree of certainty.[20] The invention of the *ch'in* is variously attributed to Fu Hsi, Shen Nung, or Shun, and its position among the crucial early deeds in the history of civilization is well established, ranking with the invention of writing and the trigrams. Several texts tell of Confucius playing the *ch'in*, especially when in a contemplative mood.[21]

A number of masters of the *ch'in* are mentioned in the *Chuang Tzu* and *Lieh Tzu*, all of whom are likewise masters of the Way. Musical mastery as demonstrated by the presence of a *ch'in* was synonymous with enlightenment, a kind of synecdoche that related aural superiority to mental or spiritual superiority in general. Interestingly, the common sensory referent in metaphors for the superior mind in early China was hearing and sound as contrasted to vision and light in the West. As Confucius said, "By age sixty, would that my ears be in tune."[22] Studies have indicated that the radical "ear" (*ehr*[g]) is etymonic and possibly phonetic in the character for "sage" (*sheng*[h]) as well as other words bearing on sagacity and perspicacity in much the same way that "vision" shares a common root with "wit" and "wisdom" in English and its ancestors.[23] Early medical theory associated the state of mind and body with auditory signals. Internal organic systems were each associated with a tone, and emotions in particular were most readily manifest in the quality of voice. The texts speak of the "sound" (*sheng*[i]) of the six emotions as if the voice were directly their own.[24] Music, being the ultimate ordering of sound, is obviously the metaphor of choice for the ultimate ordering of mind. In turn, the

g 耳　　　　　　　　　　h 聖　　　　　　　　　　i 聲

ch'in, being the most refined of musical instruments, becomes emblematic for the most refined of minds.

In both the philosophical and narrative texts, criticism of music had established a clear direction by the Han, especially in matters of typing and evaluation. In the *Analects*, where Confucius criticizes the music of Cheng, he compares it to the manner in which the color purple detracts from the luster of primary red.[25] In the *Book of Music*, Tzu-hsia comments on several types of music, that of Cheng as "lewd and corrupting," of Sung as "soft" and effeminate," of Wei as "repetitious and annoying," and the music of Ch'i as "harsh and conducive to arrogance."[26] Broadly speaking, the Confucian preference is easily related to a conservative attitude toward most instruments of civilization. With an interest in continuity and propriety in traditions, especially those important in ritual, he emphasized the careful and uninventive transmission of ancient ways.[27] Preferred music was at one with preferred behavior; it should possess a sense of balance, quietude, and easy integration into the surrounding order. Tzu-hsia criticized the four regional musics mentioned above as being "sensual," meaning that they were melodically complex and possibly performed with expanded instrumentation. Theoretically, the minimal pentatonic scale and minimal pitch variation in the melodic line were goals of good performance.[28] On these points, the Confucian position is in agreement with that of Lao Tzu and Chuang Tzu, both of whom fault even the five tones for their dulling effect on the senses and coax both the making and appreciation of art toward the side of nonaction.[29] By the Han, even the Confucian *Book of Rites* writes of music in a perfected or ultimate sense that is totally without sound:

> (Tzu-hsia says,) "Now that I have asked and received instruction in the Five Attainments, I would dare to inquire what is meant by the Three Withouts."
>
> Confucius replied, "Music without sound, Ritual without embodiment, and Mourning without garb. These are the Three Withouts."[30]

By Lu Chi's time, the idea of minimization had been exemplified in the *ch'in* lore, with popular images like the *ch'in* with broken strings, or the *ch'in* with no strings at all, the aesthete playing alone, playing to nature, playing to his own kind, or simply wandering about with his instrument, not playing at all. By the Sung, one finds reference to the aeolian *ch'in*, placed in a window or held in the woods to be strummed by the wind. In fact, the *ch'in* is a light instrument and a quiet instrument, well suited to its role for these and other reasons to be explored below.

Music is the only art form for which a record of critical consideration exists in pre-Han texts. Its primacy as a source of terminology in aesthetic evaluation is understandable from this. When critical discussions of the *Odes* ventured toward expressionist sentiments, as in the opening lines of the Mao preface, the musical component is brought to the foreground of the discussion.[31] More didactic or utilitarian considerations of the *Odes* naturally focused sharply on the texts. Significantly the *Odes*, as the origin of the genre of poetry, were described, by genre, as being virtuous and unimpeachable. The *Odes* have no depraved thoughts, according to Confucian text. One can find no equivalent to the lewd music of Cheng in discussions of early poetry. In the earliest discussion of poetry, what constituted the genre was a specific body of text, antique and venerated, by definition good. But in discussions of music, what constituted the genre was a variety of performance activities, which surely ranged from good to bad; hence music is perceived as having the potential to be good or bad. When criticism began to explore evaluation and search for refinement of evaluative norms on the practical level it was guided by the tradition of music criticism. Consideration of evaluative norms led to generalization of evaluative norms in principles defining what was aesthetic, first in music and then in art generally.

In summarizing pre-Han philosophical positions and legends about music, I do not want to convey the impression that the ideas current were simple or the thinking monolithic. There was great variety in individual's interests and great contention between views, not only along the broad Confucian-Taoist lines described above, but reaching to details of scales, tunings, instruments, and the like. By the early Han the contentious nature of much of the tradition had been translated into heated debates at court, factions arguing over the proper pitches and the proper songs and tunings for the rituals, the exact pitch of the bell standards, the proper entertainments for the court at any given season, even the proper training for the bearers of the performance arts. But in contrast, the major philosophers, divorced from particular political issues at court and from performance issues, tended to work to integrate the diversity of received theories in characteristic Han eclectic schemes. In the narrative accounts, primarily in the dynastic histories, we have the view of performed music in the Han, including the establishment of the Music Bureau for the collection of diverse musical materials, the appointment of music masters and their proclivity for the sensual and unorthodox, and the frequent suggestion that the attitude toward music at court was promiscuous and permissive. In the philosophical texts, both epigrammatic and sustained, which are epitomized by the *Treatise on the Pitchpipes and Calendar*, we have a very different view, wherein all aspects of life are fitted into a colossal cosmic taxonomy, keyed to the musical gamut and calendar. It was a system built with a passion for order and an obvious affection for complexity.[32]

In Han theory, music was a framework, providing the skeleton for a logical system organized by the numbers three, five, six, ten, and twelve. The twelve pitches (*lü*[j]) were homologous with the twelve branches, twelve annual lunations, twelve

j 律

major divisions of the tropical year, the twelve lines of the first two hexagrams, and other subjects of the duodecimal matrix.[33] The twelve tuning pitches that constituted the *lü* were generated from a sequential division of pipe lengths, were thought to be natural and absolute, and, hence, related by nature to other observable twelve-point phenomena. Han thinkers were concerned with "configurational energy" (*ch'i*[k]), it being the means by which the apparently disconnected phenomena were related. *Ch'i* was the energy that brought the sound from otherwise dead pipes, that circulated in specific configurations between heaven and earth to demarcate the periods of the tropical year, and that linked man and nature in any number of diverse ways.[34] Pitchpipe technology, which was employed in the grand search for more precision for the Han standard Huang-chung note, was also put to experimental use in the measurement of cosmic *ch'i*, one goal of which was more precision in the Han calendar. Twelve pipes of measured length were buried in the ground and observed for signs that one or another length was channeling *ch'i* at a given point in the tropical year.[35]

The measurement of cosmic *ch'i* as practiced in the Han best illustrates the relationship understood to exist between music and time, the pitchpipes and the calendar. It brings to the foreground deep-seated notions that *ch'i* could indeed be channeled, that it could be coordinately piped whereby a specific configuration was drawn through a pipe of specific length, that it connected the ancestors or other supernal forces with man, that the criteria of any particular configuration included both spatial and temporal components, and finally, that possession of good pitch and good calendars was germane to the health of the dynasty.

Han musical theory as summarized above and as presented by the excellent scholarship cited appears relentlessly mechanistic, and in fact the weightier discussions seemed infatuated with numerological concerns to the exclusion of any aesthetic ones. There are traces, however, of continuing development and refinement of aesthetic ideas. The bibliography of the *History of the Han*, based on the oldest bibliography of record, Liu Hsiang's *Ch'i lüeh chih* (Summary of Seven Classes), includes a list of music classics. Although the postscript of the list explores the "significance" (*i*[l]) of music in a mechanistic context, half of the six books in the actual list appear to be performance manuals for the *ch'in*. If these resemble what became the standard for manuals later in the tradition, they would have included a blend of instruction and lore, with relatively little emphasis on theory. Unfortunately, none of the forty-four chapters that made up the three titles survives, but an interest in performance technique and lore is evident in extant sources from the Later Han, for example, Ying Shao's *Feng-su-t'ung* (ca. 175). The *Feng-su-t'ung* has an entire section devoted to music and instruments, the introduction of which dutifully summarizes well-known points:

k 氣　　　　　　　　l 義

> Music is the means by which the sage moves heaven and earth, stirs the ghosts and spirits, settles the masses of people, and fulfills the nature of all things.[36]

After a discussion of the Five Tones, Ying Shao begins cataloging material on over twenty different instruments. Each is accorded its own paragraphs, which include brief technical descriptions of the instruments, important references to them in the classics, and important legends and lore involving them.

The *ch'in* is provided the longest entry. And its stories are among the most developed and the most significant for the later tradition. Among the stories is a detailed rendering of the important lengend of Po Ya and Chung Tzu-ch'i.

> When Po Ya played the *ch'in* and Chung Tzu-ch'i listened, Tzu-ch'i's thoughts were transported to towering mountains. He exclaimed to Po Ya, "How marvelous, with majesty akin to Mount T'ai!" But in a moment his thoughts were carried to flowing waterways. "How marvelous," he said, "bubbling and flowing like our mightiest rivers."
>
> Tzu-ch'i died, and thereupon Po Ya smashed his *ch'in* and broke its strings. Never again did the he play the *ch'in*, for he felt no one in the world was adequate to appreciate its voice.[37]

The characters in this story are traditionally placed in the sixth century B.C., and Po Ya is mentioned in the *Hsün Tzu*. There it is said he played so beautifully that even the emperor's horses looked up.[38] The story translated above, or closely related versions, is found in a number of Han collections and became a touchstone throughout later times in *ch'in* theory and practice.

The Po Ya and Chung Tzu-ch'i story is a concise example of the transitional nature of Later Han thought on music. The roots of several of its notions can be found in the earlier, cosmological context, but here they are transplanted in an emergent aesthetic one. Specifically, the idea of communication is important here, but whereas formerly it was understood as being primarily between man and supernal forces, here it is exclusively between two individuals. The emphasis is on the affective nature of communication and its potential richness. The facet of individual facility or genius is recognized, for both the performer and the listener. For Po Ya, technique is a mysterious thing, indescribable, but clearly manifest in the power of his music. The earlier concept emphasized precision of pitch and faithfulness to the ritual tradition. Chung Tzu-ch'i's eminence as a listener likewise is beyond that of Chuang Tzu's Tzu-ch'i, for whom listening was a mystic art.[39] Mystic art has been replaced by an act of emotional correspondence, or empathy, following from the fact that nature is no longer the performer, a man is. This notable shift to concern with art as a human enterprise is essential in order for music to play its role in the emergence of critical and theoretical terminology.

One more point is to be drawn from the Po Ya story, its illustration of the commutability of musical sensation and natural images. Apparently descended from the correlative thinking of the early Han, the idea has escaped the numerological framework and reappeared in an affective one. Correlation has become synesthesia, exploration of the relationship between one sense and another and between the senses and feelings. The relationship between music and feelings, for both the performer and the listener, is crucial for early aestheticians. Following is one of the few other extant stories concerning Chung Tzu-ch'i:

> One evening Chung Tzu-ch'i overheard someone playing the *ch'ing*[m] lithophone. The music evoked weighty feelings, so the next morning he sought out the player and asked, "Why, why, was your playing of the stones so grave?"
>
> The man replied, "My father killed someone and did not survive it. My mother survived, but she became a slave in a local official house. I survived, and became a musician in a local official house. A period of three years went by without my even seeing my mother. Then yesterday, I was in the marketplace and spotted her. I wanted to buy her freedom, but I have no money. I too am just the property of another house. These are the reasons for my grave feelings."
>
> Chung Tzu-ch'i said to this, "Such gravity of feeling must reside within the heart. It is not something in the hands, the chimes, or the wooden mallets. It resides in the heart, and the mallets and chimes only correlate with it."[40]

These and similar narratives are scattered throughout Han texts. One can identify in them concern with the individual and individual feelings that becomes central to the aestheticians of the early Six Dynasties. Important critical terms, like "gravity of feeling" (*pei*[n]), are given attention. And, through the association of various arts, in both theory and practice, the affinities that all have for each other come into focus. With this, a finer concept of art per se, in a human rather than broad cosmological context, is passed on.

Reading Six Dynasties criticism against the background of Han musical theory, one can appreciate the subtlety of both change and continuity in the evolving intellectual traditions. During the Chien-an Period (196–220), music was discussed almost exclusively for its expressive qualities, coinciding with the perspective of the new literary criticism associated with the Ts'ao clan. Concern for the aesthetics of contemporary poetry, best exemplified in the writings of Ts'ao P'i, is paralleled by a turning away from the discussion of musical theory and its cosmological framework toward an appreciative and critical interest in pieces and performances, and the

^m磬 ⁿ悲

naming of their desirable qualities. Yet, though the focus of the interest has changed, the terminology is essentially refurbished Han terminology. By using Han vocabulary, Six Dynasties theorists entrained Han concepts and premises, and at least began their arguments in the bedrock of earlier thought. Ts'ao P'i adopts music as the model for the ineffable dimensions of literature and returns to *ch'i*, for a tangible and demonstrable premise for his theory:

> Literature must take *ch'i* as its mainstay. And the affective manifestations of *ch'i* have particular embodiments; they cannot simply be forced. In this, a comparison may be made to music.[41]

The puissant influence of Han terminology will be obvious when we discuss the Lu Chi chapters below. Of equal if not greater significance to the shaping of early Six Dynasties theory is the influence of Han strategies of presentation or strategies of argumentation. Numerology may no longer have been the subject of the discussion, but numbers and orderly sets of terms continued to provide the structure for critical theories and texts. Veracity was found in the quinary syllogism, and the process of proof required placing a term in each of the five available spots. An affection continues for the number five, whereas twelve declines in popularity somewhat. The Five Tones become the synecdoche for music rather than the Twelve Pitches, and extensive use is made of Five Phases correlations, less of duodecimal ones.

Along with the Five Phases and Five Tones, as early as the *Book of Rites* there is a definition of "Five Defects" of music. The "Book of Music" chapter begins with a group of six emotions, into which one is moved by external things. Then the traditional Five Tones are assigned to five classes of being: lord, minister, commoner, events, and thing. Discord in each tone is related to a defect in its respective correlate. Discord in each is further related to a feeling, or a quality of perception: isolation, confusion, sorrow, grief, and anxiety. The Five Defects in this way are logically derived from the Five Tones and described with the resultant joyless emotion.[42]

There is little sustained critical evaluation of music and its nature extant from the Chien-an period or before, but there appears to have been some consensus on a group of five particulars of cultivated taste; one might call them desirable aesthetic qualities. In pioneering studies on music and literary criticism in the Six Dynasties, Jao Tsung-i writes that five qualities being discussed in contemporaneous analysis of music were borrowed by Lu Chi and made the foundation for his discussion of literary principles in the *Rhymeprose on Literature*.[43] Key terms in the discussion are *ying*,[o] *ho*,[p] *pei*, *ya*,[q] and *yen*.[r] These terms individually and in varying frequency can

[o] 應
[p] 和
[q] 雅
[r] 豔

be found in texts well before the Han, primarily used in a technical context, secondarily an affective one. Lu Chi's use of the terms is somewhat special, deriving but differing from the *Book of Rites*. Lu Chi does not name a particular feeling the listener has nor does he elaborate on the Five Tones, but he describes five qualities that music and poetry must embody in order for them to achieve the proper feelings with the proper intensity. His definitions are detailed and related to performance, not speculation. In this way, the intellectual and speculative traditions of music are linked to performance, and musical terminology is made available for utilization in the evolving aesthetic theory.

Lu Chi approaches a discussion of aesthetics in exactly the same way one approaches a discussion of an omniscient deity, by describing what it is not. The discussion occurs in chapters that Achilles Fang entitled "Purple Patches" and "Five Imperfections," because it defines five qualities of music by recourse to their characteristic defects.[44] The images of the discussion are those of isolation, loneliness, and abandonment, *ku*,[s] *tu*,[t] and *chi-mo*.[u] The *Book of Rites* argued that "Music unites," and here in its defective state it is without mate.[45] In both texts, the defects relate more closely to discernible human feelings than to the notes or qualities sought, suggesting that the positive achievement is beyond description.

Ying

Perhaps the words are cast upon diminished rhymes,
And to the farthest reach must rise alone.
Looking down there is emptiness, no friend to be found,
Looking up to vast space, no thing to be met.
Like a string out of scale, plucked alone,
Has its own voice clear, but no response.[46]

The opening stanza addresses *ying*, translated in Jao's Padua paper as "congeniality" and translated above as "response." The concept is broad, overlapping our notions of correspondence, correlation, consonance, and resonance, and describes two seemingly unrelated things that have significant interactive capabilities. The origin of the term in acoustics was sympathetic resonance, the potential of one vibrating device to "respond" to another of the same resonant frequency. Sympathetic resonance was described in detail as early as the *Kuo yü* (Tales of the States) and the *Chuang Tzu*. It was used to tune instruments, check the trueness of pitch against a standard, check the size of bells and measures, and to demonstrate the ability of one thing to act upon another at a distance without a visible connection.

^s 孤   ^t 獨   ^u 寂寞

Grand arguments for cosmic correlations to earthly events, like those found throughout the *Ch'un-ch'iu fan-lu*, appeal to *ying* or *hsiang-ying*[v] experiments to prove the potential for remote interactions.[47] With attention turning to aesthetic considerations, *ying* is reinterpreted to apply to elements within a composition and between a composition and the feelings elicited. Diminished rhymes reduce the potential for words to interact significantly with each other, an observation that has played a role in literary criticism to the present day.[48] For music to unite, the tenets of *ying* must be met.

Response and correspondence are to be found between one string and another, an instrument and another voice, a rhythmic quality or moment and another, melody and rhythm, and so forth. To some extent, there is in Lu Chi a continuation of the earlier thinking that *ying* qualities are found in art proper to the time of year and the occasion. The characteristic defect of *ying* is "smallness' (hsiao[w]). This might be described as the flatness of a tone that fails to resonate with others or the solitude of music that fails to fit with the moment, commune with nature, or move the feelings of listeners. *Ying* says that music and its components relate to counterparts, on many levels and in many ways. *Hsiao* as a defect says that the potential of art is diminished when such counterparts are not brought into significant interaction.

Ho

Perhaps the words are given to enfeebled tones,
That like frail stems, bend before full flower.
With the graceful and graceless scrambled in one form,
Good material may abound; the whole still comes forth blemished.
The horn that blares untimely from below,
Though true in pitch, finds no harmony.

Ho is translated in Jao's paper as "harmony of tone," but it might be broadened to include all facets of harmony, between each element of the music and between music and the outside. *Ho* follows from *ying*, but differs in that it describes the agreeable compatability between two things with fundamentally different natures, not simply physically detached. Musically, there is harmony between a tone and its octave or fifth, for example. Both *ying* and *ho* are concepts that recognize that counterparts must combine differences and similarities. At the point of identity, both *ying* and *ho* cease to exist.[49] Within music, *ho* describes the ability of one note to make a palatable whole with another. The characteristic defect of *ho* is "weakness" or "fraility" (*yü*[x]). It is the failure of components to energize each other in such a manner that as a whole they are greater than the sum of their parts.

[v] 相應   [w] 小   [x] 窳

Pei

Perhaps known order is abandoned and novelty embraced,
And empty space is searched for trivial things.
Words scant in feeling and poor in love,
Just blow about, without a source of life.
Weak strings under an impulsive touch,
May harmonize, but have no gravity of feeling.

The third of Lu Chi's qualities, *pei*, is translated in Jao's paper as "sadness of conveyance." *Pei* is not to emphasize melancholy, but more generally speaks to gravity of feeling, as I have translated it above, opposed to levity of feeling. *Pei* in its earliest appearances, the *Odes* and the *Analects*, describes a burden of the heart. In the former case it is a longing, in the latter a desire to express what one is incapable of expressing.[50] In the earliest occurrences defined as a burden without sound, it is later defined as a crying sound without tears.[51] As early as the *Han Fei Tzu*, gravity of sentiment was related to the powers of music: listening to the "gravest" of the modes, the Clear Chiao, caused natural disasters to be visited upon Duke P'ing of Chin and his land. The *Huai-nan Tzu* attributes to Confucius the remark, "Music at its ultimate is grave."[52] Wang Ch'ung discusses grave music in his *Lun-heng* (Balancing Discourses), and Mei Sheng mentions a grave song in his *Ch'i ch'i* (Seven Expositions). But it was Ts'ao Ts'ao himself who identified the pipings of the wind as *pei* and hence explained its affective nature:

From where within the woods comes the whistling and the strumming?
The sound of the northern winds is truly grave.

And Ts'ao Chih followed:

Turning my face to the clear wind that I might breathe and sigh,
I place my thoughts in my *ch'in's* grave strings.[53]

In the *Shuo-yüan* (Garden of Discourses), attributed to Liu Hsiang, there is a narrative exploring the relative roles of music and events in eliciting grave feelings. Yung Men-chou carries his *ch'in* to call upon Lord Meng-ch'ang, whereupon Meng-ch'ang requests that the musician play something to make him heavy of heart. Men-chou replies that if all the political and social chaos that surrounds the lord does not make him heavy of heart, it is certainly beyond the ability of his *ch'in* to do so. Lord Meng-ch'ang is persuaded and begins weeping. At this point, Men-chou takes hold of his *ch'in*, begins strumming, and reduces the lord to uncontrolled sobbing. The affinity with the Chung Tzu-ch'i story quoted above is clear. Music could serve to enrich the feeling the lord had, but it could not wholly shape his mood, especially if he were not prepared to feel the sentiment or, worse yet, were defending against it.

In the Yung Men-chou story as well as in other Han writings, there is the clear statement that the affective potential of music is not unlimited. Music can express only genuine gravity of feeling in the heart of the performer, and resonate with true gravity of feeling in the heart of the listener.[54]

Lu Chi follows this thinking, but concentrates mainly on the artist's role and the act of creating. Gravity of feeling in a poem is related to that possessed by the artist. The characteristic defect of *pei* is "hollowness" and "vacancy" (*hsü*[y]), of both surface and feeling. Technical excellence and perfection of harmony notwithstanding, those who do not possess feelings of gravity cannot play or write with *pei*.

Ya

Perhaps by galloping about, diverse things are well assembled,
And enchant by virtue of rich and varied voice.
These but delight the eye and meet the vulgar taste,
Put sound above, but music's substance low.
Ditties like "Dew Shelter" and "Mulberry Grove,"
Have grave feelings, but range beyond restraint.

The fourth quality, *ya*, is translated in Jao's paper as "restraint in expression." *Ya* referred originally to orthodox practice in composing and performing, and thus suggested the discipline, individual and social, necessary to resist new trends and foreign influence. Restraint is opposed to indulgence, orthodoxy to vulgarity and corrupt practice. Apparently in Confucius' time, *ya* meant adhering to the pentatonic scale rather than including the expanded heptatonic elaborations that periodically grew in influence. Generally speaking, what was *ya* was simple and of quiet surface, rather than complex and highly articulated, the latter being music that the *Book of Rites* refers to as "sounds of lost countries."[55] *Ya* is the encapsulation of the preference for the minimal expressed in the *Analects*, the *Book of Rites*, and Lao Tzu's frequently quoted line, "Great music is sparing in sound."[56] The characteristic defect of *ya* is called *Cheng*, identified by Confucian thinkers as the extreme example of heterodoxy.

In later times, the definitions of *ya* allowed many variations, and it was a widely considered issue during the early Six Dynasties. By and large it was detached from the ritual context in which Confucius had used it and associated with the current interests in primitive simplicity and spontaneity. If one thinks of *ya* as bearing originally on the formality of ritual performance, than its meaning is virtually inverted. Juan Chi's "Discourse on Music" contains an assertion of traditionalism in which the virtues of simplicity are related to desirable moral transformations, but it is wholly without any notion of or reference to ritual.

y 虛

The male and the female principles of the universe move easily and simply; refined music, too, is uncomplicated, The Way and its Virtue are level and plain. The Five Notes of music, too, are insipid. Refined music is uncomplicated, and so the Yin and Yang communicate naturally. It is insipid, and so all things are naturally joyous. Daily they grew in unconscious goodness and achieve their moral transformation; their customs and habits change and alter, and they are all united in the same joy-music. This was the natural way. This was music at its beginnings.[57]

The virtue of simplicity is likewise emphasized in Hsi K'ang's *Sheng wu-ai-lo lun* ("Discourse on the Nonemotional Nature of Sound") which will be examined below.

Of all the instruments known to early thinkers, the *ch'in* was the exemplar of *ya* qualities, and there is no wonder that it became the musical emblem of the Seven Sages. By the early Han, *ya* in fact became prefixed to *ch'in* in a binome, *ya-ch'in*,[z] meaning "elegant *ch'in*" or "restrained *ch'in*." Liu Hsiang offered the following explanation:

> In the expression *ya-ch'in* the character *ch'in* means "restraint" (*chin*[aa]) and the character *ya* means "correct." The superior man holds to what is correct in order to restrain himself.[58]

The three manuals of *ch'in* masters found in the bibliography of the *History of the Former Han* are *Master Lung of the Ya-ch'in*, *Master Chao of the Ya-ch'in*, and *Master Shih of the Ya-ch'in*.[59] Though none survive, we might surmise that schools worthy of having their manuals preserved were of the "refined *ch'in*."

Yen

Perhaps by clearing and emptying, true simplicity is reached,
Each enrichment and superfluity removed.
With flavor falling short of tasteless ritual broth,
It has the purity and breadth of ritual strings.
Plodding along in measured song and response,
Though restrained, this lacks artful appeal.

The fifth quality, *yen*, is translated in Jao's paper as "richness of texture." This is complementary to *ya*, and is first defined as that which lends beauty to a *ya* work. Jao points out that concern with *yen* is a striking departure from the Han view.[60] *Yen* refers to aesthetic qualities of a sensual sort, sometimes specifically embellishments or adornments, as in the introductory *yen* of a poem or story.[61] The characteristic

z 雅琴   aa 禁

defect of *yen* is "austerity," written with the character '*chih*,'[ab] familiar in the "style" vs. "substance" discussions of the era.

Without reference to particulars it is difficult to understand how the restraint prescribed by *ya* might be reconciled to the richness of texture and use of embellishments suggested by *yen*. As a critical term, *yen* was used to commend the aesthetic pleasure of listening to a particular piece of music or a particular performer. According to Jao, *yen* refers to the patterning of sound, a deduction apparently made from the implied association with *wen*.[ac] Though our initial reaction to the idea of patterning in music might be to think of rhythm or melody, we may also take it to be a subtle complexity or elaboration, unrelated to pitch, underlying the simple surface of an exemplary piece. In the case of the *ch'in* we can discern facets of the music that provide for this and hence provide a key to understanding its enduring appeal.

Performed music that is to have vitality for any audience must be innovative and evolutionary to an extent, but to have comprehensibility, innovation must be in balance with convention or tradition. It is against the background of the traditional elements, what might be called the stereotypic, that the innovative elements, the variable, have significance and aesthetic impact. Even in a culture with explicit dicta limiting innovation, music and art generally dominated by ancient rules and restraints and bound to an ideal of exact reiteration would be a deadly bore. The histories record just that complaint from time to time.

> Lord Wen of Wei asked Tzu-hsia, "When I don my formal regalia and hear performances of ancient music, my only fear is that I will fall asleep. When listening to the notes of Cheng, on the other hand, exhaustion never so much as enters my mind!"[62]

Lu Chi approaches this problem by including *yen* in his listing. The interplay of *ya* and *yen* is part of an important general problem of interplay between the stereotypic and variable in the arts of traditional societies that explicitly prize the continuity of their traditions. When the conventions of performed music require surface simplicity, as is the case of literati arts generally, we must seek for innovation and individual expression within the constraint of a simple surface. How might the patterns of music be enriched without violating the requirements of *ya*? The richness must not be an obvious intrusion into an ostensibly reiterative act. It may be inaccessible to the noninitiate, but must provide a rich feast for the connoisseur.

In orthodox music performed by the *ch'in* the solution was to constrain pitch and rhythm rigorously, as required by *ya*, but explore fully potential variations in tonal qualities and timbre. As van Gulik has shown, the *ch'in* is unsurpassed as an

ab 質   ac 文

instrument to exploit timbre variation. Within its simple pentatonic scale organization, the *ch'in* provides for a great variety in stopping, half-stopping, brushing,
touching, and strumming techniques rendering infinite variability in attack and
decay, harmonic content, vibrato, glissando, and other embellishments. To the
noninitiate, there are periods in *ch'in* performance when a flurry of hand movements
can be seen but no variation in the music perceived. Picken, Needham, and van
Gulik have all observed the importance of timbre variation in some Chinese music.
Early European visitors to China were unaccustomed to this, and we might assume
unresponsive, and felt the music to be without interest.[63] Traditional *ch'in* notation
was a tablature system recording the hand movements, not the pitches, and manuals
often had long illustrated sections showing the "hand postures" (*shou-shih*[ad]),
emphasizing the importance of this choreographic aspect of the performance.

The five aesthetic qualities reviewed above, as the Five Phases, operate in an
interlocking manner. The advances of one meet the retreats of another; the assertions
of one control the excesses of another. Excesses of *pei* are restrained by *ya*, of *ya* by
yen, of *yen* by *ya* and *ying* (variety versus sameness), of *ying* by *ho* (unison versus
harmony), and of *ho* and *ying* by *pei* (accord, correspondence, and harmony versus
loneliness and profundity of individual sentiment). Their interlocking structure
combined with the breadth of their references provides for a shifting dominant
phase, according to time, place, and individual. *Ya* provides for ritual orientation, *pei*
for lyrical orientation, and *yen* for sensual orientation.

Lu Chi was not alone in his adaptation of music terminology to broader
aesthetic issues, though we have no contemporaneous writings of equivalent detail.
The most widespread examples mirrored Ts'ao P'i's interest in *ch'i* as an analogy to
the ineffable dimension of literature. The early aesthetician considered the spiritual
dimension of art not solely in the context of inspiration, but in varied contexts,
seeking metaphors for the invisible action of objects and forces on the artist when he
produces, then the invisible action of the object or performance on the respondent.
The idea that external things "moved", were "moved by," or were "perceived by"
(*kan*[ae]) the feelings of both artist and audience was expressed over and again, but little
could be said directly about the process of that influence. The organs of perception
were related to particular stimuli. Lu Chi wrote, "Patterns interanimate to overfill
the eyes; tones effervesce to inundate the ears."[64] In the rhymeprose he has gathered
a treasury of metaphors for the mysterious processes of art. Though he does not
explicitly bring up the cannalizing of the cosmic *ch'i*, the silent pipe brought to life
with *ch'i*, the still string moved by the plucking of another string nearby, and similar
proofs, these are the ideas that inform his description of the crucial creative moment:
"tax emptiness to yield being; knock upon silence in search of tone."[65] Lu Chi

ad 手勢　　　　　　　　ae 感

favors another metaphor well known in Western examinations of the spiritual: "[Poetry] broadcasts about the diffuse fragrance of sweet blossoms."[66] The idea was dear to any sixteenth-century theorist who pondered the process by which the scent rose from the blossom and impinged upon the nose or who used "spirits" to extract the essential perfume.[67]

Unlike those who preceded them, the early Six Dynasties thinkers did not demure from attacking the most intractable problems of aesthetic process, perhaps emboldened by widespread enthusiasm for all facets of "mysterious learning" (*hsüan-hsüeh*[af]). Music is taken very broadly in the more recondite discussions, not necessarily as something that can be heard. It is important to recall the Han pronouncement that music is human and internal, sound is what is external. The five qualities under discussion, seen in this light, go beyond the description of surface features of music and poetry, or beyond a comparison of surface features between music and poetry. They point to specifics of each art form within the matrix of its own possibilities, and relate ultimately to the potentials for human creation of, and response to, art. In poetry it might be theme that gives rise to *pei*, in music it might be rhythm, but in both cases *pei* links features of the art to mind. By bringing this particular set of terms out of their earlier technical definitions into broader ones bearing on the emotional contexts of aesthetic moments, Lu Chi brings the focus more toward the mind and the experience, away from the object and performance themselves.[68] This adaptation was important in taking the terminology based in the technical aspects of a particular genre of art and making it into terminology useful for all art forms. It also made his discussion of art of germinal interest to other thinkers of his era, not simply a revival of ancient terminology.

During the Wei-Chin period, at the hub of many individual philosophical inquiries was the general interest in human emotions. In addition to discussions of art, another approach to that central issue was discussion of the sage and emotions. Did the sage have feelings, and could he be pursued as a model for ordinary men in dealing with their feelings? Another approach was discussion of language and its capacity for communicating feelings. Both of these related to the questions of feelings and art. How did art communicate feeling? Did art have emotional content inherently? Ho Yen argued that the sage was without feelings, but Wang Pi differed.[69] Wang Pi expressed confidence that words and symbols could communicate feelings, but Yin Jung differed on this point.[70] The issues were combined in discussions of music and sound to which the best thinkers put their minds. *Shih-shuo hsin-yü* (A New Account of Tales of the World) describes a journey of Wang Tao, who, when crossing the Yangtze, deigned to discuss only three subjects, one of which was the joyless and sorrowless nature of sound.[71] The ancient association between sageness and sound is rekindled in these discussions, and one finds

af 玄學

everywhere the inescapable pun between "music" (*yüeh*[ag]) and "joy" (*lo*[ah]). Hsi K'ang's "Discourse on the Nonemotional Nature of Sound" is preserved and provides a concise picture of the issues.[72]

The discourse is in the form of a catechism. An unnamed guest confronts Hsi K'ang with venerated cosmological theories of Han vintage that define the emotional correlates to the orderly sounds. He further supports these arguments with historical examples attesting to music's emotional content. Hsi K'ang rejoins that sound has specific qualities, but these qualities are not the same thing as emotions. Emotions come from within, and the connection between sound and feeling is indirect, and it is variable. That is to say, the same songs will elicit different feelings depending on the time, place, and person. The same features may have different significance and potency, depending on the culture among other things. Hsi K'ang's point is exactly what has exercised contemporary aestheticians who have argued that specific connections cannot be drawn between a piece or moment in music and a nameable feeling. Susanne Langer argues that what music represents is not feeling at all, but the morphology of feeling, which is remarkably close to Hsi K'ang's direction of thought.[73]

Hsi K'ang makes an analogy between listening to music and drinking wine. It may incline one toward a general, emotional state of mind. But the response may be very personal, sometimes resulting from a totally individual association:

> In fact, one's halls may be filled with guests. After much drinking of wine, when the *ch'in* is performed, some feel a happy elation and others sob with deep-felt sorrow. It is not that sorrow is promoted with one song and joy with another. In actuality, the notes are unchanged, but both extremes of feelings emerge together.[74]

In contrast to Han thinking, it is a distinctly humanistic position to argue that the effect of art is wholly individualistic, beyond prediction, and beyond control, even of the artist. Hsi K'ang's interlocutor retaliates by quoting Confucian text, "To change ways and transform customs, nothing is better than music."[75] Hsi K'ang has already conceded that sound may be divided into certain gross classes. What is tense conduces tenseness; what is peaceful conduces peacefulness. And here he responds with a pun, "When the eight types of instruments were brought into assembly, it brought people joy, and that was what they called 'music.'" He continues to argue that Confucius was referring to a soundless music, a higher principle of order, of which the sound we hear is only one manifestation.[76] Hsi K'ang's phraseology at this point comes from the *Book of Rites, K'ung Tzu hsien-chü* ('Confucius at Repose'), but his point is a rather forced interpretation of the passage. The weakness in logic and authority notwithstanding, his argument is an eloquent statement on the

ag 樂   ah 樂

importance of the individual mind in the aesthetic process. Even so, mind for Hsi K'ang is not an accidental or unstructured entity, but partakes of some significant correlation with cosmic order. In this he builds reasonably on the Han view:

> Musical tones have their origins in human minds, being that which intimately connects man and the cosmos, as a shadow abstracts the [three dimensional] shape or an echo corresponds to a sound.[77]

Sound has content or structure related directly to the cosmic whole, of which mind, like all things, is a part. Sound is not affective in the ordinary sense, that is, it does not cause emotion. But if it is part of an aesthetic process, it will be meaningfully coincidental with the emotional content of a given mind at a given moment.

Hsi K'ang brings to the surface what was implicit in much of the earlier theorizing about music and what was a major underpinning of early Six Dynasties aesthetic thinking. There is an overriding order of which the performer's mind, the sound, and the listener's mind are part. The order bears on what happens at each station, regardless of whether an instrument is used, whether it is played, whether it is played by a person or the wind, and whether it is heard by a person or the moon. The relationship between all elements of an aesthetic event is not direct, but through the overriding order, in a hublike arrangement. All realms are interconnected inductively, from cosmic to mundane.[78] One need not call for a muse to convey inspiration, and there was little emphasis on the medium or instrument as a conveyance between performer and audience. Rather the argument in theory was that there were no indispensable links, and to promote this notion the texts contributing to aesthetic theory continually resorted to dramatic assaults on what would seem, from the perspective of causality, to be just such an indispensable link. For example, the instrument is eliminated, the strings broken, the instrument is left untouched, the audience is absent, the sound is belittled, the brush does not reach, or the words to a poem are forgotten or abandoned. The importance of the sound or medium is so reduced that art with missing links is seen not only to be as good as any, but becomes the ideal. When the visible aspects of an aesthetic event are eliminated, for both performer and audience, the effort more than the outcome is stressed.[79] As in ritual, in music discipline is more important than sound. *Ch'in* indeed means *chin* "restraint." Confucius' Three Withouts are the ultimates of the three respective disciplines, music without sound, ritual without realization, and mourning without garb. "The sound that has sound does not go beyond a hundred *li*," states *Han-shih wai-chuan* (Han's Commentary on the Odes), "but the sound without sound spreads to the end of the world."[80] Wang Pi argued that symbols aim at ideas and words aim at symbols. Once the idea is grasped, the words and symbols may be forgotten. Forgetting the external trappings, what others might misapprehend as essential, is the sign of completed virtue.[81]

The reduction of the presence of a listener is important in other ways. When any visible listeners are absent, the emphasis falls on the self-cultivative nature of music and the relationship between the artist and nature. Musicians are often portrayed in landscape settings, sometimes without trace of an audience, sometimes holding their *ch'in* in an upright, unplayable position, and sometimes cradling it in their laps, which is also unplayable. The association between the performer and nature is not to suggest that the musician is "making" or "creating" in imitation of natural creative forces, but is rather filling, nonpurposefully, a role natural to man. If one examines the verbs used in early descriptions of making music or making poetry, they do not translate as "making" at all. The musician "holds" his *ch'in* or "embraces" it, and plays by "strumming" the strings. The poet "grasps" his brush, "selects" his words, "broadcasts" his sentiments, and eventually "traps heaven and earth in the cage of form."[82] Not only is there nothing artifactitious about the sage musician's music, but it is the means beyond all others for him to commune with nature and achieve his sagely integration.

These notions find their most compelling expression in the lore of whistling. Whistling is an exemplary sagely musical form because it is an unassisted human sound-making that unlike singing is not entangled with words. A popular story tells of Juan Chi's visit to the sage Sun Teng in the Su-men Mountains. Juan goes to interview the sage, but utterly fails to get his attention until he demonstrates his whistling technique, which was highly revered among his friends at home. Sun Teng responds to Juan Chi's whistling with a laugh and requests an encore. With this done, Juan starts down the mountain on his way home. He was halfway down the ridge, when,

> ... he heard above him a shrillness like an orchestra of many instruments, while forests and valleys re-echoed with the sound. Turning back to look, he discovered it was the whistling of the man he had just visited.[83]

The whistling of the sage was the very breath of nature, according to the T'ang author of the *Hsiao chih* (Whistling Pointers), who considered whistling a method of achieving immortality and communicating with the spirits.[84] Images of *ch'in* playing and whistling in the hills and mountains remind one that it is in nature, traveling the circuit of the four seasons, apprehending the vast complexity of the world and its objects, that the writer, according to Lu Chi, begins his artistic act.[85]

I have argued that the field of aesthetic terminology and concepts as it emerges in the early Six Dynasties is based on earlier musical terms and theory but is humanized in comparison to the mechanistic thinking of the major Han figures. That process of humanization is not a return to the social, moral, and ritual concerns of earlier Confucian texts, however. In the most general terms, art has become a potential not exclusively of man in society, not even primarily of man in society, but is rather the potential of the individual's humanity in nature. Thus in the earliest sustained discussions of aesthetics in China, one finds attention to the need for talent, for learning, and for technique in the making of art, balanced with the understanding that its ultimate origin and ultimate end are in artlessness.

1. Susanne K. Langer, *Philosophy in a New Key* (Cambridge, 1960), p. 209.

2. Discussions of the origins of music make a distinction between music as an art, early song, simple organized sound, and unorganized tonal forms. For interesting comments on the origins of music as an art, see Langer's chapter "The Genesis of Artistic Import," pp. 246–265.

3. For an introduction to the cosmological and numerological aspects of Han musical theory, see J. H. Levis, *The Foundations of Chinese Musical Art* (Peking, 1936; rpt. New York, 1964). An excellent introduction to acoustical physics and early musical theory is found in Joseph Needham, *Science and Civilization in China*, vol. 4: Physics and Physical Terminology, pt. 1: Physics (Cambridge, 1962), pp. 126–228. A study of music and musical theory in the context of early thought on the arts is in Kenneth DeWoskin, *A Song for One or Two: Music and the Concept of Art in Early China* (Ann Arbor, 1982). The review of early thought that follows in the text is largely drawn from this work.

4. Yājñavalkya Smṛti, trans. in *Ein Beitrag zur Quellenkunde des indischen Rechts*, ed. Hans Losch (Leipzig, 1927), quoted in *Sources of Indian Tradition*, ed. Wm. T. de Bary (New York, 1962), p. 274.

5. For this and other interesting examples, see E. R. Dodds, *The Greeks and the Irrational* (Berkeley, 1963), pp. 79–80.

6. *The Complete Works of Chuang Tzu*, trans. Burton Watson (New York, 1968). Chieh Yü's meeting with Confucius is found first in the *Analects* (18:5). In his three appearances in *Chuang Tzu*, attention is given to his mode of speaking (pp. 33–34, 66–67, 92–93). In English, the most common derivation given for "fool" is Latin *follis*, meaning "bellows" or "windbag." William Willeford elaborates on this: "The fool's wind scatters things and meanings, yet in the confusion reveals glimpses of a counterpole to spirit: nature with the purposes and intelligence of instinct, which, like spirit, cannot be accomodated to rational understanding." *The Fool and His Scepter* (Evanston, 1969), pp. 10–11.

7. Watson, trans., *Chuang Tzu*, p. 36. Tzu-ch'i's mind is compared to "dead ashes" when he is enraptured by the piping of Heaven.

8. Among the most interesting tales is that of Duke Ling and his visit to Duke Ping of Chin, in the *Shih chi* (Records of the Grand Historian) 24.

9. A fox, living in a family in the personna of the father, is exorcised by a chanting Taoist. Kan Pao, *Sou-shen chi* (In Search of the Supernatural), selections translated by K. DeWoskin in *Renditions* (1977), 7:111.

10. A recent and comprehensive bibliography is Fredric Lieberman, *Chinese Music: An Annotated Bibliography* (New York, 1970). Needham's chapter cited above begins with a brief review of the monuments of scholarship.

11. Bernard Karlgren, trans., *The Book of Documents* (Shu ching) (rpt. Stockholm, 1950), p. 12.

12. Henri Maspero, *La Chine antique* (Paris, 1927); trans. Frank A. Kierman, *China in Antiquity* (Amherst, 1978), pp. 274–275.

13. There is ample justification to depart from the usual translation of *li* as "ritual" in many, if not all, cases. I use the unconventional term "program" to emphasize the relationship between music, dance, and the reenactments in a broader context than a religious ritual necessarily implies. This follows early definitions of *li*, for example, in the *Shuo-wen*

chieh-tzu as the "movement of reenactment." For text describing the responsibilities of the music master, see *Chou li*, "Ch'un-kuan" 春官.

14. *Hsiao ching* (Classic of Filial Piety), 12. Throughout the "Book of Music" the comparative roles of ritual and music are discussed.

15. Fragments of three apochryphal texts on music are found in Ma Kuo-han, *Yü-han shan-fang chi-i-shu* (Redactions of Lost Texts from the Yu-han Mountain Study) (Taipei, 1967), pp. 178–180.

16. Watson, trans., *Chuang Tzu*, p. 145.

17. Ibid., pp. 156–157.

18. This is discussed in relation to poetry in James J. Y. Liu, *The Art of Chinese Poetry* (Chicago, 1962), p. 70.

19. The Way of the *Ch'in* (*Ch'in-tao* 琴道) was a way of life according to proponents. A landmark study in English is Robert van Gulik, *The Lore of the Chinese Lute* (Tokyo, 1940). Encyclopedia typically had a selection of *ch'in* stories, and there is a tradition reaching back to Han times of books devoted exclusively to the *ch'in*. *Ch'in* books were collected in *ch'in* collectanea, an important example of which is T'ang Chien-yüan, *Ch'in fu* (Taipei, 1971). Much of T'ang's material is derived from another modern collectanea, the *Ch'in-ch'ü chi-ch'eng*, compiled by the Central Academy of Music (Peking, 1963).

20. Compilations of *ch'in* legend, lore, instruction, and music were by and for devotees and hence took on characteristics of a canonical tradition, complete with sages, culture heroes, and claims to high antique origins. Because the textual traditions were highly specialized and isolated, little corroborating material is to be found outside, with the result that dating of much of the material prior to the Ming is problematic. For a detailed discussion of this problem, see DeWoskin, *A Song for One or Two*.

21. For a review of several early references, see van Gulik, *Lute*, pp. 5–8. Confucius' study of the *ch'in* with Master Shih-hsiang is found in *K'ung Tzu chia-yü* 35, and the puzzling chapter "The Old Fisherman" in *Chuang Tzu* describes Confucius playing the *ch'in* in the wilderness. Watson, trans., *Chuang Tzu*, p. 344.

22. *Lun-yü* (Analects) 2:4.

23. William G. Boltz, "Comparative Notes on the Pelliot and Ma-wang-tui Manuscripts of the *Lao-tzu*," presented at the thirtieth annual meeting of the Association of Asian Studies, Chicago, 1978.

24. Manfred Porkert, *The Theoretical Foundations of Chinese Medicine: Systems of Correspondence* (Cambridge, Mass., 1974), p. 113.

25. *Analects* 17:18.

26. *Book of Rites*, "Book of Music," trans. in Lin Yutang, *The Wisdom of Confucius* (New York, 1943), p. 241.

27. "Being a transmitter and not a maker, embracing antiquity with full faith, I compare myself to Old P'eng." *Analects* 7:1.

28. Van Gulik writes (*Lute*, p. 1) "The Lute . . . is not primarily melodical. Its beauty lies not so much in the succession of notes as in each separate note in itself. . . . Each note is an entity in itself, calculated to evoke in the mind of the hearer a special reaction. The timbre being thus of the utmost importance, there are very great possibilities of modifying the colouring of one and the same tone."

29. "The Five Colors make the eyes blind. The Five Notes make the ears deaf. The Five Flavors make the palate dull." *Tao-te ching* 12.

30. *Li chi* (Book of Rites), *K'ung Tzu hsien-chü* 孔子閒居.

31. Liu, *The Art of Chinese Poetry*, pp. 70–71.

32. An excellent background discussion is found in Fung Yu-lan, *A History of Chinese Philosophy*, trans. Derk Boode, 2 vols. (Princeton, 1952, 1953), 2:88–132, especially "The Hexagrams and Music," pp. 118–123.

33. Ibid., p. 118.

34. Porkert's thoughtful definitions of *ch'i* as energetic configuration and configurational energy are useful in approaching this difficult concept in music as well as medicine. *Theoretical Foundations*, pp. 167–176.

35. Derk Bodde, "The Chinese Cosmic Magic Known as 'Watching for the Ethers,'" in *Studia Serica Bernhard Karlgren Dedicata* (Copenhagen 1959), pp. 14–35.

36. *Feng-su-t'ung* (*Han-Wei ts'ung-shu* ed.) 6:1.

37. Ibid. 6:6–7. Other versions of the story are found in *Lieh Tzu*, "T'ang-wen" 唐問; and *Shuo yüan*, "Tsun-hsien" 尊賢.

38. Burton Watson, trans., *Hsün Tzu: Basic Writings* (New York, 1963), p. 14.

39. Watson, trans., *Chuang Tzu*, p. 36.

40. Liu Hsiang, *Hsin-hsü* (*Han-Wei ts'ung-shu* ed.) 4:13.

41. Ts'ao P'i, *Tien-lun lun-wen* (*Wen hsüan*, [Tokyo, 1971]), p. 714.

42. Lin Yutang, *Wisdom*, pp. 230–231. The same text is found in the *Records of the Grand Historian*, "Yüeh Shu" 樂書 ("Treatise on Music"), (*Chung-hua shu-chü* ed.), pp. 1181–1182.

43. Jao Tsung-i, "The Relation Between Principles of Literary Criticism of the Wei and Tsin Dynasties and Music." Paper presented to the Eleventh Conference of Young Sinologues, Padua, 1958; and "Lu Chi *Wen-fu* li-lun yü yin-yüeh chih kuan-hsi," in *Chūgoku bungaku hō* (1961), 14:22–37.

44. Achilles Fang, trans., "Rhymeprose on literature: The *Wen-fu* of Lu Chi (A.D. 261–303)," *HJAS* (1951), 14:539–542.

45. Lin Yutang, *Wisdom*, p. 234.

46. I have prepared new translations of the relevant sections of the rhymeprose here, not with the hope of improving on the two excellent translations already available, but in order to bring to the foreground the musical terminology and references. In addition to the translation by Achilles Fang cited above, the reader may consult that by Ch'en Shih-hsiang in *Anthology of Chinese Literature*, ed. Cyril Birch (New York, 1965), pp. 204–214.

47. Needham, *Science and Civilization*, 4(1):130, 134–136; for the *Kuo yü* discussion of sympathetic resonance in connection with standard pitch, see pp. 200–201.

48. Roman Jakobson, for example, has argued that proximity in sound necessarily draws words together in meaning. That is, rhyme involves the semantic relationship between the rhymed elements. "Linguistics and Poetics," in *Style in Language*, ed. T. Sebeok (Cambridge, Mass., 1960), p. 367.

49. As Wallace Stevens puts it, "Both in nature and in metaphor, identity is the vanishing point of resemblance." "Three Academic Pieces," in *The Necessary Angel* (New York, 1951), p. 72.

50. The *Analects* (7:8) uses the variant form *fei* 悱 in the expression *pu-fei pu-fa* 不悱不發 "[A student] not eager to express something within him, I cannot draw out."

51. *Tzu-hui* 字彙 definition in *Dai-Kan-Wa ji-ten* no. 10720:1.

52. *Yüeh-chi tse pei* 樂極則悲 in *Huai-nan Tzu* (rpt. Taipei, 1953) 12:19b. For the *Han Fei Tzu* passage, see Burton Watson, trans., *Han-fei-tzu: Basic Writings* (New York, 1964), pp. 54–56. There "Clear Chiao" is translated as "Pure Chueh."

53. Ts'ao Ts'ao, "K'u-han-hsing" 苦寒行, in *Ch'üan Han San-kuo Chin Nan-pei ch'ao shih*, ed. Ting Fu-pao (Taipei, 1968), p. 181. The poem is sometimes attributed to Ts'ao P'i. The second couplet is from Ts'ao Chih's *Yu-ssu fu* 幽思賦, in *Ch'üan Shang-ku San-tai Ch'in Han San-kuo Liu-ch'ao wen*, ed. Yen K'o-chün (Shanghai, 1958), p. 1124.

54. Jao Tsung-i, "Lu Chi *Wen-fu*," p. 27.

55. Ibid., p. 28.

56. *Tao-te ching* 41.

57. Donald Holzman, Poetry and Politics: The Life and Works of Juan Chi (A.D. 210–263) (Cambridge, 1976), p. 89.

58. *Wen hsüan*, Li Shan commentary to *Ch'ang-men fu* 長門賦, cited in Jao Tsung-i, "Lu Chi *Wen-fu*," p. 36, n. 28.

59. *Han shu*, "I-wen chih," 10.

60. Jao Tsung-i, "Literary Criticism," p. 5.

61. Ibid.

62. *Shih chi*, p. 1221. The same story is told in the "Book of Music," 2:24. See Lin Yutang, *Wisdom*, p. 239.

63. Needham, *Science and Civilization*, 4(1):142.

64. *Rhymeprose on Literature*, l. 117.

65. Ibid., l. 31.

66. Ibid., l. 34.

67. In *Paradise Lost*, Milton writes:
So from the root,
Springs lighter the green stalk, from thence the leaves
More aerie, last the bright consummate floure
Spirits odorous breathes: flours and their fruit
Man's nourishment, by gradual scale sublim'd
To vital Spirits aspire.... (Book 5).

68. Peter Quince says at his clavier:
Just as my fingers on these keys
Make music, so the selfsame sounds
On my spirit make a music too.
Music is feeling, then, not sound.
The *Collected Poems of Wallace Stevens* (New York, 1975), pp. 89–90.

69. *Ch'üan Shang-ku*, p. 1303.

70. Fung Yu-lan, *History*, 2:185–186.

71. Liu I-ch'ing, *Shih-shuo hsin-yü*, trans. Richard Mather, *Shih-shuo Hsin-yü: A New Account of Tales of the World* (Minneapolis, 1976), p. 102.

72. *Ch'üan Shang-ku*, pp. 1329–1333.

73. Susanne Langer, *New Key*, pp. 204–245.

74. *Ch'üan Shang-ku*, p. 1332.

75. Ibid., and n. 14 for the original record.

76. Ibid., p. 1333.

77. *Shih chi*, p. 1235.

78. Again, Porkert's investigation of medical theory is illuminating here. See pp. 55ff.

79. Wang Yang-ming wrote, "The learning of the sage and the worthy is for themselves. Its emphasis is on effort and not on effect." Wing-tsit Chan, trans., *A Sourcebook of Chinese Philosophy* (Princeton, 1969), p. 226.

80. Han Ying, *Han-shih wai-chuan*, trans. James R. Hightower (Cambridge, Mass., 1952), p. 31.

81. Fung Yu-lan, *History*, 2:184. The original expression of this notion is probably Chuang Tzu's fish trap argument, which ends: "Words exist because of meaning; once you've gotten the meaning, you can forget the words. Where can I find a man who has forgotten words so I can have a word with him." Watson, trans., *Chuang Tzu*, p. 302.

82. Fang, *Rhymeprose*, p. 533.

83. Mather, *New Account*, p. 331. See Holzman, *Poetry and Politics*, pp. 150–151 for details on whistling.

84. Holzman, *Poetry and Politics*, pp. 151–152. The earliest sustained discussion of whistling of which I am aware is Chin writer Ch'eng-kung Sui's *Hsiao fu* 嘯賦 (Rhymeprose on Whistling). Sui describes it as the ultimate sound, not depending on apparatus, not deriving from silk or bamboo, dark and mysterious enough to reach the spirits, subtle and fine enough to fathom the depths. *Ch'üan Shang-ku*, p. 1795.

85. *Rhymeprose on Literature*, ll. 1–7.

Chinese "Lyric Criticism" in the Six Dynasties

By Kang-i Sun Chang

This essay examines the nature of a major critical mode evolved in the early Chinese literary tradition, one which we may call "lyric criticism."[1] I shall focus on the aesthetic value of this literary criticism by also taking into consideration its philosophical implications. The very term "lyric criticism" may seem contradictory to some readers, in that "criticism" in the modern Western literary context generally implies conceptual judgments derived from objective analysis, which is the opposite of lyrical expression.[2] Yet the purpose of the present study is precisely to demonstrate how such a critical ideology is possible, and how it lies at the core of the Chinese literary tradition. What we call "lyric criticism" during the Six Dynasties period is the best example of an overwhelming concern with lyricism in China in genres other than lyric poetry. I shall begin by discussing some of the theoretical foundations of lyric experience in general, which in turn will elucidate the fundamental principles of this "lyric criticism."

The basis of lyricism is the poet's inner-directed private experience. By definition, private experience is nothing but a mental state experienced by an individual at a particular time and place. As a form of knowledge, private experience reaches its most profound state only when all the direct experience is reorganized and refined during a process of introspection. In the course of this "re-experience" all the elements of experience are united to form an undivided whole which is self-sufficient and self-contained. This is particularly cogent in the case of aesthetic experience, whereby initial sense impressions and feelings of an individual must be reshaped into elements of an imaginative world. This world of imagination is the culmination of the aesthetic experience, a state of true knowledge achieved through a suspended moment of consciousness in which mental act and outer reality are temporarily dissociated. But such an experience of self-realization, however real to the individual, may not be sufficiently transmitted by language itself.

Whereas analytical language is used to present objective reality and emphasizes the referent (cf. "words refer to things"),[3] symbolic language is the proper medium for representing the aesthetic experience in that it focuses on the "quality" of things. The former refers to such external distinctions as "this" and "that," while the latter deals with sensual impressions and their qualitative implications. This sort of symbolic language is especially useful in representing our mental state during creative moments. Of course, symbolic language and analytical language are not unrelated to each other with respect to methods of expression. They differ only in purpose and function—one is oriented toward external, objective, absolute truth, and the other toward the inner, subjective, relative world of imagination.

But how does symbolic language organize elements of this world of imagination? We may refer to the two axes upon which one unifies this aesthetic experience as those of the "self" and the "present." Insofar as private experience is concerned, the self and the present are the perpetual points of space-time reference against which all personal interrelations and time changes are measured. In the world of imagination, it is the qualities of subjectivity and immediacy that are paramount. If a union is accomplished when the self extends itself metonymically to embrace the outside world, then the creative process may be called, in Jakobson's terminology, "contiguity."[4] If, on the other hand, it results from a metaphorical transposition of self and object, then it may be viewed as one of "equivalence."[5] In any case, this empathic union of personal feelings and the outer world is precisely what is meant by the traditional Chinese formula *ch'ing-ching chiao-jung*.

The fact that this kind of aesthetic experience is difficult to "know" through language was keenly noted by traditional Chinese thinkers. The following passage in the *Chuang Tzu* has a particular bearing upon this problem of knowledge:

> Chuang Tzu and Hui Tzu were strolling along the dam of the Hao River when Chuang Tzu said, "See how the minnows come out and dart around where they please! That's what fish really enjoy."
>
> Hui Tzu said, "You're not a fish—how do you know what fish enjoy?"
>
> Chuang Tzu said, "You're not I, so how do you know I don't know what fish enjoy?"
>
> Hui Tzu said, "I'm not you, so I certainly don't know what you know. On the other hand, you're certainly not a fish—so that still proves you don't know what fish enjoy!"
>
> Chuang Tzu said, "Let's go back to your original question, please. You asked me how I know what what fish enjoy—so you already know I knew it when you asked the question. I know it by standing here beside the Hao."[6]

Both Chuang Tzu and Hui Tzu seemed to have understood the essential value of knowledge by experience. As to how to acquire this knowledge, the two thinkers differed widely in their views. Hui Tzu believed that since private experience cannot be known, it is impossible for one to communicate it to others. By contrast, Chuang Tzu affirmed the possibility of communication on a different level. When Chuang Tzu said, "I know it by standing here beside the Hao," he was actually referring to a level of knowledge similar to that of the aesthetic experience in which the self merges empathically into the world of external objects.[7] Only through such a process of union can men acquire both knowledge by experience and the ability to express it in language. This knowledge has the power of reaffirming the value of private judgments, in the sense that the private experience, though seemingly arbitrary on the surface, is in fact intimately known to the individual.

It should be noted that the state of union between inner self and external object, so typical of aesthetic experience, coincides precisely with the ideal world of lyric poetry. This is particularly true in the tradition of Chinese poetry where the poetic world of selfless empathy is strongly influenced by the philosophy of Chuang Tzu. One may say that what Chuang Tzu achieves in Tao is similar to what the Chinese poet accomplishes in artistic imagination.

Chuang Tzu believed that in order to achieve Tao, one must develop a certain quality of passivity called *hsin-chai* that enables one to ignore problems of knowledge and to embrace external objects with an "innocent" mind.[8] Such a union of self and objects is a state of *wu-hua* (things transformed), or that of *wu-wang* (things forgotten). As Hsü Fu-kuan put it, "This kind of empathic union brought about by Chuang Tzu's *hsin-chai* is no other than the aesthetic experience in which both subject and object are forgotten."[9]

In the view of Chuang Tzu this state of empathy (what Hsü Fu-kuan called *kung-kan*) is an expression of free play (*yu*).[10] The importance of the concept of play in Taoism may be seen from the fact that the *Chuang Tzu* opens with a chapter on "Free and Easy Playing" (*Hsiao-yao yu*). It is in the process of playing that one can be harmonious (*ho*) with all things, so as to reflect constantly on the various phases of a monistic whole.[11] Men directly perceive things but do not need to conceptualize them.

The notion of playing makes it possible for a poet to be free from purposefulness in his lyric moments. In view of this fact, many traditional Chinese poets and critics believed that empathy could be reached only when a poet forgot the purpose of his experience. The Six Dynasties poet T'ao Ch'ien (365–427), for example, expressed this idea in a couplet:

> "In things there is a real meaning
> But I have forgotten words with which to conceptualize it.[a][12]

In his chapter on "Classic Refinement" (*Tien-ya*), the Tang poet and critic Ssu-k'ung T'u (837–908) alluded to T'ao Ch'ien's philosophy:

> Fallen flowers, speechless;
> Men, as indifferent as the chrysanthemum.[b][13]

[a] 此中有眞意
欲辯已忘言

[b] 落花無言
人淡如菊

For centuries the idea of self-forgetfulness and purposelessness serves as a criterion of good poetry in the Chinese tradition. This is partly reflected in the fact that such words as "none" (*wu*), "empty" (*k'ung*), and "not knowing" (*pu-chih*) are frequently found in poems.[14] Generally a Chinese poet aims not at formulating philosophical statements, but at evoking feelings beyond words. This something "beyond" forms the basis of Chinese aesthetics.

From the above discussion one will note that although aesthetic experience itself is universal, its application differs according to culturally conditioned factors. Yet my purpose is not simply to demonstrate that aesthetic experience is essential to Chinese lyric poetry. Rather, I hope to bring to light a unique feature of Chinese literary criticism: that is, its insistence on the supreme role of the lyric experience, so much so that even nonpoetic works are judged according to their lyrical attainment. Six Dynasties "lyric criticism" can be said to be a paramount example of this emphasis on lyricism.

Like lyric poetry, "lyric criticism" is grounded on aesthetic experience. Whereas natural scenes serve as objects of contemplation for the lyric poet, a "lyric" critic treats literary works themselves as aesthetic objects. In the course of his reading experience, the critic will project his Self into the world of literature, with the aim of reaching a level of empathy comparable to that of the artistic imagination. In organizing his feelings and judgments, he may also make use of principles of poetic "contiguity" and "equivalence," so that his critical pieces will reveal the same spirit as lyric poetry. In the following pages I shall discuss how this critical mode embodies the essential qualities of Chinese lyricism, as seen in the representative works of Six Dynasties criticism—i.e. Lu Chi's (261–303) *Wen-fu*, Liu Hsieh's (ca. 465–ca. 522) *Wen-hsin tiao-lung*, and Chung Hung's (fl. 502–519) *Shih-p'in hsü*.

TYPICAL IMPRESSIONS VERSUS REFERENTIAL DESCRIPTION

Chinese critics often believed that the quality of a poet's literary style and his personality could be discerned from a typical single line or couplet (*ching-ts'e*) out of the total corpus of his work.[15] In his *Shih-p'in hsü*, Chung Hung obviously took this approach in assessing the achievements of individual poets. For example, the line by Ts'ao Chih quoted in *Shih-p'in hsü* was "Around the tall towers, sad winds in profusion" (*kao-t'ai to pei-feng*),[c] and the most typical line of Hsieh Ling-yün was believed to be "Bright moon shines upon piles of snow" (*ming-yüeh chao chi-hsüeh*).[d][16] Significantly, in such cases Chung Hung did not even mention the names of these poets, assuming that readers would immediately recall the general styles of

[c] 高台多悲風　　　[d] 明月照積雪

the poets upon reading these brief quotations. Thus, the quotations themselves function like allusions in poetry.

This tendency to dwell on the most essential qualities of objects is in keeping with an important device employed by Chinese lyric poets from as early as the *Shih ching*—namely, the use of the simple image. The structure of the simple image is similar to the syntactic pattern known as "topic and comment," in which a noun-topic is juxtaposed with a simple comment describing its most typical quality.[17] The poetic value of the simple image lies in its power to evoke endless associations regarding the essential qualities of the object in question, despite its brevity in presentation. The assumption is that readers, already acquainted with the object, will be inspired by the simple "comments" to imagine an entire range of meanings. These "comments" are sometimes like key words, as in the following lines from the *Shih ching*:

> The peach tree, how delicately beautiful (*yao-yao*),
> Brilliant (*cho-cho*) are its flowers.[e][18]

Yao-yao and *cho-cho* are brief comments describing the typical nature of the peach tree and its flowers. What is most striking here is that the original meaning of *yao-yao* (line 1) given in ancient dictionaries is simply "the appearance of the peach tree." This, of course, reveals a tautology existing in the original line. But the significance of this point is far greater than might appear at first sight—comments of this kind are used more to intensify the inner qualities of object than to elaborate on its particular features. In other words, the focus of these poetic lines is placed on the total impression of the objects in the poet's consciousness, rather than on referential details.

This particular kind of poetics was praised highly by the critic Liu Hsieh in his *Wen-hsin tiao-lung*:

> Thus, *cho-cho* describes the brilliance of peach blossoms; *i-i* depicts luxuriant willows; *kao-kao* suggests the burning face of the sun; *piao-piao* describes the image of rain and snow.... In all these, the poets have used brief expressions to sum up the whole, leaving nothing undescribed whether in their feelings or the appearance of things.[19]

Critics not only approved of the poet's tendency to use "brief expressions to sum up the whole." (*i-shao tsung-to*), they themselves also preferred to write their own remarks in a similar fashion. Thus, in his chapter "T'i-hsing," Liu Hsieh describes eight poetic styles in short, impressionistic aphorisms characteristic of such criticism:

ᵉ桃之夭夭
灼灼其華

First, elegant and graceful (*tien-ya*); second, far-ranging and profound (*yüan-ao*); third, polished and concise (*ching-yüeh*); fourth, lucid and logical (*hsien-fu*); fifth, profuse and flowery (*fan-ju*); sixth, vigorous and beautiful (*chuang-li*); seventh, fresh and extraordinary (*hsin-ch'i*); and eighth, light and trivial (*ch'ing-mi*).[20]

Elsewhere Liu Hsieh distinguished the style of Hsi K'ang (223–262) from that of Juan Chi (210–263) in quite similar language:

Hsi's emotions are pure and lofty (*ch'ing-chün*), while Juan's ideas are far-reaching and profound (*yao-shen*).[21]

As to why *ch'ing-chün* (pure and lofty) and *yao-shen* (far-reaching and profound) can sum up the quality of these two poets' works, the critic did not find an explanation necessary. Just as a lyric poet who expresses feelings in language most appropriate to his subjective experience, the critic describes his intuitive impressions on poetry by means of brief comments. Analytical language, as well as other methods of objective verification, would only be in the way here, where the immediate purpose is to recreate the aesthetic experience of reading poetry and to realize that experience through symbolic language.

Yet how can one be sure that the critic's short remarks and his selection of typical lines have indeed achieved the function of "summing up the whole," as the poets attempt to do through simple imagery? In fact, the critics themselves were fully aware of this problem, as Liu Hsieh concluded in the following statement:

It is indeed difficult to find a critic who understands a writer's innermost thoughts (*chih-yin*). It is true that personal thought is intrinsically difficult to understand; but what is still more difficult is to find someone who possesses real understanding. Barely once in a thousand years do we happen upon an understanding critic.[22]

Understanding that a *chih-yin* was not easy to find, the critics were often at pains to identify themselves with "the self" of the poets. What they were attempting to do was to lose their sense of identity at the moment of reading, the way a poet would in the creative process: the experience of an aesthetic empathy in which the power of understanding becomes so great that the critic can claim that he has fully understood the poet's work. This was why the critic Lu Chi began his *Wen-fu* with this statement:

Each time I study the works of great writers, I flatter myself I know how their minds worked.[23]

And Liu Hsieh saw the role of the poet and the critic (the ideal reader) as necessarily complementary:

The writer's first experience is his inner feeling, which he then seeks to express in words. But the reader, on the other hand, experiences the words first, and then works himself back into the feeling of the author. If he can trace the waves back to their source, there will be nothing, however dark and hidden, that will not be revealed to him.[24]

In fact, Liu's proposed key to good writing applies equally to critical writing and to poetry, as well as to other literary compositions:

> Therefore, in the art of literary writing, temperament and readiness for expression are of prime importance: that is, it is essential to keep the mind pure and tranquil so that its vitality may find spontaneous expression.[25]

MEANING BEYOND WORDS

Despite their confidence in the power of artistic expression, the critics, as mentioned above, preferred to express their feelings in brief remarks, leaving the rest to the imagination of the reader. To them the true meaning of things, like the essence of the eternal Tao, cannot be wholly captured in words. This is why the critics' expressions may be spontaneous rather than exhaustive and explanatory.

This basic idea was, of course, shared by all Chinese poets. Yet it is significant to note that although the poets realized the impossibility of converying the total meaning of Tao, they also created the symbolic device of "parallelism" (*tui*) to represent a sense of totality underlying much of Chinese thought. It is through parallelism that a poet can best present the sense of balance and mutual interrelation of things so essential to the perpetual movements of Tao. This fundamental belief may account for the continuing significance of formal parallelism in Chinese poetry, as well as the philosophical implications which go with it. Liu Hsieh's comments on parallelism support this point:

> When nature creates living beings, it endows them with limbs in pairs. The universal reason operates in such a way that nothing stands alone. The mind creates literary language, and in doing this it organizes and shapes one hundred different thoughts, making what is high supplement what is low, and spontaneously producing linguistic parallelism.[26]

We will see that Liu Hsieh himself, following the vogue of the time, wrote his *Wen-hsin tiao-lung* entirely in the style of "parallel prose." Moreover, Liu often talked about opposing concepts in terms of pairs. As we observed earlier, his distinction of eight literary styles seems somewhat mechanical at first sight, but in the mind of the critic these eight categories are intended to convey the total range of stylistic possibilities, with each style paralleling and contrasting with another:

> The graceful contrasts with the extraordinary, the profound differs from the lucid, the profuse conflicts with the concise, and the vigorous clashes with the light. When we understand these styles, we can make the roots and leaves of literary composition grow in the garden of literature.[27]

Lu Chi also expressed most of his critical thoughts about the creative process in parallel lines. Like the lyric poet who generally organizes his aesthetic experience according to the poles of temporal and spatial coordinates, Lu Chi often communicated his lyrical spirit through juxtaposition of time and space. This particular device has the effect of reinforcing the idea of totality and all-inclusiveness, as is evident from the following parallel couplet:

> He sees past and present in a moment;
> He touches the four seas in the twinkling of an eye.[f][28]

Parallelism is one of the devices used to enhance the aesthetic value of "meaning beyond words." For readers must participate in the act of imagination in order to truly appreciate the meaning of a totality made up of numerous bipolar qualities. This brings us back to the central issue in Chinese poetics—i.e. the notion that the highest ideal of Chinese literature, as Chung Hung pointed out, resides in the capacity to "give endless joy to those who taste it (*wei-chih che*), and move the heart of those who hear it (*wen-chih che*)."[29]

The lyrical quality of Six Dynasties criticism may best be seen in the concluding remarks (*tsan*) of the individual chapters of Liu Hsieh's *Wen-hsin tiao-lung*. Each of his ending statements is itself a lyrical poem, conveying the power of aesthetic experience:

> Mountains rise one behind the other, and waters meander and wind;
> Trees interlace and clouds mingle.
> Such sights before the eyes
> Stir the mind to express itself.
> "Spring days pass slowly,"
> And autumn wind "blows mournfully."
> The feeling for something is described as the giving of a gift,
> And the coming of inspiration as a response.[30]

Quite evidently the lines quoted above do not aim at literary analysis, but rather they are combined to create a poetic world in which "mountains," "waters," "trees," "clouds" become objects of aesthetic appreciation. Thus, the critic and the poet are identical during the creative process, since both of them treat artistic objects as means of acquiring self-realization.

The above discussion is not intended to suggest that traditional Chinese criticism was all lyrical, but simply to bring to light a major mode of criticism in the Six Dynasties which went hand in hand with the development of early Chinese lyric poetry. From

[f] 觀古今於須臾
撫四海於一瞬

here we will see that there existed in the Chinese literary tradition two basic approaches to the acquisition of knowledge: "lyric criticism" and "commentary." The former is closely related to aesthetic experience, and the latter to the study of objective information which may be called "scholarship." Since lyric criticism takes symbolic language as its major form of expression, it is bound to be rather impressionistic. Commentary, on the other hand, relies on analytical language to deal with problems of authorship, textual exegesis, and historical sources, and is thus explicit in its orientation. Some of the Six Dynasties sources for this second line of approach are *Mao-shih shih-i* by Kuo P'u (276–324), *Chuang Tzu chu* by Kuo Hsiang (d. ca. 310), and *Ssu-sheng p'u* by Shen Yüeh (441–513).

Such a separation of emphasis suggests that literary criticism will not always be objective, as it necessarily involves the critic's subjective experience in reading the text. Six Dynasties "lyric criticism" represents only one of the extreme cases of aesthetic experience inherent in the process of literary appreciation itself. I am not advocating here a revival of this particular critical orientation—our task today is simply to elucidate the cultural significance of early Chinese "lyric criticism" in terms of contemporary critical methodology. I believe, however, that aesthetic experience deserves our close attention in literary study, as it forms the fundamentals of literary appreciation.

1. I am grateful to Professor Yu-kung Kao of Princeton University for help in the preparation of this paper and for discussion of the ideas in it. My text is especially indebted to the two recent papers by Professor Kao: (1) "Wen-hsüeh yen-chiu ti li-lun chi-ch'ü, *Chung-wai wen-hsüeh* (December, 1978), pp. 4–21; (2) "Wen-hsüeh yen-chiu ti mei-hsüeh wen-t'i", *Chung-wai wen-hsüeh* (April, 1979, and May, 1979), pp. 4–21, and pp. 4–51.

2. This view was especially popular in the school of New Criticism which dominated the past several decades of Western literary thought.

3. For the definition of the term "referent," see John Lyons, *Introduction to Theoretical Linguistics* (London, 1968), p. 404.

4. Roman Jakobson, "Two Aspects of Language and Two Types of Aphasic Disturbances," in Roman Jakobson and Morris Halle, *Fundamentals of Language* (Leiden, 1956), pp. 55–82.

5. Ibid.

6. *Chuang Tzu: Basic Writings*, trans. Burton Watson (New York, 1964), p. 110.

7. For this point, see Chu Kuang-ch'ien, *T'an mei* (rpt. Taipei, 1958), pp. 24–33.

8. Hsü Fu-kuan, *Chung-kuo i-shu ching-shen* (The Chinese Aesthetic Spirit), 4th ed. (Taipei, 1974), p. 74.

9. Ibid.

10. Hsü Fu-kuan compared Chuang Tzu's "play" philosophy to Schiller's idea of the "play instinct" by quoting from Schiller: "Man only plays when in the full meaning of the

word he is a man, and he is only completely a man when he plays" (trans. into Chinese by Hsü, p. 63). The analogy is convincing, only that in Schiller "the play instinct" is a synthesizing power of two opposing forces—"the sensuous impulsion" and "the formal impulsion"—but there are no such opposing dual forces in Chuang Tzu's act of play. The idea of play in Chuang Tzu refers simply to a passive capacity for losing oneself in contemplation, rather than to the power of overcoming.

11. For the philosophy of the Chinese world view, see Frederick W. Mote, "The Cosmological Gulf between China and the West," in *Transition and Permanence: Chinese History and Culture*, ed. Mote and Buxbaum (Hong Kong, 1972), pp. 3–17, and Frederick W. Mote, *Intellectual Foundation of China* (New York, 1971), pp. 13–28.

12. *Ch'üan Han San-kuo Chin Nan-pei-ch'ao shih* (complete Poems of the Han, Three Kingdoms, and the Southern and Northern Dynasties), ed. Ting Fu-pao, *3 vols.* (Taipei, 1969), 1, p. 472.

13. *Shih-p'in chi-chieh*, annotated by Kuo Shao-yü (rpt. Taipei, 1974), p. 12.

14. T'ang Chün-i, *Chung-kuo wen-hua chih ching-shen chia-chih*, (The Merit of the Essence of Chinese Culture) (Taipei, 1953), p. 243.

15. Both Lu Chi and Chung Hung talked about the idea of *ching-ts'e*. See *Wen-fu* (*Fu* on Literature) and *Shih-p'in hsü* (Preface to *Shih-p'in*) in *Wei Chin Nan-pei ch'ao wen-hsüeh shih ts'an-k'ao tzu-liao* (Reference sources in Wei, Chin and the Southern and Northern Dynasties Literature, hereafter WCNP) (Peking, 1961), pp. 264 and 614.

16. See Ts'ao's poem entitled "Tsa-shih" and Hsieh's poem entitled "Sui-mu shih."

17. See Chao Yuen Ren, *A Grammar of Spoken Chinese* (Berkeley, 1968), pp. 69–70.

18. The translation is quoted with slight modification from Bernhard Karlgren, *The Book of Odes* (rpt. Stockholm, 1974), no. 6.

19. The translation is quoted with modification from Vincent Yu-chung Shih, trans., *The Literary Mind and the Carving of Dragons* (New York, 1959; rpt. in bilingual ed. Taipei, 1970), p. 349: chapter on "Wu-se" 物色.

20. Ibid., p. 222.

21. Ibid., p. 46, with modification: chapter on "Ming-shih" 明詩.

22. Ibid., p. 368, with modification: chapter on "Chih-yin" 知音.

23. Achilles Fang, trans., "Rhymeprose on Literature: The Wen-fu of Lu Chi (A.D. 261–303)", *HJAS* (1951), 14:530; rpt. in *Studies in Chinese literature*, ed. John L. Bishop (Cambridge, 1965), p. 6.

24. Vincent Yu-chung Shih, trans., p. 371, with slight modification: chapter on "Chih-yin."

25. Ibid., p. 318, with slight modification: chapter on "Yang-ch'i" 養氣.

26. Ibid., p. 270, with slight modification: chapter on "Li-tz'u" 麗辭.

27. Ibid., p. 223, with slight modification: chapter on "T'i-hsing" 体性.

28. Fang, trans., "Rhymeprose," p. 532.

29. *WCNP*, p. 604. This passage by Chung Hung reminds one of James J. Y. Liu's statement: "Chinese aesthetic theorists . . . were content with impressionistic descriptions of aesthetic experience, often drawing analogies with sensuous experience." See *Chinese Theories of Literature* (Chicago, 1975), p. 105.

30. See Vincent Yu-chung Shih, trans., p. 353, with modification: chapter on "Wu-se."

The Nature of Evaluation in the *Shih-p'in* (Gradings of Poets) by Chung Hung (A.D. 469–518)[1]

By John Timothy Wixted

The late fifth and early sixth centuries in South China mark a period of considerable ferment in literary criticism and theory. During the reign of Emperor Wu of the Liang dynasty (reg. 502–549), there appeared two major works of criticism, *Wen-hsin tiao-lung* (Elaborations on the Essence of Literature) by Liu Hsieh (465?–523),[2] and *Shih-p'in* (Gradings of Poets) by Chung Hung, as well as two major anthologies with prefaces of critical significance, *Wen hsüan* (Literary Selections) edited by Hsiao T'ung (501–531),[3] and *Yü-t'ai hsin-yung* (New Songs from the Tower of Jade) compiled by Hsü Ling (507–583).[4] The latest possible dates for their completion were, respectively, A.D. 507, 517, 527, and 537.[5]

The age was also one of social and political factions in which literary concerns were of great importance. The stage on which these interests were played out was the salon, both in the metropolitan area and in the provinces. As one scholar has recently written:

> In the salon culture, literature was the prime interest. Clannish and snobbish, unwilling or unable to sully their hands with practical affairs or associate with lesser officials, the great nobles withdrew to their literary parlor games. The romantic folk songs indigenous to the south caught the fancy of the languid aristocrat poets. New poetic techniques involving a lately rationalized tonality were tried. Literary theory became the basis of court rivalries and factionalism, and the dynasty saw the completion of the most influential canons of Chinese literary criticism.[6]

Literary skill itself was of importance, and not only as a prerequisite for gaining entrée to salons and political circles; it was also of prime importance in securing official or social advancement. An attack on a man's literary work could be tantamount to a personal or political attack.[7] This dimension to contemporary discussions of literature, though difficult to assess properly today, cannot be overlooked when examining Chung Hung's critical work.

This article will focus on the nature of evaluation in *Gradings of Poets*. In successive sections, there will be discussion of the background to Chung Hung's system of grading, the nature of the terminology he uses, the traits he focuses upon in his analyses, the standard of value implied in his criticism, the different means he employs for comparing poets, and the relationship between his work and valuation in the arts in general.

I

The biography of Chung Hung sheds some light on his background as a critic.[8] While an imperial student (*kuo-tzu sheng*) in the Yung-ming period (483–493) of the Southern Ch'i dynasty, he specialized in the *I ching* (Book of Changes). The descendant of a Chin dynasty (317–420) imperial secretary (*shih-chung*), he was himself a secretary to princes, including Hsiao Kang (503–551), the future imperial sponsor of the *New Songs from the Tower of Jade*. One of Chung Hung's two official biographies relates that he received a personal slight from the poet Shen Yüeh (441–513), the prominent advocate of formal tonal regulation in poetry; because of this, he is said to have written *Gradings of Poets* to get even—a conclusion subject to much debate among later scholars.[9]

Chung Hung's public intentions as a literary critic are outlined in the three prefaces he wrote to *Gradings of Poets*. Therein he speaks of the need for a standard of evaluation in the world of letters:

> As for officials who serve in the courts of noblemen, whenever time is left over from state discussions, they invariably turn to the topic of poetry. As each follows his individual predilections, the critique of one is at variance with that of another. The Tzu and Sheng flow indiscriminately; vermilion and purple, the pure and impure, each vies with the other. Discussions turn disputatious, and there is no reliable standard.[a][10]

In the second preface to his work, Chung Hung cites earlier critical works and finds them mostly wanting:

> Lu Chi's (261–303) *Wen fu* (Rhymeprose on Literature) is comprehensive but lacks unfavorable critiques.[11] Li Ch'ung's (fl. 323) *Han-lin lun* (Discourse on the Forest of Writing Brushes) is coherent but not incisive.[12] Wang Wei's (414–443) *Hung pao* (Vast Treasure) is tightly constructed but withholds judgments.[13] Yen Yen-chih's (384–456) discussion of literature, though done with exactitude, is hard to grasp.[14] Only Chih Yü's (d. 311) treatise on literature is detailed, yet broad and enriching; truly he is one whose words are penetrating.[15] Although these authors all discuss writing in terms of literary style and form, they do not make clear the relative merits of writers.
>
> The poetic anthologies edited by Hsieh Ling-yün (385–433) adopt whatever poems he happened upon.[16] Chang Chih's (Chin dyn.) *Wen-shih chuan* (Biographies of Literary Men) records the prose pieces he happened to have seen.[17] With the recordings of these outstanding men,

[a] 觀王公搢紳之士，每博論之餘，何嘗不以詩為口實，隨其嗜欲，商榷不同。淄澠幷泛，朱紫相奪；喧議競起，準的無依。

their concern always lay in [transmitting] the literary text; no gradings were ever made.[b][18]

Although there are significant omissions from this list, Chung Hung is correct in his basic argument that earlier works either dealt with literature theoretically, making little reference to specific writings, or were concerned with the problems of anthologizing: selecting texts and classifying them according to genre.[19]

From his remarks concluding the discussion of earlier critics, it is clear that Chung Hung will concern himself with gradings in his work. The idea for such a critique of earlier poets did not originate with him; the proximate stimulus came from an older contemporary:

> The late Liu Hui of P'eng-ch'eng (*tzu*: Shih-chang) (458–502), a man of high critical acumen, became exasperated at this confusion and intended to compile a "Gradings of Poets" for his generation. In conversation he set forth its general outline, but the work itself was never completed. Accordingly, I have been moved to write such a work.[c][20]

Chung Hung's work is distinctive for its classification of writers into three evaluative grades: "upper, middle, and lower" (*shang-*, *chung-*, *hsia-p'in*). More than one hundred twenty poets are assigned to one of these grades.[21] Specific sources for this classification system are noted by Chung Hung:

> In former times there were evaluations of men ranking them into nine categories. And the *Ch'i lüeh* (Seven Summaries) arranged scholars [into seven divisions]. Yet if one compares reputations with facts, these evaluations quite often were inappropriate.[d][22]

Chung Hung is here citing earlier nine-part and seven-part categories of arrangement or evaluation. *Seven Summaries*, the earliest bibliography in China, was compiled by Liu Hsiang (77–6 B.C.) and completed by his son Liu Hsin (d. A.D. 22). This work, extant today only in fragments, was a classified listing of books in the imperial library and contained short introdutions and critiques. Pan Ku (A.D. 32–92) drew upon it for his "I-wen chih" (Monograph on Literature) when compiling the *Han shu* (History of the Han Dynasty).[23]

Another chapter of Pan Ku's history, entitled "Ku-chin jen-piao" (A Table of Men Past and Present), assigned historical and semihistorical figures to a nine-part

b 陸機文賦，通而無貶；李充翰林，疏而不切；王微鴻寶，密而無裁；顏延論文，精而難曉；摯虞文志，詳而博贍，頗曰知言。觀斯數家，皆就談文體，而不顯優劣。至于謝客集詩，逢詩輒取，張騭文士逢文即書。諸英志錄，並義在文，曾無品第。

c 近彭城劉士章，俊賞之士，疾其淆亂，欲爲當世詩品，口陳標榜，其文未遂，感而作焉。

d 昔九品論人，七略裁士，校以賓實，誠多未值。

grading scheme: "upper, middle, and lower" categories each in turn being subdivided into three parts ("upper-upper, middle-upper, lower-upper," etc.). In his short preface to the table, Pan Ku alludes to an earlier precedent for such classificatory terms in Confucius' *Lun-yü* (Analects), and he explains the moral criteria employed in assigning figures to categories (the highest rank being reserved for those incapable of doing evil, the lowest for those incapable of doing good).[24]

From A.D. 220 onward there was instituted a system for rating all officials according to nine gradings. Office holders, termed "equitable rectifiers" (*chung-cheng*), were selected at the provincial and prefectural levels "to rate the achievements, talents, conduct, and abilities of officials from ducal ministries down to the lower officials" and to "grade them into [nine] ranks."[25]

It is no coincidence that the institution of this grading system occurred during the reign of Emperor Wen of the Wei dynasty, Ts'ao P'i (187–226), whose *Tien-lun Lun-wen* ("Essay on Literature" in *Classical Treatises*) reflected similar contemporary concerns.[26] As one modern scholar has noted: "His interest in genres was only a by-product of the typical third-century pastime of evaluating and categorizing people. The primary interest was in determining the fitness of a person for office in terms of his ability and knowledge as against the specific demands made by the office on its incumbent."[27]

Furthermore, at about this time the classification of Buddhist believers into "upper, middle, and lower" categories, as well as into nine-category subdivisions, is found in canons of Pure Land Buddhism, including the *Fo-shuo ta wu-liang-shou ching* (Aparimitayūḥ Sūtra), translated into Chinese by Saṅghavarman in 252.[28]

The interest in classifying talent for pragmatic ends gave rise to a range of works. The *Jen-wu chih* (Treatise on Personalities) by Liu Shao (190?–265), completed about 235, was a practical handbook of personality types written in an attempt to match talent with political function.[29] The later standard statement dealing with the same concerns was Chung Hui's (225–264) *Ssu-pen lun* (Treatise on the Four Basic Relations [between Natural Ability and Human Nature]).[30] By the fourth century, characterological discussion "lost much (though not all) of its political significance, and became a kind of rhetorical sport."[31] Yet parts of *Shih-shuo hsin-yü* (A New Account of Tales of the World) by Liu I-ch'ing (403–444), especially the chapter, "P'in-tsao" (Classification According to Excellence) (as well as the chapters "Shih-chien" [Insight and Judgment] and "Shang-yü [Appreciation and Praise]), provide numerous examples of traditional interest in the evaluation of character.[32]

Such earlier seven- and nine-part classification schemes, including the important tradition of characterizing and grading men of affairs, formed the background to the systems of grading and classification in the arts that became the vogue in Chung Hung's time. The earliest such examples appear to be in the field of chess. There were separate *Ch'i-p'in* (Gradings of Chess Players) by Shen Yüeh and by Liu

Hui (465–517) that predated *Gradings of Poets*.[33] Other such works in Chung Hung's general period include *Ku hua-p'in lu* (Old Record of Gradings of Painters) by Hsieh Ho (fl. 500–535),[34] *Shu-p'in* (Gradings of Calligraphers) by Yü Chien-wu (487–500),[35] and *Ku-chin shu-p'ing* (Critiques of Calligraphers Ancient and Modern) by Yüan Ang (d. 540), dated 523.[36]

Having mentioned the seven- and nine-part antecedents to his classification scheme, Chung Hung in the same preface proceeds to state something of the nature of poetic evaluation:

> As for poetic expertise, this is easier to ascertain. To draw an analogy, it is virtually the same as "sixes" or chess.[e][37]

There are shared metaphysical, social, and artistic associations between poetry and the boardgames of sixes and chess that should be pointed out in explicating the comparison Chung Hung draws in this passage.

Both chess and sixes have early associations with Chinese astronomy-astrology. Pan Ku, in his *I chih* (Essay on Chess), states the following concerning the game:

> Its significance is profound. The board must be square and true, for it acts as a simulacrum of the earth's shape; and its pathways must be true and straight, for it manifests bright virtue. Pieces are white and black, differentiating the Yin and the Yang. Spread out in their array, they aspire to the pattern of the heavens (*t'ien-wen*).[f][38]

The game of "sixes" (*[liu-]po* or "the six learned ones," referring to the number of pieces on each side) is a boardgame traceable to pre-Han times which also had early astronomical-astrological associations, "each piece being marked with one of the four animals symbolizing the four directions of space. There seems to have been a central belt of water, like the Milky Way in later systems, and when a piece arrived there it was promoted to be a 'leading piece' with greater powers."[39] The boards on which both games were played were related to the diviner's board (*shih*), upon which pieces representing heavenly bodies were thrown for prognostication.[40]

The relationship between heavenly configurations and the arrangement of their earthly counterparts in the form of pieces on game boards is analogous to that said to exist between the patternings of the cosmos (*t'ien-wen*) and their representations in writing (i.e. *wen*, "patterns"). Such concepts derive from the *I ching* (Book of Changes) and reflect the basic unitary nature of early Chinese thought, which was holistic in its view of the natural world, the latter's artistic patternings (in the form of music, writing, etc.), and the relation of both to man. In reference to literature, it

[e] 至若詩之爲技，較爾可知，以類推之，殆均博弈。

[f] 厥義深矣。局必方正，象地則也。道必正直，神明德也。棊有白黑，陰陽分也。駢羅列布，效天文也。

was given its most eloquent expression in the first chapter of Liu Hsieh's *Elaborations on the Essence of Literature*, "Yüan-tao" (On Tracing the *Tao*).[41] But even in that great work, literature is treated largely in terms which, in comparison with earlier views, are distinctly secular and nondidactic; and the metaphysical significance of a term like *wen* is carefully redirected in Liu Hsieh's formulation to serve more expressive literary concerns.[42]

Chung Hung in the opening words of his first preface pays homage to the tradition which sees the cosmic function of literature:

> It is life-breath (*ch'i*) which moves the external world, and the external world that moves us. Our sensibilities, once stirred, manifest themselves in dance and song. This manifestation illumines heaven, earth, and man and makes resplendent the whole of creation. Heavenly and earthly spirits depend on it to receive oblation, and ghosts of darkness draw upon it for secular reports. For moving heaven and earth and for stirring ghosts and spirits, there is nothing better than poetry.[g][43]

But these words, which are essentially a truncated version of the *Ta hsü* (Great Preface) to the *Shih ching* (Book of Odes) (written most probably by Wei Hung early in the first century A.D.),[44] are but a passing introductory nod to the metaphysical origins of poetry. Chung Hung's remaining prefatory remarks are distinctly nonmetaphysical in nature, and in the body of his work he takes up the task he is really concerned with, that of characterizing and grading poets.

The analogy drawn between poetry and boardgames like chess is instructive in still another respect, for by Chung Hung's time chess had become the pastime of cultivated men, being performed with no less conscious style and poise than that adopted when writing a poem. References in *A New Account of Tales of the World* show chess to be completely secular in function, the style of one player being taken as an indication of additional talent on his part, and the imperturbable demeanor of other players suggesting self-control.[45] Such anecdotes were in the tradition of characterizing and classifying one's contemporaries.

The already secularized view of poetry and chess, which surely did not lessen in the salon culture of the early sixth century, no more precluded Emperor Wu of the Liang dynasty, Chung Hung's sovereign, from opening his *Wei-ch'i fu* (Rhyme-prose on Encirclement Chess) with the statement, "The encirclement box forms a simulacrum of heaven, / Its square board patterns the earth,"[h][46] than it kept Chung Hung from speaking of poetic song as an oblation to heaven and earth and a means of communicating with spirits. Such statements were not to be taken as literal

---

[g] 氣之動物，物之感人，故搖蕩性情，形
諸舞詠。照燭三才，煇麗萬有；靈祇待
之以致饗，幽微藉之以昭告；動天地，
感鬼神，莫近于詩。

[h] 圍匳象天，方局法地。

statements of belief, but rather as allusions, rich in metaphorical implication, to the sources of their traditions.

Chung Hung probably had an additional worldly concern in mind when using the chess analogy. None of Chung Hung's commentators, in discussing the question of whether he wrote *Gradings of Poets* to settle a score with Shen Yüeh, notes the fact that Shen Yüeh had a few years previously written the work, *Gradings of Chess Players*. Figures on the contemporary scene would certainly have been aware of the possible personal implication to Chung Hung's statement, which might be paraphrased as follows: No less than Shen Yüeh, who could grade chess players, I, Chung Hung, am capable of judging the relative merits of poets (including Shen Yüeh himself).

Chess and poetry, moreover, form an analogy in that they involve skill; as such, they depend upon technique (i.e. *technē*, the kind of knowledge that is absorbed in practice).[47] Furthermore, chess and sixes, like all games, have internally structured rules and relationships, as does poetry. The analogy between writing skill and chess playing had been drawn by Chung Hung's contemporary, Liu Hsieh, in *Elaborations on the Essence of Literature*: "To have control of literary composition, its technique firmly in hand, is akin to a master chess player's being thoroughly versed in its principles."[i][48] In words consciously drawing a parallel between the two, Liu Hsieh describes the work of a writer who writes as well as a good chess player plays chess:

> As for the writing of a grand master,
> its technique has definite principles,
> and its composition is well-ordered;
> awaiting the culmination of feelings,
> it adapts its mechanisms to accord with circumstances,
> and though it shifts, what is correct is not lost.
> If its underlying principles reach the ultimate,
> and its key mechanisms enter upon the skillful,
> then meaningful flavor, full of life, will be born,
> and words having life-breath will appear in droves.[j][49]

Literature, like chess, is thus said to have its own underlying principles; it is a system of structures and relations, the disposition of whose elements must be carefully ordered, and whose key mechanisms must be managed with great flexibility and skill; furthermore, it is neither set apart from human sentiment, nor is it immutable. As such, it is what we would call an art.

Yet, although all of the elements discussed above—the metaphysical, social, and

i 執術馭篇，似善奕之窮數。
j 若夫善奕之文，則術有恆數，按部整 伍，以待情會，因時順機，動不失正。

數逢其極，機入其巧，則義味騰躍而 生，辭氣叢雜而至。

artistic—have bearing on his use of the analogy between boardgames and poetry, Chung Hung's remarks basically concern evaluation. He is saying that it is easier to grade poets than to grade men; it is virtually the same as grading chess players. Now chess playing can be graded by results: that is, by the clear-cut distinction between winning and losing. Or it can be viewed as a matter of skill or technique, and thus be judged according to how well it is performed as such. Furthermore, as a skill it can be narrowly defined, or it can be viewed in terms of more general style: that is, in terms of the way it is accompanied (or accomplished) by poise, panache, and the like. Chung Hung seems to be making the point that poetry is like chess in that it can be evaluated in terms of how well it is performed as a skill; for the most part, his actual evaluations are couched in these terms. But the personality of the poet, like the style of the chess player, can also be seen as playing a role in his work; that this is sometimes the case in Chung's critiques results almost inevitably from the kind of terminology he uses to characterize a poet's traits.

II

In describing literary traits, Chung Hung was necessarily compelled to employ expressions that were current (or would at least be comprehensible) in the language of his day. To this end, the vocabulary of terms descriptive of human nature which had been developed in the earlier characterological tradition was extended to discussions of literature by Chung Hung in *Gradings of Poets* and by Liu Hsieh in *Elaborations on the Essence of Literature*, as it was also to discussions of chess, calligraphy, and painting by critics of the age writing about them. Such works of evaluation and criticism in the arts were heirs to Liu Shao's *Treatise on Personalities*, Chung Hui's "Treatise on the Four Basic Relations [between Natural Ability and Human Nature]," and Liu I-ch'ing's *A New Account of Tales of the World*. In many passages of the latter, especially, men of social standing are shown making displays of ingenuity in trying to characterize contemporaries "in a few well-chosen, preferably abstruse and poetic words. It is in these and comparable works dealing with characterology, social intercourse, refined conversation and serious or playful 'characterization,' that we find the constant use of key terms such as *ch'i*, *ku*, *yün*, *feng*, and an elaborated, more or less technical terminology consisting of bisyllabic expressions (*sheng-ch'i*, *feng-liu*, *shen-i*, etc.). Although it is in most cases impossible to find a satisfactory English equivalent, these terms are, in general, well defined and understandable if we keep in mind that they were applied to human beings: to their 'temper,' 'air,' 'pith,' 'esprit,' 'emotionality,' and 'style,'"[50]

When applied to the arts, there was no clear-cut distinction between a man's character and his works in the usage of such terms. A man and his works had been considered inseparable in earlier Chinese thought.[51] Chung Hung's work displays this dual referential quality in many of its characterizations. (Indeed, such terms can at times refer not only to the artist and his work but also to the feeling or impression they prompt in the beholder.) Note, for example, the statement that Liu Chen's (d. 217) "true bones (*chen ku*) defy frost, while his noble air (*kao feng*) surpasses the common run."[k][52] Jen Fang (460–508) "in the extension of his [poetic] frame (*t'i*) is profound and correct; he succeeds in having the air (*feng*) of a man of affairs."[l][53] "Talent" (*ts'ai*) is a particularly rich word in these contexts, as it had been a supreme concern in the characterological tradition. Hsieh Hui-lien (397–433) "was rich in talent (*ts'ai*), incisive in thought."[m][54] Kuo P'u (276–324), "using his supreme talent (*ts'ai*), renovated the form (*t'i*) of [earlier] poetry, while Liu K'un (270–317), drawing on his pure and firm spirit (*ch'i*), consummated its beauty."[n][55] "Untrammeledness" (*i*) appears as an element in compound terms which can refer to both writer and work. Hsieh Ling-yün is described as having "surpassed [Chang Hsieh (fl. 295)] in being unrestrained (*i-tang*)."[o][56] And Yen Yen-chih, through excessive use of allusion, is said to have "gone contrary to what is distinguished (*hsiu-i*)."[p][57] The term *ch'i* ("spirit," "vital force," "life-breath," "humour"), in particular, had associations not only with earlier characterological and critical works but also with philosophical writings dating back still earlier.[58] Chung Hung uses the term when speaking of Liu K'un and Lu Ch'en (284–350): they "excelled at fashioning heart-rending language and had a pure and outstanding spirit (*ch'i*)."[q][59] And of Liu Chen, he says: "his spirit (*ch'i*) excelled his language";[r][60] "relying on his spirit (*ch'i*), he was fond of originality."[s][61]

In view of the terminology used, Chung Hung's discussions of poets are in large measure "characterizations." What is remarkable about them, the above examples to the contrary notwithstanding, is the degree to which they are focused on aspects of the poets' actual works. It should be borne in mind, however, that Chung Hung was much indebted to the earlier characterological tradition when specifying and describing a writer's traits in terms that in context are value-significant.

III

Chung Hung confers value both when he describes the specific characteristics of poets and when he assigns poets to overall categorical gradings. Before focusing on

---

k 眞骨凌霜，高風跨俗。

l 拓體淵雅，得國士之風。

m 才思富捷。

n 仗清剛之氣，贊成厥美。

o 逸蕩過之。

p 乖秀逸。

q 善爲悽戾之詞，自有清拔之氣。

r 氣過其文。

s 仗氣愛奇。

the specific traits he describes in value terms, it would be useful to say something first of the nature of valuation.

Value in the arts is relational. "Something that 'has value' must be actually or potentially worth something to somebody in some respect; outside of that relationship, it cannot have that value."[62] Or stated somewhat differently, for "an object to have value, a relation with something other than itself is needed. Value must include valuer as well as thing valued."[63]

Moreover, valuation is of particulars—relevant particulars. The more indeterminant the particulars or the more inclusive the category of particulars is upon which value is being conferred in a proposition, the less validatable it becomes; the less correspondence (i.e. truth) value it has. For example, of the two propositions, The phrasing in this line is apt, and The poetic phrasing of this poet is apt, the latter is considerably more indeterminate and difficult to validate in terms of its potential applicability. Furthermore, of the two propositions, The poetic phrasing of this poet is apt, and This is a top-grade poet, the latter is a general summary judgment that has rhetorical rather than analytical value: for example, as a prompting to readers to assign certain priorities in their reading, or as a prompting to current and future poets to write in certain ways.

There is a hierarchy of subjects found in a value proposition—a hierarchy in the inclusiveness or grossness of the subject being characterized and in the determinacy of the variables determinant of that subject. Note the differences between the following:

This phrase is good.
The phrasing in this stanza is good.
The diction in this work is good.
This work is well written.
The diction in this work is better than in that work.
This work is better written than that work.
The works by this author are well written.
The works by this author are better written than that author's works.
The writings of this period are better written than those of the period that comes after it.

Similarly, the description-valuations in Chung Hung's *Gradings of Poets* are remarkable for the differing degree of inclusiveness of their subjects. Note the range in the following:

In Juan Chi's (210–263) work, "the words are those of everyday sights and sounds."[t][64]
Ying Chü (190–252) was "good at using plain, archaic language."[u][65]

---

[t] 言在耳目之內。

[u] 善爲古語。

"Yüan Hung's (328–376) 'Poems on History,' though not fully developed in literary style, are nevertheless fresh and taut."[v][66]

Pao Chao's (405–466) "bone-joints (i.e. the poetic spirit or life force forming the basis of his work) are stronger than Hsieh Hun's (d. 412?)."[w][67]

Of Tai K'ai (Liu-Sung dyn.): "He is rich and strong in literary capability."[x][68]

Hsi K'ang (223–262) is "excessively severe and sharp."[y][69]

"Lu Chi's talent can be likened to the sea, P'an Yüeh's (247–300) to the Yangtze."[z][70]

"Lu Ch'en looked up to [Liu K'un], but did not quite reach him [in stature]."[aa][71]

Writing of the Yung-chia era (307–313) "was insipid and had little flavor";[ab][72] it had a "flat and insipid style."[ac][73]

Note that there are very few description-valuations in Chung Hung's work of the order "This phrase is good" or "This stanza is good." Specific poems are sometimes referred to as being good. But most description-valuations are made at the level of the third through fifth examples cited immediately above.

Also, one should note the relative determinacy of the qualifying predicates in Chung Hung's propositions. Some are more indeterminate than others. Compare, for example, the statement, Ts'ao Chih's (192–232) "diction is flowery and luxuriant,"[ad][74] with the one that the diction of Chang Han (258–319) and P'an Ni (d. 311) is "loftily beautiful."[ae][75] Or compare it with the statement that Hsi K'ang "is excessively severe and sharp." The latter examples seem more indeterminate.

In deciding what traits to focus on when evaluating a work (or when comparing works), it is crucial to focus on traits that are relevant to the analysis.[76] Are the traits that Chung Hung perceives in poets' works the essential ones? It would be necessary to conduct intensive analyses of the complete works of several of the poets treated by Chung Hung in order to confirm or deny that the traits recorded by him are indeed the ones most significant, essential, or revelatory of those poets' work. (And large parts of the corpus of many of the writers he refers to are no longer extant.)[77] One can note in partial support of his views, however, that later critics versed in the early poetic tradition often discern the same traits in the authors he treats as being the significant ones (and often come to the same conclusions concerning them).[78]

When focusing on the traits that Chung Hung identifies and the valuation he confers on each, it is important to keep in mind that these traits are not perceived in

[v] 彥伯詠史，雖文體未遒，而鮮明緊健。
[w] 骨節强于謝混。
[x] 才章富健。
[y] 過爲峻切。
[z] 陸才如海，潘才如江。

[aa] 中郎仰之，微不逮者矣。
[ab] 淡乎寡味。
[ac] 平淡之體。
[ad] 詞采華茂。
[ae] 文采高麗。

isolation; they are treated as significant features interrelating as constituent parts of a whole. It is rare, if ever, that these traits are identified in terms that are wholly free of valuational significance (i.e. are purely descriptive).[79] They are almost always predicated in language which explicitly (or in context) confers value. Yet the degree of value assigned a specific trait by Chung Hung varies from case to case, for the more or less significant features of poetic works differ from author to author.

"Spirit" (*ch'i*), "talent" (*ts'ai*), and "untrammeledness" (*i*) are qualities upon which Chung Hung conferred different values in different contexts. Like all value statements in the arts, these are comprised of "a descriptive proposition which has as its subject the sensible form [of what is being described] or some part of it, and some perceptible trait as its predicate."[80] That the terminology used in the above instances might be referential not only to the sensible form of a poet's work but also to the poet himself (or even his audience) does not make the statements in which they appear any less propositions of value, nor does it render them less validatable in terms of their reference to the poet's actual work, albeit their level of abstraction renders such validation quite difficult.

Other important aspects focused upon by Chung Hung, such as language and style, are more clearly referential to a poet's work, or at least to qualities perceived specifically through his work. About poetic expression, Chung Hung notes that Wang Ts'an's (177–217) is "outstanding",[af][81] Pan Chieh-yü's (48?–6? B.C.) "delicate";[ag][82] and that of the Old Poems (*ku shih*) "genial and beautiful."[ah][83] Moreover, Lu Chi is said to be "rich in phrasing,"[ai][84] and Chang Hua (232–300) "clever at using words."[aj][85]

In terms of literary style, T'ao Ch'ien's (365–427) is said to be "spare and limpid, with scarcely a surplus word";[ak][86] Kuo P'u's is "resplendent—scintillating and enjoyable";[al][87] and that of Ts'ao Chih "has both refinement and substance."[am][88] By way of comparison, the style of Chang Hua is "florid."[an][89] And Kuo P'u is spoken of as having "transformed the flat, insipid style of the Yung-chia (307–313) period."[ao][90]

Chung Hung attaches importance to the thought conveyed by the poet. The Old Poems are "sorrowful and far-reaching in thought."[ap][91] And Yen Yen-chih is said to be never frivolous: "to every word, every phrase, he conveys his intent."[aq][92] Yet of Hsieh T'iao (464–499) it is noted, "His thoughts are keen but his talents weak."[ar][93]

af 文秀。

ag 文綺。

ah 文溫以麗。

ai 詞贍。

aj 巧用文字。

ak 文體省淨，殆無長語。

al 文體相輝，彪炳可翫。

am 體被文質。

an 其體華豔。

ao 始變永嘉平淡之體。

ap 意悲而遠。

aq 一句一字，皆致意焉。

ar 意銳而才弱也。

Poetic figures are mentioned, but not in terms of the "evocative image" (*hsing*), "comparison" (*pi*), and "description" (*fu*) of the first preface (to be cited below).[94] Of Hsi K'ang it is said, "His poetic figures are clear and far-reaching."[as][95] And of Yen Yen-chih, Chung Hung states, "The figures he uses to express feeling are deep and profound."[at][96]

Straightforward expression is prized by Chung Hung. The poetry of Juan Chi is implicitly contrasted with the "patched and borrowed" phrases of highly allusive poets: "His words are those of everyday sights and sounds, yet the feelings he expresses go above and beyond the universe. So expansive, his poetry is at one with the spirit of the *Book of Odes*."[au][97] This is not to say that simple straightforwardness, unmediated by art, is considered an unqualified plus. Chung Hung says of Ts'ao P'i:

> His more than one hundred compositions are generally common and direct, like ordinary dialogue. Only with the ten or so poems including "North and west there are floating clouds,"[98] which are ample in excellence and enjoyable, does his real skill come to the fore.[av][99]

Hsi K'ang, moreover, is said to have been "unduly direct in expressing his talent."[aw][100] And Hsieh Ling-yün, "who writes down whatever strikes his eye,"[ax][101] is found guilty of prolixity.

One could go on with citations referring to other traits. But the above examples include some of Chung Hung's most recurrent concerns and serve to illustrate the nature of his statements of descriptive valuation. As one can see, most of these propositions are formulated at a fairly high level of abstraction or inclusiveness, which makes them difficult to validate. One senses that this level of statement, toward which so many of Chung Hung's description-valuations tend, is intended to communicate the nature of its subject, much in the earlier characterological tradition to which it was heir.

The traits Chung Hung notes when characterizing an individual poem or a writer's corpus have valuational significance, but it would be a mistake to rephrase them as normative statements. For example, to take Chung Hung's assertion, laudatory in context, that Hsi K'ang's "poetic figures are clear and far-reaching," and change it to the proposition, Figures in poetry *should be* clear and far-reaching, would be unwarranted. One can only rephrase Chung's statement as, Metaphors in poetry that are clear and far-reaching are generally conducive to (but by no means necessary to) good poetry. Given the wide range of traits noted with descriptive-*cum*-valuative predicates by Chung Hung, one cannot but be struck by the flexibility of his approach. It reflects the attitude of one who is willing to justify his gradings by

as 託諭清遠。

at 情喻淵深。

au 言在耳目之內，情寄八荒之表，洋洋乎會於風雅。

av 所計百許篇，率皆鄙質如偶語。惟西北有浮雲十餘首，殊美贍可翫，始見其工矣。

aw 評直露才。

ax 寓目輒書。

identifying and characterizing traits (which others may examine, and either validate or reject).[102]

Normative statements concerning what poetry should be like are found only in the prefaces to *Gradings of Poets*, not in the specific critiques. The implicit standard of value employed by Chung in his actual characterizations stands in an important relationship to the general, normative statements made in the prefaces.

IV

Chung Hung's characterizations implicitly depend upon a standard of evaluation. He himself spoke of the need for such a standard when saying of the contemporary anarchy of taste, "Discussions turn disputatious, and there is no reliable standard"; by implication, he set himself the task of fulfilling the need.

Although Chung Hung's general statements about the nature of poetry and about what constitutes good poetry, which are found in the prefaces to *Gradings of Poets*, are not applied as an explicit standard of measure in his actual characterizations, they form an important backdrop to his system of description-valuations and gradings. The general, normative statements of the prefaces contribute to his definition of poetry; the valuations of poetic traits in the body of the work are generally measured in terms of how well they perform as poetry: poetry being defined in large measure, but not entirely, by the general statements of the prefaces.

In the first of his three prefaces to *Gradings of Poets*, Chung Hung offers a definition of what he considers to be the "perfect poetry":

> Poetry has three aspects: evocative image (*hsing*), comparison (*pi*), and description (*fu*). When meaning lingers on, though writing has come to an end, this is an "evocative image." When an object is used to express a sentiment, this is "comparison." And when affairs are recorded directly, the objective world being put into words, this is "description." If one expands these three aspects and uses them judiciously, backing them up with lively force and lending them beauty of coloration, so that those who read from one's work find it inexhaustible and those who hear it are moved, this is the perfect poetry.[ay][103]

Chung Hung proceeds to stress the need for balance among the above aspects:

> If only "comparison" and "evocative image" are used, writing will suffer from density of thought; and when ideas are dense, expression stumbles. If only "description" is employed, writing will suffer from superficiality; and

---

[ay] 詩有三義焉：一曰興，二曰比，三曰賦。文已盡而意有餘，興也；因物喻志，比也；直書其事，寓言寫物，賦也。宏斯三義，酌而用之，幹之以風力，潤之以丹采，使味之者無極，聞之者動心：是詩之至也。

when thought is superficial, language becomes diffuse. Further, if one carelessly drifts back and forth among these, one's writing will be without anchoring and will suffer from prolixity.[az][104]

This makes for an interesting enough statement of the criteria that make for superlative poetry. But inasmuch as Chung Hung almost never refers to them in the body of his work, where his critiques of individual poets are contained, it is clear that he is not looking to their balanced use as an overt standard of judgment. Rather, in his prefaces he seems in large part to be paying deference to received opinion about what constitutes poetry, specifically to the aforementioned "Great Preface" to the *Book of Odes*.

Chung Hung's standard of judgment is informed most basically by his view of the nature of poetry. His conception of poetry is essentially an expressive one: namely, poetry is the direct and sincere expression of feelings personally experienced:

> Vernal breezes and springtime birds, the autumn moon and cicadas in the fall, summer clouds and sultry rains, the winter moon and fierce cold—these are what in the four seasons inspire poetic feeling. At an agreeable banquet, through poetry one can make friendship dearer. When parting, one can put one's chagrin into verse.
>
> When a Ch'u official [Ch'ü Yüan (343–277 B.C.)] is banished—
> When a Han consort [Pan Chieh-yü or Wang Chao-chün (fl. 33 B.C.)]
>   has to leave the palace—
> When white bones are strewn across the northern plain,
> And souls go chasing tumbleweed—[as in poems by Ts'ao Ts'ao (155–
>   220), Wang Ts'an, and Hsieh Chan (387–421)]
> When arms are borne in frontier camps,
> And a savage spirit overflows the border—[as in a poem by Chiang
>   Yen (444–505)]
> When the frontier traveler has but thin clothing,
> And all tears are spent in the widow's chambers—[as in the Old Poems
>   and in Ho Yen's (190–249) verse]
> When the ornaments of office are divested and one leaves the court,
> Gone, no thought of returning—[as in poems by Chang Hsieh, Yüan
>   Shu (408–453), and Shen Yüeh]
> When by raising an eyebrow a woman [Lady Li in Li Yen-nien's
>   (140–87 B.C.) poem] wins imperial favor,
> And with a second glance topples the state—

[az] 若專用比興，患在意深，意深則詞躓。　　　嬉成流移，文無止泊，有蕪漫之累矣。
若但用賦體，患在意浮，意浮則文散，

These various situations all stir the heart and move the soul. If not put into poetry, how can such sentiments be expressed? If not put into song, how can these emotions be vented? "Poetry teaches the art of sociability; it shows how to regulate feelings of resentment."[105] For giving solace to those in extreme circumstances, and for relieving the distress of those living retired from affairs, there is nothing better than poetry. So it is that among men of letters, there is none who does not take pleasure in it.[ba][106]

The expressive view of poetry manifested here by Chung Hung is only tempered by the concerns enumerated at the end of his statement and by the pragmatic ends he mentions elsewhere.[107]

It is in the same vein that Chung Hung argues forcefully against the use of allusions in poetry, their use being deemed more properly the province of non-bellettristic literature:

It has become the standard view that in writing one should use topical allusions. It is true that documents dealing with the ordering of the state should draw upon extensive erudition about ancient matters; and in making known virtuous conduct and in writing point-counterpoint arguments and memorials to the throne, one should explore past accomplishment thoroughly. But when it comes to expressing human feeling and emotion in verse, what is praiseworthy about the use of allusion? [The line by Hsü Kan (170–217)] "Thinking of you is like flowing water" merely relates what struck the eye.[108] [Ts'ao Chih's line] "The high terrace—much sad wind" simply states what was seen.[109] [The line by Chang Hua] "In the clear morning I climb Lung Peak" makes no use of allusion.[110] And as for [Hsieh Ling-yün's line] "The bright moon shines on the piled snow,"[111] could this have been derived from a canonical or historical text? Examine the best expressions past and present; the majority of them are not patched or borrowed. They all derive from the direct pursuit of the subject.

Yen Yen-chih and Hsieh Chuang (421–466), who were especially prolix and dense in the use of allusion, set the temper of their time. No wonder that during the Ta-ming and T'ai-shih reign-periods (457–464 and 465–471) writing virtually became a copybook exercise. More recently, Jen Fang, Wang Jung (467–493), and company did not value originality in diction but were given to outdoing each other in the use of

ba 若乃春風春鳥，秋月秋蟬，夏雲暑雨，冬月祁寒：斯四候之感諸詩者也。嘉會寄詩以觀，離羣託詩以怨。至于楚臣去境，漢妾辭宮；或骨橫朔野，或魂逐飛蓬；或負戈外戍，殺氣雄邊；塞客衣單，孀閨淚盡；或士有解佩出朝，一去忘返；女有揚蛾入寵，再盼傾國。凡斯種種，感蕩心靈，非陳詩何以展其義，非長歌何以騁其情？故曰：「詩可以羣，可以怨。」使窮賤易安，幽居靡悶，莫尚於詩矣。

novel allusions. From their time on, writers have increasingly made it accepted practice, so that there is not a single plainly worded line and not a single plainly worded phrase; they are all constricted and patched up with allusions. The bane to writing has been great indeed.

A writer with the high-minded goal of artlessness is seldom met with. His language devoid of elevation, a poet feels he might as well pile on allusions. Even then, if he lacks talent, he can at least display his learning. Perhaps this explains the phenomenon.[bb][112]

Chung Hung's prefatory statement of deep-seated aversion to codified tonal regulations in poetry (regardless of to what extent it may reflect personal animus toward Shen Yüeh, who was closely associated with their formulation) can be seen in the same light.[113] Namely, formalized prosodic regulations are said to interfere with the direct expression of feeling.

In his specific critiques of poets, however, except for the use of allusion, Chung Hung makes no reference to these general, normative criteria of judgment. Even regarding the use of allusion, the normative statement of Chung's preface is not applied deductively as a standard; in his actual critiques the trait is treated as one among many that affect poetic performance. Yen Yen-chih, who is characterized as having "enjoyed allusions,"[bc][114] and Jen Fang, who is said to have "used allusions at every turn,"[bd][115] are assigned by Chung Hung to the middle grade of poets. And to judge from his statements in the prefaces about the merit of "direct pursuit [of the subject] (*chih hsün*)" on the part of the author and the violence done to poetry by the dense use of allusion, one would expect Chung Hung to find Hsieh Ling-yün's poetry most wanting, since the opposite traits are discerned in his works. Yet, ascertaining that these traits are part of a greater whole and are in balance with other characteristics, Chung places Hsieh in the upper grade of poets at this higher level of valuation:

Hsieh's poetic origins go back to Ts'ao Chih. Because he mixes in the style of Chang Hsieh, he sets much store on clever resemblance, while surpassing Chang in being unrestrained. Hsieh really suffers from prolixity.

I myself feel that for such a man, whose poetic inspirations are many

bb 夫屬詞比事，乃爲通談。若乃經國文符，應資博古；撰德駁奏，宜窮往烈。至乎吟詠情性，亦何貴於用事？「思君如流水，」既是即目；「高臺多悲風，」亦惟所見；「清晨登隴首，」羌無故實；「明月照積雪，」詎出經史。觀古今勝語，多非補假，皆有直尋。顏延，謝莊，尤爲繁密，于時化之。故大明泰始中，文章殆同書抄。近任昉王元長等，詞不貴奇，競須新事，爾來作者，寖以成俗。遂乃句無虛語，語無虛字，拘攣補衲，蠹文已甚。但自然英旨，罕值其人。詞既失高，則宜加事義。雖謝天才，且表學問，亦一理乎！

bc 喜用古事。

bd 動輒用事。

and whose talent is lofty and extensive—who writes down whatever strikes his eye in such a way that, internally, it is never lacking in thought, and externally, nothing is left out—for such a man, lavishness is quite all right.

To be sure, wonderful strophes and superb couplets do appear here and there, and beautiful allusions and new sounds do incessantly converge. It is like green pines towering out from thick bushes or white jade shining amid dirt and sand—yet they cannot detract from his loftiness and purity.[be][116]

The characterization of Hsieh Ling-yün illustrates an important feature of Chung Hung's critical approach. He is apparently willing to see a greater good (in terms of poetic performance) obtaining in a whole composed to a significant degree of parts to which he is not at all well disposed.

The normative statements of the prefaces can be seen as a backdrop to the stage on which Chung Hung carries out actual critiques and gradings of poets. They reflect his general concerns and inevitably play a role in his evaluations. What is striking about the body of *Gradings of Poets* is the degree to which they are absent as explicit criteria of judgment. Even more striking is the degree to which Chung Hung sought to identify specific traits (of the sort indicated earlier in this article) that would justify his general impressions of a writer. These traits are assayed in terms of the degree to which they contribute to making a poem good as poetry: poetry being defined largely by the selfsame general statements of the prefaces, but also in good measure by the characteristics identified in the critiques which were not in those formulations, or which go counter to them, yet in context are deemed contributory to poetic quality.[117] This standard of value was suggested in Chung Hung's prefatory statement that poetic expertise can be ascertained as easily as expertise in boardgames like chess. And it is borne out in the body of *Gradings of Poets*—in the characterizations and evaluations of individual poets, and in the comparisons made between poets.

V

Discussion is in order concerning the ways Chung Hung compares one poet with another. There are four general types of comparative valuation in *Gradings of Poets*. First, there is the comparison of two poets in which a shared trait is described in language of a descriptive-valuative nature of the sort cited repeatedly above.

be　其原出於陳思，雜有景陽之體。故尚巧　　處處間起，麗典新聲，絡繹奔會。譬猶
似，而逸蕩過之，頗以繁富爲累。嶸謂　　青松之拔灌木，白玉之映塵沙，未足貶
若人興多才高，寓目輒書，內無乏思，　　其高絜也。
外無遺物，其繁富宜哉！然名章迥句，

Where specified, the sensible forms of shared traits are yet at quite a high level of inclusiveness or abstraction. For example, Shen Yüeh's "phrasing is more compact than Fan Yün's (451–503)";[bf][118] Lu Chi's "expression is inferior to that of Wang Ts'an";[bg][119] and Lu Chi's "spirit falls short of Liu Chen's."[bh][120] Where unspecified, sensible forms of a shared trait are referred to only by suggestion, propositions being formulated simply by using a descriptive-valuative predicate; such statements in particular lend themselves to broadly interpreted reference, although in context they normally refer to a writer's work. For example, Chang Hsieh is said to be "more vigorous than P'an Yüeh,"[bi][121] and Tso Ssu (d. 306?) is characterized as being "more unrefined than Lu Chi."[bj][122] The most common comparison of this latter sort, however, is the one that X-poet is "less profound" than Y-poet: P'an Yüeh is thus compared unfavorably with both Lu Chi and Tso Ssu,[123] and Fan Yün and Ch'iu Ch'ih (464–508) are found wanting beside Chiang Yen.[124]

Secondly, there is comparison of poets by metaphor or simile. The poems of a writer like Ch'iu Ch'ih are said to be "quilted patches charmingly bright, like fallen petals lying on the grass."[bk][125] This follows directly Chung Hung's characterization of Fan Yün, who is treated in the same critique: "Fan Yün's poems are bracingly nimble and smooth-turning, like a flowing breeze swirling snow."[bl][126] Aspects of two poets' work can be compared to different objects sharing some class similarity: Lu Chi's talent is likened "to the sea" and P'an Yüeh's "to the Yangtze."[127] Or two poets' work can be compared to different objects sharing little apparent similarity. Two of the most famous comparisons that appear in *Gradings of Poets*, both of which are quotes from other writers, are of this sort. One is by Hsieh Hun:

> P'an Yüeh's verse is resplendent, like embroidery being spread out; it is everywhere beautiful. Reading Lu Chi's writing is like sifting sand to find gold; here and there a gem appears.[bm][128]

The other is by T'ang Hui-hsiu (fl. 464):

> Hsieh Ling-yün's poetry is like lotus flowers coming out of the water; Yen Yen-chih's is like a mix of colors with inlays of gold.[bn][129]

Although invalidatable as value propositions, such statements are most suggestive. It is probably best to think of them—so popular in the Chinese tradition—as vague concrete approximations, poetically expressed, of traits perceived in a writer's work.[130]

bf 當詞密于范。
bg 文劣於仲宣。
bh 氣少於公幹。
bi 雄於潘岳。
bj 野於陸機。

bk 丘詩點綴映媚，似落花依草。
bl 范詩清便宛轉，如流風迴雪。
bm 潘詩爛若舒錦，無處不佳；陸文如披沙簡金，往往見寶。
bn 謝詩如芙蓉出水，顏如錯采鏤金。

A third type of comparison is that implied by contrasting the lineages ascribed to poets in terms of their style. Chung Hung begins many of his characterizations by stating the putative sources of the writer. Poetic writing is found to derive either directly from the *Book of Odes* or the *Ch'u tz'u* (Songs of the South), or indirectly from one or the other through a family tree of inheritances.[131] Thus, for example, the poetry of Yen Yen-chih is said to derive from that of Lu Chi, which is identified as going back to that of Ts'ao Chih, which in turn is said to be heir to the Kuo-feng (Airs of the States) section of the *Book of Odes*. Usually the farther removed from the founts of the poetic tradition a writer is identified as being, the poorer the grading he is likely to be assigned.[132] Thus, Ts'ao Chih and Lu Chi are included among the upper-grade poets; Yen Yen-chih is assigned to the middle grade; and Hsieh Chao-tsung (d. 483), who is said to be heir to Yen Yen-chih, is placed in the lower grade. The better the pedigree ascribed to a poet, the better his comparative position vis-à-vis other poets.

There is finally the implicit comparative valuation of poets reflected in their assignment to one of Chung Hung's three grades. Clearly, an upper-grade poet is deemed better than a middle-grade one, and both are held superior to one of the lower grade. Yet too much can be made of these grosser categories as critical tools. As has been repeatedly stressed in this article, the higher the level of abstraction, inclusiveness, or indeterminacy in a value proposition, the less force as a proposition of value it has, and the more diffuse it becomes. Rather, gradings are summary value judgments that serve other ends: e.g. those of trying to persuade the reader as to what priorities to assign in his reading and which authors to emulate in his own writing.

VI

The fact that one can disagree with the assignment of an author to one of Chung Hung's three grades while agreeing with the specifics in his critique of that writer serves only to underscore the value, *qua* criticism, of Chung Hung's approach. Let us take the example of his critique of Hsieh Ling-yün. Should we perceive and validate the same traits in Hsieh Ling-yün's work that Chung Hung found, we are not prohibited from coming to a different conclusion concerning the assignment of the writer to one of the grosser valuative categories. As is the case with any of the poets, the assignment of a grade necessarily depends upon the relative weights one gives the traits found in a writer's work, compared with other such constellations of traits in the writings of other authors. This is underscored in the case of Chung Hung's critique of T'ao Ch'ien. Later critics were dismayed at his being assigned to the middle grade of poets in *Gradings of Poets*;[133] yet few disagreed with Chung's specific characterization of the poet:

T'ao's poetry derives from that of Ying Chü, and he shares in the lively forcefulness of Tso Ssu.

His literary style is spare and limpid, with scarcely a surplus word. His earnestness is true and traditional, his verbalized inspirations supple and relaxed. When one reads his works, the fine character of the poet himself comes to mind. Ordinary men admire his unadorned directness. But lines of his like "With happy face I pour the spring-brewed wine,"[134] and "The sun sets, no clouds are in the sky,"[135] are pure and refined in the beauty of their air. How can these be merely the words of a farmer? He is the father of recluse poetry past and present.[bo][136]

One can agree with the characterization while disagreeing with the grade assignment.

Perception and valuation of significant traits is of greater value as criticism than is assignment to a gross value-fraught category, for "general summary judgments are practical in nature, and not instruments of analysis and knowledge."[137] Yet the practical, rhetorical value of summary judgments cannot be overlooked. The assignment of writers to an upper, middle, or lower grade can serve as an endorsement to insure the survival of works by certain authors; it can act as an incitement to further critical discussion of them; or it can be a prompting to readers and writers to follow certain rankings in their reading and emulation of earlier poets. Chung Hung's *Gradings of Poets* is very much a manifesto of the lattermost sort.

Yet, the assignment of past poets to grosser-level gradings can additionally serve not only as a commendation or criticism of the writers themselves, but also as a commendation or criticism of those among one's contemporaries who emulate or advocate the emulation of their writings. This, too, was surely operative in *Gradings of Poets.*

The question of contemporary implications of the work brings us back to the literary scene of the time, with its social and political factions wherein literary concerns were very much an issue. Much of the import of Chung Hung's work at this level of analysis is now lost. The reader will recall that Chung Hung found earlier seven- and nine-part evaluation schemes wanting when one compared reputations with facts. Yet, in terms of the social and literary history of his own time, it is difficult to assess the degree to which Chung Hung was himself influenced by the current reputations of the poets he graded, or to what extent the favor or disfavor they enjoyed among his powerful contemporaries affected his gradings of them. One suspects that his placement of Hsieh Ling-yün in the upper grade of poets was in large measure owing to the latter's reputation in his age. Moreover, the whole

bo 其原出於應璩，又協左思風力。文體省淨，殆無長語。篤意眞古，辭興婉愜；每觀其文，想其人德，世歎其質直。至 如「歡言酌春酒，」「日暮天無雲，」風華清靡，豈直爲田家語耶！古今隱逸詩人之宗也。

matter of Chung Hung's assigning pedigrees to the poets he treats—of the kind, Hsieh Ling-yün's "poetic origins go back to Ts'ao Chih," or T'ao Ch'ien's "poetry derives from that of Ying Chü"—suggests by implication that the grading assigned an earlier poet is being associated with his latter-day epigones among Chung Hung's contemporaries.

Regardless of the current influences Chung Hung was subject to or the nature of his own biases, *Gradings of Poets* was to survive as a critical work enjoying great prestige long after most of its contemporary implications became obscure. This fact underscores its usefulness as a critical statement read simply in terms of its own argument. One suspects that, when setting about the task of writing *Gradings of Poets*, Chung Hung cast about for categories and descriptive terms to reflect and justify his own intuitive reactions to individual poets. It was to this end that he drew upon the terminology of the earlier characterological tradition. What is significant is that he did not simply discuss poets in terms of his ultimate conclusions about them. Rather, he was intent on putting into words those elements in the poet that led to his reactions; his gradings are justified by the characterizations resulting from these description-valuations. It is this that makes Chung Hung a literary critic.

1. The author wishes to thank the Faculty Grant-in-Aid program of Arizona State University for a summer stipend to complete research on this study, as well as its Center for Asian Studies for assistance in preparing the manuscript. He also wishes to thank Dr. Achilles Fang for prior assistance with the text of the *Shih-p'in*; Dr. Ronald Egan for substantive suggestions for improving an earlier draft of this article, as well as the participants in the 1979 conference on Theories of the Arts in China, especially Dr. Susan Bush; and Dr. Hoyt Tillman, Ms. Gail Gray, Dr. Timothy Wong, Dr. David Knechtges, and Dr. Donald Gibbs for later, mostly editorial, suggestions for improvement.

The text of the *Shih-p'in* cited here is from the edition edited by Ch'en Yen-chieh, *Shih-p'in chu* (*Gradings of Poets* Annotated) (1927; rpt. Taipei, 1958 and 1960). The following additional studies and translations of the *Shih-p'in*, in particular, were consulted in the preparation of this article:

Takamatsu Takaaki (Kōmei), *Shihin shōkai* (Detailed Explication of *Gradings of Poets*) (Hirosaki, 1959).

Kōzen Hiroshi, "Shihin" (Gradings of Poets), in *Bungaku ronshū* (A Collection of Discussions of Literature), by Arai Ken and Kōzen Hiroshi (Tokyo, 1972), pp. 1–260 (hereafter cited as Kōzen).

Okamura Shigeru, "*Shihin* no jo" (The Prefaces to *Gradings of Poets*), in *Bungaku geijutsu ronshū* (A Collection of Discussions of Literature and the Arts), ed. Mekada Makoto (Tokyo, 1974), pp. 221–233.

Takagi Masakazu, *Shō Kō Shihin* (Chung Hung, *Gradings of Poets*) (Tokyo, 1978).

Hellmut Wilhelm, "A Note on Chung Hung and His *Shih-p'in*," in *Wen-lin: Studies in the Chinese Humanities*, ed. Chow Tse-tsung (Madison, Wisc., 1968), pp. 111–120.

E. Bruce Brooks, "A Geometry of the Shr̄ Pin," in *ibid.*, pp. 121–150. (hereafter cited as Brooks).

Cha Chu Whan, "On Enquiries for Ideal Poetry: An Instance of Chung Hung," *Tamkang Review* (October, 1975–April, 1976), 6(2) and 7(1):43–54.

Yeh Chia-ying and Jan W. Walls, "Theory, Standards, and Practice of Criticizing Poetry in Chung Hung's *Shih-p'in*," in *Studies in Chinese Poetry and Poetics*, vol. 1, ed. Ronald C. Miao (San Francisco, 1978), pp. 43–79.

The three prefaces and two of the three sections of gradings in the *Shih-p'in* are translated in full by John Timothy Wixted, "The Literary Criticism of Yüan Hao-wen (1190–1257)," D.Phil. Dissertation, Oxford, 1976, pp. 462–491 (q.v. for an earlier version of translations offered in this study).

All translations of the *Shih-p'in* and other works cited here are by the author, unless otherwise noted.

2. The *Wen-hsin tiao-lung* appears in a complete translation by Vincent Yu-cheng Shih, *The Literary Mind and the Carving of Dragons* (New York, 1959) (hereafter cited as Vincent Shih), and in a partial translation (five chapters) by Yang Hsien-yi and Gladys Yang, "Carving a Dragon at the Core of Literature," *Chinese Literature*, June, 1962, pp. 58–71.

Western-language studies of the work include the following:

Donald A. Gibbs, "Literary Theory in the *Wen-hsin tiao-lung*, Sixth Century Chinese Treatise on the Genesis of Literature and Conscious Artistry," Ph.D. Dissertation, Washington, 1970.

Vincent Y. C. Shih, "Classicism in Liu Hsieh's 'Wen-hsin tiao-lung,'" *Asiatische Studien/Etudes Asiatiques* (1953), 7:122–134.

Liu Shou-sung, "Liu Hsieh on Writing," *Chinese Literature*, June, 1962, pp. 72–81.

Donald A. Gibbs, "Liu Hsieh, Author of the *Wen-hsin tiao-lung*," *MS* (1970–1971), 29:117–141.

Ferenc Tökei, *Genre Theory in China in the 3rd–6th Centuries* (Budapest, 1971), pp. 81–177.

Chi Ch'iu-lang, "Liu Hsieh as a Classicist and His Concepts of Tradition and Change," *Tamkang Review* (April, 1973), 4(1):89–108.

Vincent Y. C. Shih, "Liu Hsieh's Conception of Organic Unity," *Tamkang Review* (October, 1973), 4(2):1–10.

James J. Y. Liu, *Chinese Theories of Literature* (Chicago and London, 1975), passim.

Discussion of the title of this work and how it should be translated into English is found in James R. Hightower's review of Vincent Shih's translation, *HJAS* (1959), 22:284–286; in Achilles Fang's unsigned review of the same work, *The Times Literary Supplement* (London), 4 December 1959, p. 713; in Gibbs, "Literary Theory in the *Wen-hsin tiao-lung*," pp. 84–85; and in James J. Y. Liu, *Chinese Theories of Literature*, pp. 146–147. Suggested translations of the title, in addition to those in the titles of the works by Vincent Shih, Yang Hsien-yi and Gladys Yang, and Donald Gibbs cited above, include the following:

E. R. Hughes, "The Literary Mind and Its Carving of Dragons" in *The Art of Letters: Lu Chi's "Wen fu," A.D. 302* (New York, 1951), p. 235.

Chen Shih-hsiang, "Anatomy of the Literary Mind," or "The Carving of the Dragon of the Literary Mind" ("In Search of the Beginnings of Chinese Literary Criticism," in *Semitic and Oriental Studies, A Volume Presented to William Popper on the Occasion of His*

Seventy-fifth Birthday, ed. Walter J. Fischel [University of California Publications in Semitic Philology, 11] [Berkeley and Los Angeles, 1951], p. 57).

James R. Hightower, "A Serious and Elegant Treatise on (the Art or Secret of) Literature" (rev. of Vincent Shih, pp. 284, 286).

Achilles Fang, "Dragon-carving on the Core (or Heart) of Literary Art," or "An Elaborate Presentation of the Quintessence of Literature" (rev. of Vincent Shih, p. 713).

Ch'en Shou-yi, "The Carved Dragon of the Literary Mind" (*Chinese Literature: A Historical Introduction* [New York, 1961], p. 227).

James J. Y. Liu, "Dragon Carvings of a Literary Mind" (*The Art of Chinese Poetry* [London, 1962], p. 71).

Donald Gibbs, "The Genesis and Artistry of Literature" ("Literary Theory in the *Wen-hsin tiao-lung*," p. 85).

James J. Y. Liu, "The Literary Mind: Elaborations" (*Chinese Theories of Literature*, pp. 21, 146–147).

The discussions by James R. Hightower, Achilles Fang, and James J. Y. Liu (in his latter work) are most apropos; hence the title is here rendered "Elaborations on the Essence of Literature."

3. Hsiao T'ung's preface to the *Wen hsüan* is discussed and translated by James R. Hightower, "The *Wen hsüan* and Genre Theory," *HJAS* (1957), 20:512–533; rpt. in *Studies in Chinese Literature*, ed. John L. Bishop (Harvard-Yenching Institute Series 21) (Cambridge, Mass., 1966), pp. 142–163. An abridged form of the article (including the complete translation) appears as the "Introduction" to Erwin von Zach, *Die Chinesische Anthologie*, ed. Ilse Martin Fang (Harvard-Yenching Institute Series 18) (Cambridge, Mass., 1958), pp. xiii–xvii.

4. Hsü Ling's preface to the *Yü-t'ai hsin-yung* is translated by James R. Hightower, "Some Characteristics of Parallel Prose," in *Studia Serica Bernhard Karlgren Dedicata*, ed. Søren Egerod and Else Glahn (Copenhagen, 1959), pp. 77–87; rpt. in *Studies in Chinese Literature*, ed. John L. Bishop, pp. 125–135.

5. Brooks, p. 122. The date of the compilation of the *Wen-hsin tiao-lung* is problematic.

6. John Marney, *Liang Chien-wen Ti* (Boston, 1976), p. 14. For discussion of literary groups or cliques of the Liang period, see Morino Shigeo, "Ryōsho no bungaku shūdan" (Literary Groups of the Early Liang), *Chūgoku bungaku hō* (October, 1966), 21:83–108; and Morino Shigeo, "Ryō no bungaku shūdan—Taishi Kō no shūdan o chūshin to shite" (Literary Groups in the Liang Period: Chiefly Prince Kang's Group), *Nihon Chūgoku Gakkai hō* (1968), 20:109–124.

7. Marney, *Liang Chien-wen Ti*, p. 76.

8. *Liang shu* (History of the Liang Dynasty) 49, pp. 694–697, and *Nan shih* (History of the Southern Dynasties) 72, pp. 1778–1779. (All citations of the dynastic histories are to the Chung-hua shu-chü ed. [Peking, 1959–].) Chung Hung's biography, except for a memorial on the position of military officials and quotation of the first preface to the *Shih-p'in*, is translated in full by Wilhelm, "A Note on Chung Hung," pp. 111–114. Note the suggested corrections to his translation by J. D. Jonker, rev. of *Wen-lin: Studies in the Chinese Humanities*, ed. Chow Tse-tsung, *TP* (1973), 59:279–281.

9. *Nan shih* 72, p. 989. Discussion of the charge is found in Takamatsu, pp. 182–186;

Wilhelm, pp. 114–115; Brooks, pp. 147–148; Kōzen, pp. 17–18; Takagi, p. 298; and Ch'ai Fei-fan, "Chung Hung *Shih-p'in* yü Shen Yüeh" (Chung Hung's *Gradings of Poets* and Shen Yüeh), *Chung-wai wen-hsüeh* (1975), 3(10):58–65.

10. *Shih-p'in chu*, pp. 5–6; Takamatsu, pp. 16–17; Kōzen, pp. 56–57; Okamura, p. 225; and Takagi, pp. 86–87. Cf. the translation (complete) by Brooks, pp. 124–125, and (partial) by Yeh and Walls, pp. 44–45.

For the Tzu and Sheng rivers, see A. C. Graham, trans. *The Book of Lieh-tzu* (London, 1960; rpt. 1973), p. 84.

Purple vying with vermilion is an allusion to the *Lun-yü* (Analects): *Lun-yü yin-te* (A Concordance to the Analects of Confucius) (Harvard-Yenching Istitute Sinological Index Series 16) (Peking, 1940; rpt. Taipei, 1966), 17:16, p. 36. Cf. the translations by James Legge, *Confucian Analects*, in *The Chinese Classics*, 5 vols. (rev. ed. Oxford, 1893–1895; rpt. Hong Kong, 1960). 1:326; and by Arthur Waley, *The Analects of Confucius* (London, 1938; rpt. New York, n.d.), p. 214.

11. This work appears in complete Western-language translations by five different scholars:

Georges Margouliès, *Le "Fou" dans le Wen-siuan: étude et textes* (Paris, 1926), pp. 82–97 (cf. Erwin von Zach, "Zu G. Margouliès' Uebersetzung des Wen-fu," *TP* [1928], 25:360–364). A considerably revised version appears in the author's *Anthologie raisonnée de la littérature chinoise* (Paris, 1948), pp. 419–425.

B. M. Alexéiev's Russian rendition appears in the *Bulletin de l'Académie des Sciences de l'URSS* (Classe des sciences littéraires et linguistiques) (1944), 3(4):143–164.

Chen Shih-hsiang, "Essay on Literature," in *Literature as Light against Darkness* (National Peking University Semicentennial Papers 11) (Peking, 1948), pp. 46–71. A later version appears in *Essay on Literature, Written by the Third-Century Chinese Poet Lu Chi, Translated by Shih-hsiang Chen in the Year MCMXLVIII (Revised 1952)* (Portland, Maine, 1953), pp. xix–xxx; rpt. in *Anthology of Chinese Literature, From Earliest Times to the Fourteenth Century*, ed. Cyril Birch (New York, 1965; rpt. Harmondsworth, 1967), pp. 222–232.

Hughes, *Art of Letters*, pp. 94–108 (cf. the review by Achilles Fang, *HJAS* [1951], 14:615–636).

Achilles Fang, "Rhymeprose on Literature: The *Wen-fu* of Lu Chi (A.D. 261–303)," *HJAS* (1951), 14:527–566; rpt. in *Studies in Chinese Literature*, ed. John L. Bishop, pp. 3–42.

(The best translations are those by Chen Shih-hsiang and Achilles Fang.)

Note also the following four Western-language articles on the *Wen fu*:

Chen Shih-hsiang, "Lu Chi's Life and the Correct Date of His 'Essay on Literature'" and "Some Discussion of the Translation," in *Literature as Light against Darkness*, pp. 1–21, 22–45 (not reprinted).

Chou Ju-ch'ang "An Introduction to Lu Chi's *Wen Fu*," *Studia Serica* (1950), 9:42–65.

Sister Mary Gregory Knoerle, "The Poetic Theories of Lu Chi, with a Brief Comparison with Horace's 'Ars Poetica,'" *Journal of Aesthetics and Art Criticism* (Winter, 1966), 25(2):137–143.

12. Takagi (p. 106) is followed here for the interpretation of *shu* 疏 in this passage.

Li Ch'ung's *Han-lin lun* survives only in fragments. It is referred to in the "Ching-chi chih" (Monograph on Literature) of the *Sui shu* (History of the Sui Dynasty) (35, p. 1082) as being a three-*chüan* work in the Sui, but as having been a 54-*chüan* work in the Liang. See Yen K'o-chün, *Ch'üan Shang-ku San-tai Ch'in Han San-kuo Liu-ch'ao wen* (Complete Prose Writing of Ancient Antiquity, the Three Dynasties, the Ch'in and Han Dynasties, the Three Kingdoms, and the Six Dynasties) (1894; Peking, 1958; rpt. 1965), p. 1767 (*Ch'üan Chin wen* [Complete Prose Writing of the Chin Dynasty], 53:9a–b); these passages are reprinted, with additional fragments and sources, in Hsü Wen-yü, *Wen-lun chiang-su* (Essays on Literature Explicated) (Nanking, 1937), pp. 59–65.

For studies of the work, see Toda Kōgyō, "Ri Chū no *Kanrinron* ni tsuite" (Concerning Li Ch'ung's *Discourse on the Forest of Writing Brushes*), *Daitō bunka* (July, 1937), 16:78–85; and Ch'eng Hung, "*Han-lin lun* tso-che chih-i" (An Inquiry into the Author of the *Discourse on the Forest of Writing Brushes*), *Wen shih* (October, 1962), 1:44.

13. Although a certain *Hung pao* is mentioned as being a ten-*chüan* work in the "Monograph on Literature" of the *Sui shu* (34, p. 1008), it is no longer extant.

For an early ninth-century critic's citation of a Sui dynasty work which, in turn, cites a sixth-century author's comments on the *Hung pao*, see Richard Wainwright Bodman, "Poetics and Prosody in Early Medieval China: A Study and Translation of Kūkai's *Bunkyō hifuron*," Ph.D. Dissertation, Cornell, 1978, p. 254.

14. The parallelism of this passage strongly suggests that Yen Yen-chih's "discussion of literature" is in fact the title of a work, "On Literature"; but no piece by this title exists. Perhaps Chung Hung is referring to Yen Yen-chih's *T'ing kao* (Household Announcements), fragments of which having literary interest can be found in the following: *T'ai-p'ing yü-lan* (Imperial Readings from the T'ai-p'ing Period) (Nan-hai Li shih ed., 1892) 586:2b–3c, 608:4b–5a, and 609:7a; Yen K'o-chün, pp. 2634–2637 (*Ch'üan Sung wen* [Complete Prose Writing of the Liu-Sung Dynasty] 36:4a–10b); and Ma Kuo-han, *Yü-han shan-fang chi-i-shu* (Lost Books Restored in Fragments at the Yü-han Mountain Studio) (1871 ed.; rpt. Taipei, 1967), pp. 2326–2328.

Yen Yen-chih's literary criticism is referred to by Liu Hsieh in the *Wen-hsin tiao-lung*: Wang Li-ch'i, ed., *Wen-hsin tiao-lung hsin-shu fu t'ung-chien* (Index du *Wen sin tiao lung*, avec texte critique) (Centre franco-chinois d'études sinologiques 15) (Peking, 1952; rpt. Taipei, 1968), 44, p. 114 (ll. 6ff.) (hereafter cited as *Wen-hsin tiao-lung*). Cf. the translations by Vincent Shih, p. 230; Kōzen Hiroshi, *Bunshin chōryū* (Elaborations on the Essence of Literature) (the second part of a double volume, the first part being by Ikkai Tomoyoshi, *Tō Emmei* [T'ao Yüan-ming]) (Tokyo, 1968), p. 416; Mekada Makoto, "Bunshin chōryū" (Elaborations on the Essence of Literature), in *Bungaku geijutsu ronshū*, ed. Mekada Makoto, p. 181; and Li Ching-jung, *Wen-hsin tiao-lung hsin-chieh* (New Explication of *Elaborations on the Essence of Literature*) (Tainan, 1968), p. 358.

15. Chih Yü's "treatise on literature" refers to the *Wen-chang liu-pieh chih lun* (Discussion and Notes for Literature Divided by Genre), drawn from material appended to his now lost anthology, the *Liu-pieh chi* (A Collection [of Literature] Divided by Genre): see the "Monograph on Literature" of the *Sui shu* (35, pp. 1081–1082).

Fragments of the work are assembled and their sources identified by Hsü Wen-yü, pp. 67–84. These are translated by Joseph Roe Allen III, "Chih Yü's *Discussion of Different Types of Literature*: A Translation and Brief Comment," in *Two Studies in Chinese Literary Criticism*, by Joseph Roe Allen III and Timothy S. Phelan, *Parerga* 3 (Seattle, 1976), pp. 3–36.

See also Kōzen Hiroshi, "Shi Gu *Bunshō ryūbetsu shiron kō*" (A Study of Chih Yü's *Discussion and Notes for Literature Divided by Genre*), in *Iriya kyōju Ogawa kyōju taikyū kinen Chūgoku bungaku gogaku ronshū* (*Studies on Chinese Literature and Linguistics Dedicated to Profs. Iriya Yoshitaka and Ogawa Tamaki on Their Retirement from Kyoto University*) (Kyoto, 1974), pp. 285–299; and Tōkei, *Genre Theory*, pp. 79–80.

16. Nothing remains of the three poetic anthologies by Hsieh Ling-yün cited in the "Monograph on Literature" of the *Sui shu* (35, p. 1084).

17. The *Wen-shih chuan* is frequently cited in P'ei Sung-chih's notes to the *San-kuo chih* (Record of the Three Kingdoms) and in Liu Chün's commentary to the *Shih-shuo hsin-yü* (A New Account of Tales of the World). But whereas the "Monograph on Literature" in the *Chiu T'ang shu* (Old History of the T'ang Dynasty) (46, p. 2004) as well as that in the *Hsin T'ang shu* (New History of the T'ang Dynasty) (58, p. 1481) refer to its author as Chang Chih, the *Sui shu* "Monograph on Literature" (33, p. 976) and P'ei Sung-chih (e.g. *San-kuo chih* 9, p. 280) refer to him as Chang Yin.

The work as we know it is not, as Chung Hung says, an anthology, but rather a series of biographical synopses. Perhaps these were followed by excerpts of the writers' works, in some now unknown edition.

18. *Shih-p'in chu*, p. 7; Takamatsu, pp. 45–48; Kōzen, pp. 66–70; Okamura, p. 230; and Takagi, pp. 104–111. Cf. the translation (of two phrases) by Bodman, p. 258.

Compare Chung Hung's final comment with the statement Liu Hsieh makes after enumerating the works of earlier critics: "Each of these reflects a particular corner of the field; few have even envisioned the whole open vista" (*Wen-hsin tiao-lung* 50:128 [line 10], trans. Vincent Shih, p. 5; cf. the translation by Kōzen, *Bunshin chōryū*, p. 452; Mekada, *Bungaku*, p. 210; Li Ching-jung, *Wen-hsin* p. 428; and Kuo Chin-hsi, *Wen-hsin tiao-lung i-chu shih-pa p'ien* [Translation and Commentary for Eighteen Chapters of *Elaborations on the Essence of Literature*] [Hong Kong, 1964; rpt. 1966], pp. 234–235). From the critiques that follow, it is clear that Liu Hsieh laments the fact that earlier critics fundamentally fail to examine the basic nature of literature, whereas Chung Hung is unhappy that critics have failed to discuss individual works and authors.

19. Omissions from Chung Hung's list include the following three works:

Ts'ao P'i, *Tien-lun Lun-wen* ("Essay on Literature" in *Classical Treatises*), in *Wen hsüan* (Literary Selections) (Hu K'o-chia, ed., 1809; rpt. Taipei, 1971) 52:6b–8a. The work appears in complete translations by Hughes, pp. 231–234; Ronald Miao, "Literary Criticism at the End of the Eastern Han," *Literature East & West* (1972), 16:1016–1026; and Donald Holzman, "Literary Criticism in China in the Early Third Century A.D.," *Asiatische Studien/Etudes Asiatiques* (1974), 28(2):128–131. For an informative study of the background to Ts'ao P'i's work, see Burton Watson, "Literary Theory in the Eastern Han," in *Yoshikawa hakase taikyū kinen Chūgoku bungaku ronshū* (Studies in Chinese Literature Dedicated to Dr. Yoshikawa Kōjirō on His Sixty-fifth Birthday) (Tokyo, 1968), pp. 1–13 (separate pagination). Note also T'an Chia-chien, "Shih-t'an Ts'ao P'i ti *Tien-lun Lun-wen*" (An Examination into Ts'ao P'i's "Essay on Literature" in *Classical Treatises*), *Hsin chien-she* (1964/2), pp. 93–102. P'ei Tzu-yeh, *Tiao-ch'ung lun* (Treatise on Carving Insects), in Yen K'o-chün, p. 3262 (*Ch'üan Liang wen* 53:15b–16b). For studies of the work, see Hayashida Shinnosuke, "Hai Shiya *Chōchūron* kōshō—Rikuchō ni okeru fukko bungakuron no kōzō"

(Some Thoughts on the "Treatise on Carving Insects" by P'ei Tzu-yeh: A Restorative Theory of Literature in the Six Dynasties Period), *Nihon Chūgoku Gakkai hō* (1968), 20:125–139; and John Marney, "P'ei Tzu-yeh: A Minor Literary Critic of the Liang Dynasty," *Selected Papers in Asian Studies*, vol. 1 (Western Conference of the Association for Asian Studies, Boulder, Colorado, October 10–11, 1975) (Albuquerque, 1976), pp. 161–171. Hayashida marshals evidence to assign authorship of the work to the 490s instead of the traditionally accepted date of 527–528. Thus the work would predate the major critical writings of the Liang.

Liu Hsieh, *Wen-hsin tiao-lung*. The omission of this work, so conspicuous by its absence, is "a self-conscious Confucian criticism-by-omission, a well-established historical technique in the *Spring and Autumn* [*Annals*] [*Ch'un-chiu*], as then understood" (Brooks, p. 139). See Gibbs, "Liu Hsieh," p. 131, for the work's cool contemporary reception. For a comparison of Liu Hsieh's opus with that of Chung Hung, see Kōzen Hiroshi, "*Bunshin chōryū to Shihin* no bungakukan no tairitsu" (The Contrasting Literary Views of *Elaborations on the Essence of Literature* and *Gradings of Poets*), in *Yoshikawa hakase taikyū kinen Chūgoku bungaku ronshū*, pp. 271–288; Wilhelm, pp. 117–119; and Brooks, pp. 138–139.

20. *Shih-p'in chu*, p. 6; Takamatsu, pp. 18–19; Kōzen, p. 57; Okamura, p. 225; and Takagi, pp. 87–89. Cf. the translation by Brooks, p. 125, and Yeh and Walls, p. 45.

Liu Hui, whose biography appears in the *Nan Ch'i shu* (History of the Southern Ch'i Dynasty) (48:841–843), was a minor poet assigned to the "lower grade" of poets by Chung Hung (see *Shih-p'in chu*, p. 40; Takamatsu, pp. 122–123; Kōzen, pp. 248–250; and Takagi, pp. 372–376).

21. Only writers of *shih* poetry who are no longer living are treated in his work: "Since it is only deceased poets whose work can be properly evaluated, no one who is still alive is treated here" (*Shih-p'in chu*, p. 6; Takamatsu, p. 42; Kōzen, pp. 61–62; and Takagi, pp. 95–96).

22. *Shih-p'in chu*, p. 6; Takamatsu, pp. 18–20; Kōzen, pp. 57–59; Okamura, p. 226; and Takagi, pp. 89–90.

The comparison of "guests" (i.e. reputations) with facts is an allusion to the *Chuang Tzu*: *Chuang-tzu yin-te* (A Concordance to Chuang Tzu) (Harvard-Yenching Institute Sinological Index Series, Supplement No. 20) (Peking, 1947; rpt. Cambridge, Mass., 1956), 1:2 (line 25); cf. the translation by Burton Watson, *The Complete Works of Chuang Tzu* (New York and London, 1968), p. 32.

23. *Han shu* 30:1701. For fragments of the *Ch'i lüeh*, see Yen K'o-chün, pp. 351–353 (*Ch'üan Han wen* [Complete Prose Writing of the Han Dynasty] 41:4b–7a); and Ma Kuo-han, pp. 2382–2388.

24. *Han shu* 20:861. Pan Ku cites *Lun-yü* 6:21 (p. 11), where Confucius speaks of men "above the middling sort" and "below the middling sort" (trans. Waley, p. 119; cf. Legge, 1:191), and *Lun-yü* 7:2 (p. 35), where he speaks of the "wise of the highest class" and the "stupid of the highest class" (trans. Legge, 1:318; cf. Waley, p. 209).

25. The citations are from the *Wei lüeh* (Summary of the Wei Dynasty), as quoted in *San-kuo chih* 23:661, and from the *Tzu-chih t'ung-chien* (A Comprehensive Mirror for Aid in Government) (Peking, 1956 ed.), 69:2178. Both translations are by Achilles Fang, *The Chronicle of the Three Kingdoms (220–265)*, vol. 1 (Harvard-Yenching Institute Series 6)

(Cambridge, Mass., 1952), pp. 25 and 5. Hu San-hsing (1230–1287) states in his commentary to the *Tzu-chih t'ung-chien* passage that this marks the beginning of the system of grading officials. For studies of this system, see Donald Holzman, "Les Débuts du système médiéval de choix et de classement des fonctionnaires: Les Neuf Catégories et l'Impérial et Juste," *Mélanges publiés par l'Institut des Hautes Etudes Chinoises* (Paris, 1957), pp. 387–414; Miyazaki Ichisada, *Kyūhin kanjinhō no kenkyū: Kakyo zenshi* ([Colophon title] The Mechanism of the Aristocracy in China: Installation of mandarins before the establishment of the competetive examination system) (Kyoto, 1956); and Miyakawa Hisayuki, *Rikuchōshi kenkyū* (Researches into Six Dynasties History) (Tokyo, 1956), pp. 263–335.

26. See n. 19.

27. Hightower, "*Wen hsüan* and Genre Theory," pp. 143–144. See also Wang Yao, *Chung-ku wen-hsüeh ssu-hsiang* (Medieval Literary Thought) (1951; rpt. Hong Kong, 1973), pp. 124–152.

28. Kōzen, p. 13. William Edward Soothill and Lewis Hodous, *A Dictionary of Chinese Buddhist Terms* (London, 1937; rpt. Taipei, 1962), p. 229.

29. Trans. J. K. Shryock, *The Study of Human Abilities: The Jen wu chih of Liu Shao* (American Oriental Series 11) (New Haven, 1937; rpt. New York, 1966).

30. Richard B. Mather, "Introduction," *Shih-shuo Hsin-yü: A New Account of Tales of the World* (Minneapolis, 1976), pp. xxii–xxiii.

31. E. Zürcher, "Recent Studies in Chinese Painting," rev. of *Some T'ang and Pre-T'ang Texts on Chinese Painting*, by W. R. B. Acker, *TP* (1964), 51:381.

32. Trans. Richard B. Mather (see n. 30), and Bruno Belpaire, *Anthologie chinoise des Ve et VIe siècles: Le "Che-chouo-sin-yu" par Lieou (Tsuen) Hiao-piao* (Paris, 1974). Chapter titles here follow Mather's translation.

33. The preface to Shen Yüeh's *Ch'i-p'in* is found in Yen K'o-chün, pp. 3123–3124 (*Ch'üan Liang wen* [Complete Prose Writing of the Liang Dynasty], 30:2b–3a).

Liu Hui's work is referred to in one of his official biographies as a three-*chüan* work: *Nan shih* 38, p. 989. (Note that this Liu Hui is different from the one referred to in n. 20.)

34. Hsieh Ho's work is found in Yen K'o-chün, pp. 2931–2932 (*Ch'üan Ch'i wen* [Complete Prose Writing of the Ch'i Dynasty], 25:7a–10a), and in *Mei-shu ts'ung-shu* (A Fine Arts Collectanea) (Shanghai, 1923; rpt. Taipei, 1975), 3(6):103–110. Note also the annotated edition by Yü Chien-hua, *Chung-kuo hua-lun lei-pien* (Chinese Painting Theory by Categories) (Peking, 1957; rpt. Taipei, 1975), pp. 355–367.

The *Ku hua-p'in lu* is translated in its entirety by William R. B. Acker, *Some T'ang and Pre-T'ang Texts on Chinese Painting* (Leiden, 1954), pp. 1–32. For a comparative table of five well-known English translations of the "six laws" of painting by Hsieh Ho (which appear in this work), see Michael Sullivan, *The Birth of Landscape Painting in China* (Berkeley and Los Angeles, 1962), pp. 106–107 (translations are by Osvald Sirén, Arthur Waley, Shio Sakanishi, Alexander Soper, and William Acker). Other more recent translations of the six laws appear in Edward Schafer, *Ancient China* (New York, 1967), pp. 111–123; Lin Yutang, *The Chinese Theory of Art* (New York, 1967), pp. 34–38; and Su Gin-djih, *Chinese Architecture: Past and Contemporary* (Hong Kong, 1964), p. 247. Note the additional works referred to by Lin Yutang, as well as the discussion and annotation in the following: James Cahill, "The Six Laws and How to Read Them," *AO* (1961), 4:372–381; Wen Fong, "*Ch'i-yün-sheng-tung:*

'Vitality, Harmonious Manner and Aliveness,'" *OA* (1966), n.s. 12:159–164; Wen Fong, "The First Principle of Hsieh Ho," *NPMQ* (1967), 1:7–18; and Susan Bush, *The Chinese Literati on Painting: Su Shih (1037–1101) to Tung Ch'i-ch'ang (1555–1636)* (Harvard-Yenching Institute Studies 27) (Cambridge, Mass., 1971), pp. 15–18.

35. See Yen K'o-chün, pp. 3343-3345 (*Ch'üan Liang wen* 66:6a–9b), or *Fa-shu yao-lu* (Essential Recordings on Calligraphy) (*I-shu ts'ung-pien* ed.) 2:26b–32a.

Note the following two studies of this work by Shirakawa Yoshio: "Ryō Yu Kengo *Shohin* no jobun oyobi ryakuron no kenkyū, Sono ichi" (A Study of the Preface and Short Comments in the *Gradings of Calligraphers* by Yü Chien-wu of the Liang, pt. 1), *Ōita Daigaku Kyōikugakubu kenkyū kiyō* (1977), 5(2):1–10; and "Ryō Yu Kengo *Shohin* kenkyū (A Study of *Gradings of Calligraphers* by Yü Chien-wu of the Liang), *Kokugo no kenkyū* (Ōita Daigaku) (1977), 10:105–115 [pt. 1].

36. See Yen K'o-chün, p. 3228 (*Ch'üan Liang-wen* 48:31b–32b), or *Fa-shu yao-lu* 2:32a–33b.

37. *Shih-p'in chu*, p. 6; Takamatsu, pp. 18–20; Kōzen, pp. 57–59; Okamura, p. 226; and Takagi, pp. 89–90. Cf. the translation (partial) by Cha Chu Whan, p. 43.

38. Yen K'o-chün, p. 615 (*Ch'üan Hou-Han wen* [Complete Prose Writing of the Later Han Dynasty], 26:8b); cf. the translation by Joseph Needham, *Science and Civilisation in China*, vol. 4: Physics and Physical Technology, pt. 1: Physics (Cambridge, 1962), p. 322.

Chess (called *i* 奕 by northeners and *ch'i* 棋 by southerners, according to Pan Ku in the same essay) is called *go* in Japanese. The object of the game, with 150 pieces on each side, is to surround an opponent's pieces and occupy as many cross-points as possible. For an excellent bibliography of Western-language studies of the game, see Needham, 4(1):319.

39. Ibid., 4(1):327.

40. Ibid., 4(1):321, 315 and 326–327. See also Donald J. Harper, "The Han Cosmic Board (*Shih* 式)," *Early China* (1978–1979). 4:1–10.

41. *Wen-hsin tiao-lung* 1:1–3. This chapter is translated into English, with a helpful commentary, by Gibbs, "Literary Theory in the *Wen-hsin tiao-lung*," pp. 42–57, 179–193. Cf. the complete translation by Vincent Shih, pp. 8–13, and Hughes, *Art of Letters* pp. 236–240; and the partial translation by B. Alexéiev, *La Littérature chinoise: Six conférences au Collège de France et au Musée Guimet* (Paris, 1937), pp. 24–27; Francis Woodman Cleaves, trans., L. Z. Ejdlin, "The Academician V. M. Alexeev as a Historian of Chinese Literature," *HJAS* (1947), 10:51–52; and James J. Y. Liu, *Chinese Theories of Literature*, pp. 21–25 146–148. Cf. also the translations into Japanese by Kōzen, *Bunshin chōryū*, pp. 209–213, and Mekada *Bungaku*, pp. 3–7; and into modern Chinese by Kuo Chin-hsi, *Wen-hsin*, pp. 1–13, and Li Ching-jung, *Wen-hsin* pp. 1–9.

42. Gibbs, "Literary Theory in the *Wen-hsin tiao-lung*," pp. 54–57. The terms "expressive, pragmatic, mimetic, and objective" are used by M. H. Abrams to distinguish orientations in critical theory (i.e. orientations toward the artist, the audience, the subject [or universe], or the work itself): *The Mirror and the Lamp: Romantic Theory and the Critical Tradition* (London, Oxford and New York, 1953; rpt. 1976), pp. 3–29.

43. *Shih-p'in chu*, p. 1; Takamatsu, pp. 1–2; Kōzen, pp. 22–25; Okamura, p. 233; and Takagi, pp. 31–35. Cf. the translations (complete) by Wilhelm, p. 118, and Bodman, p. 69 (cf. p. 265); and (partial) by Brooks, p. 135; Yeh and Walls, p. 50; and Wong Siu-kit, "*Ch'ing* in Chinese Literary Criticism," D. Phil. Dissertation, Oxford, 1969, p. 15.

For a discussion of *ch'i* 氣 in earlier Chinese poetics, see David Pollard, "*Ch'i* in Chinese Literary Theory," in *Chinese Approaches to Literature from Confucius to Liang Ch'i-ch'ao*, ed. Adele Austin Rickett (Princeton, 1978), pp. 43–66; James J. Y. Liu, *Chinese Theories of Literature*, pp. 12, 70–72; and Yeh and Walls, pp. 61–62.

For discussion of the word *shih* 詩 ("poetry"), see Chen Shih-hsiang, "In Search of the Beginnings of Chinese Literary Criticism," pp. 45–63; Chow Tse-tsung, "The Early History of the Word *Shih* (Poetry)," in *Wen-lin: Studies in the Chinese Humanities*, ed. Chow Tse-tsung, pp. 151–209; and Chow Tse-tsung, "Ancient Chinese Views on Literature, the *Tao*, and Their Relationship," *CLEAR* (January, 1979), 1(1):3–29.

44. See the following translations of the "Great Preface": (complete) by James Legge, *The She King, or The Book of Poetry*, in *The Chinese Classics*, 4:34–37, and Ferenc Tökei, *Naissance de l'élégie chinoise. K'iu Yuan et son époque* (Paris, 1967), pp. 85–87; (nearly complete) by Donald Gibbs, "M. H. Abrams' Four Artistic Co-ordinates Applied to Literary Theory in Early China," *Comparative Literature Today: Theory and Practice* (Proceedings of the 7th Congress of the International Comparative Literature Association, Montreal and Ottawa, 1973) (Budapest, 1979), pp. 675–679; and (partial) by James J. Y. Liu, *Chinese Theories of Literature*, pp. 64, 69, 111–112, 119–120, and Bodman, pp. 65–67, 467.

45. *Shih-shuo hsin-yü* (*SPTK* ed.; rpt. Taipei, n.d.) 5 and 6, pp. 58, 59, 63; cf. the translation by Mather, pp. 171, and 179, 183, 192.

46. Yen K'o-chün, p. 2951 (*Ch'üan Liang wen* 1:7a).

47. With *technē* (or *ars*), the conative (i.e. the exertive, which impels one toward action) dominates the cognitive (here, knowledge to do or make); the term is distinguished from *epistēmē* (or *scientia*), the disinterested exercise of intelligence, where the cognitive has become disengaged from the conative.

48. *Wen-hsin tiao-lung* 44:115 (l. 5). Cf. the translations by Vincent Shih, p. 231; Kōzen, *Bunshin chōryū*, p. 417; Mekada, *Bungaku*, p. 183; and Li Ching-jung, *Wen-hsin*, pp. 359–360.

49. *Wen-hsin tiao-lung* 44:115 (ll. 7–9). Cf. the translations by Vincent Shih, p. 232; Kōzen, *Bunshin chōryū*, p. 417; Mekada, *Bungaku* p. 183; and Li Ching-jung, *Wen-hsin*, p. 360.

50. Zürcher, p. 381. Note also the examples he cites and translates (ibid.) from *Shih-shuo hsin-yü* 8, pp. 75 (two), 79; cf. the translations by Mather, pp. 224, 226, 237.

51. Ssu-ma Ch'ien, when writing about Confucius and Ch'ü Yüan, said he could imagine what sort of men they were from their writings (*Shih chi* [Records of the Historian], 49, p. 1947 and 84, p. 2503); the latter passage is translated by Burton Watson, *Records of the Grand Historian of China: Translated from the Shih chi of Ssu-ma Ch'ien* [New York and London, 1958], 2 vols., 1:516; cf. Burton Watson, "Ssu-ma Ch'ien's Theory of Literature," in *Ssu-ma Ch'ien: Grand Historian of China* [New York, 1958], pp. 154–158).

Yang Hsiung, in his *Fa-yen* (Model Sayings), wrote: "Spoken words are the sounds of the mind, and written words are the images of the mind. When words and images take form, it becomes evident whether one is a gentleman or an ordinary man" (*Fa-yen* [*SPPY* ed.] 5:3b–4a; cf. the translations by E. von Zach, *Yang Hsiung's "Fa-yen" (Worte strenger Ermahnung): Ein philosophischer Traktat aus dem Beginn der christlichen Zeitrechnung* [*Sinologische Beiträge* (1939), 4(1); rpt. San Francisco, 1976], pp. 23–24; Bruno Belpaire, *Le Catechisme philosophique de Yang Hiong-tsé: Le "Fa-yen" de Yang Hiong-tsé* [Brussels, 1957?], pp. 44–45; and David Knechtges, *The Han Rhapsody: A Study of the "Fu" of Yang Hsiung (53 B.C.–A.D. 18)* [Cambridge, 1976], p. 94).

For additional translations of this Yang Hsiung passage and discussion of its use in Sung dynasty texts on painting and calligraphy, see James F. Cahill, "Confucian Elements in the Theory of Painting," in *The Confucian Persuasion*, ed. Arthur Wright (Stanford, 1960), p. 130, and Bush, *Chinese Literati*, pp. 20, 73. For examples of Sung dynasty allusion to Yang Hsiung's statement in which the basic argument is transformed, see Wixted, "Yüan Hao-wen," pp. 131–139 (and 395–397, 619–620).

As E. B. Brooks notes, "In Jūng Húng's [Chung Hung's] literary program ... portability of style is a kind of personal insincerity—an attitude toward style as something exterior and alienable, rather than the direct and inevitable imprint of the personality itself.... [F]ault, then, lay in possessing a style that was *not* the man" (p. 131). (Brooks makes this point in reference to Chung's critiques of Chiang Yen and T'ao Ch'ien.)

To illustrate the nature of Six Dynasties criticism, Zürcher draws the following comparison between traditional Chinese and modern Western critical attitudes: "If a modern Western critic, when invited to characterize in a few words the *paintings* of Rubens, would say 'Powerful and impetuous, he let his mind dwell on the exuberant beauty of Nature; harmonious and of classic elegance, his overflowing vitality appears from every movement of his brush,' adding, by way of further elucidation, that 'his manners were in no way inferior to those of the Ancients,' his public would hardly feel satisfied. To the medieval Chinese, it would have been a perfectly admissible piece of art criticism: a comment on the *character and personality* of an 'ancient worthy,' as observed through his works" (p. 382).

52. *Shih-p'in chu*, p. 14; Takamatsu, pp. 28–29: Kōzen, pp. 102–103; and Takagi, pp. 159–161. Cf. the translation by Yeh and Walls, p. 58.

53. *Shih-p'in chu*, p. 29; Takamatsu, pp. 78–80; Kōzen, pp. 193–194; and Takagi, pp. 289–290.

54. *Shih-p'in chu*, p. 27; Takamatsu, pp. 71–72; Kōzen, pp. 178–179; and Takagi, p. 269.

55. *Shih-p'in chu*, p. 3; Takamatsu, pp. 7–8; Kōzen, pp. 37–38; Okamura, p. 224; and Takagi, pp. 55–57.

56. *Shih-p'in chu*, p. 17; Takamatsu, pp. 38–40; Kōzen, pp. 133–134; and Takagi, pp. 191–192. Cf. the translation by Brooks, p. 139.

57. *Shih-p'in chu*, p. 25; Takamatsu, pp. 67–68; Kōzen, pp. 173–174; and Takagi, pp. 260–262. Cf. the translations by Cha Chu Whan, p. 50, and Ronald C. Egan, "The Prose Style of Fan Yeh," *HJAS* (1979), 39(2):368.

58. See n. 43.

59. *Shih-p'in chu*, p. 23; Takamatsu, pp. 60–61; Kōzen, p. 159; and Takagi, pp. 234–235. Cf. the translation (partial) by Yeh and Walls, pp. 58, 65.

60. *Shih-p'in chu*, p. 14; Takamatsu, pp. 28–29; Kōzen, pp. 102–103; and Takagi, p. 161.

61. *Shih-p'in chu*, p. 14; Takamatsu, pp. 28–29; Kōzen, pp. 102–103; and Takagi, pp. 159–160. Cf. the translation by Yeh and Walls, pp. 58, 64.

For the nonpejorative interpretation of *ch'i* 奇 as "originality," see Takagi, p. 160, and Kōzen, "*Bunshin chōryū* to *Shihin* no bungakukan no tairitsu," pp. 272–278. For an example of its problematic usage in later criticism, see Wixted, "Yüan Hao-wen," pp. 280–284, 291–292.

62. E. D. Hirsch, Jr., *The Aims of Interpretation* (Chicago and London, 1976), p. 97.

63. John M. Ellis, *The Theory of Literary Criticism: A Logical Analysis* (Berkeley, Los Angeles and London, 1974), p. 99 (quoting from his article, "Great Art. A Study in Meaning," *British Journal of Aesthetics* [1963], 3:167). See also Monroe C. Beardsley, *Aesthetics: Problems in the Philosophy of Criticism* (New York and Burlingame, 1958), pp. 510–511, 524–543, 547.

64. *Shih-p'in chu*, p. 14; Takamatsu, pp. 30–31; Kōzen, pp. 110–111; and Takagi, p. 169. Cf. the translations by Wong Siu-kit, p. 24, and Donald Holzman, *Poetry and Politics: The Life and Works of Juan Chi, A.D. 210–263* (Cambridge, 1976), pp. vii, 233.

65. *Shih-p'in chu*, p. 22; Takamatsu, pp. 56–57; Kōzen, p. 154; and Takagi, pp. 225–226. Cf. the translation by Brooks, p. 145.

66. *Shih-p'in chu*, p. 24; Takamatsu, p. 63; Kōzen, p. 165; and Takagi, pp. 243–245.

67. *Shih-p'in chu*, p. 27; Takamatsu, pp. 72–73; Kōzen, pp. 181–182; and Takagi, p. 274.

68. *Shih-p'in chu*, p. 24; Takamatsu, pp. 64–65; Kōzen, p. 167; and Takagi, pp. 248–249.

69. *Shih-p'in chu*, p. 20; Takamatsu, pp. 51–52; Kōzen, p. 145; and Takagi, pp. 212–213.

70. *Shih-p'in chu*, p. 16; Takamatsu, p. 34; Kōzen, p. 120; and Takagi, pp. 180–181. Cf. the trans. by Chou Ju-ch'ang, p. 50, and Yeh and Walls, p. 71.

71. *Shih-p'in chu*, p. 23; Takamatsu, pp. 60–61; Kōzen, pp. 159–160; and Takagi, p. 237.

72. *Shih-p'in chu*, p. 3; Takamatsu, pp. 6–7; Kōzen, pp. 35–37; Okamura, p. 223; and Takagi, pp. 51–53. Cf. the translations by Cha Chu Whan, p. 52; Jonathan Chaves, *Mei Yao-ch'en and the Development of Early Sung Poetry* (New York and London, 1976), p. 116; and Yeh and Walls, p. 50.

73. *Shih-p'in chu*, p. 23; Takamatsu, pp. 61–62; Kōzen, pp. 161–162; and Takagi, pp. 239–240. Cf. the translation by Chaves, *Mei Yao-ch'en*, p. 116.

For discussion of the term *p'ing-tan* 平淡, especially its use in Sung criticism, see ibid., pp. 114–115, and Yokoyama Iseo, "Sō shiron ni miru 'heitan no tai' ni tsuite" (On the Style of "Plainness" in the Poetical Criticism of the Sung Dynasty), *Kambun Gakkai kaihō* (1961), 20:33–40.

74. *Shih-p'in chu*, p. 13; Takamatsu, pp. 25–27; Kōzen, pp. 98–99; and Takagi, p. 151. Cf. the translations by Brooks, p. 142; Holzman, *Poetry and Politics*, p. 233; and Yeh and Walls, p. 58.

75. *Shih-p'in chu*, p. 21; Takamatsu, pp. 54–56; Kōzen, p. 151; and Takagi, pp. 223–224.

76. A most helpful discussion of the problem of valuation in the arts is provided by Elder Olson, "On Value Judgments in the Arts," *Critical Inquiry* (September, 1974), 1(1):71–90; rpt. in *"On Value Judgments in the Arts" and Other Essays* (Chicago and London, 1976), pp. 307–326.

The following is Olson's ten-point list of conditions for a sound value judgment in the arts:

1. There must be a perceptible characteristic or trait.
2. It must be essential to the work and not accidental.

3. The sensible form must be accurately perceived.

4. It must be correctly interpreted.

5. The suprasensible substructures must be grasped in their totality and in the totality of their relations as constituting the final subsumptive whole which is the form of the work.

6. The standard or criterion must represent an actual value.

7. It must be appropriate to the form.

8. It must be appropriate to the characteristic or trait.

9. The value syllogism must be a valid syllogism.

10. It must be clearly and unequivocally expressed (hence, it may contain no metaphors) (pp. 317–318).

Note that the first five conditions relate to the concept of a work, and the last five to the establishment of a judgment as such.

Reference is here made to condition 2.

77. The *Ssu-k'u ch'üan-shu tsung-mu t'i-yao* (Summary of the General Catalogue of the Imperial Library), completed in 1782, makes the following comment in reference to Chung Hung's work:

> The Liang dynasty is now more than a thousand years distant, and of the pieces left from it, the old works, nine-tenths are lost: it is improper to gather together fragments and fix the comparative merits of the literature as it was in the complete collections of that day.

([Shanghai, 1934 ed] 195:94; tr. Elizabeth Huff, "*Shih-hsüeh* by Huang Chieh: A Translation," Ph.D. Dissertation Radcliffe 1947, pp. 56–57; cf. the translation by Yeh and Walls, p. 49; also paraphrased by Wilhelm, p. 115.)

78. Note, for example, the influence of Chung Hung on the series *Lun-shih san-shih-shou* (Thirty Poems on Poetry) by the thirteenth-century poet-critic, Yüan Hao-wen. Yüan clearly draws on Chung Hung for his estimations of Ts'ao Chih, Liu Chen, Chang Hua, Juan Chi, and P'an Yüeh; regarding Liu K'un and T'ao Ch'ien, he transforms Chung's critiques into something quite different; and he takes issue with Chung Hung on the matter of Lu Chi's poetry: see Wixted, "Yüan Hao-wen," pp. 86–91, 95–97, 103–105, 108–115, 122–126, 159–163.

79. Theoretical discussion of the separability or nonseparability of description and valuation would be too involved to undertake here. See Hirsch, *Interpretation*, pp. 95–109, and Ellis, *Theory*, pp. 82, 92–93. Note especially in this regard discussion of Kant by Hirsch, pp. 98–106.

Suffice it to say that description and valuation are not easily disengaged: description invariably provokes valuation, and reflection on valuation provokes further description.

80. Olson, "*Value Judgments*" p. 323. He notes that all evaluations in the arts "must depend immediately or remotely" upon such a descriptive proposition.

81. *Shih-p'in chu*, p. 14; Takamatsu, p. 29; Kōzen, pp. 106–107; and Takagi, p. 163. Cf. the translation by Brooks, p. 143.

82. *Shih-p'in chu*, p. 13; Takamatsu, p. 25; Kōzen, pp. 95–96; and Takagi, pp. 148–149. Cf. the translation by Brooks, p. 143, and Yeh and Walls, p. 57.

83. *Shih-p'in chu*, p. 11; Takamatsu, pp. 20–21; Kōzen, p. 88; and Takagi, pp. 138–139. Cf. the translation by Yeh and Walls, p. 58.

84. *Shih-p'in chu*, p. 15; Takamatzu, pp. 31–33; Kōzen, p. 115; and Takagi, p. 172. Cf. the translation by Cha Chu Whan, p. 49, and Yeh & Walls, p. 59.

85. *Shih-p'in chu*, p. 20; Takamatsu, pp. 52–53; Kōzen, p. 147; and Takagi, pp. 215–216. Cf. the translations by Brooks, p. 143, and Anna Straughair, *Chang Hua: A Statesman Poet of the Western Chin Dynasty* (Occasional Paper 15, Faculty of Asian Studies, The Australian National University) (Canberra, 1973), p. 16.

86. *Shih-p'in chu*, p. 25; Takamatsu, pp. 66–67; Kōzen, pp. 170–172; and Takagi, p. 254. Cf. the translation by Brooks, p. 132, and Wilhelm, p. 115 (cf. Jonker, p. 281).

87. *Shih-p'in chu*, p. 23; Takamatsu, pp. 61–62; Kōzen, pp. 161–162; and Takagi, pp. 238–239.

88. *Shih-p'in chu*, p. 13; Takamatsu, pp. 25–27; Kōzen, pp. 98–100; and Takagi, pp. 152–153. Cf. the translation by Brooks, p. 142; Wong Siu-kit, p. 23; and Yeh and Walls, p. 79.

This is an allusion to the *Analects*: *Lun-yü yin-te* 6:18, p. 10; cf. Legge, 1:190, and Waley, p. 119.

89. *Shih-p'in chu*, p. 20; Takamatsu, pp. 52–53; Kōzen, p. 147; and Takagi, pp. 215–216. Cf. the translations by Brooks, p. 143, and Yeh and Walls, p. 55.

90. *Shih-p'in chu*, p. 23; Takamatsu, pp. 61–62; Kōzen, pp. 161–162; and Takagi, pp. 239–240.

91. *Shih-p'in chu*, p. 11; Takamatsu, pp. 20–21; Kōzen, p. 88; and Takagi, pp. 238–239. Cf. the translation by Yeh and Walls, p. 57.

92. *Shih-p'in chu*, p. 25; Takamatsu, pp. 67–68; Kōzen, pp. 173–174; and Takagi, pp. 259–260. Cf. the translation by Cha Chu Whan, p. 50.

93. *Shih-p'in chu*, p. 28; Takamatsu, pp. 74–75; Kōzen, p. 186; and Takagi, pp. 280–281. Cf. the translation by Bodman, p. 245.

94. *Hsing* 興 is used as an element in Chung's critiques of Chang Hua, Hsieh Ling-yün, and T'ao Ch'ien, but not in the sense used here. See Takagi, p. 216, for discussion of the problem of explicating the term *hsing-t'o* 興託 in the passage on Chang Hua. See nn. 116 and 136 for the Hsieh Ling-yün and T'ao Ch'ien passages.

See n. 103 for annotation on *fu, pi,* and *hsing.*

95. *Shih-p'in chu*, p. 20; Takamatsu, pp. 51–52; Kōzen, pp. 145–146; and Takagi, p. 214. Cf. the translation by Yeh and Walls, p. 58.

96. *Shih-p'in chu*, p. 25; Takamatsu, pp. 67–68; Kōzen, pp. 173–174; and Takagi, pp. 259–260. Cf. the translations by Wong Siu-kit, p. 24, and Yeh and Walls, p. 58.

97. *Shih-p'in chu*, pp. 14–15; Takamatsu, pp. 30–31; Kōzen, pp. 110–112; and Takagi, pp. 169–170. Cf. the translations (complete) by Holzman, *Poetry and Politics*, p. 233, and (partial) by Wong Siu-kit, p. 24, and Holzman, *Poetry and Politics*, p. vii.

98. *Wen hsüan* 29:14a; cf. the translations by Zach, *Die Chinesische Anthologie*, p. 526, and Brooks, p. 144.

99. *Shih-p'in chu*, p. 20; Takamatsu, pp. 49–51; Kōzen, pp. 142–143; and Takagi, pp. 207–209. Cf. the translation by Brooks, p. 144.

100. *Shih-p'in chu*, p. 20; Takamatsu, pp. 51–52; Kōzen, pp. 145–146; and Takagi, pp. 212–213.

The terminology is drawn from the *Analects*: *Lun-yü yin-te* 17:22, p. 37; cf. the translations by Legge, 1:330, and Waley, p. 216.

101. *Shih-p'in chu*, p. 17; Takamatsu, pp. 39–41; Kōzen, p. 133; and Takagi, pp. 193–194. Cf. the translations by Brooks, p. 139, and Yeh and Walls, p. 60.

102. Note Chung Hung's comment at the end of his second preface:

As for my promoting or demoting poets to these three gradings, it is not at all something final. I simply present this unusual framework, begging the attention of those knowledgeable in the matter.

(*Shih-p'in chu*, p. 8; Takamatsu, pp. 46–48; Kōzen, pp. 71–72; Okamura, p. 230; and Takagi, pp. 111–114. Cf. the translation [partial] by Yeh and Walls, p. 49.)

103. *Shih-p'in chu*, p. 4; Takamatsu, pp. 11–13; Kōzen, pp. 44–48; Okamura, p. 224; and Takagi, pp. 67–70. Cf. the translations (complete) by Wilhelm, p. 118; Brooks, p. 136; and Cha Chu Whan, p. 45; and (partial) by Chaves, *Mei Yao-ch'en*, p. 112; and Chen Shih-hsiang, "The *Shih-ching*: Its Generic Significance in Chinese Literary History and Poetics," *Bulletin of History and Philology* (Academia Sinica) (January, 1969), 39(1), rpt. in *Studies in Chinese Literary Genres*, ed. Cyril Birch (Berkeley, Los Angeles and London, 1974), p. 18.

Fu, pi, and *hsing* are critical terms that appear in the "Great Preface" to the *Shih ching* (see n. 44). For Western-language discussion of them, see Hightower, "*Wen hsüan* and Genre Theory," p. 519; Chen Shih-hsiang, "The *Shih-ching*: Its Generic Significance," pp. 8–41, esp. pp. 14–25; C. H. Wang, *The Bell and the Drum: "Shih Ching" as Formulaic Poetry in an Oral Tradition* (Berkeley, Los Angeles and London, 1974), p. 3; and Allen, "Chih Yü's Discussion," pp. 9–11, 17–18, 21–23.

For useful examples of *fu, pi,* and *hsing* in poetry, see Brooks, pp. 136–138.

104. *Shih-p'in chu*, p. 4; Takamatsu, pp. 11–12; Kōzen, pp. 44–49; Okamura, p. 224; and Takagi, pp. 71–72. Cf. the translations by Brooks, p. 136; Cha Chu Whan, pp. 45–46; and Yeh and Walls, p. 53.

105. The quotation is from the *Analects*: Lun-yü yin-te 17:8, p. 36; Legge, 1:323. It is from a passage of special importance in early literary theory. Note the translations and discussion by the following: Waley, p. 212; Zau Sinmay, "Confucius on Poetry," *T'ien Hsia Monthly* (September, 1938), 7(2):144–145; Ma Yau-woon, "Confucius as a Literary Critic: A Comparison with the Early Greeks," in *Essays in Chinese Studies Dedicated to Professor Jao Tsung-i* (Hong Kong, 1970), p. 20; Donald Holzman, "Confucius and Ancient Chinese Literary Criticism," in *Chinese Approaches to Literature*, ed. Rickett, pp. 36–37; C. H. Wang, pp. 4–5; James. J. Y. Liu, *Chinese Theories of Literature*, p. 109; and Vincent Y. C. Shih, "Literature and Art in 'The Analects,'" trans. C. Y. Hsu, *Renditions* (Autumn, 1977), 8:14–16.

106. *Shih-p'in chu*, pp. 4–5; Takamatsu, pp. 13–15; Kōzen, pp. 49–53; Okamura, pp. 224–225; and Takagi, pp. 72–78. Cf. the translations (partial) by Wilhelm, p. 118 (cf. Jonker, p. 281); Maureen Robertson, "... To Convey What Is Precious": Ssu-k'ung T'u's Poetics and the Erh-shih-ssu Shih P'in," in *Transition and Permanence: Chinese History and Culture, A Festschrift in Honor of Dr. Hsiao Kung-ch'üan*, ed. David C. Buxbaum and Frederick W. Mote (Hong Kong, 1972), p. 352; David E. Pollard, *A Chinese Look at Literature: The Literary Values of Chou Tso-jen in Relation to the Tradition* (Berkeley and Los Angeles, 1973), p. 9; Cha Chu Whan, pp. 43–44, 47; and Yeh and Walls, pp. 51–52.

The construing of Chung Hung's phrases as alluding to specific poems or poets here follows the Chinese and Japanese commentators noted immediately above.

107. Among the pragmatic ends of literature noted by Chung Hung is the important earlier tradition of expressing moral or political stricture in verse (see Donald Gibbs, "Notes on the Wind: The Term 'Feng' in Chinese Literary Criticism," in *Transition and Permanence*, ed. Buxbaum and Mote, pp. 285–293). Chung Hung speaks of Tso Ssu's poetry as "succeeding in the purpose of indirectly expressing stricture in verse" (*Shih-p'in chu*, pp. 16–17; Takamatsu, pp. 37–38; Kōzen, pp. 129–130; and Takagi, pp. 187–188; cf. the translations by Yeh and Walls, pp. 56, 58). Of Ying Chü, he says that "he has succeeded in the poet's aim of provoking and criticizing" (*Shih-p'in chu*, p. 22; Takamatsu, pp. 56–57; Kōzen, pp. 154–155; and Takagi, pp. 226–227). Concerning a poem by Ho Yen, he notes that "the principle of criticism through indirection is evident" (*Shih-p'in chu*, p. 21; Takamatsu, pp. 54–56; Kōzen, pp. 151–152; and Takagi, pp. 221–222). And in his critique of Yen Yen-chih, he praises certain aspects of his work, to which he adds:

> Yen also enjoys allusions, so that his writing becomes ever more constricted. Although he goes contrary to what is distinguished, his is a fine literary talent for ordering affairs of state (i.e. for the elevated documentary style).

(*Shih-p'in chu*, p. 25; Takamatsu, pp. 67–68; Kōzen, pp. 173–175; and Takagi, pp. 260–262. Cf. the translations [complete] by Cha Chu Whan, p. 50, and Egan, p. 368; and [partial] by Brooks, p. 142. The last phrase echoes Ts'ao P'i's comment, "Writing is, indeed, the great profession by which the state is ordered" [*Wen hsüan* 52:7b; cf. the translations by Hughes, p. 233; Miao, "Literary Criticism at the End of the Eastern Han," p. 1026; and Holzman, "Literary Criticism in China in the Third Century A.D.," p. 131].)

Of interest also in this regard are the statements by Chung Hung that reflect specifically affective concerns. He speaks of the Old Poems as "stirring the heart and moving the soul" (*Shih-p'in chu*, p. 11; Takamatsu, pp. 20–21; Kōzen, p. 88, and Takagi, p. 138–140; cf. the translation by Yeh and Walls, p. 57). Of Juan Chi, he says: "His poems 'On Expressing My Feelings' can release the spirit and provoke the deepest thoughts"; his poetry "makes one forget what is petty and near-at-hand and lets one attain the far-away and grand" (*Shih-p'in chu*, pp. 14–15; Takamatsu, pp. 30–31; Kōzen, pp. 110–111; and Takagi, pp. 168–170; cf. the translation by Holzman, *Poetry and Politics*, p. 233). And as earlier cited, Chung Hung spoke of the "perfect poetry" as being such that "those who read from one's work find it inexhaustible and those who hear from it are moved."

108. Ting Fu-pao, *Ch'üan Han San-kuo Chin Nan-pei-ch'ao shih* (Complete Poetry of the Han, Three Kingdoms, Chin, and Northern and Southern Dynasties) (1916; Peking, 1959; rpt. Taipei, 1968), p. 260 (*Ch'üan San-kuo shih* [Complete Poetry of the Three Kingdoms] 3:6b).

109. *Wen hsüan* 29:15a; cf. the translations by Zach, *Die Chinesische Anthologie*, p. 528; Hans H. Frankel, "Fifteen Poems by Ts'ao Chih: An Attempt at a New Approach," *JAOS* (1964), 84(1):8; and J. D. Frodsham and Ch'eng Hsi, *An Anthology of Chinese Verse: Han Wei Chin and the Northern and Southern Dynasties* (Oxford, 1967), p. 45.

110. *Pei-t'ang shu-ch'ao* (Extracts from the Northern Hall) (1888 ed.; rpt. Taipei, 1966), 157:9b.

111. Ting Fu-pao, p. 830 (*Ch'üan Sung shih* [Complete Poetry of the Liu-Sung Dynasty], 3:17b).

112. *Shih-p'in chu*, pp. 6–7; Takamatsu, pp. 42–45; Kōzen, pp. 62–66; Okamura,

pp. 229–230; and Takagi, pp. 96–104. Cf. the translations (almost complete) by Cha Chu Whan, pp. 48–49, and (partial) by Brooks, pp. 130, 141–142; Ch'en Shou-yi, p. 229; Wong Siu-kit, p. 30; Pollard, p. 92; Bodman, pp. 69–70; Marney, "P'ei Tzu-yeh," p. 168; Yeh and Walls, p. 51; Egan, p. 368; and W. L. Wong, "Selection of Lines in Chinese Poetry-talk Criticism—With a Comparison between the Selected Couplets and Mathew Arnold's 'Touchstones,'" in *China and the West: Comparative Literature Studies*, ed. William Tay, Ying-hsiung Chou, and Heh-hsiang Yuan (Hong Kong, 1980), p. 37.

Concerning "documents dealing with the ordering of the state," see n. 107.

113. For translation and discussion of Shen Yüeh's rules of prosody, see Charles D. Olney, "The Six Dynasties Poet Shen Yüeh," M. A. thesis, Columbia, 1971, pp. 18–19; E. Bruce Brooks, "Journey toward the West: An Asian Prosodic Embassy in the Year 1972," rev. of *Versification: Major Language Types*, ed. W. K. Wimsatt, *HJAS* (1975), 35:249–250; Ferenc Tōkei, "Textes prosodiques chinois au début du VIe siècle," *Mélanges de Sinologie offerts à Monsieur Paul Demiéville*, II, ed. Yves Hervouet (Paris, 1974), pp. 297–312; and Bodman, pp. 271–320.

114. *Shih-p'in chu*, p. 25; Takamatsu, pp. 67–68; Kōzen, pp. 173–175; and Takagi, pp. 260–261. Cf. the translations by Cha Chu Whan, p. 50, and Egan, p. 368.

115. *Shih-p'in chu*, p. 29; Takamatsu, pp. 78–79; Kōzen, pp. 193–195; and Takagi, p. 291.

116. *Shih-p'in chu*, pp. 17–18; Takamatsu, pp. 38–40; Kōzen, pp. 133–135; and Takagi, pp. 191–196. Cf. the translations (complete) by Brooks, p. 139, and (partial) by Yeh and Walls, pp. 59, 60, 66, 72.

Note that Chung Hung's Japanese commentators all interpret one part of this passage in the following way: "New sounds, beautiful and refined, continually converge."

117. See Olson's conditions 2–5 and 6–8 (n. 76).

Chung Hung does make reference to a standard of evaluation not directly concerned with literary performance. An appeal to authority is found in his remark concerning Chang Hua: "Men of insight regret how much womanish sentiment and how little high-spiritedness there is in his verse" (*Shih-p'in chu*, p. 20; Takamatsu, pp. 52–53; Kōzen, pp. 147–148; and Takagi, p. 217; cf. the translation by Straughair, *Chang Hua*, p. 16). Reference is made to an even wider board of critical review when, in the first of the prefaces to his work, Chung Hung says:

> Slicked down, fatty sons from noble families, embarrassed lest their compositions not come up to par, spend all day fiddling with revisions and half the night crooning. In their estimation, their verses are outstanding; but a consensus of opinion finds them flat and pedestrian.

(*Shih-p'in chu*, p. 5; Takamatsu, pp. 15–17; Kōzen, pp. 53–55; Okamura, p. 225; and Takagi, pp. 80–82; cf. the translation by Cha Chu Whan, p. 47.) And although Chung Hung spoke of Li Ch'ung's critical treatise as being "coherent but not incisive" (see n. 12), he also states, "The *Discourse on the Forest of Writing Brushes* being a sound discussion, Lu Chi is praised therein as being more profound than P'an Yüeh" (*Shih-p'in chu*, p. 16; Takamatsu, p. 33; Kōzen, p. 120; and Takagi, pp. 180–181; cf. the translation by Yeh and Walls, p. 71).

For discussion of the circularity implicit when an appeal is made directly or indirectly to the standard of authority, see Olson, "*Value Judgments*," p. 316, and Beardsley, *Aesthetics*, pp. 548–549.

118. *Shih-p'in chu*, p. 30; Takamatsu, pp. 80–82; Kōzen, pp. 196–197; and Takagi, p. 297. Cf. the translation by Wilhelm, p. 115.

119. *Shih-p'in chu*, p. 15; Takamatsu, pp. 31–33; Kōzen, pp. 115–116; and Takagi, p. 174.

120. *Shih-p'in chu*, p. 15; Takamatsu, pp. 31–33; Kōzen, pp. 115–116; and Takagi, p. 174. Cf. the translation by Yeh and Walls, pp. 56, 58 (see also pp. 64–65).

121. *Shih-p'in chu*, p. 16; Takamatsu, pp. 35–36; Kōzen, pp. 124–125; and Takagi, pp. 182–184.

122. *Shih-p'in chu*, p. 17; Takamatsu, pp. 37–38; Kōzen, pp. 129–130; and Takagi, pp. 187–189.

123. *Shih-p'in chu*, pp. 16, 17; Takamatsu, pp. 33–37, 37–38; Kōzen, pp. 119–121, 129–130; and Takagi, pp. 179–180, 187–189. Cf. the translation (of the former) by Yeh and Walls, p. 71.

124. *Shih-p'in chu*, p. 29; Takamatsu, pp. 77–78; Kōzen, p. 192; and Takagi, pp. 287–288.

125. *Shih-p'in chu*, p. 29; Takamatsu, pp. 77–78; Kōzen, p. 192; and Takagi, p. 287. Cf. the translation by Robertson, p. 333, and Yeh and Walls, pp. 66, 73 (cf. Paul W. Kroll, rev. of *Studies in Chinese Poetry and Poetics*, vol. 1, ed. Ronald C. Miao, *CLEAR* [January, 1980], 2[1] : 148).

126. *Shih-p'in chu*, p. 29; Takamatsu, pp. 77–78; Kōzen, p. 192; and Takagi, pp. 286–287. Cf. the translation by Robertson, p. 333, and Yeh and Walls, pp. 66, 73.

127. See n. 70.

128. *Shih-p'in chu*, p. 16; Takamatsu, pp. 33–34; Kōzen, pp. 119–121; and Takagi, p. 180. Cf. the translation by Robertson, p. 332, and Yeh and Walls, pp. 66, 70, 71 (see also p. 68).

The passage also appears in the *Shih-shuo hsin-yü* (4 : 44; cf. the translation by Mather, p. 136), where it is attributed to Sun Ch'o (320–377).

129. *Shih-p'in chu*, p. 26; Takamatsu, pp. 67–68; Kōzen, pp. 173–175; and Takagi, pp. 263–264. Cf. the translation by Yeh and Walls, p. 66 (see also pp. 68, 70, 72) (cf. Kroll, p. 148).

The passage also appears, in somewhat altered form, in the *Nan shih* (34 : 881), where it is attributed to Pao Chao; cf. the translation by Adele Austin Rickett, *Wang Kuo-wei's "Jen-chien tz'u-hua": A Study in Chinese Literary Criticism* (Hong Kong, 1977), pp. 88–89.

T'ang Hui-hsiu is treated by Chung Hung in the section on "lower grade" poets (see *Shih-p'in chu*, p. 37; Takamatsu, pp. 111–113; Kōzen, pp. 232–234; and Takagi, pp. 346–348; cf. the translation by Brooks, p. 133).

130. Note discussion of this by Robertson, pp. 332–333, and Yeh and Walls, pp. 67–71. Cf. Elder Olson's conditions 9 and 10 for a sound proposition of value (n. 76).

131. Note the filiation charts provided by Takamatsu, pp. 161–162; Brooks, p. 140; Kōzen, p. 16; and Takagi, p. 15. Note also the discussion of Chung Hung's filiation of writers by Wilhelm, pp. 115–116; Brooks, passim; and Yeh and Walls, pp. 45–48.

132. Presumably the description-valuations following the statements of filiation stand in relation to the latter much as they stand in relation to the gradings proper, as justifications of them. The assignment of filiations, moreover, like the assignment of gradings, can be viewed more as a rhetorical than an analytical device.

133. It may be in reference to this that the Sung poet Mei Yao-ch'en (1002–1062) wrote: "Loving to discuss the poetry of past and present, / Laughing at Chung Hung in our critical judgments" (*Wan-ling hsien-sheng chi* [Collection of the Wan-ling Gentleman] [*SPTK* ed.] 57:6a; trans. Chaves, *Mei Yao-ch'en*, p. 117; cf. the other, less pejorative references to Chung Hung in Mei Yao-ch'en's verse cited by Chaves, pp. 116–117). For critiques of Chung Hung by Yeh Meng-te (1077–1148) and Wang Shih-chen (1643–1711), see Huff, pp. 53–56, and Yeh and Walls, pp. 48–49 (for the latter only). For these and other citations of Chung's critics, see Takagi, pp. 22–23. The following are two studies of Chung Hung's placement of T'ao Ch'ien: Wang Shu-min, "Lu Chung Hung p'ing T'ao Yüan-ming shih" (On Chung Hung's Critique of T'ao Yüan-ming's Poetry); *Hsüeh yüan* (1948), 2(4):68–69; and Shu Chung-cheng, "*Shih-p'in* wei-shen-ma chih T'ao Ch'ien yü chung-p'in" (Why the *Gradings of Poets* Places T'ao Ch'ien in the "Middle Grade"), *Kuo-li Cheng-chih Ta-hsüeh hsüeh-pao* (May, 1975), 31:1–12. Cf. in this regard Brooks' comments on portability of style (cited in n. 51) and the "crafty" nature of hermit poets (p. 133).

134. *Wen hsüan* 30:4b, trans. James Robert Hightower, *The Poetry of T'ao Ch'ien* (Oxford, 1970), p. 229; cf. the translations by Zach, *Die Chinesische Anthologie*, p. 545; and William Acker, *T'ao the Hermit* (London, 1952), p. 99 (rpt. in *Anthology of Chinese Literature*, ed. Birch, p. 203).

135. *Wen hsüan* 30:27a; trans. Hightower, *The Poetry of T'ao Ch'ien*, p. 180; cf. the translations by Zach, *Die Chinesische Anthologie*, p. 568, and Brooks, p. 132.

136. *Shih-p'in chu*, p. 25; Takamatsu, pp. 65–67; Kōzen, pp. 169–172; and Takagi, pp. 251–258. Cf. the translations (complete) by Wilhelm, p. 115 (cf. Jonker, p. 281), and Brooks, p. 132, and (partial) by Yeh and Walls, pp. 54, 56, and Cahill, "Confucian Elements in the Theory of Painting," p. 123.

Concerning the line, "When one reads his works, the fine character of the poet himself comes to mind," cf. n. 51.

In speaking of the "unadorned directness" of T'ao's poetry, Chung Hung is using language from the *Analects*: *Lun-yü yin-te* 12:20, p. 24; cf. the translation by Legge I:259, and Waley, p. 168.

See Brooks' interpretation of the final two lines of the critique as being pejorative (pp. 132–134).

137. Ellis, *Theory*, p. 102.

V / Two Sung Views of the Arts

Su Shih's Reading of the *Chung yung*

By Christian Murck

I

In this paper my aim is to translate and examine closely the *Chung yung lun* (Discussion of the *Doctrine of the Mean*), a three-part essay written by Su Shih (1037–1101) in his early twenties. My hypothesis is that Su Shih's distinctive approach to this important Confucian text deepens our understanding of his aesthetics by helping situate artistic activity in the context of his personal approach to self-cultivation generally.

Su Shih's famous appreciations of Wen T'ung (1019–1079) often suggest that his friend was able to embody the Way through his art, to create images intuitively and spontaneously, with a generative force analogous to that of the cosmos. In one essay Su Shih distinguishes things that have constant form from those that may lack constant form but have constant principle. Form is dependent on technical expertise and may be created by artisan painters, but principle is harder to grasp.

> In bamboos and rocks, and leafless trees, Yü-k'o can be truly said to have grasped their principle: now they are alive and now dead, now twisted and cramped, and now regular and luxuriant. In the roots and stems, joints and leaves, in what is sharp and pointed or veined and striated, there are innumerable changes and transformations never once repeated; yet each part fits its place, and is in harmony with divine creation and accords with man's conceptions. Is it not because of what the accomplished scholar has lodged in it?[1]

In another essay, which quotes Su Ch'e's "Ink Bamboo Prose Poem" in which Wen T'ung reluctantly admitted that he was a "man of the Way,"[2] Su Shih discussed Wen T'ung's technique of painting:

> When bamboo comes into being, it is only an inch-long shoot, but the joints and leaves are all in it. It develops from cicada chrysalises and snake scales to swords drawn out eight feet, because this development was immanent in it. Now when painters do it joint by joint and add to it leaf by leaf, will this be bamboo? Thus, in painting bamboo one must first have the perfected bamboo in mind. When one takes up the brush and gazes intently, one sees what one wants to paint. Then one rises hurriedly

and wields the brush to capture what one sees. It is like the hare's leaping up and the falcon's swooping down; if there is the slightest slackening, then the chance is gone. Yü-k'o taught me in this way, and I could not achieve it but understood the way it should be done.[3]

The technique here lies primarily in achieving a certain state of mind, such that the bamboo is fully realized in the mind before a single stroke is on the paper, and the actual painting is done in utter intensity like the hare leaping for its life or the falcon dropping onto its prey. Su Shih has studied with the master and intellectually grasped the idea, but cannot attain the spontaneity and intensity necessary to put it into practice; this is expressed as a lack of unity: "inner and outer are not one, mind and hand are not in accord."[4] Wen T'ung's greatness as a painter of bamboo does not lie in his technical skill, or his elite status, or his education, or his personality, though all these are not irrelevant, but in his capacity to see the perfected bamboo in his mind, and spontaneously and decisively to realize that insight in the physical action of wielding the brush. The perception that leads to painting and the act itself present a microcosm in which the same transformative forces are at work that appear in the wider cosmos. The painting itself presents to an observer the traces, the physical marks, which enable an appreciation of the artist's creativity.

The question of representation in painting is given a new dimension when considered in this light. Su Shih was the author of the famous lines:

> If anyone understands painting in terms of formal likeness,
> His understanding is close to that of a child.
> If when someone composes a poem it must be a certain poem,
> He is definitely not a man who knows poetry.
> There is one basic rule in poetry and painting;
> Natural skill and pure freshness.[a][5]

Approached as a technical problem in art history, it is not easy to relate these lines to the visual evidence, which suggests that Northern Sung painters in general were more concerned with representing reality faithfully than later painters in the Yüan and Ming, who often cited Su's poem. The poem is, to begin with, deliberately paradoxical and humorous; many people then as now no doubt discussed painting in terms of whether or not it "looked like" its subject matter, and in a society where the occasional poem was a matter of high convention, poets were often asked for poems on set themes or set rhymes. In rejecting the truisms, Su Shih is not saying that formal likeness is unimportant or irrelevant, rather he is suggesting that there is another level of concern of even greater importance. The key to that level is the last line, which proclaims that in both poetry and painting the effort or skill of the artist must be "heavenly," i.e. natural, rather than bound by artificial technical conven-

[a] 天工與清新

tions or requirements. And the result must have a quality of purity and freshness; it must strike the reader or viewer as familiar and yet new in its particularity, just as a mountain seen for the first time is familiar as a mountain yet strange as that mountain, or the sadness of parting is always similar yet always different with each parting. The artist is thus called once again by Su Shih to embody creatively the Way. Of course he must also be able to make a poem rhyme, or his bamboo recognizably a bamboo, but technical skill does not determine whether the result is satisfying, it is only a means. The purpose of painting requires more than representation; representation of a bamboo in the art of Wen T'ung is a medium for allowing human feeling its full creative function in the cosmos. The pedestrian connoisseur may approach the painting at a childlike level, but one who is a "man of the Way" will understand the artist's deeper intention.

For the reasons outlined above, the artist is not to be considered simply a maker of images; rather, painting is related to the other shaping acts of the imagination, and all are understood in the totality of a man's being:

> Yü-k'o's literary work is the least of his virtue and his poetry, the minor part of his writing. What is not used up in poetry overflows to become calligraphy and is transformed to become painting: both are what is left over from poetry. Those who appreciate his poetry and literary work are increasingly few. As for those who love his virtue as they love his painting—alas![6]

Virtue here connotes the power of the Way manifested in a particular individual, the virtue through which he is able to work creatively, as well as his moral character.

In all of these scattered comments on the arts, I suggest, the discussion of technical questions insistently points to a general aesthetic stance, and furthermore raises broader philosophical issues. How is artistic activity related to the "accomplished scholar," the "man of the Way"? Wen T'ung's art is evidently of a special character, but how did he develop it? What is its relevance to other men? to ethics? to spiritual commitment? In answering such questions, Su Shih's interpretation of the *Chung yung* provides important evidence. Before turning to the essay itself, a brief description of the circumstances under which it was written may clarify its importance in Su's life, and the intellectual discourse to which it contributed.

II

In the early part of 1057, Su Shih and his brother Su Ch'e (1039–1112) passed the *chin-shih* examination directed by Ou-yang Hsiu (1007–1072). This was a controversial examination marked by the successful imposition of questions emphasizing classics and history which the examiners expected to be discussed in ancient style prose. Candidates who had prepared themselves through the now discredited literary curriculum bitterly attacked Ou-yang Hsiu, but he and the advocates of the ancient style carried the day. One of the reasons was the widely admitted brilliance of the candidates successful under the new standards, including the Su brothers.[7] After their examination success, the Su family was forced to withdraw from the capital because of the death of their mother, but their reputation had been established and grew with the wider circulation of their writings. Four years later, the brothers were presented for a special *hsien-liang fang-cheng*[b] examination, Su Shih under the sponsorship of Ou-yang Hsiu, and Su Ch'e under that of Ssu-ma Kuang (1019–1086). Candidates were required to submit in advance a group of fifty essays, half on history and classics, half on the analysis of current policy. They were then examined: on one day six five-hundred character essays on classical problems were required; on another day the emperor set a contemporary problem for a three-thousand character response. In the course of the Northern Sung dynasty, the first two ranks in this examination were never awarded, the third rank was achieved by only four men, the fourth rank was the lowest passing grade, and the fifth rank was failure. Su Shih was ranked third; his brother almost failed because of his sharp criticism of the court, but the personal intervention of Emperor Jen-tsung preserved a fourth-rank pass.[8] Su Shih's portfolio is particularly interesting because we see the confident young *shih-tai-fu*[c] presenting himself; he clearly selected topics which would demonstrate the range of his concerns, his intellectual confidence, and his masterly prose style. Su Shih offers the reader an intellectual self-portrait which must bulk large in any general attempt to characterize his thought. Here our purpose is a narrower one, to focus specifically on the *Chung yung lun*.

The *Chung yung* was the only major text of the Confucian tradition given lengthy treatment by Su Shih in his examination portfolio. This chapter of the *Li chi* was particularly important in the Confucian resurgence of the Northern Sung. One famous incident concerned the philosopher Chang Tsai (1020–1077), who as a youth enjoyed discussing military strategy. Calling upon the reformer Fan Chung-yen (989–1052), who had had military experience in border posts, Chang raised his favorite topic, but Fan startled him by saying, "Confucians have their own ethical teaching in which to delight; why are you concerned with military affairs?" Fan then urged him to study the *Chung yung*.[9] This story's currency may be explained by the several important orientations it suggests: Confucian learning is presented as more important for a young man than practical skills in statecraft, a chapter from a classic is singled out rather than a later Confucian work such as the *Analects* or *Mencius*, and the chapter offers a Confucian metaphysical perspective of interest to thinkers familiar with Buddhism. Subsequently, Chang Tsai's nephews Ch'eng Hao (1032–

[b] 賢良方正　　　　　[c] 士大夫

1085) and Ch'eng I (1033–1107) studied with him, and they too became interested in the *Chung yung*, though neither wrote a separate commentary on it.[10] It remained for Chu Hsi to establish the *Chung yung* as one of the Four Books, and to specify its relation to the other three as parts of a comprehensive Neo-Confucian synthesis.

In the eleventh century, however, that synthesis had not yet taken form, and interpretation of the *Chung yung* reflected the full intellectual range of the period. Among those who wrote on it was Ssu-ma Kuang, the distinguished historian and official, who focused on the ideas of centrality and harmony found in the opening chapter.[11] The *Chung yung* had long served eclectic thinkers to link Buddhism and Taoism with Confucianism. Confucian commentators have been mentioned above; the text was approached in the eleventh century from the Buddhist side by the monk Ch'i-sung (d. 1072).[12] In 1061, when Su Shih was preparing the essays in his examination portfolio, it was not surprising that he chose to write on the *Chung yung*; this text was one of those at the heart of the intellectual ferment of the day.

III

The first part of the *Chung yung lun* opens with a revealing comment on the state of the Confucian understanding of the Way:

> How extreme is the difficulty of understanding the Way! Those who discuss its obvious characteristics are stuck in shallowness and unclear; those who discuss its subtleties are vastly overflowing and cannot be verified. These faults began with Confucians of former times who sought the Way of becoming a sage and attained nothing. They then devoted themselves to composing incomprehensible writings, almost as though saying, "Later generations will regard me as profoundly knowledgeable." Later Confucians saw that they were hard to understand, and, not knowing their vacuousness and lack of attainment, considered them profoundly creative regarding the Way. Ashamed of themselves for their inability, [these later Confucians] followed along and echoed them, saying, "It is so." Deceiving one another they thought was loftiness; growing used to one another they thought was profundity. And the Way of the sages was day by day farther away. From the time Tzu-ssu wrote the *Chung yung*, Confucians all have looked back to it as the explanation of the nature[d] and the mandate.[e] Alas! How could such as Tzu-ssu have been their type of person?[13]

[d] 性　　　　　　　　　　[e] 命

If those who seek the way of the sages find themselves in difficult straits both when they discuss its obvious characteristics, and when they attempt to unravel its subtleties, what would Su Shih advise them to do? Perhaps their common mistake is in attempting to "understand" the Way, and communicate that understanding in written form, but Su's alternative to understanding is not yet clear. Moreover, in the context of this opening stance, what are we to make of his attitude toward Tzu-ssu? Tzu-ssu is seemingly not one of the castigated "later Confucians," but the *Chung yung* is usually regarded as a text which significantly develops Confucian spirituality, a view which Su Shih himself recognizes when he says that all Confucians after Tzu-ssu look to the *Chung yung* for the explanation of the nature and the mandate. In what way is it different from other writings?

For amplification of this opening passage, a useful source is another essay in the group, entitled *Tzu-ssu lun* (Discussion of Tzu-ssu). This begins with the statement that Confucius was not concerned with writing, and thus never established doctrines, but simply was a sage. Su remarks, "The way of Confucius can be followed yet cannot be spoken of, can be known yet cannot be discoursed upon."[14] It is precisely for this reason that Confucius, who did not struggle over trivial theoretical details, is universally recognized as a sage. Following Confucius, Su continues, there were not only attacks from outside the school by such men as Chuang Tzu, Mo Tzu, Han Fei Tzu, etc., but even more painful, inner divisions among Confucians. These Su Shih traces to Mencius:

> Mencius said, "Man's nature is good." Therefore Hsün Tzu said, "Man's nature is bad," and Yang Tzu further said, "Man's nature is a mixture of good and bad." Mencius had already established his doctrine of goodness, therefore Hsün Tzu had to present his doctrine of badness. That human nature was either good or bad had already been established by the two masters, therefore Yang Tzu, too, had to present his doctrine of the mixture of good and bad. In forming doctrines it is not refinement which is sought, rather the aim is to be different from others, thus there appears a multitude of theories and one cannot know where it will stop.[15]

Mencius, of course, was traditionally presumed to have studied under a disciple of Tzu-ssu, thus placing him in a direct line of descent from Confucius.[16]

The major point of Su Shih's *Tzu-ssu lun* turns on this relationship: he argues that Mencius was inferior to Tzu-ssu, not in his understanding of the Way, but in his rhetorical expression of that understanding.

> What Mencius said about the goodness of the nature all came out of his teacher Tzu-ssu's book; Tzu-ssu's book was entirely the subtle words and sincere doctrines of the sage. Mencius obtained it, but did not use it well; he was able to speak of its Way, but he did not know the purpose of its words.[17]

To demonstrate his point, Su Shih quotes a passage on the Way from *Chung yung* 12:

> Men and women of simple intelligence can share its knowledge; and yet in its utmost reaches, there is something which even the sage does not know. Men and women of simple intelligence can put it into practice; and yet in its utmost reaches there is something which even the sage is not able to put into practice.[18]

What Su Shih admires in this passage is its inclusiveness, its assertion that the Way is accessible and grounded in the common experience and capacity of men, yet also has a profundity that cannot be exhausted even by a sage. He suggests a connection between this line of thought in *Chung yung* and Mencius:

> Since this is so, then commiseration is enough for humanity,[f] yet humanity does not stop with commiseration. Shame and dislike are enough for rightness,[g] yet rightness does not stop with shame and dislike. Is this not the reason Mencius propounded the doctrine of the good nature? Tzu-ssu said that the Way of the sage came from that which the whole world is able to do, and Mencius said that all the people of the world could practice the Way of the sage. There is no difference between them, yet Tzu-ssu found his evidence in the Way of the sage, and Mencius found his evidence in the men of the world. Therefore the conflicting arguments of later generations all come out of Mencius, and Tzu-ssu's theory is agreed to by the whole world and rejected by none. After this one realizes Tzu-ssu's correctness in discussion.[19]

Su Shih's *Tzu-ssu lun* is itself rhetorically brilliant. It deftly proceeds from one apparently unexceptionable statement to another, lucid and full of common sense, arriving at a conclusion which doesn't require him to demonstrate the falsity of Mencius's position, yet nevertheless generally repudiates the entire Mencian enterprise. "There is no difference between them," yet the distinction Su Shih makes is not simply one of nuance and method, or, rather, nuance and method are everything.

If one accepted Su's point of view, the implications for Confucianism would be far-reaching; for example, it would necessitate a revaluation of the concept of the true transmission of the Way.[h] [20] When Su Shih wrote, of course, the position of Mencius was much less firmly fixed than it later became; indeed there was a current of criticism of Mencius in Northern Sung thought little noticed in later periods. The claim to inherit the Mencian tradition in Su Shih's view would simply reveal the claimant as lacking understanding of Mencius's standing in the Confucian tradition; he would hardly be accepted as an authentic spokesman for the sagely Way.

[f] 仁　　　　　[g] 義　　　　　[h] 道統

The weakness of Su Shih's essay as a philosophical argument is as striking as its rhetorical strength. He is surely correct in arguing that one might derive the position that the nature is good from chapter twelve of the *Chung yung*; in that common men and women share in the knowledge and practice of the Way, their nature may be considered good. But Su Shih does not acknowledge that Mencius is facing a problem which is not addressed by his supposed source, namely, whether the Way is spontaneously generated within the nature so that the nature itself is characterized by this activity and must be understood as morally good, or whether the Way is implanted in the nature by some outside force, such as customs handed down from earlier generations, so that the nature might be characterized as morally neutral, mixed, or bad. The problem raised by Mencius has occupied a central position in the Confucian tradition to such an extent that one might well argue that it was the renewal of serious interest in the Mencian problematic that first marked the depth of the renascence of Confucian spirituality in Northern Sung. Mencius provided for Northern Sung thinkers such as the Ch'eng brothers and for subsequent Neo-Confucians a positive basis for moral self-cultivation. If Su Shih seriously proposed that all discussion of these issues be judged by the standard of universal acquiesence and the avoidance of disputation which he credits to Tzu-ssu, then one might suspect the result would be to paralyze moral philosophy as an intellectual and spiritual endeavor. The question then arises, what basis for moral practice would he provide? How should one proceed to follow the Way of the sage? These issues are not addressed in his *Tzu-ssu lun*, but they are important in the *Chung yung lun*.

Returning to the first part of that essay at the point where we left it above, we find Su Shih, having sketched his stance toward discussions of the Way and Tzu-ssu's position in it, ready to turn to the *Chung yung* proper:

> Now, having formerly attempted to discuss it, the *Chung yung* is an incomplete text left by Confucius. Its essential subjects are three only. These three are what the Duke of Chou and Confucius followed in being sages, and its empty phrases and overgrown extensions are the cause of Confucians writing essays.[21]

Su Shih read the version of the *Chung yung* in the *Li chi*, rather than that divided into thirty-three chapters by Chu Hsi which has been standard within Neo-Confucianism since the twelfth century, and which most modern scholars use. For the sake of convenient reference, this paper anachronistically uses Chu Hsi's chapter numbers, which make it easier to discuss the structure of the work concisely. Chu Hsi attributes chapter one to Tzu-ssu, and considers it a general summary of the tradition handed down to him. Chapters two through eleven are quotations from Confucius, whose purpose Chu explains as illustrating chapter one. Chapter twelve is again Tzu-ssu, and it is followed by another block of chapters quoting Confucius, chapters thirteen through twenty. Chapter twenty is in many ways the high point of the *Chung yung*, a long discourse on government seen as a problem of moral practice within human society, what Tu Wei-ming has called the "fiduciary community."[22] Chapter twenty-one is a pithy statement by Tzu-ssu of the relationship between *ch'eng*[i] (sincerity, integrity, reality) and *ming*[j] (enlightenment, brilliance, understanding).[23] Chapters twenty-two through thirty-three are attributed to Tzu-ssu by Chu, and treated as expanding chapter twenty-one in his commentary.[24] Writing a century before this fully articulated Neo-Confucian approach to the structure of the *Chung yung*, Su Shih simply notes that a body of material left by Confucius has now been completely fleshed out by Tzu-ssu; the reader's problem is to grasp the essential message of the text, and the reader stands warned against being tempted by its "empty phrases" into producing the "incomprehensible writings" of later Confucians.[25]

Su Shih advises the reader:

> Therefore I have eliminated its empty phrases and seized upon the three [essentials]. It first discusses how sincerity and enlightenment are entered; next it discusses how one begins in following the Way of the sages, inferring from this arrival at its ultimate end; and it ends by placing it within centrality and its practice.[26] I believe that the Way of the sages is generally manifest here. The *Li chi* says, "From sincerity to enlightenment is called the nature. From enlightenment to sincerity is called education. Given sincerity, there will be enlightenment, and given enlightenment, there will be sincerity."[27]

The passage from the *Chung yung* quoted here addresses a central paradox in Confucian spirituality. It is asserted that human nature is what is imparted by heaven, that following the nature comprises the Way, and that the movement from *ch'eng* to *ming* describes the dynamic structure of man's nature. From this point of view, being true to our heaven-imparted nature is the basic spiritual task. On the other hand, it is also asserted that cultivating the Way is an educational process, and that if one learns properly, the reverse movement, from *ming* to *ch'eng*, occurs. From this point of view, the fundamental spiritual task might be considered intellectual, that is, moral learning. While such learning requires a deep personal commitment, and takes the development of the nature as its subject matter, it nevertheless requires teachers, texts, and the external authority of a received tradition. As in chapter twelve, the *Chung yung* elsewhere always fruitfully preserves this dual emphasis: "Therefore the gentleman honors the moral nature and follows the path of study and inquiry."[28] In Northern Sung and subsequently, a key to differentiating among the range of positions is the attitude toward this problem of the thinker under consideration. Su Shih isolates this passage for analysis because it bears crucially on the theoretical and practical program of the text and its interpretative tradition.

In the remainder of the first part of the *Chung yung lun*, Su Shih considers *ch'eng*

i 誠　　　　　　　　　　j 明

and *ming*, exploring their relation as the first of the three essential subjects treated by the text. He says:

> As for sincerity, what is it? It is what is called "delighting in it" (*lo chih*[k]), for delighting in it one will naturally be faithful, therefore it says, "Sincerity." As for enlightenment, what is it? It is what is called "knowing it" (*chih chih*[l]), for knowing it one reaches the goal, therefore it says, "Enlightenment." Only the sage has not reached knowing while he has already entered into delighting. That which is entered first is the host, and awaits the rest, therefore this delighting is the host. In the case of a worthy, he has not reached delighting while already entering knowing. That which is entered first is the host, and awaits the rest, therefore this knowing is the host. When delighting is the host, there are things which are not known, but knowing is always practiced. When knowing is the host, although nothing is not known, there are things which cannot be practiced. The Master said, "To know it is not as good as to love it, and to love it is not as good as to take delight in it."[29] Knowing it and delighting in it—this is the distinction between the worthy and the sage. Loving it is the means by which the worthy seeks sincerity. The gentleman in learning is cautious[30] about his beginning. Why? Because that which he enters first is important. Knowing a great deal, yet still being unable to take delight is thus not as good as apprehension due to not knowing. Of people's likes and dislikes, none are as strong as liking beauty and disliking ugliness; this is the sincerity of the sage. Therefore it is said, "From sincerity to enlightenment is called the nature."[31] Confucius grew older and loved learning. When he went to Chou and observed the rites, he inquired of Lao Tan and Ch'ang Hung, and afterwards was enlightened regarding the rites and music.[32] When he studied the *Book of Changes* after turning fifty, probably there also were things known late in life, but that he had earlier attained sagehood was simply due to delighting in it.[33] When Confucius was in difficulty between Ch'en and Ts'ai, and inquired of Tzu-lu and Tzu-kung, the two masters were discontent and Tzu-kung even wanted to compromise.[34] These two masters were not unknowing; they had not yet reached a way of delighting in it. Moreover, Tzu-lu was able to face death in Wei, yet was unable not to be discontent between Ch'en and Ts'ai: how could this be the fault of his knowledge? Therefore the reason these disciples accompanied Confucius's travels was not solely seeking to listen to what they had not previously heard, rather it was seeking to delight in what they already had. Being enlightened yet not sincere, though they may hold fast to what they have, they will be upset without knowing how

[k] 樂之   [l] 知之

to secure it. If they don't know how to secure it, then one can be with them in peace, but cannot be with them in worry or adversity. It is when worry and adversity arrive that the difference between sincerity and enlightenment can be seen. Considered from this point of view, how can the gentleman not be sincere.[35]

Here we see Su Shih, following his conservative view of the text as an incomplete legacy from Confucius, rather than as an extension of the Confucian teaching, offering an interpretation based on a reading of the *Analects*. Priority is given to delighting in the Way, and this is understood as explaining the *Chung yung*'s concept of *ch'eng*. *Ming* is rather narrowly interpreted as having an intellectual grasp of the way, an abstract and detached knowledge which proves wanting in times of crisis. Considering the life of Confucius as an exemplar of following the Way of the sage, Su Shih finds support for his thesis in Confucius' humble pursuit of knowledge, which continued throughout his life even after he may be said to have become a sage, and in his equanimity in adversity. Confucius' life was rooted in his passionate attachment to the Way, whereas the two disciples had studied under Confucius but not yet attained his sincerity. Su Shih's understanding of *ch'eng* thus emphasizes its element of joyous and active commitment to the Way, which transforms and fully realizes the self as rational, scholarly inquiry cannot.

The argument that the difference between *ch'eng* and *ming* can best be seen in the crucible of action, when facing a direct threat to physical well-being, typifies Su Shih's temperament. His father Su Hsün made his literary reputation in large part through historical analyses of strategists and heroes of the Warring States period,[36] and Su Shih's examination essays, carrying on the mode of inquiry of his father, include discussions of events in the *Tso chuan*, and of personalities such as Kuan Chung, Su Wu, Han Fei, and Chu-ko Liang. In the opening part of the *Chung yung lun*, it is in the family tradition that Su Shih presents the sage as capable of heroism; the gentleman who wishes to follow the Way must regard the sage's sincerity, his delighting in the Way against all odds, as fundamental. Throughout his subsequent career, Su sustained a commitment to political action despite repeated defeats; in the privation of his periods of exile, he struggled, for the most part successfully, to secure himself psychologically. In the *Chung yung lun* the youthful, ambitious scholar-official articulated an ideal of joyful commitment which proved able to support him in later years, though it gradually acquired an increasing admixture of detachment and fatalism.

In the second section of his essay, devoted to "the beginning in following the Way of the sage," Su Shih pivots the argument on the concept of enlightenment:

In the gentleman's desire for sincerity, nothing is more useful than enlightenment. Considered from its roots, the Way of the sage entirely emerges from human feelings. Not following the roots, but anticipating the final growth, then it will be believed that the sage to some extent must force himself to practice vigorously, and that it is not something in which human feeling delights. If such is the case, though one may desire to be sincere, his way is without a starting point, therefore I say, "Nothing is more useful than enlightenment." It causes our mind to awaken, know what it should be, and seek its pleasure.[37]

The strong validation given here to human feelings and to pleasure contrasts with a view of moral self-cultivation as requiring intense effort, part of which might be considered self-disciplinary. The *Chung yung* itself, for example, says:

> Study it extensively, inquire into it accurately, think it over carefully, sift it carefully, and practice it earnestly.... If another man succeed by one effort, you will use a hundred efforts. If another man succeed by ten efforts, you will use a thousand efforts.[38]

Yet in the Confucian tradition the effort to realize sagehood is the completion and flowering of man, an autochthonous process rather than a coercive process. In the classical tradition Mencius emphasized this most strongly, but it runs throughout Confucianism so that even in Hsün Tzu, with his rejection of the goodness of human nature and his emphasis on the necessity of the socializing power of ritual and inherited norms, there is a vision of the mind inherently having the capacity to perceive the moral value of civilization. Hsün Tzu could therefore argue with conviction equal to Mencius's, though on different grounds, that every man had the potential to become a sage. Su Shih stands within this general tradition in rejecting forced or artificial effort, but in the context of the eleventh century his project is clearly to direct attention away from the problem of defining exactly what constitutes the effort to become a sage, much less exhorting his readers toward vigorous practice. Rather enlightenment, "knowing it," is important because the mind is awakened to its true, appropriate pleasures, in which human feelings delight, and thus the "final growth" of sincerity, "loving it," sends down roots.

In the thought of Ch'eng I, the Mencian position became the basis of the effort called for by the *Chung yung*, and the *Great Learning* provided a specific series of steps leading to self-cultivation and then to ordering family, state, and world. In 1056, as a student at the national academy under Hu Yüan (993–1059), Ch'eng I wrote his famous essay "A Treatise on What Yen Tzu Loved to Learn." Its opening sections deal with the same problem Su Shih discusses above:

> In the school of Confucius, there were three thousand pupils. Yen Tzu alone was praised as loving to learn. It is not that the three thousand scholars had not studied and mastered the Six Classics such as the *Book of Odes* and the *Book of History*. Then what was it that Yen Tzu alone loved to learn? Answer: It was to learn the Way of becoming a sage.

Can one become a sage through learning? Answer: Yes. What is the way to learn? Answer: From the essence of life accumulated in Heaven and Earth, man receives the Five Agents in their highest excellence. His original nature is pure and tranquil. Before it is aroused, the five moral principles of his nature, called humanity, righteousness, propriety, wisdom, and faithfulness, are complete. As his physical form appears, it comes into contact with external things and is aroused from within. As it is aroused from within, the seven feelings, called pleasure, anger, sorrow, joy, love, hate, and desire, ensure. As feelings become strong and increasingly reckless, his nature becomes damaged. For this reason the enlightened person controls his feelings so that they will be in accord with the Mean. He rectifies his mind, nourishes his nature. This is therefore called turning the feelings into the [original] nature. The stupid person does not know how to control them. He lets them loose until they are depraved, fetter his nature, and destroy it. This is therefore called turning one's nature into feelings.

The way to learn is none other than rectifying one's mind and nourishing one's nature. When one abides by the Mean and correctness and becomes sincere, he is a sage. In the learning of the superior man, the first thing is to be clear in one's mind and to know where to go and then act vigorously in order that one may arrive at sagehood. This is what is meant by "sincerity resulting from enlightenment."[39]

In Ch'eng I's moral psychology, the seven feelings damage the purity and tranquillity of one's original nature unless they are controlled, and the vigorous action he calls for is directed at governing the feelings in order to develop toward sagehood. At the conclusion of his essay, Ch'eng I relates his general argument about learning to a critique of the literary culture of his day in a way that must have been unsettling to many:

... in later years people thought that sagehood was basically due to inborn knowledge and could not be achieved through learning. Consequently the way to learn has been lost to us. Men do not seek within themselves but outside themselves and engage in extensive learning, effortful memorization, clever style, and elegant diction, making their words elaborate and beautiful. Thus few have arrived at the Way. This being the case, the learning of today and the learning that Yen Tzu loved are quite different.[40]

Ch'eng thus draws a sharp distinction between moral learning, directed at self-cultivation and the spiritual aim of sagehood, and a superficial learning aimed at acquiring information useful for passing civil service examinations, or a polished style and a name in the literary world.

Whether Su Shih had read Ch'eng I's essay, written four years prior to his own, is not clear. Yet it is evident that the piece was circulating among the same men to whom the Sus were presenting their own writings when they came to the capital in 1057. In the event, Su Shih was among those who rejected both the critique of feeling, and the insistence on a redefinition of learning.

Su Shih is neither hedonistic nor solipsistic in his validation of feelings. As a concrete example immediately makes clear, he anticipates that human feelings will, if properly known and understood, lend support to social custom and ameliorate the coercive element in the Confucian concept of ritual:

> As for the teaching of the five constants today, only ritual seems to coerce men. How is this? Human feelings all love pleasure and dislike suffering, yet today we always make them afraid to sprawl when sitting, and take bending the back like a chiming stone in a hundred bows to be ritual.[41] Human feelings are all delighted by riches and rank and ashamed of poverty and lowliness, yet today we always make them afraid to exalt themselves, and take humility[42] and restraint as ritual. Ordinary dishes are convenient, sacrificial vessels are honored. Clothing worn at home is convenient, court robes and caps are honored. Sorrow is desired to end quickly, yet we extend [mourning] to three years. Happiness is desired to never end, yet it does not last until the end of the day. This is how ritual coerces men, yet it is an error of looking at the final growth. Why not return to its roots and think it over? Now I think that bending the back like a chiming stone is not as preferable as the ease of standing erect, and if it is simply ease which is sought, then standing is not as preferable as sitting, sitting is not as preferable as sprawling, sprawling is not as preferable as reclining, and reclining all the time I may as well be naked and not be concerned [about other's opinions].[43] If I went naked and were unconcerned, I would inevitably come to detest it. Nor would only I detest it, the ordinary men and women of the world would all detest it. Having come to detest it, then that tendency must necessarily end in bending the back like a chiming stone in a hundred bows. Speaking of it in this way, then bending the back like a chiming stone in a hundred bows is born simply in the moment of desiring not to be naked. How could this be so only for bending the back like a chiming stone in a hundred bows? Everything which is said to coerce people must have its origin. Distinguishing its origin and extending it from there to its ultimate end, this is called enlightenment.[44]

Enlightenment is thus a process of tracing the connections between human feelings and fully articulated social ritual, but Su Shih insists on beginning from feeling. If the process is reversed, if ritual is studied as an end in itself instead of as a means of giving full and harmonious expression to feeling, then it must become coercive. By insisting on the direct, conscious connection between feeling and ritual, Su Shih implies a flexible attitude toward any particular ritual; given a different degree of enlightenment, different people might behave in different ways and still be following the Way of the sage.

The conclusion of the second part of the *Chung yung lun* develops a passage from the text emphasizing the universality of the Way:

> Therefore the *Li chi* says, "The Way of the gentleman is broad and therefore hidden. Men and women of simple intelligence can share its knowledge; and yet in its utmost reaches there is something which even the sage does not know. Men and women of simple intelligence can put it into practice, and yet in its utmost reaches, there is something which even the sage is not able to put into practice." [45] If the Way of the gentleman is analyzed from its beginning and discussed, then the words are brief; being brief, there is enlightenment. If it is analyzed in reverse and then considered, then the words are broad; being broad, [the Way] is hidden. The gentleman wishes it were not hidden, therefore he begins from that which common men and women have in abundance, and extends it to reach that which the sage cannot match; taking up the easiest things in the world and penetrating to the most difficult, he makes the world being at ease with the most difficult no different from [being at ease with] the easiest. Mencius said, "Here is a basketful of rice and a bowlful of soup. Getting them will mean life; not getting them will mean death. When these are given with abuse, even a wayfarer would not accept them; when these are given after being trampled upon, even a beggar would not accept them. Yet when it comes to ten thousand bushels of grain one is supposed to accept without asking if it is in accordance with the rites or if it is right to do so. What benefit are ten thousand bushels of grain to me? .... Formerly I would not accept when it was a matter of life or death, now I do it for the sake of the enjoyment of friends, wives and concubines. This way of thinking is known as losing one's original heart." [46] Not accepting ten thousand bushels is a difficulty of princes and great men, yet if we take the refusal of the wayfarer or the begger, and weigh them in the balance, how are they different from the capability of common men and women penetrating and reaching to what the sage cannot come up to. Thus all who follow this theory are seeking to be at ease with the most difficult, and devoting themselves to the desire to be sincere. Everyone in the world wishes to be sincere, yet they do not obtain its theory, therefore all this is offered as the theory of sincerity. [47]

So this section of Su's essay, which began with *ming*, has returned to dwell again on *ch'eng*. Enlightenment provides a method (a way) to attain sincerity, and its secret lies in beginning from that which is common, simple, and easy, and realizing that in moral terms the problems faced at this level are essentially similar to the problems which are apparently much more complex and intractable. Thus the beggar and the statesman face the same issue of integrity, when each is offered a compromising gift; that the gift is a basketful of rice and a bowlful of soup in the one case, and ten thousand bushels of grain in the other is unimportant, and the enlightened man in each case is free to be sincere.

Su Shih's interpretation of the opening of chapter twelve of the *Chung yung*, "The Way of the gentleman is broad and hidden," contrasts sharply with that of the Ch'eng-Chu school. For Su, what is broad about the Way of the gentleman is the verbiage that appears when the Way is described from its full development rather than from its simple beginning. And this verbiage unfortunately obscures truth that is accessible to all if properly approached. Chu Hsi regards *fei erh yin*[m] as a characterization of the Way itself, "broad and yet hidden," rather than as a critique of the discussion of the Way. Chu defines the key terms within the framework of a familiar duality:"*Fei* is breadth of function; *yin* is subtlety of substance." He continues:

> The Way of the gentleman close at hand begins in the room of husband and wife, and far removed extends to what cannot be exhausted in heaven and earth or the sages. In its greatness nothing is outside it, in its minuteness nothing fits inside it; it may be called broad (*fei*). However, the reason its principle is as it is, is hidden (*yin*) and unseen.[48]

In this view, the Way itself is subtle and unfathomable in essence, but broad, comprehensive, and concrete in its social and natural manifestations. For Chu Hsi, the phrase does not contain the admonitions to keep one's words brief, begin from what common people abundantly have, and seek to be at ease with the most difficult.

In the final part of the *Chung yung lun*, Su Shih turns to the concept of centrality and its practice that is at the heart of the text. One of the major passages in the *Chung yung* relates feelings and their expression to this concept:

> Before the feelings of pleasure, anger, sorrow, and joy are aroused it is called centrality. When these feelings are aroused and each and all attain due measure and degree, it is called harmony. Centrality is the great foundation of the world, and harmony is its universal path.[49]

This passage generated intense discussion in the Ch'eng-Chu school, and one might expect that Su Shih, with his strong emphasis on feelings, would attempt to explicate

[m] 費而隱

it. He does not. Instead, he considers the idea of centrality primarily in general terms as related to conduct, action, and balancing concrete choices faced by one who seeks to act according to the Way. The final section of his essay opens:

> Though the gentleman be able to delight in it, if he does not know centrality and its practice, then his Way will necessarily be exhausted. The *Li chi* says, "There are gentlemen who act in accordance with the Way, but give up when they have gone half way. But I can never give up."[50] It is not that the gentleman's faith in the Way is not earnest; it is not that he has not reached the stage of vigorously practicing it. He has attained the one-sided and forgotten centrality, and is unable to travel peacefully in the comprehensive road until the end of a day. Though he does not wish to give it up, how can he possibly attain it.[51] The *Li chi* says, "Confucius said, 'I know why the Way is not pursued. The intelligent go beyond it and the stupid do not come up to it,'"[52] Is going beyond more difficult, or returning to centrality more difficult? It would seem that going beyond is more difficult, but there are those in the world able to go beyond yet not able to [hit] centrality, therefore returning to centrality is what is [truly] difficult. The *Li chi* says, "The world, the states, and the families can be put in order. Ranks and emoluments can be declined. A bare, naked weapon can be trampled upon. But centrality cannot [easily] be attained."[53] Since to exceed it is impermissible, and not to come up to it is impermissible, is it just such an [impasse]? No. Mencius says, "Holding on to the middle is closer to being right,[54] but to do this without the proper measure is no different from holding to one extreme."[55] The *Book of Documents* says, "Those who do not come up to the highest excellence, and yet do not involve themselves in crime, let the sovereigns receive."[56] It also says, "Seeing this perfect excellence, turn to this perfect excellence."[57] And the *Li chi* says, "The gentleman [exemplifies] centrality because, as a gentleman, he can maintain centrality at any time."[58] The ruler's excellence includes that which is not excellent, yet rests on excellence. Always maintaining centrality includes that which is not central, yet returns to centrality. I think that when centrality and its practice reach this point it is especially difficult, thus[59] there is the inferior man's centrality and its practice. Including that which is not central, yet returning to centrality, this is the Way, the reason the gentleman always maintains centrality, and the cause of the inferior man's having no caution. The *Li chi* says, "The inferior man acts contrary to centrality and its practice because as an inferior man he has no caution."[60]

The question here is whether centrality is to be considered a narrow ground of utterly correct action, neither inadequate nor excessive in any way. Su Shih argues that it should be understood more broadly. Thus the ruler in accepting those who are not perfect demonstrates his own centrality; the gentleman who always maintains the mean must adapt to changing circumstances with a sense of the "proper measure." As a standard of behavior centrality is therefore not narrow or fixed, but flexible and dependent on the exercise of cautious judgment. Sh Shih's strategy for exercising judgment rests on the principle of inclusiveness. The gentleman determines centrality by including the peripheral; the center is maintained by a continuous process of perceiving the dual poles in any situation (what constitutes "not coming up to" and "exceeding") and accommodating both.

The indeterminacy of centrality not only makes it difficult to attain and maintain, it also makes it vulnerable to misuse:

> Alas! The Way is difficult to speak of and there are inferior men who, because they closely resemble it, steal its name. The sage is concerned and apprehensive, thus he ponders it repeatedly and speaks of it without becoming satiated. How is it that this Way is certainly what is appropriated by inferior men for their own advantage? The superior man sees danger and is able to die, but he makes an effort and does not die, because he seeks union with centrality and its practice. The inferior man is greedy for profit and by chance avoids it, yet he too wants to use the name of centrality and its practice for his private advantage. This is the reason Confucius and Mencius disliked the "good villager." "If a man is praised for his honesty in his village, then he is an honest man wherever he goes." "He shares with others the practices of the day and is in harmony with the sordid world." He says, "The ancients! Why must they walk along in such solitary fashion? Being in this world, one must behave in a manner pleasing to this world. So long as one is good, it is all right."[61] Considering the ancients foolish and what the present generation approves of perfectly adequate, does he not closely resemble centrality and its practice? Therefore Confucius said, "I dislike purple for fear it might be confused with vermilion; I dislike weeds for fear they might be confused with the rice plant."[62] Why is this? He disliked their confusing resemblance. Truly centrality and its practice are difficult to speak of. The gentleman who wishes to devote himself to this must not follow its appearances, but seek its flavor: this is its inward spring. The *Li chi* says, "There is no one who does not eat and drink, but there are few who can really know flavor."[63]

Su Shih thus advises caution: the *Chung yung* may often be claimed as a pretext by inferior men; appearances may prove deceptive. The implication once again is that social convention, including common standards of morality, does not necessarily comprise centrality and commonality; they may on the contrary be more firmly grasped on occasion by the solitary gentleman who does not please the world.

Su Shih's reading of the *Chung yung* can be summarized in terms of the three issues he posed at the beginning of his essay. First, on entering sincerity and enlightenment, he argues that sincerity, understood as delighting in the Way, is fundamental to sagehood. Enlightenment is a process that continues unabated even after reaching sagehood, as shown by the example of Confucius' continuing curiosity and desire to learn, but it is not the fundamental characteristic of the sage, therefore the gentleman wishes to be sincere. Second, on the gentleman's beginning in following the Way, he argues that enlightenment, understood as the process of tracing the development of human feelings into the ritualized patterns readily observable in society, is the appropriate beginning because it awakens the mind to what it ought to be, and leads it to seek its pleasure according to that standard. Thus enlightenment is a way of nurturing the appropriate expression of feelings, and leads eventually to delighting in the Way and to sincerity. The structure of Su Shih's essay, with its balanced consideration first of the movement from *ch'eng* to *ming*, and then of the movement from *ming* to *ch'eng*, exemplifies the point made in the third section, where centrality is understood as practicing a process of inclusion. The formal expression of thought, the rhetorical stance, the flow of gracefully parallel phrases demand attention as themselves pivoting on a "center" intuitively grasped by the reader rather than explicitly delineated by the writer. The transition between sincerity and enlightenment, or enlightenment and sincerity, remains unspecified. One might derive a static structure from Su's essay by suggesting that enlightenment is chronologically prior to sincerity, but ontologically operating on a lower level than sincerity, but Su himself would resist any such statement. By placing the Way within the context of centrality, Su Shih emphasizes a certain indeterminacy, a need for flexibility, subtlety, and caution, and both proposes and demonstrates a technique for finding the center in the flux of life.

Considered as a philosophical essay, the *Chung yung lun* has many of the same weaknesses as the *Tzu-ssu lun*; the reader feels a reluctance in Su Shih to grapple with the issues raised by the text, and his arguments lead rather quickly to the benign assertion that nothing more can be said. A comparison with the writings of the Ch'eng-Chu school on the *Chung yung* demonstrates not merely a more detailed commentary, but a more powerful, unified theoretical structure. To evaluate Su Shih by this standard ignores his explicit rejection of it; tightly reasoned philosophical structures in Su Shih's opinion misrepresent the nature of the Confucian Way, and mislead those who want to follow it. In his own terms, then, Su's reading of the *Chung yung* offers an alternative to what he conceived of as overly dry intellectualism. I would suggest that the alternative implied may best be described as aesthetic, and that the *Chung yung lun* must be understood in the context of making and responding to art.

Su Shih's emphasis on human feelings as the source of the Way of the sage, and on delighting in the Way as the essence of its practice, suggests that one who wishes to realize himself in the Way faces above all a problem of sensitivity and perception.

He must be awake to his own feelings, to the centrality of feeling in man, and of man in the natural world. He must "know the sound" (*chih yin*[n]) so familiar from anecdotes about the *ch'in*; both phrases center on the necessity of sensitive appreciation to the creative process. This is a quality essential to the artist both in his own work, and in his audience, for an art based on centrality and commonality of feeling demands for its own completion sympathetic response from another. Su Shih's extraordinary appreciations of Wen T'ung, discussed briefly above, demonstrate his creative participation in Wen's art.

Human feelings are not hermetically self-referential for Su Shih; they stand in relation to and are part of, both the social world and the cosmos. Su Shih's response to the cosmos is determined by the belief that it is constantly changing, a ceaseless self-generation that ineluctably destroys everything and simultaneously surges with new creation. Although the cosmos is not personified, all phenomena are interconnected, and subject to the same processes, including human phenomena. The link between transcience and the perpetuity of regular patterns of change, for which the seasonal rotation often serves as a metaphor, may be traced back to the *I ching* and to *Chuang Tzu*, and has been important in Chinese moral philosophy, science, and aesthetics.

Su Shih repeatedly voices in both prose and poetry the melancholy and exhilaration felt by a man sensitive to the cosmos. Here is part of an essay recording the Riding Vacuity Pavilion (*Ling-hsu t'ai*[o]):

> The disappearance and rise, completion and destruction of things cannot be known. Formerly there were weeds and uncultivated fields, covered by frost and dew, the hiding place of foxes and snakes. At that time, how could one have known there would be a Riding Vacuity Pavilion? Disappearance and rise, completion and destruction alternate without end, thus the return of the pavilion to desolate fields and wild grasses is entirely unknowable. Once I tried climbing the pavilion with its master and looked out: to the east was the Ch'i-nien Hall of the To-ch'üan Palace of Duke Mu of Ch'in, to the south were the Ch'ang-yang and Wu-tso Palaces of Emperor Wu of Han, to the north were the Jen-shou Palace of the Sui and the Chiu-ch'eng Palace of the T'ang. I thought of the time of their splendor: heroic and beautiful, how could their strength and immovability been merely one hundred times that of the pavilion! Yet after a few generations, seeking their traces one finds nothing surviving but broken tiles and crumbling walls; they are already transformed to millet and brambles, wasteland and farms. How much more likely for this pavilion. If even this pavilion cannot be relied upon to last, how much more will the accomplishments and failures of human affairs be fleeting.

[n] 知音　　　　　　　　[o] 凌虛台

> Whoever seeks to overawe the age and be sufficient in himself is mistaken. Perhaps there is something in the world which may be relied upon, but it is not the survival or disappearance of this pavilion.[64]

Su Shih here meditates on historical ruins—seen in his mind's eye rather than physically—and wittily reminds the builder of the pavilion that however grand and solid it seems, it too faces an uncertain future. Yet there is also a striking continuity of man and his works in the cosmos; the vast palaces of the past are replaced not by a natural world with no trace of man, but by "millet and brambles, wasteland and farms." Moreover, as if to echo and mock their grandiloquence, a humble pavilion, a new man-made structure, has appeared to look over their ruins. Man is thus part of both the destructive and the renewing force of history; the two are in fact one.

To delight in the Way assumes a new force when considered as man's response to the cosmos. Su Shih is fully aware of the challenge presented. Thus the joyful optimism of the conclusion to the *First Prose Poem on the Red Cliff*—"There are the endless treasures of the creator (*tsao-wu-che*[P]), here for you and me to enjoy together!"[65]—gives way to the darker mood of the poet's climb up the cliff in the *Second Prose Poem on the Red Cliff*:

> Tucking up my robe, I began to climb, picking my way along the steep embankment, pushing tangled grass, straddling rocks the shape of tigers, clambering over roots twisted like dragons. I pulled my way up to the eagle's precarious nest, and looked down into the hidden falls of the river god. My two friends couldn't keep up.
>
> I gave a long, shrill whoop. Trees and grass shook and swayed, the mountains rang, the valley echoed. A wind came up, roiling the water, and I felt a chill of sadness, a shrinking fear. I knew with a shudder that I couldn't stay there any longer.[66]

In the first prose poem Su Shih celebrates the human capacity to enjoy the transformations of nature together with like-minded friends, even in the awareness of their own impermanence. In the second, he has left human companionship behind, confronts the natural world directly and shakes it at his will. The defiant whoop is an act of bravado, perhaps even of hubris, for it ascribes to man a larger creative role in the cosmos than he can sustain, and so the poet returns to his friends. Together they drift, allowing the current to determine their resting place. Suddenly, in the stillness of the night, a long crane cuts overhead, and harshly cries out. This is the famous passage often portrayed in the illustrations of the prose poem. It is aptly chosen, for the crane breaks the silence just as the poet did earlier and similarly becomes the focal point of a moment of extreme beauty and transcience; the poet in the tiny boat below, given no warning of this natural transmutation of his action,

P 造物者

must be understood as responding instantly and deeply. The scene is thus a classic conjoining of artist and cosmos, and it has all the more power because the poet does not tell us his specific thoughts or reactions as the crane passes. But we know the crane's impact, because the poet later dreams of meeting a Taoist immortal and suddenly realizing that the crane was the transformed immortal. Yet even the dream is ambiguous: questioned, the immortal merely laughs and disappears; the poet starts awake and peers out the door, but sees no sign of him. Here, what is permanent? What is real?

In a larger sense, even the "shrinking fear" of the second poem, and the mysterious moment when the poet's response to the crane cannot be put into words, take their place as parts of an aesthetic whole, an expression of feeling organized by the consciousness of the poet. In the creativity of the artist, then, may be found a sustainable role, or "self," for man within the cosmos. Man may not be able to be the *tsao-wu-che* of the cosmos, for just as that is not an anthropomorphic concept it is not possible to deify man in its image, but he can nevertheless exercise the same transforming power.

This paper was written while the author was a member of the Society of Fellows in the Humanities, Columbia University. Comments from colleagues at the Conference on Theories of the Arts in China were helpful in the revision of that preliminary version. Peter Bol, Princeton University, generously shared drafts of his own work on Su Shih, and commented perceptively on mine. In addition, I am grateful for suggestions made by James T. C. Liu, F. W. Mote, and Willard Peterson.

1. Su Shih, *Ching-chin Tung-p'o wen-chi shih-lüeh* (Su Shih's Collected Prose), compiled by Lang Yeh (Peking, 1957) (hereafter *Collected Prose*) 4, pp. 49–50. Translation emended from Susan Bush, *The Chinese Literati on Painting: Su Shih (1037–1101) to Tung Ch'i-ch'ang (1555–1636)* (Cambridge, Mass., 1971), p. 42.

2. Su Ch'e, *Luan-ch'eng chi* (SPTK) 17:8b; cited and partially translated by Bush, *Chinese Literati*, p. 37.

3. *Collected Prose* 49, p. 813; trans. Bush, *Chinese Literati*, p. 37.

4. Ibid.

5. Su Shih, *Chi-chu fen-lei Tung-p'o hsien-sheng shih* (edited and annotated edition of Su Shih's Poetry) (SPTK) 11:29a; trans. Bush, *Chinese Literati*, pp. 26 and 32. I have translated the last line more literally than Bush, who renders it "Natural genius and originality."

6. Su Shih, *Tung-p'o ch'üan-chi* (SPPY) 21:12b–13a; trans. Bush, *Chinese Literati*, p. 12. I have rendered *te* (德) as "virtue" rather than "accomplishment."

7. James T. C. Liu, *Ou-yang Hsiu: An Eleventh Century Neo-Confucianist* (Stanford, 1967), pp. 150–152 vividly describe the 1057 examination.

8. George C. Hatch, "Su Shih," in *Sung Biographies*, ed. Herbert Franke (Wiesbaden, 1976), pp. 909–912. Hatch's long article is the best general study in English of Su Shih's life and thought.

9. *Sung shih* (Peking, 1977) 427, p. 12723. Cited by W. T. Chan, *A Source Book in Chinese Philosophy* (Princeton, 1963), p. 496.

10. A work titled *Chung yung i* (中庸義) is attributed to Ch'eng Hao in the *Sung shih* bibliographic treatise, but W. T. Chan has accepted Chu Hsi's view that this was actually written by Lü Ta-lin. See *Sung shih* 202, p. 5049; Chu Hsi, *Chu Tzu ta-ch'üan* (SPPY ed.) 75:26b–27a; and *A Sung Bibliography*, ed. Yves Hervouet (Hong Kong, 1978), p. 50.

11. A work titled *Liu-chia Chung yung ta hsüeh chieh-i* (六家中庸大學解義) by Ssu-ma Kuang et al., is listed in *Sung shih* 202, p. 5050. No such title is found in the *Ssu-k'u t'i-yao*, and it seems not to be extant. It may simply have reprinted Ssu-ma Kuang's essay "On Centrality and Harmony" along with similar short works by five others. See *Wen-kuo Wen-cheng Ssu-ma kung wen-chi* (Ssu-ma Kuang's Collected Prose) (SPTK ed.) 71:13a–15b. In that essay he comments, "This centrality and harmony are a single thing. In nourishing it, it is central; in applying it, it is harmonious. Thus [the text] says, 'Centrality is the great foundation of the world, and harmony its universal path.'" He then links this passage to others in the Confucian tradition dealing with the cultivation of the mind, his sources including the *Book of Documents, Analects, Mencius,* and others. From Su Shih's point of view, the opinions expressed are unexceptionable. The interpretation of the relation between centrality and harmony set forth in the opening passage of the *Chung yung* was of greater interest to Ch'eng I, and developed into a major theoretical problem for Chu Hsi. See Mou Tsung-san, *Hsin-t'i yü hsing-t'i* (The Substance of Mind and the Substance of Human Nature), 3 vols. (Taipei, 1968), 2:350–384, 3:42–447. For Ssu-ma Kuang, as for Su Shih, the passages posed few difficulties, further evidence of their remoteness from the concerns of Ch'eng and Chu.

12. See the comments of W. T. Chan on the attraction of Taoists and Buddhists to the *Chung yung* in *A Source Book*, pp. 95–96. On Ch'i-sung's commentary, see Jan Yun-hua's article in Hervouet, ed., *A Sung Bibliography*, p. 386.

13. In this paper, *Collected Prose* is cited for the *Chung yung lun*. Edited and annotated by Lang Yeh, this work was presented to the throne in 1173, and carries a preface by Emperor Hsiao-tung (r. 1162–1189). Imperial sponsorship was part of the Southern Sung policy of claiming the cultural heritage of the Northern Sung, and reversing the cultural policies of Ts'ai Ching and Emperor Hui-tsung. The late Northern Sung proscription on Su Shih's works was thus lifted and replaced by special imperial honors. Honoring Su Shih may also be taken as an indication that the Ch'eng-Chu school had not yet achieved a dominant position at court. The examination portfolio is found in *Collected Prose* in chapter 4–8 and 15–19. In other editions, the examination porfolio is gathered together under the title *Ying-chao chi* (應詔集), as in the *Tung-p'o ch'üan-chi* (SPPY ed.), and the *Su Tung-p'o chi* (Basic Sinological Series). Comparing the *Tung-p'o ch'üan-chi* (hereafter TPCC) and *Collected Prose*, there are minor textual variants in *Chung yung lun*, which are noted below. For a discussion of the various editions of Su Shih's collected works, see George Hatch, "*Tung-p'o ch'i-chi*" in Hervouet, *A Sung Bibliography*, pp. 396–398.

14. *Collected Prose* 6, p. 83. Cf. *Analects* 8:9: "The Master said, 'The common people

can be made to follow a path but not to understand it.'" Trans. D. C. Lau, *The Analects*
(Harmondsworth, 1979), p. 93.

15. *Collected Prose* 6, p. 84.

16. Ssu-ma Ch'ien, *Shih chi* (Peking, 1959) 74, p. 2343.

17. *Collected Prose* 6, p. 84.

18. Trans. Chan, *A Source Book*, p. 100. In all translations from the *Chung yung* I have consulted Chan, but occasionally emended to fit Su Shih's interpretation, or the immediate context.

19. *Collected Prose* 6, pp. 84–85. The allusion in the second sentence of this passage is to *Mencius* 2A:6: "The feeling of commiseration is enough for humanity; the feeling of shame and dislike is enough for rightness...."

20. Chu Hsi, *Chu Tzu ta-ch'üan*, "Chung yung chang-chü hsu," 76:22a–b provides a succinct summary. Mencius is seen as the direct heir of Tzu-ssu, and there is a long hiatus broken by the emergence of the Ch'eng brothers, who are the heirs of Mencius. This concept was derived from Ch'eng I, who called his brother the first to represent the authentic Way after Mencius. See his *I-ch'uan wen-chi* (伊川文集) in the *Erh-Ch'eng ch'üan-shu* (The Complete Works of the Two Ch'eng Brothers) (*SPPY* ed.) 7:1a–7b. Cited by W. T. Chan, *Reflections on Things at Hand* (New York, 1967), p. xxx. Ch'eng I in turn derived it from Han Yü. See Fung Yu-lan, *A History of Chinese Philosophy*, trans. Derk Bodde, 2 vols. (Princeton, 1952, 1953), 2:409–410.

21. *Collected Prose* 4, p. 50.

22. Tu Wei-ming, *Centrality and Commonality: An Essay on Chung-yung* (Honolulu, 1976), pp. 52–99. I am also indebted to Professor Tu for suggesting in a conversation several years ago that Su Shih's emphasis on feelings would be an interesting subject for study.

23. Tu provides a useful discussion of the term *ch'eng* in ibid., pp. 106–109, and chapter 4, "The Moral Metaphysics," *passim*. In the view of the frequent English translation of *ch'eng* as "sincerity," it is particularly important to take note that *ch'eng* is not simply a personal virtue or principle of psychological balance; rather it is conceived as the ground of a moral order shared by both heaven and man, and therefore leads both to self-realization, and to identification with heaven, and in fact implies transcending this duality. Consider *Chung yung* 22: "Only those who are absolutely sincere (*ch'eng*) can fully develop their nature. If they can fully develop their nature, they can fully develop the nature of others. If they can fully develop the nature of others, they can then fully develop the nature of things. If they can fully develop the nature of things, they can then assist in the transforming and nourishing process of Heaven and Earth, they can thus form a trinity with Heaven and Earth." Tr. Chan, *A Source Book*, p. 108.

24. See Chu Hsi, *Chung yung chang-chü* (rpt. Taipei n.d.), introductory notes and *passim*.

25. Modern textual criticism must deal with attribution of the text to Tzu-ssu, or any single author, with the question of its date, and with the authenticity of the quotations from Confucius, but Su Shih accepted traditional views on all these problems, so they did not influence his reading of the text.

26. *Chung yung* is translated "centrality and its practice" here because I believe Su Shih probably accepted Cheng Hsuan's (A.D. 127–200) gloss: "The *Chung yung* records the practical application of centrality and harmony. *Yung* (庸) is practice (*yung* 用)." Quoted in

Chu Pin, *Li-chi hsün-tsuan* (Collected Glosses to the *Li-chi*) (*SPPY* ed.) 31 : 1a. Translating the term from the Neo-Confucian point of view, I would prefer "centrality and commonality," following Tu, *Centrality and Commonality*, pp. 20–21.

27. *Collected Prose* 4, p. 50. *Chung yung* 21, translation emended from Chan, *A Source Book*, p. 107.

28. See *Chung yung* 1, 12, and 27.

29. *Analects* 6 : 18, tr. Chan, *A Source Book*, p. 30.

30. *TPCC* reads *shen* (慎) for *chin* (謹).

31. *Chung yung* 12, tr. Chan, *A Source Book*, p. 100. On liking and disliking, see *Analects* 4 : 6, and *Mencius* 1B : 5, 5A : 1, and 7A : 8.

32. *TPCC* substitutes the name of another music teacher, Shih Hsiang (師襄). The visit to Chou is described in *K'ung Tzu chia-yü* (Stories from the School of Confucius), "Kuan Chou" (*SPPY* ed.), 3 : 1b.

33. *Analects* 7 : 16.

34. *K'ung Tzu chia-yü*, "Tsai o," 5 : 5b–6b.

35. *Collected Prose* 4, pp. 50–51.

36. George C. Hatch, "Su Hsün," in Franke, *Sung Biographies*, pp. 885–900. See also his doctoral dissertation, "The Thought of Su Hsün (1009–1066): An Essay in the Social Meaning of Intellectual Pluralism in Northern Sung" (Seattle: University of Washington, 1972) for an extended analysis of Su Hsün's thought.

37. *Collected Prose* 4, p. 52.

38. *Chung yung* 20, tr. Chan, *A Source Book*, p. 107.

39. Trans. Chan, *A Source Book*, pp. 547–548. The *locus classicus* for Yen Yüan being praised for loving learning is *Analects* 6 : 2. The original text of Ch'eng's essay is in *Erh Ch'eng ch'üan-shu* (*SPPY* ed.), "I-ch'uan wen-chi" 4 : 1a–2a. I am indebted to Peter Bol for pointing out its importance in this context.

40. Trans. Chan, *A Source Book*, p. 550.

41. There are allusions here to two passages in *Chuang Tzu*. In chap. 18, "Perfect Happiness": "Chuang Tzu's wife died. When Hui Tzu went to convey his condolences, he found Chuang Tzu sitting with his legs sprawled out, pounding on a tub and singing." Trans. Burton Watson, *The Complete Works of Chuang Tzu* (New York, 1968), pp. 191–192. In chap. 21, "The Old Fisherman": Tzu-lu says, ". . . now this old fisherman, pole in hand, presents himself in front of you, and you double up at the waist, as bent as a chiming stone, and bow every time you reply to his words—this is going too far, isn't it?" Trans. Watson, *Chuang Tzu*, p. 351. The old fisherman had just been sharply criticizing rigidity in following ritual.

42. *TPCC* reads *rang* (讓) for *hsün* (遜).

43. There were, of course, famous models in Chinese history for calculated eccentricity and disregard for convention. Su may have been thinking of the Chin period figure Kuang I and his friends, for example. See *Chin shu* (Peking, 1974), 49, p. 1385: "To avoid disorder he crossed the Yangtze River, and again depended on Fu-chih. When he first arrived Fu-chih together with Hsieh K'un, Juan Fang, Pi Cho, Yang Man, Heng I, and Juan Fu, with hair let down and naked, had been locked in a room half-drunk for several days. [Kuang] I knocked at the door seeking entry, but the doorkeeper paid no attention, so [Kuang] I immediately

took his clothes off outside the door, stuck his head through a dog's burrow, and spying them, called out loudly. Surprised, Fu-chih said, 'No one else could do that; it must be my friend Meng-tsu [i.e. Kuang I].' He quickly called for him to come in, and then they drank together day and night without stopping."

44. *Collected Prose* 4, pp. 52–53.

45. *Chung yung* 12, trans. Chan, *A Source Book*, p. 100.

46. *Mencius* 6A:10, trans. D. C. Lau (Harmondsworth, 1970), p. 166.

47. *Collected Prose* 4, p. 53.

48. Chu Hsi, *Chung yung chang-chü*, pp. 7–8, commentary on ch. 12.

49. *Chung yung* 1, trans. emended from Chan, *A Source Book*, p. 98. See also Tu, *Centrality and Commonality*, pp. 1–7 on this chapter.

50. *Chung yung* 11, trans. Chan, *A Source Book*, p. 100.

51. TPCC reads *yeh* (耶) for *yeh* (邪).

52. *Chung yung* 4, trans. Chan, *A Source Book*, p. 99.

53. *Chung yung* 9, trans. Chan, *A Source Book*, p. 99.

54. *TPCC* drops the particle *chih* (之).

55. *Mencius* 7A:26, trans. Lau, p. 188.

56. *Book of Documents*, "Hung Fan," trans. James Legge, *The Chinese Classics*, 5 vols. (Oxford, 1890s; rpt. Hong Kong, 1960), 3:329.

57. Ibid.

58. *Chung yung* 2; trans. Chan, *A Source Book*, p. 99.

59. *TPCC* drops *ku* (故).

60. *Chung yung* 2; trans. Chan, *A Source Book*, p. 99. *Collected Prose* 4, p. 54.

61. *Mencius* 7B:37; trans. Lau, p. 203. This is part of a discussion between Wan Tzu and Mencius on *Analects* 17:13: "The Master said, 'The good villager is the thief of virtue.'" Su Shih has excerpted and rearranged the passage from Mencius.

62. *Mencius* 7B:37; see also, *Analects* 17:18: "The Master said, 'I dislike purple for displacing vermillion. I detest the tunes of Cheng for corrupting classical music. I detest clever talkers who overturn states and noble families." Trans. Lau, *Analects*, p. 146.

63. *Chung yung* 4; trans. Chan, *A Source Book*, p. 99. *Collected Prose* 4, pp. 54–55.

64. *Collected Prose* 48, p. 807.

65. *Collected Prose* 1, p. 4; trans. Burton Watson, *Su Tung-p'o: Selections from a Sung Dynasty Poet* (New York, 1965), p. 90.

66. *Collected Prose* 1, p. 5; trans. Watson, *Su Tung-p'o.* p. 92.

Chiang K'uei's Treatises on Poetry and Calligraphy

By Shuen-fu Lin

Kuo Shao-yü regards the Southern Sung period as a great divide in the history of Chinese literary criticism. He observes that, prior to the Southern Sung, emphasis was put on the theorizing of the nature, and the clarification of general concepts, of literature, while the critical treatment of literary works itself occupied only a place of secondary importance. This situation was reversed during the period from the Southern Sung to the late Ch'ing. Along with the interesting shift of focus, the expression of ideas tended to be more systematic also.[1] In general, Kuo Shao-yü's brief observations are perceptive and helpful; they are perhaps applicable to other areas of aesthetics as well. Here I do not intend to examine or to expand upon them in terms of the entire field of Chinese aesthetics. I want simply to study the development of a comparatively more "objective, systematic, and pragmatic" approach to the arts by focusing on the treatises on poetry and calligraphy written by the poet-recluse, composer, and critic Chiang K'uei (ca. 1155–ca. 1221) whose work and career exemplified the aesthetic convictions and aspirations of his age.[2] We know that traditional Chinese critics, with very few exceptions, usually preferred the intuitive, impressionistic, and unsystematic approach to the arts that had relied on a fusion, rather than a dichotomy, of subject and object. In the light of this prevailing trend, the new development that gradually came to fruition in the late Sung must be considered important.

CHIANG K'UEI'S TREATISES ON POETRY

Despite his vast learning as a scholar and the variety of his talent as an artist, Chiang K'uei is not a prolific writer. His poetry criticism consists of merely two brief prefaces to the collection of his *shih* poetry and *Shih shuo*[a] (A Discourse on Poetry), totaling some half a dozen pages in the Chinese original.[3] Yet meager as they may appear, these three treatises must be ranked among the most important documents in the history of Sung poetics. From these few pages one can obtain a clear sense of the state of *shih* poetry in the late Sung, of Chiang K'uei's own aesthetic ideals, and of the development of literary criticism at this time. I shall devote my attention chiefly to Chiang K'uei's critical theory and practice in their historical context.

[a] 詩說

According to Hsia Ch'eng-t'ao's research, Chiang K'uei's critical and scholarly works were probably all done during the decade after he took residence in Hang-chow in 1196.[4] His collected *shih* poetry was printed around 1204, so the two prefaces must have been written around this date. In his preface to "A Discourse on Poetry," he related that he had received the treatise from a Taoist immortal on a visit to the Southern Mountain (Mt. Heng in modern Hunan Province) in the year 1186. This story is obviously fictitious—Chiang K'uei may have been imitating the manner in which the Five Dynasties painter Ching Hao presented his famous *Pi-fa chi*.[5] Considering the crisscrossing of ideas and purposes, the prefaces to his poetry collection and the "Discourse" probably date from the same period in Chiang K'uei's career. Moreover, the "Discourse" must represent the essence of several decades of experience in studying and writing poetry.

There are two seemingly incongruous principal ideas running through Chiang K'uei's entire poetry criticism. One is that great poetry must be spontaneous and natural, completely free from any self-conscious efforts. The other is that a true poet must attend to self-cultivation and to learning the methods and skill in poetry. The incongruity between the two is only apparent and not real because in his poetics the former is an ideal to be attained through meticulous cultivation advocated in the latter. The ideal is in keeping with the mainstream of traditional Chinese literary theory which views great poetry as the supreme, spontaneous expression of man's feeling and spirit.[6] The rigorous process of cultivation is more typical of Sung, and especially of late Sung, temperament. Although Chiang K'uei's contribution to Chinese literary criticism lies mainly in this latter aspect, I shall first take a look at the relationship in his theory between the traditional ideal of spontaneity and the mastery of the technical aspect.

The first preface to his collected *shih* poetry begins with the following statement:

> Poetry was originally without styles; the three hundred pieces in the *Shih ching* (Odes) were all spontaneous sounding of the flutes of heaven. When it came down to the reign period of the "Yellow Beginning" (A.D. 220–226) and down to the present day, poets have different natural endowments, so what they have produced has also been different. As a result, some people who are not discerning have regarded it captivating that the poetry of each poet has its own style.[7]

The word I have translated as "style" is *t'i*[b] which carries the basic meaning of "body," "form," "substance," and "style." Chiang K'uei is not trying to dispense with form and style in poetry entirely here. Rather, his purpose is to set forth at the outset a concept of poetry at the ideal level of creative spontaneity as a corrective

b 體

of contemporary more mechanistic theory which emphasizes imitation of previous models. Chiang K'uei lived at the time when the influence of the Chiang-hsi school of poetry, which stresses derivation from past masters, was still being strongly felt.[8] He admits in the subsequent passages that he himself tried to imitate Huang T'ing-chien (1045–1105), founder of the Chiang-hsi school, until all of his creativity was stifled.[9] He then became "enlightened to the fact that imitation is a fault and that one will achieve more if he does not imitate any previous master."[10] It is indicated that the greatest of his senior contemporary poets, Yang Wan-li (1124–1206), Lu Yu (1125–1210), Fan Ch'eng-ta (1126–1193), Yu Mao (1127–1194), and Hsiao Te-tsao (fl. late twelfth century), were all in agreement with him on the need to try to evolve one's own poetry.[11] Chiang K'uei attacks, then, not poetic styles but a mechanistic conception of poetry.

The phrase the "spontaneous sounding of the flutes of heaven" contains an allusion to the chapter *Ch'i-wu lun*[c] (The Equality of Things) in the *Chuang Tzu*. In the story about Nan-kuo Tzu-ch'i, three kinds of flutes are mentioned: flutes of earth, of men, and of heaven.[12] The flutes of earth refer to the sound produced by the various hollows found on earth; the flutes of men refer to the sound produced by man-made instruments like pipes and flutes. Of the flutes of heaven, Nan-kuo Tzu-ch'i says, "Blowing on the ten thousand things in a different way, so that each can be itself—all take what they want for themselves, but who does the sounding?" As Burton Watson has observed, the flutes of heaven do not refer to something distinct from the other two types of flute but to their natural and spontaneous functioning.[13] In light of this allusion, it is clear that Chiang K'uei uses the *Odes* to illustrate the spontaneous functioning of the poetic psyche. The songs in this anthology are great not because they are primitive, simple, and natural but because their art is so supreme that they actually transcend all perceptible forms. The following remark in the "Discourse" clearly supports this argument: "All the three hundred songs in the *Odes* leave no trace in their praise, satire, admonition, and grievance. One should meet the hearts of their authors with one's own heart."[14] Chiang K'uei may very well have the *Odes* in mind when he talks about poetry of the highest order elsewhere in the "Discourse":

> When a poem is neither marvelous nor strange, stripped of all verbal ornamentation, and is something which one knows to be superb without realizing why, this is called the high subtlety of spontaneity.[15]

Since Chiang K'uei, like many Chinese critics, idealizes the past as a source of authority and inspiration, it is natural that emulating the ancients becomes an important issue in his poetics. The following passage from the second preface to his collected poetry deals with this problem:

[c] 齊物論

> In writing poetry, to seek to be in harmony with the ancients is not as good as to seek to be different from them. To seek to be different from the ancients is not as good as to be unable not to harmonize with and not to differ from them without actually seeking to do so. Because one sees poetry, he who formerly sought to be in harmony with the ancients will now seek to be different from them. When the time comes that he does not see poetry any more, he will reach the state in which he is unable not to harmonize with and not to differ from the ancients without seeking to do so. For him poetry will come like the wind, will stop like the rain, will be like a seal that stamps on the ink clay, or will be like water that fills a vessel. Is this what Su Shih (1037–1101) called "unable not to write?"[16]

The central point here is still creative spontaneity. Unlike the first preface, however, a poet's individual creativity is now brought into dynamic relation with his tradition. When a poet has reached this level of achievement, whatever he writes will not only be entirely his own but also in total harmony with the quality of the ancients. For him writing poetry will be an inevitable and spontaneous act within an appropriate framework. Chiang K'uei takes as an example Su Shih who has said that his writing "always goes wherever it should go and rests wherever it is unable not to rest."[17] The reference to Su Shih is informative, as he represents the Sung ideal of a great literati artist whose natural talent has been well tempered by traditional norms. By putting emphasis on cultivating spontaneity of the individual talent within certain norms, Chiang K'uei's critical theory is actually quite dynamic. By contrast, for instance, the important thirteenth-century critical text *Ts'ang-lang shih-hua* is more rigid in its theory about modeling upon the ancients.[18]

It is interesting that when a poet reaches the state of spontaneity, he is described as someone who "does not see poetry any more." Underlying this statement is an allusion to that famous story about Butcher Ting in the *Chuang Tzu* who is able to cut up oxen without looking at them.[19] The reason Butcher Ting is able to reach such heights in his skill is that what he cares about is *tao*, the Way, that goes beyond sheer skill. But *tao* is to be sought in the practice of the skill, the experience itself of cutting up oxen. Hsü Fu-kuan is correct in saying that the Butcher Ting story illustrates two key ideas in Chuang Tzu's philosophy: first, the dissolving of the dichotomy between self and object; second, the concept of *tao* essentially designates a kind of aesthetic spirit that is absolutely free.[20] It should be clear from the preceding discussion that both of these ideas underpin Chiang K'uei's theory of great poetry and of the ideal poet.

Not to be ignored is that Butcher Ting's fantastic skill presupposes a complete and thorough knowledge of his object, the ox. This knowledge is not of a scientific kind that entails meticulous dissection and analysis, but of an aesthetic kind, to be obtained by an intuitive grasp of the inner workings of the whole object as it is. Butcher Ting's thorough knowledge of the ox is prerequisite to his empathetic identification with the object. Without this knowledge, he would never be able to go beyond skill and enter the realm of *tao* which, paradoxically, being absolutely free, transcends all knowledge. In the same manner, the poet has to go through this necessary prior stage of "seeing poetry" before he arrives at the ultimate goal of spontaneity.

It is precisely in order to provide the aspiring poet with a more accessible path for reaching this goal that Chiang K'uei wrote the "Discourse," as he says in the very last statement of the treatise:

> This treatise on poetry is not written for those who are able to write poetry but is written for those who are not yet able in order to make them able to write poetry. Since only when one is able to write poetry can he exhaust my theories, it is also written for those who are able to write poetry already. However, if one regards my discourse as exhaustive and will not reach a level of attainment through self-effort, can he be sufficiently called a person capable of writing poetry? Among the worthies to come, will there be some who can still discern the flavors after one kind of water is poured into another, or forget about the trap once the rabbit is caught? Alas! will people in the future not heavily blame me too [for having written this discourse]?[21]

The cautious and circuitous tone this passage has to do with the fact that Chiang K'uei does not want his reader to take his treatise to be a mechanical "how-to-do-it" manual and ignore his higher ideal of reaching psychic spontaneity through self-effort. The remark about someone "who can discern the flavors after one kind of water is poured into another" alludes to an anecdote in the *Shuo-fu*[d] chapter of the *Lieh Tzu* in which I-ya is said to have this unusual ability.[22] This allusion is used to caution the reader to find out for himself the true meaning of the "Discourse." The remark that follows this allusion is drawn from the concluding statement in the chapter *Wai-wu*[e] (External Things) in the *Chuang Tzu* in which the author advises the reader to forget the words once their meaning are understood in the same manner as one can cast aside the trap and the snare when the fish and the rabbit are caught.[23] The "Discourse" provides, as do the fish trap and the rabbit snare, a convenient means to an end. But to become a great artist one cannot rely on a technical manual. By alluding to the two Taoist texts, Chiang K'uei hopes that an aspiring poet can grasp the meaning of his theory and then cast the "Discourse" aside in order to reach a higher region of attainment.

Having reviewed the more general aspects of Chiang K'uei's poetics, we can now examine in greater detail the "Discourse," his major contribution to Chinese poetry criticism. The "Discourse" grows out of an already long tradition of poetic

d 說符   e 外物

treatises, especially the late T'ang treatises which are diversely named *shih-ko*,[f] *shih-li*,[g] *shih-chüeh*,[h] and so on, and the vast number of the new critical genre of the Sung period, the *shih-hua*. It consists of a long preface and thirty separate statements of varying lengths. Despite its somewhat fragmented character it surpasses all previous treatises of the T'ang and Sung periods as a serious, lucid, and relatively comprehensive treatment of the art of writing poetry. Unlike most surviving T'ang treatises, Chiang K'uei's "Discourse" does not indulge in the use of exalted, impressionistic, and highly metaphorical language or in presenting a profusion of categories of "parallelisms," of "poetic ideas," of "poetic forces," etc., which tend to dazzle more than instruct the reader. Nor does it resemble the casual, amateur manner of previous Sung works in the *shih-hua*[i] format that randomly record anecdotes about poets together with the authors' own thoughts on the art of poetry. Chiang K'uei's "Discourse" is the most important Southern Sung treatise on poetry before the appearance of the more monumental works of the thirteenth century such as Yen Yü's *Ts'ang-lang shih-hua* and Chang Yen's *Tz'u yüan*. The achievement of the "Discourse" is due, in part, to the growing sophistication of the *shih-hua* genre and to the increasing professionalism of the poet–critic. More important, it also reflects the increasing objective tone that has prevailed in late Sung culture, especially since the late twelfth century.[24]

I have mentioned that, traditionally, poetry had been regarded as the supreme expression of man's feeling and spirit. Because of the dominance of this theory, traditional Chinese critics are in the habit of seeing the attributes of a poem as extensions of the author's personality. As Maureen Robertson has pointed out, during the T'ang period, however, many critics began to talk about poetry "in terms of its artistic components and its intrinsic aesthetic appeals, without mentioning specific poets at all."[25] Indeed, as in Ssu-k'ung T'u's *Erh-shih-ssu shih-p'in* (Twenty-four Modes of Poetry), "styles began to be distinguished for the first time as objective phenomena, not primarily as extensions of individual personalities."[26] Nevertheless, at this early stage of Chinese literary criticism, a clear notion of a poem as an organic entity is lacking and poetry is not yet observed with objective detachment. Thus Ssu-k'ung T'u's exposition is poetic rather than analytic, and the late T'ang manuals that discuss artistic components of style often indulge in arbitrary distinctions of patterns with no sense of overall structure. The subsequent Sung critics on poetry and prose make a significant advance in this respect. Frequently one can see in the *shih-hua* and in discussion of prose the attempt to approach the text as an entity in itself from a structural point of view. Chiang K'uei's well-rounded definition of poetry as an objective entity, to which we will now turn, represents the maturation of centuries of a new development.

[f] 詩格

[g] 詩例

[h] 詩訣

[i] 詩話

The "Discourse" begins with the following statement:

> In general, a poem has its aura, form and appearance, blood vessels, and resonance and deportment. One must make the aura expansive but one can lose in being vulgar. One must make the form and appearance vast but one can lose in being unrestrained. One must make the blood vessels penetrating but one can lose in being obvious. One must make the resonance and deportment untrammeled but one can lose in being frivolous.[27]

The definition of a poem in terms of the four vital things of "aura" (*ch'i-hsiang*[j]), "form and appearance" (*t'i-mien*[k]), "blood vessels" (*hsüeh-mo*[l]), and "resonance and deportment" (*yün-tu*[m]) is reminiscent of a definition of an essay given by the Northern Sung prose writer Li Chien of the late eleventh and early twelfth centuries. Li Chien says, "A piece of prose cannot be found lacking in any of these four things: "form" (*t'i*), "intent" (*chih*[n]), "material force" (*ch'i*[o]), and "resonance" (*yün*[p]).[28] The near identity of these two sets of terms suggests a strong debt Chiang K'uei might have owed to the earlier writer. However, the disparity in two key terms, namely *ch'i-hsiang* and *chih*, leads to an important difference between their conceptions with regards to the literary work.

In his explanation of the four vital components of prose, Li Chien has relied heavily on the metaphor of the human body. He compares a piece of prose that does not have a "form" to a man without ears, eyes, a mouth, and a nose; that does not have "intent" to a man who has these organs without knowing their function; that does not have "material force" to a man who knows the functions of these organs but lacks the vital spirit that must run through them; and that does not have "resonance" to a vulgar man who, though complete, alive, and strong, lacks personal grace.[29] We know that it has been the habit of Chinese critics long before the Sung to view literature as living organisms. In fact, Ch'ien Chung-shu has argued that organicism (or "animism" as he calls it) is one characteristic in which Chinese literary criticism differs from that of the West.[30] Terms like *ch'i*, *ku*[q] (bone), *li*[r] (strength), *shen*[s] (spirit), *mo*[t] (veins), *sui*[u] (marrow), *wen-hsin*[v] (the heart of writing), and *chü-yen*[w] (the eye of a line) are, indeed, legion in early critical writings. But they usually appear more or less in isolated contexts. More important, frequently some of these terms are used simultaneously to refer to both the writer's personality and his work. It is remarkable that Li Chien has presented an organic

j 氣象
k 體面
l 血脉
m 韻度
n 志

o 氣
p 韻
q 骨
r 力
s 神

t 脉
u 髓
v 文心
w 句眼

definition that is at once simple and comprehensive. Here I shall examine his concept of *chih* in particular, since his other three concepts are similar to those used by Chiang K'uei.

In Li Chien's usage, *chih* refers to the author's intellectual and moral discernment which enables him to determine what is right or wrong, what to take or to abandon, to follow the Way of the sages, and to depart from vulgar customs.[31] Defined as such, *chih*, then, refers to what James J. Y. Liu has called "mind's intent" or "moral purpose"[32] of the author that serves as the regulating or guiding force at the time when a piece of prose is being written. In Li Chien's theory, *chih* appears to be an *external* element that "knows" (or "does not know") and regulates the functions of the vital organs of a piece of prose. Consequently, the writing itself, though metaphorically conceived as living organism, still remains an extension of the personality and character of the author. Li Chien has come very close to defining the literary text as an objective entity, but his adherence to the traditional theory regarding literature as extension of man's personality has prevented him from achieving the new view.

Chiang K'uei also relies on the metaphor of the human organism, but he does so by stressing the observable aspects of man. This can be seen in the three terms that correspond to Li Chien's theory. By adding *mien* (face, appearance) to *t'i* (body, form), and *tu* (measure) to *yün* (resonance), Chiang K'uei has indeed made these two constituents more readily perceptible. Similarly, the use of *hsüeh-mo* (blood vessels) instead of the more elusive *ch'i* (ether, breath of life, matter energy) makes a significant difference in perceptibility. Metaphorically, *t'i-mien* refers to the framework or overall structure of a poem, *hsüeh-mo* to the force that maintains its inner harmony and vitality, and *yün-tu* to the rhythm and grace that it carries. What, then, is *ch'i-hsiang* which I have rendered "aura"?

The compound term *ch'i-hsiang* is not often found in critical writings prior to the Sung period. Separately, of course, they do occur frequently in early Chinese criticism. This is especially true of the word *ch'i*, one of the most important concepts in Chinese philosophy and aesthetics. In an excellent article, David Pollard has provided the following concise description of its basic meanings:

> In Chinese cosmology, *ch'i* is what the world is made of, the "vapor" out of which sensible things condense, primordial matter-energy. In relation to human beings it is the "breath" we breathe out, which, when linked with "blood" stands for physical vitality (*hsüeh-ch'i*[x]), when linked with "endowment" gives the sense of inherited constitution (*ch'i-ping*[y]).[33]

When this *ch'i* is made manifest in nature, literature, customs, or an individual, it is perceived as "atmosphere," "climate," "manner," or "style."[34] *Hsiang* means

---

[x] 血氣   [y] 氣稟

a resemblance, a representation, an outward sign, or an image of a phenomenon, event, idea, or underlying principle. *Hsiang* constitutes one essential part of the *Book of Changes*, referring to the representations of all phenomena in the world. In poetry treatises, *hsiang* usually denotes the image, the part that provokes in the reader a mental picture. For instance, Ssu-k'ung T'u uses the word in his "Twenty-four Modes of Poetry" several times to mean the image, the observable part of a poem, beyond which a poet can convey what is otherwise inexpressible.[35]

The few occurrences of *ch'i* and *hsiang* used as a compound in pre-Sung texts that I have come across all seem to refer to either simply "climate" or, by the natural analogy, to "atmosphere" in literature. For example, Kūkai speaks of the "sceneries of dusk and dawn, and the [changing] climates of the four seasons,"[36] and Chiao-jan says "that [the fact] the atmosphere is all embracing and harmonious (*ch'i-hsiang yin-yün*[z]) is a result of a profound understanding of form."[37] In the *Shan-shui lun* traditionally attributed to Wang Wei (701–761), in the statement "the viewer must first look at its vital image and then distinguish whether it is clear or murky," the term *ch'i-hsiang* is restricted to representation of the natural phenomenon.[38]

Northern Sung writers began to give *ch'i-hsiang* a more variegated significance. Jen Tan says of Yen Shu (991–1055) that, when he writes about wealth, he does not mention gold, jade, or embroidery, but only presents a general aura of it.[39] In a letter to a nephew, Su Shih says, "In writing, when young, one must make the manner lofty and steep (*ch'i-hsiang cheng-jung*[aa]); when one becomes old and more skillful, he then can create blandness (*p'ing-tan*[ab])."[40] In a letter to a friend, Huang T'ing-chien comments that using unusual expressions will make the writing's manner weary and decrepit.[41] In these instances, *ch'i-hsiang* is indeed used almost in the same way as in Southern Sung texts to mean "aura" or "outward manifestation." But on the whole, its use as a critical concept is rather limited and incidental. Writers continue to use the word *ch'i* by itself as the main concept to describe the vitality of an author's personality.

In the Southern Sung, however, *ch'i-hsiang* emerges as an important concept in the writings of at least several major critics such as Chu Hsi (1130–1200), Chiang K'uei, and Yen Yü. In the *Ts'ang-lang shih-hua*, Yen Yü frequently uses it in his evaluation of *shih* poetry of the various periods from the late Han to the Sung Dynasty.[42] The reason for the curious rise of the term is probably related to the development of the rationalistic wing of Neo-Confucianism. Can it be sheer coincidence that Ch'eng I (1033–1107), who inaugurated this dominant trend in Neo-Confucian thought, started to use it as a key concept, though not for the purpose of literary criticism?

Ch'i-hsiang is used by Ch'eng I in the context of observing and investigating the characters and constitutions of the sages and the worthies. He says, "Wherever one

z 氣象氳氲　　　　　　aa 氣象崢嶸　　　　　　ab 平淡

reads the *Analects of Confucius*, apart from trying to understand the words, one must recognize the *ch'i-hsiang* of the sages and worthies."[43] Again he uses the term in his discussions of the passages in the *Analects* in which Confucius and a few disciples are engaged in the "expressions of one's wishes" (*yen chih*[ac]).[44] The "expression of one's wishes" is a pedagogical technique that Confucius often used to observe his disciples' characters, inherited constitutions, and personal and intellectual capacity for action. To recognize the *ch'i-hsiang* of a sage or a worthy is to recognize the outward manifestation of his personality. Confucius is said to carry the aura of heaven-and-earth.[45] Thus *ch'i-hsiang* becomes more than just the manner: it is the total manifestation, or the vital presence, of the sage's entire being, that can be actualized in an expression. To experience such an aura of a sage can help a student emulate him. The observation of a sage's *ch'i-hsiang*, therefore, provides the rationalistic thinker one more empirical approach than introspection alone to the problems of knowledge and self-cultivation.

Chu Hsi, the great Southern Sung thinker and follower of Ch'eng I's orientation of thought, extends the term *ch'i-hsiang* to a wider range of application. He uses it in his evaluation of historical and contemporary personalities, in his discussion of cannonical texts, as well as in his criticism of poetry, prose, and the other arts. The occurrences of *ch'i-hsiang* in the *Chu Tzu yü-lei* (Classified Conversations of Master Chu) are indeed numerous. There can be no doubt that the observation of *ch'i-hsiang* constitutes an essential part in Chu Hsi's epistemological method that stresses the observation of things. It must be pointed out that he is more concerned with the moral cultivation of a writer. So even though he is quite competent in analyzing verbal structure and techniques, he seldom talks about *ch'i-hsiang* in complete isolation from the personality of an author.

Returning now to Chiang K'uei's "Discourse," it is clear that his pragmatic approach and his conception of poetry are in keeping with Ch'eng I's and Chu Hsi's insistence on the observation of things as the basis of knowledge and self-cultivation. A poem is conceived by him as an organic entity that can be directly observed in detachment, no longer simply an extension of its author's personality. Further, *ch'i-hsiang* is not just an outward manifestation, a realization in words, of a man's inherited constitution, virtue, or vitality. It is something that an author can actually "make" to appear "expansive" or "vulgar." This view contrasts sharply with Liu Hsieh's (sixth century) theory of *Yang ch'i*[ad] (Cultivating *ch'i*) which is, in fact, a method of holding back and releasing the *ch'i* within oneself, a method somewhat comparable to Taoist breath control.[46] It also contrasts with Su Ch'e's (1039–1112) belief that skill in writing cannot be learned, while *ch'i*, the vital spirit, can be acquired through cultivation which essentially entails visiting great sights and meeting great men.[47] Even when Su Shih says, "In writing, when young, one must

ac 誌   ad 養氣

make the manner lofty and steep; when one becomes old and more skillful, he then can create blandness," he is still not talking about composition in isolation from the vitality and personality of an author. This is not to say that Chiang K'uei ignores cultivation or that he does not think a poet's personality can ever affect his poetry. The following statements will illustrate his attitude:

> The suffocation or obstruction of one's thought is due to the imperfection of one's cultivation. One should remedy it with learning.

> The language of a poet has its particular flavor. This is like the twenty-four modes in music, each mode having its own rhyme and tone which are the basis of that mode. Although the language of an imitator can resemble that of a master, the resonance of the original will be lost.[48]

The awareness of cultivation and of individual talent and temperament has not prevented him from examining the skill in poetry. On the contrary, he believes that learning can remedy the imperfection of one's cultivation. Moreover, through learning, one can eventually achieve an even higher goal, as he says, "Calmness and alacrity (*ch'en-cho t'ung-k'uai*[ae]) are qualities of being natural. To be spontaneously natural and to have learned to be natural are the same as being natural."[49] By viewing a poem as an entity in itself which is then analyzed into four vital constituents, Chiang K'uei has provided a more tangible way of learning the poetic craft.

Most of the "Discourse" is devoted to discussions of the defects and methods of poetry. It touches on the practical matters such as overall structure, parallelism, allusion, exposition of ideas, narration of events, ornamentation, closure. The comments are always very specific and to the point. Even when Chiang K'uei is talking about those qualities which remain somewhat elusive in traditional criticism, his explanation is always lucid and directly relevant to the poem itself. An example will suffice to illustrate this point:

> There are four kinds of high subtlety in poetry. The first is the high subtlety of principle. The second is the high subtlety of idea. The third is the high subtlety of imagination. The fourth is the high subtlety of spontaneity. When a poem is seemingly obstructed but is in fact continuous, this is called the high subtlety of principle. To set forth an event which takes the reader by surprise is called the high subtlety of idea. To write out secrecy and delicacy, like showing the bottom of a transparent pool, is called the high subtlety of imagination. When a poem is neither marvelous nor strange, stripped of all verbal ornamentation, and is something which one knows to be superb without realizing why, this is called the high subtlety of spontaneity.[50]

[ae] 沉著痛快

May we not assume that Chiang K'uei's more objective attitude toward the poem enables him to concentrate on the practical aspects of composition and to write with such clarity and concreteness as found in the above passage? The four qualities described here can be read as four varieties of high subtlety in poetry. They can also be read as forming a sequence of four levels of increasing artistic depth and marvel. The order can be said to parallel that of progressing from "seeing poetry" to "not seeing poetry any more," discussed in a previous section. In the last analysis, Chiang K'uei's objective approach to poetry and his high ideal of effortless spontaneity are not contradictory but complementary.

CHIANG K'UEI'S *Hsü Shu-p'u*

In 1203 Chiang K'uei wrote his famous long colophon on the *Pao-mu chih* by Wang Hsien-chih (344–388), inscribed on a brick which was unearthed in the spring of 1202.[51] Chiang K'uei mentioned in the colophon that he had been studying and practicing calligraphy for thirty years.[52] Therefore, by the time he first began doing scholarly research in calligraphy in 1201, he had already had several decades of experience in the practice of the art.[53] Although he did not achieve a lasting fame as a great artist in the history of Chinese calligraphy, he was highly regarded as an accomplished calligrapher by late Sung and early Yüan writers.[54] It is important to know these facts before we examine his calligraphy treatises. For his achievement as a critic of calligraphy depends as much on his knowledge of the art's entire history as on his vast experience as a practicing artist.

All of his writings on calligraphy were done between the years of 1202 and 1209. They consist of a handful of colophons on a few copies of Wang Hsi-chih's (303?–361?) *Lan-t'ing hsü*, a colophon on *Pao-mu chih*, written in 1203, the *Chiang-t'ieh p'ing*, completed in 1203, of which six out of twenty chapters have survived, and the *Hsü Shu-p'u*.[55] The last work in this list, published in 1208, was one of the very last treatises on calligraphy he had written, and certainly represents the distilled essence of his reflections on the theory and practice of Chinese calligraphy. Because of its more general and theoretical nature, I have specifically chosen it for discussion of late Sung aesthetics.

The title *Hsü Shu-p'u* means "A Sequel to the *Shu-p'u*," the important text written by the early T'ang calligrapher Sun Kuo-t'ing (648?–703?). However, it is neither a supplement to, nor an exposition in simpler language of, what Sun Kuo-t'ing has said in the *Shu-p'u*, as some scholars have erroneously suggested.[56] With the purpose of providing calligraphy students with a standard guide, Sun Kuo-t'ing attempts to present a synthetic review of the development of the works of a few major figures, and of the subjective and objective conditions that concern the practicing calligrapher. It is in this sense of offering a new synthetic review of the art for aspiring artists of his time that Chiang K'uei's treatise is called a "sequel" or "succession" to the early T'ang text. In theoretical framework, in conception of the art, and in critical methodology, the *Hsü Shu-p'u* is actually quite different from the T'ang predecessor.

Commenting on the shortcomings of previous treatises on calligraphy, the major Northern Sung scholar and artist Mi Fu (1051–1107), whose critical works on calligraphy have greatly influenced Chiang K'uei, says in his *Hai-yüeh ming-yen*:

> Reading through the treatises on calligraphy by previous worthies, I find the evidences they provide preposterous and the comparisons they make bizarre and forced. What kind of expressions are the like of "a dragon leaps through the gate of heaven" or "a tiger reclines in the phoenix chamber"? Sometimes they try so hard to be clever in their choice of words that they have departed far from the methods. These are no help to the learner at all. Therefore, what I say is meant only to guide people into calligraphy and I will not use exalted language.[57]

These criticisms are no doubt exaggerated. Nonetheless, they do apply to a general tendency in pre-Sung texts. For all the profound insights and practical instructions it offers, Sun Kuo-t'ing's *Shu-p'u*, written in elaborate parallel prose, cannot avoid indulging in such verbal extravagances. Just as in poetry criticism, Sung writers generally adopt the already well-established, plainer *ku-wen* prose as a medium in their treatises. Along with the rise of *chin-shih hsüeh*,[af] the "study of metal and stone," and the practice of writing colophons, they also further advance the methodology in the study of calligraphy. Chiang K'uei's *Hsü Shu-p'u* clearly reflects these important developments in Sung scholarship.

The *Hsü Shu-p'u* excels previous calligraphy texts in at least three interconnected aspects: its systematic and comprehensive theoretical framework, its conception of the written word as an objective entity, and its remarkably rigorous techniques of structural analysis. Mi Fu must be given credit for his pioneer effort in analyzing details and for some of his general comments on the development of calligraphy which have influenced Chiang K'uei. I shall have more to say on this later. Suffice it to say here that Mi Fu's original contributions are presented in the fashion of random jottings resembling the practice of the *shih-hua* writers mentioned earlier. Let us now turn to examine each of the three aspects in greater detail.

The *Hsü Shu-p'u* is divided into twenty sections, two of which have only the headings and no descriptions. The first ten sections deal with broader issues, focusing on the three basic scripts—the regular (*chen*), the cursive (*ts'ao*), and the running (*hsing*), and the problems of using the brush and the ink relevant to them. Discussed also are the problems of writing with vermilion and of copying by tracing or in a

[af] 金石學

freehand manner. Section ten, entitled "Feeling and Temperament," consists of four long quotations from the *Shu-p'u*, which are concerned with a practicing calligrapher's cultivation and all the internal and external conditions that confront him at work. Significantly, this section complements the rest of the treatise which is oriented toward an analysis of calligraphy itself. The "General Comment" which begins the treatise discusses in concise structural terms the origins of the three basic scripts in the various early forms of writing, the seal (*chuan*), the *pa-fen*, the flying white (*fei-pai*), and the draft cursive (*chang-ts'ao*). He states that each of the three basic scripts has its own form and it is difficult for the calligrapher to master all of them. However, a good calligrapher must practice until he is familiar with different styles. Although the *Hsü Shu-p'u* is focused on the three basic styles from the Wei-Chin period onward, Chiang K'uei does not want the reader to ignore the early developments. Apart from being a preface to the entire work, this "General Comment" also adds a historical dimension. The last ten, or rather, eight, sections are devoted to analysis of specific structural principles or components of calligraphy: blood vessels, squareness and roundness, balance, configuration, spaciousness and denseness, prevailing spirit, slowness and briskness, and brush-tips. One remarkable feature of these detailed sections is that Chiang K'uei always related his structural analysis to the general prevailing spirit or rhythmic vitality of calligraphy. Thus the *Hsü Shu-p'u* is a systematic and comprehensive treatment of all the relevant aspects, both large and small, of the regular, the cursive, and the running styles of calligraphy. This systematic framework is further enhanced by a coherent sense of the history of calligraphy. Having been influenced by Mi Fu's predispositions, Chiang K'uei is very critical of the transformations T'ang calligraphers have brought forth and hopes to restore the "untrammeled spirit" (*p'iao-i-chih-ch'i*[ag]) of Wei-Chin masters.[58] This view is, of course, not without his strong bias, but it is, nevertheless, a view derived from his inductive study of the development of Chinese calligraphy.

The following passage from section two on the regular script contains an interesting conception of the written word:

> The length, size, tilt, straightness, spaciousness and denseness of the characters are by nature variegated. How can one make them uniform? For instance, the elongation of the character *tung* 東, the shortness of the character *hsi* 西, the smallness of the character *k'ou* 口, the largeness of the character *t'i* 體, the tilt of the character *p'eng* 朋, the straightness of the character *tang* 黨, and the spaciousness of the character *ch'ien* 千, and the denseness of the character *wan* 萬. When characters have many strokes, they should be made lean; when they have few strokes, they should be made plump. The loftiness of the calligraphy of the Wei-Chin period lies in its completion of the authentic form of each character without involving any subjective imposition (of the artist).[59]

[ag] 飄逸之氣

This passage comes after Chiang K'uei's attack on the "even and square" characteristic of T'ang regular script. Chiang K'uei associates the "untrammeled spirit" with the more natural style and "vulgarity" with calligraphy that has been "fitted into the compass and the square." He then concludes the passage with the interesting view that each character has its own "authentic form" (*chen-t'ai*[ah]) that must not be violated by the artist's "subjective opinion" (*ssu-i*[ai]). Clearly the written word is here conceived as an objective entity, itself dynamic and autonomous. The task of the calligrapher is nothing but to bring its "authentic form" to full realization. Despite its startling freshness, this view of the written character is not entirely novel in Chinese thought.

In an excellent article on the legend of Ts'ang Chieh, the inventor of Chinese writing, Jonathan Chaves has ably examined the traditional Chinese idea that writing originates in nature. He quotes an interesting passage from Wang An-shih (1021–1086) to illustrate this belief:

> While characters were made by man, in their origin they actually come from nature. Phoenixes and birds have patterns, and the Chart from the River had diagrams. These were not created by man; man merely imitated them. Thus, such positions as above and below, within and without, beginning and end, front and back, center and side, left and right, are all configurations of nature.[60]

These remarks come from an official report to the emperor presenting a book called *Tzu shuo* (Explanation of Characters) Wang An-shih himself compiled.[61] What Wang An-shih is concerned with here is not the ontological status of the written word but the extension of the primordial patterns of nature. It is not unlike the early organic theory of literature which views literature as an extension of the writer's personality discussed in an earlier context. The famous T'ang scholar Chang Huai-kuan (mid-9th c.) is not yet talking about the ontological status of the written word either, when he says:

> Plants and trees all attend to their own spirit of life, unwilling to be buried or concealed. How much more should this be true of birds and beasts, of human beings? The countenances of fierce beasts and birds of prey are different from one to the other: the Way of calligraphy models upon this.[62]

The idea of a unique form inherent in each character may be implicit here, but Chang Huai-kuan's main argument is that calligraphy must model upon the diversity of life in nature in order to produce variegated vitality.

In the paragraph quoted previously, Chiang K'uei is, in fact, much influenced by Mi Fu's distaste for T'ang calligraphers' attempt to make characters uniform in size. The association of Yen Chen-ch'ing's regular script with vulgarity has also been

ah 眞態　　　ai 私意

raised by Mi Fu in his *Hai-yüeh ming-yen*.[63] That particular text also contains the following astonishing words:

> When the clerical script (*li*) was established in calligraphy, the archaic methods of the large seal script (*ta-chuan*) were largely destroyed. The small and large seal scripts (*chuan-chou*) allow the forms of the characters to be big or small in size. Therefore, one can know from them the shapes of the hundred things which are alive, moving, all well-rounded, each self-sufficient in its own way. The clerical script began to have the tendency to enlarge or reduce the sizes of the characters (to make them uniform) and the methods of the Three Dynasties were lost.[64]

It would be a mistake, I believe, to equate Mi Fu's idea with Chiang K'uei's conception of the written word as an entity in itself. Mi Fu is commenting on the more pictographic forms of the seal script which bear close resemblance to natural shapes of things. He has not completely broken away from the traditional view that writing is an extension of those vital and self-sufficient forms in nature. But it cannot be denied that Chiang K'uei's concept of the character as an objective entity has developed out of this traditional view.

Chiang K'uei's concept of the word is not restricted to the regular script alone. In point of fact, he already indicates in the "General Comment" that the regular, the cursive, and the running scripts all have their inviolable forms. The following comments on the cursive script can further illustrate his attitude:

> The forms of the cursive script are like man's sitting, reclining, walking, standing, bowing complaisantly, quarreling in anger, taking a boat, galloping on a horse, singing, dancing, and beating his chest and stamping his feet in extreme grief. All these transformations of attitudes are not casually formed. Moreover, the form of a character itself usually has many transformations, involving beginnings and correspondences. There is a principle governing the ways in which one begins a character and completes it with the corresponding strokes.... In Wang Hsi-chih's calligraphy, the characters *hsi-chih* 羲之, *tang* 當, *te* 得, *shen* 深, and *wei* 慰 are the most numerous—each of them appearing several tens of times. The transformations of each of these are different from each other but they also resemble each other in a certain way. It can be said that Wang Hsi-chih is capable of "following his heart's desire without overstepping the boundary."[65]

By use of the example of Wang Hsi-chih's works, Chiang K'uei is saying that a character can involve many transformations because of the specific contexts it is in but they all reveal one underlying structural principle. To be sure, this idea probably reflects the general Sung interest in universal laws. But it can also mean that each character in the cursive script also has its authentic form that cannot be violated. His last remark alludes, of course, to Confucius' famous statement about his spiritual attainment at the age of seventy.[66] After a lifetime of self-cultivation and appropriation of social norms, Confucius was able to attain spontaneity. The implied comparison in the allusion is very important, and should be read in light of Chiang K'uei's comment of the "authentic form" of the regular script discussed previously. Wang Hsi-chih is able to achieve such heights in his art because he has abandoned his subjective opinion, and has thus appropriated the correct forms of the characters. In Chiang K'uei's view, therefore, Wang Hsien-chih cannot match his father in achievement precisely because he has not done this:

> Since Wang Hsien-chih the handling of the brush has often been defective. Within a character the long and short strokes are placed together, the tilted and the straight are juxtaposed, and the plump and the lean are mixed. The calligraphers seek grace after the forms of the characters have been made. These trends have become worse in recent times.[67]

Wang Hsien-chih is here criticized for his defective handling of the brush which is clearly a result of not observing the correct form of a character.

It is natural to expect Chiang K'uei, who insists on the ontological status of the written word, to focus his critical attention on the aesthetic object itself. Indeed, the entire *Hsü Shu-p'u* is oriented toward providing an objective description in structural terms of Chinese calligraphy, especially of the period from the Wei-Chin through the Northern Sung times. There are two passages in the Hsü Shu-p'u which indicate the close relation of Chiang K'uei's approach to calligraphy to his concept of the written word as an objective entity:[68]

> A beginner must not avoid the tracing of texts because it will teach him how to control his hand and will help him to succeed more easily. The texts must all be the famous works of ancient masters which one can place on a bench or a desk or hang beside his seat in order to gaze at them day and night, contemplating the principles behind the manipulation of the brush, before he sets out to copy by tracing or in a freehand.

> It has been said that, in doing outline tracing, one should put the model text upside down, so that one will not allow any subjective opinion to intervene.

Although these statements are concerned with the problem of copying the works of previous masters as a form of training, they actually can be applied to describe his usual objective and thorough method in studying calligraphy.

The *Hsü Shu-p'u* shows that Chiang K'uei is most capable of analyzing the minute details of brushwork, configurations of elements, and overall structure without ignoring the larger issues of style, historical development, and calligraphy's "prevailing spirit." No matter how brief, the conclusions he makes all appear to rely upon his own careful inductive research. The following two passages from his discussion of the "eight methods" (*pa-fa*[aj]) of the regular script will serve as an example:[69]

> The *t'iao* (lift) and the *t'i* (hook) are the pace of a character and must be made weighty and solid. The *t'iao* and *t'i* of Chin calligraphers sometimes carry a tilted downstroke or extend outward horizontally. Yen Chench'ing and Liu Kung-ch'üan began to produce these two strokes with the vertical brush-tip which caused the untrammeled spirit to disappear.

> The turning (*chuan*[ak]) and the folding (*che*[al]) strokes are the methods of the square and the round. By and large, the regular script uses the folding stroke while the cursive script used the turning stroke. In making a folding stroke one must halt the brush briefly, a technique that produces strength in writing. In making a turning stroke one must avoid any obstruction (in the movement of the brush). If the brush is obstructed the calligraphy will lack vigor. But only with some turning strokes will the regular script be continuous and only with some folding strokes will the cursive script be vigorous. This is something that one cannot afford not to know.

There are, in these passages, simple, but reasonably precise, descriptions of four strokes, discussions of the methods of their execution, and analysis of dynamic spirit of calligraphy in terms of the handling of structural elements. Relying on a rigorous examination of the handling and the configurations of elements in the works of Wei-Chin masters, Chiang K'uei has covered both technical aspects and the inner dynamics and vitality of calligraphy. One can find many discussions of brush methods, or even specifically of the eight methods, written by T'ang and Sung scholars, selected in the *Shu-yüan ying-hua*, compiled by Ch'en Ssu around midthirteenth century. Few of them, if any, can match Chiang K'uei's descriptions in being simple, down to earth, specific, and comprehensive in relating small technical details to broader structural principles.[70]

I would like to close this brief review of Chiang K'uei's *Hsü Shu-p'u* with a mention of a very minor work of his on the Ting-wu version of Wang Hsi-chih's masterpiece, the *Lan-t'ing hsü*. The work is a continuation of Mi Fu's pioneer attempt to describe the ways in which some of the strokes or radicals in this text are executed.[71] It was much admired by Chou Mi (1232–1298), the late Sung and early Yüan poet-scholar-connoisseur who included it in his *Ch'i-tung yeh-yü*. The work consists of nineteen brief notes, of which the following two can serve as an illustration:[72]

aj 八法   ak 轉   al 折

The bottom horizontal stroke of the radical *k'ou* 口 in the character *ho* 和 extends slightly outward.

The foot of the character *shih* 事 extends outward aslant without making an upward lift.

In the history of Chinese calligraphy, no single work has attracted more critical attention from scholars than Wang Hsi-chih's *Lan-t'ing hsü*. Yet among the vast number of comments and colophons on this text written by scholars through the Sung or even later, we cannot find anything, except Mi Fu's occasional comments, that has dealt with details in such a meticulous manner.[73] One might object to analysis of this sort as being trivial, but that would be to misunderstand completely the rigor and objectivity of his critical method.

CONCLUSION

Chiang K'uei's treatises on poetry and calligraphy demonstrate a remarkable consistency in his conception of the arts, in his aesthetic ideal, and in his conviction that the methodological approach will eventually bring a full realization of such a conception and ideal. Throughout traditional Chinese history, the most creative thinkers, critics, and artists have persistently relied on the idea of a spontaneously self-generating and self-regulating cosmos as a metaphor for ideal self-realization and artistic expression. Chiang K'uei's references to the *Odes*, the *Chuang Tzu*, Su Shih, and Wang Hsi-chih illustrate that he is in keeping with this dominant ideal. What is new in his theory, and in much of late Sung aesthetics, is the greater emphasis on the pragmatic approach to the problem of composition and on observation of works of art in detachment as prerequisite to the attainment of spontaneous expression. What is also new is his more "academic" attitude in presenting a systematic and objective structure of discourses on these theoretical issues and on the arts themselves.

In preparing this revised version of a paper presented at the Conference on Theories of the Arts in China, the author has received great benefit from the corrections and comments suggested by conference participants. The many comments made by Susan Bush, James J. Y. Liu, Christian Murck, Maureen Robertson and Tu Wei-ming are especially appreciated.

1. Kuo Shao-yü, *Chung-kuo wen-hsüeh p'i-p'ing shih* (A History of Chinese Literary Criticism) 2 vols. (Shanghai, 1948), 2:1–2.

2. Shuen-fu Lin, *The Transformation of the Chinese Lyrical Tradition: Chiang K'uei and Southern Sung Tz'u Poetry* (Princeton, 1978). See especially "Introduction," pp. 3–48.

3. For the "Prefaces," see Hsia Ch'eng-t'ao, ed., *Po-shih shih tz'u chi* (Collected *Shih* and *Tz'u* Poetry of Po-shih) (Hong Kong, 1972) (henceforth *Shih tz'u chi*), pp. 1–2; for the "Discourse," see ibid., pp. 65–69.

4. Hsia Ch'eng-t'ao, ed., *Chiang Po-shih tz'u pien-nien chien-chiao* (A Collated and Chronologically Arranged Edition of Chiang Po-shih's *Tz'u* Poetry) (Taipei, 1967) (henceforth *Chien-chiao*), pp. 233–234.

5. See Kiyohiko Munakata, *Ching Hao's Pi-fa-chi: A Note on the Art of the Brush* (Ascona, 1974), pp. 11–16.

6. This dominant theory was condensed in the statement *shih yen chih* or "poetry expresses intents." The early more elaborate exposition of this theory can be found in the "Major Preface" to the *Mao Shih*. James J. Y. Liu has provided a concise discussion of the concept in his *Chinese Theories of Literature* (Chicago, 1975), pp. 67–70.

7. *Shih tz'u chi*, p. 1.

8. See Hsia Ch'eng-t'ao's preface to the *Chien-chiao*, pp. 3–5.

9. *Shih tz'u chi*, p. 1.

10. Ibid.

11. Ibid.

12. Kuo Ch'ing-fan, *Chuang tzu chi-shih* (Collected Commentaries on the *Chuang tzu*) 2 vols. (Taipei, 1962), 1:45–50.

13. Burton Watson, trans., *The Complete Works of Chuang Tzu* (New York, 1968), p. 37.

14. *Shih tz'u chi*, p. 67.

15. Ibid., p. 68.

16. Ibid., p. 2.

17. Su Shih, *Ching-chin Tung-p'o wen-chi shih-lüeh* (Taipei, 1960) 46, pp. 779–780.

18. Yen Yü constantly talks about "modeling upon High T'ang poets." See the first chapter *shih-pien* in Kuo Shao-yü, ed., *Ts'ang-lang shih-hua chiao-shih* (A Collated and Annotated Edition of the *Ts'ang-lang shih-hua*) (Peking, 1962), pp. 1–43.

19. Watson, *Chuang Tzu*, pp. 50–51.

20. Hsü Fu-kuan, *Chung-kuo i-shu ching-shen* (The Chinese Aesthetic Spirit) (Taipei, 1976), p. 53.

21. *Shih tz'u chi*, p. 69.

22. Chang Chan, ed., *Lieh tzu chu-shih* (A Commentary on the *Lieh Tzu*) (Taipei, 1966), pp. 143–144.

23. Watson, *Chuang Tzu*, p. 302.

24. For more detailed discussion, see my *The Transformation of the Chinese Lyrical Tradition*, "Introduction."

25. Maureen A. Robertson, "'To Convey What Is Precious': Ssu-k'ung T'u's Poetics and the Erh-shih-ssu Shih P'in," in *Transition and Permanence: Chinese History and Culture*, eds. David Buxbaum and Frederick W. Mote (Seattle, 1972), p. 331.

26. Ibid.

27. *Chien-chiao*, p. 66.

28. Li Chien's remarks are quoted in Chang Tzu, *Shih-hsüeh kuei-fan* (Standards for the Education of an Official) (Taipei, 1972), 33:5b–7b.

29. Ibid., 6a–7a.

30. Ch'ien Chung-shu, "One Special Characteristic of Traditional Chinese Literary Criticism," *Wen-hsüeh tsa-chih* (1937), 1(4):1–22. This article is in Chinese.

31. Chang, *Shih-hsüeh kuei-fan*, p. 6a.

32. Liu, *Chinese Theories of Literature*, p. 68.

33. David Pollard, "*Ch'i* in Chinese Literary Theory," in *Chinese Approaches to Literature from Confucius to Liang Ch'i-ch'ao*, ed. Adele Austin Rickett (Princeton, 1978), p. 45.

34. Ibid.

35. Robertson, "To Convey What Is Precious," p. 331.

36. Kūkai, *Bunkyo hifuron* (Peking, 1975), p. 138.

37. Hu Chen-heng, *T'ang-yin kuei-ch'ien* (Shanghai, 1957), p. 6.

38. Shen Tzu-ch'eng, ed., *Li-tai lun-hua ming-chu hui-pien* (A Collection of Famous Treatises on Painting through the Ages) (Taipei, n.d.), p. 32.

39. Quoted in Chang, *Shih-hsüeh kuei-fan*, 33:4b–5a.

40. Ibid., 32:9a.

41. Ibid., 33:2a.

42. Kuo, *Ts'ang-lang shih-hua chiao-chu*, see especially the section on *shih-p'ing*, pp. 129–189.

43. Chu Hsi, *Ssu-shu chi-chu* (Collected Commentaries on the Four Books) (Taipei, 1959), p. 53.

44. Ibid., pp. 53, 81.

45. Ibid., p. 53.

46. Pollard, "*Ch'i*," p. 57.

47. Ibid., p. 58.

48. *Shih tz'u chi*, pp. 68, 69.

49. Ibid., p. 68.

50. Ibid.

51. Yeh Shao-weng, *Ssu-ch'ao wen-chien-lu* (Records of Experiences during Four Reigns) (n.p., n.d.), *wu-chi*, 6a–13a.

52. Ibid., 9b.

53. Chiang K'uei's scholarly research on calligraphy began when a friend gave him a copy of the catalogue *Chiang-t'ieh*. See Chiang K'uei's preface to his *Chiang-t'ieh p'ing* (*TSCC*, vol. 1599), pl. 1.

54. See Hsia Ch'eng-t'ao's review of late Sung and early Yüan views on Chiang K'uei's calligraphy in his *Chien-chiao*, pp. 286–287.

55. Ibid., pp. 241–245.

56. See for instance, Teng San-mu, *Shu-fa hsüeh-hsi pi-tu* (A Required Reading for Students of Calligraphy) (Hong Kong, 1962), pp. 2–3.

57. Mi Fu, *Hai-yüeh ming-yen* (ISTP, II), p. 1.

58. For Mi Fu's view of T'ang calligraphy, see ibid., pp. 1–3.

59. Chiang K'uei, *Hsü Shu-p'u* (*TSCC* vol. 1622), p. 1.

60. Jonathan Chaves, "The Legacy of Ts'ang Chieh: The Written Word as Magic," *OA* (1977), n.s. 22(2):203.

61. Wang An-shih, *Wang Lin-ch'uan chi* (Taipei, 1961), 56, p. 354.

62. Chang Huai-kuan, "Shu i" (A Critique of Calligraphy) in Chang Yen-yüan, ed.,

Fa-shu yao-lu (A Collection of Important Treatises on Calligraphy) (*TSCC* vol. 1626), p. 66.

63. Mi, *Hai-yüeh ming-yen*, pp. 2–3.

64. Ibid., p. 3.

65. Chiang, *Hsü Shu-p'u*, p. 3.

66. Chu, *Ssu-shu chi-chu*, p. 37.

67. Chiang, *Hsü Shu-p'u*, p. 2.

68. Ibid., pp. 5 and 6.

69. Ibid., p. 2.

70. Ch'en Ssu, *Shu-yüan ying hua* (Fine Flowers from the Garden of Calligraphy) (Shanghai, 1919). See especially the first two *chüan*.

71. Lothar Ledderose, *Mi Fu and the Classical Tradition of Chinese Calligraphy* (Princeton, 1979), pp. 102–103, no. 19.

72. Chou Mi, *Ch'i-tung yeh-yü* (Words of a Rustic from Ch'i-tung) (Taipei, 1969), p. 175.

73. See for instance, Sang Shih-ch'ang's *Lan-t'ing k'ao* in *Fa-t'ieh k'ao* (ISTP, VII), ed. Yang Chia-lo (Taipei, 1967).

VI / Issues in Ming Criticism

Alternate Routes to Self-Realization in Ming Theories of Poetry

By Richard John Lynn

The archaist movement (*fu-ku*[a]) which centered around the *ch'ien-hou ch'i-tzu*[b] (Former and Latter Seven Masters) dominated the world of literature in China during most of the fifteenth and sixteenth centuries and continued to exert a powerful influence throughout the rest of the traditional era. It is characterized by a dictum attributed to Li Meng-yang (1472–1529) that "prose (*wen*) must be like that of the Ch'in (221–207 B.C.) or the Han (206 B.C.–A.D. 220), and poetry (*shih*) must be like that of the High T'ang,"[1] The archaists believed the T'ang to be the "classic" era of poetry, and in this they can in large part be regarded as "neoclassical formalists," although there was much more to their critical views and their creative efforts. There was another major movement in Ming criticism and poetic practice which, in contrast to the archaists, advocated a very different view of poetry. This movement culminated in the Kung-an school led by Yüan Hung-tao (1568–1610) and his brothers and was carried on into the early Ch'ing by Ch'ien Ch'ien-i (1582–1664). It argued that the freedom of individual expression represented the true essence of poetry and opposed the archaists' strict adherence to T'ang models. These anti-archaists or expressionists were, in fact, very fond of the poetry of the Sung era (960–1279), something the archaists deplored and against which they warned the student of poetry. The anti-archaists believed that Sung poetry incorporated much originality, individualism and honest expression, qualities they thought were lacking in the archaist practice of emulating models drawn exclusively from the T'ang. Also, since they viewed the entire tradition in terms of individual poets rather than in terms of period styles, the anti-archaists' interpretation of what T'ang poetry was is strikingly different from that of the archaists. The archaists saw it as a repository of absolute truths valid for all time, but the anti-archaists viewed it simply as an assemblage of poets, ardent and intense, whose honest expression of emotions and sensibilities continued to live on in the poetry they had written.

The anti-archaists all seemed to have the greatest antipathy for the two works that did most to fashion the basic tenets of the archaist movement: Yen Yü's (ca. 1180–ca. 1235) *Ts'ang-lang shih-hua*, which became the archaist theoretical manual, and Kao Ping's (1350–1423) *T'ang-shih p'in-hui*, which was the archaist practical guidebook to the "essence" of the "true" T'ang style.[2] Although the *Ts'ang-lang shih-hua* is a complex and manifold text, I believe that it essentially engages in five

[a] 復古　　　　　[b] 前後七子

different arguments:[3] (1) The poetry of the High T'ang masters is the perfect realization of the true Law or *Dharma* of poetry (*shih-fa*[c]) which consists of the inseparable combination of manner (the *way* by which a poem comes into being) and medium (the *kind* of language through which the poem articulates itself). Manner must be completely spontaneous and "natural," and the medium must be formally "correct" (*cheng*[d]), i.e. indistinguishable from examples of poetry of the High T'ang era.[4] (2) Perfect poetry depends upon spontaneity, and this spontaneity is best understood in terms of a concept Yen borrows from Ch'an (Zen) Buddhism, *wu*[e] (enlightenment). The poets of the High T'ang had *t'ou-ch'e chih wu*[f] (thoroughly penetrating enlightenment) in the sense that they were capable of first assimilating or internalizing the rules (*fa*[g]) of poetry which they learned from the best poets of the earlier tradition and then *unlearning* or *transcending* those rules and the tradition to become masters in their own right.[5] (3) Not all of T'ang poetry is worthy of emulation, since after the High T'ang poetry underwent a *pien*[h] (deviation) and *some* Middle T'ang (766–834) and Late T'ang (835–907) poetry are products of "false enlightenment," analogous to *P'i-chih Sheng*[i] (*Pratyeka Yāna*), the erroneous method of attempting to attain individual enlightenment in isolation without any teacher and apart from the true *P'u-sa Sheng*[j] (*Bodhisattva Yāna*), or to *Sheng-wen Sheng*[k] (*Srāvaka Yāna*), the equally erroneous method of attempting to attain enlightenment through the (mere) chanting of the scriptures and listening to doctrine.[6] Reasoning analogously, Yen seems to mean that the "deviant" poetry of the Middle and the Late T'ang eras tends both to an "unorthodox" interest in the idiosyncratic peculiarities of individual emotionalism and to a self-indulgent formal mannerism which necessarily violates the correct (*cheng*) rules laid down by the orthodox (*cheng*) tradition of poetry.[7] (4) To a considerable extent, the *Ts'ang-lang shih-hua* is a diatribe against Sung dynasty poetry in general and in particular against the poetry of the Chiang-hsi school. Yen Yü condemns Sung poetry essentially on two grounds: it is not "enlightened" (spontaneous), and thereby fails in respect to poetic *manner*, and it does not embody the true *fa* (the rules = the Way or *Dharma*) of poetry, that is, it fails in respect to the *kind* of language proper to correct/orthodox poetry. High T'ang poetry, in his view, involves limitless suggestion, connotation and implication; it is free from the limitations of literal-minded, rational language and thought, and it is utterly spontaneous and transcends all traces of craft. By contrast, these are the very qualities he believes Sung poetry to lack, and he condemns most of it as a crude, clumsy, self-conscious and craft-ridden failure, reserving approval only for those poets of the early Sung such as Ou-yang Hsiu (1007–1072) and Mei Yao-ch'en (1002–1060) who stayed close to proper T'ang

c 詩法	f 透徹之悟	i 辟支乘
d 正	g 法	j 菩薩乘
e 悟	h 變	k 聲聞乘

models. Huang T'ing-chien (1045–1105), as founder of the Chiang-hsi school and thus principal instigator of everything wrong with Sung poetry, reaped only his extreme disapprobation, and Su Shih (1037–1101), who may have been undeniably "spontaneous," nevertheless did much to establish the Sung dynasty style of poetry with all its tendencies to prosy discourse and, as such, placed himself beyond the pale of Yen's orthodoxy as well.[8] (5) In addition to these assertions concerning the manner of poetic composition and the medium of its articulation, Yen also argues that the poets of the High T'ang are perfect models for emulation because of the heightened powers of perception and the heightened personal character of expression that come across in their poetry. Although he never explicitly says so, he implies in a number of passages that the poets of the High T'ang represent the pinnacle of cultural/moral excellence; they are for him the great cultural heroes of the tradition whose perceptions of and insights into reality are thoroughly penetrating and infinite in their implications[9] and whose personal characters share such perfectly estimable qualities as "bravery," "power," "restraint," "magnanimity," etc.[10] Their poetry, as such, deserves emulation not only for its formal features but for the salutary effects it will have on the characters of the emulators; emulation is, in fact, a form of self-cultivation, a deliberate cultural/moral conditioning in which the emulator attempts to identify with and internalize both the style and the character of ideal cultural types. It is more than likely that in this respect Yen was very much influenced by contemporary developments in Neo-Confucianism which stressed a similar emulation-based procedure for the acquisition of sagehood.[11]

There is no manifesto corresponding to the *Ts'ang-lang shih-hua* for the anti-archaist/expressionist position in poetry, no basic theoretical text to which we can trace the essential tenets of the Kung-an school. Expressionism as a view of the nature and function of poetry actually had a very long and complex development before the Ming era, as well as earlier in the Ming itself, and the Kung-an school can be regarded in large part as an heir to an extensive tradition rather than the initiator of a new trend.[12] The most significant way in which the anti-archaists/expressionists differed from the archaists was that they did not make any value distinction between "proper" poetic and "improper" prosy language in poetry. Thus, they appreciated a great deal of Sung dynasty poetry and, for many of them, Su Shih became their great hero. In effect, they denied the orthodox-heterodox dichotomy, the High T'ang/non-High T'ang distinction upon which Yen Yü built his whole edifice of poetic "truth." Their Way or *Dharma* of poetry is thus very much broader than that of the archaists, as the poetry of the High T'ang does not constitute its sole standard of excellence. As long as poetry is spontaneous and the true expression of individual feeling and real experience, it receives their approval. No era of poetry and no particular group of poets need provide exclusive and universal models for emulation; these can come from any era, including the Sung. In fact, emulation itself plays a far less important role in their view of poetry; there is a far looser relationship between the student of poetry and his models than in the archaist view, and spontaneity to them means something quite different from the spontaneity of the archaists. They believed in the spontaneous expression of the "natural" man unencumbered by any burden of learning, cultivation or discipline, so the archaists' conception of High T'ang *fa* (Law/Way/*Dharma*) with all its implications for self-transcendency and heightened sensibilities and perceptions meant little or nothing to them.[13] "True" poetry in their view, is to be found or discovered in the poet's own person and is not something to be learned or cultivated in relation to an identification with the accomplishments of others, with an "orthodox" tradition. Both the archaists and the anti-archaists/expressionists regarded poetry as a route to self-realization, but their respective routes differed radically, with the archaists insisting that poetry be learned from without, from identifying with and then transcending a tradition, and the anti-archaists insisting that poetry be discovered from within, from liberating the natural powers of perceptions, feelings and articulation that are inherent in each individual.

The survey which follows attempts to bring to light the essential features of both views. The archaists will be treated first, then the anti-archaists/expressionists, and a final section will contrast and compare the two and try to suggest what effect the two views had on the later tradition of Chinese literature as a whole.

The intellectual climate of the early Ming was particularly conducive to the development of archaism. The dynasty's founder, Chu Yüan-chang (T'ai-tsu), and his advisors made great efforts to utilize notions of legitimacy, based upon claims of cultural and political orthodoxy, as means to bolster political, social and economic control and overall reconsolidation and unity. It was this climate that fostered Kao Ping's *T'ang-shih p'in-hui*, for, like the many other scholarly and literary projects of this time—the *Hung-wu cheng-yün* (Correct Rhymes as Established During the Hung-wu Era) (1375) and the *Ta-Ming lü* (Law Code of the Great Ming Dynasty) (final version promulgated in 1398), for example—Kao's work attempted to establish, in the form of a guidebook, the correct (*cheng*) interpretation of a particular tradition, in its case the tradition of T'ang poetry. Although it was not produced under imperial auspices, this private project later received the Yung-lo Emperor's approval, and Kao, who had been a commoner, was appointed directly to the Han-lin Academy as a *tai-chao* (compiler) because of it.[14]

Kao belonged to a circle of poets, the so-called "Ten Talents of Fukien," led by Lin Hung (ca. 1340–ca. 1400) which was dedicated to reestablishing the golden age of the T'ang dynasty. It not only wished to recover the standards of the T'ang but also wanted to purge contemporary poetry of what it considered to be the lingering decadence of the poetry of the Yüan era, heterodox poetry which either was permeated with an extravagant mannerism modeled upon that of the Late T'ang or consisted of a hybrid mixture of T'ang and Sung elements.[15] Kao's anthology, with its classified selections headed by critical introductions, was compiled as a practical, illustrated guide to what he considered the "true" T'ang style—it is his attempt to put together an anthology which illustrates, in concrete examples, the critical assertions made by Yen Yü.[16] With it, the student of poetry could hope to find his way through all of T'ang poetry to what constituted its orthodox core, and, by emulating this core, achieve the same results himself. Moreover, this emulation was not meant to be restricted to formal considerations alone but also included the cultivation or shaping of personality, sensibilities and character. That Kao meant the student of poetry to model himself personally upon the heroic proportions, the refined personalities and the magnanimous characters of the poets of the High T'ang, viewing them as ideal cultural types, is obvious from some of the things he said in the critical sections of the *T'ang-shih p'in-hui*, for example:

> There is no more flourishing poetry than that of the T'ang, and none more respected than that of the High T'ang. Critics regard only Tu [Fu] [712–770] and Li [Po] [701–762] as the very best, but besides them there are also some ten-odd poets whom we can call *ming-chia*[l] (Famous Masters) . . . . Regard the refined elegance (*ch'ing-ya*[m]) of Hsiang-yang [Meng Hao-jan] [689–740], the exquisite delicacy (*ching-chih*[n]) of Yu-ch'eng [Wang Wei] [701–761], the genuine earnestness (*chen-shuai*[o]) of Ch'u Kuang-hsi [fl. ca. 742], the startling charm (*sung-chün*[p]) of Wang Chiang-ning [Wang Ch'ang-ling] [d. ca. 756], the strong moral fiber (*ch'i-ku*[q]) of Kao Ta-fu [Kao Shih] [d. 765], the remarkable independence (*ch'i-i*[r]) of Ts'en Chia-chou [Ts'en Shen] [fl. ca. 760], the serene nobility (*ch'ung-hsiu*[s]) of Li Ch'i [fl. ca. 742], the otherworldliness (*ch'ao-fan*[t]) of Ch'ang Chien [fl. ca. 749], the carefree contentment (*hsien-k'uang*[u]) of Liu Sui-chou [Liu Ch'ang-ch'ing] [709–ca. 780], the chaste magnificence (*ch'ing-shan*[v]) of Ch'ien K'ao-kung [Ch'ien Ch'i] [fl. ca. 766], how tranquil and profound (*ching erh shen*[w]) is Wei [Wei Ying-wu] [ca. 735–ca. 835], how warm and intimate (*wen erh mi*[x]) is Liu [Liu Tsung-yüan] [773–819]! For all these poets, it is a matter of the noble ethers, which pervade the mountains and waters of the entire world, condensing at a particular time and producing men. Oh, how glorious they were! I present them all here as "Famous Masters". . . . If the student wishes to seek out the correct/orthodox (*cheng*) source of poetry and follow its flow, it will suffice to look over [these masters]![17]

The qualities attributed to all these poets of the High T'ang "style" (that it is a style and not a simple chronological period is obvious from the fact that Kao includes in it such later figures as Wei Ying-wu and Liu Tsung-yüan) have as much to do with

l 名家	q 氣骨	u 閑曠
m 清邪	r 奇逸	v 清贍
n 精緻	s 沖秀	w 青而深
o 眞率	t 超凡	x 溫而密
p 聳俊		

personal character as with formal features—the two seem actually to be inseparable entities; style makes the man, and the man is his style. By emulating these poets, the student of poetry cultivates himself in such a way that he, through identifying with them, hopes to become an ideal cultural type himself.

The later sections of Kao's anthology attempt to gather together representative works of Middle and Late T'ang Poets which, in his opinion, still preserve something of the orthodoxy of the High T'ang in spite of the general trend to manneristic heterodoxy that characterizes these periods. The two poets he considers the outstanding examples of this for the Middle T'ang are Han Yü (768–824) and Meng Chiao (751–814), whose poetry he places in a category called *cheng-pien*[y]—orthodox innovation or innovation which still stays within the bounds of orthodoxy:

> Now observe how broad and cultured (*po-ta erh wen*[z]) Ch'ang-li [Han Yü] was, how he upheld and promoted the *Six Confucian Classics* and how he searched throughout the writings of his worthy predecessors for appropriate materials. His poetry gallops at full tilt with vehement vigor or is as if it were a precipitous peak bursting upward sheer and straight, like earth-shaking thunder and sky-splitting lightning, like thousands and thousands of foot-soldiers and cavalry charging helter-skelter in every direction, or as if it were an oceanlike flood that no one can stop. Moreover, such poems as his *Ch'iu-huai* ("Autumn Longing") and *Mu-hsing ho-t'i-shang* ("An Evening Stroll atop the River Dike") in spirit and structure (*feng-ku*[aa]) are somewhat like works of the Chien-an era [196–220], but their new sound (*hsin-sheng*[ab]) is completely different. This is innovation within the bounds of orthodoxy (*cheng-chung chih pien*[ac]). When Tung-yeh [Meng Chiao] was young, he cherished an upright nature (*keng-chieh*[ad]) and was resolute in spite of the deprivation he suffered in filthy poverty. Late in life, having finally achieved a lofty rank in the examinations, he was appointed to office and made a *wei* (commandant). His poetry is lean yet capable of providing a pattern to the thought (*ch'iung erh yu li*[ae]), and, although his bitter tone is lonely and desolate (*k'u-tiao ch'i-liang*[af]), as soon as it emerges from his breast it is free from parsimonious overtones (*wu lin-ssu*[ag]). As for his pieces in the ancient ballad form (*ku yüeh-fu*), when one has chanted them and savored them for a time, he will realize that they have more than enough piognancy (*yü-pei*[ah]). This, too, is innovation within the bounds of orthodoxy.[18]

y 正變	ac 正中之變	af 苦調凄涼
z 博大而文	ad 耿介	ag 無吝色
aa 風骨	ae 窮而有理	ah 餘悲
ab 新聲		

Kao seems to have a much wider view of T'ang poetry than Yen Yü, since he saw much more good in Middle and Late T'ang poetry—for instance, Yen had nothing but contempt for Meng Chiao and condemned him for what he considered to be his self-indulgent and petty emotionalism and his mannered affectations in poetic style.[19] Nevertheless, Kao, like Yen, in his overall treatment of T'ang poetry employs the term *pien* (which was translated as "innovation" in the above passage) in a pejorative sense, as "deviation" or "degeneration," something used primarily to describe the decline of poetry after the High T'ang era:

> Alas! In the aftermath of the disaster of the T'ien-pao era [i.e. the rebellion of An Lu-shan] the Ethers of the Three Luminaries and the Five Sacred Mountains dispersed, and the characters of the men of the times fell short of completion, and thus the style of literary art began to degenerate (*pien*). During this time, Liu Ch'ang-ch'i, Ch'ien Ch'i, Wei Ying-wu, and Liu Tsung-yüan appeared one after the other, each contributing to a fine chorus of poetry, and managed to keep up the standards of their predecessors.... However, after them modern-style verse (*chin-t'i*[ai]) became somewhat overcomplicated (*p'o-fan*[aj]) and drew further and further away from the old sounds.[20] ... After the renaissance of the Yüan-ho Era [806–820], literary style began to disintegrate (*san*[ak]), and the orthodox school (*cheng-p'ai*[al]) was not continued. The more people followed inferior learning, the fainter became the old sounds....[21]

The core of Kao's anthology is, of course, the poetry of the High T'ang—that of the Early T'ang is included merely as anticipatory to it, that of the Late T'ang as its decline. This view is put succinctly in one of the subsidiary prefaces to the anthology by Wang Ch'eng (1370–1415), another of the "Ten Talents of Fukien":

> It is now seven or eight hundred years that T'ang poetry is with us, and finally we have an anthology of it here with which we can be completely satisfied, since no precious pearl has been discarded and no priceless piece of jade has been left out.... I once heard Man-shih [Kao Ping] discuss poetry in the following way: 'Poetry has taken the following course from the *300 Odes*: That of the Han and the Wei was such that *chih*[am] (substance) outweighed *wen* (form), that of the Six Dynasties was such that the blossoms [i.e. formal beauty] outdid the fruit [i.e. substance/subject matter], and that which struck a mean between these two extremes and which completely realized the style (*t'i*[an]) of the authors of the *Odes* is only the poetry of the T'ang. However, since periods differ from one another, so what poets write differs as well. The prosodic art of the Early T'ang was

ai 今體	ak 散	am 質
aj 頗繁	al 正派	an 體

not yet pure (*ch'un*[ao]), while the bad habits of the Late T'ang resulted in mean and lowly works (*pei-hsia*[ap]). That which stands out unique and lofty, truly worthy of esteem, is only the High T'ang![22]

The upshot of all this for the contemporary world of poetry of the early Ming was that there could be only one kind of poetry for anyone to write, that which emulated the poetry of the High T'ang. It was then that this view really took hold of the Chinese tradition, a hold which had many challengers over the next five centuries but which never completely lost its grip. We shall now see how it was expanded and rendered more sophisticated at the hands of the Former and Latter Seven Masters, the Ming archaists proper.

Li Meng-yang is remembered primarily as a formalist and arch-proponent of the High T'ang style, but in his critical remarks on poetry there is much that is also concerned with self-realization. The two aspects, role of self in poetry, on the one hand, and poetic form, on the other, seem, in his view, to reciprocate and generate each other in such a way that remarks made about the one often apply to the other:

> Poetry is something by which one expresses his *chih*[aq] (mind's/heart's intent) while remaining in harmony with the Way, and so in it we value *wan*[ar] (gentle persuasiveness) but not *hsien*[as] (precipitousness), *chih* (substance) but not *mi*[at] (flashy show), *ch'ing*[au] (straightforward emotion) but not *fan*[av] (intricacy), and *jung-hsia*[aw] (harmonious fusion of elements) but not *kung-ch'iao*[ax] (conscious craft). This is why it is said that once one hears the music [i.e. poetry] a person makes, he will know the quality of that person's virtue. Thus, I am able to discern the broad divisions possible in the *yin*[ay] (tone) of poetry, namely *chuang*[az] (dignity) vs. *pi*[ba] (biased argument), *chien*[bb] (simplicity) vs. *ch'ih*[bc] (extravagance), and *fu*[bd] (sincerity) vs. *fu*[be] (frivolity). When the tradition of poetry reached the likes of Yüan [Chen], Po [Chü-i], Han [Yü], Meng [Chiao], P'i [Jih-hsiu], and Lu [Kuei-meng], there began endless squabbling, and, even after hundreds of thousands of words, not one of them would yield to the other. How is this any different from going into the marketplace and clawing for gold or getting up on the stage and posturing a role! Are there such who, when they see someone wearing a scholar's cap and jade pendants at his waist, do not grow timid, cast down their pens and run away! Why is this so? It is because they are ashamed at not being *chün-tzu*[bf] (true gentlemen)![23]

ao	純	au	情	ba	詖
ap	卑下	av	繁	bb	簡
aq	志	aw	融洽	bc	侈
ar	宛	ax	工巧	bd	孚
as	嶮	ay	音	be	浮
at	靡	az	莊	bf	君子

Li is saying, in effect, that the successful poem is the meeting place of the ideal poet as person and the ideal verbal medium of expression, where the poet realizes himself as an ideal cultural type *through* articulating his character, sensibilities, emotions, and ideas in the approved form of verse, the High T'ang style—that moment of perfection before poetry "degenerated" at the hands of such Middle and Late T'ang poets as Po Chü-i, Meng Chiao, etc. Thus, learning to write "correct" poetry is meant to be an educational experience for the student of poetry, for it enables him to acquire culturally approved personal, moral, and intellectual qualities, qualities modeled upon the greatest poet-personalities of the past. This all suggests that there is a profound commitment to words, to the linguistic medium of poetry, in the sense that words are regarded as an effective, perhaps the most effective, vehicle of self-cultivation, the way one learns how to become a "great man." [24] Also, like Yen Yü and Kao Ping before him, Li Meng-yang disparages the self-centered mannerism of the Middle and Late T'ang eras; in fact, he is far closer to Yen than to Kao, since he voices such contempt for post-High T'ang poets. Consequently, his spectrum of possibilities for "correct" models of emulation is correspondingly narrower.

Most of the criticism left to us from the Former Seven Masters consists of remarks concerned with formal features of poetry, so-called "correct" models for emulation and the need to identify with "orthodox" poetic tradition. This situation changes considerably with the Latter Seven Masters a generation or so later, for with them, especially in the critical writings of Hsieh Chen (1495–1574), there is a very great deal which is concerned with such problems as self-realization, the nature of imitation/emulation, the relationship between the individual and the tradition, and the nature of literary creativity. Like Li Meng-yang, Hsieh was concerned with what constituted qualities to be esteemed in poetry:

> In *t'i* (style) we esteem *cheng-ta*[bg] (correctness and magnificence); in *chih* (mind's/heart's intent) we esteem *kao-yüan*[bh] (loftiness and profundity); in *ch'i*[bi] (spirit) we esteem *hsiung-hun*[bj] (nobility and power); and in *yün*[bk] (tone) we esteem *chüan-yung*[bl] (what excites interest and fascination). If one does not cultivate the basic natures of these four dimensions, he will lack the means to express their truth, and if one is not enlightened about them, he will lack the means to enter into their wonders (*miao*[bm]). [25]

These four dimensions seem to refer as much to qualities of personality as they do to formal style, and the perfect state of their realization, the level at which they become "wondrous," is something attained when the individual poet first identifies with, and then transcends, the tradition:

bg 正大
bh 高遠
bi 氣

bj 雄渾
bk 韻

bl 雋永
bm 妙

The Great Way [of Poetry] is nothing other than the sum of what derives from the masters of the High T'ang. Therefore, dragging the lower borders of my scholar's gown and wearing straw sandals, I began with what is central and correct (*chung-cheng*[bn]) and was very careful to step everywhere the feet of those ancients had fallen. Later, when I had become a master in my own right, I was like a bee which had taken nectar from hundreds of different flowers to make honey; although the flavor of each nectar originally differed, my honey became such that one could not distinguish among them in it.[26]

The ideal poet's expression, then, is a composite derivation of all the correct models of the tradition which transcends its own composition, and, as far as both formal and expressive features are concerned, individuality is something to be learned from the tradition, derived out of it. As such, the student of poetry has the chance of becoming the equal of the greatest poets of the past:

Study in turn the works of each of the fourteen masters [of the High T'ang], for all of them can be models for you. You should select the very best pieces from their collected works and set them down together as an anthology, which you then should read over again and again in order to capture their *shen-ch'i*[bo] (expressive qualities), chant them in order to obtain their *sheng-tiao*[bp] (audio qualities), and savor them in order to condense (*p'ou*[bq]) their essences (*ching-hua*[br]). Once you manage to do these three essential things, your creative powers will attain an undifferentiated whole (*tsao hu hun-lun*[bs]), no longer will you need to make statues of the "Banished Immortal" [Li Po] or paint portraits of Shao-ling [Tu Fu], and the myriad things of existence will form one self with you, and men who lived throughout countless ages will form one mind with you (*fu wan-wu i-wo yeh ch'ien-ku i-hsin yeh*[bt]).[27]

Here Hsieh advocates the study of poetry as a kind of mystic exploration of all time, space, and human experience, as a means to expand the self and achieve a cosmic individuality in which all things are one. Grand claims for the potential of poetry indeed! Important also is the idea that the student of poetry can become the equal of the greatest poets who ever lived, Li Po and Tu Fu. However, there is no rivalry here but the discovery of the route to enlightenment and sharing there, with Li and Tu, the same set of expanded sensibilities, emancipated consciousness, and perfect powers of articulation. Hsieh's view of individuality accordingly does not at all see it in the ordinary sense of the word, one individual among scores of other equally individual

bn 中正
bo 神氣
bp 聲調

bq 裒
br 精華
bs 造乎渾淪

bt 夫萬物一我也
千古一心也

individuals, but in terms of a universal monism in which one individual merges and discovers his place, and, in so doing, his powers of consciousness, expression, and articulation become limitless. The poets of the High T'ang were, he believes, able to achieve this, and, by assimilating their best works as his own, the student of poetry can achieve it as well. Moreover, far more is involved than the simple imitation of past masters:

> If poetry lacks *shen-ch'i* (expressive qualities), even if it were to capture the likenesses of the sun and the moon, it would have no light itself. One who studies Li [Po] and Tu [Fu] must not merely restrict himself to what the words say but must also follow his natural inclination and read them so deeply that, after a long time, he will obtain them [i.e. Li's and Tu's *shen-ch'i*] as well. This is the method of appropriating spirits and assimilating souls (*t'i hun she po*[bu]).[28]

Approaching this from the opposite point of view, Hsieh was also careful to advise the student not to confuse his own self-centered individuality with what he as an individual poet had achieved, with the truly enlightened self:

> If one can manage to avoid complacency in the composition of poetry, this will lead to the Embryo of Great Literary Accomplishment (*ta-ya chih p'ei*[bv]), and, although one might have ascended to the Very Highest Vehicle (*shang-sheng*[bw]), [i.e. write poetry in the High T'ang style], it would be even more marvelous if, being in possession of the Correct Dharma Eye, one were to adopt a critical attitude toward it. One should be diligent so as to advance it, take pains so as to refine it, and be modest so as to bring it to full realization. If one is able to win approval for it throughout the whole world (*ju t'ien-hsia chih mu*[bx]), he then can know that it will please people forever (*pai-shih chih mu k'o-chih*[by])![29]

The greatest poetry wins approval among everyone forever, and such poetry, says Hsieh, cannot be limited to the mere restrictions operating for the poet who would indulge his individual tastes, his individual sensibilities, and powers of apprehension and articulation at the expense of the self-transcendent universality which is its real requirement.

There are other statements in Hsieh's critical writings which refer to these concerns, but we will turn to another of the Latter Seven Masters, Wang Shih-chen (1526–1590), to round out this survey of archaist criticism. Like Hsieh, Wang was greatly concerned with the relationship between the individual and the tradition and with the nature of creativity. The following passage, although it deals with prose,

bu 提魂攝魄
bv 大雅之胚

bw 上乘
bx 入天下之目

by 百世之目可知

can illuminate several principal features of the archaist attitude toward literary art in general:

> Li Hsien-chi [Li Meng-yang] admonished people not to read any prose written after the T'ang Dynasty. At first, I thought this far too narrow a view, but now I believe it to be correct. If one's learning is too heterogeneous, when he begins to write himself, of course, he will find confusion waiting for him at the tip of his brush, and it will be difficult to spur it on. Moreover, when he does an imitation of a particular piece of writing, while it might be easy to let his brush run on, he will begin to feel uneasy about it, and the marks of conscious craft will become all too apparent; it will certainly not be the hand of a master artist at work. From now on I plan to be just like someone who purges his innards with three bushels of pure lime, that is, I should daily take up the *Six Classics*, the *Rites of Chou*, the *Mencius*, the *Lao Tzu*, the *Chuang Tzu*, the *Lieh Tzu*, the *Hsün Tzu*, the *Kuo yü*, the *Tso chuan*, the *Chan-kuo tz'u*, the *Han-fei Tzu*, the *Li sao*, the *Lü-shih ch'un-ch'iu*, the *Huai-nan Tzu*, the *Shih chi*, the *Han shu* of the Pan family, and, as for the writers from the Western Han up through Han [Yü] and Liu [Tsung-yüan], I should make a discriminating selection of the very best of their works, and I should read all of these so thoroughly that I shall begin to swim in them and so let their infusive power flow vast and full in me. Then, when I have occasion to write, I shall be totally able to follow the inclinations of my inner creative powers (*i shih hsin chiang*[bz]), my spirit (*ch'i*) will surge forth in complete harmony with my intent (*i*[ca]), and my intuitive powers will form a unity with the objects of perception (*shen yü ching ho*[cb]). Breaking off then in new directions, I shall whip up my horse and drive, silently receiving directions from within myself, and, whether it be through palaces or mountainous forests, or even through the Great Desert which swallows men's tracks, how wonderful that will be! There are people in the world now who understand that they should approve of antiquity and disparage the present, but if it [i.e. creative talent] only comes hither after having been summoned and only goes yon after having been led to do so, such people have already fallen to the level of enlightenment of the second order (*ti-erh-i*[cc]).[30]

Here Wang asserts that the true realization of creativity, of self and of its articulation, depends upon the successful assimilation of correct (*cheng*) models from the orthodox (*cheng*) tradition of literature. Without this tradition, the individual writer, left to his

bz 一師心匠   cb 神與竟合

ca 意   cc 第二義

own resources, stands no chance of achieving anything meaningful and worthwhile, either as a person or as a composer of literature. Whatever resources the individual might have, these are held only in potential and can never be truly realized through any kind of self-generating process but must depend for their organization, operation, and success totally upon the tradition which first purges all impurities and then nourishes the potential goodness which remains.

This conception of the relationship between the individual and the tradition is stated forcibly in Yen Yü's *Ts'ang-lang shih-hua*[31] and occurs often in archaist formulations of literary theory throughout the Ming and Ch'ing eras.[32] However, while this fundamental concept was unquestioned and the implications drawn from it were unchallenged within the archaist movement itself, there still persisted throughout the Ming a countertradition of expressionism which advocated a very different kind of self-realization. We shall now turn to the anti-archaists/ expressionists and see how their own tradition culminated in the polemical stance of the Kung-an school at the end of the Ming.

Kuo Shao-yü suggests that the expressionism of the Kung-an school can be traced back through Ming poetry to the late Yüan and early Ming figure Yang Wei-chen and quotes two passages from Yang's writings which reveal the importance he places on the role of individual personality in poetry:

> Poetry is man's *hsing-ch'ing*[cd] (personal nature), and, since each person has a personal nature, each person is capable of poetry—so how could what one learns from a teacher ever become the poetry of the individual poet himself!...[33] Poetry is a product of language, and language is a product of the will (*chih*). Each individual person has a will and a mode of language through which he creates poetry—something never arrived at by means of following what another person has already done.[34]

In fact, Yang seems to have indentified the nature of poetry with the personal nature of the poet itself:

> The criteria (*p'in*[ce]) for evaluating poetry are no different from those used to evaluate individual persons. A person has a particular facial expression, a particular bodily structure, a particular personal nature, and a particular spirit (*shen-ch'i*), and the way a poem is unsightly or beautiful or good or bad is established in exactly in the same terms. The *Feng* and the *Ya* [i.e. the *Classic of Poetry*, the *Odes*] developed in time into the *Sao* [the *Elegies of Ch'u, Ch'u-tz'u*] which in turn developed into the poetry of the *Nineteen Ancient Poems*, and these in their turn developed into the poetry of T'ao [Ch'ien] [365–427], then Tu [Fu] and the two Li's [Li Shang-yin (ca. 813–858) and Li Ho (791–817)]. Here the *ch'ing-hsing*[cf] (personalities) of

cd 性情   ce 品   cf 情性

the poets involved are not *yeh*^{cg} (vulgar), and their *ch'i* (spirits) are not *ch'ün*^{ch} (common), therefore the *ku-ko*^{ci} (formal structures) are not *pi*^{cj} (inferior), and the *mien-mu*^{ck} (formal expressive features) are not *lou*^{cl} (ugly). Alas! These poetic qualities failed to be carried on by successors, and, as far as the poetry of the Ch'i dynasty [479–502], the Liang [502–557], the Late T'ang, and that of Sung is concerned, since the formal expressive features became increasingly ugly and the formal structures kept becoming more and more inferior, one can guess what became of the personalities and spirits involved! Alas! If one were to study poetry in terms of that of the Late T'ang or the end of the Sung and still wish to approximate that of T'ao, Tu, and the Two Li's while hoping to draw close to the *Sao* and the *Ya*, such a person would encounter insurmountable obstacles! However, as far as personality and spirit in poetry are concerned, no distinction can be made between those of antiquity and those of modern times, and, if one can get at the personalities and spirits of the ancients, he will find their poetry there as well. Nevertheless, if one fails to recognize the consistency of the formal expressive features, it would be nonsense to expect to be able to get at the formal structures and even more nonsense to expect to get at the personalities involved. Failing that, of course, it would be most nonsensical to expect to get at the spirits that lie at the bottom of everything else![35]

Yang seems to be defining poetry in dualistic terms. Just as human beings are composed of supraphysical personalities and spirits, on the one hand, and physical facial expressions and physical statures, on the other, so poems are imbued with personal/spiritual qualities which become manifest through formal expressive features and formal structures. Note that Yang does not insist upon any set of so-called "perfect" models for poetic emulation and, in fact, declares that no distinctions can be made between the personal and spiritual qualities of poets of antiquity and his own age. With him, formal imitation does not play the all-important role it did with the archaists; he warned against it and viewed the poetry of a variety of eras as all equally valid for the revelation of the individual selves involved—such poems are excellent because of the personal qualities of the poets. For the archaists, "correct" poetry shaped the man as a "correct" ideal type, whereas for Yang, the poet as individual man shapes his poems as correlatives of his own inner self. The archaists approached poetry from the outside in; Yang reversed this and approached it from the inside out—as long as poetry is the true expression of the individual poet and the individual poet is *intrinsically* a person of fine human qualities, that poetry will be approved. Form, as such, will be "true" or "correct" as long as it serves as an effective vehicle for the expression of real personal qualities.

^{cg} 野	^{ci} 骨骼	^{ck} 面目
^{ch} 羣	^{cj} 庳	^{cl} 鄙

Kao Ch'i (1336–1374) is remembered perhaps more as a technical virtuoso who could imitate a great variety of (primarily) T'ang poets (and thus a figure who considerably influenced the development of archaism) than as an advocate of expressionism. Nevertheless, the expression of strongly felt emotion was one of the cornerstones of his theory of poetry:

> The essentials of poetry are three: 'formal style' (ko[cm]), 'meaning' (i), and 'gusto' (ch'ü[cn]): that is all. Formal style is that by which one distinguishes the form (t'i); meaning is that by which one conveys the feeling (ch'ing); gusto is that by which one reaches the miraculous (miao).[36] If formal styles are not distinguished, then one will degenerate into corrupt vulgarity and the whole idea of learning from the ancients will be perverted. If feeling is not conveyed, then one will fall into empty superficiality and the substance by which one might move people will be too shallow. If the miraculous is not attained, then one will drift into the commonplace and the atmosphere (feng[co]) necessary to transcend the ordinary will be too weak.... Yüan-ming [T'ao Ch'ien] excelled at expressing the happiness and freedom of life in the country but could not celebrate the glory of life at court; Ch'ang-chi [Li Ho] was skillful at expressing the unusual but lacked the means to sing of the charms of a garden in the hills. In both cases this is a failure to master all of what poetry can be. Therefore, one must take as his teachers all those who excelled at one particular kind of poetry and imitate them as circumstances demand (sui shih mo ni[cp]), waiting for the time to arrive when one's mind and heart fuses with all of them (tai ch'i-shih chih hsin-jung[cq]) so that he can realize his own potential all at once (hun-jan tzu-ch'eng[cr]), begin to be able to establish a reputation in his own right, and avoid the failing of being overly biased in favor of one kind of poetry.[37]

This view seems to strike a balance between the expressionists and the archaists, since it advocates the expression of genuine emotion and the true inner world of the poet, on the one hand, while still insisting upon the practice of selective imitation of past masters, on the other. Also, inspiration and the genuiness of personal experience are essential ingredients of the poetic act. Kao seems to suggest that one learns how to feel and to express his own emotions and "gusto" by learning from, and identifying with, the great poets of the past, and that there is a kind of emotive and spiritual continuum which transcends time and space and is universal to all men. How close this all is to the view of a Hsieh Chen is impossible to say, since Kao's expressionism ran so deep and was, in spite of his pluralistic emulation of earlier poets, so individual to him.

cm 格
cn 趣

co 風
cp 隨事摹擬

cq 待其時至心融
cr 渾然自成

Archaism during the Ming was to a great extent a phenomenon associated with high-ranking officials and their immediate followers. Li Tung-yang (1447–1516) was a transitional figure between the *t'ai-ko-t'i*[cs] (chancellery style of poetry) of the early Ming and the archaist poets of the next generation, and he was a grand secretary. Several of the Former Seven Masters, Li Meng-yang among them, were his disciples, and they, as did the majority of the Latter Seven Masters of the next generation, attained high office as well. Although the influence of these poet-officials reached far and wide outside officialdom, many poets, scattered throughout the empire, resisted this influence and continued to write an obviously expressionistic kind of poetry, inspired often by a fondness for Sung dynasty poetry, something quite out of keeping with archaist taste for the T'ang. Such poets were sometimes to be found among the prominent painters of the day such as Shen Chou (1427–1509), who emulated poets who were anathema to the archaists—Po Chü-i, Su Shih, and Lu Yu (1125–1210). Even the most brief survey of Shen's poetry reveals where his interests lay: with the simple and direct description of everyday life and the casual and easy self-expression of the sensibilities associated with that kind of life, all very much in the Sung "style." Among Shen's fellow countrymen (Wu district, Suchou) was Tu Mu (1459–1525), a famous collector of rubbings of stone and metal inscriptions, art connoisseur, and minor poet whose remarks on poetry were collected together as the *Nan-hao shih-hua*. Tu's work seems untouched by archaist influence, for in it favorable references to Sung and Yüan poetry abound, that of the High T'ang is de-emphasized, if anything, and Middle and Late T'ang poets are treated with respect. Although one entry deals with Yen Yü's analogy between poetry and Ch'an in considerable detail, it concentrates on the problem of the nature of spontaneity and completely ignores Yen's concept of "orthodoxy" in poetry with all the implications which became so important later for the archaists.[38] Another critic contemporary with the Former Seven Masters who adopted a stance similar to Tu's was Ho Meng-ch'un (1474–1536), whose *Yü-tung shih-hua* reveals a fondness for Sung dynasty poetry and its simple and direct expressionism.[39] I suspect that further reading in critical works of the early sixteenth century would reveal that these tendencies were even more widespread. In any event, there seems to be enough evidence that the influence of the archaists did not extinguish a continuing tradition of expressionism, a tradition which, as we shall see, extended directly to the more outspoken and articulate critics of the middle and late Ming who deliberately advocated an anti-archaist position and who glorified the straightforward expression of the natural self.

It has been suggested that there were three major factors during the Ming that led to the extreme expressionism of the Kung-an school: the influence of the philosophy of individualism which was making such an impact at the time,

cs 臺閣體

especially that of Li Chih (1527–1602) and to some extent also that of Chiao Hung (1541–1620); the influence of contemporary dramatists such as Hsü Wei (1521–1593) and T'ang Hsien-tsu (1550–1616), whose classical verse and remarks on poetry as well as their dramas were thoroughly oriented toward the glorification of individualism and the exaltation of strongly felt emotion; and the influence of contemporary poets such as Yü Shen-hsing (1545–1608) and Kung Nai (*chin-shih* of 1601) who advocated originality, expressionism, and individuality in poetry and who strongly opposed the views of the archaists.[40]

The radical philosophy of Li Chih, his iconoclasm, and his uncompromising individualism have been studied in considerable detail in various English language publications,[41] and his influence upon the Kung-an school has also received appropriate attention.[42] Thus we need not go into these here, except to say that Li's thought is probably best understood in terms of the general trend in Ming philosophy to emancipate the individual from tradition and to define the individual self as an autonomous entity, a trend that began in earnest with Ch'en Hsien-chang (1428–1500) and Wang Shou-jen (1472–1529) several generations earlier.[43] Li's own thought represents a more radical development of Ch'en's and Wang's thought. Whereas they attempted to reinterpret the Confucian tradition in their own terms (much like existential theologians have tried to reinterpret traditional Christianity and "renew" it in terms of "experiential truth"), Li became the complete iconoclast, rejected the basic assumptions and sanctions of the tradition, and attempted to create a new view of self and society based upon his own subjective awareness of self and his own objective knowledge of the way *he saw* human society operate, both in the past through history and in the present through his own experience of it. For him the most valued, indeed sacred, thing in all human existence is the *t'ung-hsin*[ct] (childlike mind), that pristine state of mind which manages to remain untouched by the "lies" of the tradition and the manipulation of those lies by current society. He advocated the autonomous self as the highest good, and it was inevitable that his thought should have influence in the contemporary world of letters, poetry included.

Hsü Wei is better known as a dramatist, painter, and calligrapher than as a poet, but his poetry was highly appreciated by the Kung-an school of the next generation, as this critique of him written by Yüan Hung-tao reveals:

> Since Weng-ch'ang [Hsü Wei] had not managed to satisfy his ambitions in officialdom, he began to lead a dissolute life with wine and liquor and indulged his passion for scenery, traveling all over Ch'i, Lu, Yen, and Chao and even seeing as much of the Northern Desert as he could. From the things he saw—mountains running, seas standing, desert sands rising, thunder scudding, rain crashing, and trees falling—and, whether he found

ct 童心

himself in secluded forests or great cities, any sight which could startle and surprise him, be it people, fish, or birds, all these did he manage to convey in his poetry. Moreover, in his breast he harbored a fully vital spirit that was inextinguishable. He was imbued with the sadness of a hero who had lost his way and who had no gate he might cross so to rest his feet. As a result, the composition of his poetry is either like angry shouting or like happy laughter, like water roaring through a canyon, like a seedling thrusting up through the earth, like a widow's night cries, like a homesick traveler getting up in the cold. Although his formal style is rather poor, his innate creativity (*chiang-hsin*[cu]) always emerges naturally. He had the spirit of an upright and honest man, someone who all those who take on feminine airs and serve as lackies never dare hope to be.[44]

A reading of Hsü's poetry reveals the essential correctness of Yüan's remarks; he was indeed primarily interested in the violence and extremes of nature, society, and the self. Agitation, crisis, and profound emotion are the chief characteristics of his work, and this Dionysian aspect stands in great contrast to the Apollonian art of the archaists. Hsü wanted his poetry to shock and rouse his readers, and he expected the poetry of others to do the same thing to him:

When I had a go at reading the selection of poetry you [a certain Hsü Pei-k'ou] had sent to me, it succeeded in making me feel as if icy water had been poured down my back—a fantastic shock all at once! This really is the kind of poetry that inspires one (*hsing*[cv]), makes one observe (*kuan*[cw]), makes one fit for company (*ch'ün*), and is able to express grievances (*yüan*[cx]).[45]

The qualities of *hsing*, *kuan*, *ch'ün*, and *yüan* were, of course, supposedly attributed by Confucius to the *Odes*, that font of the entire Chinese tradition of poetry,[46] and Hsü here affirms his basic view of poetry that it must be made out of the stuff that jolts the reader into a heightened awareness of himself and his world and that it electrifies him in such a way that he is compelled to feel what the poet himself felt in the writing.

Since Hsü's view of poetry was founded upon the intense and individual response of the poet to life, he had to deplore the practice of imitation:

Someone might learn to make bird calls, but, even though the sounds he makes are exactly like a bird's, his nature (*hsing*[cy]) will still be that of a man. Likewise, if a bird learns to make the sounds of human speech, even though it might sound just as if it were a man, its nature will still be that of a bird. It is impossible to deny that there certainly is a difference between

cu 匠心   cw 觀   cy 性

cv 興   cx 怨

them! This is exactly the situation as regards those of our contemporaries who try to write poetry. Such people do not express what they themselves have experienced but plagiarize what others have already written, saying that "this particular piece is in that particular style, and that particular piece is not, while this line resembles that particular poet, and that line does not." Although such people might be very skillful and really manage to do imitations to an extraordinary degree, each one of them as individuals cannot be anything other than a bird trying to make human speech![47]

T'ang Hsien-tsu was a prolific poet in the *shih* form, but he left almost no poetry criticism. However, both he and Hsü Wei seem to have largely thought of all literary art as one and did not, as far as their basic assumptions were concerned, greatly distinguish among verse (*shih*), lyrics (*tz'u*), drama (*ch'ü*), and prose (*wen*).[48] This flexible, almost indifferent, attitude to generic form, of course, set them and the Kung-an school at complete odds with the archaists for whom form always played a key role in almost any theoretical discussion. Therefore, it is likely that whatever T'ang says about the function and nature of any literary form will apply as well to poetry. In fact, in all such remarks he makes about literature he maintains a remarkable consistency of view which stresses the sanctity of impulse, the independence of personal expression, and the absolute inadequacy of imitation as a mode of literary art. The following passage is typical:

The world is dominated by old Confucian scholars with whom it is impossible to discuss literary art (*wen*). Their ears have not heard much, their eyes have not seen much, yet they spew forth their superficial and prejudiced opinions. Just look at the prose in the world today, and you will think that how could there ever be prose again after this! I say that the miraculous (*miao*) qualities of prose do not result from following another's example and becoming exactly like him. Rather, they come naturally in an unconscious flash of spiritual inspiration (*tzu-jan ling-ch'i huang-hu erh lai pu-ssu erh chih*[cz]). Uncanny and amazing, this is a state to which none can give a name, not anything with which one ordinarily can manage to identify. When Su Tzu-chan [Su Shih] painted withered trunks, bamboos, and rocks, he broke completely with painters of both the past and his present, and the style of his paintings became all the more marvelous. In fact, if one were to assess his paintings solely in terms of painting style, it almost appears that they do not even have one! The painters of the Mi family [Mi Fu (1052–1107) and his son Mi Yu-jen (1086–1165)], as far as landscape and figure painting are concerned, did not do much formal planning but, with the mere sketching of a few brushstrokes, made the

[cz] 自然靈氣恍惚而來不思而至

depiction of things vividly come to life (*hsing-hsiang wan-jan*[da]). By contrast, if they had tried to bring things off by means of conscious planning, they would never have achieved such beauty as they did. Thus, one can, through the seemingly trifling skills of brush and ink, enter into the Divine and become confirmed as a Sage (*ju shen cheng sheng*[db]). Since I am not a learned person, who will explain all this to me![49]

Not only do T'ang's critical views transcend the boundaries between the different literary forms, they also transcend the field of literature itself and apply as well to the visual arts. For him, all art is one, and what really matters—all that matters—is spontaneity and the genuine expression of the individual self.

The basic tenets of literary theory held by the Kung-an school have received extensive treatment elsewhere, and many of the most important passages in the critical writings of the school have already been translated and annotated and do not have to be dealt with again here.[50] Actually, there was not so much that was new in Yüan Hung-tao, his brothers, and their followers; their iconoclastic attitude toward High T'ang poetry, their fondness for Sung dynasty poetry, their wide-ranging taste for highly individual expressionist poetry from all over the tradition, their insistence upon the authenticity of poetic expression itself, and finally their glorification of the natural instincts and the innate qualities unique and original with each individual—all these are to be found scattered throughout the earlier Ming expressionists such as those we have been examining and were also suggested, at least in part, in the radical thought of Li Chih and Chiao Hung, if not in their "existential" and "experiential" forerunners Ch'en Hsien-chang, Wang Shou-jen, and their immediate followers. What the members of the Kung-an school did was to render all these features into a far more constant and coherent view of literature and to write a great deal of very original poetry and prose that exemplified in concrete form the theoretical principles involved. As an identifiable school, this group of writers was able to make the kind of impact on the Chinese world of letters at large which earlier expressionists as individuals had failed to do, and, as a deliberate and conscious countermovement to the established archaists, it not only breathed new life into Ming literature but also had a genuinely positive effect upon much of the best of Ch'ing literature as well.

The hardy individualism of the Ming expressionists, with all its distrust of tradition, did not outlive the end of the Ming dynasty, and by the early Ch'ing a resurgence of the archaist tradition was all too apparent.[51] However, the seventeenth century saw the development of an expanded, more open-ended attitude toward poetry and a movement which might be called "progressive" or "reformed" archaism or neoclassicism, for then poets and critics attempted to reconcile the individual with the tradition so that each could contribute to an increased and more

da 形象宛然　　　　　db 入神證聖

profitable appreciation of the other.[52] By the eighteenth century this trend had collapsed, and an almost complete triumph of archaism in its most sterile and suffocating form had asserted itself. It appears that the odds were against a successful implementation of an individualist/expressionist view of poetry, or even the development of a lasting positive regard for the salutary effect such a view would have on a tradition of poetry which largely remained rooted in archaism. The weight of tradition itself and the general distrust of the "un-cultivated" individual which seems to have operated throughout much of later Chinese history combined to orient students of poetry, generation after generation, to the archaist conception of poetry. The tendency to escape from freedom and all the responsibilities freedom entails is strong in any civilization, and traditional China, of course, was no exception. The archaists offered set formulae, a fixed discipline, and, most importantly, a promise that their way was the way to the emancipation of genius and the fulfillment of self. During most of the time they held sway over the world of letters they were well organized and had the support and sanction of the state with whose views concerning self and society they largely concurred. Authoritarian state ideology and archaism seem to have had a great deal in common. With the former, the individual self apart from the acculturating influence of the approved tradition was considered a positive danger and threat to stability and continuity of the status quo; with the latter, the individual poet apart from the shaping influence of the approved tradition was equally considered a threat, for he could subvert the whole apparatus by which the intelligensia (the practicing poet was more often than not either an office-holding bureaucrat or an aspirant to such position), through participation in literary culture, were made to conform to "approved" ideal social types. Nevertheless, the spark of true individualism caught fire at times, as in the late Ming with the Kung-an school, or, at least, inspired the traditional-minded to expand the tradition in such a way as to allow a more individually expressive poetry to take shape, as that, for instance, of the mid-Ch'ing poet Wang Shih-chen (1634–1711).[53]

As far as creativity within archaism is concerned, it could be considered in much the same light as that within the classical and various neoclassical movements in literature of the Western tradition. There are several parallels. For example, both archaism and neo-archaism in China and classicism and neoclassicism in the West identified a body of approved, supposedly "first-rate" works which were to form the nucleus of humanistic-aesthetic training. Then, both, in order to protect this nucleus, derided and made every effort to suppress "popular" elements in contemporary literature, elements that were seen as diluting and adulterating the "purity" of the classical works. Also, both identified and attempted to emulate a definite period of literary development, a period that supposedly had attained the ultimate perfection in literary art. Finally, and more problematic, is what seems to have been similar attitudes toward the nature and function of *mind* in the creative process. In both the mind was seen as essentially a *passive* entity, something to be shaped by models and conditioned by tradition rather than as something that creates works *ex nihilo*. The active and intrinsically self-sufficient creative mind, on the other hand, is generally associated with romanticism in the Western tradition, and in this respect at least, Western romanticism and the expressionist/anti-archaist movement of the later Chinese tradition appear to have something in common, as well as sharing a common emphasis on the roles of expressionism and individualism in the creative process. By contrast, the systematic cultivation of the self in terms of "perfect" models and its articulation in generation after generation of exemplary works in their own right are the cornerstones of both classicism/neoclassicism in the West and in the archaist/neo-archaist tradition in China. The vast differences between the two cultural/intellectual traditions notwithstanding, a case can be made, I believe, for comparing the two literary traditions in this way, though more detailed analysis would surely encounter problems of very considerable complexity.

Finally, as far as self-realization is concerned, we have seen that during the Ming two essentially different routes to such a state were suggested and encouraged in much of the critical writings on poetry of the time. The archaists insisted that self-realization was something to be learned from without and internalized through a process of emulation of supposedly self-realized and great masters of the past, and the anti-archaists/expressionists insisted that self-realization was something to be discovered within and liberated through the spontaneous exercise of the expressive faculties innate in the natural man. We might also draw a parallel here between these two contrasting views which occur within the tradition of literary theory during the Ming and the two different views of self-realization held by Ch'eng-Chu orthodoxy (like the archaists) and the radical philosophy of individualism associated with Wang Shou-jen and his "school" (like the anti-archaists/expressionists) within the development of Ming Neo-Confucianism.[54] This also would result in having to deal with complex and extensive issues, the scope of which is so great that I cannot treat them here.

1. From Li's biography in *Ming-shih* (History of the Ming Dynasty) (*Po-na-pen*) 286:12b.

2. Cf. Ch'ien Ch'ien-i, *Yu-hsüeh chi* (*SPTK* ed.) 15:127b–128a.

3. A discussion of the analogy and a translation of all pertinent passages appears in Richard John Lynn, "Ts'ang-lang's Discussions of Poetry," in *Sources of Neo-Confucianism*, ed. Irene Bloom (to be published by the Columbia University Press).

4. Yen Yü, *Ts'ang-lang shih-hua chiao-shih* (A Collated and Annotated Edition of Ts'ang-lang's Discussions of Poetry), collated and annotated by Kuo Shao-yü, (Peking, 1962), p. 127. A translation of the complete work, a fine pioneering effort, was done by

Günther Debon into German, *Ts'ang-lang's Gespräche über die Dichtung: ein Beitrag zur Chinesische Poetik* (Wiesbaden, 1962).

5. *Ts'ang-lang shih-hua*, p. 10.

6. Ibid; see also Kuo Shao-yü, n. 9, p. 12 and ann. pp. 15–20.

7. Ibid, pp. 24, 136, 162, 179.

8. Ibid, p. 24.

9. Ibid, pp. 24, 162, for example.

10. Ibid, pp. 235–236.

11. See Richard John Lynn, "Orthodoxy and Enlightenment: Wang Shih-chen's Theory of Poetry and its Antecedents," *The Unfolding of Neo-Confucianism*, ed. W. T. de Bary (New York and London, 1975), pp. 219–230.

12. See Jonathan Chaves' paper in this volume and James J. Y. Liu, *Chinese Theories of Literature* (Chicago, 1975), pp. 67–68.

13. See Ch'ien Ch'ien-i's denunciation of the *Ts'ang-lang shih-hua* and the archaists, *Yu-hsüeh chi* 15:127b–128a.

14. *Ming-shih* 286:2a–b.

15. See the biographical notice on Yang Wei-chen in *Dictionary of Ming Biography*, ed. L. C. Goodrich and Chaoying Fang (New York, 1976), p. 1551.

16. Kao Ping, *Li-tai ming-kung hsü-lun* (Discussion [of Poetry] by Famous Figures Throughout the Ages), in *T'ang-shih p'in-hui* (A Classified Anthology of T'ang Poetry) (ed. of 1628–1644); see also Kao's own preface to this work.

17. Kao Ping, *Wu-yen ku-shih hsü-mu* (Introduction to Five-Syllabic Ancient-Style Verse), in *T'ang-shih p'in-hui*, *Ming-chia* (Famous Masters), 6b–7a.

18. Kao Ping, *Wu-yen ku-shih hsü-mu*, *Cheng-pien* (Orthodox Innovation), 11b–12a.

19. *Ts'ang-lang shih-hua*, p. 179.

20. Kao Ping, *Wu-yen ku-shih hsü-mu*, *Chieh-wu* (Retracers), 9b.

21. Kao Ping, *Wu-yen ku-shih hsü-mu*, *Yü-hsing* (Lingering Echoes), 12a.

22. Wang Ch'eng, preface to *T'ang-shih p'in-hui*, 6a–b.

23. Li Meng-yang, *Yü Hsü-shih lun wen shu* (A Letter to Mr. Hsü in Which I Discuss Literary Art); quoted in Kuo Shao-yü, *Chung-kuo wen-hsüeh p'i-p'ing shih* (A History of Chinese Literary Criticism) (Hong Kong, n.d.), p. 302.

24. See Lynn, "Orthodoxy and Enlightenment," pp. 218–219.

25. Hsieh Chen, *Ssu-ming shih-hua* (*Hsü li-tai shih-hua* ed.) 1:3b.

26. Hsieh Chen, *Ssu-ming shih-hua* 3:5b.

27. Ibid. 3:8b.

28. Ibid. 2:6b.

29. Ibid. 3:12b.

30. Wang Shih-chen, *I-yüan chih-yen* (Goblet Words from the Garden of Art) (*Hsü li-tai shih-hua* ed.) 1:9b–10a.

31. *Ts'ang-lang shih-hua*, pp. 1, 10–11, 23–25.

32. See Richard John Lynn, "Tradition and Individual: Ming and Ch'ing Views of Yüan Poetry," *JOS* (1977), 15(1):1–19; this article appears in a slightly different version in *Chinese Poetry and Poetics*, ed. Ronald C. Miao (San Francisco, 1978), pp. 321–375.

33. Yang Wei-chen, *Li Chung-yü shih hsü* (Preface to the Poetry of Li Chung-yü),

Tung-wei-tzu wen-chi, 7, quoted in Kuo, *Chung-kuo wen-hsüeh p'i-p'ing shih*, p. 278.

34. Yang Wei-chen, *Chang Pei-shan ho T'ao-chi hsü* (Preface to Chang Pei-shan Echoing Poetry from the Collected Works of T'ao [Ch'ien]), *Tung-wei-tzu wen-chi*, 7, quoted in *Chung-kuo wen-hsüeh p'i-p'ing shih*, p. 278.

35. Yang Wei-chen, *Chao-shih shih-lu hsü* (Preface to the Poetry of Mr. Chao), *Tung-wei-tzu wen-chi*, 7, quoted in *Chung-kuo wen-hsüeh p'i-p'ing shih*, p. 279.

36. With a few minor changes, the translation up to this point follows that to be found in Liu, *Chinese Theories of Poetry*, p. 89.

37. Kao Ch'i, *Tu-an chi hsü* (Preface to the *Tu-an chi*), *Fu-tsao chi*, 2, quoted in *Chung-kuo wen-hsüeh p'i-p'ing shih*, p. 287.

38. Tu Mu, *Nan-hao shih-hua* (*Hsü li-tai shih-hua* ed.), 3a–b.

39. See Aoki Masaru, *Shina bungaku shisō shi* (Tokyo, 1943), p. 149.

40. Kuo, *Chung-kuo wen-hsüeh p'i-p'ing shih*, p. 348.

41. See Wm. Theodore de Barry, "Individualism and Humanitarianism in Late Ming Thought," in *Self and Society in Ming Thought*, ed. W. T. de Bary and the Conference and Ming Thought (New York and London, 1970), pp. 188–225.

42. See Liu, *Chinese Theories of Literature*, pp. 78–79, 81–82, 86–87, 134, and Jonathan Chaves, *Pilgrim of the Clouds: Poems and Essays from Ming China* (New York, 1978), pp. 11–25.

43. It may even be possible to trace this trend back farther to thinkers such as Wu Yü-pi (1392–1469) and Hu Chü-jen (1434–1484) who were still closely associated with Ch'eng-Chu orthodoxy; see Wing-tsit Chan, "The Ch'eng-Chu School of Early Ming," in *Self and Society in Ming Thought*, pp. 29–50, and Hellmut Wilhelm, "On Ming Orthodoxy," *MS* (1970–1971), 29:1–26.

44. Yüan Hung-tao, *Yüan Chung-lang wen-ch'ao* (*Yüan Chung-lang ch'üan-chi* ed.), p. 1.

45. Hsü Wei, *Hsü Wen-ch'ang san-chi* (*Ming-tai i-shu-chia chi hui-k'an* ed.), 16:43b.

46. See Liu, *Chinese Theories of Literature*, p. 109.

47. Hsü Wei, *Hsü Wen-ch'ang san-chi*, 19:8a.

48. See Kuo, *Chung-kuo wen-hsüeh p'i-p'ing shih*, pp. 354–359.

49. T'ang Hsien-tsu, *Ho-ch'i hsü*, *Yü-ming-t'ang wen-chi*, 5, quoted in *Chung-kuo wen-hsüeh p'i-p'ing shih*, p. 359.

50. See Liu, *Chinese Theories of Poetry*, pp. 79–81; Lynn, "Tradition and the Individual," pp. 7–9; Chaves, *Pilgrim of the Clouds*, pp. 16–17, etc.

51. See Lynn, "Tradition and the Individual," pp. 10–11.

52. Ibid., pp. 11–16.

53. See Richard John Lynn, *Tradition and Synthesis: Wang Shih-chen as Poet and Critic* (Ph.D. dissertation, Stanford, 1971).

54. See Lynn, "Orthodoxy and Enlightenment," pp. 219–236.

The Panoply of Images: A Reconsideration of the Literary Theory of the Kung-an School

By Jonathan Chaves

I

The so-called Kung-an school of late Ming writers consisted of the three Yüan brothers, Yüan Tsung-tao (1560–1600), Yüan Hung-tao (1568–1610), and Yüan Chung-tao (1570–1624)—all of whom came from Kung-an *hsien* in Hupei, whence the name of the school—as well as the circle of their friends, primarily T'ao Wang-ling (1562–1609), Chiang Ying-k'o (1556–1605), and Huang Hui (1554–1612). There are two prevalent views of this group of poets and essayists: (1) To their critics, they were wildly unconventional rebels against the orthodoxy of the prevailing literary trend in Ming poetry, namely that advocated by the Former and Latter Seven Masters (*ch'ien, hou ch'i tzu*), but their work easily degenerated into vulgarity or "precious fun-poking." This view has found a recent expression in Ch'en Shou-yi, *Chinese Literature: A Historical Introduction,*[1] although Ch'en does balance it with some guarded praise for certain of Yüan Hung-tao's works. (2) To their modern admirers, they were Chinese romantics, champions of personal expression in literature, and of individualism as opposed to imitation. This view was put forth with great vigor in the 1920s and 30s by Chou Tso-jen,[2] and after him by Lin Yutang in several articles in his magazine, *Jen-chien shih* (*This Human World*); Lin also expressed his admiration for Yüan Hung-tao in certain of his English-language books, most notably *The Importance of Living* (1937) and *The Importance of Understanding* (1960).[3] (Lin seems also to have seen the Kung-an writers as humorists or wits.) More recently, this view informs the most thorough study of the school to date, Hung Ming-shui's Ph. D. dissertation, *Yüan Hung-tao and the Late Ming Literary and Intellectual Movement* (Madison, Wisc. 1974).[4]

I would maintain that the first of these two views trivializes the Kung-an writers, while the second, although it does present part of the truth concerning them, ultimately distorts our understanding of the full range of their achievement. Elsewhere I intend to argue in detail against the use of the term "romantic" for these men or indeed for any traditional Chinese writers. Here, by concentrating on the main ideas of Yüan Hung-tao—the central figure in the school—and his circle, I hope to show that the truth is more complex. Far from being wild rebels, the Kung-an writers produced some of the most cogently argued, thought-provoking statements on literary theory in the entire Chinese tradition. These are found in essays and letters which are written with a passionate intensity, a refreshing clarity of thought, and a frequently mordant wit. Whereas many Chinese critics concentrate their primary message into two–character terms whose ultimate meaning is almost always impossible to pin down, the Kung-an writers, while also employing certain key terms, write with such evident desire to communicate that in their best essays and letters every line contributes to the dynamic progress of the argument. For those accustomed to struggling with the ambiguities of classical Chinese rhetoric, the result can be breath-taking—almost like a sword cutting swiftly through the proverbial knot.

Upon careful reading of the Kung-an writers, these surprises emerge: (1) Yüan Hung-tao et al. were *not* adamantly opposed to the main figures among the orthodox masters. They recognized the quality of much of their work, and reserved their contempt primarily for the lesser followers of the masters. (2) Certain key concepts were actually *shared* by the orthodox masters and the Kung-an writers, primarily the notion that poetry can embody a deeper reality innate within the phenomena of existence. In other words, in the Kung-an school, both the "expressive" and "metaphysical" theories can be found,[5] and the latter is often presented in the *very same terms* used by the orthodox writers. (3) The Kung-an writers never completely rejected the principle of learning from the past, even from the High T'ang poets the imitation of whom was a central tenet in orthodox gospel. They simply felt one should broaden one's horizons, and learn from other periods— primarily mid- and late T'ang, and Sung—as well, and that what one should learn from them was not narrow formalism, but the courage to be true to one's own feelings and perceptions, and to evolve a style appropriate to those feelings and perceptions. (4) The Kung-an writers were not only interested in self-expression, although it was certainly a major theme for them. They were profoundly concerned with the relationship of art and nature, with the art of poetry per se—indeed, with creativity itself. They recognized certain common factors underlying the aesthetics of poetry, painting and calligraphy, while at the same time advising that one specialize in one particular form of expression. On all these issues, they have a good deal to say which is of considerable interest, but the door to understanding will remain closed if we continue to see them merely as a reaction against the orthodox tradition, or as self-centered "romantics."

Let us examine these points in some detail. Here are statements by various members of the Kung-an school on the orthodox tradition, particularly the concept of *fu-ku* ("return to antiquity"):

> *Yüan Hung-tao (from his preface to the collected works of Chiang Ying-k'o):* In recent times, certain men of letters have started to advocate a theory of *fu-ku* so as to overcome it [i.e. the problem of the increasing decadence of literature]. Now as far as "*fu-ku*" is concerned, it is a correct idea. But their practice has led to the extreme of considering plagiarism to be *fu-ku*—imitating every word and every line, and then forcing these

into some kind of unity, rejecting the scenes before their very eyes and instead adopting obsolete phrases.[6]

Yüan Tsung-tao: K'ung-t'ung [Li Meng-yang (1472–1529), one of the Former Seven Masters], not realizing [that the great writers of the past did not imitate each other], imitated every work of theirs, calling this a "return to the orthodox," and later men of letters see this practice as an established precedent, and honor it as an axiomatic mandate. Whenever they see that a writer has a single phrase which does not resemble the works of the ancients, they curse him roundly as a follower of an "evil, unorthodox way." They do not realize that for K'ung-t'ung to imitate past literature as an individual engaged in his own creative work was not really reprehensible, but when this individual's practice was handed down to become the practice of hundreds, then error became compounded and the practice degenerated rapidly into something not even worth taking into consideration. Moreover, K'ung-t'ung's essays contain a great many of his own ideas, and in their depiction of events and expression of feelings, they frequently are quite realistic....[7]

Yüan Chung-tao: With the Hung [-chih] and Chia [-ching] periods [i.e. 1488–1505, 1522–1566], certain scholar-officials [i.e. the Former Seven Masters] advocated *fu-ku* ["return to antiquity"] as a means to reform the vulgar, prolix practices of contemporary literature—and this was not a bad idea! But what with plagiarism and the use of conventionalized diction, it became the seedbed of degeneration. The later officials [i.e. the Latter Seven Masters] took this over as their doctrine, and without striving for "meaning and flavor" (*i-wei*[a]), they only imitated words and lines, holding to an extremely narrow view, and establishing theories with great pride. Their students, men of little understanding, followed them in these blameworthy practices....[8]

Chiang Ying-k'o: In the present dynasty, those who have discussed poetry—men like Li K'ung-t'ung [Li Meng-yang] and Li Yü-lin [Li P'an-lung (1514–1570), one of the Latter Seven Masters]—have been known in the world for the vigor of their movement to return to antiquity (*fu-ku*). Now these two gentlemen, while they certainly possessed vigor in their return to antiquity, also possessed the flaw of becoming bogged down in antiquity!...[9]

Elsewhere, Chiang Ying-k'o expresses his admiration for the poetry and prose of Li Meng-yang, Wang Shih-chen (1526–1590), Hsieh Chen (1495–1575), Li P'an-lung, Tsung Ch'en (1525–1560), and Ho Ching-ming (1483–1521), all of them major orthodox masters.[10] In each case, Chiang strives for a balanced view, telling what he likes and what he does not like in the writer he is discussing.

[a] 意味

If we evaluate the above statements without any preconceptions as to the literary scene in late Ming China, an unexpected perspective emerges: Yüan Hung-tao and the other important figures in the Kung-an school, far from being wild rebels against orthodoxy, were serious literary critics capable of carefully weighing the pros and cons of an idea, or the positive and negative aspects of any given writer. They were aware of the reformist component in the historical *fu-ku* concept,[11] and they were in sympathy with it, but they were also deeply disturbed by the excesses to which blind emulation of past writers could lead. In this respect, they were remarkably similar to the circle of Northern Sung scholars which centered around Ou-yang Hsiu (1007–1072). Ou-yang and his friends were upset by what they regarded as the excessive artificiality of the so-called Hsi-k'un[b] school of poetry which had flourished earlier in the Sung dynasty, but they certainly recognized the considerable talents of the chief Hsi-k'un poets, primarily Yang I (974–1020) and Liu Yün (971–1031), blaming the excesses of their movement on their minor followers.[12] In addition, Ou-yang and his circle employed the *fu-ku* concept creatively, hoping to revitalize Sung poetry by drawing inspiration from the great writers of the past. For these reasons, it would not be inappropriate to suggest that an essential sympathy of views existed among the Ou-yang Hsiu circle, the best of the orthodox masters of the Ming dynasty, and the Kung-an school of the late Ming.

It is worth noting that when Yüan Chung-tao, who died in 1624 and thus outlived the other Kung-an writers by twelve or more years, realized that certain followers of his brother, Hung-tao, were misunderstanding his vision, he chided them with characteristic honesty: "Men of understanding corrected them [i.e. the practices of the orthodox masters], and did not refrain from depicting any emotion, or from using any scene. But some of them could not avoid casting off conventionalized diction only to tend toward vulgarity!"[13] Yüan may have in mind the notorious Ching-ling[c] school, primarily Chung Hsing (1574–1624) and T'an Yüan-ch'un (1586–1631). The poetry of these men, which is actually diametrically opposed to that of the Kung-an poets, seems virtually incomprehensible in its awkward diction. But Chung and T'an were regarded as followers of Yüan Hung-tao in that they, too, were rebelling against the orthodox emulation of High T'ang poetry alone. The main point for us is that just as the Kung-an writers could recognize the good aspects of the very poets they were opposed to, so were they capable of seeing the negative aspects of writers thought of as being on their own side.

Chung-tao spends a good deal of time in some of his most important polemical essays correcting what he regards as excesses within the Kung-an camp. Again, this is the posture not of a wild-eyed rebel, but of a serious critic concerned with striking a sensible balance.

b 西崑   c 竟陵

II

When we turn to the Kung-an writers' views on what it is that literature communicates, we find that while the "expressive" concept is clearly of major importance for them (more will be said on this later)—as it certainly was *not* for the orthodox masters—they also held what I believe must be considered the "metaphysical" view (in Liu's sense) as well.

Richard John Lynn, in an important study, has demonstrated the extent to which the orthodox school derived its ideas and terminology from the *Ts'ang-lang shih-hua* of Yen Yü (1180–1235).[14] One of the key terms in that text is *hsing-ch'ü*,[d] which Lynn translates as "inspired interest." In one passage, Yen Yü uses this term to characterize the poetry of the High T'ang, while in another, it is one of his five principles of poetics, where, according to Lynn, it "represents the faculty or function of the poet's vision—his intuitive cognition."[15] This, of course, is the cornerstone of the orthodox/metaphysical school. Now, in one of Yüan Hung-tao's major statements on literature, the *Hsü Ch'en Cheng-fu hui-hsin chi*[e] (Preface to the "Intuition Collection" of Ch'en Cheng-fu),[16] Yüan centers his discussion around the second word in this compound, *ch'ü*: "That which is difficult for people to obtain is *ch'ü*. *Ch'ü* is something like the colors of a mountain, the flavor (*wei*) of a river, the luster of a flower, the gesture of a woman. Even a good talker can't come up with a description of it; only one who has intuition (*hui-hsin-che*[f]) can comprehend it." Later, he castigates those who attempt to experience *ch'ü* by collecting antiques, or devoting themselves to incense or tea: "These have nothing to do with the spiritual feeling (*shen-ch'ing*[g]) [of *ch'ü*]." Clearly, *ch'ü* here is something more than "flair" (Pollard) or "zest" (Lin Yutang). It is the ineffable essence at the heart of things, and even partakes of a spiritual quality. It is also a quality in the mind or soul of one who perceives *ch'ü* in the outer world, in keeping with the dualistic function of many Chinese critical terms, i.e. their applicability both to some quality in the *world* and to the same quality in the mind of the perceiver. As Lynn says, speaking of the compound *hsing-ch'ü* (and of another compound including the word *hsing*), *ch'ü* implies "an inspired awareness of the ultimate reality of things."[17] How appropriate, then, that Ch'en Cheng-fu, "one who has a profound understanding of *ch'ü*,"[18] as Yüan says, should have named his book, "*Intuition*" Collection.

The word *ch'ü*, both alone and in various compounds, occurs frequently in Kung-an writings. Yüan Hung-tao, in a letter to a friend, says that the only good Six Dynasties poets were T'ao Ch'ien (365–427) and Hsieh Ling-yün (385–433), and that T'ao had "the *ch'ü* of poetry" (*shih-ch'ü*).[19] Here, and elsewhere, one is tempted to translate *ch'ü* as "essence." In another passage, Yüan tries to determine what it is

d 興趣
e 敍陳正甫會心集

f 會心者
g 神情

that distinguishes the creative individual (whether poet, painter; or calligrapher) from ordinary people, and concludes that it is the "*ch'ü* of a remarkable person" (*i-jen chih ch'ü*[h]).[20]

Yüan Tsung-tao, in a poem, praises the southern Sung poet, Lu Yu (1125–1210) for "having *ch'ü* just like that of Yüan [Chen (779–831)] and Po [Chü-i (772–846)]."[21] Interestingly, Lu Yu himself used the word *ch'ü* in a passage contrasting the T'ang poets Ts'en Shen (715–770) and Wei Ying-wu (b. 737): "The heroic and expansive *ch'ü* of the former and the calm and tranquil *ch'ü* of the latter are entirely different."[22] Here, and in Tsung-tao's usage, *ch'ü* comes close to meaning "style." i.e. the "essence" of that which distinguishes a given poet's work. Tsung-tao's poem also speaks of the flavor, *wei*, of Lu's poetry, and it is worth noting that the two words, *ch'ü* and *wei*, are combined in the compound *ch'ü-wei* as used by Ssu-k'ung T'u (837–908), in many respects the "grandfather" of the orthodox/metaphysical school. In his letter to Wang Chia,[23] Ssu-k'ung applies the term *ch'ü-wei* to the poets Wei Ying-wu and Wang Wei (701–761).

The word *ch'ü* is also used in the more conventional sense of "pleasure," without any particular reference to literature. Tsung-tao recalls that "Chou-wang [i.e. T'ao Wang-ling] spoke with feeling about the *ch'ü* [pleasure] he once experienced watching the moon at West Lake. We looked at each other, sighing in appreciation for a long time."[24] Even here, though, the "pleasure" in question involved penetrating to the deepest level of the experience, a process which lies at the heart of the Kung-an conception of creativity. This use, too, of the word is not without precedent. A good example occurs in a poem by Wei Ying-wu about visiting the quarters of a Buddhist monk:[25] "As I give myself to the pleasure (*ch'ü*) of serenity, I feel at odds with the world of dust." Here, also, the word *ch'ü* has a quasi-religious sense which it never entirely loses.

Finally, it might be noted that the use of *ch'ü* alone to mean "the essence of an experience or of a work of art" was common early in the Ming dynasty. One of the major early Ming poets, Chang Yü (1333–1385), who is not known as a literary theorist, seems to have had a particular fondness for it. He uses it to indicate "essence":

Buddhism: Now I understand the profundity of the meaning and essence (*ch'ü*) of the Empty Gate.[26]

Literature: Calmly, I sit with the books of the ancients, open a volume, and find new essence (*ch'ü*).[27]

Painting: The royal descendant [i.e. the Yüan dynasty painter, Chao Yung (1289–ca. 1360)] while still a young man painted this essence (*ch'ü*) from his heart.[28]

Calligraphy: [Of the calligrapher, Sung K'o (1327–1387)] The marvelous-

[h] 異人之趣

ness of your work comes close to [that of the great calligraphers,] Chung [Yu (151–230)] and Wang [Hsi-chih (303–379)]; how profound the essence (*ch'ü*)![29]

The Kung-an writers knew and admired the work of Chang Yü, as well as that of the other three poets who, together with him, made up the Four Worthies of Early Ming Poetry. In the words of Chiang Ying-k'o, "At the dawn of our dynasty, such men as Kao [Ch'i (1336–1374)], Yang [Chi (ca. 1334–ca. 1383)], Chang [Yü], and Hsü [Pen (d. 1379/80)] truly wrote poets' poetry!"[30] Chang Yü also anticipates the Kung-an writers' application of a given term not only to literature, but to calligraphy, painting, and philosophy as well.

By following a train of thought inspired by a key term in one of Yüan Hung-tao's seemingly iconoclastic essays, we have found that Kung-an theory in this respect at least was consistent with a certain tradition within Ming literary thought, and Chinese literary thought in general. The same conclusion could have been reached by tracking down the histories of at least half a dozen other such terms.

Another key term in the Kung-an vocabulary is *chen*,[i] "real," "true," "authentic." It is frequently contrasted with *wei*,[j] "fake," "phony." Li Chih (1527–1602), the individualist thinker who was a friend of the Yüan brothers and may have both exercised considerable influence on them and been influenced by them, speaks of "phony" men who produce "phony writings,"[31] and there can be little doubt that he has in mind the orthodox masters and their followers. Yüan Hung-tao, in a letter to an unnamed friend,[32] asks why it is that people would prefer to have "authentic" (*chen*) modern art works, such as a painting by Shen Chou (1427–1509) or a calligraphy by Chu Yüan-ming (1461–1527), rather than fakes of old art works, such as a painting by Chao Meng-fu (1254–1322) or an ancient bronze. He concludes that it is precisely the quality of *chen*, "authenticity," that the modern works possess which makes them prized (in a culture which otherwise prizes antiquity).

The Kung-an writer who placed greatest emphasis on the concept of *chen* in poetry was Chiang Ying-k'o. "In writing poetry," he tells us, "first seek the real (*chen*); don't start by seeking a T'ang style."[33] Another passage is of particular interest:[34]

> When one writes poetry, if it is real (*chen*) poetry, although each and every poem may not be lovely (*chia*[k]), they will all possess essence (*ch'ü*). If these poems originate in falseness (*chia*[l]), some of them may still be lovely, but even though they are lovely, they will lack essence. Consider a scholar-official of our class, with official robe and broad sash: even if his

i 眞
j 僞
k 佳
l 假

face be unattractive and his appearance unprepossessing, people will always respect him. They will respect his realness (*chen*). Now imagine an actor, handsome and imposing. Give him an official robe and broad sash to wear, and he will indeed look quite impressive and noble. And yet people will look down at him. They will look down at his falseness (*chia*).

Chiang goes on to relate that the great Neo-Confucian thinker, Wang Yang-ming (1472–1528) once said of a man's work that it resembled the writings of various great writers of the past. The man was greatly pleased, failing to realize that Wang was actually damning with faint praise. He had *merely* achieved an imitative likeness, like that of the actor dressed up as an official, not the quality of *chen*, i.e. a style of his own.

But *chen* means more here than "real" as opposed to "fake." It also implies, again, a *deeper* reality beneath surface appearances, and therefore is similar to *ch'ü*. It should be recalled that the definition of *chen* in the *Shuo-wen chieh-tzu* dictionary written by Hsü Shen and completed in 121 is: "[What occurs when] an immortal transforms his physical form and ascends to heaven (*hsien-jen pien hsing erh teng t'ien yeh*[m])."[35] This is the sense that the word has in its many Taoist usages, e.g. "*chen jen*," "true man," or "immortal." An interesting use of *chen* in art criticism occurs in the *Pi-fa chi*, a text attributed to the great painter, Ching Hao (? after 870–? ca. 935).[36] In the translation of Kiyohiko Munakata, who argues persuasively for the traditional attribution of the text, one key passage reads, "Lifelikeness means to achieve the form of the object but to leave out its *spirit*. Reality (*chen*) means that the forces of both *spirit* and *substance* are strong (*ssu che to ch'i hsing i ch'i ch'i; chen che ch'i chih chü sheng*[n])."[37] Here a crucial distinction is drawn between mere objective realism (*ssu*), which does succeed in capturing an external likeness, and *chen*, which is here seen to comprise both external and internal, or spiritual, values. The term *ch'i*, translated "spirit" here, is also used by the Kung-an writers. Yüan Hung-tao speaks of the *ch'i* (or "spirit-vitality" in this context) of poetry declining age by age.[38] T'ao Wang-ling says that "Literature obtains its spirit-vitality (*ch'i*) from dynamism (*tung*[o])."[39] He then goes on to draw a parallel with painting. Chiang Ying-k'o brings together *ch'i* and the already familiar term *wei* ("flavor"), and applies them to the works of the orthodox master, Tsung Ch'en: "Tsung Tzu-hsiang [i.e. Tsung Ch'en] suffers only from excessive mysteriousness; he is not founded in reality. And yet his prose style has much of Tung-p'o's [Su Shih (1037–1101)] spirit-flavor (*ch'i-wei*)."[40]

The closeness of the terms *chen* and *ch'ü*, and the association of both with a quasi-religious sense of being, is indicated by a poem of Chang Yü, the early Ming poet praised by Chiang Ying-k'o in a passage already translated. The poem,[41]

[m] 仙人變形而登天也
[n] 似者得其形遺其氣。眞

者氣質俱盛。

[o] 動

entitled *To Hermit Wu*, opens with these lines: "This hermit-gentleman embodies *real essence*; / floating, floating—he loves the immortals of old! (*yin-weng yün chen-ch'ü; p'iao-p'iao huai ku hsien*[P])." The poem goes on to describe Wu as a Taoist-alchemist. Elsewhere, Chang Yü applies the same compound, *chen-ch'ü*, to poetry, demonstrating the flexibility of many of these terms. This poem is called, *In Answer to a Painter Who Asked Me About Poetry*: "Would you know the real essence (*chen-ch'ü*) of poetry?/ It is quite different from your painting!"[42]

The idea that poetry uncovers or communicates a "reality" (one is almost tempted to use Carlos Castaneda's term, "separate reality") or essence innate in things cannot help but remind us of the orthodox school's use of the Ch'an Buddhist term, *wu*,[q] "enlightenment." Lynn argues strongly that Yen Yü, in *Ts'ang-lang shih-hua*, and the orthodox masters after him, merely used Ch'an and its terminology metaphorically.[43] It presented them with a convenient set of hierarchical levels on which to arrange the various periods of literary history, or various degrees of achievement in poetic art. When Lynn speaks, however, of poetry which "attempts to express a state in which the reality of self merges in submission to the larger reality of Nature as a whole,"[44] we would seem to be quite close indeed to the *substance* of the Ch'an enlightenment experience—that is to say, these men may indeed have used Ch'an terms as analogues, but at the same time they do seem to have believed that the actual act of poetic perception was in some fashion actually similar, or even identical to, the enlightenment experience! Now, the Kung-an writers also use the term *wu*, but they use it sparingly. Here is an example drawn from Yüan Chung-tao's *Preface to the Collected Works of Yüan Chung-lang*: "[Hung-tao] was naturally endowed with a remarkable genius, differing from the men of this world as immortals differ from commoners. His learning [or philosophy] (*hsüeh-wen*[r]) derived from consulations [with monks] and enlightenment (*ts'an-wu*[s])."[45] T'ao Wang-ling says of essay writing that "although this is a minor art, it does possess divine mechanisms (*shen-chi*[t]) and must be mastered through enlightenment (*wu te chih*[u])."[46] But by and large, these passages are the exception rather than the rule. It may be that the very association of Ch'an ideas with the orthodox writers led the Kung-an school to downplay them, or it is possible that they avoided Ch'an formulations because they were profoundly involved with a very different mode of Buddhism, namely, the popular, devotional "Pure Land" school.[47] Nevertheless, the use of such terms as *chen, ch'i, ch'ü, shen* (as in *shen-chi* above), etc., leaves little room for doubt that for the Kung-an writers, too, at least one of the functions of literature was to embody or communicate a perception of innate reality, through a process similar in some fashion to religious meditation.

P 隱翁蘊眞趣，飄飄懷古
仙。
q 悟

r 學問
s 參悟

t 神機
u 悟得之

III

One area where the Kung-an school really appears to part company with the traditionalists is in its rejection of excessive reliance on imitation, and, as a corollary of this, its advocation of the idea that the poem springs from the coming together of the poet's own heart or mind, on the one hand, and the external world, on the other. The case against the importance of imitation is argued at greater length and with greater frequency than any other issue in Kung-an polemics. A good example is the essay, *Imitating the Poems of the Ancients*, by Chiang Ying-k'o[48] who proves himself here as elsewhere one of the most dynamic polemicists among the Kung-an writers:

The old *yüeh-fu* poems and old *shih* poems had titles based on their contents, and they were written about contemporary events. Examples are *Your Horse is Tan* (*Chün ma huang*), *The Pheasant is Mottled* (*Chih-tzu pan*), *We Cut Grass and Spread Nets* (*I ju chang*), *Since Your Departure* (*Tzu chün chih ch'u i*).[49] These poems were naturally superior—but poets of our present dynasty just take the titles of these poems, write a poem of their own in imitation of each original, and call this "returning to antiquity" (*fu-ku*). But the ancients were writing in their own times, about their own contemporary events, which then gave rise to certain emotions and, in turn, the appropriate words to describe them. We may try to imitate these poems, but this is not the same period as theirs, and the events they described are not taking place now: how can the emotions they felt arise in us? And yet we make ourselves write out poems of our own on these themes! Even if they are well executed, it is like a skillful worker or capable artisan who molds some clay, carves some wood and produces an exact image of a man which nevertheless totally lacks the vital spirit of a real man. Why should this be prized? And if mere similitude in itself is not worth much, how about something which fails to achieve even similitude?

Furthermore, if one must imitate each and every *yüeh-fu*—*Your Horse is Tan*, *The Pheasant is Mottled*, etc.—then why hold back from imitating such poems as the *Ospreys* (*Kuan chü*) and the *Locusts* (*Chung ssu*)?[50] Could it be that the old *yüeh-fu* and the old *shih* poems are more ancient than the Three Hundred Poems?

From this we can see that imitating the poems of the ancients is of no use. We may pile up our imitations, filling rooms of shelves and furniture, spending months and years at it, but this will not help us become known as writers. Now if we look at the song-poems of Li [Po (701–762)] and Tu [Fu (712–770)], such as *Song of Mount Lu* (*Lu-shan yao*) and *The Roads to Shu are Hard* (*Shu tao nan*),[51] and *Song of Mei-p'o* (*Mei-p.o hsing*), *Song of Watching the Fishermen* (*Kuan ta-yü ko*), *Song of Binding the Chicken* (*Fu-chi hsing*), and *Song of My Thatched Roof Being Destroyed by the Autumn Wind*

(*Mao-wu wei ch'iu-feng so p'o ko*),[52] we find that all of them, along with their titles, are based on actual events of the time, and of course they are supreme masterpieces of all time. It is for this reason that [Li and Tu] are heroes among poets. If this is so, then any poet who cannot come up with his own approach, and who obsequiously limits himself to the poem titles and themes established in the past, calling this "returning to antiquity," is truly a louse living in somebody else's pants!

Chiang's position appears to be fairly "cut and dry." Other Kung-an statements, however, give us a somewhat more complicated picture. In a letter to a friend,[53] Yüan Hung-tao has this to say:

> I have read your fine collection of poems—they are fresh, original, and have a strong beauty. Not a single poem falls into the well-worn paths of recent practice, so I know you are not one to follow in the footsteps of others! And yet Hsing Shao-ch'ing, in his preface to your book, says of you that you are one who models (*fa*[v]) himself directly on the T'ang dynasty, without doing so through the intermediaries, Wang [Shih-chen] and Li [P'an-lung]. Now this statement is quite correct—but I would add that while it goes without saying that Wang and Li are not worth modeling oneself on, even if one models oneself directly on the T'ang poets, one is still being like Wang and Li! The marvelousness of the T'ang poets lies precisely in the fact that they did *not* model themselves (*wu-fa*[w]) on anyone! For example, the T'ang poets felt there was no need to model oneself on the Six Dynasties, Han and Wei poets. And even though they admired such poets as Shen [Ch'üan-ch'i (650–712)] and Sung [Chih-wen (656–712)], Li [Po] and Tu [Fu], they were utterly unwilling to model their work after that of these poets. This is why the T'ang was the supreme period in all of antiquity!
>
> You possess profound mystical insight, and so you have modeled yourself on the nonmodeling of the T'ang! This is a point not brought out in Shao-ch'ing's preface, so I have added it for him.

One is reminded of the constant protestations of the existentialists, Sartre and Camus, that there is no God: ultimately, they "protest too much," and we begin to feel that the idea of God actually obsesses them. Similarly, Yüan Hung-tao's thoughts constantly return to the achievements of the great T'ang poets, even in contexts, such as this one, in which he is arguing *against* emulation of their work. He never actually attacks the substance of their poetry—on the contrary, he has great admiration for it. What he is saying is that one should not blindly imitate Li Po or Tu Fu, which is what the orthodox masters, such as Wang Shih-chen and Li P'an-lung, appear to be calling for (or at least what their school has degenerated into in the

v 法   w 無法

hands of their followers). But one should certainly derive inspiration from what may be called the individualist spirit of the T'ang poets, their refusal to model themselves on anyone else. And he is calling attention to an irony in the orthodox position: the mainstream poets of the Ming were emulating poets who themselves disdained to emulate anyone! Yüan would have agreed completely with the formulation of the contemporary American poet and critic, Robert Bly, in a recent interview:[54] "When a man or woman succeeds in grasping what his or her master has done, and breaking through it, he doesn't create something artificial. He enters through his bellybutton into the interior space inside himself. And there, to everyone's surprise, are new kinds of grass and new kinds of trees...."

Elsewhere, Yüan Hung-tao shows that this concept can also apply to the art of painting. In an important passage, he describes a visit he and his elder brother Tsung-tao paid to the great painter and art critic, Tung Ch'i-ch'ang (1555–1636):[55]

> Once, when Po-hsiu [Yüan Tsung-tao] and I were visiting Tung Hsüan-tsai [Tung Ch'i-ch'ang], Po-hsiu asked, "Of the major figures in the recent world of painting, such as Wen Cheng-ming (1470–1559), T'ang Po-hu [T'ang Yin (1470–1523)], and Shen Shih-t'ien [Shen Chou], can it be said that they possess something of the brush-style (*pi-i*[x]) of the old masters?" To this, Hsüan-tsai replied, "There are recent painters in whom not a single brushstroke differs from the old masters—now, actually, they are *unlike* the old masters, and one might even say this is not painting." I was amazed to hear this, and exclaimed, "These are the words of one who has perceived the Tao!" For the good painter learns from things, not from other painters. The good philosopher learns from his mind, not from some doctrine. The good poet learns from the panoply of images (*sen-lo wan-hsiang*[y]), not from writers of the past. When one models oneself on the [poets of the] T'ang dynasty, it is not a question of modeling one's technique (*chi-ko*[z]), lines and words on theirs. One models oneself on the spirit of their *not* being like the Han [poets], or the Wei [poets], or the Six Dynasties [poets]. This is the true "modeling."

Here again is the kind of paradoxical formulation for which China had a tradition going back to the Taoist classics.

IV

It follows that Yüan Hung-tao and his circle, in addition to the "metaphysical" notion of literature which we have already discussed, held also to an "expressive"

---

x 筆意   y 森羅萬象   z 機格

view. Accordingly, they frequently use the verb, *shu*[aa] (to express), in characterizing what it is that the writer does. Here are some characteristic passages:

> *Yüan Hung-tao*: In general, [Yüan Chung-tao] expresses his individual innate sensibility (*tu shu hsing-ling*[ab]), without being constricted by conventionalized diction. He is unwilling to write a thing that does not flow out from his own breast![56]
>
> *Yüan Chung-tao*: He [a certain "Master Fu-ching"] is neither T'ang nor Sung; he directly expresses (*shu*) that which it is his intention to say, without any desire for fame in "carving dragons" or "embroidering tigers."[57]
>
> *Huang Hui*: They [the Eight Masters of Prose] boldly cast off hackneyed phrases and express (*shu*) their individual perceptions.[58]
>
> *T'ao Wang-ling*: [One should] express (*shu*) that which is most moved [i.e. one's emotions].[59]

It further follows that there will be a correlation between a writer's individual *personality* and his *style*. In a truly remarkable passage, Chiang Ying-k'o provides one of the clearest expressions of this concept in all of Chinese literary criticism:[60]

> Poetry is based on the nature and emotions (*hsing-ch'ing*[ac]). If a poem is a real (*chen*) poem, then a single reading will suffice to bring the poet's nature and emotions [i.e. personality] before one's eyes. On the whole, if the poetry is expansive, the poet must be openhearted. If the poetry is weighty, the poet must be serious. If the poetry is unrestricted, the poet must be a free spirit. If the poetry has a limpid beauty, the poet must be a person of good spirits. If the poetry is withered and gaunt, the poet must be cold and repressed. If the poetry is rich and full, the poet must be generous and giving. If the poetry is mournful, the poet must be depressed. If the poetry is elegiac, the poet must be of noble sentiment. If the poetry is untrammeled, the poet must be of heroic temperament. If the poetry is lofty and pure, the poet must be cultivated. If the poetry is ordered, the poet must be strict and disciplined.
>
> This is comparable to the flowering peach tree, plum tree and apricot tree. By looking at the blossoms one can tell the tree they came from. As for plagiarists, they are "deer who cover themselves with tigerskins" and have no discrimination. For example, a poet who speaks of himself as old when he is not actually old, poor when he is not actually poor, or sick when he is not actually sick, is a robber of Tu Fu's house! A poet who never drinks a single cup of wine, but says, "Three hundred cups a day!" who never spends a cent, but says, "Tens of thousands of cash with a

aa 抒，攄   ab 獨抒性靈   ac 性情

sweep of the hand!" is a pickpocket stealing from Li Po! From these examples, others can be deduced. When such poets say their work is based on their nature and emotions, they miss the mark by over a thousand miles!

As powerful as such statements as this undoubtedly are, they should not lead us to conclude that for the Kung-an writers individual personality was the only determinant of literary style. It is a sign of the seriousness and creative thinking of these men that they also developed what amounts to a kind of Zeitgeist theory. As Yüan Hung-tao puts it, "I'd go so far as to say that they [the Sung poets] *could* not have written in the T'ang manner, and that the evolution of the spirit of the age is what made this so. Similarly, the T'ang *could* not have followed the *Literary Anthology* style...."[61] A particularly cogent presentation of this view is given by Huang Hui, in a preface he wrote to a newly printed collection of writings by the so-called Eight Masters of Prose, i.e. Han Yü (768–824), Liu Tsung-yüan (773–819), Ou-yang Hsiu, Su Hsün (1009–1066), Su Shih, Su Ch'e (1039–1112), Tseng Kung (1019–1083), and Wang An-shih (1021–1086).[62] Huang follows the conventional version of literary history when he states that prose writing declined after the Han dynasty and was then revived twice, first by Han Yü, and later by the Sung masters. What is interesting, however, is his feeling that this was the result of "a natural tendency (*tzu-jan chih shih*[ad])." "Isn't it true," Huang asks rhetorically, "that literature follows the vicissitudes of the times?" And to stress this point, he argues that there *were* others who attempted to revive the great tradition, but "there was no one to echo their singing," and so "in the end, they could not vastly expand beyond their own borders." As an example, he refers to Mu Hsiu (979–1032), a man who admired Han Yü and Liu Tsung-yüan and attempted to create a revival of interest in their work early in the Sung dynasty, but apparently the times were not right, and such an event had to await the emergence of the generation of Ou-yang Hsiu.

From this perspective on literary history, Huang derives a refreshingly optimistic theory:

> As I see it, from ancient times the destiny of the nation has consisted of an alternation of low points and high points, darkness and light. That which is chaotic becomes stabilized. The fragmented becomes unified.... If the prose writing of the T'ang dynasty did not reach its peak in the Chen-kuan (627–649) and K'ai-yüan (713–741) periods, but did reach a peak in the Yüan-ho (806–820) period, and if the prose writing of the Sung dynasty did not reach its peak in the Yung-hsi (984–987) and Ch'ien-hsing (1022) periods, but did reach a peak in the Chia-yu (1056–1085) period, then how can we know that the writers of literature

ad 自然之勢

which is "decadent and thorny" are not the predecessors of a peak period? We may even be in such a period now!

Such a conception stands in stark contrast with the orthodox "golden age" view that prose literature reached its height in the Han dynasty, and poetry in the High T'ang period, and that the achievements of these periods can never be equaled again, let alone surpassed. Freed from this constricting scenario, Yüan Hung-tao and his friends were able to appreciate the full gamut of literary styles created by writers of the mid- and late T'ang periods, as well as the Sung dynasty. Yüan Hung-tao was probably the first, and possibly the only, writer in traditional China to express the opinion that Su Shih was the greatest poet of all time: "Han [Yü], Liu [Tsung-Yüan], Yüan [Chen] and Po [Chü-i] may have been the 'Sages of Poetry,' but Su was the 'God of Poetry!'"[63] Yüan's elder brother, Tsung-tao, admired Po Chü-i and Su Shih so much that he named his studio *Po-Su chai* ("Studio of Po and Su") after them. In passage after passage of their writings, the Kung-an poets revel in the multiplicity of styles that flourished in the mid- and late T'ang, and in the Sung. As Chung-tao writes (in the second preface to his own collected works, dated 1623),[64]

> Poetry never flourished more than it did in the T'ang. Now the reason that people speak of "Flourishing T'ang" (*sheng T'ang*) is precisely because the T'ang poets achieved great artistry in *different* styles, and yet this ultimately did not prevent their works from being transmitted. The weighty seriousness of Tu Kung-pu [Tu Fu] and the brilliance of Li Ch'ing-lien [Li Po] are almost diametrically opposed, but this is because each of them was approaching poetry from his own angle so as to express his own talent to the full, to the point where their light still shines untarnished today.... Even such poets as.... Lu T'ung (d. 835), Li Ho (791–817), and Meng Chiao (751–814) all strived with each other, locking horns in a great struggle for strangeness and artfulness in their time, and yet the men of letters of their time did not criticize and reject them for the bizarre tendencies in their work! This is precisely why T'ang was able to "flourish!"

In all the above statements, the Kung-an writers are attempting to counter the orthodox view that only certain High T'ang poets should be emulated, with a more flexible conception: there are a great many stylistic options in literature, just as there are many different personality types, as well as different historical and social circumstances. A given age can achieve greatness in literature only if it has the capacity to appreciate stylistic variety (although on a more general level, there is a certain energy in a given period which is close to what might be called "Zeitgeist"). The T'ang and Sung were admirable not because they created unalterable models which must be followed for all time, but, on the contrary, because of their tolerance for true creativity, even where it led to eccentricity.

V

In his otherwise excellent discussion of Yüan Hung-tao, Kuo Shao-yü inexplicably maintains that Yüan held to a conception of "pure art" (or as a Westerner might say, "art for art's sake"), "separated from reality."[65] In fact, one of the basic tenets of the Kung-an school was that art must reflect concrete reality, as opposed to some completely imaginary realm, or idealized antiquity. Chiang Ying-k'o makes this clear in a brief note on Tu Fu:[66]

> After Tu Shao-ling [Tu Fu] moved to K'uei-chou, his poetry became monumental and expansive, vastly different from his previous work. It was not that he intentionally changed his style, but rather that the landscape of Szechwan was naturally striking and awe-inspiring, and Shao-ling was able to capture the spirit of this realm (hsiang-ching ch'uan-shen[ae]). Thus, when one reads these poems, the mountains and streams appear in perfect clarity before one's eyes! This is what is called "being as effortless as the spring silkworms spinning their cocoons;" he is faithful to the forms of actual things (sui-wu hsiao-hsing[af]). One can call him a real (chen) poet, a real master of the writer's brush!

Similarly, in speaking of T'ang poetry in general, Chiang says, "The poems on climbing mountains for the view written by the T'ang poets are all suited to (ch'eng[ag]) the actual mountains and streams [which they describe].... The men of letters of our own dynasty have also written many poems on climbing for the view, but if one were to pick out lines from them and hang them up as matched couplets, could they possibly be as precisely suited to the actual mountains and streams as are the T'ang examples?"[67]

Yüan Hung-tao, during a trip to various famous scenic spots in Chekiang, writes,

> When I first came to Ling-yen Temple, I suspected that the poem about this place by Sung Chih-wen would turn out to be inaccurate; I felt that the ancients, when they selected scenes (ching[ah]), were like the modern writers who pick [images] indiscriminately. But when I climbed to T'ao-kuang Cloister, I realized for the first time that in such of his phrases as "along the Che River," "above the vast sea," "grabbing creepers," and "scooped-out wooden bowls," each word conjured up a picture of this place, something other old poets could not achieve.[68]

ae 象境傳神   ag 稱
af 隨物肖形   ah 景

Similarly, Yüan Tsung-tao attacks the followers of Li Meng-yang for using archaic official titles rather than their modern equivalents, or the old place names instead of those in contemporary use, so that "if the reader does not consult a universal gazetteer, he will hardly ever realize what place is being discussed!"[69] (Yüan gives Li himself credit for using modern place names.)

All these passages—and others like them—indicate that in the Kung-an conception, *poetry must reflect the concrete reality of an actual place as experienced by the poet*, and the first Chiang Ying-k'o quotation (on Tu Fu in Szechwan) goes further to suggest that *the actual scene will naturally inform a true poet's work with stylistic qualities appropriate to the successful characterization of that scene*. This is what a modern critic might refer to as "sense of place." The poet can be seen as a medium through whom the world manifests its inner self. Yüan Hung-tao's extensive travels, which resulted in his superb *yu-chi*, or "travel essays," were undertaken as a kind of pilgrimage to spots which might provide him with poetic inspiration in this sense. One might even see his travels as having foreshadowed the famous journeys of the Japanese *haiku* poet, Bashō (1644–1694), recorded in the latter's masterpiece, *Oku no hosomichi*, and his other travel diaries. It is even conceivable that Bashō knew something of Yüan experiences, as Yüan's complete writings became known in Japan when the Ming loyalist, Ch'en Yüan-yün (1587–1671) introduced the monk-poet Gensei (1623–1668) to them.[70] Gensei's own poetry, written in Chinese, was influenced by that of Yüan.

When Chiang Ying-k'o speaks of Tu Fu's creative energy as "being as effortless as the spring silkworms spinning their cocoons," he is expressing another important idea in Kung-an theory: creativity in art and literature is ultimately like the creative process in nature itself. Passages in the Kung-an writers where this idea is brought forth are legion. To give just one example, Yüan Hung-tao writes, "When wind touches the waters, ripples form. When sunlight strikes the mountains, vapors arise. Even Ku [K'ai-chih (ca. 344–406)] and Wu [Tao-tzu (b. ca. 700)—Ku and Wu were two famous painters] could not have created such scenes."[71]

This fundamentally Taoist view—that nature is the supreme artist—was shared to some extent by the orthodox masters. In the words of Li Meng-yang (as translated by James J. Y. Liu),[72] "The ancients used rules, which were not invented by them but really created by Nature. Now, when we imitate the ancients, we are not imitating them but really imitating the natural laws of things." But it is of interest that the stress here is on rules and imitation, whereas the Kung-an writers were more fascinated by the actual creative transformations of nature, in search of which Yüan Hung-tao undertook his travels.

Perhaps related to the association of creative power with the Tao is a tolerance for *flaws* in creative work, even the idea that sometimes the flaws are the most interesting part! This is reminiscent of the Taoist paradox, which sees value in that which most people reject, but it also can be assimilated to the notion that the manifestations of nature are not "artificially" polished. In the *Tao-te ching*, this idea finds expression in the contrast between the "Uncarved Block" (*p'u*[ai]) and the "implements" into which it may be carved. "He [the Sage] returns to the state of the Uncarved Block. Now when a block is sawed up it is made into implements; but when the Sage uses it, it becomes Chief of all Ministers. Truly, 'The greatest carver does the least cutting.'"[73] It is in this context that we must understand such remarkable passages as the following, from Yüan Hung-tao's preface to the collected works of his younger brother, Chung-tao:[74]

> At times, his emotions and the scene would come together, and in an instant he would produce a thousand words, as naturally as the rivers flow east, enough to take one's breath away! In these writings of his, there are some lovely (*chia*) passages, and there are also flawed (*tz'u*[aj]) passages. Now of the lovely passages we need say nothing, but even the flawed passages contain many highly individual and creative phrases full of innate honesty, and as far as I am concerned, I particularly love these flawed parts! Indeed, the so-called "lovely" passages cannot help but make me resentful of their ornamental prettiness and conventionality—this is because the author had not yet completely freed himself from the mechanical practices of modern men of letters!

The assertion here that the "flaws" are actually the best things in Chung-tao's work—because they are the most creative and honest—is reminiscent of Chuang Tzu's ability to find true beauty in the crooked tree, as opposed to the straight, perfectly proportioned tree, and also of the affection of Chinese painters and garden designers for fantastic rocks pockmarked with bizarre holes. Underlying this conception is the age-old feeling that creativity inheres ultimately in the natural world itself, and that the true artist is he who opens himself to that creativity, with all its strange manifestations.

The last quotation from Yüan Hung-tao mentioned the coming together (*hui*) of the poet's emotion (*ch'ing*) and the scene (*ching*). Our discussion has shown that the Kung-an school recognized both the expression of the poet's emotions and the penetration of the inner reality of the world ("scene") as key functions of poetry. Chiang Ying-k'o provides a link between the two by using the term *ching-chieh*[ak] (world, from the Sanskrit, *viṣaya*) in a way which anticipates Wang Kuo-wei by centuries.[75] In his important essay, *Ch'iu chen*[al] (Seeking the Real) Chiang writes:[76]

> In any poetry—whether it be based on narration of an event, or on lyrical emotion, whether it be about some particular object or scene—

ai 朴，樸
aj 疵
ak 境界
al 求眞

there will naturally be an immediately present "world" (*ching-chieh*) which must be depicted and represented, and this should be revealed with the greatest clarity, so that the sight and hearing of anyone who reads it will feel a renewed freshness.

The word *ching*[am] alone occurs frequently in traditional Chinese literary criticism and is often difficult to distinguish from *ching*[an] (scene). An early usage occurs in Ssu-k'ung T'u's (837–908) *Ehr-shih-ssu shih-p'in* (The Twenty-four Modes of Poetry). The eighteenth of these is entitled *shih ching*,[ao] (real scene or realm of reality).[77] This in turn is echoed by Yüan Chung-tao's use of the phrase *chen ching shih ch'ing*[ap] in the 1618 preface to his own works[78] ("The ancients . . . had true scenes and real feelings" in their writings). But Chiang's explanation of the phrase *ching-chieh* makes it clear that this term actually refers to a conjunction or fusion of emotion and scene to create a world in the poem which reflects or embodies both the poet's emotion and the scene or experience which inspired it. Such a view obviously is far less simplistic than the usual characterizations of Kung-an literary thought.

VI

The conception of creativity that emerges from the works of the Kung-an writers is applicable to other forms of aesthetic expression besides literature. T'ao Wang-ling develops elaborate parallels between literature and calligraphy, and literature and painting: "Literature is like painting in that neither is any good unless it captures the spirit-principle (*shen-li*[aq])."[79] Yüan Hung-tao, in his extraordinary text on flower arrangement, draws a comparison between this art and both painting and literature; "Flower arrangements should not be too dense or too sparse. One should use no more than two or three varieties. The regulation of their height and density is comparable to composition in painting. . . . The forms and postures should be natural, like the prose of Tzu-chan [Su Shih] or the poetry of Ch'ing-lien [Li Po]—not restricted by parallelism: this is the true 'order!'"[80]

We have already seen that the Yüan brothers were friends of Tung Ch'i-ch'ang. In a letter to Tung, Yüan Hung-tao praises him for his ability to achieve mastery in philosophy, poetry, painting and calligraphy:

> I have lamented the fact that there are few multitalented men in the world, and yet you do seem to have them all! Discussions of the "nature" and of "fate," poetry, calligraphy, painting—in the past, only Wang Yu-ch'eng [Wang Wei] and Su Yü-chü [Su Shih] combined these talents. But

am 境
an 景

ao 實境
ap 眞境實情

aq 神理

Mo-chieh [Wang Wei] lacked any reputation for "practicing by the pond" [i.e. for calligraphy], and P'o-kung [Su Shih], when he did dab with his brush [to paint] could only do withered bamboo and craggy rocks. If I place you in the ranks of Wang and Su, the men of our time will certainly say I know what I'm talking about![81]

This high praise is all the more remarkable for the fact that the Kung-an writers appear to have believed that, in general, one should strive for excellence in just one form of expression. Chiang Ying-k'o argues forcefully for specialization in either poetry or prose, without mixing the two,[82] and Yüan Hung-tao himself seems to have been disturbed by the extent to which Wang Yang-ming, whom he otherwise admired, adulterated his Neo-Confucian thought with Ch'an-derived elements.[83] But these men recognized the ultimate unity of the creative force, and certainly gave credit when it was due to such a figure as Tung Ch'i-ch'ang.

Not unexpectedly, Tung Ch'i-ch'ang shared with the Kung-an school a feeling that the fundamental wellsprings of inspiration must be found, not in old masters, but in nature: "Painters may take the old masters as their teachers, and this does count as a Superior Vehicle, but beyond this one must make nature ["heaven and earth"] one's master. Every morning one should observe the transformations of clouds and mists, keeping away from mountains in paintings. When one walks in the mountains, and sees strange trees, one must grasp them from all four sides.... When one has thoroughly observed them, then one will naturally transmit their spirit [in one's paintings]...."[84]

Elsewhere, Tung echoes Yüan Hung-tao's experience of understanding a poem (painting) through actually viewing the scene which inspired it:

Mi Yüan-hui [Mi Yu-jen (1074–1153)] painted a picture called *White Clouds Over the Hsiao and Hsiang Rivers*, and he inscribed on it these words:
   "Clearing after a night of rain,
      morning clouds about to appear:"
this is what it looks like.

   I purchased this scroll from Hsiang Hui-po and carried it about wherever I went. Once, when my boat was moored in Lake Tung-t'ing, and the slanting sunlight filtered into my cabin, I gazed out at the great vastness—the cloud formations in the broad sky, so strange and marvelous!—and realized that this was like an inkplay in the Mi family style!...[85]

For Tung Ch'i-ch'ang, as for the writers of the Kung-an school, the time had come to revitalize a major Chinese tradition by going back to the ultimate root of all art and literature in the Chinese conception: nature. There is some irony in the fact that Tung's actual paintings are, if anything, among the most "abstract" and intellectualized in all of Chinese art, but at least the Kung-an poets and essayists carried this theory into practice, creating some of the most lively poetry and prose of Ming dynasty China.

I wish to acknowledge here the assistance of the National Endowment for the Humanities and the American Council of Learned Societies in connection with the research for, and preparation of, this paper.

1. Ch'en Shou-yi, *Chinese Literature: A Historical Introduction* (New York, 1961), pp. 513–517. The phrase, "precious fun-poking" occurs on p. 517.

2. For Chou Tso-jen's interest in the Kung-an school, see David E. Pollard, *A Chinese Look at Literature* (Berkeley and Los Angeles, 1973), pp. 79–81, 158–166. Pollard points out (p. 158) that Chou antedated Lin Yutang in his interest in the school.

3. See C. T. Hsia, *A History of Modern Chinese Fiction*, 2nd ed. (New Haven and London, 1971), pp. 132–134; Lin Yutang, *The Importance of Living* (New York, 1937), p. 154 and *passim*; Lin Yutang, *The Importance of Understanding* (Cleveland and New York, 1960), pp. 112–113, 329.

4. See p. 2, n. 5 of Hung's dissertation for his use of the word "romanticism."

5. For these terms, see James J. Y. Liu, *Chinese Theories of Literature* (Chicago, 1975), *passim*.

6. Yüan Hung-tao, *Yüan Chung-lang ch'üan chi* (The Complete Works of Yüan Hung-tao) (Taipei, 1964), *wen-ch'ao*, p. 7.

7. Yüan Tsung-tao, *Yüan Po-hsiu ch'üan chi* (The Complete Works of Yüan Tsung-tao) (Shanghai, 1936), p. 163. For another rendition of the same passage, see Hung, *Yüan Hung-tao*, pp. 169–171.

8. Yüan Chung-tao, *K'o-hsüeh-chai shih wen chi* (Collected Poetry and Prose from the Jeweled Snow Pavilion) in the *Chung-kuo wen-hsüeh chen-pen ts'ung-shu* (Shanghai, 1936), *wen-chi*, p. 26.

9. Chiang Ying-k'o, *Hsüeh-t'ao hsiao-shu* (A Little Book of Snowy Waves) (Shanghai, 1948, with author named by his *tzu*, Chin-chih), p. 1.

10. Ibid., pp. 9–10, 48–49.

11. For a good discussion of the *fu-ku* concept, see Stephen Owen, *The Poetry of Meng Chiao and Han Yü* (New Haven and London, 1975), pp. 8–23.

12. For a more detailed discussion, see Jonathan Chaves, *Mei Yao-ch'en and the Development of Early Sung Poetry* (New York and London, 1976), pp. 75–76.

13. Yüan Chung-tao, *wen-chi*, p. 31.

14. Richard John Lynn, "Orthodoxy and Enlightenment: Wang Shih-chen's Theory of Poetry and its Antecedents," in *The Unfolding of Neo-Confucianism*, ed. Wm. Theodore de Bary and the Conference on Seventeenth-Century Chinese Thought (New York and London, 1975), pp. 217ff.

15. Ibid., pp. 226 and 261, n. 59.

16. Yüan Hung-tao, *wen-ch'ao*, p. 5. Partial translations in Pollard, *A Chinese Look at Literature*, pp. 79–80, and Lin Yutang, *The Importance of Understanding*, pp. 112–113.

17. Lynn, "Orthodoxy and Enlightenment," p. 227.

18. Yüan Hung-tao, *wen-ch'ao*, p. 5.

19. Yüan Hung-tao, *ch'ih-tu*, p. 42.

20. Yüan Hung-tao, *sui-pi*, p. 10.

21. Yüan Tsung-tao, *Yüan Po-hsiu ch'üan chi*, p. 27.

22. Lu Yu, *Lu Fang-weng ch'üan chi* (Complete Works of Lu Yu) (Hong Kong, n.d.), *Lao-hsüeh-an pi-chi* (Jottings from the Studio for Learning in Old Age), 3, p. 16.

23. As quoted in Suzuki Torao, *Shina shiron shi* (A History of Chinese Poetry Criticism) (Tokyo, 1927), pp. 138–139.

24. Yüan Tsung-tao, *Yüan Po-hsiu ch'üan chi*, p. 176.

25. Wei Ying-wu, *Wei Su-chou chi* (Collected Works of Wei Ying-wu) (*SPPY* ed.) 7:11a. For other examples by Wei, see Thomas P. Nielson, *A Concordance to the Poems of Wei Ying-wu* (San Francisco, 1976), p. 183.

26. Chang Yü, *Ching-chü chi* (Life-in-Tranquility Collection) (*SPTK* ed.) col. 3, 5:3b.

27. Ibid. 1:42b.

28. Ibid. 1:42b–43a.

29. Ibid. 5:1b.

30. Chiang Ying-k'o, *Hsüeh-t'ao hsiao-shu*, p. 9.

31. See Wm. Theodore de Bary, "Individualism and Humanitarianism in Late Ming Thought," in *Self and Society in Ming Thought*, ed. W. T. de Bary and the Conference on Ming Thought (New York and London, 1970), p. 195.

32. Yüan Hung-tao, *ch'ih-tu*, p. 14.

33. Chiang Ying-k'o, *Hsüeh-t'ao hsiao-shu*, p. 4.

34. Ibid., p. 12.

35. Hsü Shen, *Shuo-wen chieh-tzu* (Explanation of Words, Explication of Characters) (Hong Kong, 1969), 8, p. 168.

36. Kiyohiko Munakata, *Ching Hao's "Pi-fa-chi:" A Note on the Art of the Brush* (Ascona, 1974). The dates given for Ching Hao are based on Munakata's discussion (see pp. 55–56).

37. Ibid., pp. 12 and 21. The emphases are the translator's.

38. Yüan Hung-tao, *ch'ih-tu*, p. 20.

39. T'ao Wang-ling, *Hsieh-an chi* (Collection of the Studio for Retirement) 5 vols. (Taipei, 1976), 1:434–436.

40. Chiang Ying-k'o, *Hsüeh-t'ao hsiao-shu*, p. 10.

41. Chang Yü, *Ching-chü chi* 1:30b.

42. Ibid. 4:8b.

43. Lynn, "Orthodoxy and Enlightenment," p. 222 and *passim*.

44. Ibid., p. 253.

45. Yüan Chung-tao, *wen-chi*, p. 89.

46. T'ao Wang-ling, *Hsieh-an chi*, 5:2339.

47. For this, see Kristin Yü Greenblatt, "Chu-hung and Lay Buddhism in the Late Ming," in *The Unfolding of Neo-Confucianism*, pp. 93–138.

48. Chiang Ying-k'o, *Hsüeh-t'ao hsiao-shu*, pp. 4–5. The translation is complete.

49. The first three of these come from the *Eighteen Cymbal Songs* (*Nao ko* 鐃歌) of the Han dynasty. The last is one of five poems entitled *Thoughts in the Boudoir* (*Shih-ssu* 室思) by the late Han poet, Hsü Kan (171–216).

50. Poems from the *Book of Songs* (the "Three Hundred Poems").

51. Poems by Li Po. *Lu shan kao* 廬山高 in Chiang's text is properly *Lu shan yao* ... 謠 (*Song of Mount Lu* ...). A poem entitled *Lu shan kao* does exist, but it was written by Ou-yang Hsiu. The title *Shu tao nan* 蜀道難 actually did occur prior to Li Po, although Li's use of it is certainly highly imaginative and fits Chiang's criterion of originality. See Hans H. Frankel, "*Yüeh-fu* Poetry," in *Studies in Chinese Literary Genres*, ed. Cyril Birch (Berkeley, Los Angeles, and London, 1974), pp. 100–104.

52. Poems by Tu Fu. For *hsien* 羨 in the text, read *mei* 渼.

53. Yüan Hung-tao, *ch'ih-tu*, pp. 42–43.

54. Wayne Dodd, "Robert Bly—An Interview," *The Ohio Review* (December, 1978), 19(3):39.

55. Yüan Hung-tao, *wen-ch'ao*, p. 9.

56. Ibid., *wen-ch'ao*, p. 5.

57. Yüan Chung-tao, *wen-chi*, p. 45.

58. Huang Hui, *Huang T'ai-shih i-ch'un-t'ang i-kao* (Manuscript of Recovered Writings from the Joy-in-Spring Hall of Scholar Huang) (Taipei, 1976), p. 166.

59. T'ao Wang-ling, *Hsieh-an chi*, 1:380.

60. Chiang Ying-k'o, *Hsüeh-t'ao hsiao-shu*, pp. 11–12.

61. Yüan Hung-tao, *ch'ih-tu*, p. 20.

62. Huang Hui, *Huang T'ai-shih*, pp. 163–167.

63. Yüan Hung-tao, *ch'ih-tu*, p. 42.

64. Yüan Chung-tao, *shih-chi*, first preface, p. 1 after title page.

65. Kuo Shao-yü, *Chung-kuo wen-hsüeh p'i-p'ing shih* (History of Chinese Literary Criticism) (Hong Kong: Hung-chih shu-tien, n.d.; originally published 1964), pp. 372, 377–378.

66. Chiang Ying-k'o, *Hsüeh-t'ao hsiao-shu*, p. 7.

67. Ibid., pp. 20–21.

68. Yüan Hung-tao, *yu-chi*, pp. 14 and 15 (for two slightly different versions of the same text).

69. Yüan Tsung-tao, *Yüan Po-hsiu ch'üan chi*, p. 163.

70. See Iriya Yoshitaka, *En Kōdō* [Yüan Hung-tao], in the series, *Chūgoku shijin senshū* (Anthology of Works by Chinese Poets), series II (Tokyo, 1963), introduction, pp. 12–13, and Burton Watson, *Japanese Literature in Chinese*, 2 vols. (New York, 1975–1976), 2:13 and 31.

71. Yüan Hung-tao, *wen-ch'ao*, p. 10. See also *yu-chi*, pp. 34–34.

72. James J. Y. Liu, *The Art of Chinese Poetry* (Chicago, 1962), p. 80.

73. *Tao te ching*, ch. 28, as translated by Arthur Waley, *The Way and Its Power* (pb. ed., New York, n.d.), p. 178.

74. Yüan Hung-tao, *wen-ch'ao*, p. 5.

75. See Liu, *Art of Chinese Poetry*, p. 84.

76. Chiang Ying-k'o, *Hsüeh-t'ao hsiao-shu*, p. 4.

77. Ssu-k'ung T'u, *Erh-shih-ssu shih-p'in* (The Twenty-four Modes of Poetry), *Li-tai*

shih-hua, ed. Ho Wen-huan (rpt., Taipei, 1959), 4b–5a.

78. Yüan Chung-tao, *shih-chi*, 2nd preface, p. 2.

79. T'ao Wang-ling, *Hsieh-an chi*, 1:433. See also pp. 377, 378–379, 434–435.

80. Yüan Hung-tao, *sui-pi*, p. 20. For another rendition of this passage, and a partial translation and paraphrase of the rest of Yüan's text on flower arrangement, see Lin Yutang, *The Importance of Living*, pp. 310–316.

81. Yüan Hung-tao, *ch'ih-tu*, p. 73.

82. Chiang Ying-k'o, *Hsüeh-t'ao hsiao-shu*, pp. 29–30.

83. See Yüan Hung-tao, *ch'ih-tu*, pp. 60 and 71.

84. This passages appears in the *Hua-shuo*, a text attributed both to Mo Shih-lung (ca. 1540–1587) and to Tung Ch'i-ch'ang. See the edition of the text in *Mei-shu ts'ung-k'an*, 4 vols. (Taipei, 1956–1965), 3:298. For the view that the *Hua-shuo* is actually by Tung Ch'i-ch'ang rather than Mo Shih-lung, see Fu Shen, "A Study of the Authorship of the '*Hua-shuo*': A Summary," *Proceedings of the International Symposium on Chinese Painting*, Taipei, 1972, pp. 85–112. The passage in question also occurs in the *Hua-yen*, a text unquestionably written by Tung Ch'i-ch'ang: in *Mei-shu ts'ung-k'an*, 1:284.

85. Tung Ch'i-ch'ang, *Hua-yen*, p. 290.

The "Wild and Heterodox School" of Ming Painting

By Richard Barnhart

In the late sixteenth century, a particularly abusive critical dismissal of six recent and/or contemporary painters was published in works attributed to several well-known scholars of art. Under the heading *Hsieh-hsüeh,*[a] "The Heterodox School," in the *K'ao-p'an yü-shih* (Leisure Affairs in Retirement) ascribed to T'u Lung (1542–1605), this terse view is expressed:

> As for such painters as Cheng Wen-lin, Chang Fu-yang, Chung Li, Chiang Sung, Chang Lu, Wang Chao and the like, they constitute the heterodox school of painting, reaching pretentiously for an attitude of wildness (*t'u ch'eng k'uang-t'ai*[b]) but achieving nothing.[1]

The same passage is found in texts attributed to Hsiang Yüan-pien (1525–1596), by Kao Lien (ca. 1575), and by Wen Chen-heng (1585–1645).[2] Subsequently, the concept of a "wild and heterodox school" was incorporated into the accepted history of Ming painting with the publication of Hsü Ch'in's *Ming-hua lu* (Record of Ming Painters) in the early Ch'ing period.[3]

Examination of the critical and theoretical attitudes underlying the phrase "wild and heterodox" suggests that its formulation is a reflection of significant changes in the course of Ming painting and theory. As "wildness" in art and life is attacked, the virtues of moderation are affirmed. As heterodoxy is denied, an increasingly rigorous orthodoxy is propagated. Professionalism is shown to be inferior to scholarly amateurism, and a large realm of artistic activity is found inappropriate and undesirable.

In another focus, formulation of the expression "wild and heterodox" antedates and anticipates the development of Tung Ch'i-ch'ang's "Theory of the Northern and Southern Schools of Landscape Painting," and firmly plants the latter in the context of sixteenth-century art and theory—in which, otherwise, Tung expressed relatively little interest.

WILDNESS IN MING PAINING

In style and technique, what is herein called "wildness" seems to have begun in what were either the late or merely the more spontaneous works of Tai Chin

[a] 邪學   [b] 徒逞狂態

1. Tai Chin (1388–1462), "Fishermen on the River." Section of a handscroll, ink and colors on paper, height 46 cm. Courtesy of the Freer Gallery of Art, Smithsonian Institution, Washington, D.C.

2. Wu Wei (1459–1508), "Pleasures of Fishermen." Section of a handscroll, ink and colors on paper, height 27.2 cm. Ching Yüan Chai Collection.

3. Shih Chung (1438–ca. 1517), "Snow over the Hall of the Immortal of the Hsiang River." Hanging scroll, ink on paper, 142.5 × 32.3 cm. Private collection.

4. Chang Lu (ca. 1464–ca. 1538), "Training a Crane at the Taoist Monastery."
Hanging scroll, ink on silk, 140 × 97 cm. Hashimoto Collection, Takatsuki, Japan.

(1388–1462), and to have developed in the art of Wu Wei, Lin Liang, Shih Chung, Hsü Lin, and Kuo Hsü, as well as Chang Fu-yang, Chung Li, Chiang Sung, Wang Chao, Chang Lu, Chu Pang, and others. The painters favoring this mode were nearly all professional masters. A few had sporadic, uneven associations with the court (only Lin Liang was a successful court painter), but most were independent master-painters. There is some reason to think that they were as dissatisfied with the limitations of academic art as with those of the literati tradition. A number of them were known as poets, calligraphers, or dramatists. As painters, they are described as "attacking directly," "brushing furiously," "splashing and dripping"—suggesting that they were pushing their professional skills into a realm something akin to pure process, or spontaneous creation. Their techniques can be described by few of the familiar terms ("ax-cut" strokes occasionally, "Mi-dots," the "boneless" style), but generally demand such vague equivalents as "scribbly" or "splashy."[4] Beneath their scribbles and splashes, however, lies great skill, the skill of the virtuoso, working near the boundary of conscious planning—"trusting the brush," achieving the unexpected and the failed as well as the brilliant and daring.

The phenomenon, broadly approached, extends across a wide spectrum, embracing calligraphy, personal behavior, attitudes toward the past and toward correctness and orthodoxy, and reaching into fundamental philosophical and aesthetic preferences.

Before the phrase "wild and heterodox" was coined, the idea of wildness, craziness, or impetuousness meant by the word *k'uang*[c] had held a largely positive meaning among artists. The relatively tolerant original Confucian attitude is suggested in a passage from the *Analects*:

> The Master said: If I cannot get men who steer a middle course to associate with, I would far rather have the impetuous (*k'uang*) or the timid. For the impetuous at any rate assert themselves; and the timid have this at least to be said for them, that there are things they leave undone.[5]

Wildness or impetuousness in this context is at least preferable to other extremes if one is unable to attain the Confucian center. Perhaps a reflection of these priorities is the fact that many professional painters of the Ming period chose to become professional and to emulate the ideal of *k'uang* only after attempting, or beginning, a life aimed at the traditional literati ideal.

It is in the *Chuang Tzu*, however, that the fullest expression of unconventionality and wildness as a positive ideal is found. Descriptions of the naked painter, the wheelwright Pien, the carver Ting, and the woodcarver Ch'ing define art as the spontaneous release of disciplined skill in unconscious harmony with the Tao, and the artist as teacher of kings cloaked in the guise of unconventionality or ordinariness.[6]

c 狂

With reference to this identity, as James Cahill has pointed out, a number of Ming painters had adopted *k'uang* and related words such as *ch'ih*[d] (stupid or crazy) and *hsien*[e] (transcendent immortal) as parts of their artistic names.[7] Kuo Hsü called himself "Pure and Wild" (*Ch'ing-k'uang*). Tu Chin took the name "Ancient and Wild" (*Ku-k'uang*); and both Kuo Hsü and Sung Teng-ch'un were popularly known as *K'uang-sheng*, or "The Wild Master." Shih Chung called himself "Stupid" or "Crazy Old Man" (*Ch'ih-weng*), and Sun Lung was known as "Stupid in Everything," or "Completely Stupid" (*Tu-ch'ih*). Wu Wei was "Little Immortal" (*Hsiao-hsien*); Ch'en Tzu-ho was "Wine-Immortal" (*Chiu-hsien*); Cheng Wen-lin was "Crazy Immortal" (*Tien-hsien*); Hsü Lin was "Bearded Immortal" (*Jan-hsien*), and Hsieh Shih-ch'en was *Ch'u-hsien*,[f] or "Immortal of the Useless Tree" after the familiar passage in *Chuang Tzu*.[8]

There are other indications of Taoist affinities in the lives of many of these artists. Chang Fu-yang was a Taoist priest, associated with the Taoist style of landscape painting defined by Fang Ts'ung-i, himself a Taoist priest of the Yüan period.[9] Shih Chung, the "Crazy Old Man," was also associated with the Fang T'sung-i style, and was clearly a Taoist in life and philosophy. A biographer described him as a man "of irrepressible nature, who rode around on a buffalo, his feet bare, wearing Taoist robes, with yellow flowers tied to his waist."[10] And of Wu Wei, the "Little Immortal," his friend Chang Ch'i observed: "In the evening sun among the red leaves he sits along / Throwing aside the Confucian classics to read the Taoist books."[11]

It may also be observed that the largest single group of indentifiable images in the figure paintings of Wu Wei and his follower, Chang Lu, is formed of the pantheon of popular Taoist immortals: Lao Tzu, Chuang Tzu, Li T'ieh-kuai and Liu Hai-hsien, Tung-fang Shuo, "The Immortal of the Northern Sea," and the assorted images of the mythological imagination.[12]

The attitudes of these men toward the act of painting could also be understood as reflecting a Taoist rather than Confucian ideal of art, at least insofar as the concepts defined so well by James Cahill as "Confucian elements in the theory of painting" may be said to suggest a philosophically Confucian practice of art among scholars.[13] The descriptions left us of the "wild" masters in the art of painting define an attitude far from the restrained, "even and pale" disengagement of the *wen-jen* ideal. Most vivid is the familiar story of Wu Wei, staggering drunk into the presence of Emperor Hsien-tsung and "splashing and rubbing," abruptly painting a picture of pines in the wind so powerful and compelling that it left all present shaken and pale.[14] Wang Chao is described as "pouring black ink over a piece of silk," and then modulating it with a brush filled with water to create a picture of "Sunrise."[15] Of Wu Wei's contemporary, Ch'en Tzu-ho, it is said, "He was fond of wine and skilled

---

d 癡   e 仙   f 樗仙

at painting. After he was drunk he would brandish his brush, making landscapes, figures, flowers and animals, and all were remarkable beyond compare."[16]

In a poem written on one of his landscape paintings, Shih Chung touches upon other concerns of the unconventional masters.

> All of my life I have lived, a failure, here in the river country,
> Poetry and wine have been my companions, to make me drunk and crazy (*tsui k'uang*[g]).
> I sketch a scroll of clouds and mist to dissipate the day,
> Obtain a bite of wind and moon . . . (characters illegible)
> Nature of course knows nothing of skill or awkwardness,
> And reason differs from man to man.
> I wish for a connoisseur as capable as Nan-kung,
> But nowadays how many even recognize Su or Huang?[17]

"Drunk and crazy," evidently, describes the attitudes of many of the "wild" masters, and may also recall the drunken, iconoclastic "untrammeled" masters of T'ang and Sung.[18]

If it is not surprising to see in Shih Chung's poem reference to Mi Fu—often the ideal of the discerning connoisseur, and creator of the Mi-style of ink-wash landscape, the tradition to which Shih very loosely belonged—perhaps less expected is the reference to Su Shih and Huang T'ing-chien, particularly in an age that valued T'ang poetry over Sung.[19] They are evoked primarily to suggest the ignorance among Shih's contemporaries of the qualities and attitudes he admired, but Su Shih was a favorite image in the painting of the "wild" masters, along with the Taoist immortals, and was evidently a significant ideal for those who espoused a free and independent manner in the fifteenth and sixteenth centuries.[20] Su's ebullient, heroic attitude toward art, sometimes encouraged by wine, was a familiar one in the popular imagination, and his description of the spirit of his own writing as an "inexhaustible spring" surging forth is among the most vivid expressions of an irrepressible, spontaneous celebration of the creative act.[21]

That these concepts of spontaneity and unconscious release were held high by the artists we are considering is indicated repeatedly in their biographies. Of Wang Chao, one of the original "wild and heterodox" painters, it is said,

> He described his brushwork as free and surging like the sea or the clouds, and he therefore took the name, "Sea-clouds" (Hai-yün).[22]

Chang Lu's approach to painting is described by a friend:

> When he saw the heights of the mountains or the depth of valleys, the surge and flow of springs and streams, the interweavings of trees and

g 醉狂

rocks, the flight of the birds or the swimming of the fish, he would stare long in concentration. Then he would stretch out the silk and sit quietly, searching his thoughts for true understanding (*shen-hui*) [of these natural phenomena]. When ideas came he would throw up his arms and leap up [to begin]. He used his brush just as Heaven created all things, without stopping from beginning to end.[23]

Wu Wei "was often inspired when he was drunk, and would brandish his brush and splash his ink with abandon, completing a painting in an instant. He wielded his brush as if it were flying.... His techniques and ideas were bold and free, like a dragon leaping or a phoenix soaring.... impossible to restrain."[24]

As techniques and attitudes of boldness, freedom and spontaneity were being developed by several major painters of the fifteenth and sixteenth centuries, wildness was also being nurtured toward its greatest expression in calligraphy. "Wild-cursive" (*k'uang-ts'ao*) writing enjoyed its most important revival in the hands of Chu Yün-ming (1460–1526) at just the time that Wu Wei and Shih Chung were most celebrated for their eccentric wildness. Explaining Chu's enjoyment of the boldest and most spontaneously expressive form of calligraphy, his friend Wang Ch'ung wrote, "His nature and personality are bold and direct, and he has no patience for strictness and reserve. Therefore in his calligraphy he produced more mad cursive and large scrolls."[25]

Wang Ch'ung knew Chu Yün-ming intimately, and his observation of the relationship between personality and the choice of artistic styles and aesthetic modes suggests still another aspect of the "wild and heterodox" phenomenon. Of Chung Li's personality we read, "On summer days he would often sit in contemplation in the woods, barefoot, hair unkempt, holding a white feather fan. If he saw people he would often pay them no attention. They often laughed at him as 'an immortal' (*hsien*), but he seemed not to hear."[26] Chang Fu-yang, the Taoist-priest painter, is described as "a man of free and irrepressible nature."[27] Wang Chao was a man of "powerful physique and great strength," fond of the military arts and of sword dancing, "bold, free, and ungovernable" in personality. "He drank great quantities of wine through his nose, and called it "elephant drinking.'"[28] Shih Chung was "heroic and ungovernable."[29] And Wu Wei's reckless, impatient student, Sung Teng-ch'un, was "found of wine and devoted to heroism, a skilled archer and horseman."[30]

These attributes of physical strength, boldness of action and of manner, heroic spirit, skill in the martial arts, heavy drinking, eccentricity, and great personal pride only in part recall the old "untrammeled" masters; the strain of personal heroism and physical courage running through these biographies appears to define a quite different personal ideal, and one that will be seen to be reflected in many ways in the paintings of the "wild and heterodox" masters.

THE ORIGINS OF THE THEORY OF THE WILD AND HETERODOX SCHOOL

The later sixteenth-century scholars who fashioned the expression "wild and heterodox" did not do so without critical and theoretical preparation. Two slightly earlier men, in particular, Li K'ai-hsien (1502–1568)[31] and Ho Liang-chün (1506–1573),[32] had established a framework within which the later terminology could be easily constructed. Approaching painting from diametrically opposite points of view—Li favoring the professionals and court painters, Ho the scholars and amateurs—both men nonetheless shared a distaste for the tendencies soon to be characterized as wild and heterodox; and both were equally outspoken in denouncing them.

Li K'ai-hsien

The reader coming for the first time upon Li K'ai-hsien's judgments of Ming painters active up until 1545, when his text, the *Chung-lu hua-p'in* (Li K'ai-hsien's Critique of Painting),[33] was completed, can only be startled to find Shen Chou ranked in the fourth category (out of six), fifteenth overall, and well behind such painters as T'ao Ch'eng, Tu Chin, Hsia Ch'ang, Chou Ch'en, and Lü Chi, not to mention Tai Chin and Wu Wei, whom Li regarded as the two greatest masters of the dynasty. Li's description of Shen Chou's painting, "like a priest in a mountain forest, with nothing to offer but dryness and blandness" (*k'u-tan*),[h][34] may have been eccentric, but in fact his general rating of Ming painters is probably not so very different from the views of most scholars of art at the time. Tai Chin seems to have been nearly universally regarded as the greatest painter of the age, and Wu Wei was not far behind.[35]

Nearly all of the painters admired by Li K'ai-hsien were professional painters. Traditional, i.e. Sung-like, skills—fluidity and strength of brushwork, mastery in the use of ink, spontaneity, versatility, and a vivid sense of reality—were the qualities most admired by Li,[36] and they naturally were mainly the achievement of professionals. Li was not blind to the very different qualities of the scholarly styles, however, and Ni Tsan and another fourteenth-century scholar, Chuang Lin, alone occupy his second category, ranking fifth and sixth overall.[37] Both represented "purity" (*ch'ing*) to Li, and he likens Ni Tsan's art to an elegant table-top plant, slight and small, but worth keeping in a jade vase. The style of Chuang Lin is described as "like the color of the mountains in early autumn, just after a fine rain has cleared, bringing pleasure to the mind of the hermit and inspiration to the poet."

Li lists as the "four faults" of painting stiffness, dryness, muddiness, and lack of

[h] 枯淡

strength in brushwork.[38] He obviously also had a sharp eye for what he regarded as pretentiousness, and believed that the art of painting had reached its apogee in the Sung dynasty. The decline thereafter was only briefly interrupted by Ni Tsan and Chuang Lin in the Yuan period, and by the achievement of Tai Chin, Wu Wei, T'ao Ch'eng, and Tu Chin during the Ming—an achievement seen by him as the successful emulation of Sung.

Even though he attempts various approaches toward a system, Li K'ai-hsien's criteria are nowhere very clearly or systematically stated. We may detect in his critical survey a preference, however, for describing faults in terms of Buddhist monks and Taoist priests, wearing colorful costumes and paraphernalia but leaving a stench in the nostrils, or sitting stupidly facing the wall, waiting for enlightenment to strike. The best he can say of such types is that, like Shen Chou, they might be dry and bland.

He describes Chiang Tzu-ch'eng's painting as "like an Indian monk, his entire body clothed in precious objects, yet giving off a putrid odor." Hsia Ch'ang is "like a monk in a rustic temple, sitting facing the wall, hoping to become immortal." Lin Liang "is like the sticks on a wood-gatherer's back or the dried wood at the bottom of a stream—carpenters wouldn't even look at it."[39] Kuo Hsü "is like an old Confucian trying to learn farming; his strength is not equal to his fellows' and he grows more weeds than grain." Wang Chih is likened to an inept carpenter: "his blade can't find the right places and his design lacks any quality whatever." Chung Li "is like a placard hung in a Taoist monastery; the characters are big and the ink thick, but all one sees are lines like black worms."[40] Wang E "is like an official of the Five Dynasties, his hat is of black silk but his person is that of a butcher."[41]

Li was not in general favorable toward free or sketchy styles, with the important exception of that of Wu Wei, who was considered second in stature only to Tai Chin, and likened to Hsiang Yü winning the great battle at Chü-lu, "his heroic spirit bursting out, crowning his age."[42] Of the artists soon to be characterized as wild and heterodox, Li is almost wholly contemptuous. To a critic who esteemed the Sung standard above all, such men as Chung Li, Chang Lu, Kuo Hsü, and Shih Chung seemed merely coarse, crude, and vulgar. Although he does not use the word academic, it was the refined academic tradition of Sung and its Ming revival that Li considered supreme. The "wild" painters, to him, violated this ideal, failing to reach the correct standard of professional accomplishment, and were to be rejected.

Ho Liang-chün

Ho was only a few years younger than Li K'ai-hsien, but he must have completed his notes on painting, *Ssu-yu-chai hua-lun* (Theories of Painting from the

Studio of the Four Friends)[43] about twenty-five years after the publication of Li's *Hua-p'in*. While Li rarely expresses concrete reasons for his judgments, Ho is systematic and thorough, never leaving any doubt as to the theoretical foundations of his thought.

As compared with Li and what I believe was common opinion in the earlier Ming period, Ho assumes that even the most gifted professional painter (*hang-chia*[i]) must be inferior to the best of the scholar-amateurs (*li-chia*[j]). This view he demonstrates in a comparison between Tai Chin—"the best of the professionals"—and Wen Cheng-ming, ranked only third in his list of scholar-painters. Tai, he notes, is *only* a painter, "limited by his personal qualities" (*hsien-yü jen-p'in*[k]), while Wen is not only as skillful as the professionals but possesses the additional virtues and achievements of the scholar.[44] In assessing the great masters of Ming painting, he is therefore careful to assess the professionals separately from the scholars, having already established the innate superiority of his own class. The leading professionals he then lists in order as Tai Chin, Wu Wei, Tu Chin, and Chou Ch'en; while the leading scholar-amateurs are said to be Shen Chou, T'ang Yin [sic!], Wen Cheng-ming, and Ch'en Shun.[45] With Tai Chin and Shen Chou heading their lists, this is probably the beginning of the now familiar dichotomy between the Tai-Che and Shen-Wu camps, although the names Che and Wu are not used, and the theoretical distinction here drawn is strictly between the professional and the scholar-amateur.

In "praising" Tai Chin elsewhere, Ho adds an additional qualification in declaring him "the leading hand among the academicians" (*yüan-t'i chung ti-i shou*[l]),[46] effectively implying that all of the artists most admired by Li K'ai-hsien belonged only to a lower order of achievement, not to be compared with that of any of the leading scholars.

Most crucial in Ho's thought is his dedication to clarifying the "orthodox tradition" (*cheng-mai*[m]).[47] The basis of this issue is stated simply by Ho, quoting unnamed "men of the past": "The first requirement is that one's personal character be lofty; the second requirement is that one's tradition of learning be ancient" (*i-hsü jen-p'in kao, erh-hsü shih-fa ku*[n]).[48] A slightly different way of phrasing the second requirement is offered by Kao Lien, who is probably the original author of the expression "wild and heterodox." In praising Chao Meng-fu he writes, "In everything he modeled himself upon the ancients, without a single heterodox brushstroke."[49]

Now, it is evident that the word heterodox takes concrete meaning only with reference to the orthodox, and to the specific identity of the "orthodox tradition." Orthodoxy in literature had been a preoccupation of scholars since at least the publication of Yen Yü's theory of poetry in the Southern Sung period. Yen Yü's

i 行家
j 利家

k 限於人品
l 院體中第一手

m 正脈
n 一須人品高　二須師法古

dictum, "There is a Heterodox and an Orthodox Way" (*Tao yu hsieh-cheng*[o]), along with his definitions of the Lesser and Greater Vehicles, the Northern and Southern traditions, and "wild-fox heterodoxy," was presumably the *locus classicus* of the endless discussion of orthodoxy in Ming literary thought, as it now became for art theorists.[50] It is a mark of the openness and receptivity of earlier artists, critics, and theorists that so little interest in orthodoxy was expressed at any time prior to the sixteenth century. Even in the most confused and complicated eras, at the junction of Sung and Yüan, for example, orthodoxy and heterodoxy were scarcely broached as matters of interest or importance. Huang Kung-wang, it is true, did cite heterodoxy as one of the four qualities it was very important for all painters to avoid,[51] but without definition of orthodoxy, and in the company of "sweetness," "vulgarity," and "derivativeness," the term does not seem to have had a powerful philosophical or historical base. Otherwise, by comparison with the attitude that prevailed from the late Ming period on, broad tolerance of diverse styles, techniques, personalities, and ideas appear to have characterized the earlier centuries.

With Li K'ai-hsien and Ho Liang-chün a new era opens. It speaks eloquently of the changed climate to contrast Ho's two major criteria of artistic superiority—lofty personal character and correct tradition, with Su Shih's major criteria—natural genius and originality (*t'ien-kung yü ch'ing-hsin*[p]).[52] Ho again and again returns to correctness of tradition:

> In landscape painting . . . Kuan T'ung and Ching Hao form one school, Tung Yüan and Priest Chü-jan another school, and Li Ch'eng and Fan K'uan still another. Coming to Li T'ang, he too forms a school. In these several masters, brush strength and spirit-consonance are all complete. Later painters who were able to follow them constitute the correct tradition (*cheng-mai*).
>
> As for Ma Yüan and Hsia Kuei of the Southern Sung, they too were famous masters . . . but their art after all is merely the academic style.[53]
>
> Because [the Yüan scholar-painters] were all lofty men, they were ashamed to serve the Barbarian Yüan, and instead sought their hopes in retirement. They wandered daily among the mountains and rivers, thus profoundly understanding their nature and appearances. Furthermore, their styles all came from Ching, Kuan, Tung, and Chü and their tradition is therefore the correct one (*ch'üan-p'ai yu cheng*[q]). How could they thus not far surpass their predecessors![54]
>
> Shen Chou's style of painting derives from Tung Yüan and Chü-jan, and he also devoted himself to copying the works of the Four Great Yüan

[o] 道有邪正 [p] 天工與清新 [q] 伝派又正

Masters, attaining the *samādhi* of them all. His craftsmanship is therefore lofty and distant, his brush and ink pure and rich, and his graded washes saturated with the Primal Spirit![55]

Such recent Chekiang painters as Shen Shih, Ch'en Hao, and Yao I-kuan, however, have not the slightest affiliation with correct traditions (*ch'u wu so shih-ch'eng*[r]), merely recklessly smearing and rubbing away—and then have the nerve to paint big pictures as gifts for people! What a laugh!

As for the likes of Chiang Sung and Wang Chih of Nanking and Chang Lu of the North, I would be ashamed to wipe my table with their paintings![56]

Thus very closely, Ho Liang-chün, like Tung Ch'i-ch'ang a native of Hua-t'ing, anticipates the "Southern school" of his fellow-townsman, defining an "orthodox tradition" from the Northern Sung masters through Chao Meng-fu, Kao K'o-kung, and the Four Great Masters of Yüan, to Shen Chou and Wen Cheng-ming, i.e. the "Wu school." This great tradition of scholar-amateurs is distinguished by its faithfulness to its own heritage, and is constituted solely of men of "lofty personal character"—no court painters (except Li T'ang),[57] no professionals, no one who did not derive his style from Tung-Chü, Ching-Kuan, or Li-Fan.

A separate, "capable" class is set aside for the "academic style," the Southern Sung and Ming court painters who, while not "orthodox" or of "lofty character," did adhere to a standard.

Lastly, not recognized by school or other classification, but fit not even to wipe a dirty table with, are Chang Lu, Chiang Sung, Kuo Hsü, Shen Shih, Ch'en Hao, and the others. These last, men of inferior personal character, neither adhering to the orthodox heritage nor meeting the artistic standards of correctness, are said to merely recklessly smear and rub, and to make big pictures!

It then remained only to coin the name "Wild and Heterodox" for those who chose to be neither orthodox nor academic, and this was done almost immediately by Kao Lien, T'u Lung, and/or Hsiang Yüan-pien.

THE MYTH OF THE PROFESSIONAL PAINTER

In defining the correct tradition of painting for his time and class, Ho Liang-chün was of course severely limiting the possible range of stylistic, expressive, and social avenues open to artists who wished to be seriously considered by writers on art. His comments on a contemporary, Hsieh Shih-ch'en, suggest some of these limitations:

[r] 初無所師承

... Hsieh Shih-ch'en, called Ch'u-hsien, is another skillful painter. He has quite a lot of gall (p'o yu tan-ch'i[s]), and is able to do big hanging scrolls. However, his brush and ink both are muddy, and he is a man of vulgar personal character. The San-ssu in Hang-chou asked him to go there and do a painting for them, and he responded by asking a very high price! The fellow gives off a bad stench.[58]

As Ho suggests, Hsieh liked to paint very large pictures, as well as the albums and handscrolls favored by scholar-artists. Paintings of large vision and physical size had of course been favored by many Sung and Yüan masters, as well as by the Ming academic and professional painters; but they had become increasingly upopular among scholar-amateurs who had come to associate large pictures with vulgarity, obviousness, pretentiousness, and painting-to-order, drawing upon a tradition of scholarly opinion going back to the Sung period.[59] Ho Liang-chün repeatedly belittles the vulgarity and pretentiousness of Ming painters and collectors who admired large-scale works or sets of hanging scrolls.[60]

Large-scale paintings generally required silk rather than paper as a painting surface, and the use of silk in turn made demands on painters that, increasingly, only professionals could meet. Silk, for example requires controlled, elaborate, ink-wash manipulation, because of the tendency of wash to flow over, rather than to be absorbed by, silk. Scholar-amateurs preferred absorbent paper, and rarely had the inclination to master ink-wash techniques.

Silk also requires a vigorous, hard, biting brushline that will cut into the intractable silk surfaces; hence, the ubiquitous description of the brushwork of painters on silk from Li Ssu-hsün to Tai Chin and Chang Lu as "strong, hard, vigorous, cutting."[61] Scholar-painters had developed a preference, on the contrary, for calligraphy-based concepts and types of brushwork suitable for paper, and described in such terms as "an awl scratching sand," "a seal stamping clay," and "a rain-stained wall"[62]—all evoking subtle, conceptual ideals of restraint, evenness, centeredness, and reserved strength: the "Confucian elements" of Chinese painting, These Confucian modes of brushwork were neither congenial nor appropriate to painters who chose to work in the old, monumental, visionary mode of the Sung artist, and it is interesting that there still were a few such painters in the sixteenth century.

When Ho Liang-chün wrote his diatribes against those who violated the "orthodox tradition," the two most capable and acclaimed artists of this bold, large-scale vision were, in fact, Hsieh Shih-ch'en—whose "muddy" brush and ink, vulgarity, pretentiousness, and commercialism Ho found distasteful, and Chang Lu—whose pictures Ho refused to dirty his watebasket with.

In his comments on Hsieh Shih-ch'en, Ho raises the issue of what might be

---

[s] 頗有膽氣

called "the myth of the professional painter." He was clearly outraged that a man graced by a request for his painting would have the vulgarity of character to demand a high price for his work. He also classified the arch-professional, T'ang Yin, among the scholar-amateurs. Scholars like Ho were far more comfortable with the belief that decent professional painters, like Tai Chin, would prefer to starve rather than to submit to the demeaning commercialism necessary to a successful career—witness, the still-perpetuated myth of Tai Chin's impoverished death.[63] Contemporary facts indicate that he was universally acclaimed as the greatest painter of his age, that he was praised and celebrated by the leading scholars of the nation, that his smallest work was prized like gold, and that he can only have died after a long life amidst public honors and the full trappings of success.[64] And yet the fiction of a dismal end continues. Obviously, to many scholars, there was neither romance nor honor in the death of a successful professional painter.

The great popularity of so many professional painters during the middle Ming period is in fact a noteworthy artistic and social phenomenon.[65] One could scarcely recall a more colorful group of eccentric individualists than the succession of painters including Tai Chin, Wu Wei, Shih Chung, Chung Li, Wang Chao, Hsü Lin, T'ang Yin and the others. Often celebrated at court, patronized grandly by poets, scholars, merchants, and lords, acclaimed in popular song, drama, and fiction, they lived on the skill or genius of their art and the fascination of their diverse personalities—despite the disdain of some scholars.

The professionals as a group did not write extensively on art, and we must for the most part rely upon indirect evidence for their attitudes, and their reactions to the kind of criticism we have introduced. One important exception is Chang Lu, a central figure in the original "wild and heterodox" group, whose painting seems to have regularly offended scholarly critics. His attitude toward literary criticism was one that we might suspect a great many professional painters shared, even if very few scholars would record it, namely, that as scholars the critics knew nothing of the art of painting and would better say nothing of it. Chang's views are recorded by his friend and biographer, Chu An-k'an:

> The Master often grieved, "There have been so few true connoisseurs of art in past or present. This is because there are so many people who do not know how to paint, and so few who do. Now, of course, people who do not know how to read haven't the means by which to appreciate literature, or to admire calligraphy; how, then, could it be possible for men who do not know how to paint to understand anything about painting? Even men of the very highest natural genius can get no more than the general outline. But as to the strength or weakness of brushwork, or the clearness or muddiness of ink-wash tonalities, these things they can never know at all. It is like the carpenter Pien carving a wheel, or the carver Ting

releasing the flesh from the bone—there are things that go even beyond brush and ink.[66]

Given this attitude, it is perhaps less surprising that Chang Lu should be the subject of the most vigouous criticism the scholars could bring to bear. The pure painters, like Tai Chin, Wu Wei, and Chang Lu had enough shortcomings already, not being scholars or degree-holders, but for them to assert that they actually understood more about painting than a learned scholar was to go too far. The elaborate attention given to the old question of the relative meritis of mere aficionados of painting (*hao-shih chia*[t]) versus the true connoisseurs (*chien-shang chia*[u]) by late Ming and Ch'ing art scholars[67] was probably sparked by this same attitude, and was aimed at establishing that they were the natural and proper arbiters of artistic achievement—not mere painters.

AESTHETIC QUALITIES OF THE "WILD AND HETERODOX SCHOOL"

The aesthetic approved by Ho Liang-chün was that associated with scholar-painters and poets since the Sung dynasty. It is loosely described in such terms as "even and pale" (*p'ing-tan*[v]), "lofty and antique" (*kao-ku*[w]), "elegant beauty" (*hsiu-mei*[x]); by the personal attributes of *shen-yün*[y]; by the social status of scholar-amateur; and by association with the correct tradition. The artist of this kind did not paint to order, or for any vulgar person; he did not paint on a large scale or, mostly, on silk; he was never obvious; and he did not evince intensity of emotion or passionate involvement with art on any level.

These attributes and qualities, turned completely over, had been the ideals of the "Wild and Heterodox" group, and of many other Ming painters. They acknowledged no "orthodox" tradition. They were nearly all professional painters, artists-for-hire; they often preferred large-scale paintings on silk or even walls. They favored wildness and strangeness over scholarly elegance, obviousness over subtlety, drama or melodrama over "the even and pale," boldness over restraint, and, breaking the restrictions of correctness and uprightness of personal manner and behavior, they preferred willful eccentricity and wildness in character and person-ality over the Confucian ideal, in life as in art. There is every indication that they were absolutely serious about these ideals, and dedicated to their realization in art.

If the deep foundations of such attitudes and ideals lie mostly in the Taoist tradition of thought, there is also a fascinating current of individualist thought in art going back at least to the Six Dynasties calligrapher who boasted, "Regret not that

t 好事家
u 鑒賞家

v 平淡
w 高古

x 秀美
y 神韻

my writing does not resemble the Two Wangs, regret instead that theirs does not resemble mine!''—an attitude quoted happily many times by Tao-chi.[68] In the early Ming period, the painter, Wang Li, was perhaps the most eloquent and influential spokesman for originality based upon nature rather than ancient models; and as he regarded the Southern Sung academic masters as the epitome of creative genius, his impact on early Ming art was doubly significant. Wang devoted himself to capturing the forms and spirit of the Hua Mountains, but only succeeded when he went to the mountains themselves:

> At that moment I thought no more of commonly accepted school manners. There schools and rules have all been established and made famous by men; am I alone not a man, who can make his own rules?[69]

Wang Li's treatises on painting, among the most thoughtful in art theory, undoubtedly exerted considerable influence during the Ming period, and were highly praised at the end of the dynasty by Wang Shih-chen.[70]

And if we are indeed to see a relationship between ideas of personal courage and heroism on the one hand, and bold individuality on the other, then we may consider the comments on painting by the early Ming martyr, Lien Tzu-ning:[71]

> Now as for the art of painting, there have been many specialists and great masters who have been able to exhaust the subtleties of formal representation, but only a few men of surpassing genius whose vision extends far beyond the dust of the mundane world have been able to attain the realm of meanings, nature and emotion, those far distant reaches touched by Nature's Creativity that are beyond normal understanding. Meng Tzu said, "The Great Workman can teach people how to use the compass and square, but he cannot teach them skill." In Chuang Tzu's story of the carpenter Pien he says, "I cannot teach it to my own son, and he cannot learn it from me." This is the kind of thing painting is. It is something the heart-mind must grasp and the hand respond to, though the heart and hand are not conscious of it, and still less can it be expressed in words, or by imitating works of art. Imitating the works of the old masters is like limiting oneself to the dust and the dirt, or the husks and chaff, without ever reaching the truth (*chen*[z]).[72]

The pursuit of truth or reality in painting might be the subject of another lengthy paper, but I would here note only the consistency with which the biographies of the "Wild and Heterodox" painters suggest their rejection of the imitation of old models in favor of the quest for reality.[73] Their paintings, in the long range of art history, represent the sixteenth-century embodiment of Kuo Hsi's old dictum, that

z 眞

the best landscape paintings are those in which one may wander or live,[74] and they were still creating new ways to make vivid and plausible the phenomena and experience of the natural world.

These issues of reality, originality, and individuality extend to other personal and artistic ideals. While Li K'ai-hsien, for example, favored the professional traditions and skills, like "good drawing"—to only slightly misuse that term—and a sense of reality, he also singled out Wu Wei for the "heroic spirit" (*meng-ch'i*[aa]) of his art, something Li felt made him stand out above everyone else in his age. This quality of the "heroic spirit" is related closely to individuality, and extends, too, into the realm of expression and aesthetic standards. A number of critics have addressed the issue.

After Tung Ch'i-ch'ang had fashioned his "Theory of the Northern and Southern Schools of Landscape Painting," generally avoiding the realm of expression and style related to the "heroic spirit," the Ch'ing literary critic Wang Shih-chen (1634–1711) took exception:

> Recent painters revere only the Southern School, and avoid such painters as Fan K'uan, Li Ch'eng, Ching Hao, and Kuo Hsi. This is because they particularly enjoy the elegant and rich (*hsiu-jun*[ab]), but fear the heroic and strange (*hsiung-ch'i*[ac]). I am not willing to accept this theory. Have they not thought that the historians Ssu-ma Ch'ien and Pan Ku, the writers Han Yü and Liu Tsung-yüan, the poets Tu Fu and Han Yü, and Li Meng-yang and Ho Ching-ming of recent times all belong to the Northern School?[75]

The "heroic spirit" had been embodied in the art of many of the great Northern Sung landscape painters, and it may be seen too in the art of such Yüan masters as Wu Chen and Wang Meng. In the Ming, heroic expression is found in the art of only a few men: Tai Chin, Wu Wei, Shih Chung, Chung Li, Chang Lu, Hsieh Shih-ch'en, Wang Chao. They are, in the main, the "Wild and Heterodox" masters, as suggested by another Ch'ing critic, Yü Chih, writing of a painting by Chang Lu:

> This style of painting must be appreciated for its broad, vast scope, and its heroic, powerful spirit (*hsiung-wei chih ch'i*[ad]). Where brush and ink reach, it is like the wind sweeping or lightning flashing, suddenly covering a thousand li with a force that sweeps all else before it. There is nothing here of the bitterness of self-restriction or measured ink, but only the purity of Natural Creation not availing of human strength....[76]

Yet another aspect of the artistic alternative to the elegant taste of the scholar is suggested in an account of one of the "wild" painters reported by Ho Liang-chün:

aa 猛氣
ab 秀潤

ac 雄氣
ad 雄偉之氣

Once at Hsü Lin's house I saw a hanging scroll by Tu Chin of the "Thunder Gods." The figures were over a foot high, and there were seven or eight of them in a group. Some held huge axes, others flaming torches, and still others thunderbolts. Their appearances were all strange and old-fashioned, completely lacking in what used to be called "elegant beauty." Certainly a strange work! Hsü would hang it in his central hall on the Day of the Dragon-boat Festival, or on the 15th of the 7th month, and startle his guests by saying, "This is Tu Chin's *Wang-ch'uan t'u!*" [77]

Hsü Lin, one suspects, was suggesting something rather profound with his comparison of Tu Chin's haunting, powerful image of other-worldly forces with the revered artistic icon of the *wen-jen* tradition, suggesting that the lofty taste of the scholars was taking them far from another, equally interesting realm, of the strange and old, the dramatic and vigorous. Hsü it is certain, pursued an artistic goal very different from those of other scholars, as his own free and spirited paintings indicate. [78]

One sixteenth-century critic who very nearly admits a preference for the alternate culture of boldness, wildness, spontaneity, originality, and the heroic spirit, is Wang Shih-chen (1526–1590). [79] Wang identified closely with the literati ideals of Wu-hsien, except, significantly, in his preference for Sung over Yüan painting, but nonetheless was drawn to such masters as Tai Chin, Wu Wei, and even Chang Lu. Unlike most of his literary contemporaries, Wang also admired Su Shih. [80] As a classicist, perhaps, Wang found it convenient to see Wu Wei and Chang Lu as followers of Wu Tao-tzu; at any rate he could appreciate the characteristics of their art in that context. [81] Unlike Ho Liang-chün, whom he knew, Wang considered Tai Chin the leading painter of the dynasty, ranking him first in his list of biographies, and pointedly adding the comment, "As the common saying has it, he was a professional with the virtues of the amateurs," [82] something Ho had specifically denied in his comparison of Tai Chin with Wen Cheng-ming. The reason for placing Tai Chin above even Shen Chou was Wang's belief that Tai was the more original of the two. Compare the following comments:

Wen-chin's origins come from Kuo Hsi, Li T'ang, Ma Yüan and Hsia Kuei, but his finest achievements for the most part come from himself (*miao-ch'u to tzu fa chih*[ae]).

[Shen Chou] was able to transform and go in and out among all of the famous masters of Northern Sung and Yüan, but only with Tung Yüan, Chü-jan, and Li Ch'eng did he find particular personal correspondence. He produced a few of his own ideas (*hsiao i chi-i fa chih*[af]), and when he happened to be successful I suspect that even those masters could not surpass him. [83]

ae 妙處多自發之   af 稍以己意發之

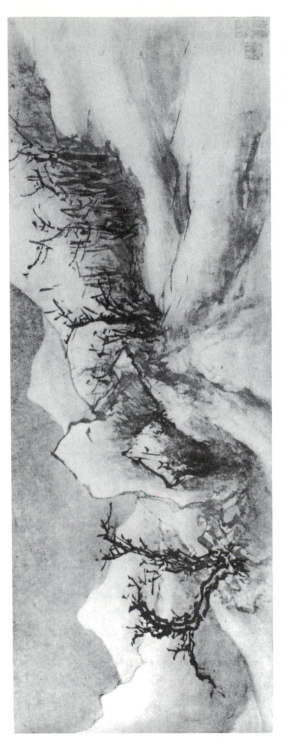

5. Chiang Sung, "Winter Landscape," from "Landscapes of the Four Seasons." Section of a handscroll, ink and light colors on paper, height 23 cm. Museum für Ostasiatische Kunst, Berlin–West.

6. Lin Liang, "The Autumn Hawk." Hanging scroll, ink and colors on silk,
136.8 × 74.8 cm. National Palace Museum, Taipei, Taiwan, R.O.C.

7. Chung Li, "Scholar Watching a Waterfall." Hanging scroll, ink and colors on silk, 175.8 × 103.5 cm. Anonymous loan, The Art Museum, Princeton University.

8. Chu Pang, "Strolling Alone in Empty Mountains." Hanging scroll, ink on paper, 161 × 91.5 cm. The Art Museum, Princeton University, Du Bois S. Morris Collection.

The contrast here between "for the most part" and "a few" is too neat to be anything but deliberate, and offers the unusual example of a late Ming scholar-critic, unconcerned with literati orthodoxy, determining the stature and rank of painters without concern for social status, solely on the clear grounds of originality.

As for the "wild" masters, Wu Wei and Chang Lu, Wang is also very even-handed:

> As a figure painter, Wu Wei evolves from the unrestrained brushwork of Wu Tao-tzu. He was not very good at planning, but his remarkably untrammeled and free manner is moving. Landscape elements, trees, and rocks are all done with the "ax-cut stroke," and are enormously strong and vigorous. His style is suited to painting on the walls of ancestral temples, or on large standing screens, but I fear it is inappropriate for small scrolls or album leaves.

> Among those who carried on Wu Wei's manner, Chang Lu is best known. However, he missed the refinement and freedom of Wu's style, catching only its firmness and muscular strength. Northerners value his works as great treasures. [Nowadays] genuine works and forgeries are all mixed up, and ugly imitators have flourished. Wu Wei too, did not escape the encumberance of this evil path.[84]

> Hsieh Shih-ch'en ... was also a quite able painter of standing screens and large hanging scrolls. His paintings have spirit and vigor, but also suffer from finickyness. He, too, distantly continues the traditions of Tai Chin and Wu Wei.[85]

Wang's critique adds up to a reasonably complete description of a positive artistic ideal, one formed of originality, boldness of vision and technique, large scale, freedom, muscular strength, and vigor of brushwork. Chan Ching-feng, a younger contemporary of Wang and evidently influenced by him, was also extremely sympathetic to the goals of the professional and wild masters, and attacked as narrow regional bias the Suchou preference for Shen Chou over Tai Chin.[86] His description of a group of paintings by Wu Wei offers a tantalizing glimpse of an art form that was disappearing and a precise formulation of its power and originality:

> In the Lung-ku Temple in Nanking there were once four corridor walls painted by Wu Wei. First was Po Chü-i in Ch'an meditation; second was Su Shih in meditation: third was Bodhidharma crossing the Yangtze; and fourth was Confucius, Lao Tzu, and Śākyamuni. The walls were over twenty feet wide and more than forty feet high! The figures, objects, mountains, rocks, and trees truly spread irresistibly from earth to heaven! If Ma Yüan or Hsia Kuei could see them they would be awed. In their

paintings, each brushstroke is concentrated and precise; as for Wu Wei, he totally abandons himself, attacking directly and brushing furiously—and yet there is not a single detail in which the spirit does not soar and the essence penetrate. Only perhaps in the Confucius, Lao Tzu, and Śākyamuni was there a slight decline, One can imagine that it was the last of the four to be done, and that by then both his inspiration and his strength were exhausted ... By the end of the Lung-ch'ing/beginning of the Wan-li period [1513 ff.] the walls were in complete ruin; nowadays not even the corridors are there.[87]

FROM "WILD AND HETERODOX" TO THE CHE AND NORTHERN SCHOOLS

Late in the sixteenth century, the term Che school began to be used to describe the Southern-Sung inspired academic and professional painting of the Ming period, and it was followed quickly by the Northern school of Tung Ch'i-ch'ang.[88] Tung himself had relatively little to say about Ming painting, but it is clear from the sequence that his historical theory is merely the capstone to an interpretation that had first found scholar-amateurs superior to professionals, then defined a precise orthodox tradition of scholar-painters and a separate category of academic art, and finally set aside a separate class for the "wild and heterodox," all in the context of sixteenth-century painting.

It goes beyond my scope to follow this development further, but the ultimate theory among scholars in the generation of Tung Ch'i-ch'ang held all Ming painters except the scholar-amateurs to be "heterodox." The sequence is seen in comments, first, by Hsieh Chao-che, and then by Shen Hao:

> At the beginning of the dynasty Tai Chin was acclaimed as a famous painter. However, his personal character and style were crude and inferior. But since the other painters of the time, like Wu Wei and Chiang Tzu-ch'eng did not even come up to Tai, his fame dominated the period. Once Shen Chou appeared, Tai Chin was obliterated....[89]

Shen Hao, recalling Yen Yü, in a discussion called "The Division of Schools," made the final correction:

> The Northern school ... coming down to Tai Chin, Wu Wei, and Chang Lu daily progressed toward "fox-ch'an," and the robes and rice-bowl [fell into] the dust the dirt.[90]

"*Fox-ch'an*" is merely an abbreviation of Yen Yü's "wild-fox heterodoxy," and virtually all Ming painting but the true school of Suchou is now smeared with the brush of heterodoxy. The "wild" masters thus became merely the worst of a bad lot, and what had flourished as an individualistic approach to art and expression was seen only to have mocked and reviled correctness and orthodoxy.

The inability of some scholars to tolerate what they came to regard as these excesses is nowhere better illustrated than by the critical fate of Chu Yün-ming's "wild-cursive" calligraphy. The generation of Tung Ch'i-ch'ang and Mo Shih-lung, preoccupied with orthodoxy, correctness, and classical models, found Chu's wild-cursive "eccentric and vulgar," "undisciplined and free, loose and careless," sometimes "losing the principles of brushwork," and finally "abandoned and not without 'wild-fox' heterodoxy." To this point, there is a very close parallel with the critical appraisals of the wild painters, but the scholars of calligraphy went further, and declared ultimately that all such works were simply crude forgeries—that Chu Yün-ming had never done anything so vulgar or excessive![91]

Were I competent to do so, I would attempt to explore the relationship of these developments in art to others in literature and philosophy. Certainly one is struck by apparent parallels in the evolution of the Wang Yang-ming school and in literary theory. Wang Shih-chen, for example, sounds very much like Ho Liang-chün and Kao Lien on art when he discusses the excesses of Wang Yang-ming's followers:

> [They] flourished and spread throughout the land in the Chia-ching (1522–1566) and Lung-ch'ing (1567–1572) periods. What led finally to their great excesses was that they used their lecturing to serve the cult of heroism, and used the cult of heroism to indulge their unrestrained selfishness. Their arts had basically nothing to them that might rouse men to action, and lacking any real conviction or concern they joined in beating the drums, blowing their horns, flapping their wings, drawing crowds together and flashing here and there, until ... everything rotted apart and it could not be put together again.[92]

A comparison with heroism, wildness, and excess in painting is probably too superficial, but even so, one is struck by the apparent contrast between Wang's views here on thought and action, on the one hand, and his seemingly very different attitude, generally favorable, toward the heroic, wild school of painting represented by Chang Lu and Wu Wei. The differences would appear to indicate in this case at least that the realm of art occupied a separate sphere, and that the categories of scholarship, art, literature, and philosophy had such different status, goals, traditions, and ideals that they did not closely overlap. One would draw the same conclusion at the intersection of Tung Ch'i-ch'ang, Yüan Hung-tao, and Li Chih.[93]. On the evidence of Tung's art and theory, it does not seem likely that the philosopher understood the painter, or the painter the writer. I could be wrong, but it seems to me that the individualistic thought of Li Chih and Yüan Hung-tao is not far from the individualism of the "Wild and Heterodox" painters, nor from Lien Tzu-ning or Wang Li, and is most richly developed in art and theory by Tao-chi.[94]

1. T'u Lung, *K'ao p'an yü-shih* (*ISTP* ed.) 2, p. 32.

2. Hsiang Yüan-pien (attributed to), *Chiao-ch'uang chiu-lu* (*ISTP* ed.), p. 41; Kao Lien, *Yen-chien ch'ing-shang chien* (*ISTP* ed.), p. 192; Wen Chen-heng, *Ch'ang-wu chih* (*ISTP* ed.) 5, p. 33, at the end of the section called "Famous masters." The four texts cited in notes 1 and 2 are included in volumes 28 and 29 of *ISTP*, *Kuan-shang hui-lu*, volumes 1 and 2. Of the four, only the latter two have not been questioned as to authorship. See the biographies of T'u Lung and Hsiang Yüan-pien in *Dictionary of Ming Biography*, ed. L. C. Goodrich and Chaoying Fang, 2 vols. (New York, 1976) (hereafter *DMB*), and the discussion of the problems of these texts and the authorship of the phrase "Wild and Heterodox" in Suzuki, Kei, *Mindai Kaigashi no kenkyū: Seppa* (Studies in Ming Painting: the Che school) (Tokyo, 1968) (hereafter Suzuki), n. 312. Judging from the comments of the early Ch'ing collector, Ku Fu, cited by Suzuki, Kao Lien may have been the originator of the term, but it was quickly associated with other texts and authors as well, and was obviously common currency in the later sixteenth century.

3. Hsü Ch'in, *Ming-hua lu* (*HSTS* ed.) 3, pp. 32–33 (in the entry on Chiang Sung).

4. These are the terms used by James Cahill in *Parting at the Shore* (New York and Tokyo, 1978) (hereafter Cahill, *Parting*), *passim*. Biographical information concerning the painters mentioned here is found in Suzuki; and in Cahill, *Parting*, especially pp. 45–53, 97–134, and 135–166. The plates accompanying this article illustrate the art of a few of the "wild and heterodox" masters.

5. *The Analects of Confucius*, trans. and ann. Arthur Waley (New York, 1938), p. 177. I have modified the translation. My thanks to Tu Wei-ming for suggesting this reference.

6. *Chuang Tzu*, chaps. 21, 13, 3, and 19. For translations, see James R. Ware, trans., *The Sayings of Chuang Chou* (New York, 1963), pp. 29, 93, 127, 141.

7. Cahill, *Parting*, pp. 163–166.

8. *Chuang Tzu*, chap. 1 (Burton Watson, trans., *Chuang Tzu: Basic Writings*, New York and London, pp. 29–30).

9. The Yüan "Taoist style" of painting has been defined most closely by Chiang I-han; see his articles on Wu Po-li, *NPMQ* (Spring, 1974), 8(3):51–62; and Teng Tzu-fang, *ibid.* (Summer, 1973), 7(4):49–85.

10. This description is found in the biographical notes appended to Li K'ai-hsien's *Chung-lu hua-p'in* by his friend and fellow townsman, Hu Lai-kung, p. 68 in the *ISTP* edition.

11. In Wu's epitaph, written in 1508 (Suzuki, n. 266). Chang Ch'i (1499 *chin-shih*) was asked to write the epitaph by a son of the painter who brought family records and documents for the purpose.

12. The largest selection of reproductions of paintings by the "wild" masters is Suzuki Kei, *Ri To, Ba En, Ka Kei* (Li T'ang, Ma Yüan, Hsia Kuei), *Suiboku bijutsu taikei*, vol. 2 (Tokyo, 1974). For others, see Cahill, *Parting*, pls. 44 and 56; Richard Barnhart, "Survivals, Revivals and the Classical Tradition of Chinese Figure Painting," *Proceedings of the International Symposium on Chinese Painting* (Taipei, 1970), pp. 143–210, pls. 22–23.

13. James Cahill, "Confucian Elements in the Theory of Painting," in *The Confucian Persuasion*, ed. Arthur Wright (Stanford, 1966), pp. 115–140.

14. From his biography in *Wu-sheng-shih shih* (History of Soundless Poetry) trans. in

Osvald Sirén, *Chinese Painting: Leading Masters and Principles*, 7 vols. (New York and London, 1955–1958), 4:135.

15. *Hsiu-ning-hsien chih* (Gazetteer of Hsiu-ning Country), quoted in Suzuki, n. 328.

16. *Fu-chien t'ung-chih* (Gazetteer of Fukien), quoted in Suzuki, n. 342.

17. This is the poem written on the "Landscape" reproduced in Cahill, *Parting*, pl. 67, and transcribed in *Shih-ch'ü pao-chi*, 1st ed., 39, p. 20.

18. Shūjuō Shimada, trans. James Cahill, "Concerning the 'I-p'in' Style of Painting," *OA* (1961), n.s. 7:66–74; (1962), 8:130–137; (1964), 10:3–10. At the end of his study, Shimada specifically refers to the "tendencies toward wildness and unrestraint in the Che School of the Ming dynasty" as later appearances of the I-p'in style and philosophy.

19. On the preference of Ming writers for T'ang, see especially Richard John Lynn, "Orthodoxy and Enlightenment: Wang Shih-chen's Theory of Poetry and its Antecedents," in *The Unfolding of Neo-Confucianism*, ed. Wm. Theodore de Bary and the Conference on Seventeenth-Century Thought (New York and London, 1975), pp. 217–269.

20. See, for example, Cahill, *Parting*, color pl. 7; Suzuki, figs. 108 and 133. There are also other paintings of Su Shih in various collections, including one (46–152) attributed to Wu Wei in the Art Museum, Princeton University. Suzuki has suggested that Ch'en Tzu-ho's "Drunken Rider" may be "Tung-p'o Returning Home Drunk"; see Suzuki, n. 342.

21. Kōjirō Yoshikawa, *An Introduction to Sung Poetry*, trans. Burton Watson, (Cambridge, 1967), p. 102; and Su Shih, *Chi-chu fen-lei Tung-p'o hsien-sheng shih* (edited and annotated edition of Su Shih's Poetry (*SPTK*), 11:21b, quoted and trans. Susan Bush, *The Chinese Literati on Painting: Su Shih (1037–1101) to Tung Ch'i-ch'ang (1555–1636)* (Cambridge, Mass., 1971), p. 35.

22. *Hsiu-ning-hsien chih* (Gazetteer of Hsiu-ning hsien), quoted in Suzuki, n. 326.

23. Chu An-k'an, *Chang P'ing-shan hsien-sheng*, (Master Chang Lu) in *Ming wen-hai*, ed. Huang Tsung-hsi (*Ssu-k'u ch'üan-shu* VII [rpt. Taipei, 1977], 313–388), 64, pp. 3–6.

24. Ni Yüeh, *Sung Wu Tz'u-weng huan ch'ao hsü*, (Preface on Seeing Wu Wei off to Court), quoted in Suzuki, n. 277.

25. Quoted in Shen C. Y. Fu, *Traces of the Brush* (Yale University, 1977), p. 214.

26. *Shang-yü-hsien chih* (Gazetteer of Shang-yü Country), quoted in Suzuki, n. 314.

27. From a colophon dated 1526, by Lu Shih-tao, attached to the *San-ts'ai li-ch'ü t'u* attributed to Chang Fu-yang; see Suzuki, n. 323.

28. *Hsiu-ning-hsien chih*, quoted in Suzuki, n. 326.

29. *Chiang-ning-fu chih* (Gazetteer of Chiang-ning Prefecture), quoted in Suzuki, n. 262.

30. Suzuki, n. 9.

31. Biography in *DMB*.

32. Biography in *DMB*.

33. I have used the *Mei-shu ts'ung-shu* edition reproduced in *ISTP*, vol. 12, *Ming-jen hua-hsüeh lun-chu, pt. 1*.

34. Ibid., p. 48 (for the description) and pp. 55–56 (for the critical ranking).

35. Critical assessments of Tai Chin are collected in Suzuki, pp. 15–23 and nn. 12–41.

36. *Chung-lu hua-p'in*, pp. 50–52 for the "six essentials of painting."

37. Ibid., p. 55 and p. 47.

38. Ibid., pp. 52–54 for the "four faults of painting."

39. Ibid., p. 48.

40. Ibid., p. 49.

41. Ibid., p. 50.

42. Ibid., p. 47.

43. I have used the *Mei-shu ts'ung-shu* edition reproduced in *ISTP*, vol. 12, *Ming-jen hua-hsüeh lun-chu*, pt. 1. For a discussion of the text and its dating, see Ho Liang-chün's biography in *DMB*.

44. Ho Liang-chün, *Ssu-yu-chai hua-lun*, p. 44. The same distinction was drawn earlier by Wu K'uan (1436–1504) between Shen Chou and Tai Chin; see Suzuki, n. 18.

45. Ho, *Ssu-yu-chai hua-lun*, p. 43.

46. Ibid., p. 44.

47. Ibid., p. 39; and see below for further discussion.

48. Ibid., p. 37. The original author of the passage was Chiang K'uei; see Shuen-fu Lin's article in this volume.

49. Kao Lien, *Yen-chien ch'ing-shang chien* (*ISTP*, vol. 28), p. 186.

50. Yen Yü, his theory, and his influence on Ming literary critics are discussed by Richard John Lynn in his study of orthodoxy in the Ming and early Ch'ing periods; see n. 19. For orthodoxy in painting, focused on the seventeenth century, see James Cahill, "The Orthodox Movement in Early Ch'ing Painting," in *Artists and Traditions*, ed. Christian F. Murck (Princeton, 1976), pp. 169–181. Particularly relevant to this paper is his appendix, "The Orthodox View of Orthodoxy."

51. Huang Kung-wang, *Hsieh shan-shui chüeh* (The Secrets of Landscape Painting) (Peking, 1962 ed.), p. 6.

52. Quoted in Bush, *Chinese Literati*, p. 26.

53. Ho, *Ssu-yu-chai hua-lun*, p. 39.

54. Ibid., pp. 36–37.

55. Ibid., pp. 44–45.

56. Ibid., p. 47.

57. Li T'ang is the only name in Ho's list that was later dropped from the Orthodox succession. His presence probably owes to the fact that his style was extremely influential in Suchou scholarly circles, especially to T'ang Yin, but also to Wen Cheng-ming, as well as the popular Suchou professionals. After a generation, his name was dropped, and T'ang Yin's clouded by association with professionalism. See Cahill, "The Orthodox Movement in Early Ch'ing" (cited in n. 50), pp. 177–181, for relevant texts.

58. Ho, *Ssu-yu-chai hua-lun*, p. 40.

59. Li Kung-lin, for example, is said to have prided himself on never painting anything as vulgar as large scrolls or paired sets, according to Teng Ch'un, *Hua chi* (Peking, 1963 ed.) 9, p. 117. Chao Hsi-ku, the thirteenth-century connoisseur, maintained, contrary to all evidence, that great masters did not paint on a large scale, or with any deliberation, but only casually, when moved by spontaneous inspiration. See Bush, *Chinese Literati*, p. 112. Mi Fu (*Hua-shih*, *ISTP* ed., p. 24) boasts, "I no longer paint large pictures!" as Susan Nelson reminded me.

60. Ho, *Ssu-yu-chai hua-lun*, pp. 37–38, and his discussion of Hsieh Shih-ch'en, p. 40.

61. For example, Bush, *Chinese Literati*, p. 170, quoting Shen Hao. See also Yü Chien-

hua, *Chung-kuo shan-shui-hua te nan-pei-tsung lun* (The Theory of the Northern and Southern Schools of Chinese Landscape Painting) (Shanghai, 1961), pp. 8–19.

62. The types and qualities of brushwork preferred by scholar-painters are discussed by Wen Fong, "Tung Ch'i-ch'ang and the Orthodox Theory of Painting," *NPMQ* (January, 1968), 2(3):1–26.

63. Sirén, *Chinese Painting*, 4:128–129; Cahill, *Parting*, p. 47.

64. The story of Tai's impoverished death began among his admirers in the Ming period, but is contradicted by Tu Ch'iung's earlier biographical notes and other contemporary writing. See Suzuki, pp. 15–23; and Ch'en Fang-mei, *Tai Chin yen-chiu* (M.A. Thesis, Taiwan University, 1974).

65. Tu Ch'iung says of Tai Chin after his retirement to Hangchou, "his fame became even greater, and those who sought his paintings considered even a single brushstroke as precious as gold" (Suzuki n. 35). Of Chang Lu, Wang Shih-chen wrote, "Northerners prize his works as if they were the rarest treasures" (ibid., n. 338). See also the biography of another successful professional, Hsü Lin, in *DMB*.

66. Quoted by Chu An-k'an in his biography; see n. 23.

67. Li K'ai-hsien (*Chung-lu hua-p'in*, p. 63), Ho Liang-chün (*Ssu-yu-chai hua-lun*, pp. 27–28), T'u Lung (*K'ao-p'an yü-shih*, *ISTP* ed., p. 31), Kao Lien (*Yen-chien ch'ing shang chien*, pp. 187ff.), Hsiang Yüan-pien (*Chiao-ch'uang chiu-lu*, *ISTP* ed., pp. 39–40), and Wen Chen-heng (*Ch'ang-wu chih*, *ISTP* ed., p. 31) are a few of the late Ming scholars who discuss this old question, which continues to occupy orthodox scholars through the Ch'ing period.

68. Marilyn and Shen Fu, *Studies in Connoisseurship* (Princeton, 1973), p. 55.

69. Osvald Sirén, *The Chinese on the Art of Painting* (New York and Hong Kong, 1963), p. 122. Wang's writings are discussed on pp. 121–122, and in Cahill, *Parting*, pp. 5–7. The original texts are included in *PWCSHP* 16.

70. Wang Shih-chen, *Yen-chou shan-jen ssu-pu-kao, hsü-kao* (Collected Works) 138:1a–b. For other appreciations of Wang Li see *PWCSHP* 86.

71. Biography in *DMB*.

72. Sirén, *The Chinese on the Art of Painting*, p. 152. My translation, based upon the text in *PWCSHP* 16, differs somewhat.

73. In addition to the biographical notes above, see Suzuki, p. 230; and Cahill, *Parting*, p. 130, on Chang Lu's "Fisherman under a Cliff."

74. Kuo Hsi, *Lin-ch'uan kao-chih*, trans. S. Sakanishi, *An Essay on Landscape Painting* (London, 1959), p. 34.

75. Quoted in Yü Chien-hua, *Chung-kuo shan-shui-hua te nan-pei-tsung lun*, p. 48.

76. Ibid., p. 52.

77. Ho, *Ssu-yu-chai hua-lun*, pp. 45–46.

78. Cahill, *Parting*, pl. 49.

79. Biography in *DMB*. His opinion of Wang Li was cited above in n. 71.

80. See the biography by Barbara Yoshida-Krafft in *DMB*, p. 1403. According to views expressed at the Breckinridge Conference, however, this opinion may be exaggerated.

81. Perhaps Wang was consciously echoing Su Shih, who had eloquently praised the "heroic spirit" of Wu Tao-tzu (see my "Survivals, Revivals" referred to in. n. 12, above).

82. Wang Shih-chen, *I-yüan chih-yen* 155:16b.

83. Ibid. 155:16b–17a.

84. Ibid. 155:17b.

85. Ibid. 155:19a.

86. Chan Ching-feng, *Tung-t'u hsüan-lan pien (MSTS* ed.) 2, pp. 110–111. Susan Nelson called this passage to my attention, and I am most grateful.

87. Ibid. 4, p. 201.

88. Bush, *Chinese Literati*, pp. 172–179.

89. Hsieh Chao-che, *Wu-tsa-tsu*, quoted in Suzuki, n. 2.

90. Shen Hao, *Hua-chu*, text quoted in *HLTK*, 1:134.

91. Fu, *Traces of the Brush*, pp. 214–215.

92. Quoted in Wm. Theodore de Bary, "Individualism and Humanitarianism in Late Ming Thought," in *Self and Society in Ming Thought*, ed. Wm. Theodore de Bary and the Conference on Ming Thought (New York and London, 1970), p. 178.

93. Discussed by Nelson Wu, "Tung Ch'i-ch'ang (1555–1636): Apathy in Government and Fervor in Art," in *Confucian Personalities*, ed. Arthur Wright and Denis Twichett (Stanford, 1962), pp. 260–293.

94. James Cahill seems to suggest a similar conclusion in his "The Orthodox Movement in Early Ch'ing Painting" (see n. 50) especially in the concluding comments on p. 181. For Tao-chi's theories, see Marilyn and Shen Fu, *Studies in Connoisseurship*, pp. 51–58.

I would like to acknowledge with gratitude and affection the contributions to my understanding of Ming painting made by graduate students in a seminar that I gave at Princeton University in the fall of 1979. Their industry and lively intelligence are reflected in many ways in this paper and, to the following, I extend my thanks: Elizabeth Brotherton, Pao-chen Ch'en, Shou-ch'ien Shih, and Caron Smith.

I-p'in in Later Painting Criticism

By Susan E. Nelson

From the T'ang dynasty on, the term *i* ("free" or "untrammeled") has occupied an important place in literature devoted to the art of painting. Its specific meanings, connotations, and value implications varied considerably over time and according to individual users; it certainly had as wide a range of meaning as any term in the critical literature. Its meaning in T'ang and Sung criticism has been the subject of illuminating studies;[1] its sense in later criticism, however, has not yet been examined.

The two early texts which include important passages on the "untrammeled" style in painting describe it in terms of radical experimentalism and willful rejection of convention. The *T'ang-ch'ao ming-hua lu*, written by Chu Ching-hsüan around the middle of the ninth century, lists three men in an "untrammeled class' (*i-p'in*) of masters who rejected orthodox methods and therefore had to be set apart from the conventional three classes of *shen* ("divine" or "inspired"), *miao* ("wonderful"), and *neng* ("competent"). Two of them, Wang Mo and Li Ling-sheng, are said to have painted in an impulsive, spontaneous way, using abbreviated, sketchy brushstrokes and unleashing their thoughts and gestures with the help of wine. Most extreme was Wang Mo, who

> ... when he was sufficiently drunk, would spatter the ink onto the painting surface. Then, laughing and singing all the while, he would stamp on it with his feet and smear it with his hands, besides swashing and sweeping it with the brush.[2]

In Huang Hsiu-fu's *I-chou ming-hua lu* (prefaced in 1006), only one painter, Sun Wei of the late ninth century, is classed in the *i* rank; he, too, is described as careless and abandoned by nature. The text mentions that he did not drink to excess; the reference to his drinking habits seems at least as telling as the point about his moderation.[3]

In addition to the untrammeled masters' uninhibited character and painting style, both texts dwell upon their high-minded temperament. Li Ling-sheng, according to the *T'ang-ch'ao ming-hua lu*, would never defer to to the rich and powerful, maintaining an uncorrupted independence; the *I-chou ming-hua lu* says the same of Sun Wei. Both texts suggest that it was this unconcern with recognition and rewards that allowed the untrammeled painters to undertake their risky formal experiments, "disdaining" (as Huang Hsiu-fu put it) the careful detail and meticulousness in drawing that presumably would have ensured worldly success. Though he acknowledges that it is rough and unpolished, "clumsy in the laying out of squares and circles," Huang nonetheless sees in *i* painting an element of order and reason, for in the end "the forms are complete." This completeness, not to be explained in terms of conventional painting discipline, is a projection of the artist's inner life; and so "it cannot be imitated; for its source is the expression of ideas."[4] In its original sense, *i* referred to the condition of retirement from official life, with implications of relaxed leisure, release from protocol and obligations, and imperviousness to the lures of advancement;[5] many of the *i* painters also had Taoist affiliations. The high regard in which this lofty independence and nonchalance was held is reflected in Huang Hsiu-fu's decision to place the *i* rank above the other three.

This kind of painting was not to hold the critics' admiration indefinitely; by the twelfth century, a change in the view and evaluation of the *i-p'in* took place. Teng Ch'un in his *Hua chi* (prefaced in 1176) claims to approve of the untrammeled painters in general, but he does not really express enthusiasm for any of them. Of those after Sun Wei, in his view, the best could just be "tolerated," while others were simply terrible. He scoffs at their aspirations to "loftiness," and seems to consider their supposed high-minded unconcern for convention little more than unruliness and posey eccentricity.[6] The value of disengagement and disdain for worldly approval, of course, is not impugned; but the recognized *i-p'in* painters' wild and perverse methods had evidently lost some of their appeal. From this time on, views about "freedom" in painting were never quite the same.

Teng Ch'un himself offers an explanation for this shift: the influence of Emperor Hui-tsung (1082–1135), who preferred and patronized more orderly, finished painting. The real reason, however, cannot be so specifically pinpointed; it was a broad and growing taste for understatement and tact in painting. Artists inspired by this taste generally tended to shun the wild ways of men like Wang Mo, but they constituted a variety of new movements. The kind of painting favored by Hui-tsung—choice, demure, discreet—was one of these. Others preserved some of the improvisational quality of the old *i-p'in* while avoiding its sense of immoderation; these trends, associated with a group of late eleventh- and early twelfth-century "scholars," were to culminate in the "literati painting" (*wen-jen hua*) of the Yüan period.[7]

In post-Yüan painting criticism, *i* is a common term. Many and varied paintings, of course—"Southern school" paintings in general, and especially those of Yüan times—might suggest the adjective *i* to a Ming or Ch'ing critic. The term was in constant use, and it is certainly not possible to account for the associations every writer was drawing on every time someone or something is described as *i*. But despite the looseness of its meaning, it had, of course, certain generally accepted connotations. The present broad review of the critical literature from the sixteenth to the eighteenth centuries allows us to identify those connotations, and reveals that the adjective had undergone a fundamental change in meaning. Much of the sense it had carried in connection with the early *i* masters was lost, while it picked up new meanings quite divorced from the image of Wang Mo and his fellows.

As had the earlier, the later painters designated as *i* inclined to a sketchy way with the brush, for this was perhaps the natural stylistic concomitant of an "untrammeled" state of mind. In T'ang, however, abrupt and sketchy brushwork was new and exceptional, and may have been enough to bring its practitioners together under the notion of a loose but identifiable style. By later times, sketchiness in itself was far too common and diverse in its manifestations to stand as the distinguishing feature of a style. The *i-p'in* was reserved for a much more limited category. Not included in this category were the painters perhaps closest to the T'ang eccentrics in their bold and aggressive brushwork. These artists tended to be professionals rather than "retired," and their kind of spontaneity was no longer thought to stem from "loftiness;" they are almost never described as *i*.[8] The *i-p'in* of later criticism was made up of a different sort of painter. Like the T'ang *i-p'in*, it was an extremely small and exclusive group; so small, in fact, that its individual members not only represented, but actually in large part determined, the new definition of *i* painting.

I

The later *i-p'in* had a core of only two members: the Sung painter Mi Fu (1052–1107) and the Yüan man Ni Tsan (1301–1374). A well-known passage by the late Ming painter and connoisseur Tung Ch'i-ch'ang (1555–1636) sums this up:

> Old Yü's [Ni Tsan's] painting at the time of the last dynasty can be called of the untrammeled class. . . . Among Sung men, Mi Hsiang-yang [Mi Fu] was beyond the beaten path; the others all came out of a mold. There were many able Yüan men, but they carried on the dictates of the Sung methods, merely adding a little solitary and relaxed feeling. Wu Chung-kuei [Wu Chen] had an abundance of inspiration; Huang Tzu-chiu [Huang Kung-wang], an especially marvelous quality; Wang Shu-ming [Wang Meng] mastered the former ways. But these three all had a conventional, practiced air to their brushwork. Yün-lin [Ni Tsan] alone was old-fashioned, unassertive, and natural. He was the only one after Mad Mi.[a][9]

[a] 迂翁畫在勝國時可稱逸品……宋人中米襄陽在蹊逕之外，餘皆從陶鑄而來。元之能者雖多，然稟承宋法，稍加蕭散耳。

吳仲圭大有神氣，黃子久特妙風格，王叔明奄有前規。而三家皆有縱橫習氣。獨雲林古淡天然。米癲後一人而已。

Aside from Mi, the Sung painters all conformed to the same pattern; aside from Ni, the Yüan painters, however distinguished, had copied the Sung and were tainted with a "practiced air." This was true even of the other three of the so-called "four great Yüan masters," Wu Chen (1280–1354), Huang Kung-wang (1269–1354), and Wang Meng (ca. 1310–1385). Tung Ch'i-ch'ang evidently took the meaning of *i* in this absolute sense.

All great artists, of course, were thought to have accomplished something personal and unprecedented within the framework of received traditions. The best of these were painters of the "inspired" (*shen*) class; for the achievement of freedom on the basis of perfected training was the acknowledged rule of the study of the art. Even Mi Fu and Ni Tsan, the artists thought to epitomize "freedom" most completely, were sometimes discussed within this pattern of assimilation and transcendence. They had recognized debts to former men; certain aspects of their painting were seen as derivative, and they could be placed within the established painting lineages.[10]

All the same, although these painters could be seen within an art-historical framework, they (and they alone) could also be seen without it. The distinctive aspect of their painting—what made it *i*—was seen not as a "transformation" (*pien*), as it was with other great or greater but not as "untrammeled" painters, but as something altogether new.

Ni Tsan seems to have had a special place in his heart for Mi Fu. Numerous colophons of his are recorded on paintings by Mi, and he named one of his libraries in honor of the Sung man. This admiration extended to Mi's follower Kao K'o-kung (1248–1310), and his words of generous praise for Kao were well remembered by later critics. One of Ni's associates during his twenties was Kuo Pi (1301–1355), a painter strongly influenced by Mi, and Kuo may have been partly responsible for drawing Ni's attention to Mi Fu; but Ni's interest certainly went beyond the academic to a recognition of a spiritual kinship. There were, after all, remarkable correspondences in temperament and personal habits between the two men. Both were obsessively clean, given to wearing antique dress, and of a legendary cranky haughtiness.[11]

The kinship between them was recognized by Ni's contemporaries. His good friend Chang Yü (1283–1350) suggested it in the colophon he composed for a work Ni painted in 1349, which he compared to the painting of Mi Fu and his son, Mi Yu-jen (1086–1165);[12] and again in his inscription to an anonymous portrait of Ni, where Chang wrote: "in spirit, he is companion to Hai-yüeh [Mi Fu]."[13] Chang's understanding of this spiritual friendship is explained further in a comment by another member of Ni's circle, Yüan Hua (1316–after 1376). Yüan inscribed a 1368 painting of Ni's with a poem that concludes, "Ni Yü is like Mad Mi." He went on to add in prose:

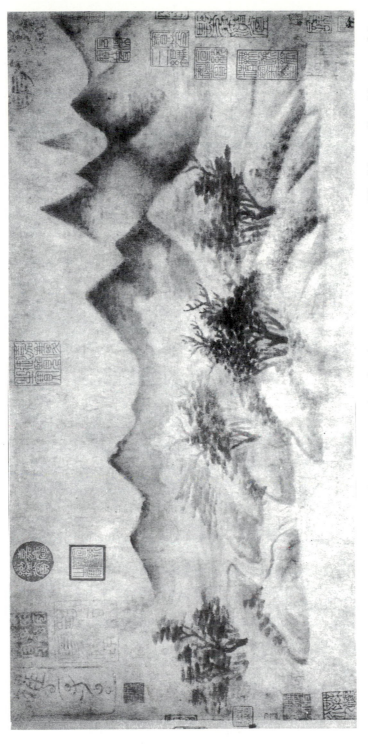

1. Mi Yu-jen (1086–1165) "Cloudy Mountains." Handscroll, ink on paper, 27.5 × 57 cm. The Metropolitan Museum of Art, Gift of J. Pierpont Morgan, by exchange, 1973.

> My late friend Chang Chen-chü [Chang Yü] of Chien-a pointed out that Mi Nan-kung [Mi Fu] had a passion for cleanliness, and all his paintings and calligraphy were scrolls of small size; in recent times, Ni Yün-lin [Ni Tsan] is the only one who closely resembles him. Mi called himself "Tien" [mad] so I will call Ni "Yü" [eccentric]. Today, looking at his surviving paintings, they all equal [Mi].[b][14]

A third Yüan man, Ku Meng, also made the connection between Mi and Ni in a poem on a Ni painting, and gave the same reason as that later developed by Tung Ch'i-ch'ang: the two masters' disengagement and relaxed approach.

> As it happened the inkslab was ready, he [Ni] sketched in a relaxed way. How could the dots and washes resemble those of the artisan painters?...
> One finds oneself thinking of Mi Nan-kung.[c][15]

Tung Ch'i-ch'ang was therefore echoing a long-standing recognition of a resemblance between Mi and Ni in his passage singling them out as the only two perfectly unconventional and truly natural painters. In fact, throughout Ming and Ch'ing writing on painting, Mi and Ni are mentioned together with a persistence that leaves no doubt they were seen as the two masters who, after T'ang, had been able to paint as if art had no history.

The pairing of the names of Mi and Ni must, however, give one pause. Whatever their personal likenesses, the painting styles of the two men were radically different from one another—in fact, to the Chinese critic, they represented two poles on a recognized continuum of technique, that of "brush" and "ink." Mi Fu's painting has not survived, but the historical image of his style (which is what counts for an understanding of the critics' views) is well established through an abundance of copies and derivative works. Representative of the historically accepted image is a painting attributed to his son, Mi Yu-jen, who was said to have adopted his father's style (fig. 1). Conical mountains rise and fall like waves, separated and partly obscured by dense bands of mist. A humid, hazy effect is achieved through Mi's distinctive method of building up the forms with masses of wet, overlapping dots, denser where the mists are thinner, paler and even more thinly layered where they are thicker. This technique is used with great consistency throughout the painting, so that there is hardly a line anywhere—hardly a place where the brush has been pulled any distance across the surface. In Chinese critical terminology, this painting exemplifies the use of "ink" and the styles of the two Mi are often spoken of as "moist."

In marked contrast is the style of the painter Tung Ch'i-ch'ang called "the only

[b] 向客張貞居澗阿，言米南宮有潔癖。善畫，但作小幅。近代惟倪雲林頗近之。米以顛名，余故以迂名倪。觀今遺墨故

筆及之。

[c] 偶因滌硯寫從容，點染那能似畫工……令人猛憶米南宮。

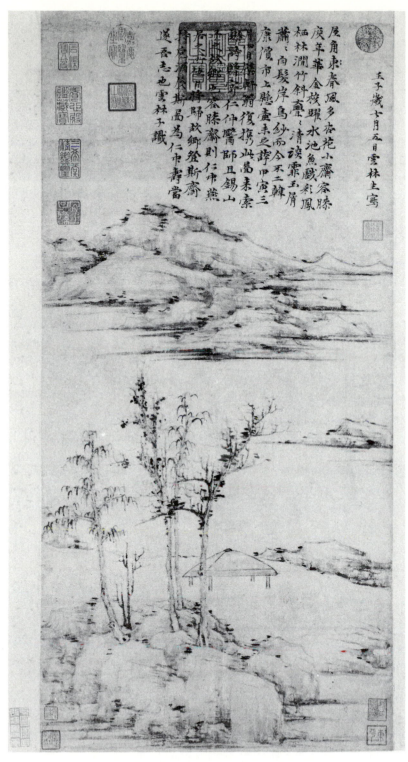

2. Ni Tsan (1301–1374), "Jung-hsi Studio," dated 1372 and
1374. Hanging scroll, ink on paper, 74.7 × 35.5 cm. National
Palace Museum, Taipei, Taiwan, R.O.C.

man after Mad Mi''—Ni Tsan. ''The Jung-hsi Studio'' (1372), a masterpiece of his late years, is a skeletal construction of thin, bony lines etched with a dry, scratchy brush (fig. 2). There are no effects of atmosphere whatever and variety in ink tonalities is kept to a narrow range. The sense of line—the trace of the drawn brush, the fiber, the contour—dominates; even where dots, suggestive of foliage, are set down, the brush is pulled briefly so the very dots verge on becoming lines. In contrast to the ''ink'' of the two Mis, Ni's painting is a supreme example of the use of ''brush,'' and he was said to have been ''sparing of ink as if it were gold.'' Tung Ch'i-ch'ang recognized the radical dissimilarity between the two styles, but still insisted on their basic kinship. In the following comment, he appended the name of Kao K'o-kung to those of the two Mis, since Kao was one of their outstanding followers. He refers here to ''scholar's painting,'' *shih-fu hua*, with which *i-p'in* had come to be partly identified:

> The Yüan men took Mi Yüan-chang [Mi Fu] the father and his son and President Kao Fang-shan [Kao K'o-kung] to be [the main exponents of] scholar's painting. But Ni Yüan-chen [Ni Tsan] also deserves to be ranked in the same group with Mad Mi. Although their achievements are different, their distant feeling is the same.[d16]

However dissimilar the formal means of the two painters in conception and execution, they were alike in their radical manipulations of both natural imagery and brush technique. Mi departed from tradition in his abandonment of the range of established *ts'un* (texture-strokes) whose creation, diversification, and refinement had been one of the great cumulative achievements of the landscape painting of the two centuries preceding his own time. The highly charged dots of the Mi style represent bold transmutations of the image and an unabashed exploration of the potentials of ink. Ni Tsan also, although he painted at a time when many artists were experimenting with calligraphic manipulations and abstractions, probably carried these attempts further than any, playing with linear design and kinetic motion in a way that testified to a greater nonchalance toward nature. Like Mi's, his brushwork seemed exceptionally untypecast—to use Tung Ch'i-ch'ang's term, unmolded.

However, to some other critics, Mi and Ni had undermined the strength of traditional and proven values, substituting flimsy personal mannerisms—a criticism similar to that Teng Ch'un had leveled against the degenerate *i* masters of late T'ang and early Sung. Hsieh Chao-che (1567–1624) may represent those who saw the two painters not as admirably spontaneous but as coarse and unbalanced. A traveler and administrator, Hsieh was not primarily a critic of art, but painting along with much else fell within his wide-ranging interests, and in the following passage he gives a

[d] 元人以米元章父子與高房山侍郎爲士夫畫。然倪元鎮又當爲米顚配享。雖功力　　不同遠韻則一。

reasoned presentation of views that may be found suggested more fleetingly here and there throughout the critical literature. Recapitulating the history of landscape painting, he describes an evolution whose point of departure in early T'ang was a rather stiff minuteness. Experiments with very wet and very dry brushwork, he seems to imply, led to a freer and more relaxed style which, however, was still based on control, observation, and disciplined taste. This was the pinnacle, reached in the tenth and eleventh centuries, after which a decline set in. The agents of this decline were Mi Fu and Ni Tsan.

> Although there was landscape [painting] in the early T'ang, it still tended toward the fine and workmanlike. For instance, the brushwork of Li Ssu-hsün and Wang Mo-chieh [Wang Wei] was fine down to the minutest detail. When it came to Wang Hsia [Wang Mo], there was the beginning of "splashed ink" (*p'o-mo*), and Hsiang Jung first used dryness and sharp definition. Coming down to Ching Hao and Kuan T'ung, a transformation to simple and natural high-distance scenes was perfected.... When it came to Sung, the generation of Tung Yüan, Li Ch'eng, Kuo Hsi, and Fan K'uan emerged, fresh and relaxed in a way that had no precedents. Still, in structure their work was fine and closely wrought; in composition, it had proportion and balance; in their handling of intense and dilute, far and near, there was nothing that was not fitting. It was definitely not something that could be managed by the loose or impetuous.

> Then Mi Yüan-chang [Mi Fu] studied Wang Hsia but did not attain his spirit; Ni Yüan-chen [Ni Tsan] used a dry brush but was lacking in vividness. Since then the sort who cover up their clumsiness and cultivate an abrupt style have all been emulating one another, and so people speak of "painting ideas" and no longer strive for precision and workmanship. Thus did painting rise and fall.[e17]

Tung Yüan and the others represented to Hsieh an ideal blend of relaxation and control. After them, Mi Fu used *p'o-mo* and Ni Tsan a dry technique; but (unlike Wang Mo and Hsiang Jung, the T'ang experimenters with wet and dry) their work seemed to lack proportion and a certain harmony or inner core. This set painting on the path to the present lack of discipline and vision.

There were really two things about Mi and Ni that bothered Hsieh. For one, he

---

e 唐初雖有山水，然尚精工。如李思訓王摩詰之筆，皆細入毫芒。至王洽始爲潑墨，項容始尚枯硬。逮夫荊浩關仝，一變爲平淡高遠之致。……全宋董源李成郭熙范寬輩出，天眞橫逸，上無古人矣。然其結構精密，位置適均，濃淡遠近，無不合宜。固非草率造次所可辦也。自朱元章學王洽而不得其神，倪元鎭用枯筆而都無色澤。於是藏拙取捷之輩，轉相摹倣。自謂畫意不復求精工矣。此亦繪事升降之會也。

disliked the extremism of their styles, which he thought limited and one-sided. Mi was wet and splashy, without a controlling conception; Ni was dry and thin, without richness and vitality. He felt each of them had mastered a technique but lacked depth, resonance, and a guiding, unifying idea. In the second place, he did not admire their spontaneity. Earlier artists, he pointed out—men of the Five Dynasties and Sung—had had "free" qualities still wedded to judgment and standards of excellence.[18] The spontaneity of Mi and Ni was dangerously offhanded, "loose and impetuous," and opened the way to careless and undisciplined imitation.

II

Both Mi Fu and Ni Tsan were in fact very widely imitated. The distinctive simplicity and minimalism of their styles was an irresistible temptation, perhaps especially to the inexperienced. Neither involved the impressive (if often misprized) accomplishments of arresting or charming effects, meticulous or illusionistic description, or the command of a wide range of model styles. The severe technical limitations each master was thought to have worked under, pushing a chosen approach to its limit and arriving at an exaggerated and instantly recognizable effect, made his style appear quite finite and compact as a subject of study. Besides, their superior "relaxation"—the total and pristine independence from tradition considered necessary to the creation of such fresh and personal styles—enjoyed a great prestige and invited emulation. Of all the major masters' styles, theirs were among the most often copied, eventually becoming the most codified and formularized.

The flood of imitations no doubt provoked, and continued in spite, or even as a result, of the development of a focal theme in the later literature on untrammeled painting: the argument that it could not be imitated. This point had been made earlier by Huang Hsiu-fu ("it cannot be imitated, for its source is the expression of ideas"), but now became the subject of much more intense interest. It was, of course, understood that every great artist's work had certain personal qualities that could never be reproduced; but with Mi and Ni, the painting style had been so radically reduced that it seemed to consist of nothing that was not personal; there was nothing left over in the public domain.

The argument that Mi's and Ni's styles were inimitable was launched from two angles. One confronted the question of the seeming simplicity and bluntness of their means. Close and sympathetic inspection, according to this argument, would take the viewer past this obvious signature effect to subtle undertones, which added complementary dimensions to the painting's surface uniformity, leaving it complex and paradoxically many-sided in its expressive effect.

The other approach was more theoretical in nature. It had to do with the principle that, since the real content of each man's style was "freedom," by definition it could not be imitated. One cannot follow independence; one cannot learn to be unpracticed; one cannot acquire naïveté. Imitation necessarily involved acts of study and discipline that were directly at odds with the process of making a "free" painting.

Li Jih-hua (1565–1635), for one, a thoughtful commentator contemporary with Tung Ch'i-ch'ang, addressed himself to explaining the complexity and paradoxical completeness of these seemingly one-sided styles. "Nan-kung's [Mi Fu's] [painting] has a rainy, misty look, but the bone [structure] is naturally spare and elegant; Yün-lin [Ni Tsan] is solitary and mild, but his energy (*ch'i*) is naturally great and vast."[19] He was in total disagreement with Hsieh Chao-che, who saw Ni as lacking in "vividness;" to Li, Ni's reticent painting conveyed a sense of depth and vitality. His point about Mi, likewise, was to stress that there was more to him than met the eye. Though his painting looks wet and mistily ill-defined, it actually has a sense of the "brush" and a strong and wiry underlying structure.

This notion appears persistently not only in passages in which the names of Mi and Ni are linked, but also in those devoted to each of the two masters individually. The hidden "bone" in Mi's superficially indistinct brushwork was a frequent theme in the writing he inspired throughout the Ch'ing dynasty. Ch'ien Tu (1763–1844) insisted that "in the Mi family's misty trees and mountain ranges there still are fine strokes; each layer is clearly distinguished"[20] and Shen Tsung-ch'ien, in his treatise prefaced 1781, wrote that "mists and clouds fill the scroll, but really it is the excellence of the brush dots that serves to support the inky vapors," a point that modern men miss;[21] Sheng Ta-shih (1771–?) scoffed at "wet and washy" imitators of Mi who use "plenty of ink and no brush," and don't realize that in his method "pure sharpness pierces through; in every stroke the bone can be seen."[22] The point throughout is the same. Mi's apparent technical simplicity was really based on a firm, masterly structure and his seeming offhandedness on strong underlying ideas. Because his imitators did not see or were unable to recreate this fundamental strength and clarity, they fell into meaningless mannerisms. Tung Ch'i-ch'ang was well aware of this danger. He himself, he said, rarely practiced the Mi style "for fear of slipping into facility."[23] Elsewhere he wrote,

> In recent times, common artists make some brush dots and this is immediately acclaimed as Mi-style mountains. How ridiculous! Yüan-chang [Mi Fu] looked with disdain upon the ages past and did not yield place to Yu-ch'eng [Wang Wei]; could he have casually and indulgently opened a comfortable shortcut for later men?[f][24]

A closely parallel critical theme revolved around the barren effect of Ni Tsan's

f 近來俗子點筆，便是稱米家山，深可笑　　湊泊開後人護短逕路耶？
也。元章睥睨千古，不讓右丞，可容易

style. The extreme dryness of his brush technique, the frail and almost leafless state of his trees, the absence of figures—an absence which a lonely, deserted pavilion made all the more noticeable—all contributed to an air of desolation, which in the forgeries and copies soon circulating in considerable numbers sometimes became thoroughly disagreeable. Ni's reputation for supreme high-mindedness certainly encouraged viewers to think positively about even the most vapid paintings in his style, but they were not to everybody's taste, and a few independent-minded writers voiced their doubts. Hsieh Chao-che criticized Ni as lackluster, wanting in "vividness." Echoes of this view can occasionally be found in catalogues of painting and calligraphy, such as Chang Ch'ou's (1577–1643) *Ch'ing-ho shu-hua fang* of the early seventeenth century, and Ku Fu's *P'ing-sheng chuang-kuan* (prefaced 1692) of the late. Chang placed Ni in a group of Yüan painters he considered inferior to Chao Meng-fu (1254–1322), Huang Kung-wang, and Wang Meng. "I have carefully examined them [Ni and his like] and savored them intimately," he wrote; "they have a one-sided sort of excellence, not a fully rounded ability." [25] Ku Fu felt Ni had "gone too far in sparing the ink." [26] Describing Ni's deserted scenes, he said:

> [These paintings] have no lasting flavor. How could they achieve the natural quality of an empty courtyard where several trees have been planted and old fist-shaped stones have been amassed, where clustered bamboo flourish in abundance, with the winds passing, the rain approaching, the mists parting, and the moon traversing?[g][27]

The rebuttal to this view was that Ni's empty scenes paradoxically conveyed the fruitful amplitude and "natural quality" of the well-stocked, atmosphere-filled garden Ku Fu described as their antithesis. Chang Ch'ou himself, in a more pro-Ni frame of mind, wrote that even though Ni husbanded ink as if it were gold, his effect was still "glossy and rich";[28] and Yün Shou-p'ing (1633–1690), a painter and thoughtful commentator whose appreciation of Ni Tsan was especially keen, said that though Ni might paint only "one tree and one rock, there was the flavor of a thousand peaks and ten thousand valleys." [29] Comments of this sort are almost invariably accompanied by the observation, parallel to that on Mi's followers, that later imitators had completely failed to grasp these qualities; Mi's were too "wet and washy," and Ni's, as the great early Ch'ing painter and art theorist Tao-chi (1641– ca. 1720) said, "have imitated only the dry and desolate or the thinnest parts and consequently their copies have no far-reaching spirit." Tao-chi wrote this comment on a Ni-style painting of his own in which the typical Ni Tsan composition and motifs seen in "The Jung-hsi Studio" are executed with a very wet brush, as if seeking to bring Ni's rich inner content to the surface.[30]

g 一覽無餘味矣，何如空庭種樹幾株，堆　　　　月轉之為，得自然也。
　朴古拳石，而多栽叢竹，風過雨來烟開

It was not, however, only the run-of-the-mill imitator who was thought unable to grasp what underlay Ni's "thinness." A famous anecdote has it that the great Ming painter Shen Chou (1427–1509) was able to master the styles of all the great Yüan masters but Ni, who eluded him, by his own admission, through the paradoxical completeness of his seemingly simple means.[31] With an almost ritualistic regularity later painters personally tested, and concurred with, the notion of Ni's inimitability. Shen's equally renowned student Wen Cheng-ming (1470–1559) wryly compared one of his own attempts to "studying at Han-tan,"[32] where hopeful scholars were said to lose their old accomplishments while failing to master new ones. Wen's friend and follower Lu Chih (1496–1576), whose dry and angular brushwork was strongly influenced by Ni Tsan, wrote a long inscription to a painting of 1567, now in the Cleveland Museum, recounting his efforts to imitate Ni from youth to the present painting and his feelings of alternating success and failure; he was not displeased by Wen Cheng-ming's opinion that he had "barely succeeded in achieving some resemblance."[33] As a matter of fact, the surviving oeuvres of each of these artists include outstanding paintings in the Ni style; but in their own opinion, with which critics generally agreed, they had quite missed the essential qualities of his art. By the seventeenth century, the notion that imitation of Ni's style was singularly difficult was firmly established.

There were a few critics who claimed that "it was through effort and study that [Ni] attained his appearance of utter naturalness."[34] This interpretation of Ni's style, however, represents more or less the established notion of how any traditional master achieved his seemingly natural control and command. The majority of critics did not subscribe to the view that Ni was a diligent worker who had produced his distinctive style through "effort and study." His special ease and spontaneity was not inimitable because it was founded on effort; that would not make it inimitable, merely hard to imitate. It was inimitable because it was *not* founded on effort; it came naturally.

Convictions about this quality in Ni's style and appreciation for it found especially clear expression in the writings of two early Ch'ing painter-critics, Yün Shou-p'ing and Wang Yüan-ch'i (1642–1715). The inimitable spontaneity of Ni's style made a strong impression on Yün. He repeated the story about Shen Chou's lack of success and quoted Tung Ch'i-ch'ang's comment that, compared to Ni, even Huang Kung-wang had a practiced and conventional air.[35] Elsewhere, Yün mentions his own inadequacy and that of his relative Yün Hsiang (1568–1655), a painter who was said to have been preoccupied with Ni Tsan in his old age. They had "deliberated over" and "practiced" Ni's brushwork for years, Yün said, "without attaining its spontaneous and relaxed quality."[36] He here suggests the basic dilemma of those who emulate Ni: study will not lead to, in fact will prevent, spontaneity. As he said in another context, "Naiveté is the one thing that cannot be achieved by deliberate intention; this is *i-p'in*. . . . It is just this that Ni Yü called 'sketching the relaxed feelings in my breast.'"[37]

Wang Yüan-ch'i also dwelt on the question of Ni's spontaneity, which was to be achieved effortlessly or not at all. "In studying painting," he wrote, "when it comes to [the style of] Yün-lin, one must not use one drop of effort; it is in between having an intention and not having one."[38] Wang marveled at Ni's absence of will or conscious imposition of control, and effortlessness antithetical to the acts of study and imitation. In another comment elaborating on Tung Ch'i-ch'ang's passage about "the only one after Mad Mi" translated above, Wang wrote:

> The various masters of Sung and Yüan each came out of a set pattern. Only the Lofty Scholar [Ni Tsan] washed away in one stroke the accumulations of tradition, and emptied out everything. He was the first in the "untrammeled" class. This was not a created method. By not using effort, he did that which those who are good at using effort cannot achieve.[h][39]

Wang concludes this passage with some remarks on Ni's inimitability and his own failed attempts.

III

In view of the strength and all but universal acceptance of the notion that the untrammeled masters' styles were the most inimitable of all, it is striking to note the critical evaluation of the best known of their imitators. In principle, *i* presumed the artist's complete unpredictability and uniqueness, his disengagement from the genealogies of art history. Nonetheless, the notion of *i* became intimately allied to the formal techniques of Ni Tsan and Mi Fu. With rare exceptions, the names other than Mi or Ni commonly encountered in groupings surrounding the concept of *i* in later times are those of their imitators, associates, or the few whose painting struck critics as similar to their personal formal styles. Their followers, theoretically in an untenable position, were actually at quite an advantage. While critics constantly stressed the inimitability of the untrammeled masters, the reproduction of the styles of Mi or Ni seemed at the same time to trigger the notion of *i* in the viewer's mind as readily as other stylistic conventions triggered "Tung Yüan school" or "blue-green style."

Among the contemporaries of Mi Fu and his son were two painters who may have been influenced by them. These were Chao Ling-jang (fl. ca. 1080–1100) and Ma Ho-chih (fl. ca. 1140–1190). Both Chao and Ma—perhaps especially Chao—shared Mi Fu's preference for low, intimate, haze-filled scenery; both used a pointillistic brush technique for foliage. Broad, wet strokes of "broken ink" appear

h 宋元諸家，各出機杼。惟高士一洗陳迹，空諸所有，爲逸品中第一，非觕爲是法也。於不用工力之中，爲善用工力者所莫能及。

in some of their works; one of Ma's extant paintings has mountains outlined in ragged strokes recalling T'ang *i-p'in* techniques, while in an album leaf of a marshy shore with lake birds, Chao used loose wet strokes of the same derivation to suggest spits of land and rocks protruding from shallow water.[40] The scale of the dotting in Chao's foliage, though, is finer than Mi's, and the "broken" strokes at the water's edge are thoroughly incorporated into a scene whose overall effect is neat, delicate, and finished, with none of Mi's sense of expansiveness.

Chao's technical resemblances to Mi, however, triggered a powerful association, and he—and Ma—are frequently ranked together with Mi in the rarified, unaccountable *i-p'in*. Tung Ch'i-ch'ang's friend Ch'en Chi-ju (1558–1639), for instance, in listing the painters throughout history who stood apart from both the academic and the scholarly traditions, names (for the period after the tenth century) "the senior and junior Mis, Ma Ho-chih, Kao K'o-kung, and Ni Tsan; these are like men of another realm, who do not consume 'smoke and fire,' altogether of a different makeup."[41] Tung Ch'i-ch'ang included Chao Ling-jang in a similar grouping, describing Ni's style as "an untrammeled style, generally of the same school as Mi Hsiang-yang [Mi Fu] and Chao Ta-nien [Chao Ling-jang]."[42] Tung also wrote that, among Sung men, Chao and Ma were of the *i* class and should be considered the "source" of Ni Tsan.[43] Elsewhere, he spoke of Chao's as "true Sung scholar's painting; this school was later transmitted to Ni Yün-lin."[44] It seems that Chao and Ma, though actually painters quite different from Mi, were drawn into his orbit through certain occasional formal resemblances and came to be credited with "untrammeled" qualities which might not have been seen in their styles otherwise.

This effect is more prounced when it comes to Mi's Yüan followers, Kao K'o-kung and Fang Ts'ung-i (ca. 1301–1393). These two were certainly not judged to be among the "common artists" Tung Ch'i-ch'ang held up to scorn who "make some brush dots" and consider themselves masters of the Mi style; those were rather the mostly nameless authors of shapeless inky scenes many of which still circulate under the names of Mi Fu or Mi Yu-jen themselves—or of Kao or Fang. Kao K'o-kung's high ranking among painters dates back to his own day, and was reinforced by the praise which Chao Meng-fu and Ni Tsan had paid him. Chao had called Kao his own better, and Ni had said Huang Kung-wang (whom most regarded as supreme) could not dream of matching Kao.[45]

Though Chao's and Ni's judgments might be questioned (and indeed have been),[46] Kao and Fang were certainly painters of stature. Their debts to Mi lay generally in the depiction of rather symmetrical rounded or conical mountains with mist and the technique of massing of dots in place of reliance on line. Each had a quite distinctive artistic personality, different from Mi and from one another: Kao somewhat eclectic and essentially conservative, achieving in his landscapes a quiet, handsome, and solid effect, well-proportioned and well-integrated; Fang animating his scenes with a dynamic inner life, mountains and brushstrokes seeming to quiver and glow. It was recognized that, using ideas borrowed from Mi Fu, Kao and Fang had accomplished something personal. Their achievements fell, in other words, within the traditional pattern of study and innovation of important masters throughout painting history.

The vitality and magnetism of Mi Fu's image was such, however, that the individuality of Kao and Fang tended to become blurred in the eyes of later men. Those examples or aspects of their painting that were closest to Mi were the best remembered, and Ming and Ch'ing paintings done in imitation of them or "in their spirit" are often indistinguishable from imitations of Mi. Critics linked them very closely to Mi as sharing the main formal features of his style.

When it came to the theoretical inimitability of Mi's untrammeled qualities, of course, the notion logically applied to the attempts of Kao and Fang (and, for that matter, of Mi's son Yu-jen) as well as to those of more pedestrian copyists. The instantly recognizable borrowings from Mi are incontrovertible evidence of the study and sophistication supposedly antithetical to pure spontaneity. It was largely the absence of such obviously derivative elements in his own painting that led to Mi's ranking in the *i-p'in*.

The general drift of critical opinion, however, was to see Kao and Fang as untrammeled themselves, sharing in Mi's sublime disengagement and also in his inimitability. It may be recalled that Tung Ch'i-ch'ang, who defined Mi's painting as not coming out of a "mold," spoke of Kao—a distinctly "molded" painter, whatever his virtues—together with Mi in a passage on the scholarly *yün* quoted above, and Ch'en Chi-ju placed him with Mi, Ni, and Ma Ho-chih in a realm beyond traditions.

This view was established at least by the time of Wang Shih-chen (1526–1590), the prominent scholar of the generation preceding Tung's, who named Mi's Yüan followers as members of the untrammeled group. Wang was a classicist by taste, and he resisted the vogue for Yüan painting, with its informality and relaxed sketchiness. About the untrammeled painters, supposedly the most relaxed and informal of all, he naturally felt especially strong reservations. He set Ni, Kao, and Fang apart from the artists he recognized as the best of Yüan; he wrote of the two Mis, Kao, and Ni as simple and sketchy painters, concluding that, though they belonged in the un-trammeled class, "they were not true masters."[47] Chang Ch'ou, too, criticized Kao along with Ni Tsan in a group of painters with a "one-sided sort of excellence," while in another context and a different mood, Chang wrote that of all the landscape painters in history "only the works of the two Mis, Kao, and Ni are simple, mild, and surpassingly relaxed (*i*) in a way that cannot be imitated. Truly rare and unique!"[48] Shen Tsung-ch'ien wrote of Fang in the same terms as Chang had of Kao:

> As for Mi Yüan-chang [Mi Fu], Ni Yün-lin [Ni Tsan], and Fang Fang-hu [Fang Ts'ung-i], those of their works that have come down to us are all

nothing more than the most unassuming scenes; but their flavor of purity and peaceful relaxation (*i*), the workings of their ever-changing misty suggestiveness—this is what later men have striven desperately to imitate, but few have matched them.[i49]

Kao and Fang were credited, in other words, with Mi-like unlearned and unlearnable, "untrammeled" qualities.

Yün Shou-p'ing's comments may stand for similar ones voiced by many seventeenth- and eighteenth-century critics. Alluding to Chao Meng-fu's and Ni Tsan's praise of Kao K'o-kung, he wrote about Kao's inimitability. "Even Ou-po [Chao Meng-fu] and I-feng [Huang Kung-wang] found it hard to match the spiritual quality of Fang-shan [Kao]. How can later students ford his turbulent banks?"[50] And again,

> Kao Shang-shu's [Kao K'o-kung's] "Night Mountains" really cuts free of the beaten path of brush and ink, and attains the subtle essence of the two Mis. It is not easy to study.... Take old Ch'ih's [Huang Kung-wang's] rare spontaneity; even this was not conceded by Yüan-chen [Ni Tsan] [to match Kao's]. What of the fashionable artists of today![j51]

Yün saw Fang Ts'ung-i in the same light, as totally free from a "practiced air." He describes this unpracticed quality actually as a consequence of Fang's "practice" of Mi Fu's style:

> Fang-hu [Fang Ts'ung-i] used the ink-play of Mi Hai-yüeh [Mi Fu], following his idea ... entirely washing away the practiced air of painting. This is why former men placed the "untrammeled class" higher than the "inspired class."[k52]

The cases of these Mi Fu followers illustrate the process of narrowing the notion of *i* that took place in later times. While a simple definition of the term as a descriptive adjective would broadly note "retirement," informality and freedom, in practice Mi's style came to be seen as the way to express informality and freedom, and *i* was used to refer to the "Mi style" as well as the values the style was thought to embody.

Of painters in the Ni style, many were described as untrammeled in the same way as Kao K'o-kung and Fang Ts'ung-i. Ts'ao Chih-po (1271–1355), for instance, is occasionally found in this company of artists who supposedly transcended everything that could be studied—evidently because of certain similarities his style bore to

i 且如米元章，倪雲林，方方壺諸人，其所傳之跡，皆不過平平之景，而其清和宕逸之趣，縹緲靈變之機，後人縱竭心力以擬之，鮮有合者。

j 高尚書夜山圖，眞絕去筆墨畦徑，得二米之精微，殆不易學。⋯⋯以癡翁之奇逸，猶不爲元鎭所許，況時流哉。

k 方壺用米海嶽墨戲隨意⋯⋯洗盡縱橫習氣，故昔人以逸品置神品之上也。

that of his friend Ni Tsan, whom he was thought to have followed.[53] Ni's other followers, such as the masters of the seventeenth-century Anhui school, are persistently described as *i* by the critics; if they are not actually classified in the exclusive *i-p'in* along with two Mis, Ni, Kao, and Fang, this was mainly because they were men of post-Yüan times and therefore not "ancients." It should by no means suggest that Ni's style was any less firmly identified with *i* than Mi's.

What was known of Ni's unbending nature and uncompromising tastes reinforced the notion of his high-minded purity. So did his statements expressing disregard for the opinions of others and even for the integrity of the object in nature—painting "merely to sketch the exceptional exhilaration in my breast, that's all"—which every later painter and connoisseur knew by heart.[54] Ni was often referred to simply as Kao-shih, "the Lofty Scholar." His style, of course, was the ultimate evidence; for through his extremely unified and well-knit imagery—brush and ink as well as composition and motifs contributing to a compelling frosty, stellar quality—the ideas of purity and loftiness reached a high level of aesthetic realization. It seemed a fitting—to some, perhaps, the only—manner of expression for a pristine temperament with nothing to conceal and no nervous afterthoughts betraying an imperfect degree of "relaxation."[55] His severe, terse, monochromatic style possessed the same magnetic power as Mi Fu's, drawing into the *i* category paintings that markedly shared its formal characteristics; perhaps to an even greater extent, in fact, Ni remade the notion of *i* in his own image.

The currency of this view may be gauged by the efforts many critics made to discredit it, protesting, with Yün Shou-p'ing, that "one should not discuss lofty relaxation (*i*) in terms of the complexity or simplicity of brush and ink."[56] Yün went on to cite Ni Tsan as the extreme of "simplicity," contrasting him to the "complex" painter Wang Meng. The case of Wang Meng, in fact, sheds an illuminating sidelight on the identification of *i* with Ni's style. Wang was, among the major Yüan masters, the one most rarely described as *i* in later criticism. This was no coincidence; the restlessness and density of his brushwork, his eclectic mastery of ancient styles, his massive and crowded compositions with their flourishing and vigorous air were all diametrically opposed to the sparseness, severity, and minimalism of his contemporary Ni Tsan. The rare examples of Wang's work that occasionally earn the adjective *i* seem often to have been uncharacteristically Ni Tsan-like. One, for instance, was described by Wu Ch'i-chen in his catalogue prefaced in 1677 as "simple and *i* . . . altogether without his [Wang's] usual method."[57] Shao Sung-nien, a late Ch'ing cataloguer, called another painting strikingly at variance with Wang's usual "strange peaks, weird rocks, tall pines, and flourishing trees" done in "fine and dense, rich and strong" brushwork. Instead, this work had "a pure faraway [feeling] and sparse quality. This is *i-p'in*."[58] Much as Wang Meng was admired, his typical painting did not share in the cool emptiness which had come to be seen as the natural vehicle for the *i* spirit.

It was Ni in particular whom the critic T'ang Chih-ch'i (1579–1651) singled out in an interesting and ambitious passage in which he undertakes to define *i*. T'ang attempts a wholly theoretical definition, but in the end he gives it up; with his concluding sentence, he seeks to animate his abstractions with the example of the master he considers the outstanding exponent of *i*—Ni Tsan.

> Of the wonders of landscape [painting], the antique, the arresting, the fully realized, the harmonious—these [qualities] are easy to identify. Only the term *i* is extremely difficult to analyze. When it comes to *i*, there may be a pure *i*, an elegant *i*, a refined *i*, a subtle *i*, a profound *i*. Granted that there may be different kinds of *i*, nothing has ever been *i* and murky, *i* and vulgar, *i* and indecisive or base. Think of it in these terms, and you will exhaust the varying manifestations of *i*. Although *i* verges on the bizarre, really it is without any intention of being bizarre. Although it never departs from harmoniousness, still it goes far beyond harmoniousness. As for its brush and ink, they advance correctly and stop promptly; as for its hills and valleys, they have an everyday and ordinary character. The observer experiences, with a shiver, new insights; and, with serene joy, spontaneous appreciation. This indeed is what all artists have admired all along, but have never been able to get a hand at. Truly, it is hard to put into words. As for master Yüan-chen [Ni Tsan], one can only sigh in admiration.[159]

While T'ang Chih-ch'i seems to want to bring out the range and variety of the manifestations of *i*, he is actually describing something rather limited and specific. The adjectives he chooses skirt the notions of exuberance, adventurousness, and the outpouring of feeling to center on refinement, subtlety, appropriateness, and understatement. He denies its bizarrerie, and affirms its unwavering balance (*yün*).

IV

From Wang Mo's uproarious spattering and stamping to the "refined," "subtle" quality of Ni Tsan's "everyday" scenes; plainly the sense of the term *i* in later criticism differed in significant ways from what is known of pre-Sung untrammeled painting. "Loftiness," of course, was a characteristic of both groups of

[1] 山水之妙，蒼古奇峭，圓渾韻動則易知。唯逸之一字，最難分解。蓋逸有清逸，有雅逸，有俊逸，有隱逸，有沉逸。逸縱不同，從未有逸而濁，逸而俗，逸而模稜卑鄙者。以此想之，則逸之變態盡矣。逸雖近於奇，而實非有意為奇。雖不離乎韻，而更有邁於韻。其筆墨之正行忽止，其丘壑之如常少異，令觀者冷然別有意會，悠然自動欣賞。此固從來作者都想慕之，而不可得入手，信難言哉。吾於元鎮先生，不能不嘆服云。

painters; this was the condition that freed them of convention and allowed them to develop styles uncannily free of the hackneyed, the timeworn, the predictable. *I* retained this sense of "retirement" from the exigencies and proprieties of the workaday world.

In the enjoyment of this freedom, the T'ang *i-p'in* painters had been rebellious and aggressively experimental. Wang Mo, in Chu Ching-hsüan's description, seemed to be exploding with wine and ink; Li Ling-sheng and Sun Wei, if less unruly, still were insolent and roughly independent. The later *i-p'in* artists are not described in these terms; they were rather detached, aloof, unconcerned. The understated feeling of their painting has occasionally been described as subdued or restrained, words which imply a lack of "freedom."[60] To most viewers what it projected, however, was rather the calm and equanimity of an artist who feels no need to push himself, who is free of anxieties and pressures. If the T'ang *i* was a release of the inner impulses from outer restraints (aptly translated "untrammeled"), the *i* of later times took the form of the disengagement of the inner sensibilities from outer compulsions (perhaps better rendered "relaxed"). Wang Mo's liberated impulses, therefore, burst forth, while Ni Tsan's seemed rather to straighten, to achieve balance.

Essentially, what had taken place in this shift in the understanding of untrammeled painting was the subsuming of the notion of "freedom" within the broader scope of "scholar's painting." Certain scholarly values had been associated with the T'ang eccentrics, for only men of a certain education and disposition were thought to be capable of the attitudes they expressed; but the idea of scholar's painting really crystallized later, within the mid-Sung movements mentioned above, around the distinguished circle of Mi Fu who, with his contemporaries Wen T'ung (d. 1079), Su Shih (1037–1101), Li Kung-lin (ca. 1049–1106), and others, departed from the representational concerns of mainstream painting of the eleventh century and embraced new ideals of expression. These were the scholars, and their painting was scholar's painting. It encompassed a rather wide range of styles, opening a broad path for posterity; it included, for instance, an erudite kind of archaistic painting, involving a careful, formal manner and the use of bright colors and even gold. The branch with which we are concerned, however, drew instead on certain of the stylistic innovations of the earlier *i-p'in* artists, such as free and sketchy brushwork, which were appropriate to a relaxed, informal approach and in keeping with expressive intentions.

Mi Fu was one who had debts to the old eccentrics. He was an admirer of the eleventh-century *i* painter Sun Chih-wei and was said to have occasionally used implements other than the brush for painting, a method first tried by the T'ang *i-p'in* artists in an effort to rid their work of a professional look.[61] In his use of broad wet dots and renunciation of fine outlines, he was widely recognized (by Hsieh Chao-che, among others) as heir to the *p'o-mo* technique of such artists as Wang Mo. His style, or its later stereotype, expressed something of an aggressive or impulsive spirit lingering from the T'ang, and Shimada has accordingly included Mi in the heritage of T'ang *i-p'in*.[62]

Teng Ch'un, however, writing in the late twelfth century, did not name Mi Fu or any of his circle as members of the *i-p'in*, for Mi's painting had another side as well. Like the other scholar-painters of his day, he espoused a set of ideals having little to do with those of the T'ang independents: the importance of the study of ancient models; the superiority of modest, small-format painting; the appreciation of *p'ing-tan* ("blandness"), an understated, unobtrusive flavor. He drew at least as much on Tung Yüan, the tenth-century landscapist later taken as the patriarch of literati painting, as on the T'ang *i* masters.[63] Mi's painting represents in part a transformation of the old untrammeled styles into forms that harmonized with the nascent scholarly tastes and that could be perpetuated under them.

Mi Fu stood at the turning point of the evolution just described. The later phase of this evolution, however—the one dominated by prestigious scholarly ideals— came to quite eclipse the earlier. By Ming and Ch'ing times the T'ang *i* painters were dim images indeed. As historical figures they were for the most part as obscure as the Sung scholars were illustrious; few if any of their works were to be seen, and they are seldom mentioned at all in later criticism. By *i-p'in*, most critics meant to designate the scholarly *i-p'in* of Mi Fu and Ni Tsan, and Mi Fu is accordingly often seen as the originator or first major exponent of the *i-p'in* style. The following passage on enfranchisement from convention and fashion, by Yün Shou-p'ing, exemplifies this view:

> Not to follow the trodden path is called having a scholarly air; not to go in for the taste of the time is called being of untrammeled quality. The creation of this current began with the two Mis and attained a peak in the Yüan period, spilling over to the beginning of Ming. Consider its brush and ink; they are outstanding for relaxed spontaneity. Savor its flavor; it excels for a lonely plainness. Although it rejects the square and avoids the round [regular drawing, probably with straightedge and compass], still it is extremely lovely and complete.[m][64]

In his last sentence, Yün paraphrases Huang Hsiu-fu's description of the *i* style ("clumsy in the laying out of squares and circles . . . yet the forms are complete") written a century before Mi Fu's time. All the same, Yün traces the *i* movement no further back than Mi.

The various notions that Yün Shou-p'ing brings together here represent the

[m] 不落畦徑，謂之士氣，不入時趣，謂之逸格。其創制風流，昉于二米，盛于元季，泛濫明初。稱其筆墨，則以逸宕為上；咀其風味，則以幽澹為工，雖離方遯圓，而極妍盡態。

main characteristics of *i* as it was understood by later critics. Related to T'ang was the unconventional quality, the "relaxed spontaneity" of the style; but this now found expression in "lonely plainness," in the chaste severity cherished by the scholarly tradition. In this passage, Yün uses the terms *i-ko* and *shih-ch'i* as if they were interchangeable. He also seems to have fallen prey to the very misconception he enjoined critics against in a passage quoted above, that of equating *i* with a spare simplicity. The firm association of this constellation of ideas—freedom from convention, *i*, scholarliness, and bare emptiness—appears elsewhere in his own writing, as in this description of a Yüan painting:

> The common, dusty, conventional ways of painters are here entirely swept away, there is only a desolate chilly scene.... [This] is called the "scholarly air" and the "untrammeled class."[n][65]

The birth of scholar's painting marked the end of the old *i-p'in*, for it brought about a separation between the bold and expansive T'ang brushwork and the notion of loftiness. The associations of high-mindedness and independence were now absorbed by the new scholarly current, along with some of the old techniques of abbreviation. What was left—the rougher, more eruptive aspect of T'ang *i-p'in* brushwork—while still called *i* by Teng Ch'un, soon lost that honorable name. No longer associated with loftiness, it seemed all empty bluster. Its later practitioners, such as the Ch'an painters of Southern Sung and Yüan and the "Wild and Heterodox" masters of Ming, were noticed with aversion or not at all by critics committed to the values of scholarliness and of *i* in its new guise.

1. Shūjirō Shimada, trans. James Cahill, "Concerning the *I-p'in* style of Painting," I–III, *OA* (1961), n.s. 7:66–74; (1962), 8:130–137; and (1964), 10:19–26 (hereafter "Concerning the *I-p'in*"). Other aspects of early *i* painting have been pointed out by Alexander C. Soper; see "Shih-k'o and the *I-p'in*," *AAA* (1975–1976), 29:6–22. For the literati tradition of art theory, to which ideas about the *i-p'in* were related, see Susan Bush, *The Chinese Literati on Painting: Su Shih (1037–1101) to Tung Ch'i-ch'ang (1555–1636)* (Cambridge, Mass., 1971).

This study has greatly benefited from the comments of the participants in the conference; I am particularly indebted to the suggestions of Richard Barnhart and James Cahill.

2. Translated in Shimada, "Concerning the *I-p'in*," I, p. 68. The entire treatise has been translated in Alexander C. Soper "T'ang Ch'ao Ming Hua Lu: Celebrated Painters of the T'ang Dynasty by Chu Ching-hsüan of T'ang," *AA* (1958), 21:204–230; for the untrammeled painters, see pp. 228–229. The third man in Chu Ching-hsüan's *i* class, Chang Chih-ho, is described mainly in terms of character; his style is only lightly touched upon. In other

[n] 畫家塵俗蹊徑盡爲掃除，獨有荒寒一境⋯所謂士氣逸品。

sources, however, there are records of his drunkenness and erratic painting methods; see "Concerning the *I-p'in*," I, pp. 68–69.

3. *I-chou ming-hua lu*, *WSHY* 9:1a. Huang called the *i-p'in* the *i-ko*.

4. Ibid. 9 *mu* (Introduction): 1a.

5. Shimada believes all four were in fact "retired" ("Concerning the *I-p'in*," II, p. 137).

6. Teng Ch'un, *Hua chi*, *WSHY* 8:33b–34a. See the translation in Robert J. Maeda, *Two Sung Texts on Chinese Painting and the Landscape Styles of the 11th and 12th Centuries* (New York and London, 1978), p. 92.

7. For Yüan painting and the artists of that period discussed in this study, see James Cahill, *Hills beyond a River: Chinese Painting of the Yüan Dynasty, 1279–1368* (New York and Tokyo, 1976).

8. See Richard Barnhart's study in this volume: "The 'Wild and Helterodox School' of Ming Painting."

9. Tung Ch'i-ch'ang, *Hua ch'an-shih sui-pi* (1798 ed.) (hereafter *HCS*) 2:18a–b.

10. Mi Fu occupied a crucial spot in the transmission of the literati tradition, which he was thought to have received from the tenth-century masters Tung Yüan and Chü-jan and passed on to the four Yüan masters. For Ni Tsan's artistic indebtedness, see my study of seventeenth-century views on Ni and his models: "Rocks Beside a River: Ni Tsan and the Ching-Kuan Style in the Eyes of Seventeenth-Century Critics," *AAA* (1980), 33:65–88.

Tung Ch'i-ch'ang's somewhat ambivalent views on this subject are expressed in a passage where he straddles the positions of placing Ni within established traditions and in a separate untrammeled group. He wrote:

> Ni Yü [Ni Tsan] at the time of the last dynasty was famous throughout the world for his poetry and painting. He rated himself not lower than Huang Kung-wang and Wang Shu-ming [Wang Meng]. He said: "This painting of mine thoroughly attains the ideas handed down from Ching [Hao] and Kuan [T'ung]; it is not something that Wang Meng could have seen in his dreams." But in determining his ranking, it should be called an untrammeled style. It is generally of the same school as Mi Hsiang-yang [Mi Fu] and Chao Ta-nien [Chao Ling-jang]. It's true that he was really a brother to Huang and Wang. (*HCS* 2:9a–10b.) 倪迂在勝國時以詩畫名世。其自標置不在黃公望王叔明下。有云：我此畫深得荊關遺意；非王蒙輩所能夢見也，然定其品當稱逸格，盖米襄陽趙大年一派耳。於黃王真伯仲不虛也。

Tung also made some observations on the need for technical mastery as a stepping-stone to the freedom of Wang Mo and Mi Fu; see Wen Fong's discussion in "Tung Ch'i-ch'ang and the Orthodox Theory of Painting," *NPMQ* (January, 1968), 2(3):14.

11. Both also took their possessions to live on boats, a connection Chu-tsing Li has noted in *Sung Biographies: Painters*, ed. Herbert Franke (Wiesbaden, 1976), p. 3 Temperamental likenesses such as these may account for the typical absence of figures from both men's landscapes. For Ni Tsan's eccentric personality, see the anecdotes collected by Ku Yüan-ch'ing (1487–1565) in *Yün-lin i-shih*, in *Tse-ku-chai ch'ung-ch'ao*, ed. Ch'en Huang (Shanghai, 1824), 6, p. 46. Portions of these have been translated in A. W. E. Dolby, "Ni Tsan: Unconventional Artist of the Yüan Dynasty," *OA* (1973), 19:429–432.

12. Recorded in many texts, e.g. Chang Ch'ou, *Ch'ing-ho shu-hua fang*, 4 vols. (rpt.

1763 ed., Taipei, 1975) (hereafter *CHSHF*), *lü* : 42a.

13. This painting is now in the National Palace Museum, Taipei; see Chang Kuang-pin, *Yüan ssu ta chia* (Taipei, 1975), pp. 63–64 (Chinese) and 75–76 (English).

14. The painting which bears this inscription, *Yü-hou k'ung-lin*, now in the National Palace Museum, Taipei, has been the subject of an article by Kao Mu-sen, "Shih-tsung *Yü-hou k'ung-lin* kuan-k'uei Ni Tsan chung-nien hua-feng" (The Problem of *Empty Grove After Rain* and the Style of Ni Tsan's Middle Age), *NPMQ* (Autumn, 1978), 13(1):67–68 (Chinese) and 15–37 (English). See also Chang Kuang-pin, *Yüan ssu ta chia*, pp. 53–54 (Chinese) and 61–62 (English).

15. Quoted in Pien Yung-yü (1645–1702), *Shih-ku-t'ang shu-hua hui-k'ao*, 4 vols. (Taipei, 1958), 4:246.

16. Quoted by Chang Ch'ou, *Chen-chi jih-lu* (1918 ed.), 1:36b–37a.

17. Hsieh Chao-che, *Wu tsa tsu*, in *Kuo-hsüeh chen-pen wen-k'u* 13, ed. Chin-hsia-ko chu-jen (pseud.), 20 vols. (Shanghai, 1953), 16:280–281. This and other portions of Hsieh's comments on art have been translated by Lin Yutang in *The Chinese Theory of Art* (London, 1967), pp. 127–136.

18. Hsieh's understanding of Hsiang Jung's art is at odds with most early sources, which suggest that Hsiang was an inky painter like Wang Mo, who is sometimes said to have been his student.

19. Li Jih-hua, *Chu-lan hsü-hua ying*, *ISTP*, 18:144. The passage goes on to mention Huang Kung-wang in similar terms.

20. Ch'ien Tu, *Sung-hu hua-i*, *HLTK*, 2:477.

21. Shen Tsung-ch'ien, *Chieh-chou hsüeh-hua pien* (Peking, 1962), p. 50.

22. Sheng Ta-shih, *Hsi-shan wo-yu lu*, *HLTK*, 1:415.

23. *HCS* 2:23b–24b.

24. Ibid. 2:17b. This comment, incidentally, forms part of a passage on Ni Tsan and on certain subtleties in his style that his imitators had not grasped, illustrating once more the way critics' thoughts tended to flow back and forth between the two masters.

25. *CHSHF*, *lü* : 13b. Compare Wang Shih-chen's comment on Mi Fu, quoted by Wai-kam Ho: "This gentleman admittedly had style, but he was one-sided and semi-skilled" ("Li Ch'eng and the Mainstream of Northern Sung Painting," *Proceedings of the International Symposium on Chinese Painting* [Taipei, 1972], p. 256).

26. Ku Fu, *P'ing-sheng chuang-kuan* (Shanghai, 1962) 9:85.

27. Ibid. 9:93–94. Ku's daring view of the ephemeral appeal of Ni's painting directly opposed the widespread opinion voiced by the mid-seventeenth-century writer Ku Ning-yüan that "other famous paintings, after they have hung on the wall for a few days, suddenly have a tired look; as for old Yü's, one can't bear to take them down even after months and years" (quoted in Wang Chi-ch'ien, "Ni Yün-lin chih hua," *NPMQ* [January, 1967], 1[3]:43).

28. *CHSHF*, *lü* : 48b. A very similar statement was made in Ch'ien Tu, *Sung-hu hua-i*, *HLTK*, 2:477.

29. Yün Shou-p'ing, *Ou-hsiang-kuan hua-pa*, in *Hua-hsüeh hsin-yin*, ed. Ch'in Tsu-yung (Shanghai, 1918) (hereafter *OHK*), 5:7b–8a. An identical statement is attributed to Wang Hui in Wang Chi-ch'ien, "Ni Yün-lin chih hua," *NPMQ* 1(3):43.

30. Translated and reproduced in Sherman E. Lee and Wai-kam Ho, *Chinese Art Under the Mongols: The Yüan Dynasty (1279–1368)* (Cleveland, 1958), p. 53. See also Wang Yüan-ch'i's comments on Ni's misguided imitators who, overdoing his severe brushwork, produce a crotchety and dessicated effect (*Lü-t'ai t'i-hua kao*, *HLTK*, 1:221).

31. For one retelling, see Ho Liang-chün, *Ssu-yu-chai hua-lun*, *MSTS*, 3:3:44. Chu-tsing Li has suggested that this anecdote forms the core of the legend of Ni's inimitability: see *A Thousand Peaks and Myriad Ravines: Chinese Paintings in the Charles A. Drenowatz Collection*, 2 vols. (Zurich, 1974), 1:48–49. Shen Chou also commented on the difficulty of imitating Ni, and the failure of the early Ming painter Wang Fu (1362–1416) to do so, in a passage quoted in Yü Chien-hua, *Chung-kuo hua-lun lei-pien* (Chinese Painting Theory by Categories), 2 vols. (Peking, 1957), 2:707. Incidentally, Tung Ch'i-ch'ang said he had seen a successful Ni-style Shen Chou: see *HCS* 2:38b.

32. *Wen Cheng-ming hui-kao* (Shanghai, 1929), 6:63. Yün Shou-p'ing, too, wrote, "If you study Yün-lin, you can't avoid the ridicule of Han-tan" (*OHK* 6:9b). The allusion is to Chuang-tzu's story about youths from the state of Yen sent to Han-tan in Chao who failed to learn the accomplishments of Chao and moreover forgot the native talents of Yen.

33. The inscription is translated by Wai-kam Ho in Sherman E. Lee, *The Colors of Ink* (New York, 1974), p. 115.

34. Fang Hsün (1736–1799), *Shan-ching-chü hua-lun*, *HLTK*, 2:453. Fang elsewhere wrote that *i-p'in* painting, which was achieved by transcending the three other classes, was beyond the reach of "those who have no skill or application and are ignorant of the six methods" (ibid., 2:449). Wang Shih-chen, in a colophon for a Ni painting, had written that there was a great deal of skill and effort behind its seeming naiveté: see *Yen-chou shan-jen t'i-pa*, *Yen-chou shan-jen ssu-pu kao* (Ming, Shih-ching-t'ang ed.) 137:18a. The same view appears in a comment by Ch'en Hung-shou (1599–1652) to the effect that, just as painstaking masters may achieve a natural quality, those known for sketchiness still need discipline. "For example, old Ni's strokes, though only a handful, all have forethought and orderliness" (quoted by Ch'en Chuan [fl. early eighteenth century] in *Yü-chi shan-fang hua wai-lu*, *MSTS*, 1[8]:134–135).

35. *OHK* 5:15a. Yün is alluding to the passage in Tung's *HCS* 2:20b.

36. *OHK* 5:7a.

37. Ibid. 6:12b. The same point was made by Li Jih-hua, who wrote that, without relaxed feelings in one's own breast, one could never successfully adopt Ni's style which had been born of the master's unconcern with questions of skill and clumsiness and of his "relaxed feelings" (quoted in Yü Chien-hua, *Chung-kuo hua-lun lei-pien*, 1:130).

38. Wang Yüan-ch'i, *Lü-t'ai t'i-hua kao*, *HLTK*, 1:231.

39. Ibid., p. 228. Or, as Sheng Ta-shih—who was well acquainted with Wang Yüan-ch'i's thought—wrote: "What those with ability are not able to do, those without ability are able to do" (*Hsi-shan wo-yu lu*, *HLTK*, 1:399).

40. Chao's and Ma's paintings are reproduced in Richard M. Barnhart et al., *Tō Gen, Kyonen* (*Bunjinga suihen*, 2) (Tokyo, 1977), pl. 74 and 76. The similarities between the styles of Chao Ling-jang and Mi Fu have been commented upon by Max Loehr in "Apropos of Two Paintings by Mi Yu-jen," *AO* (1959), 3:172–173 and by Robert Maeda, who also mentions Ma Ho-chih in "The Chao Ta-nien Tradition," *AO* (1970), 8:251–252.

41. Quoted by Yü Chien-hua, *Chung-kuo shan-shui-hua te nan-pei-tsung lun* (The Theory of the Northern and Southern Schools of Chinese Landscape painting) (Shanghai, 1963), p. 11.

42. *HCS* 2:9b–10a. This passage is translated more fully in n. 10.

43. See Fu Shen's discussion in "A Study of the Authorship of the Hua-shuo," *Proceedings of the International Symposium on Chinese Painting*, p. 96.

44. *HCS* 2:8a. Yün Shou-p'ing compared Chao and Ni in terms of the intimate compositions and farway feelings their painting had in common (*OHK* 6:8b). The sixteenth-century commentator Chan Ching-feng (ca. 1600) linked Chao to Mi in a comment raising doubts about whether or not the "cloudy mountains" style was really as original as people thought. Describing an album leaf by Chao labeled "after a T'ang man," Chan noted, "I see that cloudy mountains did not originate with Mi Yüan-chang [Mi Fu]. Evidently the T'ang men already had this method, and Ta-nien [Chao Ling-jang] and Yüan-chang merely transmitted it" (Chan Ching-fèng, *Tung-t'u hsüan-lan pien* [Peking, 1947] 3:31b). Chan did not accept the notion of the *i* masters' completely unpracticed quality. In the same passage, he also pointed out that since there are no figures in this leaf, "we can see that not to draw figures in landscape was not something that Ni Yüan-chen [Ni Tsan] originated." (He made the same observation in ibid., 1:18a–b.)

45. Ni's statement appears in his colophon to Huang's *Yü-i t'u*; see Cahill, *Hills Beyond a River*, p. 89. (For representative paintings by Kao and Fang, see pl. 19 and 59 of that book.) Comments by Chao Meng-fu attesting to Kao's mastery of the Mi style are recorded in *CHSHF, lü*:1b and in Pien Yung-yü, *Shih-ku-t'ang shu-hua hui-k'ao*, 4:188–189. The latter passage has been translated and discussed by H. C. Chang, "Inscriptions, Stylistic Analysis, and Traditional Judgment in Yüan, Ming, and Ch'ing Painting," *AM* (December, 1959), n.s. 7:215–216. In another comment, Chao called a Kao K'o-kung landscape "the prime viewing experience of a lifetime" (*p'ing-sheng chuang-kuan*), the phrase later taken by Ku Fu as the title of his catalogue: see *CHSHF, lü*:4a–b.

46. One critic who found it unjustifiable was Chang Ch'ou; he believed Ni was trying to incite Huang "to push himself to the limit of his abilities," and could not really have considered Kao the better painter: see ibid., *lü*:10b–11a.

47. Wang Shih-chen, *I-yüan chih-yen fu-lu, Yen-chou shan-jen ssu-pu kao* 155:14a–b and 6b. It may be that the author of the *Chieh-tzu-yüan hua-chuan* was directly taking issue with Wang's deprecating view when he wrote of Kao, Ni, and Fang in a near-paraphrase that "though they belong in the *i* class, they were also outstanding masters" (Wang Kai, ed., *Chieh-tzu-yüan hua-chuan* ["Mustard-seed Garden Painting Manual"], 3 pts.; pt. 1 [prefaced in 1679], facs. rpt., Peking, 1979, 1:20). In the same vein is the late eighteenth-century T'ang-tai's passage stressing that Yüan masters such as Ni, Kao, and Fang, "although they are called *i-p'in*, are actually members of the same family" with Huang, Wang, Wu, and Chao Meng-fu (*Hui-shih fa-wei, HLTK*, 1:238); and Tung Ch'i-ch'ang's insistence that the untrammeled Ni "was really a brother to Huang and Wang": see n. 10, above.

48. *CHSHF, lü*:1a.

49. Shen Tsung-ch'ien, *Chieh-chou hsüeh-hua pien*, p. 62.

50. *OHK* 6:6a.

51. Ibid. 6:9a–b.

52. Ibid. 6:5a. Fang Ts'ung-i was famous as a Taoist, and this links him to the T'ang *i-p'in* painters in ways not shared by Mi, Ni, and the other later *i* artists.

53. Yün Shou-p'ing grouped Ni, Ts'ao, Kao, and Mi (ibid. 5:14b); and T'ang-tai, paraphrasing Wang Shih-chen on the Yüan *i* masters, added Ts'ao's name, and set up a Yüan circle of Kao, Ni, Ts'ao, and Fang (*Hui-shih fa-wei*, *HLTK*, 1:238). For a discussion of Ts'ao's style establishing the unlikelihood that he actually did follow Ni, see Chu-tsing Li, "*Rocks and Trees and the Art of Ts'ao Chih-po*," *AA* (1960), 23:153–208. Li describes a process of loss of individuality similar to what happened with Kao and Fang. The result was that imitations and forgeries of Ts'ao Chih-po make him out to be more like Ni than he actually was.

54. Ni's well-known passage on bamboo painting is translated in Bush, *Chinese Literati*, p. 134. According to an anecdote reported by Shen Hao (fl. 1630–1650): "Once by candle-light [Ni] did some bamboo and trees, and felt quite pleased with himself; the next morning on arising he spread it out and looked at it, and it was not a bit like bamboo! Laughing, Yü said, 'It is no easy matter to reach a point of total non-resemblance!'" (*Hua-chu, HLTK*, 1:140.)

一日燈下作竹樹，傲然自得。曉起展視，全不似竹。迂笑曰：全不似處，不容易到耳。

55. As it was phrased in the *Chieh-tzu yüan hua-chuan*: "Where other masters use their brush in a fretful muddy way, they are still able to conceal one or two faulty strokes; but with Yün-lin [Ni Tsan], in those places where there are no strokes there is still 'painting,' and wrong strokes can never be concealed." (*Chieh-tzu-yüan hua-chuan*, 1:3:28a.)

在他家用筆煩溽猶可藏得一二敗筆，雲林則於無筆處尚有畫在。敗筆總不能藏。

A recent study describes the currency of the "dry linear" style in the seventeenth century: see Fu Shen, "Ming Ch'ing chih chi te k'o-pi kou-lao feng-shang yü Shih-t'ao te tsao-ch'i tso-p'in," *Hsiang-kang Chung-wen ta-hsüeh Chung-kuo wen-hua yen-chiu-so hsüeh-pao* (1976), 8(2):579–603; English summary, "An Aspect of Mid-seventeenth Century Chinese Painting: The 'Dry Linear' Style and the Early Work of Tao-chi," pp. 604–615. Fu discusses the contribution to this tradition of both Ni and Huang Kung-wang. Huang, however, presented an image much more complex than Ni's including qualities of freshness, vigor, amplitude, and uncanny communion with the workings of creation. It was mainly when his name is paired with Ni's that the "dry linear" aspect of his style is stressed.

56. *OHK* 5:2b. See also Shen Hao on density and simplicity as irrelevant to scholarliness and relaxation (*i*) (*Hua chu, HLTK*, 1:140). Chang Shih's complaint that "superficial men take ink monochrome and color to distinguish elegant from vulgar" (*Hua t'an, HLTK*, 1:424–425) and Chang Keng's (1685–1760) that "those who discuss the scholarly air [in painting] nowadays are only taking it for dry brush and sparing ink" (*P'u-shan lun-hua, HLTK*, 1:270–271) have a parallel sense.

57. Wu Ch'i-chen, *Shu-hua chi* (Shanghai, 1963), p. 192.

58. Shao Sung-nien, *Ku-yüan ts'ui lu* (Shanghai, 1904) 2:31a.

59. T'ang Chih-ch'i *Hui-shih wei-yen, HLTK*, 1:111.

60. See, for instance, Richard Barnhart's reference to the "restrained, 'even and pale' disengagement of the *wen-jen* ideal" ("Wild and Heterodox", following ref. 13 in the text) and the passage he quotes on "the bitterness of self-restriction or measured ink" (ibid., at ref. 76).

61. Shimada, "Concerning the *I-p'in*," III, p. 20. Su Shih also was evidently fond of Sun Wei and painted with the frayed ends of sugar canes; see ibid., III, p. 24, and Nicole Vandier-Nicolas, *Art et sagesse en Chine: Mi Fou (1051–1107)* (Paris, 1963), p. 208.

62. "Concerning the I-p'in," III, pp. 19–20, 24.

63. This was a widely recognized fact. See the observations of Tung Ch'i-ch'ang on the subject in *HCS* 2:5a, 24b, and 26a. In one place, Tung linked Mi's cloudy mountain style to both Wang Mo and Tung Yüan (ibid. 2:30b–31a). There may be reason to suppose that Tung Yüan was, in turn, drawing upon some of the more small-scaled or pointillistic aspects of T'ang *i-p'in* brushwork such as that which Li Ling-sheng seems to have practiced.

64. *OHK* 5:4a. In passages quoted above, Tung Ch'i-ch'ang also used *i* and "scholar's painting" interchangeably (see refs. 42–44) although Ch'en Chi-ju kept them separate (see ref. 41).

65. *OHK* 6:5b.

Contributors

RICHARD BARNHART is Professor of the History of Art at Yale University. He is currently studying the Sung emperor Hui-tsung's collection of painting and calligraphy, and writing a history of Northern Sung landscape, an area in which he has published extensively.

SUSAN BUSH, a Resident Associate in Research at the John King Fairbank Center for East Asian Research, Harvard University, has authored *The Chinese Literati on Painting: Su Shih (1037–1101) to Tung Ch'i-ch'ang (1555–1636)* as well as various articles on Six Dynasties and Jürchen Chin art.

KANG-I SUN CHANG is Assistant Professor of Chinese Literature at Yale University. She is the author of *The Evolution of Chinese Tz'u Poetry: From Late T'ang to Northern Sung*, and of a number of English and Chinese articles on Chinese poetry.

JONATHAN CHAVES is Associate Professor of Chinese at the George Washington University. Among his publications in the fields of Chinese poetry, calligraphy, and aesthetics are *Heaven My Blanket, Earth My Pillow*, and *Mei Yao-chen and the Development of Early Sung Poetry*, as well as *Pilgrim of the Clouds*, nominated for the National Book Award in Translation in 1979.

KENNETH DeWOSKIN is Associate Professor of Chinese Language and Literature at the University of Michigan and also Associate Director of the Center for Chinese Studies at Ann Arbor. His interests include Chinese literature, aesthetics, and music, and he has published several textual studies of Six Dynasties narrative and *A Song for One or Two: Music and the Concept of Art in Early China*.

JOHN HAY is Assistant Professor of Chinese Art at Harvard University. His special field is Chinese painting, focusing on Sung and Yüan landscape in particular, and he has written several works on Chinese art and archaeology, including *Ancient China*.

LOTHAR LEDDEROSE, Professor of the History of East Asian Art at Heidelberg University, has done research in the areas of Chinese calligraphy, painting, and art theory. His writings include *Mi Fu and the Classical Tradition of Chinese Calligraphy*. At present he is studying the representation of hells and paradises in Chinese and Japanese art.

SHUEN-FU LIN is Associate Professor of Chinese Literature at the University of Michigan. His writings on T'ang and Sung poetry and literature include *The Transformation of the Chinese Lyrical Tradition: Chiang K'uei and Southern Sung Tz'u Poetry*.

RICHARD JOHN LYNN was the head of the Department of Chinese at Macquarie University, Sydney, Australia. He is the author of *Kuan Yün-Shih, Chinese Literature: A Draft Bibliography in Western European Languages*, and numerous articles on Chinese poetry, literary criticism, and intellectual history. He is currently working on a complete translation of the *Ts'ang-lang shih-hua* by Yen Yü.

KIYOHIKO MUNAKATA is Associate Professor of Art and Design at the University of Illinois at Urbana-Champaign. He has written several studies on early Chinese art theory and landscape painting, among them *Ching Hao's Pi-fa-chi: A Note on the Art of the Brush*.

CHRISTIAN MURCK is in international banking at Manufacturers Hanover Trust Company. Editor of *Artists and Traditions: The Uses of the Past in Chinese Culture*, his major scholarly interests are in the cultural history of the Sung and Ming dynasties.

SUSAN E. NELSON is Assistant Professor in Fine Arts at Indiana University in Bloomington. She is the author of a number of studies on Ming and Ch'ing art criticism, including a dissertation of 1978 for Harvard University on "Ni Tsan and the Image of Yüan Painting in the Seventeenth Century."

MAUREEN ROBERTSON is Associate Professor of Far Eastern Language and Literature and Comparative Literature at the University of Iowa. Her writing and research have been primarily in the field of T'ang poetry and poetics.

TU WEI-MING is Professor of Chinese History and Philosophy at Harvard University. Among his publications on cultural history and philosophy are *Neo-Confucian Thought in Action—Wang Yang-ming's Youth* and *Humanity and Self-Cultivation: Essays in Confucian Thought*.

JOHN TIMOTHY WIXTED is Assistant Professor of Asian Languages at Arizona State University, where he teaches Chinese and Japanese language and literature. He has published *The Song-Poetry of Wei Chuang (836–910)*, and *Poems on Poetry: Literary Criticism by Yuan Hao-wen (1190–1257)*.

PAULINE YU is Associate Professor in the Humanities Program at the University of Minnesota. She is the author of *The Poetry of Wang Wei: New Translations and Commentary* and a number of articles on Chinese and comparative poetry and poetics.

Glossary for Chinese and Japanese Texts in the Notes

An Ch'i 安岐, *Mo-yüan hui-kuan*
墨園彙觀

Aoki Masaru 青木正児, *Shina bungaku
shisō shi* 支那文学思想史

Ch'ai Fei-fan 柴非凡, "*Chung Hung
Shih-p'in yü Shen Yüeh*" 鍾嶸詩品與
沈約, *Chung-wai wen-hsüeh* 中外文學

Chan Ching-feng 詹景鳳, *Tung-t'u hsüan-
lan-pien* 東圖玄覽編

Chang Chih (Yin) 張隲(隱), *Wen-shih
chuan* 文士傳

Chang Ch'ou 張丑, *Chen-chi jih-lu*
眞蹟日錄; *Ch'ing-ho shu-hua-fang*
清河書畫舫

Chang Heng 張衡, "*Hsi-ching fu*"
西京賦; "*Tung-ching fu*" 東京賦

Chang Huai-kuan 張懷瓘, "(*P'ing shu*)
Yao-shih-lun" (評書) 藥石論; "*Shih-t'i
shu-tuan*" 十體書斷; "*Shu i*" 書議

Chang Keng 張庚, *P'u-shan lun-hua*
浦山論畫

Chang Kuang-pin 張光賓, *Yüan ssu ta chia*
元四大家

Chang Shih 張式, *Hua-t'an* 畫譚

Chang Tzu 張鎡, *Shih-hsüeh kuei-fan*
仕學規範

Chang Yen-yüan 張彥遠, *Fa-shu yao-lu*
法書要錄; *Li-tai ming-hua chi* 歷代明
畫記

Chang Yü 張羽, *Ching-chü chi* 靜居集

Chao I 趙一, *Fei ts'ao-shu* 非草書

Ch'en Chuan 陳譔, *Yü-chi shan-fang hua
wai-lu* 玉几山房畫外錄

Ch'en Fang-mei 陳芳妹, "*Tai Chin yen-
chiu*" 戴進研究

Ch'en Huang 陳璜, *Tse-ku-chai ch'ung-
ch'ao* 澤古齋重鈔

Ch'en San-li 陳三立, *Lu-shan chih fu-k'an*
廬山志副刊 in *Lu-shan ku-chin yu-chi
ts'ung-ch'ao* 廬山古今遊記叢鈔

Ch'en Shih-tao 陳師道, *Hou-shan shih-hua*
後山詩話

Ch'en Shun-yü 陳舜俞, *Lu-shan chi*
廬山記

Ch'en Ssu 陳思, *Shu-yüan ying hua*
書苑英華

Ch'en Tsung-chou 陳從周, "*Shao-hsing
ta-yü-ling chi Lan-t'ing tiao-ch'a chi*"
紹興大禹陵及蘭亭調查記, *Wen-wu*
文物

Ch'en Yen-chieh 陳延傑, *Shih-p'in chu*
詩品注

Cheng Hsüan 鄭玄, *Mao-shih cheng-i*
毛詩正義

Ch'eng Hao 程顥, Ch'eng I 程頤, *Erh-
Ch'eng ch'üan-shu* 二程全書

Ch'eng Hung 程弘, "*Han-lin lun tso-che
chih-i*" 翰林論作者質疑, *Wen shih*
文史

Chia-ku wen-pien 甲骨文編

Chiang K'uei 姜夔, *Chiang-t'ieh p'ing*
絳帖平; *Hsü Shu-pu* 續書譜

Chiang-ning fu-chih 江寧府志

Chiang Shao-shu 姜紹書, *Wu-sheng-shih
shih* 無聲詩史

Chiang Ying-k'o 江盈科, *Hsüeh-t'ao
hsiao-shu* 雪濤小書

(*Chiao-cheng*) *San-fu huang-t'u* (校正)
三輔黃圖

Ch'ien Ch'ien-i 錢謙益, *Yu-hsüeh chi*
有學集

Ch'ien Tu 錢杜, *Sung-hu hua-i* 松壺畫憶

Chih Yü 摯虞, *Wen-chang liu-pieh chih lun*
文章流別志論 app. to *Liu-pieh chi*
流別集

Chin shu 晉書

Chin-tai pi-shu 津逮秘書, comp. Mao
Chin 毛晉

Ch'in-ch'ü chi-ch'eng 琴曲集成

Ch'in Tsu-yung 秦祖永, *Hua-hsüeh hsin-
yin* 畫學心印

Ching-chi chih 經籍志, in *Sui shu* 隋書

Chiu T'ang shu 舊唐書

Chou i 周易

Chou li 周禮

Chou-li chu-shu 周禮注疏

Chou Mi 周密, *Ch'i-tung yeh-yü*

齊東野語

Chou shu 周書

Chou Tun-i 周敦頤, *T'ung-shu, wen-tz'u* 通書, 文辭

Chu An-k'an 朱安沠, *Chang P'ing-shan hsien-sheng* 張平山先生

Chu Hsi 朱熹, *Chu Tzu ta-ch'üan* 朱子大全; *Chu Tzu yü-lu* 朱子語錄; *Chung yung chang-chü* 中庸章句; *Ssu shu chi-chu* 四書集註

Chu Kuang-ch'ien 朱光潛, *T'an mei* 談美

Chu Pin 朱彬, *Li-chi hsün-tsuan* 禮記訓纂

Chu Tung-jun 朱東潤, *Chung-kuo wen-hsüeh p'i-p'ing shih ta-kang* 中國文學批評史大綱

Chu Tzu-ch'ing 朱自清, *Shih yen chih pien* 詩言志辨

Ch'üan Ch'i wen 全齊文; *Ch'üan Chin wen* 全晉文; *Ch'üan Han wen* 全漢文; *Ch'üan Hou-Han wen* 全後漢文; *Ch'üan Liang wen* 全梁文; *Ch'üan Sung wen* 全宋文; *Ch'üan T'ang wen* 全唐文; see Yen K'o-chün 嚴可均

Ch'üan San-kuo shih 全三國詩; *Ch'üan Sung shih* 全宋詩; *Ch'üan T'ang shih* 全唐詩; see Ting Fu-pao 丁福保

Chuang Su 莊肅, *Hua-chi pu-i* 畫繼補遺

Chuang Tzu 莊子

Chuang-tzu yin-te 莊子引得

Ch'un-ch'iu fan-lu 春秋繁露

Chung Hung 鍾嶸, *Shih-p'in (hsü)* 詩品(序)

Chung yung i 中庸義

Erh-chiao lun 二教論 in *Taishō issai kyō kankō kai* 大正一切経刊行会

Erh ya 爾雅

Fan Ning 范寧, "Wen-pi yü wen-ch'i" 文筆與文氣, *Kuo-wen yüeh-k'an* 國文月刊

Fan Wen-lan 范文瀾, *Wen-hsin tiao-lung chu* 文心雕龍註

Fan Yeh 范曄, "Yü-chung yü chu sheng-chih shu" 獄中與諸甥姪書

Fang Hsün 方薰, *Shan-ching-chü hua-lun* 山靜居畫論

Feng-su t'ung (-i) 風俗通義

Fu-chien t'ung-chih 福建統志

Fu Shen 傅申, "Ming Ch'ing chih chi te k'o-pi kou-lao feng-shang yü Shih-t'ao te tsao-ch'i tso-p'in" 明清之際的渴筆勾勒風尚與石濤的早期作品, *Hsiang-kang chung-wen ta-hsüeh Chung-kuo wen-hua yen-chiu-so hsüeh-pao* 香港中文大學中國文化研究所學報

Fukunaga Mitsuji 福永光司, *Geijutsu ronshū* 芸術論集 (*Chūgoku bunmei sen* 中国文明選)

Gumyōshū kenkyū 弘明集研究

Han Ang 韓昂, *T'u-hui pao-chien hsü-pien* 圖繪寶鑑續編

Han shu 漢書

Han-Wei ts'ung-shu 漢魏叢書

Han Ying 韓嬰, *Han-shih wai-chuan* 韓詩外傳

Hatano Takeshi 畑野武司, "'Sō Hei gasansui jo' no tokushitsu" 宗炳 "画山水序" の特質, *Chūgoku chūsei bungaku kenkyū* 中国中世文学研究

Hayashi Minao 林巳奈夫, "Sengokujidai no gazomon" 戦国時代の画像文, *Kōkogaku zasshi* 考古学雑誌

Hayashida Shinnosuke 林田慎之助, "Hai Shiya Chōchūron kōshō—Rikuchō ni okeru fukko bungakuron no kōzō" 裴子野雕虫論考証—六朝における復古文学論の構造, *Nihon Chūgoku gakkai hō* 日本中国学会報

Ho Liang-chün 何良俊, *Ssu-yu-chai hua-lun* 四友齋畫論

Ho Wen-huan 何文煥, *Li-tai shih-hua* 歷代詩話

Hoshigawa Kiyitaka 星川清孝, *Koshi gen* 古詩源 (*Kanshi taishi* 漢詩大系)

Hou Jen-chih 侯仁之, "Pei-hai kung-yüan

yü Pei-ching ch'eng" 北海公園與
北京城
Hou K'ang 侯康, *Wen-pi k'ao* 文筆考
Hsi-ching tsa-chi 西京雜記
Hsia Ch'eng-t'ao 夏承燾, *Chiang Po-shih
tz'u pien-nien chien-chiao* 姜白石詞編年
箋校, *Po-shih shih tz'u chi* 白石詩詞集
Hsiang Yüan-pien 項元汴, *Chiao-ch'uang
chiu-lu* 蕉窗九錄
Hsiao ching 孝經
Hsiao I 蕭繹, *Li-yen p'ien hsia* 立言篇下 in
Chin-lou Tzu 金樓子
Hsiao T'ung 蕭統, (*Chao-ming*) *Wen-hsüan*
(*hsü*) (昭明) 文選 (序)
Hsieh Chao-che 謝肇淛, *Wu tsa tsu*
五雜組 in *Kuo-hsüeh chen-pen wen-k'u*
國學珍本文庫
Hsieh Chen 謝榛, *Ssu-ming shih-hua*
四溟詩話
Hsin T'ang shu 新唐書
Hsiu-ning-hsien chih 休寧縣志
Hsü Ch'in 徐沁, *Ming-hua lu* 明畫錄
Hsü Fu-kuan 徐復觀, *Chung-kuo i-shu
ching-shen* 中國藝術精神
Hsü Shen 許慎, *Shuo-wen* (*chieh-tzu*)
說文 (解字)
Hsü Wei 徐渭, *Hsü Wen-ch'ang san-chi*
徐文長三集
Hsü Wen-yü 許文雨, *Wen-lun chiang-su*
文論講疏
Hsün Tzu 荀子
Hu Chen-heng 胡震亨, *T'ang-yin kuei-
ch'ien* 唐音癸籤
Hu Ying-lin 胡應麟, *Shih sou* 詩藪
Hua-lun ts'ung-k'an 畫論叢刊, comp. Yü
An-lan 于安瀾
Hua-shih ts'ung-shu 畫史叢書, comp. Yü
An-lan 于安瀾
Huai-nan Tzu 淮南子
Huang Chieh 黃節, *Shih-hsüeh* 詩學
Huang-fu Mi 皇甫謐, *Kao-shih chuan*
高士傳
Huang Hsiu-fu 黃休復, *I-chou ming-hua lu*
益州名畫錄

Huang Hui 黃輝, *Huang T'ai-shih i-ch'un-
t'ang i-kao* 黃太史怡春堂逸稿
Huang Kung-wang 黃公望, *Hsieh shan-
shui chüeh* 寫山水訣
Huang-ti nei-ching su-wen 黃帝內經素問 in
I-t'ung cheng-mo ch'üan-shu 醫統正脈
全書
Huang Tsung-hsi 黃宗羲, *Ming wen-hai*
明文海
Hui-chiao 慧晈, *Kao-seng chuan* 高僧傳
Hui-yüan 惠遠, *K'uang-shan chi* 匡山集;
Lu-shan lüeh-chi 廬山略記; "Sha-men
pu ching wang-che lun" 沙門不敬
王者論; "Yu shan chi" 遊山記

Ikkai Tomoyoshi 一海知義, *Tō Enmei*
陶淵明
Iriya Yoshitaka 入矢義高, *En Kōdō*
袁宏道 (*Chūgoku shijin senshū*
中国詩人選集)
I-shu ts'ung-pien 藝術叢編, comp. by
Yang Chia-lo 楊家駱

Jao Tsung-i 饒宗頤, "Lu Chi *Wen-fu* li-
lun yü yin-yüeh chih kuan-hsi" 陸機
文賦理論與音樂之關係, *Chūgoku
bungaku hō* 中國文學報
Juan Fu 阮福, *Wen-pi k'ao* 文筆考
Juan Yüan 阮元, "Shu Liang Chao-ming
t'ai-tzu *Wen-hsüan hsü* hou" 書梁昭明
太子文選序後, "Wen-yen shuo"
文言說 in *Yen-ching-shih san-chi*
掔經室三集; "Wen-yün shuo" 文韻說
in *Yen-ching-shih hsü-chi* 掔經室續集

Kaizuka Shigeki 貝塚茂樹, Kohara
Hironobu 古原宏伸, *Ōi* 王維 (*Bunjinga
suihen* 文人画粋編)
Kan Pao 干寶, *Sou-shen chi* 搜神記
Kao Ch'i 高啓, *Tu-an chi hsü* 獨庵集序
Kao Lien 高濂, *Yen-chien ch'ing-shang chien*
燕間清賞箋
Kao Mu-sen 高木森, "Shih-ts'ung *Yü-hou
k'ung-lin* kuan-k'uei Ni Tsan chung-

nien hua-feng" 試從「雨後空林」管窺倪瓚中年畫風

Kao Ping 高棅, "Li-tai ming-kung hsü-lun" 歷代名公叙論, "Wu-yen ku-shih hsü-mu" 五言古詩叙目, in *T'ang-shih p'in-hui* 唐詩品彙

Kao Yu-kung 高友工, "Wen-hsüeh yen-chiu ti li-lun chi-ch'u" 文學研究的理論基礎, "Wen-hsüeh yen-chiu ti mei-hsüeh wen-ti" 文學研究的美學問題

Kimata Tokuo 木全德雄, "Eon to Sōhei o megutte" 慧遠と宗炳をめぐって

Kimura Eiichi 木村英一, *Eon kenkyū* 慧遠研究

Kobayashi Taichirō 小林太市郎, *Chūgoku kaigashi ronkō* 中国絵画史論考

Kosugi Kazuo 小杉一雄, "Asuka jidai ni okeru zōzan no genryū ni tsuite" 飛鳥時代に於ける造山の源流に就って, *Hōun* 宝雲

Kōzen Hiroshi 興膳宏, *Bunshin chōryū* 文心彫龍; "*Bunshin chōryū to Shihin* no bungakukan no tairitsu" 文心彫龍と詩品の文學觀の対立; "*Shihin*" 詩品 in *Bungaku ronshū* 文学論集, ed. Arai Ken 荒井健; "Shi Gu *Bunshō ryūbetsu shiron kō*" 摯虞文章流別志論考, *Iriya kyōju Ogawa kyōju taikyū kinen Chūgoku bungaku gogaku ronshū* 入矢教授小川教授退休記念中国文学語学論集

Ku Fu 顧復, *P'ing-sheng chuang-kuan* 平生壯觀

Ku-kung chi-k'an 故宮季刊

Ku Tsu-yü 顧祖禹, *Tu-shih fang-yü chi-yao* 讀史方輿紀要

Ku Yüan-ch'ing 顧元慶, *Yün-lin i-shih* 雲林遺事

Kūkai 空海, *Bunkyō hifuron* 文鏡秘府論, ed. Chou Wei-te 周維德

K'ung Tzu chia-yü 孔子家語

Kuo Chin-hsi 郭晉稀, *Wen-hsin tiao-lung i-chu shih-pa p'ien* 文心雕龍譯注十八篇

Kuo Ch'ing-fan 郭慶藩, *Chuang Tzu chi-shih* 莊子集釋

Kuo Hsi 郭熙, *Lin-ch'üan kao-chih* 林泉高致

Kuo Shao-yü 郭紹虞, *Chung-kuo li-tai wen-lun hsüan* 中國歷代文論選; *Chung-kuo wen-hsüeh p'i-p'ing shih* 中國文學批評史; *Shih-p'in chi-chieh* 詩品集解; *Ts'ang-lang shih-hua chiao-shih* 滄浪詩話校釋

Lao Tzu, Tao-te ching 老子道德經

Li chi 禮記

Li Ching-jung 李景濚, *Wen-hsin tiao-lung hsin-chieh* 文心雕龍新解

Li Han 李漢, *Ch'ang-li hsien-sheng chi-hsü* 昌黎先生集序

Li Jih-hua 李日華, *Chu-lan hsü-hua-yin* 竹嬾續畫賸; *Liu-yen-chai erh-pi* 六硯齋二筆

Li K'ai-hsien 李開先, *Chung-lu hua-p'in* 中麓畫品

Li Meng-yang 李夢陽, "Fou-yin hsü 缶音序 in *K'ung-t'ung hsien-sheng chi* 空同先生集; "Yü Hsü-shih lun wen shu" 與徐氏論文書

Li Po 李白, *Li T'ai-po ch'üan-chi* 李太白全集

Li Tung-yang 李東陽, "Ching-ch'uan hsien-sheng shih-chi hsü" 鏡川先生詩集序, "Ch'un-yü-t'ang kao-hsü" 春雨堂稿序, "P'ao-weng chia-ts'ang chi-hsü" 鮑翁家藏集序 in *Huai-lu-t'ang chi wen-(hou-)kao* 懷麓堂集文(後)稿; *Lu-t'ang shih-hua* 麓堂詩話

Liang shu 梁書

Lieh Tzu 列子

Lieh Tzu chu-shih 列子註釋, ann. Chang Chan 張湛

Liu (Ch'ung-ch'un) Ta-chieh 劉(崇純)大杰, *Chung-kuo wen-hsüeh fa-chan shih* 中國文學發展史

Liu Hsiang 劉向, *Hsin-hsü* 新序

Liu I-ch'ing 劉義慶, *Shih-shuo hsin-yü* 世說新語, ann. Liu Chün 劉峻

Liu Shih-p'ei 劉師培, *Chung-kuo chung-ku wen-hsüeh-shih chiang-i* 中國中古文學講義

Liu T'ien-hui 劉天惠, *Wen-pi k'ao* 文筆考

Liu Tsung-yüan 柳宗元, "Ta-li p'ing-shih Yang-chün wen-chi hou-hsü" 大理評事楊君文集後序

Liu Yin 劉因, *Ching-hsiu hsien-sheng wen-chi* 靜修先生文集

Lo Ken-tse 羅根澤, *Chou Ch'in Liang-Han wen-hsüeh p'i-p'ing shih* 周秦兩漢文學批評史; *Chung-kuo wen-hsüeh p'i-p'ing shih* 中國文學批評史

Lo-yang ch'ieh-lan chi chiao-shih 洛陽伽藍記校釋

Lu Chi 陸機, *Wen-fu* 文賦

Lu-shan chi-lüeh 廬山記略

Lu Yu 陸游, *Lao-hsüeh-an pi-chi* 老學庵筆記 in *Lu Fang-weng ch'üan-chi* 陸放翁全集

Lü-shih ch'un-ch'iu 呂氏春秋

Lun-yü 論語

Lun-yü yin-te 論語引得

Ma Kuo-han 馬國翰, *Yü-han shan-fang chi-i-shu* 玉函山房輯佚書

Matsumoto Tamotsu 松本保, *Jōdo no niwa (Taiyō niwa to ie shiriizu)* 浄土の庭（太陽庭と家シリーズ）

Mei-shu ts'ung-shu 美術叢書, comp. Teng Shih 鄧實

Mei Yao-ch'en 梅堯臣, *Wan-ling chi* 宛陵集

Mekada Makoto 目加田誠, *Bunshin chōryū* 文心彫龍 (*Bungaku geijutsu ronshū* 文学芸術論集)

Meng Tzu (Mencius) 孟子

Mi Fu 米芾, *Hai-yüeh ming-yen* 海岳名言, *Hua shih* 畫史

Ming shih 明史

Miyakawa Hisayuki 宮川尚志, *Rikuchōshi kenkyū* 六朝史研究

Miyazaki Ichisada 宮崎市定, *Kyūhin kan-jinhō no kenkyū: Kakyo zenshi* 九品官人

法の研究—科挙前史

Mizuno Seiichi 水野清一, "Kandai no senkai ishō ni tsuite" 漢代の仙界意匠について

Mo ching 脈經

Mo Shih-lung 莫是龍, *Hua shuo* 畫說

Morino Shigeo 森野繁夫, "Ryō no bungaku shūdan—Taishi Kō no shūdan o chūshin to shite" 梁の文学集団—太子綱の集団を中心として; "Ryōsho no bungaku shūdan" 梁初の文学集団

Morohashi Tetsuji 諸橋轍次, *Dai Kan-Wa ji-ten* 大漢和辞典

Mou Tsung-san 牟宗三, *Hsin-t'i yü hsing-t'i* 心體與性體

Murakami Yoshimi 村上嘉実, "Rikuchō no teian" 六朝の庭園, *Kodaigaku* 古代学; "Tōto Chōan no Ōshitsu teien" 唐都長安の王室庭園, *Kansai Gakuin shigaku* 関西学院史学

Nagahiro Toshio 長廣敏雄, *Rikujo jidai bijutsu kenkyū* 六朝時代美術の研究

Nakamura Shigeo 中村茂夫, *Chūgoku garon no tenkai* 中国画論の展開

Nan-Ch'i shu 南齋書

Nan shih 南史

Obi Kōichi 小尾郊一, *Chūgoku bungaku ni arawareta shizen to shizenkan—chūsei bungaku o chūshin to shite* 中国文学に現われた自然と自然観—中世文学を中心として

Okamura Shigeru 岡村繁, "Shihin no jo" 詩品の序

Pan Ku 班固, "Hsi-tu fu" 西都賦, "Tung-tu fu" 東都賦

Pao Ken-ti 包根弟, *Yüan shih yen-chiu* 元詩研究

Pei-t'ang shu-ch'ao 北堂書鈔

P'ei Tzu-yeh 裴子野, *Tiao-ch'ung lun* 雕蟲論

P'ei-wen-chai shu-hua-p'u 佩文齋書畫譜,

comp. Sun Yüeh-pan 孫岳頒

P'ei-wen yün-fu 佩文韻府

Pien Yung-yü 卞永譽, *Shih-ku-t'ang shu-hua hui-k'ao* 式古堂書畫彙考

San-kuo chih 三國志, ann. P'ei Sung-chih 裴松之

Sang Shih-ch'ang 桑世昌, "Lan-t'ing k'ao" 蘭亭考

Seng-chao 僧肇, *Chu Wei-mo-chi ching* 注維摩詰經

Seng-yu 僧祐, *Hung-ming chi* 弘明集

Shan-hai ching 山海經

Shang-yü-hsien chih 上虞縣志

Shao Sung-nien 邵松年, *Ku-yüan ts'ui-lu* 古緣萃錄

Shen Hao 沈顥, *Hua-chu* 畫麈

Shen Tsung-ch'ien 沈宗騫, *Chieh-chou hsüeh-hua-pien* 芥舟學畫編

Shen Tzu-ch'eng 沈子丞, *Li-tai lun-hua ming-chu hui-pien* 歷代論畫名著彙編

Sheng Ta-shih 盛大士, *Hsi-shan wo-yu-lu* 溪山臥游錄

Shih ching 詩經

Shih-ch'ü pao-chi, ch'u pien 石渠寶笈初編

Shirakawa Shizuka 白川静, *Kōkotsubun no sekai* 甲骨文の世界

Shirakawa Yoshio 白川義郎, "Ryō Yu Kengo *Shohin* kenkyū" 梁庾肩吾「書品」研究, *Kokugo no kenkyū* 国語の研究; "Ryō Yu Kengo *Shohin* no jobun oyobi ryakuron no kenkyū, Sono ichi" 梁庾肩吾書品の序文および略論の研究その一, *Ōita Daigaku Kyōikugakubu kenkyū kiyō* 大分大学教育学部研究紀要

Shodō zenshū 書道全集

Shou-shan ken-yüeh 壽山艮嶽 in *Yün-ku tsa-chi* 雲谷雜記

Shu ching 書經

Shu Chung-cheng 舒衷正, "*Shih-p'in* wei-shen-ma chih T'ao Ch'ien yü chung-p'in" 詩品爲什麼置陶淵明於中品, *Kuo-li Cheng-chih ta-hsüeh hsüeh-*

pao 國立政治大學學報

Shuo-fu 說郛, comp. T'ao Tsung-i 陶宗儀

Shuo-yüan 說苑

Ssu-k'u ch'üan-shu chen-pen pieh-chi 四庫全書珍本別輯

Ssu-k'u ch'üan-shu tsung-mu t'i-yao 四庫全書總目提要

Ssu-k'ung T'u 司空圖, *Erh-shih-ssu shih-p'in* 二十四詩品; "Yü Li-sheng lun-shih shu" 與李生論詩書

Ssu-ma Ch'ien 司馬遷, *Shih chi* 史記

Ssu-ma Hsiang-ju 司馬相如, "Shang-lin fu" 上林賦

Ssu-ma Kuang 司馬光, *Wen-kuo Wen-cheng Ssu-ma kung wen chi* 溫國文正司馬公文集

Ssu-pu pei-yao 四部備要, comp. Kao Yeh-hou 高野侯

Ssu-pu ts'ung-k'an 四部叢刊, comp. Chang Yüan-chi 張元濟

Su Ch'e 蘇轍, *Luan-ch'eng chi* 欒城集

Su Ngo 蘇鶚, *Tu-yang tsa-pien* 杜陽雜編

Su Shih 蘇軾, "*Chung yung* lun" 中庸論; *Chi-chu fen-lei Tung-p'o hsien-sheng shih* 集註分類東坡先生詩; *Ching-chin Tung-p'o wen-chi shih-lüeh* 經進東坡文集事略; *Su Tung-p'o chi* 蘇東坡集; *Tung-p'o ch'üan-chi* 東坡全集

Sugimura Yūzō 杉村勇造, *Chūgoku no niwa* 中国の庭

Sugiyama Shinzō 杉山信三, *Fujiwarashi no Ujidera to sono inke* 藤原氏の氏寺とその院家 (*Nara Kokuritsu Bunkazai Kenkyū-jo gakuhō* 奈良国立文化財研究所学報)

Sun Ch'o 孫綽, "Yu T'ien-t'ai shan fu" 遊天台山賦; *Yü tao lun* 喻道論

Sun Hsiao-hsiang 孫筱祥, "Pei-hai kung-yüan ti yüan-lin i-shu" 北海宮苑的園林藝術

Sun Tzu 孫子

Sung shih 宋史

Sung shu 宋書

Suzuki Kei 鈴木敬, *Mindai kaigashi no kenkyū: Seppa* 明代絵画史研究：浙派;

Ri To, Ba En, Ka Kei 李唐，馬遠，夏珪
(*Suiboku bijutsu taikei* 水墨美術大系）

Suzuki Torao 鈴木虎雄, *Shina shiron shi* 支那詩論史

Ta-yeh tsa-chi 大業雜集

T'ai-p'ing yü-lan 太平御覽

Takagi Seiichi 高木正一, *Shō Kō Shihin* 鍾嶸詩品

Takamatsu Takaaki (Kōmei) 高松亨明, *Shihin shōkai* 詩品詳解

T'an Chia-chien 譚家健, "Shih-t'an Ts'ao P'i ti *Tien-lun Lun-wen*" 試談曹丕的典論論文, *Hsin chien-she* 新建設

Tanaka Dan 田中淡, "Zuichō kenchikuka no sekkei to kōshō" 隋朝建築家の設計と考証

Tanaka Toyozō 田中豊蔵, *Chūgoku bijutsu no kenkyū* 中国美術の研究

T'ang Chien-yüan 唐健垣, *Ch'in fu* 琴府

T'ang Chih-ch'i 唐志契, *Hui-shih wei-yen* 繪事微言

T'ang Chün-i 唐君毅, *Chung-kuo wen-hua chih ching-shen chia-chih* 中國文化之精神價值; *Yüan tao* 原道 in *Chung-kuo che-hsüeh yüan-lun* 中國哲學原論

T'ang Hsien-tsu 湯顯祖, "Ho-ch'i hsü" 合奇序, *Yü-ming-t'ang wen-chi* 玉茗堂文集

T'ang Hou 湯垕, *Hua-chien* 畫鑑

T'ang-tai 唐岱, *Hui-shih fa-wei* 繪事發微

T'ao Wang-ling 陶望齡, *Hsieh-an chi* 歇庵集

Teng Ch'un 鄧椿, *Hua chi* 畫繼

Teng San-mu 鄧散木, *Shu-fa hsüeh-hsi pi-tu* 書法學習必讀

Teng Shih-liang 鄧仕樑, *Liang-Chin shih-lun* 兩晉詩論

Ting Fu-pao 丁福保, *Ch'ing shih hua* 清詩話; *Ch'üan Han San-kuo Chin Nan-pei-ch'ao shih* 全漢三國晉南北朝詩

Toda Kōgyō 戶田浩曉, "Ri Chū no Kanriron ni tsuite" 李充の翰林論について, *Daitō bunka* 大東文化

Ts'ao P'i 曹丕, *Tien-lun Lun-wen* 典論論文

Tso chuan 左傳

Tsu Pao-ch'üan 祖保泉, *Ssu-k'ung T'u shih-p'in chu-shih chi i-wen* 司空圖詩品注釋及譯文

Tsung Ping 宗炳, "Hua shan-shui hsü" 畫山水序; *Ming fo lun* 明佛論

Ts'ung-shu chi-ch'eng 叢書集成, comp. Wang Yün-wu 王雲五

Tu Mu 都穆, *Nan-hao shih-hua* 南濠詩話

Tu Mu 杜牧, "Tu Tu Han chi" 讀杜韓集

Tu-shih yin-te 杜詩引得

T'u Lung 屠隆, *K'ao-p'an yü-shih* 考槃餘事

Tung Ch'i-ch'ang 董其昌, *Hua-ch'an-shih sui-pi* 畫禪室隨筆; *Hua-chih* 畫旨; *Hua-yen* 畫眼; *Jung-t'ai chi (pieh-chi)* 容臺集（別集）

Tzu-chih t'ung-chien 資治通鑑, ann. Hu San-hsing 胡三省

Wang An-shih 王安石, *Wang Lin-ch'uan chi* 王臨川集

Wang Ch'eng 王偁, *T'ang-shih p'in-hui hsü* 唐詩品彙序

Wang Chi-ch'ien 王季遷, "Ni Yün-lin chih-hua" 倪雲林之畫

Wang Chia 王嘉, *Shih-i chi* 拾遺記

Wang Kai 王概, *Chieh-tzu-yüan hua-chuan* 芥子園畫傳

Wang Kuo-wei 王國維, *Jen-chien tz'u hua* 人間詞話

Wang Li-ch'i 王利器, *Wen-hsin tiao-lung hsin-shu (fu t'ung-chien)* 文心雕龍新書(附通檢); "Wen-pi hsin-chieh" 文筆新解

Wang Meng-ou 王夢鷗, *Li-chi chin-chu chin-i* 禮記今註今譯

Wang Shih-chen 王世貞 *I-yüan chih-yen* 藝苑卮言, *Yen-chou shan-jen t'i-pa* 弇州山人題跋 in *Yen-chou shan-jen ssu-pu-kao* 弇州山人四部稿; *Wang-shih hua-yüan* 王氏畫苑 in *Wang-shih shu-*

hua yüan 王氏書畫苑

Wang Shu-min 王叔岷, "Lun Chung Hung p'ing T'ao Yüan-ming shih" 論鍾嶸評陶淵明詩, Hsüeh yüan 學原

Wang Yao 王瑤, Chung-kuo wen-hsüeh ssu-hsiang 中古文學思想

Wang Yüan-ch'i 王原祁, Lu-t'ai t'i-hua-kao 麓台題畫稿

Wei Chin Nan-pei-ch'ao wen-hsüeh-shih ts'an-k'ao tzu-liao 魏晉南北朝文學史參考資料

Wei lüeh 魏略

Wei Ying-wu 韋應物, Wei Su-chou chi 韋蘇州集

Wen Chen-heng 文震亨, Ch'ang-wu chih 長物志

Wen Cheng-ming hui-kao 文徵明彙稿

Wen-pi shih ping te-shih 文筆十病得失

Wu Ch'i-chen 吳其貞, Shu-hua chi 書畫記

Wu Ch'iao (Shu) 吳喬(殳), Wei-lu shih-hua 圍爐詩話

Wu Shih-ch'ang 吳世昌, "Wei-Chin feng-liu yü ssu-chia yüan-lin" 魏晉風流與私家園林, Hsüeh-wen yüeh-k'an 學文月刊

Wu Tsung-tz'u 吳宗慈, Lu-shan chih 廬山志

Yamada Keiji 山田慶児, Chūgoku no kagaku to kagakusha 中国の科学と科学者

Yamashita Ryūji 山下龍二, Yōmeigaku no kenkyū 陽明学の研究

Yang Hsiung 揚雄, Fa-yen 法言; "Yü-lieh fu" 羽獵賦

Yang Shu-ta 楊樹達, Han-tai hun-sang li-su k'ao 漢代婚喪禮俗考

Yang Wei-chen 楊維楨 "Chang Pei-shan ho T'ao-chi hsü" 張北山和陶集序, "Li

Chung-yü shih hsü" 李仲虞詩序 in Tung-wei-tzu wen-chi 東維子文集

Yen K'o-chün 嚴可均, Ch'üan Shang-ku San-tai Ch'in Han San-kuo Liu-ch'ao wen 全上古三代秦漢三國六朝文

Yen Yen-chih 顏延之, T'ing kao 庭誥

Yen Yü 嚴羽, Ts'ang-lang shih-hua 滄浪詩話

Yin Fan 殷璠, Ho-yüeh ying-ling chi 河岳英靈集, in T'ang-jen hsüan T'ang-shih 唐人選唐詩

Yokoyama Iseo 橫山伊勢雄, "Sō shiron ni miru 'heitan no tai' ni tsuite" 宋詩論にみる平淡の体について, Kanbun Gakkai kaihō 漢文学会会報

Yoshikawa hakase taikyū kinen Chūgoku bungaku ronshū 吉川博士退休記念中国文学論集

Yü Chien-hua 俞劍華, Chung-kuo hua-lun lei-pien 中國畫論類編; Chung-kuo shan-shui-hua te nan-pei-tsung lun 中國山水畫的南北宗論; Li-tai ming-hua chi 歷代名畫記 · Shih T'ao Hua-yü-lu 石濤畫語錄

Yü Ying-shih 余英時, "Han-Chin chih chi shih chih hsin tzu-chüeh yü hsin ssu-ch'ao" 漢晉之際士之新自覺與新思潮, Hsin-ya hsüeh-pao 新亞學報

Yüan Chung-tao 袁中道, K'o-hsüeh-chai shih wen chi 珂雪齋詩文集

Yüan Hao-wen 元好問, Lun-shih san-shih-shou 論詩三十首

Yüan Hung-tao 袁宏道, "Yüan Chung-lang wen-ch'ao" 袁中郎文鈔, Yüan Chung-lang ch'üan chi 袁中郎全集

Yüan Tsung-tao 袁宗道, Yüan Po-hsiu ch'üan chi 袁伯修全集

Yün Shou-p'ing 惲壽平, Ou-hsiang-kuan hua-pa 甌香館畫跋

Index-Glossary

Library of Congress Cataloging in Publication Data

Main entry under title:
Theories of the arts in China.

Papers presented at a conference sponsored by the Committee on Studies of Chinese
Civilization of the American Council of Learned Societies held June 6–12, 1979, at the
Breckinridge Public Affairs Center of Bowdoin College, York, Maine.
Includes index.
1. Arts, Chinese—Congresses.   I. Bush, Susan.   II. Murck, Christian   III. American
Council of Learned Societies. Committee on Studies of Chinese Civilization.
NX583.A1T48 1983   700'.1   83-42551
ISBN 0-691-04020-6